INTEGRATING BUSINESS WITH TECHNOLOGY

By completing the projects in this text, students will be able to demonstrate business knowledge, application software proficiency, and Internet skills. These projects can be used by instructors as learning assessment tools and by students as demonstrations of business, software, and problem-solving skills to future employers. Here are some of the skills and competencies students using this text will be able to demonstrate:

Business Application skills: Use of both business and software skills in real-world business applications. Demonstrates both business knowledge and proficiency in spreadsheet, database, and Web page/blog creation tools.

Internet skills: Ability to use Internet tools to access information, conduct research, or perform online calculations and analysis.

Analytical, writing and presentation skills: Ability to research a specific topic, analyze a problem, think creatively, suggest a solution, and prepare a clear written or oral presentation of the solution, working either individually or with others in a group.

Business Application Skills

BUSINESS SKILLS	SOFTWARE SKILLS	CHAPTER
Finance and Accounting		
Financial statement analysis	Spreadsheet charts	Chapter 2*
	Spreadsheet formulas	Chapter 10
	Spreadsheet downloading and formatting	
Pricing hardware and software	Spreadsheet formulas	Chapter 5
Technology rent vs. buy decision Total Cost of Ownership (TCO) analysis	Spreadsheet formulas	Chapter 5*
Analyzing telecommunications services and costs	Spreadsheet formulas	Chapter 7
Risk assessment	Spreadsheet charts and formulas	Chapter 8
Retirement planning	Spreadsheet formulas and logical functions	Chapter 11
Capital budgeting	Spreadsheet formulas	Chapter 14
		Chapter 14*
Human Resources		
Employee training and skills tracking	Database design Database querying and reporting	Chapter 13*
Job posting database and Web page	Database design Web page design and creation	Chapter 15
Manufacturing and Production		
Analyzing supplier performance and pricing	Spreadsheet date functions Database functions Data filtering	Chapter 2
Inventory management	Importing data into a database Database querying and reporting	Chapter 6
Bill of materials cost sensitivity analysis	Spreadsheet data tables Spreadsheet formulas	Chapter 12*
Sales and Marketing		
Sales trend analysis	Database querying and reporting	Chapter 1

*Dirt Bikes Running Case on Companion Web Site

Management Information Systems

MANAGING THE DIGITAL FIRM

ELEVENTH EDITION

GLOBAL EDITION

Kenneth C. Laudon
New York University

Jane P. Laudon
Azimuth Information Systems

Library of Congress Cataloging-in-Publication Information is available.

Executive Editor: Bob Horan
International Acquisitions Editor: Laura Dent
Editorial Director: Sally Yagan
Editor in Chief: Eric Svendsen
Product Development Manager: Ashley Santora
Editorial Assistant: Christina Rumbaugh
Editorial Project Manager: Kelly Loftus
Executive Marketing Manager: Patrick Leow
Marketing Manager: Anne Fahlgren
Permissions Project Manager: Charles Morris
Senior Managing Editor: Judy Leale
Production Project Manager: Karalyn Holland
Senior Operations Specialist: Arnold Vila
Operations Specialist: Benjamin Smith
Senior Art Director: Janet Slowik
Cover Designer: Bobby Starnes
Cover Illustration/Photo: Merve Poray/Shutterstock Images
Manager, Rights and Permissions: Zina Arabia
Manager: Visual Research: Beth Brenzel
Image Permission Coordinator: Angelique Sharps
Composition: Azimuth Interactive, Inc.
Full-Service Project Management: Azimuth Interactive, Inc.
Printer/Binder: Courier/Kendallville
Typeface: 10.5/13 ITC Veljovic Std Book

Credits and acknowledgments borrowed from other sources and reproduced, with permission, in this textbook appear on appropriate page within text (or on page 641).

If you purchased this book within the United States or Canada you should be aware that it has been wrongfully imported without the approval of the Publisher or the Author.

Microsoft® and Windows® are registered trademarks of the Microsoft Corporation in the U.S.A. and other countries. Screen shots and icons reprinted with permission from the Microsoft Corporation. This book is not sponsored or endorsed by or affiliated with the Microsoft Corporation.

Pearson Education Ltd., London
Pearson Education Singapore, Pte. Ltd
Pearson Education, Canada, Ltd
Pearson Education-Japan
Pearson Education Australia PTY, Limited

Pearson Education North Asia, Ltd., Hong Kong
Pearson Educación de Mexico, S.A. de C.V.
Pearson Education Malaysia, Pte. Ltd.
Pearson Education Upper Saddle River, New Jersey

10 9 8 7 6 5 4
ISBN-13: 978-0-13-609368-8
ISBN-10: 0-13-609368-X

About the Authors

Kenneth C. Laudon is a Professor of Information Systems at New York University's Stern School of Business. He holds a B.A. in Economics from Stanford and a Ph.D. from Columbia University. He has authored twelve books dealing with electronic commerce, information systems, organizations, and society. Professor Laudon has also written over forty articles concerned with the social, organizational, and management impacts of information systems, privacy, ethics, and multimedia technology.

Professor Laudon's current research is on the planning and management of large-scale information systems and multimedia information technology. He has received grants from the National Science Foundation to study the evolution of national information systems at the Social Security Administration, the IRS, and the FBI. Ken's research focuses on enterprise system implementation, computer-related organizational and occupational changes in large organizations, changes in management ideology, changes in public policy, and understanding productivity change in the knowledge sector.

Ken Laudon has testified as an expert before the United States Congress. He has been a researcher and consultant to the Office of Technology Assessment (United States Congress), Department of Homeland Security, and to the Office of the President, several executive branch agencies, and Congressional Committees. Professor Laudon also acts as an in-house educator for several consulting firms and as a consultant on systems planning and strategy to several Fortune 500 firms.

At NYU's Stern School of Business, Ken Laudon teaches courses on Managing the Digital Firm, Information Technology and Corporate Strategy, Professional Responsibility (Ethics), and Electronic Commerce and Digital Markets. Ken Laudon's hobby is sailing.

Jane Price Laudon is a management consultant in the information systems area and the author of seven books. Her special interests include systems analysis, data management, MIS auditing, software evaluation, and teaching business professionals how to design and use information systems.

Jane received her Ph.D. from Columbia University, her M.A. from Harvard University, and her B.A. from Barnard College. She has taught at Columbia University and the New York University Graduate School of Business. She maintains a lifelong interest in Oriental languages and civilizations.

The Laudons have two daughters, Erica and Elisabeth, to whom this book is dedicated.

Brief Contents

4

Complete Contents

Chapter 4   Ethical and Social Issues in Information Systems 148

Chapter 8   Securing Information Systems 320

Part Three Key System Applications for the Digital Age 363

Chapter 12   Enhancing Decision Making 474

BUSINESS CASES AND INTERACTIVE SESSIONS

Here are some of the business firms you will find described in the cases and Interactive Sessions of this book:

Chapter 1: Information Systems in Global Business Today
NBA Teams Make a Slam Dunk with Information Technology
Virtual Meetings: Smart Management
UPS Competes Globally with Information Technology
Is Second Life Ready for Business?

Chapter 2: Global E-Business: How Businesses Use Information Systems
Hyperone: Solutions to Achieve Business Objectives
Air Canada Takes Off with Maintenix
El-Alamein for Printing and Packaging Goes Digital
Modernization of NTUC Income

Chapter 3: Information Systems, Organizations, and Strategy
EBay Fine Tunes Its Strategy
Can Technology Save Soldiers' Lives in Iraq?
Can Detroit Make the Cars Customers Want?
Soundbuzz's Music Strategy for Asia-Pacific

Chapter 4: Ethical and Social Issues in Information Systems
Ethical Issues Facing the Use of Technologies for the Aged Community
Green IT at Wipro
Flexible Scheduling at Wal-Mart: Good or Bad for Employees?
Should Google Organize Your Medical Records?

Chapter 5: IT Infrastructure and Emerging Technologies
Cars.com's IT Infrastructure Drives Rapid Business Growth
Computing Goes Green (Pomona Valley Hospital Medical Center, Hewlett Packard)
Salesforce.com: Software-As-A-Service Goes Mainstream
Amazon's New Store: Utility Computing

Chapter 6: Foundations of Business Intelligence: Databases and Information Management
Can HP Mine Success from an Enterprise Data Warehouse?
The Internal Revenue Service Uncovers Tax Fraud with a Data Warehouse
The Databases Behind MySpace
Trouble with the Terror Watch List Database (FBI)

Chapter 7: Telecommunications, the Internet and Wireless Technology
Virgin Megastores Keeps Spinning with Unified Communications
Should Network Neutrality Continue? (YouTube, Time Warner Cable, Comcast)
Monitoring Employees on Networks: Unethical or Good Business? (Potomac Hospital, Ajax Boiler)
Google Versus Microsoft: Clash of the Technology Titans

Preface

We wrote this book for business school students who wanted an in-depth look at how business firms use information technologies and systems to achieve corporate objectives. Information systems are one of the major tools available to business managers for achieving operational excellence, developing new products and services, improving decision making, and achieving competitive advantage.

When interviewing potential employees, business firms often look for new hires who know how to use information systems and technologies for achieving bottom-line business results. Regardless of whether you are an accounting, finance, management, operations management, marketing, or information systems major, the knowledge and information you find in this book will be valuable throughout your business career.

We have made every effort to ensure the currency and authority of cases and examples used through this text. You will find in this book that cases and data have 2008 sources. The research literature as well as professional publications form an important foundation for our work.

WHAT'S NEW IN MIS?

Plenty. In fact, there's a whole new world of doing business using new technologies for managing and organizing business operations. What makes the MIS field the most exciting area of study in schools of business is the continuous change in technology, management, and business processes (Chapter One describes these changes in more detail).

A continual stream of information technology innovations is transforming the traditional business world. Examples include the emergence of cloud computing, the growth of a mobile digital business platform, and, not least, the use of social networks by managers to achieve business objectives. Most of these changes have occurred in the last few years. These innovations are enabling entrepreneurs and innovative traditional firms to create new products and services, develop new business models, and transform the day-to-day conduct of business. In the process, some old businesses, even industries, are being destroyed while new businesses are springing up.

For instance, the emergence of online music stores—driven by millions of consumers who prefer iPods and MP3 players—has forever changed the older business model of distributing music on physical devices, such as records and CDs. Online video rentals are similarly transforming the old model of distributing films through theaters and then through DVD rentals at physical stores. New high-speed broadband connections to the home have supported these two business changes.

E-commerce is back, generating over $250 billion in revenues in 2008, and growing at 15 percent a year. It is forever changing how firms design, produce and deliver their products and services. E-commerce has reinvented itself again, disrupting the traditional marketing and advertising industry and putting major media and content firms in jeopardy. MySpace and Facebook, along with other social networking sites such as YouTube, PhotoBucket, and Second Life, exemplify the new face of e-commerce in the 21st Century. They sell services. When we think of e-commerce we tend to think of selling physical products. While this iconic vision of e-commerce is still very powerful and the fastest growing form of retail in the U.S., growing up alongside is a whole new value stream based on selling services, not goods. It's a services model of e-commerce. Information systems and technologies are the foundation of this new services-based e-commerce.

Likewise, the management of business firms has changed: With new mobile phones, high-speed wireless Wi-Fi networks, and wireless laptop computers, remote salespeople on the road are only seconds away from their managers' questions and oversight. Managers on the move are in direct, continuous contact with their employees. The growth of enterprise-wide information systems with extraordinarily rich data means that managers no longer operate in a fog of confusion, but instead have online, nearly instant, access to the really important information they need for accurate and timely decisions. In addition to their public uses on the Web, wikis and blogs are becoming important corporate tools for communication, collaboration, and information sharing.

THE ELEVENTH EDITION: THE COMPREHENSIVE SOLUTION FOR THE MIS CURRICULUM

Since its inception, this text has helped to define the MIS course around the globe. This edition continues to be authoritative and exceptionally up-to-date, but is also more customizable, flexible, and geared to meeting the needs of different colleges, universities, and individual instructors. This book is now part of a complete learning package that includes the core text and an extensive Companion Web site.

The core text consists of 15 chapters with hands-on projects covering the most essential topics in MIS. The Companion Web site provides more in-depth coverage of chapter topics, video cases, career resources, additional case studies, supplementary chapter material, interactive quizzes, and data files for hands-on projects.

THE CORE TEXT

The core text provides an overview of fundamental MIS concepts using an integrated framework for describing and analyzing information systems. This framework shows information systems composed of management, organization, and technology elements and is reinforced in student projects and case studies.

Chapter Organization

Each chapter contains the following elements:
- A chapter-opening case describing a real-world organization to establish the theme and importance of the chapter
- A diagram analyzing the opening case in terms of the management, organization, and technology model used throughout the text
- A series of Learning Objectives

A diagram accompanying each chapter-opening case graphically illustrates how management, organization, and technology elements work together to create an information system solution to the business challenges discussed in the case.

- Two Interactive Sessions with Case Study Questions and MIS in Action projects
- A Hands-on MIS Projects section featuring two Management Decision Problems, a hands-on application software project, and a project to develop Internet skills
- A Learning Tracks section identifying supplementary material on the Companion Web site
- A chapter Review Summary keyed to the Learning Objectives
- A list of Key Terms that students can use to review concepts
- Review Questions for students to test their comprehension of chapter material
- Discussion Questions raised by the broader themes of the chapter
- Video Cases (available on the Companion Web site)
- A Collaboration and Teamwork project to develop teamwork and presentation skills, with options for using open-source collaboration tools
- A chapter-ending case study for students to apply chapter concepts

KEY FEATURES

We have enhanced the core text to make it more interactive, instructor-friendly and leading-edge. The eleventh edition includes the following new features:

Business-Driven with Business Cases and Examples

The text helps students see the direct connection between information systems and business performance. It describes the main business objectives driving the use of information systems and technologies in corporations all over the world: operational excellence; new products and services; customer and supplier intimacy; improved decision making; competitive advantage; and survival. In-text examples and case studies show students how specific companies use information systems to achieve these objectives.

We use only current (2008) examples and cases from business and public organizations throughout the text to illustrate the important concepts in each chapter. All the case studies describe well-known companies and organizations that are familiar to students, such as Google, Facebook, Coca-Cola, Wal-Mart, eBay, the NBA, Procter & Gamble, and JetBlue.

Student Learning-Focused

Student Learning Objectives are organized around a set of study questions to focus student attention. Each chapter concludes with a Review Summary and Review Questions organized around these study questions.

Interactivity

There's no better way to learn about MIS than by doing MIS! We provide different kinds of hands-on projects where students can work with real-world business scenarios and data, and learn first-hand what MIS is all about. These projects heighten student involvement in this exciting subject.

- **New Management Decision Problems**. Two new Management Decision Problems per chapter teach students how to apply chapter concepts to real-world business scenarios requiring analysis and decision making.

- **New Collaboration and Teamwork Projects.** Each chapter features a collaborative project that encourages students working in teams to use Google Sites, Google Docs, and other open-source collaboration tools. The first team project in Chapter One asks students to build a collaborative Google Site.

- **Hands-on MIS Projects**. Each chapter concludes with a Hands-on MIS Projects section containing three types of projects: two Management Decision Problems, a hands-on application software exercise using Microsoft Excel or Access, and a project that develops Internet business skills.

- **Interactive Sessions**. Two short cases in each chapter have been redesigned as Interactive Sessions to be used in the classroom (or on Internet discussion boards) to stimulate student interest and active learning. Each case concludes with two types of activities: *Case Study Questions* and *MIS in Action*. The *Case Study Questions* provide topics for class discussion, Internet discussion, or written assignments. *MIS in Action* features hands-on Web activities for exploring more deeply the issues discussed in the case.

- **Thirty New Video Cases.** Students learn from stories and videos. To enable video learning, we've put together a new collection of video cases. Each chapter has two business video cases (30 videos in all) which are available on the Companion Web site. Case study questions link the videos to chapter concepts.

Two real-world business scenarios per chapter provide opportunities for students to apply chapter concepts and practice management decision making.

Management Decision Problems

1. Applebee's is the largest casual dining chain in the world, with 1970 locations throughout the U.S. and nearly 20 other countries worldwide. The menu features beef, chicken, and pork items, as well as burgers, pasta, and seafood. The Applebee's CEO wants to make the restaurant more profitable by developing menus that are tastier and contain more items that customers want and are willing to pay for despite rising costs for gasoline and agricultural products. How might information systems help management implement this strategy? What pieces of data would Applebee's need to collect? What kinds of reports would be useful to help management make decisions on how to improve menus and profitability?

Improving Decision Making: Using Databases to Analyze Sales Trends

Software skills: Database querying and reporting
Business skills: Sales trend analysis

Effective information systems transform data into meaningful information for decisions that improve business performance. At the Laudon Web site for Chapter 1, you can find a Store and Regional Sales Database with raw data on weekly store sales of computer equipment in various sales regions. A sample is shown below, but the Web site may have a more recent version of this database for this exercise. The database includes fields for store identification number, sales region number, item number, item description, unit price, units sold, and the weekly sales period when the sales were made. Develop some reports and queries to make this information more useful for running the business. Try to use the information in the database to support decisions on which products to restock, which stores and sales regions would benefit from additional marketing and promotional campaigns, which times of the year products should be offered at full price, and which times of the year products should be discounted. Modify the database table, if necessary, to provide all of the information you require. Print your reports and results of queries.

> Students practice using software in real-world settings for achieving operational excellence and enhancing decision making.

I -	Store -	Sales Re(-	Item I -	Item Descrip -	Unit Pr -	Units S -	Week Enc -
1	1	South	2005	17" Monitor	$229.00	28	10/27/2008
2	1	South	2005	17" Monitor	$229.00	30	11/24/2008
3	1	South	2005	17" Monitor	$229.00	9	12/29/2008
4	1	South	3006	101 Keyboard	$19.95	30	10/27/2008
5	1	South	3006	101 Keyboard	$19.95	35	11/24/2008
6	1	South	3006	101 Keyboard	$19.95	39	12/29/2008
7	1	South	6050	PC Mouse	$8.95	28	10/27/2008
8	1	South	6050	PC Mouse	$8.95	3	11/24/2008
9	1	South	6050	PC Mouse	$8.95	38	12/29/2008
10	1	South	8500	Desktop CPU	$849.95	25	10/27/2008
11	1	South	8500	Desktop CPU	$849.95	27	11/24/2008
12	1	South	8500	Desktop CPU	$849.95	33	12/29/2008
13	2	South	2005	17" Monitor	$229.00	8	10/27/2008
14	2	South	2005	17" Monitor	$229.00	8	11/24/2008
15	2	South	2005	17" Monitor	$229.00	10	12/29/2008
16	2	South	3006	101 Keyboard	$19.95	8	10/27/2008
17	2	South	3006	101 Keyboard	$19.95	8	11/24/2008
18	2	South	3006	101 Keyboard	$19.95	8	12/29/2008
19	2	South	6050	PC Mouse	$8.95	9	10/27/2008

Record: 1 of 96   No Filter   Search

Improving Decision Making: Using Intelligent Agents for Comparison Shopping

Software skills: Web browser and shopping bot software
Business skills: Product evaluation and selection

This project will give you experience using shopping bots to search online for products, find product information, and find the best prices and vendors.

You have decided to purchase a new digital camera. Select a digital camera you might want to purchase, such as the Canon PowerShot SD 950 or the Olympus Stylus 1200. To purchase the camera as inexpensively as possible, try several of the shopping bot sites, which do the price comparisons for you. Visit My Simon (www.mysimon.com), BizRate.com (www.bizrate.com), and Google Product Search. Compare these shopping sites in terms of their ease of use, number of offerings, speed in obtaining information, thoroughness of information offered about the product and seller, and price selection. Which site or sites would you use and why? Which camera would you select and why? How helpful were these sites for making your decision?

> Each chapter features a project to develop Internet skills for accessing information, conducting research, and performing online calculations and analysis.

Each chapter contains two Interactive Sessions on Management, Organizations, or Technology using real-world companies to illustrate chapter concepts and issues.

INTERACTIVE SESSION: ORGANIZATIONS

TURNER SPORTS NEW MEDIA MARRIES TV AND THE INTERNET

Turner Sports New Media is the online division of Turner Broadcasting System, a collection of TV networks assembled by billionaire Ted Turner. TBS was founded in the 1970's by Turner and has since grown into a prominent media company with diverse holdings, including CNN, TBS, TNT, and Cartoon Network. Turner Sports New Media was founded by Turner's sports division's chief, David Levy, in response to the growing popularity of broadband video. Predicting that broadband video would damage Turner's TV business, Levy focused on making deals to manage the Web rights of various sports leagues and to unite TV and the Internet in creative ways.

Turner Sports New Media has established itself as an innovator through its ability to combine TV and the Web more successfully than rivals. Turner's success allows them to both sell more ads and persuade sports leagues such as the PGA Tour and NASCAR to pay Turner millions per year to run their Web operations. Turner's formula is to provide rich, interactive features that use TV and the Web simultaneously to enhance the viewer's experience.

In 2003, Turner lacked the number of Web clients it has today, with only NASCAR.com under their management. By 2006, they had added pga.com and pgatour.com, and in early 2008 they reached an agreement with the NBA to jointly manage nba.com, which has 5.5 million unique monthly visitors. Their latest target is Major League Soccer's Web operations, which, oddly enough, are managed by Major League Baseball. Turner earns fees for managing the sites and splits ad revenues with each league. With each site that Turner Sports New Media manages, their goal is to get fans switching between TV and unique features on their desktops or laptops. For example, pgatour.com visitors can watch play on certain holes, watch a certain player, aerial views of the course, and get tips from pros on the site while events are in progress.

Many sports leagues don't like to relinquish control of their Web sites to outside organizations, preferring to handle their Web operations themselves to avoid paying fees to organizations like Turner Sports New Media. The NFL recently reacquired rights to its Web site back from CBS. But Turner's value proposition to sports leagues is a compelling one. The league's official site will benefit from Turner's reach and the Web's relationship with consumers. Turner's experience with running Web sites is extensive, as is their track record for success in increasing site traffic and developing innovative interactive applications. Marketers can place ads in multiple formats (TV and the Internet).

Turner's oldest client is NASCAR, and the recent contract extension signed between the two suggests that NASCAR is more than happy with Turner's results. NASCAR.com has been one of the top three sports league sites on the Internet in the past few years. Since Turner assumed control of the league's Web rights, the site has seen double-digit growth in page views and an increase in average monthly unique visitors of 25 percent over the last 7 years. Over the past calendar year the site had 1.4 billion page views. Turner will continue to operate NASCAR.com through 2014, collaborating in content creation, e-commerce, and race ticket sales. Turner will continue to have oversight over news content, broadband coverage, wireless platforms, video downloads, and ad sales, and will seek to provide fans with better information and NASCAR merchandise.

Turner has implemented a wide array of cutting-edge applications and offerings to NASCAR.COM, including TrackPass, its most interactive feature. TrackPass is a premium service that consists of several interactive applications, including TrackPass Scanner, TrackPass Pit Command, and TrackPass RaceView. RaceView renders each car digitally and offers a multitude of camera angles and viewing options for each and every car and driver. Users can pause, rewind, and replay live races and listen to any driver's in-car audio, in addition to a variety of other features that give the viewer unparalleled customization over how they watch and enjoy each race.

Other features that Turner has implemented on NASCAR.com include a 24-hr news center, live streaming for some races, a social networking 'community' section, an extensive video library, live and interactive broadband shows, and a merchandise superstore.

Turner's contract extension with the NBA extends the longest-running partnership between a league and programming network in professional sports to a whopping 32 years. The contract also grants

---

MIS in Action projects encourage students to learn more about the companies and issues discussed in the case studies.

CASE STUDY QUESTIONS

1. Describe the unique features of e-commerce technology illustrated in this case.

2. How does the Web enhance the TV businesses for the companies discussed in this case? How does it add value?

3. Why is NASCAR TrackPass a good example of Turner Sports New Media's value to sports league sites?

4. Do you think Turner Sports New Media will continue to grow steadily? Why or why not?

MIS IN ACTION

Visit PGA.com, PGATour.com, or NASCAR.com, explore the Web site, and then answer the following questions.

1. What unique features of e-commerce technology can you find on the site? What purposes do they serve?

2. How does the Web site promote TV viewing? How does it create value for the company?

Customization and Flexibility: New Learning Track Modules

Our Learning Tracks feature gives instructors the flexibility to provide in-depth coverage of the topics they choose. A Learning Tracks section at the end of each chapter directs students to short essays or additional chapters on the Laudon Companion Web site. This supplementary content takes students deeper into MIS topics, concepts and debates; reviews basic technology concepts in hardware, software, database design, telecommunications, and other areas; and provide additional hands-on software instruction. The Eleventh Edition includes new Learning Tracks on Business Process Management, Cloud Computing, Web 2.0, The Booming Job Market in IT Security, Hot New Careers in E-Commerce, Computer Forensics, Sarbanes-Oxley, Service Level Agreements, Building a Web Page, Excel Pivot Tables, Capital Budgeting for Information Systems, and additional coverage of Computer Hardware and Software technology.

AUTHOR-CERTIFIED TEST BANK AND SUPPLEMENTS

- **Author-Certified Test Bank.** The authors have worked closely with skilled test item writers to ensure that higher level cognitive skills are tested. Test bank multiple choice questions include questions on content, but also include many questions that require analysis, synthesis, and evaluation skills.

- **New Annotated Interactive PowerPoint Lecture Slides**. In addition to illuminating key concepts, class slides include four to five Interactive Sessions where students are encouraged to discuss in class the cases in the chapter or related issues in MIS, management, and business. The faculty slides are annotated with teaching suggestions and author comments.

Globalization

This edition has even more global emphasis than previous editions. New material on globalization (Chapter 1), global workgroup collaboration (Chapter 2), software localization (Chapter 15), global security threats (Chapter 8), global supply chains (Chapter 9), global marketplaces (Chapter 10), and offshore outsourcing (Chapter 11), accompanied by numerous examples of multinational and non-U.S. companies, show how to use IS in a global business environment.

New Leading-Edge Topics:

This edition includes new coverage of the following leading-edge topics:
Cloud computing
Web 2.0 and Web 3.0
Collaboration systems and tools
SaaS (Software as a Service)
Globalization
Virtual worlds
Widgets
Web mining and text mining
Unified communications
Unified threat management
Business uses of wikis, blogs, and social networking
Service level agreements
Software localization

COMPANION WEB SITE

The Laudon/Laudon text is supported by an excellent Web site at http://www.pearsonglobaleditions.com/laudon that reinforces and enhances text material with Learning Tracks supplements, the Dirt Bikes U.S.A. running case, the complete set of video cases, data files for the Hands-on MIS Projects, Career Resources and Digital Portfolio guide, an Interactive Study Guide, International Resources, additional case studies, and a special PowerPoint slide show on IT Careers custom-prepared by Ken Laudon. The Web site features a secure password-protected faculty area from which instructors can download the Instructor's Manual and suggested answers to the Hands-on MIS Projects. The site has an improved online syllabus tool to help professors add their own personal syllabi to the site in minutes.

Career Resources

The Companion Web site offers extensive Career Resources, including job-hunting guides and instructions on how to build a Digital Portfolio demonstrating the business knowledge, application software proficiency, and Internet skills acquired from using the text.   The portfolio can be included in a resume or job application or used as a learning assessment tool for instructors.

INSTRUCTIONAL SUPPORT MATERIALS

Image Library

The Image Library is an impressive resource to help instructors create vibrant lecture presentations. Almost every figure and photo in the text is provided and organized by chapter for convenience.   These images and lecture notes can be imported easily into Microsoft PowerPoint to create new presentations or to add to existing ones.

Instructor's Manual

The Instructor's Manual features not only answers to review, discussion, case study, and collaboration and teamwork project questions but also an in-depth lecture outline, teaching objectives, key terms, teaching suggestions, and Internet resources. This supplement can be downloaded from the secure faculty section of the Laudon Web site.

Test Item File

The Test Item File is a comprehensive collection of true-false, multiple-choice, fill-in-the-blank, and essay questions. The questions are rated by difficulty level and the answers are referenced by section. An electronic version of the Test Item File is available in TestGen and TestGen conversions are available for BlackBoard or WebCT course management systems. All TestGen files are available for download at the Instructor Resource Center.

Annotated PowerPoint Slides

Electronic color slides created by Azimuth Interactive Corporation, Inc., are available in Microsoft PowerPoint. The slides are annotated using the Notes section of PowerPoint slides. The notes provide teaching hints for instructors and conceptual background. The slides illuminate and build on key concepts in the text. Faculty can download the PowerPoint slides from the Web site.

Microsoft Office Tutorial Software

For instructors seeking application software training to use with this text, Pearson is pleased to offer student training in Microsoft Office 2007. This item is not available as a stand-alone item but can be packaged with the Laudon/Laudon text at an additional charge. Contact your local Pearson representative for more details.

ACKNOWLEDGMENTS

The production of any book involves valued contributions from a number of persons. We would like to thank all of our editors for encouragement, insight, and strong support for many years. We thank Bob Horan for guiding the development of this edition and Kelly Loftus for her role in managing the project.

We praise Karalyn Holland for overseeing production for this project. Our special thanks go to our supplement authors for their work. We are indebted to William Anderson for his assistance in the writing and production of the text and to Megan Miller for her help during production. We thank Diana R. Craig for her assistance with database topics.

Special thanks to colleagues at the Stern School of Business at New York University; to Professor Edward Stohr of Stevens Institute of Technology; to Professors Al Croker and Michael Palley of Baruch College and New York University; to Professor Lawrence Andrew of Western Illinois University; to Professor Lutz Kolbe of the University of Gottingen; to Professor Walter Brenner of the University of St. Gallen; to Professor Detlef Schoder of the University of Cologne; to Professor Donald Marchand of the International Institute for Management Development; and to Professor Daniel Botha of Stellenbosch University who provided additional suggestions for improvement. Thank you to Professor Ken Kraemer, University of California at Irvine, and Professor John King, University of Michigan, for more than a decade's long discussion of information systems and organizations. And a special remembrance and dedication to Professor Rob Kling, University of Indiana, for being my friend and colleague over so many years.

We also want to especially thank all our reviewers whose suggestions helped improve our texts. Reviewers for this edition include the following:

Kamal Nayan Agarwal, *Howard University*
David Bradbard, *Winthrop University*
Richard Clemens, *West Virginia Wesleyan College*
Jason Chen, *Gonzaga University*
Kungwen Chu, *Purdue University Calumet*
Albert Cruz, *National University*
Warren W. Fisher, *Stephen F. Austin State University*
Bobby Granville, *Florida A&M University*
Michelle Hepner, *University of Central Oklahoma*
Rui Huang, *Binghamton University, SUNY*

Al Lederer, *University of Kentucky*
Mary Reed, *Jamestown College*
Eliot Rich, *SUNY University at Albany*
Leasa Richards-Mealy, *Columbia College*
Richard S. Segall, *Arkansas State University*
Lanny Wilke, *Montana State University- Northern*
Karen L. Williams, *University of Texas at San Antonio*
Paul Witman, *California Lutheran University*

We also want to thank the following international case contributors and reviewers:

Case Contributors:

Ahmed Elragal, German University in Cairo
Lesley Land, University of New South Wales
Neerja Sethi and Vijay Sethi, Nanyang Technological University

International Reviewers:

Ibrahim Al-Jabi, King Fahd University of Petroleum and Minerals
Michael Chalhoub, Lebanese American University
Sherif Kamal, American University in Cairo
Nader Nada, Arab University for Science and Technology
Suresh Subramoniam, Prince Sultan University

K.C.L.
J.P.L.

PART ONE

Organizations, Management, and the Networked Enterprise

Part One introduces the major themes of this book, raising a series of important questions: What is an information system and what are its management, organization, and technology dimensions? Why are information systems so essential in businesses today? How can information systems help businesses become more competitive? What broader ethical and social issues are raised by widespread use of information systems?

Chapter 1

Information Systems in Global Business Today

NBA TEAMS MAKE A SLAM DUNK WITH INFORMATION TECHNOLOGY

Basketball is a very fast-paced, high-energy sport but it's also big business. Professional teams that belong to the National Basketball Association (NBA) pay each of their players an average of $5 million per year. For that amount of money, member teams expect a great deal and are constantly on the watch for ways of improving their performance. During an 82-game season, every nuance a coach can pick up about a weakness in an opponent's offense or in the jump shot of one of his own players will translate into more points on the scoreboard, more wins, and ultimately more money for the team.

Traditional basketball game statistics failed to capture all of the details associated with every play and were not easily related to videotapes of games. As a result, decisions about changes in tactics or how to take advantage of opponents' weaknesses were based primarily on hunches and gut instincts. Coaches could not easily answer questions such as "Which types of plays are hurting us?" Now professional basketball coaches and managers are taking their cues from other businesses and learning how to make decisions based on hard data.

A company called Synergy Sports Technology has found a way to collect and organize fine-grained statistical data and relate the data to associated video clips. Synergy employs more than 30 people to match up video of each play with statistical information on which players have the ball, what type of play is involved, and the result.

Each game is dissected and tagged, play by play, using hundreds of descriptive categories, and these data are linked to high-resolution video.

Coaches then use an index to locate the exact video clip in which they are interested and access the video at a protected Web site. Within seconds they are able to watch streaming video on the protected site or they can download it to laptops and even to iPods. One NBA team purchased iPods for every player so they could review videos to help them prepare for their next game.

For example, if the Dallas Mavericks have just lost to the Phoenix Suns and gave up too many fast-break points, the Mavericks coach can use Synergy's service to see video clips of every Phoenix fast break in the game. He can also view every Dallas transitional situation for the entire season to see how that night's game compared with others. According to Dallas Mavericks owner Mark Cuban, "the system allows us to look at every play, in every way, and tie it back to stats. So we can watch how we played every pick and roll, track our success rate, and see how other teams are doing it."

The service helps coaches analyze the strengths and weaknesses of individual players. For example, Synergy's system has recorded every offensive step of the Mavericks' Dirk Nowitzki since he joined the NBA in 1998. The system can show how successfully he is driving right or left in either home or away games, with the ability to break games and player performance into increasingly finer-grained categories. If a user clicks on any statistic, that person will find video clips from the last

three seasons of 20, 50, or even 2,000 plays that show Nowitzki making that particular move.

About 14 NBA teams have already signed up for Synergy's service, and are using it to help them scout for promising high school and international players. Although nothing will ever replace the need to scout players in person, the service has reduced NBA teams' skyrocketing travel costs.

Sources: Scot Petersen, "Dunking the Data," *eWeek*, June 16, 2008; Randall Stross, "Technology to Dissect Every Dunk and Drive," *The New York Times*, April 29, 2007; and www.nba.org, accessed July 27, 2008.

The challenges facing NBA teams show why information systems are so essential today. Like other businesses, professional basketball faces pressures from high costs, especially for team member salaries and travel to search for new talent. Teams are trying to increase revenue by improving employee performance, especially the performance of basketball team members.

The chapter-opening diagram calls attention to important points raised by this case and this chapter. Management was unable to make good decisions about how to improve the performance of teams and of individual players because it lacked precise data about plays. It had to rely on "best guesses" based on videotapes of games. Management found a new information system to provide better information.

The information system is based on a service provided by Synergy Sports Technology. Synergy staff members break down each game into a series of plays and then categorize each play by players, type of play, and the outcome. These data are tagged to the videos they describe to make the videos easy to search. NBA coaches and management can analyze the data to see which offensive and defensive moves are the most effective for each team player. Team members themselves can use iPods to download the videos to help them prepare for games. This innovative solution makes it possible for basketball management to use objective statistical data about players, plays, and outcomes to improve their decision making about what players should or shouldn't do to most effectively counter their opponents.

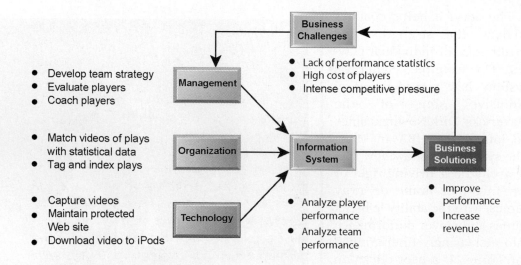

1.1   THE ROLE OF INFORMATION SYSTEMS IN BUSINESS TODAY

I t's not business as usual in America anymore, or the rest of the global economy. In 2008, American businesses will spend about $840 billion on information systems hardware, software and telecommunications equipment. In addition, they will spend another $900 billion on business and management consulting and services—much of which involves redesigning firms' business operations to take advantage of these new technologies. Figure 1-1 shows that between 1980 and 2007, private business investment in information technology consisting of hardware, software, and communications equipment grew from 32 percent to 51 percent of all invested capital.

As managers, most of you will work for firms that are intensively using information systems and making large investments in information technology. You will certainly want to know how to invest this money wisely. If you make wise choices, your firm can outperform competitors. If you make poor choices, you will be wasting valuable capital. This book is dedicated to helping you make wise decisions about information technology and information systems.

HOW INFORMATION SYSTEMS ARE TRANSFORMING BUSINESS

You can see the results of this massive spending around you every day by observing how people conduct business. More wireless cell phone accounts were opened in 2008 than telephone land lines installed. Cell phones, BlackBerrys, iPhones, e-mail, and online conferencing over the Internet have all become essential tools of business. Fifty-eight percent of adult Americans have used a cell phone or mobile handheld device for activities other than voice communication, such as texting, emailing, taking a picture, looking for maps or directions, or recording video (Horrigan, 2008).

By June, 2008, more than 80 million businesses worldwide had dot-com Internet sites registered (60 million in the U.S. alone) (Versign, 2008). Today 138 million Americans shop online, and 117 million have purchased on line. Every day about 34 million Americans go online to research a product or service.

In 2007, FedEx moved over 100 million packages in the United States, mostly overnight, and the United Parcel Service (UPS) moved 3.7 billion packages worldwide. Businesses sought to sense and respond to rapidly changing customer demand, reduce inventories to the lowest possible levels, and achieve higher levels of operational efficiency. Supply chains have become more fast-paced, with companies of all sizes depending on just-in-time inventory to reduce their overhead costs and get to market faster.

As newspaper readership continues to decline, more than 64 million people receive their news online. About 67 million Americans now read blogs, and 21 million write blogs, creating an explosion of new writers and new forms of customer feedback that did not exist five years ago (Pew, 2008). Social networking sites like MySpace and Facebook attract over 70 and 30 million visitors a month, respectively, and businesses are starting to use social networking tools to connect their employees, customers, and managers worldwide.

FIGURE 1-1   INFORMATION TECHNOLOGY CAPITAL INVESTMENT

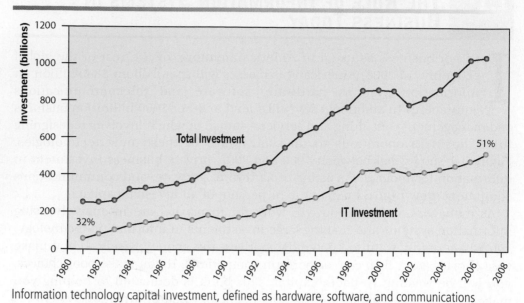

Information technology capital investment, defined as hardware, software, and communications equipment, grew from 32 percent to 51 percent of all invested capital between 1980 and 2008.

Source: Based on data in U.S. Department of Commerce, Bureau of Economic Analysis, *National Income and Product Accounts*, 2008.

E-commerce and Internet advertising are booming: Google's online ad revenues surpassed $16.5 billion in 2007, and Internet advertising continues to grow at more than 25 percent a year, reaching more than $28 billion in revenues in 2008.

New federal security and accounting laws, requiring many businesses to keep e-mail messages for five years, coupled with existing occupational and health laws requiring firms to store employee chemical exposure data for up to 60 years, are spurring the growth of digital information now estimated to be 5 exabytes annually, equivalent to 37,000 new Libraries of Congress.

WHAT'S NEW IN MANAGEMENT INFORMATION SYSTEMS?

Lots! What makes management information systems the most exciting topic in business is the continual change in technology, management use of the technology, and the impact on business success. Old systems are being creatively destroyed, and entirely new systems are taking their place. New industries appear, old ones decline, and successful firms are those who learn how to use the new technologies. Table 1-1 summarizes the major new themes in business uses of information systems. These themes will appear throughout the book in all the chapters, so it might be a good idea to take some time now and discuss these with your professor and other students. You may want to even add to the list.

In the technology area there are three interrelated changes: (1) the emerging mobile digital platform (think iPhones, BlackBerrys, and tiny Web-surfing netbooks), (2) the growth of online software as a service, and (3) the growth in "cloud computing" where more and more business software runs over the Internet. Of course these changes depend on other building-block technologies described in Table 1-1, such as faster processor chips that use much less power.

TABLE 1-1 WHAT'S NEW IN MIS

CHANGE	BUSINESS IMPACT
TECHNOLOGY	
Cloud computing platform emerges as a major business area of innovation	A flexible collection of computers on the Internet begins to perform tasks traditionally performed on corporate computers.
More powerful, energy efficient computer processing and storage devices	Intel's new PC processor chips consume 50% less power, generate 30% less heat, and are 20% faster than the previous models, packing over 400 million transistors on a dual-core chip.
Growth in software as a service (SaaS)	Major business applications are now delivered online as an Internet service rather than as boxed software or custom systems.
Netbooks emerge as a growing presence in the PC marketplace, often using open source software	Small, lightweight, low-cost, energy-efficient, net-centric sub-notebooks use Linux, Google Docs, open source tools, flash memory, and the Internet for their applications, storage, and communications.
A mobile digital platform emerges to compete with the PC as a business system	Apple opens its iPhone software to developers, and then opens an Applications Store on iTunes where business users can download hundreds of applications to support collaboration, location-based services, and communication with colleagues.
MANAGEMENT	
Managers adopt online collaboration and social networking software to improve coordination, collaboration, and knowledge sharing	Google Apps, Google Sites, Microsoft's Office Sharepoint and IBM's Lotus Connections are used by over 100 million business decision makers worldwide to support blogs, project management, online meetings, personal profiles, social bookmarks, and online communities.
Business intelligence applications accelerate	More powerful data analytics and interactive dashboards provide real-time performance information to managers to enhance management control and decision making.
Managers adopt millions of mobile tools such as smartphones and mobile Internet devices to accelerate decision making and improve performance	The emerging mobile platform greatly enhances the accuracy, speed, and richness of decision making as well as responsiveness to customers.
Virtual meetings proliferate	Managers adopt telepresence video conferencing and Web conferencing technologies to reduce travel time and cost while improving collaboration and decision making.
ORGANIZATIONS	
Web 2.0 applications are widely adopted by firms	Web-based services enable employees to interact as online communities using blogs, wikis e-mail, and instant messaging services. Facebook and MySpace create new opportunities for business to collaborate with customers and vendors.
Telework gains momentum in the workplace	The Internet, wireless laptops, iPhones, and BlackBerrys make it possible for growing numbers of people to work away from the traditional office. 55 percent of U.S. businesses have some form of remote work program.
Outsourcing production	Firms learn to use the new technologies to outsource production work to low wage countries.
Co-creation of business value	Sources of business value shift from products to solutions and experiences and from internal sources to networks of suppliers and collaboration with customers. Supply chains and product development become more global and collaborative; customer interactions help firms define new products and services.

YouTube, iPhones and Blackberrys, and Facebook are not just gadgets or entertainment outlets. They represent new emerging computing platforms based on an array of new hardware and software technologies and business investments. Besides being successful products in their own right, these emerging technologies are being adopted by corporations as business tools to improve management and achieve competitive advantages. We call these developments the "emerging mobile platform."

Managers routinely use so-called "Web 2.0" technologies like social networking, collaboration tools, and wikis in order to make better, faster decisions. Millions of managers rely heavily on the mobile digital platform to coordinate vendors, satisfy customers, and manage their employees. For many if not most U.S. managers, a business day without their cell phones or Internet access is unthinkable.

As management behavior changes, how work gets organized, coordinated, and measured also changes. By connecting employees working on teams and projects, the social network is where works gets done, where plans are executed, and where managers manage. Collaboration spaces are where employees meet one another—even when they are separated by continents and time zones. The strength of cloud computing, and the growth of the mobile digital platform means that organizations can rely more on telework, remote work, and distributed decision making. Think decentralization. This same platform means firms can outsource more work, and rely on markets (rather than employees) to build value. It also means that firms can collaborate with suppliers and customers to create new products, or make existing products more efficiently.

All of these changes contribute to a dynamic new global business economy. In fact, without the changes in management information systems just described, the global economy would not succeed.

GLOBALIZATION CHALLENGES AND OPPORTUNITIES: A FLATTENED WORLD

In 1492 Columbus reaffirmed what astronomers were long saying: the world was round and the seas could be safely sailed. As it turned out, the world was populated by peoples and languages living in near total isolation from one another, with great disparities in economic and scientific development. The world trade that ensued after Columbus's voyages has brought these peoples and cultures closer. The "industrial revolution" was really a world-wide phenomenon energized by expansion of trade among nations.

By 2005, journalist Thomas Friedman wrote an influential book declaring the world was now "flat," by which he meant that the Internet and global communications had greatly reduced the economic and cultural advantages of developed countries. U.S. and European countries were in a fight for their economic lives, competing for jobs, markets, resources, and even ideas with highly educated, motivated populations in low-wage areas in the less developed world (Friedman, 2006). This "globalization" presents both challenges and opportunities.

A growing percentage of the economy of the United States and other advanced industrial countries in Europe and Asia depends on imports and exports. In 2009, more than 33 percent of the U.S. economy results from foreign trade, both imports and exports. In Europe and Asia, the number exceeds 50 percent. Many Fortune 500 U.S. firms derive half their revenues from foreign operations. For instance, more than half of Intel's revenues in 2006 came from overseas sales of its microprocessors. Toys for chips: 80 percent of the toys sold in the U.S. are manufactured in China, while about 90 percent of the PCs manufactured in China use American-made Intel or Advanced Micro Design (AMD) chips.

It's not just goods that move across borders. So too do jobs, some of them high-level jobs that pay well and require a college degree. In the past decade the U.S. lost several million manufacturing jobs to offshore, low-wage producers. But manufacturing is now a very small part of U.S. employment (less than 12 percent). In a normal year, about 300,000 service jobs move offshore to lower wage countries, many of them in less-skilled information system occupations, but also including "tradable service" jobs in architecture, financial services, customer call centers, consulting, engineering, and even radiology.

On the plus side, the U.S. economy creates over 3.5 million new jobs a year, and employment in information systems, and the other service occupations listed above, has expanded in sheer numbers, wages, productivity, and quality of work. Outsourcing has actually accelerated the development of new systems in the United States and worldwide.

The challenge for you as a business student is to develop high-level skills through education and on-the-job experience that cannot be outsourced. The challenge for your business is to avoid markets for goods and services that can be produced offshore much less expensively. The opportunities are equally immense. You will find throughout this book examples of companies and individuals who either failed or succeeded in using information systems to adapt to this new global environment.

What does globalization have to do with management information systems? That's simple: everything. The emergence of the Internet into a full-blown international communications system has drastically reduced the costs of operating and transacting on a global scale. Communication between a factory floor in Shanghai and a distribution center in Rapid Falls, South Dakota, is now instant and virtually free. Customers now can shop in a worldwide marketplace, obtaining price and quality information reliably 24 hours a day. Firms producing goods and services on a global scale achieve extraordinary cost reductions by finding low-cost suppliers and managing production facilities in other countries. Internet service firms, such as Google and eBay, are able to replicate their business models and services in multiple countries without having to redesign their expensive fixed-cost information systems infrastructure. Half of the revenue of eBay (as well as General Motors) in 2009 originates outside the United States. Briefly, information systems enable globalization.

THE EMERGING DIGITAL FIRM

All of the changes we have just described, coupled with equally significant organizational redesign, have created the conditions for a fully digital firm. A digital firm can be defined along several dimensions. A **digital firm** is one in which nearly all of the organization's *significant business relationships* with customers, suppliers, and employees are digitally enabled and mediated. *Core business processes* are accomplished through digital networks spanning the entire organization or linking multiple organizations.

Business processes refer to the set of logically related tasks and behaviors that organizations develop over time to produce specific business results and the unique manner in which these activities are organized and coordinated. Developing a new product, generating and fulfilling an order, creating a marketing plan, and hiring an employee are examples of business processes, and the ways organizations accomplish their business processes can be a source

INTERACTIVE SESSION: MANAGEMENT

VIRTUAL MEETINGS: SMART MANAGEMENT

For many businesses, including investment banking, accounting, law, technology services, and management consulting, extensive travel is a fact of life. The expenses incurred by business travel have been steadily rising in recent years, primarily due to increasing energy costs. In an effort to reduce travel expenses, many companies, both large and small, are using videoconferencing and Web conferencing technologies.

A June 2008 report issued by the Global e-Sustainability Initiative and the Climate Group estimated that up to 20 percent of business travel could be replaced by virtual meeting technology.

A videoconference allows individuals at two or more locations to communicate through two-way video and audio transmissions at the same time. The critical feature of videoconferencing is the digital compression of audio and video streams by a device called a codec. Those streams are then divided into packets and transmitted over a network or the Internet. The technology has been plagued by poor audio and video performance in the past, usually related to the speed at which the streams were transmitted, and its cost was prohibitively high for all but the largest and most powerful corporations. Most companies deemed videoconferencing as a poor substitute for face-to-face meetings.

However, vast improvements in videoconferencing and associated technologies have renewed interest in this way of working. Videoconferencing is now growing at an annual rate of 30 percent. Proponents of the technology claim that it does more than simply reduce costs. It allows for 'better' meetings as well: it's easier to meet with partners, suppliers, subsidiaries, and colleagues from within the office or around the world on a more frequent basis, which in most cases simply cannot be reasonably accomplished through travel. You can also meet with contacts that you wouldn't be able to meet at all without videoconferencing technology.

The top-of-the-line videoconferencing technology is known as telepresence. Telepresence strives to make users feel as if they are actually present in a location different from their own. Telepresence products provide the highest-quality videoconferencing available on the market to date. Only a handful of companies, such as Cisco, HP, and Polycom, supply these products. Prices for fully equipped telepresence rooms can run to $500,000.

Companies able to afford this technology report large savings. For example, technology consulting firm Accenture reports that it eliminated expenditures for 240 international trips and 120 domestic flights in a single month. The ability to reach customers and partners is also dramatically increased. Other business travelers report tenfold increases in the number of customers and partners they are able to reach for a fraction of the previous price per person. Cisco has over 200 telepresence rooms and predicts that it saves $100 million in travel costs each year.

Videoconferencing products have not traditionally been feasible for small businesses, but another company, LifeSize, has introduced an affordable line of products as low as $5,000. Reviews of the LifeSize product indicate that when a great deal of movement occurs in a frame, the screen blurs and distorts somewhat. But overall, the product is easy to use and will allow many smaller companies to use a high-quality videoconferencing product.

There are even some free Internet-based options like Skype videoconferencing and ooVoo. These products are of lower quality than traditional videoconferencing products, and they are proprietary, meaning they can only talk to others using that very same system. Most videoconferencing and telepresence products are able to interact with a variety of other devices. Higher-end systems include features like multi-party conferencing, video mail with unlimited storage, no long-distance fees, and a detailed call history.

Companies of all sizes are finding Web-based online meeting tools such as WebEx, Microsoft Office Live Meeting, and Adobe Acrobat Connect especially helpful for training and sales presentations. These products enable participants to share documents and presentations in conjunction with audioconferencing and live video via Webcam. Cornerstone Information Systems, a Bloomington, Indiana business software company with 60 employees, cut its travel costs by 60 percent and the average time to close a new sale by 30 percent by performing many product demonstrations online.

Before setting up videoconferencing or telepresence, it's important for a company to make sure it really needs the technology to ensure that it will be a profitable venture. Companies should determine how their employees conduct meetings, how they communicate and with what technologies, how much travel they do, and their network's capabilities. There are still plenty of times when face-to-face interaction is more desirable, and often traveling to meet a client is essential for cultivating clients and closing sales.

Videoconferencing figures to have an impact on the business world in other ways, as well. More employees may be able to work closer to home and balance their work and personal lives more efficiently; traditional office environments and corporate headquarters may shrink or disappear; and freelancers, contractors, and workers from other countries will become a larger portion of the global economy.

Sources: Steve Lohr, "As Travel Costs Rise, More Meetings Go Virtual," *The New York Times*, July 22, 2008; Karen D. Schwartz, "Videoconferencing on a Budget," *eWeek*, May 29, 2008; and Jim Rapoza, "Videoconferencing Redux," *eWeek*, July 21, 2008; Mike Fratto, "High-Def Conferencing At a Low Price," *Information Week*, July 14, 2008; Marianne Kolbasuk McGee, "Looking Into The Work-Trend Crystal Ball," *Information Week*, June 24, 2008; Eric Krapf, "What's Video Good For?", *Information Week*, July 1, 2008.

CASE STUDY QUESTIONS

1. One consulting firm has predicted that video and Web conferencing will make business travel extinct. Do you agree? Why or why not?

2. What is the distinction between videoconferencing and telepresence?

3. What are the ways in which videoconferencing provides value to a business? Would you consider it smart management? Explain your answer.

4. If you were in charge of a small business, would you choose to implement videoconferencing? What factors would you consider in your decision?

MIS IN ACTION

Explore the WebEx Web site (www.webex.com) and note all of its capabilities for both small and large businesses, then answer the following questions:

1. List and describe its capabilities for small-medium and large businesses. How useful is WebEx? How can it help companies save time and money?

2. Compare WebEx video capabilities with the video-conferencing capabilities described in this case.

3. Describe the steps you would take to prepare for a Web conference as opposed to a face-to-face conference.

of competitive strength. (A detailed discussion of business processes can be found in Chapter 2.)

Key corporate assets—intellectual property, core competencies, and financial and human assets—are managed through digital means. In a digital firm, any piece of information required to support key business decisions is available at any time and anywhere in the firm.

Digital firms sense and respond to their environments far more rapidly than traditional firms, giving them more flexibility to survive in turbulent times. Digital firms offer extraordinary opportunities for more flexible global organization and management. In digital firms, both time shifting and space shifting are the norm. *Time shifting* refers to business being conducted continuously, 24/7, rather than in narrow "work day" time bands of 9 A.M. to 5 P.M. *Space shifting* means that work takes place in a global workshop, as well as within national boundaries. Work is accomplished physically wherever in the world it is best accomplished.

A few firms, such as Cisco Systems and Dell Computers, are close to becoming digital firms, using the Internet to drive every aspect of their business. Most other companies are not fully digital, but they are moving toward close digital integration with suppliers, customers, and employees. Many firms, for example, are replacing traditional face-to-face meetings with "virtual" meetings using videoconferencing and Web conferencing technology. The Interactive Session on Management provides more detail on this topic.

STRATEGIC BUSINESS OBJECTIVES OF INFORMATION SYSTEMS

What makes information systems so essential today? Why are businesses investing so much in information systems and technologies? In the United States, more than 23 million managers and 113 million workers in the labor force rely on information systems to conduct business. Information systems are essential for conducting day-to-day business in the United States and most other advanced countries, as well as achieving strategic business objectives.

Entire sectors of the economy are nearly inconceivable without substantial investments in information systems. E-commerce firms such as Amazon, eBay, Google, and E*Trade simply would not exist. Today's service industries—finance, insurance, and real estate, as well as personal services such as travel, medicine, and education—could not operate without information systems. Similarly, retail firms such as Wal-Mart and Sears and manufacturing firms such as General Motors and General Electric require information systems to survive and prosper. Just like offices, telephones, filing cabinets, and efficient tall buildings with elevators were once the foundations of business in the twentieth century, information technology is a foundation for business in the twenty-first century.

There is a growing interdependence between a firm's ability to use information technology and its ability to implement corporate strategies and achieve corporate goals (see Figure 1-2). What a business would like to do in five years often depends on what its systems will be able to do. Increasing market share, becoming the high-quality or low-cost producer, developing new products, and increasing employee productivity depend more and more on the kinds and quality of information systems in the organization. The more you understand about this relationship, the more valuable you will be as a manager.

Specifically, business firms invest heavily in information systems to achieve six strategic business objectives: operational excellence; new products, services, and business models; customer and supplier intimacy; improved decision making; competitive advantage; and survival.

FIGURE 1-2   THE INTERDEPENDENCE BETWEEN ORGANIZATIONS AND INFORMATION SYSTEMS

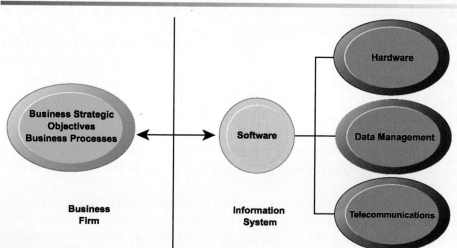

In contemporary systems there is a growing interdependence between a firm's information systems and its business capabilities. Changes in strategy, rules, and business processes increasingly require changes in hardware, software, databases, and telecommunications. Often, what the organization would like to do depends on what its systems will permit it to do.

Operational Excellence

Businesses continuously seek to improve the efficiency of their operations in order to achieve higher profitability. Information systems and technologies are some of the most important tools available to managers for achieving higher levels of efficiency and productivity in business operations, especially when coupled with changes in business practices and management behavior.

Wal-Mart, the largest retailer on Earth, exemplifies the power of information systems coupled with brilliant business practices and supportive management to achieve world-class operational efficiency. In 2007, Wal-Mart achieved close to $379 billion in sales—nearly one-tenth of retail sales in the United States—in large part because of its RetailLink system, which digitally links its suppliers to every one of Wal-Mart's stores. As soon as a customer purchases an item, the supplier monitoring the item knows to ship a replacement to the shelf. Wal-Mart is the most efficient retail store in the industry, achieving sales of more than $28 per square foot, compared to its closest competitor, Target, at $23 a square foot, with other retail firms producing less than $12 a square foot.

New Products, Services, and Business Models

Information systems and technologies are a major enabling tool for firms to create new products and services, as well as entirely new business models. A **business model** describes how a company produces, delivers, and sells a product or service to create wealth.

Today's music industry is vastly different from the industry in 2000. Apple Inc. transformed an old business model of music distribution based on vinyl records, tapes, and CDs into an online, legal distribution model based on its own iPod technology platform. Apple has prospered from a continuing stream of iPod innovations, including the iPod, the iTunes music service, and the iPhone.

Customer and Supplier Intimacy

When a business really knows its customers, and serves them well, the customers generally respond by returning and purchasing more. This raises revenues and profits. Likewise with suppliers: the more a business engages its suppliers, the better the suppliers can provide vital inputs. This lowers costs. How to really know your customers, or suppliers, is a central problem for businesses with millions of offline and online customers.

The Mandarin Oriental in Manhattan and other high-end hotels exemplify the use of information systems and technologies to achieve customer intimacy. These

With its stunning multi-touch display, full Internet browsing, digital camera, and portable music player, Apple's iPhone set a new standard for mobile phones. Other Apple products have transformed the music and entertainment industries.

hotels use computers to keep track of guests' preferences, such as their preferred room temperature, check-in time, frequently dialed telephone numbers, and television programs, and store these data in a giant data repository. Individual rooms in the hotels are networked to a central network server computer so that they can be remotely monitored or controlled. When a customer arrives at one of these hotels, the system automatically changes the room conditions, such as dimming the lights, setting the room temperature, or selecting appropriate music, based on the customer's digital profile. The hotels also analyze their customer data to identify their best customers and to develop individualized marketing campaigns based on customers' preferences.

JC Penney exemplifies the benefits of information systems-enabled supplier intimacy. Every time a dress shirt is bought at a Penney store in the United States, the record of the sale appears immediately on computers in Hong Kong at the TAL Apparel Ltd. supplier, a giant contract manufacturer that produces one in eight dress shirts sold in the United States. TAL runs the numbers through a computer model it developed and then decides how many replacement shirts to make, and in what styles, colors, and sizes. TAL then sends the shirts to each Penney store, bypassing completely the retailer's warehouses. In other words, Penney's shirt inventory is near zero, as is the cost of storing it.

Improved Decision Making

Many business managers operate in an information fog bank, never really having the right information at the right time to make an informed decision. Instead, managers rely on forecasts, best guesses, and luck. The result is over- or underproduction of goods and services, misallocation of resources, and poor response times. These poor outcomes raise costs and lose customers. In the past decade, information systems and technologies have made it possible for managers to use real-time data from the marketplace when making decisions.

For instance, Verizon Corporation, one of the largest regional Bell operating companies in the United States, uses a Web-based digital dashboard to provide managers with precise real-time information on customer complaints, network performance for each locality served, and line outages or storm-damaged lines. Using this information, managers can immediately allocate repair resources to affected areas, inform consumers of repair efforts, and restore service fast.

Information Builders' digital dashboard delivers comprehensive and accurate information for decision making. The graphical overview of key performance indicators helps managers quickly spot areas that need attention.

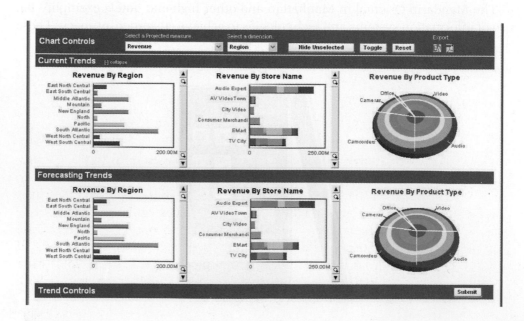

Competitive Advantage

When firms achieve one or more of these business objectives—operational excellence; new products, services, and business models; customer/supplier intimacy; and improved decision making—chances are they have already achieved a competitive advantage. Doing things better than your competitors, charging less for superior products, and responding to customers and suppliers in real time all add up to higher sales and higher profits that your competitors cannot match.

Perhaps no other company exemplifies all of these attributes leading to competitive advantage more than Toyota Motor Company. Toyota has become the world's largest auto maker because of its high level of efficiency and quality. Competitors struggle to keep up. Toyota's legendary Toyota Production System (TPS) focuses on organizing work to eliminate waste, making continuous improvements, and optimizing customer value. Information systems help Toyota implement the TPS and produce vehicles based on what customers have actually ordered.

Survival

Business firms also invest in information systems and technologies because they are necessities of doing business. Sometimes these "necessities" are driven by industry-level changes. For instance, after Citibank introduced the first automatic teller machines (ATMs) in the New York region in 1977 to attract customers through higher service levels, its competitors rushed to provide ATMs to their customers to keep up with Citibank. Today, virtually all banks in the United States have regional ATMs and link to national and international ATM networks, such as CIRRUS. Providing ATM services to retail banking customers is simply a requirement of being in and surviving in the retail banking business.

There are many federal and state statutes and regulations that create a legal duty for companies and their employees to retain records, including digital records. For instance, the Toxic Substances Control Act (1976), which regulates the exposure of U.S. workers to more than 75,000 toxic chemicals, requires firms to retain records on employee exposure for 30 years. The Sarbanes–Oxley Act (2002), which was intended to improve the accountability of public firms and their auditors, requires certified public accounting firms that audit public companies to retain audit working papers and records, including all e-mails, for five years. Many other pieces of federal and state legislation in healthcare, financial services, education, and privacy protection impose significant information retention and reporting requirements on U.S. businesses. Firms turn to information systems and technologies to provide the capability to respond to these

1.2 PERSPECTIVES ON INFORMATION SYSTEMS

So far we've used *information systems* and *technologies* informally without defining the terms. **Information technology (IT)** consists of all the hardware and software that a firm needs to use in order to achieve its business objectives. This includes not only computer machines, disk drives, and handheld mobile devices, but also software, such as the Windows or Linux operating systems, the Microsoft Office desktop productivity suite, and the many thousands of computer programs that can be found in a typical large firm. "Information systems" are more complex and can be best be understood by looking at them from both a technology and a business perspective.

WHAT IS AN INFORMATION SYSTEM?

An **information system** can be defined technically as a set of interrelated components that collect (or retrieve), process, store, and distribute information to support decision making and control in an organization. In addition to supporting decision making, coordination, and control, information systems may also help managers and workers analyze problems, visualize complex subjects, and create new products.

Information systems contain information about significant people, places, and things within the organization or in the environment surrounding it. By **information** we mean data that have been shaped into a form that is meaningful and useful to human beings. **Data**, in contrast, are streams of raw facts representing events occurring in organizations or the physical environment before they have been organized and arranged into a form that people can understand and use.

A brief example contrasting information and data may prove useful. Supermarket checkout counters scan millions of pieces of data from bar codes, which describe each product. Such pieces of data can be totaled and analyzed to provide meaningful information, such as the total number of bottles of dish detergent sold at a particular store, which brands of dish detergent were selling the most rapidly at that store or sales territory, or the total amount spent on that brand of dish detergent at that store or sales region (see Figure 1-3).

Three activities in an information system produce the information that organizations need to make decisions, control operations, analyze problems, and create new products or services. These activities are input, processing, and output (see Figure 1-4). **Input** captures or collects raw data from within the organization or from its external environment. **Processing** converts this raw input into a meaningful form. **Output** transfers the processed information to

FIGURE 1-3   DATA AND INFORMATION

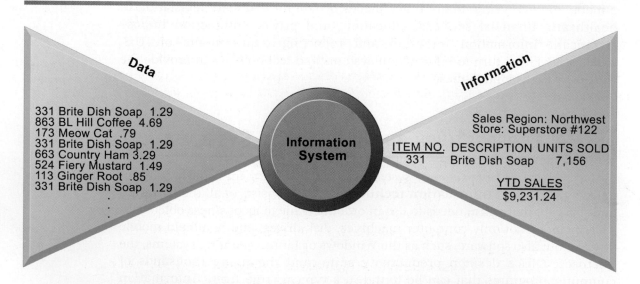

Raw data from a supermarket checkout counter can be processed and organized to produce meaningful information, such as the total unit sales of dish detergent or the total sales revenue from dish detergent for a specific store or sales territory.

FIGURE 1-4   FUNCTIONS OF AN INFORMATION SYSTEM

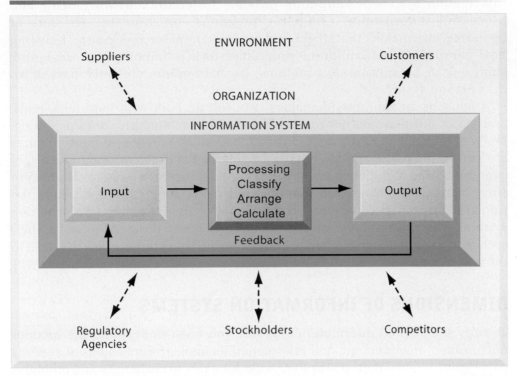

An information system contains information about an organization and its surrounding environment. Three basic activities—input, processing, and output—produce the information organizations need. Feedback is output returned to appropriate people or activities in the organization to evaluate and refine the input. Environmental actors, such as customers, suppliers, competitors, stockholders, and regulatory agencies, interact with the organization and its information systems.

the people who will use it or to the activities for which it will be used. Information systems also require **feedback**, which is output that is returned to appropriate members of the organization to help them evaluate or correct the input stage.

In the NBA teams' system for analyzing basketball moves, there are actually two types of raw input. One consists of all the data about each play entered by Synergy Sports Technology's staff members—the player's name, team, date of game, game location, type of play, other players involved in the play, and the outcome. The other input consists of videos of the plays and games, which are captured as digital points of data for storage, retrieval, and manipulation by the computer.

Synergy Sports Technology server computers store these data and process them to relate data such as the player's name, type of play, and outcome to a specific video clip. The output consists of videos and statistics about specific players, teams, and plays. The system provides meaningful information, such as the number and type of defensive plays that were successful against a specific player, what types of offensive plays were the most successful against a specific team, or comparisons of individual player and team performance in home and away games.

Although computer-based information systems use computer technology to process raw data into meaningful information, there is a sharp distinction between a computer and a computer program on the one hand, and an information system on the other. Electronic computers and related software programs are the technical foundation, the tools and materials, of modern information systems. Computers provide the equipment for storing and processing information. Computer programs, or software, are sets of operating instructions that direct and control computer processing. Knowing how computers and computer programs work is important in designing solutions to organizational problems, but computers are only part of an information system.

A house is an appropriate analogy. Houses are built with hammers, nails, and wood, but these do not make a house. The architecture, design, setting, landscaping, and all of the decisions that lead to the creation of these features are part of the house and are crucial for solving the problem of putting a roof over one's head. Computers and programs are the hammer, nails, and lumber of computer-based information systems, but alone they cannot produce the information a particular organization needs. To understand information systems, you must understand the problems they are designed to solve, their architectural and design elements, and the organizational processes that lead to these solutions.

DIMENSIONS OF INFORMATION SYSTEMS

To fully understand information systems, you must understand the broader organization, management, and information technology dimensions of systems (see Figure 1-5) and their power to provide solutions to challenges and problems in the business environment. We refer to this broader understanding of information systems, which encompasses an understanding of the management and organizational dimensions of systems as well as the technical dimensions of systems, as **information systems literacy**. **Computer literacy**, in contrast, focuses primarily on knowledge of information technology.

The field of **management information systems (MIS)** tries to achieve this broader information systems literacy. MIS deals with behavioral issues as well

FIGURE 1-5   INFORMATION SYSTEMS ARE MORE THAN COMPUTERS

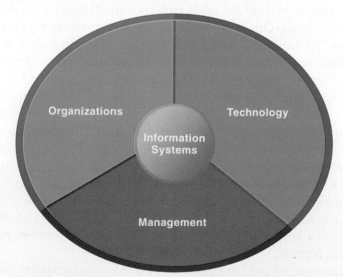

Using information systems effectively requires an understanding of the organization, management, and information technology shaping the systems. An information system creates value for the firm as an organizational and management solution to challenges posed by the environment.

as technical issues surrounding the development, use, and impact of information systems used by managers and employees in the firm.

Let's examine each of the dimensions of information systems—organizations, management, and information technology.

Organizations

Information systems are an integral part of organizations. Indeed, for some companies, such as credit reporting firms, without an information system, there would be no business. The key elements of an organization are its people, structure, business processes, politics, and culture. We introduce these components of organizations here and describe them in greater detail in Chapters 2 and 3.

Organizations have a structure that is composed of different levels and specialties. Their structures reveal a clear-cut division of labor. Authority and responsibility in a business firm are organized as a hierarchy, or a pyramid structure. The upper levels of the hierarchy consist of managerial, professional, and technical employees, whereas the lower levels consist of operational personnel.

Senior management makes long-range strategic decisions about products and services as well as ensures financial performance of the firm. **Middle management** carries out the programs and plans of senior management and **operational management** is responsible for monitoring the daily activities of the business. **Knowledge workers**, such as engineers, scientists, or architects, design products or services and create new knowledge for the firm, whereas **data workers**, such as secretaries or clerks, assist with paperwork at all levels of the firm. **Production or service workers** actually produce the product and deliver the service (see Figure 1-6).

FIGURE 1-6   LEVELS IN A FIRM

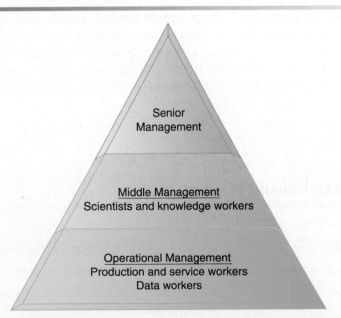

Business organizations are hierarchies consisting of three principal levels: senior management, middle management, and operational management. Information systems serve each of these levels. Scientists and knowledge workers often work with middle management.

Experts are employed and trained for different business functions. The major **business functions**, or specialized tasks performed by business organizations, consist of sales and marketing, manufacturing and production, finance and accounting, and human resources (see Table 1-2). Chapter 2 provides more detail on these business functions and the ways in which they are supported by information systems.

An organization coordinates work through its hierarchy and through its business processes, which are logically related tasks and behaviors for accomplishing work. Developing a new product, fulfilling an order, or hiring a new employee are examples of business processes.

Most organizations' business processes include formal rules that have been developed over a long time for accomplishing tasks. These rules guide employees in a variety of procedures, from writing an invoice to responding to customer complaints. Some of these business processes have been written down, but others are informal work practices, such as a requirement to return telephone calls from co-workers or customers, that are not formally documented. Information systems automate many business processes. For instance, how a customer receives credit or how a customer is billed is often determined by an information system that incorporates a set of formal business processes.

Each organization has a unique **culture**, or fundamental set of assumptions, values, and ways of doing things, that has been accepted by most of its members. You can see organizational culture at work by looking around your university or college. Some bedrock assumptions of university life are that professors know more than students, the reasons students attend college is to learn, and that classes follow a regular schedule.

Parts of an organization's culture can always be found embedded in its information systems. For instance, UPS's concern with placing service to the customer first is an aspect of its organizational culture that can be found in the company's package tracking systems, which we describe later in this section.

Different levels and specialties in an organization create different interests and points of view. These views often conflict over how the company should be run and how resources and rewards should be distributed. Conflict is the basis for organizational politics. Information systems come out of this cauldron of differing perspectives, conflicts, compromises, and agreements that are a natural part of all organizations. In Chapter 3, we examine these features of organizations and their role in the development of information systems in greater detail.

TABLE 1-2 MAJOR BUSINESS FUNCTIONS

FUNCTION	PURPOSE
Sales and marketing	Selling the organization's products and services
Manufacturing and production	Producing and delivering products and services
Finance and accounting	Managing the organization's financial assets and maintaining the organization's financial records
Human resources	Attracting, developing, and maintaining the organization's labor force; maintaining employee records

Management

Management's job is to make sense out of the many situations faced by organizations, make decisions, and formulate action plans to solve organizational problems. Managers perceive business challenges in the environment; they set the organizational strategy for responding to those challenges; and they allocate the human and financial resources to coordinate the work and achieve success. Throughout, they must exercise responsible leadership. The business information systems described in this book reflect the hopes, dreams, and realities of real-world managers.

But managers must do more than manage what already exists. They must also create new products and services and even re-create the organization from time to time. A substantial part of management responsibility is creative work driven by new knowledge and information. Information technology can play a powerful role in helping managers design and deliver new products and services and redirecting and redesigning their organizations. Chapter 12 treats management decision making in detail.

Technology

Information technology is one of many tools managers use to cope with change. **Computer hardware** is the physical equipment used for input, processing, and output activities in an information system. It consists of the following: computers of various sizes and shapes (including mobile handheld devices); various input, output, and storage devices; and telecommunications devices that link computers together.

Computer software consists of the detailed, preprogrammed instructions that control and coordinate the computer hardware components in an information system. Chapter 5 describes the contemporary software and hardware platforms used by firms today in greater detail.

Data management technology consists of the software governing the organization of data on physical storage media. More detail on data organization and access methods can be found in Chapter 6.

Networking and telecommunications technology, consisting of both physical devices and software, links the various pieces of hardware and transfers data from one physical location to another. Computers and communications equipment can be connected in networks for sharing voice, data, images, sound, and video. A **network** links two or more computers to share data or resources, such as a printer.

The world's largest and most widely used network is the **Internet**. The Internet is a global "network of networks" that uses universal standards (described in Chapter 7) to connect millions of different networks with more than 1.4 billion users in over 230 countries around the world.

The Internet has created a new "universal" technology platform on which to build new products, services, strategies, and business models. This same technology platform has internal uses, providing the connectivity to link different systems and networks within the firm. Internal corporate networks based on Internet technology are called **intranets**. Private intranets extended to authorized users outside the organization are called **extranets**, and firms use such networks to coordinate their activities with other firms for making purchases, collaborating on design, and other interorganizational work. For most business firms today, using Internet technology is both a business necessity and a competitive advantage.

The **World Wide Web** is a service provided by the Internet that uses universally accepted standards for storing, retrieving, formatting, and displaying information in a page format on the Internet. Web pages contain text, graphics, animations, sound, and video and are linked to other Web pages. By clicking on highlighted words or buttons on a Web page, you can link to related pages to find additional information and links to other locations on the Web. The Web can serve as the foundation for new kinds of information systems such as UPS's Web-based package tracking system described in the following Interactive Session.

All of these technologies, along with the people required to run and manage them, represent resources that can be shared throughout the organization and constitute the firm's **information technology (IT) infrastructure**. The IT infrastructure provides the foundation, or *platform*, on which the firm can build its specific information systems. Each organization must carefully design and manage its information technology infrastructure so that it has the set of technology services it needs for the work it wants to accomplish with information systems. Chapters 5 through 8 of this text examine each major technology component of information technology infrastructure and show how they all work together to create the technology platform for the organization.

The Interactive Session on Technology describes some of the typical technologies used in computer-based information systems today. United Parcel Service (UPS) invests heavily in information systems technology to make its business more efficient and customer oriented. It uses an array of information technologies including bar code scanning systems, wireless networks, large mainframe computers, handheld computers, the Internet, and many different pieces of software for tracking packages, calculating fees, maintaining customer accounts, and managing logistics.

Let's identify the organization, management, and technology elements in the UPS package tracking system we have just described. The organization element anchors the package tracking system in UPS's sales and production functions (the main product of UPS is a service—package delivery). It specifies the required procedures for identifying packages with both sender and recipient information, taking inventory, tracking the packages en route, and providing package status reports for UPS customers and customer service representatives.

The system must also provide information to satisfy the needs of managers and workers. UPS drivers need to be trained in both package pickup and delivery procedures and in how to use the package tracking system so that they can work efficiently and effectively. UPS customers may need some training to use UPS in-house package tracking software or the UPS Web site.

UPS's management is responsible for monitoring service levels and costs and for promoting the company's strategy of combining low cost and superior service. Management decided to use computer systems to increase the ease of sending a package using UPS and of checking its delivery status, thereby reducing delivery costs and increasing sales revenues.

The technology supporting this system consists of handheld computers, bar code scanners, wired and wireless communications networks, desktop computers, UPS's central computer, storage technology for the package delivery data, UPS in-house package tracking software, and software to access the World Wide Web. The result is an information system solution to the business challenge of providing a high level of service with low prices in the face of mounting competition.

INTERACTIVE SESSION: TECHNOLOGY

UPS COMPETES GLOBALLY WITH INFORMATION TECHNOLOGY

United Parcel Service (UPS) started out in 1907 in a closet-sized basement office. Jim Casey and Claude Ryan—two teenagers from Seattle with two bicycles and one phone—promised the "best service and lowest rates." UPS has used this formula successfully for more than 90 years to become the world's largest ground and air package-distribution company. It is a global enterprise with more than 425,000 employees, 93,000 vehicles, and the world's ninth largest airline.

Today UPS delivers more than 15 million parcels and documents each day in the United States and more than 200 other countries and territories. The firm has been able to maintain leadership in small-package delivery services despite stiff competition from FedEx and Airborne Express by investing heavily in advanced information technology. UPS spends more than $1 billion each year to maintain a high level of customer service while keeping costs low and streamlining its overall operations.

It all starts with the scannable bar-coded label attached to a package, which contains detailed information about the sender, the destination, and when the package should arrive. Customers can download and print their own labels using special software provided by UPS or by accessing the UPS Web site. Before the package is even picked up, information from the "smart" label is transmitted to one of UPS's computer centers in Mahwah, New Jersey, or Alpharetta, Georgia, and sent to the distribution center nearest its final destination. Dispatchers at this center download the label data and use special software to create the most efficient delivery route for each driver that considers traffic, weather conditions, and the location of each stop. UPS estimates its delivery trucks save 28 million miles and burn 3 million fewer gallons of fuel each year as a result of using this technology.

The first thing a UPS driver picks up each day is a handheld computer called a Delivery Information Acquisition Device (DIAD), which can access one of the wireless networks cell phones rely on. As soon as the driver logs on, his or her day's route is downloaded onto the handheld. The DIAD also automatically captures customers' signatures along with pickup and delivery information. Package tracking information is then transmitted to UPS's computer network for storage and processing. From there, the information can be accessed worldwide to provide proof of delivery to customers or to respond to customer queries. It usually takes less than 60 seconds from the time a driver presses "complete" on a DIAD for the new information to be available on the Web.

Through its automated package tracking system, UPS can monitor and even re-route packages throughout the delivery process. At various points along the route from sender to receiver, bar code devices scan shipping information on the package label and feed data about the progress of the package into the central computer. Customer service representatives are able to check the status of any package from desktop computers linked to the central computers and respond immediately to inquiries from customers. UPS customers can also access this information from the company's Web site using their own computers or wireless devices such as cell phones.

Anyone with a package to ship can access the UPS Web site to track packages, check delivery routes, calculate shipping rates, determine time in transit, print labels, and schedule a pickup. The data collected at the UPS Web site are transmitted to the UPS central computer and then back to the customer after processing. UPS also provides tools that enable customers, such Cisco Systems, to embed UPS functions, such as tracking and cost calculations, into their own Web sites so that they can track shipments without visiting the UPS site.

UPS is now leveraging its decades of expertise managing its own global delivery network to manage logistics and supply chain activities for other companies. It created a UPS Supply Chain Solutions division that provides a complete bundle of standardized services to subscribing companies at a fraction of what it would cost to build their own systems and infrastructure. These services include supply chain design and management, freight forwarding, customs brokerage, mail services, multimodal transportation, and financial services, in addition to logistics services.

Hired Hand Technologies, a Bremen, Alabama-based manufacturer of agricultural and horticultural equipment, uses UPS Freight services not only to track shipments but also to build its weekly manufacturing plans. UPS provides up-to-the-minute information about exactly when parts are arriving within 20 seconds.

Sources: United Parcel Service, "Powering Up the Supply Chain," *UPS Compass*, Winter 2008 and "LTL's High-Tech Infusion," *UPS Compass*, Spring 2007; Claudia Deutsch, "*Still Brown, but Going High Tech*," *The New York Times*, July 12, 2007; and www.ups.com, accessed July 26, 2008.

CASE STUDY QUESTIONS

1. What are the inputs, processing, and outputs of UPS's package tracking system?

2. What technologies are used by UPS? How are these technologies related to UPS's business strategy?

3. What problems do UPS's information systems solve? What would happen if these systems were not available?

MIS IN ACTION

Explore the UPS Web site (www.ups.com) and answer the following questions:

1. What kind of information and services does the Web site provide for individuals, small businesses, and large businesses? List these services and write several paragraphs describing one of them, such as UPS Trade Direct or Automated Shipment Processing. Explain how you or your business would benefit from the service.

2. Explain how the Web site helps UPS achieve some or all of the strategic business objectives we described earlier in this chapter. What would be the impact on UPS's business if this Web site were not available?

IT ISN'T JUST TECHNOLOGY: A BUSINESS PERSPECTIVE ON INFORMATION SYSTEMS

Managers and business firms invest in information technology and systems because they provide real economic value to the business. The decision to build or maintain an information system assumes that the returns on this investment will be superior to other investments in buildings, machines, or other assets. These superior returns will be expressed as increases in productivity, as increases in revenues (which will increase the firm's stock market value), or perhaps as superior long-term strategic positioning of the firm in certain markets (which produce superior revenues in the future).

Using a handheld computer called a Delivery Information Acquisition Device (DIAD), UPS drivers automatically capture customers' signatures along with pickup, delivery, and time card information. UPS information systems use these data to track packages while they are being transported.

We can see that from a business perspective, an information system is an important instrument for creating value for the firm. Information systems enable the firm to increase its revenue or decrease its costs by providing information that helps managers make better decisions or that improves the execution of business processes. For example, the information system for analyzing supermarket checkout data illustrated in Figure 1-3 can increase firm profitability by helping managers make better decisions on which products to stock and promote in retail supermarkets.

Every business has an information value chain, illustrated in Figure 1-7, in which raw information is systematically acquired and then transformed through various stages that add value to that information. The value of an information system to a business, as well as the decision to invest in any new information system, is, in large part, determined by the extent to which the system will lead to better management decisions, more efficient business processes, and higher firm profitability. Although there are other reasons why systems are built, their primary purpose is to contribute to corporate value.

From a business perspective, information systems are part of a series of value-adding activities for acquiring, transforming, and distributing information that managers can use to improve decision making, enhance organizational performance, and, ultimately, increase firm profitability.

The business perspective calls attention to the organizational and managerial nature of information systems. An information system represents an organizational and management solution, based on information technology, to a

FIGURE 1-7   THE BUSINESS INFORMATION VALUE CHAIN

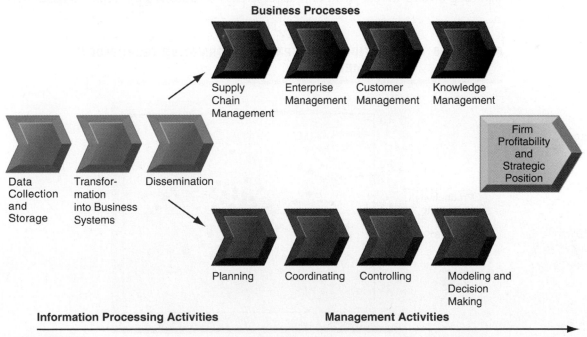

From a business perspective, information systems are part of a series of value-adding activities for acquiring, transforming, and distributing information that managers can use to improve decision making, enhance organizational performance, and, ultimately, increase firm profitability.

challenge or problem posed by the environment. Every chapter in this book begins with short case study that illustrates this concept. A diagram at the beginning of each chapter illustrates the relationship between a business challenge and resulting management and organizational decisions to use IT as a solution to challenges generated by the business environment. You can use this diagram as a starting point for analyzing any information system or information system problem you encounter.

Review the diagram at the beginning of this chapter. The diagram shows how the NBA's systems solved the business problem presented by intense competitive pressures of professional sports, the high cost of professional basketball players, and incomplete data on team and player performance. Its system provides a solution that takes advantage of computer capabilities for processing digital video data and linking them to team and player data. It helps NBA coaches and managers make better decisions about how to best use the talents of their players in both offensive and defensive maneuvers. The diagram also illustrates how management, technology, and organizational elements work together to create the systems.

COMPLEMENTARY ASSETS: ORGANIZATIONAL CAPITAL AND THE RIGHT BUSINESS MODEL

Awareness of the organizational and managerial dimensions of information systems can help us understand why some firms achieve better results from their information systems than others. Studies of returns from information technology investments show that there is considerable variation in the returns firms receive (see Figure 1-8). Some firms invest a great deal and receive a great deal (quadrant 2); others invest an equal amount and receive few returns (quadrant 4). Still other firms invest little and receive much (quadrant 1), whereas others invest little and receive little (quadrant 3). This suggests that

FIGURE 1-8 **VARIATION IN RETURNS ON INFORMATION TECHNOLOGY INVESTMENT**

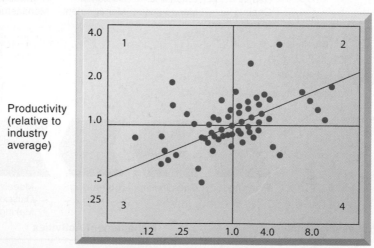

Although, on average, investments in information technology produce returns far above those returned by other investments, there is considerable variation across firms.

Source: Based on Brynjolfsson and Hitt (2000).

investing in information technology does not by itself guarantee good returns. What accounts for this variation among firms?

The answer lies in the concept of complementary assets. Information technology investments alone cannot make organizations and managers more effective unless they are accompanied by supportive values, structures, and behavior patterns in the organization and other complementary assets. Business firms need to change how they do business before they can really reap the advantages of new information technologies.

Some firms fail to adopt the right business model that suits the new technology, or seek to preserve an old business model that is doomed by new technology. For instance, recording label companies refused to change their old business model which was based on physical music stores for distribution rather than adopt a new online distribution model. As a result, online legal music sales are dominated not by record companies but by a technology company called Apple Computer.

Complementary assets are those assets required to derive value from a primary investment (Teece, 1988). For instance, to realize value from automobiles requires substantial complementary investments in highways, roads, gasoline stations, repair facilities, and a legal regulatory structure to set standards and control drivers.

Recent research on business information technology investment indicates that firms that support their technology investments with investments in complementary assets, such as new business models, new business processes, management behavior, organizational culture, or training, receive superior returns, whereas those firms failing to make these complementary investments receive less or no returns on their information technology investments (Brynjolfsson, 2003; Brynjolfsson and Hitt, 2000; Davern and Kauffman, 2000; Laudon, 1974). These investments in organization and management are also known as **organizational and management capital**.

TABLE 1-3 COMPLEMENTARY SOCIAL, MANAGERIAL, AND ORGANIZATIONAL ASSETS REQUIRED TO OPTIMIZE RETURNS FROM INFORMATION TECHNOLOGY INVESTMENTS

Organizational assets	Supportive organizational culture that values efficiency and effectiveness Appropriate business model Efficient business processes Decentralized authority Distributed decision-making rights Strong IS development team
Managerial assets	Strong senior management support for technology investment and change Incentives for management innovation Teamwork and collaborative work environments Training programs to enhance management decision skills Management culture that values flexibility and knowledge-based decision making.
Social assets	The Internet and telecommunications infrastructure IT-enriched educational programs raising labor force computer literacy Standards (both government and private sector) Laws and regulations creating fair, stable market environments Technology and service firms in adjacent markets to assist implementation

Table 1-3 lists the major complementary investments that firms need to make to realize value from their information technology investments. Some of this investment involves tangible assets, such as buildings, machinery, and tools. However, the value of investments in information technology depends to a large extent on complementary investments in management and organization.

Key organizational complementary investments are a supportive business culture that values efficiency and effectiveness, an appropriate business model, efficient business processes, decentralization of authority, highly distributed decision rights, and a strong information system (IS) development team.

Important managerial complementary assets are strong senior management support for change, incentive systems that monitor and reward individual innovation, an emphasis on teamwork and collaboration, training programs, and a management culture that values flexibility and knowledge.

Important social investments (not made by the firm but by the society at large, other firms, governments, and other key market actors) are the Internet and the supporting Internet culture, educational systems, network and computing standards, regulations and laws, and the presence of technology and service firms.

Throughout the book we emphasize a framework of analysis that considers technology, management, and organizational assets and their interactions. Perhaps the single most important theme in the book, reflected in case studies and exercises, is that managers need to consider the broader organization and management dimensions of information systems to understand current problems as well as to derive substantial above-average returns from their information technology investments. As you will see throughout the text, firms that can address these related dimensions of the IT investment are, on average, richly rewarded.

1.3 CONTEMPORARY APPROACHES TO INFORMATION SYSTEMS

The study of information systems is a multidisciplinary field. No single theory or perspective dominates. Figure 1-9 illustrates the major disciplines that contribute problems, issues, and solutions in the study of information systems. In general, the field can be divided into technical and behavioral approaches. Information systems are sociotechnical systems. Though they are composed of machines, devices, and "hard" physical technology, they require substantial social, organizational, and intellectual investments to make them work properly.

TECHNICAL APPROACH

The technical approach to information systems emphasizes mathematically based models to study information systems, as well as the physical technology and formal capabilities of these systems. The disciplines that contribute to the technical approach are computer science, management science, and operations research.

Computer science is concerned with establishing theories of computability, methods of computation, and methods of efficient data storage and access. Management science emphasizes the development of models for decision-making and management practices. Operations research focuses

FIGURE 1-9   CONTEMPORARY APPROACHES TO INFORMATION SYSTEMS

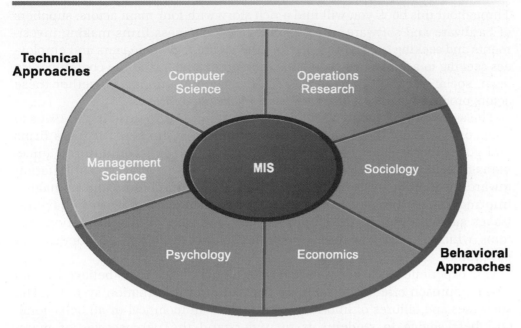

The study of information systems deals with issues and insights contributed from technical and behavioral disciplines.

on mathematical techniques for optimizing selected parameters of organizations, such as transportation, inventory control, and transaction costs.

BEHAVIORAL APPROACH

An important part of the information systems field is concerned with behavioral issues that arise in the development and long-term maintenance of information systems. Issues such as strategic business integration, design, implementation, utilization, and management cannot be explored usefully with the models used in the technical approach. Other behavioral disciplines contribute important concepts and methods.

For instance, sociologists study information systems with an eye toward how groups and organizations shape the development of systems and also how systems affect individuals, groups, and organizations. Psychologists study information systems with an interest in how human decision makers perceive and use formal information. Economists study information systems with an interest in understanding the production of digital goods, the dynamics of digital markets, and understanding how new information systems change the control and cost structures within the firm.

The behavioral approach does not ignore technology. Indeed, information systems technology is often the stimulus for a behavioral problem or issue. But the focus of this approach is generally not on technical solutions. Instead, it concentrates on changes in attitudes, management and organizational policy, and behavior.

APPROACH OF THIS TEXT: SOCIOTECHNICAL SYSTEMS

Throughout this book you will find a rich story with four main actors: suppliers of hardware and software (the technologists); business firms making investments and seeking to obtain value from the technology; managers and employees seeking to achieve business value (and other goals); and the contemporary legal, social, and cultural context (the firm's environment). Together these actors produce what we call *management information systems.*

The study of management information systems (MIS) arose in the 1970s to focus on the use of computer-based information systems in business firms and government agencies. MIS combines the work of computer science, management science, and operations research with a practical orientation toward developing system solutions to real-world problems and managing information technology resources. It is also concerned with behavioral issues surrounding the development, use, and impact of information systems, which are typically discussed in the fields of sociology, economics, and psychology.

Our experience as academics and practitioners leads us to believe that no single approach effectively captures the reality of information systems. The successes and failures of information are rarely all technical or all behavioral. Our best advice to students is to understand the perspectives of many disciplines. Indeed, the challenge and excitement of the information systems field is that it requires an appreciation and tolerance of many different approaches.

The view we adopt in this book is best characterized as the **sociotechnical view** of systems. In this view, optimal organizational performance is achieved by jointly optimizing both the social and technical systems used in production.

Adopting a sociotechnical systems perspective helps to avoid a purely technological approach to information systems. For instance, the fact that information technology is rapidly declining in cost and growing in power does not necessarily or easily translate into productivity enhancement or bottom-line profits. The fact that a firm has recently installed an enterprise-wide financial reporting system does not necessarily mean that it will be used, or used effectively. Likewise, the fact that a firm has recently introduced new business procedures and processes does not necessarily mean employees will be more productive in the absence of investments in new information systems to enable those processes.

In this book, we stress the need to optimize the firm's performance as a whole. Both the technical and behavioral components need attention. This means that technology must be changed and designed in such a way as to fit organizational and individual needs. Sometimes, the technology may have to be "de-optimized" to accomplish this fit. For instance, mobile phone users adapt this technology to their personal needs, and as a result manufacturers quickly seek to adjust the technology to conform with user expectations. Organizations and individuals must also be changed through training, learning, and planned organizational change to allow the technology to operate and prosper. Figure 1-10 illustrates this process of mutual adjustment in a sociotechnical system.

FIGURE 1-10   A SOCIOTECHNICAL PERSPECTIVE ON INFORMATION SYSTEMS

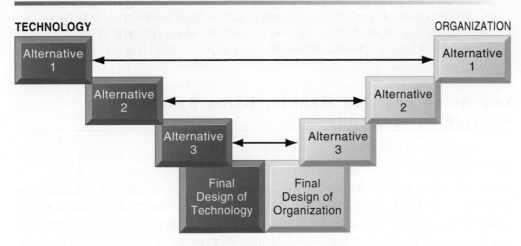

In a sociotechnical perspective, the performance of a system is optimized when both the technology and the organization mutually adjust to one another until a satisfactory fit is obtained.

1.4   HANDS-ON MIS PROJECTS

The projects in this section give you hands-on experience in analyzing financial reporting and inventory management problems, using data management software to improve management decision making about increasing sales, and using Internet software for developing shipping budgets.

Management Decision Problems

1. Snyders of Hanover, which sells more than 78 million bags of pretzels, snack chips, and organic snack items each year, had its financial department use spreadsheets and manual processes for much of its data gathering and reporting. Hanover's financial analyst would spend the entire final week of every month collecting spreadsheets from the heads of more than 50 departments worldwide. She would then consolidate and re-enter all the data into another spreadsheet, which would serve as the company's monthly profit-and-loss statement. If a department needed to update its data after submitting the spreadsheet to the main office, the analyst had to return the original spreadsheet and wait for the department to re-submit its data before finally submitting the updated data in the consolidated document. Assess the impact of this situation on business performance and management decision making.

2. Dollar General Corporation operates deep discount stores offering housewares, cleaning supplies, clothing, health and beauty aids, and packaged food, with most items selling for $1. Its business model calls for keeping costs as low as possible. Although the company uses information systems (such as a point-of-sale system to track sales at the register), it deploys them very sparingly to keep expenditures to the minimum. The company has no automated method for keeping track of inventory at each store. Managers know approximately how many cases of a particular product

the store is supposed to receive when a delivery truck arrives, but the stores lack technology for scanning the cases or verifying the item count inside the cases. Merchandise losses from theft or other mishaps have been rising and now represent over 3 percent of total sales. What decisions have to be made before investing in an information system solution?

Improving Decision Making: Using Databases to Analyze Sales Trends

Software skills: Database querying and reporting
Business skills: Sales trend analysis

Effective information systems transform data into meaningful information for decisions that improve business performance. At the Laudon Web site for Chapter 1, you can find a Store and Regional Sales Database with raw data on weekly store sales of computer equipment in various sales regions. A sample is shown below, but the Web site may have a more recent version of this database for this exercise. The database includes fields for store identification number, sales region number, item number, item description, unit price, units sold, and the weekly sales period when the sales were made. Develop some reports and queries to make this information more useful for running the business. Try to use the information in the database to support decisions on which products to restock, which stores and sales regions would benefit from additional marketing and promotional campaigns, which times of the year products should be offered at full price, and which times of the year products should be discounted. Modify the database table, if necessary, to provide all of the information you require. Print your reports and results of queries.

Store & Region Sales Database1							
II ▾	Store ▾	Sales Reg ▾	Item I ▾	Item Descrip ▾	Unit Pr ▾	Units S ▾	Week Enc ▾
1	1	South	2005	17" Monitor	$229.00	28	10/27/2008
2	1	South	2005	17" Monitor	$229.00	30	11/24/2008
3	1	South	2005	17" Monitor	$229.00	9	12/29/2008
4	1	South	3006	101 Keyboard	$19.95	30	10/27/2008
5	1	South	3006	101 Keyboard	$19.95	35	11/24/2008
6	1	South	3006	101 Keyboard	$19.95	39	12/29/2008
7	1	South	6050	PC Mouse	$8.95	28	10/27/2008
8	1	South	6050	PC Mouse	$8.95	3	11/24/2008
9	1	South	6050	PC Mouse	$8.95	38	12/29/2008
10	1	South	8500	Desktop CPU	$849.95	25	10/27/2008
11	1	South	8500	Desktop CPU	$849.95	27	11/24/2008
12	1	South	8500	Desktop CPU	$849.95	33	12/29/2008
13	2	South	2005	17" Monitor	$229.00	8	10/27/2008
14	2	South	2005	17" Monitor	$229.00	8	11/24/2008
15	2	South	2005	17" Monitor	$229.00	10	12/29/2008
16	2	South	3006	101 Keyboard	$19.95	8	10/27/2008
17	2	South	3006	101 Keyboard	$19.95	8	11/24/2008
18	2	South	3006	101 Keyboard	$19.95	8	12/29/2008
19	2	South	6050	PC Mouse	$8.95	9	10/27/2008

Record: I◄ ◄ 1 of 96 ► ►I ►✶ No Filter Search

Achieving Operational Excellence: Using Internet Tools to Budget for Shipping Costs

Software skills: Internet-based software
Business skills: Shipping cost budgeting

You are the shipping clerk of a small firm that prints, binds, and ships popular books for a midlevel publisher. Your production facilities are located in Albany, New York (ZIP code 12250). Your customers' warehouses are located in Irving, Texas (75015); Charlotte, North Carolina (28201); Sioux Falls, South Dakota (57117); and Portland, Oregon (97202). The production facility operates 250 days per year. Your books are usually shipped in one of two sized packages:

- Height: 9 inches, Length: 13 inches, Width: 17 inches, Weight: 45 pounds
- Height: 10 inches, Length: 6 inches, Width: 12 inches, Weight: 16 pounds

The company ships about four of the 45-pound boxes to each of the warehouses on an average day and about eight 16-pound boxes.

Your task is to select the best shipper for your company. Compare three shippers, such as FedEx (www.fedex.com), UPS (www.ups.com), and the U.S. Postal Service (www.usps.gov). Consider not only costs but also such issues as delivery speed, pickup schedules, drop-off locations, tracking ability, and ease of use of the Web site. Which service did you select? Explain why.

LEARNING TRACK MODULES

The following Learning Tracks provide content relevant to topics covered in this chapter:

1. How Much Does IT Matter?
2. Information Systems and Your Career

Review Summary

1. *How are information systems transforming business and what is their relationship to globalization?*

   E-mail, online conferencing, and cell phones have become essential tools for conducting business. Information systems are the foundation of fast-paced supply chains. The Internet allows many businesses to buy, sell, advertise, and solicit customer feedback online. Organizations are trying to become more competitive and efficient by digitally enabling their core business processes and evolving into digital firms. The Internet has stimulated globalization by dramatically reducing the costs of producing, buying, and selling goods on a global scale. New information system trends include the emerging mobile digital platform, online software as a service, and cloud computing.

2. *Why are information systems so essential for running and managing a business today?*

   Information systems are a foundation for conducting business today. In many industries, survival and the ability to achieve strategic business goals are difficult without extensive use of information technology. Businesses today use information systems to achieve six major objectives: operational excellence; new products, services, and business models; customer/supplier intimacy; improved decision making; competitive advantage; and day-to-day survival.

3. *What exactly is an information system? How does it work? What are its management, organization, and technology components?*

   From a technical perspective, an information system collects, stores, and disseminates information from an organization's environment and internal operations to support organizational functions and decision making, communication, coordination, control, analysis, and visualization. Information systems transform raw data into useful information through three basic activities: input, processing, and output.

   From a business perspective, an information system provides a solution to a problem or challenge facing a firm and represents a combination of management, organization, and technology elements. The management dimension of information systems involves issues such as leadership, strategy, and management behavior. The technology dimension consists of computer hardware, software, data management technology, and networking/telecommunications technology (including the Internet). The organization dimension of information systems involves issues such as the organization's hierarchy, functional specialties, business processes, culture, and political interest groups.

4. *What are complementary assets? Why are complementary assets essential for ensuring that information systems provide genuine value for an organization?*

   In order to obtain meaningful value from information systems, organizations must support their technology investments with appropriate complementary investments in organizations and management. These complementary assets include new business models and business processes, supportive organizational culture and management behavior, appropriate technology standards, regulations, and laws. New information technology investments are unlikely to produce high returns unless businesses make the appropriate managerial and organizational changes to support the technology.

5. *What academic disciplines are used to study information systems? How does each contribute to an understanding of information systems? What is a sociotechnical systems perspective?*

   The study of information systems deals with issues and insights contributed from technical and behavioral disciplines. The disciplines that contribute to the technical approach focusing on formal models and capabilities of systems are computer science, management science, and operations research. The disciplines contributing to the behavioral approach focusing on the design, implementation, management, and business impact of systems are psychology, sociology, and economics. A sociotechnical view of systems considers both technical and social features of systems and solutions that represent the best fit between them.

Key Terms

Review Questions

1. How are information systems transforming business and what is their relationship to globalization?

   • Describe how information systems have changed the way businesses operate and their products and services.

   • Identify three major new information system trends.

   • Describe the characteristics of a digital firm.

   • Describe the challenges and opportunities of globalization in a "flattened" world.

2. Why are information systems so essential for running and managing a business today?

   • List and describe six reasons why information systems are so important for business today.

3. What exactly is an information system? How does it work? What are its management, organization, and technology components?

   • Define an information system and describe the activities it performs.

   • List and describe the organizational, management, and technology dimensions of information systems.

   • Distinguish between data and information and between information systems literacy and computer literacy.

   • Explain how the Internet and the World Wide Web are related to the other technology components of information systems.

4. What are complementary assets? Why are complementary assets essential for ensuring that information systems provide genuine value for an organization?

   • Define complementary assets and describe their relationship to information technology.

   • Describe the complementary social, managerial, and organizational assets required to optimize returns from information technology investments.

5. What academic disciplines are used to study information systems? How does each contribute to an understanding of information systems? What is a sociotechnical systems perspective?

   • List and describe each discipline that contributes to a technical approach to information systems

   • List and describe each discipline that contributes to a behavioral approach to information systems.

   • Describe the sociotechnical perspective on information systems.

Discussion Questions

1. Information systems are too important to be left to computer specialists. Do you agree? Why or why not?

2. If you were setting up Web sites for NBA teams, what management, organization, and technology issues might you encounter?

Video Cases

You will find video cases illustrating some of the concepts in this chapter on the Laudon Web site along with questions to help you analyze the cases.

Collaboration and Teamwork: Creating a Web Site for Team Collaboration

Form a team with three or four classmates. Then use the tools at Google Sites to create a Web site for your team. You will need to a create a Google account for the site and specify the collaborators (your team members) who are allowed to access the site and make contributions. Specify your professor as the viewer of the site so that person can evaluate your work. Assign a name to the site. Select a theme for the site and make any changes you wish to colors and fonts. Add features for project announcements and a repository for team documents, source materials, illustrations, electronic presentations, and Web pages of interest. You can add other features if you wish. Use Google to create a calendar for your team. After you complete this exercise, you can use this Web site and calendar for your other team projects.

Is Second Life Ready for Business?
CASE STUDY

Second Life is a 3D virtual online world created by former RealNetworks CTO Philip Rosedale through Linden Lab, a company he founded in San Francisco in 1999. The world is built and owned by its users, who are called residents. Over 14 million people have signed up to be residents of Second Life's world, also known as the Grid. In July 2008, the usage stats on Second Life's Web site (www.secondlife.com) showed that close to 1.1 million residents had logged in over the previous sixty days. Second Life runs over the Internet using special software that users download to their desktops.

Second Life is not a game. Residents interact with each other in a 3-D social network. They can explore, socialize, collaborate, create, participate in activities, and purchase goods and services. The Second Life Web site says that its world is similar to a massively multiplayer online role playing game (MMORPG) but distinct in that it allows nearly unlimited creativity and ownership over user-created content. When logged in, residents take on a digital persona, called an avatar. Each user may customize his or her own avatar, changing its appearance, its clothing, and even its form from human to humanoid or something altogether different.

Second Life has its own virtual economy and currency. The currency is the Linden Dollar, or Linden for short, and is expressed as L$. There is an open market for goods and services created on the Grid. Residents may acquire Lindens this way, or by using currency exchanges to trade real-world money for Lindens. The Linden has a real-world value, which is set by market pricing and tracked and traded on a proprietary market called the LindeX. A very modest percentage of residents earns a significant profit from dealing in the Second Life economy. One user, known on the Grid as Anshe Chung, has accumulated enough virtual real estate that she could sell it for an amount of Lindens equaling US$1 million. More common are the residents who gross enough to cover the expense of their participation in the world. According to statistics issued by Second Life, 389,108 residents spent money on the Grid during June 2008.

Basic membership in Second Life is free and includes most of the privileges of paid membership, except the right to own land. Residents with Premium memberships are eligible to own land on the Grid.

The largest lots, or Entire Regions, measure 65,536 square meters (about 16 acres) and incur a monthly land use fee of US $195.

Residents create content for the Grid using tools provided by Second Life. For example, the software includes a 3-D modeling tool that enables users to construct buildings, landscapes, vehicles, furniture, and any other goods they can imagine. A standard library of animations and sounds enables residents to make gestures to one another. Basic communication is performed by typing in the manner of an instant message or chat session.

Users may also design and upload their own sounds, graphics, and animations to Second Life. Second Life has its own scripting language, Linden Scripting Language, which makes it possible for users to enhance objects in the virtual world with behaviors.

Although the concept of a 3-D virtual world is in its infancy, this has not stopped businesses, universities, and even governments from jumping into the fray to see what a virtual world has to offer. The hope is that Second Life will be a birthing ground for new industries and transform business, commerce, marketing, and learning the same way that the Web did in the late twentieth and early twenty-first centuries.

The advertising and media industries have been early proponents of the technology, opening virtual offices to facilitate internal communications and to position themselves at the forefront of the digital landscape in order to recruit tech-savvy employees. A Second Life presence may convince potential clients that an advertising agency is on the cutting edge of technology, and therefore able to market to consumers who are there as well.

Crayon is a new-media marketing firm that has purchased an island on the Grid, named crayonville, to serve as its primary office. With employees scattered in real-world offices on both sides of the Atlantic, crayonville provides the firm with a new way to bring everyone together, even if the employees are represented by avatars. Crayon leaves its conference room open to the public unless matters of client confidentiality come into play. Employees communicate by text message and with Skype Internet telephony.

Television and media companies such as CNN and BBC have used Second Life to attract viewers who have forsaken television for the Internet or to offer existing viewers a new medium for interacting with their brands.

What about Second Life would encourage companies like IBM to invest $10 million in exploring the possibilities of virtual business? For one, it can offer the following to support important business functions like customer service, product development, training, and marketing: a three-dimensional space in which a user can interact with visual and auditory content; custom content that can be altered and animated; a persistent presence that remains intact for future work even when users log off; and a community where like-minded people can gather to pursue activities of mutual interest.

IBM employees use their avatars to attend meetings in virtual meeting rooms where they can see PowerPoint slides while reading the text of a meeting or lecture or listen to it via a conference call. Virtual attendees can use instant messaging to send questions and receive answers from other avatars or the lecturer. Lynne Hamilton, who runs professional development classes for IBM's human resources (HR) department, uses Second Life for orienting new employees located in China and Brazil. An HR avatar will give a talk and then respond to text questions from the new employees.

Sears, American Apparel, Dell, Circuit City, and Toyota established a presence on Second Life. These retailers' expectations had been low, but they believed their virtual presence could enhance their brand image and provide new insights into how people might act in the online realm. However, as of the writing of this case, their virtual stores were mostly empty or had shut their doors. The social aspect of the shopping experience is not yet present.

While it is too soon for companies to obtain a return on their investment in Second Life, some have instantly recognized the value of user-created content, user investment, and user input, and the cost-savings of leveraging all for new business opportunities. Prototyping in a virtual world is fast and cheap. Crescendo Design, a residential designer in Wisconsin, uses Second Life's 3-D modeling tools to give clients an inside view of their homes before they are constructed. Clients can suggest changes that would not be obvious from working from traditional blueprints, and the designer avoids mistakes that would be expensive to fix if made in the real world.

Institutions of higher education have created virtual "campuses" where students and faculty can meet for real-time classwork or to hold informal discussions related to their classes. Second Life is a particular boon to distance learning. Insead, an international business school with real-world classes in France and Singapore is building a virtual campus with rooms for virtual classroom lectures, research laboratories, and lounge areas for students to meet with professors, potential employers, and fellow classmates. Instead's Second Life presence will help it reduce travel and physical building expenses while bringing together students and professors from across the globe. Eventually students will be able to download documents, work in teams, and meet alumni online. The Stockholm School of Economics and Duke Corporate Education are also experimenting with Second Life.

Companies such as Hewlett-Packard and global management consultancy Bain and Company, have experimented with Second Life for screening prospective hires. Job seekers create an avatar representing themselves and communicate with executives of prospective employers by exchanging instant text messages. Some interviewees and employers reported trouble designing and controlling the movements of their avatars, and companies still need to interview their final selections face to face. But participating companies have found Second Life useful for narrowing the pool of candidates and trimming recruitment expenses.

From a popularity standpoint, Second Life is far behind social networks such as MySpace, Facebook, and YouTube, which are accessible through a familiar Web browser and do not require any additional software. A user who is willing to take the steps necessary to download and install the Second Life Viewer may find that his or her computer does not meet Second Life's minimum or recommended system requirements. This last factor is especially important for businesses that may need to reconfigure the systems of a large number of employees in order to get them on the Grid.

Sources: Dave Greenfield, "Doing Business in the Virtual World," *eWeek*, March 10, 2008; David Talbot, "The Fleecing of the Avatars," *Technology Review*, January/February 2008; Don Clark, "Virtual World Gets Another Life," *The Wall Street Journal*, April 3, 2008; Andrew Baxter, "Second Life for Classrooms," *Financial Times*, February 29, 2008; Kamales Lardi-Nadarajan, "Synthetic Worlds," *CIO Insight*, March 2008; Alice LaPlante, "Second Life Opens for Business,"*Information Week*, February 26, 2007; Anjali Athavaley, "A Job Interview You Don't Have to Show Up For," *The Wall Street Journal*, June 20, 2007; Linda Zimmer, "How Viable is Virtual Commerce?" *Optimize Magazine*, January 2007; Mitch Wagner, "What Happens in Second Life, Stays in SL," *Information Week*, January 29, 2007.

CASE STUDY QUESTIONS

1. How can Second Life provide value to businesses that use it?

2. What kinds of businesses are most likely to benefit from a presence on Second Life? Why?

3. Considering what you have learned about Second Life, how could you, as an individual, create a modest start-up business on the Grid? What goods would you sell? Why would this be a good choice of product? What, in simple terms, would your business plan be? Why would it work?

4. Visit eBay on the Web and see what Second Life items you can find listed for auction. How would you rate the activity surrounding these items? Are you surprised by what you see? Why or why not?

5. What obstacles does Second Life have to overcome in order to become a mainstream business tool? Does it face fewer or more obstacles to become a mainstream educational tool? To what do you attribute the difference?

6. Would you like to interview for a job using Second Life? Why or why not?

7. Is Second Life a precursor of how business will be conducted in the future or a corporate experiment? Justify your answer.

Chapter 2

Global E-Business: How Businesses Use Information Systems

HYPERONE: SOLUTIONS TO ACHIEVE BUSINESS OBJECTIVES

Hyperone is the first fully Egyptian, combined hypermarket-department store in the country, covering 40,000 square meters in the Sheikh Zayed District, a suburb of Cairo. Established in 2005, the chain's success speaks for itself; it employs more than 1,600 people and has an average of 45,000 visitors a day.

Hypermarkets use economies of scale to keep prices low. Their business model is based on low overheads, a result of expansive stores located on the outskirts of cities (where property prices are lower) coupled with sales of large volumes of goods at low profit margins. The savings are passed along to the consumer. As Hyperone continues to move into big retail prominence, the IT structure of the organization played a major role in this success story. Hyperone's management has adopted a strategic plan for information systems. Three key people, the CEO, the Information Systems Consultant, and the Information Systems Manager worked hard on achieving the seven major objectives of the plan. The objectives were:

Support daily operations: Create an effective, accurate, integrated and error free automated system to support the complex and dynamic daily operations

Support customer satisfaction: Hyperone is keen to provide better quality products at low costs and a high standard of service through the analysis of sales and the understanding of the client's data after recording it in databases.

Attract and retain distinguished employees: Because the human element is a major factor of success, Hyperone took the necessary steps to maintain these elements by providing training, paying competitive salaries, and also providing an adequate work environment.

Support decision making: Raise the productivity of the institution through the support of decision-making by means of reliance on standard indicators called performance indicators or ballot results.

Reinforce the direct and electronic relationship with suppliers: One of the characteristics of the retail trade is the huge number of suppliers. This incited a lot of senior retail stores to focus on those suppliers and improve their relationship with them.

Reduce risk of operations: The use of information systems in different sectors of the store, and its functions and departments, made it very important to achieve a high degree of reliability so that it can perform smoothly. Accordingly, a unit was created within the Information systems department to achieve this goal.

Reliance on advanced technology: The competition amongst retailers in recent years is for the acquisition of advanced technology and to activate it in the service of the store, its customers and suppliers. Therefore, it became one of the strategic objectives at Hyperone.

Sources: Hyper Dreams (http://www.businesstodayegypt.com/article.aspx?ArticleID=7869), Business Today, February 2008. Hyperone IT Master Plan, 2008.

The case of Hyperone shows the capacity of information systems to address typical business problems such as day-to-day operations support and decision-making support. The scale of Hyperone's business can extend to a global scale if people, organization and technology components are properly addressed in order to achieve the planned business strategy laid down for Hyperone. These components address both internal business operations as well as external and inter-organizational issues necessary for global operations.

- Case contributed by Dr Ahmed Elragal, German University in Cairo

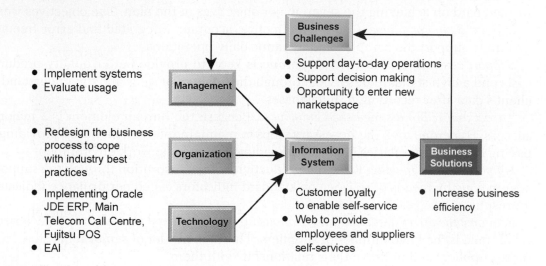

2.1   BUSINESS PROCESSES AND INFORMATION SYSTEMS

In order to operate, businesses must deal with many different pieces of information about suppliers, customers, employees, invoices, and payments, and of course their products and services. They must organize work activities that use this information to operate efficiently and enhance the overall performance of the firm. Information systems make it possible for firms to manage all their information, make better decisions, and improve the execution of their business processes.

BUSINESS PROCESSES

Business processes, which we introduced in Chapter 1, refer to the manner in which work is organized, coordinated, and focused to produce a valuable product or service. Business processes are concrete workflows of material, information, and knowledge—sets of activities. Business processes also refer to the unique ways in which organizations coordinate work, information, and knowledge, and the ways in which management chooses to coordinate work.

To a large extent, the performance of a business firm depends on how well its business processes are designed and coordinated. A company's business processes can be a source of competitive strength if they enable the company to innovate or to execute better than its rivals. Business processes can also be liabilities if they are based on outdated ways of working that impede organizational responsiveness and efficiency.

Every business can be seen as a collection of business processes. Some of these processes are part of larger encompassing processes. Many business processes are tied to a specific functional area. For example, the sales and marketing function would be responsible for identifying customers, and the human resources function would be responsible for hiring employees. Table 2-1 describes some typical business processes for each of the functional areas of business.

TABLE 2-1 EXAMPLES OF FUNCTIONAL BUSINESS PROCESSES

FUNCTIONAL AREA	BUSINESS PROCESS
Manufacturing and production	Assembling the product
	Checking for quality
	Producing bills of materials
Sales and marketing	Identifying customers
	Making customers aware of the product
	Selling the product
Finance and accounting	Paying creditors
	Creating financial statements
	Managing cash accounts
Human resources	Hiring employees
	Evaluating employees' job performance
	Enrolling employees in benefits plans

Other business processes cross many different functional areas and require coordination across departments. For instance, consider the seemingly simple business process of fulfilling a customer order (see Figure 2-1). Initially, the sales department would receive a sales order. The order will pass first to accounting to ensure the customer can pay for the order either by a credit verification or request for immediate payment prior to shipping. Once the customer credit is established, the production department has to pull the product from inventory or produce the product. Then the product will need to be shipped (and this may require working with a logistics firm, such as UPS or FedEx.) A bill or invoice will then have to be generated by the accounting department, and a notice will be sent to the customer indicating that the product has shipped. Sales will have to be notified of the shipment and prepare to support the customer by answering calls or fulfilling warranty claims.

What at first appears to be a simple process, fulfilling an order, turns out to be a very complicated series of business processes that require the close coordination of major functional groups in a firm. Moreover, to efficiently perform all these steps in the order fulfillment process requires a great deal of information. The required information must flow rapidly both within the firm—with business partners, such as delivery firms—and with the customer. Computerized information systems make this possible.

HOW INFORMATION TECHNOLOGY ENHANCES BUSINESS PROCESSES

Exactly how do information systems enhance business processes? Information systems automate many steps in business processes that were formerly performed manually, such as checking a client's credit, or generating an invoice and shipping order. But today, information technology can do much more. New technology can actually change the flow of information, making it possible for many more people to access and share information, replacing

FIGURE 2-1   THE ORDER FULFILLMENT PROCESS

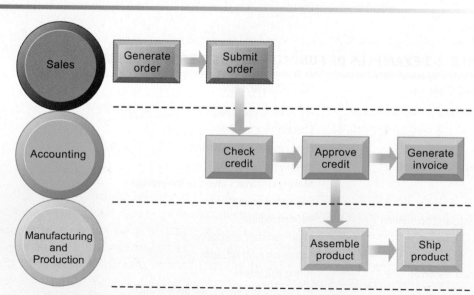

Fulfilling a customer order involves a complex set of steps that requires the close coordination of the sales, accounting, and manufacturing functions.

sequential steps with tasks that can be performed simultaneously, and eliminating delays in decision making. It can even transform the way the business works and drive new business models. Ordering a book online from Amazon.com or downloading a music track from iTunes are entirely new business processes based on new business models that would be inconceivable without information technology.

That's why it's so important to pay close attention to business processes, both in your information systems course and in your future career. By analyzing business processes, you can achieve a very clear understanding of how a business actually works. Moreover, by conducting a business process analysis, you will also begin to understand how to change the business to make it more efficient or effective. Throughout this book we examine business processes with a view to understanding how they might be changed, or replaced, by using information technology to achieve greater efficiency, innovation and customer service.

2.2 TYPES OF INFORMATION SYSTEMS

Now that you understand business processes, it is time to look more closely at how information systems support the business processes of a firm. Because a business may have hundreds or even thousands of different business processes, and because there are different interests, specialties, and levels in an organization, there are different kinds of systems. No single system can provide all the information an organization needs.

A typical business organization will have systems supporting processes for each of the major business functions—systems for sales and marketing, manufacturing and production, finance and accounting, and human resources. You can find examples of systems for each of these business functions in the Learning Tracks for this chapter. Functional systems that operated independently of each other are becoming a thing of the past because they could not easily share information to support cross-functional business processes. They are being replaced with large-scale cross-functional systems that integrate the activities of related business processes and organizational units. We describe these integrated cross-functional applications in Section 2.3.

A typical business firm will also have different systems supporting the decision making needs of each of the main management groups we described earlier. Operational management, middle management, and senior management each use a specific type of system to support the decisions they must make to run the company. Let's look at these systems and the types of decisions they support.

TRANSACTION PROCESSING SYSTEMS

Operational managers need systems that keep track of the elementary activities and transactions of the organization, such as sales, receipts, cash deposits, payroll, credit decisions, and the flow of materials in a factory. **Transaction processing systems (TPS)** provide this kind of information. A transaction processing system is a computerized system that performs and records the daily routine transactions necessary to conduct business, such as sales order entry, hotel reservations, payroll, employee record keeping, and shipping.

The principal purpose of systems at this level is to answer routine questions and to track the flow of transactions through the organization. How many parts are in inventory? What happened to Mr. Williams's payment? To answer these kinds of questions, information generally must be easily available, current, and accurate.

At the operational level, tasks, resources, and goals are predefined and highly structured. The decision to grant credit to a customer, for instance, is made by a lower-level supervisor according to predefined criteria. All that must be determined is whether the customer meets the criteria.

Figure 2-2 illustrates a TPS for payroll processing. A payroll system keeps track of money paid to employees. An employee time card with the employee's name, Social Security number, and number of hours worked per week represents a single transaction for this system. Once this transaction is input into the system, it updates the system's file, or database (see Chapter 6), that permanently maintains employee information for the organization. The data in the system are combined in different ways to create reports of interest to management and government agencies and to send paychecks to employees.

Managers need TPS to monitor the status of internal operations and the firm's relations with the external environment. TPS are also major producers of information for the other types of systems. For example, the payroll system illustrated in Figure 2-2, along with other accounting TPS, supplies data to the company's general ledger system, which is responsible for maintaining records of the firm's income and expenses and for producing reports such as income statements and balance sheets. It also supplies employee payment history data

FIGURE 2-2   A PAYROLL TPS

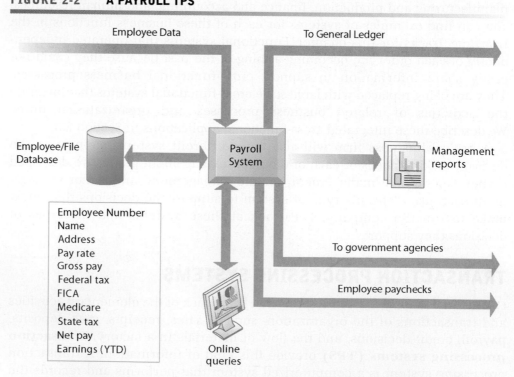

A TPS for payroll processing captures employee payment transaction data (such as a time card). System outputs include online and hard-copy reports for management and employee paychecks.

for insurance, pension, and other benefits calculations to the firm's human resource systems and employee payment data to government agencies such as the U.S. Internal Revenue Service and Social Security Administration.

Transaction processing systems are often so central to a business that TPS failure for a few hours can lead to a firm's demise and perhaps that of other firms linked to it. Imagine what would happen to UPS if its package tracking system were not working! What would the airlines do without their computerized reservation systems? (See the chapter-ending case study on JetBlue.)

MANAGEMENT INFORMATION SYSTEMS AND DECISION-SUPPORT SYSTEMS

Middle management needs systems to help with monitoring, controlling, decision-making, and administrative activities. The principal question addressed by such systems is this: Are things working well?

In Chapter 1, we defined management information systems as the study of information systems in business and management. The term **management information systems (MIS)** also designates a specific category of information systems serving middle management. MIS provide middle managers with reports on the organization's current performance. This information is used to monitor and control the business and predict future performance.

MIS summarize and report on the company's basic operations using data supplied by transaction processing systems. The basic transaction data from TPS are compressed and usually presented in reports that are produced on a regular schedule. Today, many of these reports are delivered online. Figure 2-3 shows how a typical MIS transforms transaction-level data from inventory, production, and accounting into MIS files that are used to provide managers with reports. Figure 2-4 shows a sample report from this system.

FIGURE 2-3   **HOW MANAGEMENT INFORMATION SYSTEMS OBTAIN THEIR DATA FROM THE ORGANIZATION'S TPS**

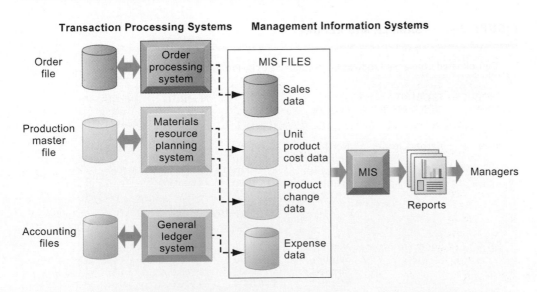

In the system illustrated by this diagram, three TPS supply summarized transaction data to the MIS reporting system at the end of the time period. Managers gain access to the organizational data through the MIS, which provides them with the appropriate reports.

MIS serve managers primarily interested in weekly, monthly, and yearly results, although some MIS enable managers to drill down to see daily or hourly data if required. MIS generally provide answers to routine questions that have been specified in advance and have a predefined procedure for answering them. For instance, MIS reports might list the total pounds of lettuce used this quarter by a fast-food chain or, as illustrated in Figure 2-4, compare total annual sales figures for specific products to planned targets. These systems generally are not flexible and have little analytical capability. Most MIS use simple routines, such as summaries and comparisons, as opposed to sophisticated mathematical models or statistical techniques.

Decision-support systems (DSS) support nonroutine decision making for middle management. They focus on problems that are unique and rapidly changing, for which the procedure for arriving at a solution may not be fully predefined in advance. They try to answer questions such as these: What would be the impact on production schedules if we were to double sales in the month of December? What would happen to our return on investment if a factory schedule were delayed for six months?

Although DSS use internal information from TPS and MIS, they often bring in information from external sources, such as current stock prices or product prices of competitors. These systems use a variety of models to analyze data, or they condense large amounts of data into a form in which decision makers can analyze them. DSS are designed so that users can work with them directly; these systems explicitly include user-friendly software.

An interesting, small, but powerful DSS is the voyage-estimating system of a subsidiary of a large American metals company that exists primarily to carry bulk cargoes of coal, oil, ores, and finished products for its parent company. The firm owns some vessels, charters others, and bids for shipping contracts in the open market to carry general cargo. A voyage-estimating system calculates financial and technical voyage details. Financial calculations include ship/time costs (fuel, labor, capital), freight rates for various types of cargo, and port expenses. Technical details include a myriad of factors, such as ship cargo

FIGURE 2-4   SAMPLE MIS REPORT

Consolidated Consumer Products Corporation Sales by Product and Sales Region: 2009

PRODUCT CODE	PRODUCT DESCRIPTION	SALES REGION	ACTUAL SALES	PLANNED	ACTUAL versus PLANNED
4469	Carpet Cleaner	Northeast	4,066,700	4,800,000	0.85
		South	3,778,112	3,750,000	1.01
		Midwest	4,867,001	4,600,000	1.06
		West	4,003,440	4,400,000	0.91
	TOTAL		16,715,253	17,550,000	0.95
5674	Room Freshener	Northeast	3,676,700	3,900,000	0.94
		South	5,608,112	4,700,000	1.19
		Midwest	4,711,001	4,200,000	1.12
		West	4,563,440	4,900,000	0.93
	TOTAL		18,559,253	17,700,000	1.05

This report, showing summarized annual sales data, was produced by the MIS in Figure 2-3.

capacity, speed, port distances, fuel and water consumption, and loading patterns (location of cargo for different ports).

The system can answer questions such as the following: Given a customer delivery schedule and an offered freight rate, which vessel should be assigned at what rate to maximize profits? What is the optimal speed at which a particular vessel can optimize its profit and still meet its delivery schedule? What is the optimal loading pattern for a ship bound for the U.S. West Coast from Malaysia? Figure 2-5 illustrates the DSS built for this company. The system operates on a powerful desktop personal computer, providing a system of menus that makes it easy for users to enter data or obtain information.

This voyage-estimating DSS draws heavily on analytical models. Other types of DSS are less model driven, focusing instead on extracting useful information to support decision making from massive quantities of data. For example, Intrawest—the largest ski operator in North America—collects and stores vast amounts of customer data from its Web site, call center, lodging reservations, ski schools, and ski equipment rental stores. It uses special software to analyze these data to determine the value, revenue potential, and loyalty of each customer so managers can make better decisions on how to target their marketing programs. The system segments customers into seven categories based on needs, attitudes, and behaviors, ranging from "passionate experts" to "value-minded family vacationers." The company then e-mails video clips that would appeal to each segment to encourage more visits to its resorts.

Sometimes you'll hear DSS referred to as *business intelligence systems* because they focus on helping users make better business decisions. You'll learn more about them in Chapters 6 and 12.

The Interactive Session on Technology describes another example of a system for decision support. Air Canada adopted Maintenix software for its aviation maintenance program to help schedule and organize aircraft maintenance work. Try to identify the decision-support applications detailed in the case and the kinds of decisions they support.

FIGURE 2-5   VOYAGE-ESTIMATING DECISION-SUPPORT SYSTEM

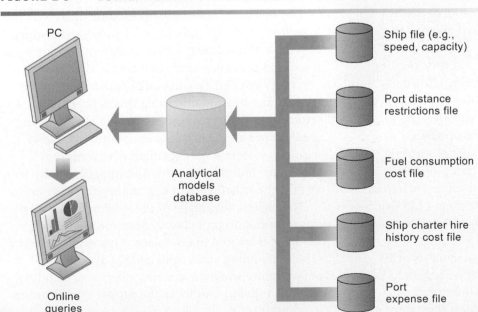

This DSS operates on a powerful PC. It is used daily by managers who must develop bids on shipping contracts.

INTERACTIVE SESSION: TECHNOLOGY

AIR CANADA TAKES OFF WITH MAINTENIX

Air Canada is Canada's most prominent airline. It is the largest provider of scheduled passenger services in the Canadian market, the Canada-U.S. trans-border market, and in the international market to and from Canada. The airline serves over 33 million customers annually and provides direct passenger service to over 170 destinations on five continents. But the company's information systems had plenty of room for improvement. When Air Canada technicians worked on planes, they used several different legacy software packages installed over the past 15 years. The systems weren't able to interact with one another or with finance and inventory systems. The inefficiencies of these systems were costing Air Canada the time of its engineers and money that could have been used on maintaining its planes, instead of needlessly maintaining excess inventory.

Air Canada turned to Mxi Technologies for help in addressing these problems. Mxi is renowned in the airline industry for its Maintenix software package, which provides integrated, intelligent aviation MRO (maintenance, repair, and operations) software to aviation organizations hoping to improve productivity. The benefits of Maintenix that interested Air Canada were enhanced visibility of fleet-wide data, timelier decision-making, support of its currently existing business model, and increased operational efficiencies.

Maintenix provides a system platform that is accessible via the Web and easy to deploy to all stations around the world. Mxi claims that their software reduces repetitive tasks and time chasing missing or incomplete information by allowing maintenance, engineering, and finance divisions to easily share information. Maintenix can supply data to the company's existing enterprise resource planning (see Section 2.3) and financial software, and Air Canada plans to link it up with its PeopleSoft finance and human resource applications. Wireless deployment also makes Maintenix more effective, since aviation technicians, equipment, and parts are always on the move.

The Maintenix software package consists of six different modules, which are separate segments of the product that interconnect. Airlines deploying Maintenix can choose which modules they want to use, as well as whether they want full or partial installation of those modules. The six modules are maintenance engineering, line maintenance, heavy maintenance, shop maintenance, materials management, and finance. Air Canada chose to fully implement the maintenance engineering, line maintenance, and materials management modules. The airline chose to only partially implement the heavy maintenance, shop maintenance, and finance modules because a separate contractor that also maintains Air Canada planes handles those tasks.

The maintenance engineering module is the foundation of the Maintenix system. It is used to establish the configuration hierarchy, rules, and maintenance program that all of the other modules depend upon. Through this module, the airline can set up a "logical configuration", which describes aircraft components, part relationships, and compatibility rules.

Line maintenance involves matching a dynamic list of maintenance work requirements against finite resources at varying locations within a flight schedule that is constantly undergoing change. The module includes line station planning applications, which are designed to schedule maintenance and allocate work, based on the capabilities of the line station facilities as well as the aircrafts' scheduled locations. For example, this module allows Air Canada to ensure that qualified technicians are available before they schedule maintenance.

The materials management module deals with the logistically complex process of ensuring availability of parts without overstocking. Maintenix ensures that the minimum amount of each part is always in inventory without causing engineers to be short on parts at any time. Maintaining this delicate balance is critical in order to maximize revenue and achieve greater operational efficiencies. Maintenix allows wireless, real-time management of inventory, automates routine activities, and integrates fully with an airline's existing inventory management systems.

The biggest advantage of the system is that all of this information provided by Maintenix's various modules is located in one place. This results in more rapid scheduling and avoids pitfalls of poorly organized information systems, such as scheduling work to a station that lacks the proper qualifications to accomplish it.

One example of how Maintenix will increase Air Canada's efficiency might be as follows. An Air

Canada technician requests a part he needs for maintenance from supply. Maintenix automatically processes the request. If the required part is available, Maintenix automatically reserves it and the appropriate personnel are immediately informed that the part is ready to be picked for issue. In the meantime, the technician is easily able to track the status of his part requests and is made aware once the part is ready to be collected. If any change happens and the part is unavailable, Maintenix will notify the technician. As a result, technicians can accomplish more maintenance work as opposed to managing details that Maintenix is now handling via automation. This leads to increased productivity and increased profitability. The system is expected to be fully implemented by 2010.

Sources: Greg Meckbach, "Air Canada to Overhaul Maintenance Software," *ComputerWorld Canada*, April 18, 2008; "Air Canada Selects Maintenix for Fleetwide Implementation," Reuters, April 15, 2008; "Maintenix Product Overview," www.mxi.com, May 2008.

CASE STUDY QUESTIONS

1. What problems does Air Canada hope that Maintenix will solve?
2. How does Maintenix improve operational efficiency and decision-making?
3. Give examples of three decisions supported by the Maintenix system. What information do the Maintenix modules provide to support each of these decisions?

MIS IN ACTION

Visit the Mxi Technologies Web site (www.mxi.com) and examine the Maintenix modules for heavy maintenance, shop maintenance, and finance modules. Then answer the following questions:

1. How could an airline benefit from implementing these modules?
2. Give an example of a decision that each of these modules supports.

EXECUTIVE SUPPORT SYSTEMS FOR SENIOR MANAGEMENT

Senior managers need systems that address strategic issues and long-term trends, both in the firm and in the external environment. They are concerned with questions such as these: What will employment levels be in five years? What are the long-term industry cost trends, and where does our firm fit in? What products should we be making in five years? What new acquisitions would protect us from cyclical business swings?

Executive support systems (ESS) help senior management make these decisions. ESS address nonroutine decisions requiring judgment, evaluation, and insight because there is no agreed-on procedure for arriving at a solution. ESS present graphs and data from many sources through an interface that is easy for senior managers to use. Often the information is delivered to senior executives through a **portal**, which uses a Web interface to present integrated personalized business content. You will learn more about other applications of portals in Chapters 10 and 11.

ESS are designed to incorporate data about external events, such as new tax laws or competitors, but they also draw summarized information from internal MIS and DSS. They filter, compress, and track critical data, displaying the data of greatest importance to senior managers. For example, the CEO of Leiner Health Products, the largest manufacturer of private-label vitamins and supplements in the United States, has an ESS that provides on his desktop a minute-to-minute view of the firm's financial performance as measured by working capital, accounts receivable, accounts payable, cash flow, and inventory. The information is presented in the form of a digital dashboard, which displays on a single screen graphs and charts of key performance indicators for managing a company. **Digital dashboards** are becoming an increasingly popular feature of ESS.

Figure 2-6 illustrates a model of an ESS. It consists of workstations with menus, interactive graphics, and communications capabilities that can be used to access historical and competitive data from internal corporate systems and external databases such as Dow Jones News/Retrieval or the Gallup Poll. More details on leading-edge applications of DSS and ESS can be found in Chapter 12.

The Interactive Session on Organizations describes real-world examples of several of these types of systems used by a company that is attempting to revamp its IT infrastructure. Note the types of systems illustrated by this case and the role they play in improving both operations and decision making.

2.3 SYSTEMS THAT SPAN THE ENTERPRISE

Reviewing all the different types of systems we have just described, you might wonder how a business can manage all the information in these different systems. In fact, getting all the different kinds of systems in a company to work together has proven to be a major challenge. There are several solutions to this problem.

ENTERPRISE APPLICATIONS

One solution is to implement **enterprise applications**, which are systems that span functional areas, focus on executing business processes across the business firm, and include all levels of management. Enterprise applications

FIGURE 2-6   MODEL OF AN EXECUTIVE SUPPORT SYSTEM

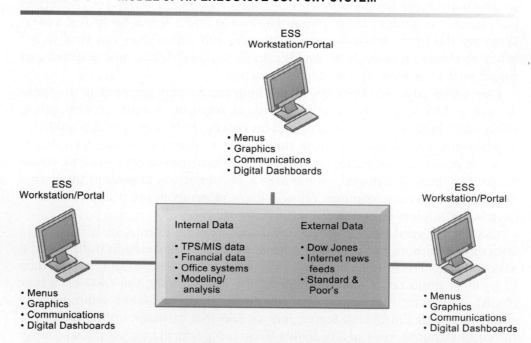

This system pools data from diverse internal and external sources and makes them available to executives in an easy-to-use form.

INTERACTIVE SESSION: MANAGEMENT

EL-ALAMEIN FOR PRINTING AND PACKAGING GOES DIGITAL

Founded in 1921, El-Alamein is one of the leading companies in the Middle East in the printing and packaging industry. With head-quarters (HQ) located in Alexandria, El-Alamein occupies an area of 40,000 square meters and employs more than 700 employees. El-Alamein has managed to obtain international quality certificates including: ISO 9001, ISO 14001, ISO OHSAS 18001, and BRC/IOP. The company has two main Strategic Business Units (SBUs): offset factory as well as a flexible factory.

"Since 1921, El-Alamein Co. led the revolution of the Printing and Packaging industry in Egypt. El-alamein is the approved supplier to the biggest international companies in the fast food industry. The company produces paper cups for cold and hot drinks as well as ice-cream packages with their different shapes and sizes. The company also produces eight-cornered carton boxes to pack sandwiches and burgers, in addition to different shapes and sizes of fried potatoes boxes. The company produces wrapping paper for sandwiches and fast food, and produces printed multi-layered paper bags by using automatic heat sealing for the bottom and side-seams."

The company faces many challenges: there isn't a reliable infrastructure, network, servers, storage or PCs; there isn't an IT/IS department in the organization chart; competitors have taken serious steps in becoming digitally enabled, and information loss has taken many shapes for example lost orders, inaccurate inventory, and lack of integration between functional departments.

Until June 2006 the company had never had an IT department and relied on separate PCs with end-user designed excel sheets to facilitate the work duties. The company CEO decided to go digital from July 2006 and the company had to establish several infrastructural components such as the computer network, a backup system and security policy.

Once the IT infrastructure had been successfully implemented, this enabled the implementation of various systems including time and attendance systems. This saved a lot of lost working hours and has been linked to the ERP.

Having an attractive and informative website has become a major need for many companies, especially those targeting the international market. El-Alamein is no different, which is the reason why the company has developed a website (www.elalamein.net). The website helps many functional departments including marketing, HR, sales, and customer services.

After reviewing different Enterprise Resource Planning (ERP) systems and scoring them against the company requirements, Oracle E-Business Suite was chosen as the best ERP to meet the company information and business requirements. Those requirements were taken from end-users, as well as various department heads. An implantation vendor was selected to start the project. The modules chosen to help automate the business processes were: Oracle Financials, inventory management, manufacturing, sales and marketing, order-management, and procurement. To ensure ERP implementation success, Elalamein focused on the following business process requirements; project management documentation; post-implementation performance measurement; CEO and IT Consultant involvement in the project steering committee, and adequate training and change management. After one year of implementation, only two modules went live: the financial and HR modules. Remaining modules are due to go live within one year.

The project has experienced some difficulties, the foremost being the resistance to change from heads of departments. To reduce the risk the company has taken the following three steps. First, identify key persons from all functional areas who will act as change agents and take the responsibility of persuading other employees of the importance of the system. Second, train users to use the new system and understand how the new business processes will be affected; and third foster end-user project participation by involving more employees than just senior management in the decision, analysis, and implementation.

Employee turnover can cost organizations a lot of money in terms of production time, and retraining especially when key persons are involved, and El-alamein faced that challenge many times during implementation. The company lost six key persons in a period of six months. This has resulted in delay in those functional areas, and the repetition of some steps during the analysis and setup phases.

After two years of implementing various technologies and solutions, El-Alamein has reduced investment risks, strengthened process integration, improved productivity and enhanced the efficiency of inventory handling. With these IT investments, the company has established strategic relationships with multinational companies.

The establishment of El-alamein IT/IS has resulted in an increase in company value by more than EGP 10 million. This is nearly five times what has been spent so far on IT/IS, making the return on investment of IT/IS over 500 percent.

Sources: www.elalamein.net.

CASE STUDY QUESTIONS

1. What systems are described here? What valuable information do they provide?
2. What are the risks facing El-Alamein in implementing the ERP system? How do you evaluate the actions taken from their side to mitigate those risk factors?
3. What value did the IT/IS investments add to El-Alamein?

MIS IN ACTION

Visit Teradata's website (www.teradata.com) and read about enterprise data warehousing. Then answer the following questions:

1. Do you think that Teradata could be beneficial to El-Alamein?
2. If El-Alamein decided to implement data warehousing, will Teradata be sufficient for them or will they require other software?
3. What do you think of the integration between ERP and data warehousing in terms of the benefits it can deliver to El-Alamein?

• Case contributed by Dr Ahmed Elragal, German University in Cairo

help businesses become more flexible and productive by coordinating their business processes more closely and integrating groups of processes so they focus on efficient management of resources and customer service.

There are four major enterprise applications: enterprise systems, supply chain management systems, customer relationship management systems, and knowledge management systems. Each of these enterprise applications integrates a related set of functions and business processes to enhance the performance of the organization as a whole. Figure 2-7 shows that the architecture for these enterprise applications encompasses processes spanning the entire organization and, in some cases, extending beyond the organization to customers, suppliers, and other key business partners.

FIGURE 2-7   ENTERPRISE APPLICATION ARCHITECTURE

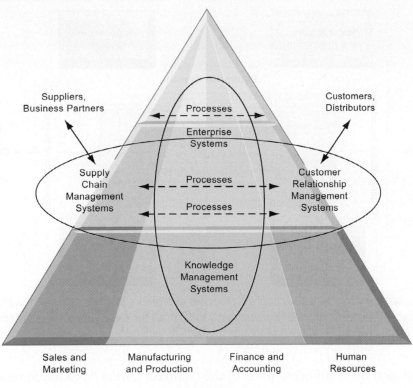

Enterprise applications automate processes that span multiple business functions and organizational levels and may extend outside the organization.

Enterprise Systems

A large organization typically has many different kinds of information systems built around different functions, organizational levels, and business processes that cannot automatically exchange information. This fragmentation of data in hundreds of separate systems degrades organizational efficiency and business performance. For instance, sales personnel might not be able to tell at the time they place an order whether the ordered items are in inventory, and manufacturing cannot easily use sales data to plan for new production.

Enterprise systems, also known as *enterprise resource planning (ERP)* systems, solve this problem by collecting data from various key business processes in manufacturing and production, finance and accounting, sales and marketing, and human resources, and storing the data in a single central data repository. Information that was previously fragmented in different systems can be easily shared across the firm to help different parts of the business work more closely together (see Figure 2-8).

For example, when a customer places an order, the data flow automatically to other parts of the company that are affected by them. The order transaction triggers the warehouse to pick the ordered products and schedule shipment. The warehouse informs the factory to replenish whatever has depleted. The accounting department is notified to send the customer an invoice. Customer service representatives track the progress of the order through every step to inform customers about the status of their orders. Improved coordina-

FIGURE 2-8 **ENTERPRISE SYSTEMS**

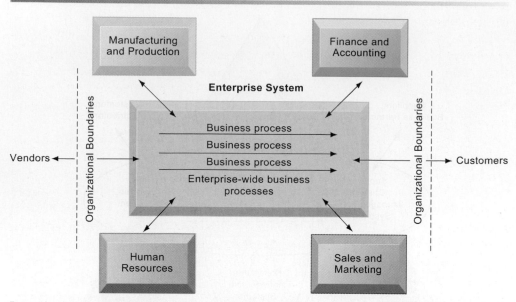

Enterprise systems integrate the key business processes of an entire firm into a single software system that enables information to flow seamlessly throughout the organization. These systems focus primarily on internal processes but may include transactions with customers and vendors.

tion between these different parts of the business lowers costs while increasing customer satisfaction.

Air Liquide, the world's leading supplier of industrial and medical gases, operates more than 500 production sites worldwide, 250 of which are in Europe. Over the years, the company had implemented a large variety of systems to serve these sites. Acquisitions of new subsidiaries added to the number of systems the company maintained; at one time, the company had 800 individual applications running across Europe. This patchwork of uncoordinated local systems prevented Air Liquide from easily shipping products across European national borders, which EU safety standards allowed. Implementing mySAP ERP software allowed the company to centralize business processes that had previously been handled locally or nationally and replace its tangled legacy systems with centralized integrated software supporting the activities of the company as a whole. Air Liquide now has a common set of applications, consistent business processes, and integrated master data, while still allowing international subsidiaries some measure of flexibility to adapt to local conditions (SAP AG, 2007).

Supply Chain Management Systems

Supply chain management (SCM) systems help businesses manage relationships with their suppliers. These systems help suppliers, purchasing firms, distributors, and logistics companies share information about orders, production, inventory levels, and delivery of products and services so that they can make better decisions about how to organize and schedule sourcing, production, and distribution. The ultimate objective is to get the right amount of their products from their source to their point of consumption with the least amount of time and with the lowest cost.

Supply chain management systems are one type of **interorganizational system** because they automate the flow of information across organizational boundaries. You will find examples of other types of interorganizational information systems throughout this text because such systems make it possible for firms to link electronically to customers and to outsource their work to other companies.

Figure 2-9 illustrates supply chain management systems used by Haworth Incorporated, a world-leading manufacturer and designer of office furniture. Haworth's 15 North American manufacturing facilities are located in North Carolina, Arkansas, Michigan, Mississippi, Texas, Ontario, Alberta, and Quebec. These facilities supply inventory to distribution centers in Michigan, Pennsylvania, Georgia, and Arkansas.

Haworth's Transportation Management System (TMS) examines customer orders, factory schedules, carrier rates and availability, and shipping costs to produce optimal lowest-cost delivery plans. These plans are generated daily and updated every 15 minutes. The TMS works with Haworth's Warehouse Management System (WMS), which tracks and controls the flow of finished goods from Haworth's distribution centers to its customers. Acting on shipping plans from TMS, WMS directs the movement of goods based on immediate conditions for space, equipment, inventory, and personnel. Haworth uses special "middleware" software to link its TMS and WMS to order entry, manufacturing planning, and shipping systems and to pass customer orders, shipping plans, and shipping notifications among the applications.

Customer Relationship Management Systems

Customer relationship management (CRM) systems help firms manage their relationships with their customers. CRM systems provide information to coordinate all of the business processes that deal with customers in sales, marketing, and service to optimize revenue, customer satisfaction, and customer retention. This information helps firms identify, attract, and retain the most profitable customers; provide better service to existing customers; and increase sales.

CRM systems consolidate and integrate customer information from multiple communication channels—telephone, e-mail, wireless devices, retail outlets, or the Web. Detailed and accurate knowledge of customers and their preferences helps firms increase the effectiveness of their marketing campaigns and provide higher-quality customer service and support.

FIGURE 2-9   EXAMPLE OF A SUPPLY CHAIN MANAGEMENT SYSTEM

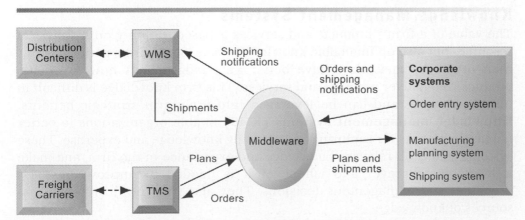

Customer orders, shipping notifications, optimized shipping plans, and other supply chain information flow among Haworth's Warehouse Management System (WMS), Transportation Management System (TMS), and its back-end corporate systems.

Illustrated here are some of the capabilities of Salesforce.com, a market-leading provider of on-demand customer relationship management (CRM) software. CRM systems integrate information from sales, marketing, and customer service.

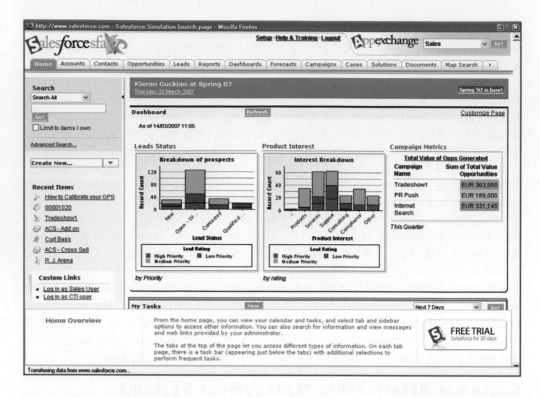

For example, Saab U.S.A., which imports and distributes vehicles to U.S. dealerships, used CRM applications for automotive dealers from Oracle-Siebel Systems to integrate data that were distributed among systems supporting its dealer network, a customer service assistance center, and a lead management center. The CRM systems provide a 360-degree view of each Saab customer, including prior service-related questions and all the marketing communication the customer had ever received. The systems provide detailed information to measure the sales results of specific leads, and target leads are directed more precisely to the right salespeople at the right dealerships. Since the CRM applications were implemented, Saab's follow-up rate on sales leads has increased from 38 to 50 percent and customer satisfaction rose from 69 to 75 percent.

Knowledge Management Systems

The value of a firm's products and services is based not only on its physical resources but also on intangible knowledge assets. Some firms perform better than others because they have better knowledge about how to create, produce, and deliver products and services. This firm knowledge is difficult to imitate, unique, and can be leveraged into long-term strategic benefits. **Knowledge management systems (KMS)** enable organizations to better manage processes for capturing and applying knowledge and expertise. These systems collect all relevant knowledge and experience in the firm, and make it available wherever and whenever it is needed to improve business processes and management decisions. They also link the firm to external sources of knowledge.

KMS support processes for acquiring, storing, distributing, and applying knowledge, as well as processes for creating new knowledge and integrating it into the organization. They include enterprise-wide systems for managing and distributing documents, graphics, and other digital knowledge objects; systems for creating corporate knowledge directories of employees with special areas of expertise; office systems for distributing knowledge and information; and knowledge work systems to facilitate knowledge creation. Other knowledge management applications use intelligent techniques that codify knowledge for use by other members of the organization and tools for knowledge discovery that recognize patterns and important relationships in large pools of data.

We examine enterprise systems and systems for supply chain management and customer relationship management in greater detail in Chapter 9 and cover knowledge management applications in Chapter 11.

INTRANETS AND EXTRANETS

Enterprise applications create deep-seated changes in the way the firm conducts its business, and they are often costly to implement. To coordinate their activities, many different departments and employees must change the way they work and the way they use information. Companies that do not have the resources to invest in enterprise applications can still achieve some measure of information integration by using intranets and extranets, which we introduced in Chapter 1.

Intranets and extranets are really more technology platforms than specific applications, but they deserve mention here as one of the tools firms use to increase integration and expedite the flow of information within the firm, and with customers and suppliers. Intranets are internal networks built with the same tools and communication standards as the Internet and are used for the internal distribution of information to employees, and as repositories of corporate policies, programs, and data. Extranets are intranets extended to authorized users outside the company. We describe the technology for intranets and extranets in more detail in Chapter 7.

An intranet typically centers on a portal that provides a single point of access to information from several different systems and to documents using a Web interface. Such portals can be customized to suit the information needs of specific business groups and individual users if required. They may also feature e-mail, collaboration tools, and tools for searching internal corporate systems and documents.

For example, SwissAir's corporate intranet for sales provides its salespeople with sales leads, fares, statistics, libraries of best practices, access to incentive programs, discussion groups, and collaborative workspaces. The intranet includes a Sales Ticket capability that displays bulletins about unfilled airplane seats around the world to help the sales staff work with colleagues and with travel agents who can help them fill those seats.

Companies can connect their intranets to internal company transaction systems, enabling employees to take actions central to a company's operations, such as checking the status of an order or granting a customer credit. SwissAir's intranet connects to its reservation system.

Extranets expedite the flow of information between the firm and its suppliers and customers. SwissAir uses an extranet to provide travel agents with fare data from its intranet electronically. GUESS Jeans allows store buyers to order merchandise electronically from ApparelBuy.com. The buyers can use this extranet to track their orders through fulfillment or delivery.

COLLABORATION AND COMMUNICATION SYSTEMS: "INTERACTION" JOBS IN A GLOBAL ECONOMY

With all these systems and information, you might wonder how is it possible to make sense out of them? How do people working in firms pull it all together, work towards common goals, and coordinate plans and actions? Information systems can't make decisions, hire or fire people, sign contracts, agree on deals, or adjust the price of goods to the marketplace.

The number of people who perform these tasks in a firm is growing. A recent report from the consulting firm McKinsey and Company argued that 41 percent of the U.S. labor force is now composed of jobs where interaction (talking, e-mailing, presenting, and persuading) is the primary value-adding activity. Blue collar production jobs are now down to 15 percent of the labor force, and transactional jobs—filling out forms or reports or accepting payments) are now 25 percent of the labor force. Moreover, the "interaction" jobs are the fastest-growing: 70 percent of all new jobs created since 1998 are "interaction" jobs.

With globalization, firms have teams around the globe in different time zones working on the same problem, so the need for continuous interaction and communication around the clock has greatly expanded. Working 24/7 is not just a problem for call centers, but involves a much larger group of managers and employees than in the past.

Jobs such as sales representative, marketing manager, stock analyst, corporate lawyer, business strategist, or operations manager require sharing information and interacting with other people. Here are some business decisions that require knowledge based on collaboration and interaction:

- How much should we charge for this service?
- What kind of discount should we give this customer who is considering our competitor?
- Should we sign a three-year contract with a vendor, or would we be safer with a one-year contract?
- Should we make a special deal with our largest distributor, or work with all distributors on an equal basis?
- Should we put our price list on the Web site where our competitors can see it?
- Where should we be looking for new lines of business?

The answers to these questions generally cannot be found in structured information systems such as those we have described earlier in this chapter. True, these systems help managers and employees by making essential information available. But what's needed to complete these decisions is face-to-face interaction with other employees, managers, vendors, and customers, along with systems that allow them to communicate, collaborate, and share ideas.

We now briefly introduce some of the enterprise-wide information system solutions used by business firms for this purpose. They include Internet-based collaboration environments, e-mail and instant messaging (IM), communication via cell phones and other mobile devices, social networking, wikis, and virtual worlds. Chapters 7, 10, and 11 describe these solutions in greater detail.

In the past, these collaboration and communication systems were not considered an essential part of the information systems field, or even an IT management concern. Today this has changed, and our view of information systems is extended to include these vital management tools.

Internet-Based Collaboration Environments

Teams of employees who work together from many different locations around the world need tools to support workgroup collaboration. These tools provide storage space for team documents, a space separate from corporate e-mail for team communications, group calendars, and an audio-visual environment where members can "meet" face to face in a live video conference (see the Chapter 1 Interactive Session on Management). Products such as IBM's Lotus Sametime and Internet conferencing systems such as WebEx, Microsoft Office Live Meeting, and Adobe Acrobat Connect are especially helpful.

E-mail and Instant Messaging (IM)

Worldwide, there are an estimated 210 billion legitimate e-mail messages sent each day with about 80 billion originating in the United States. One in six people in the world use e-mail. There are also about 12 billion instant messages sent every day, 8 billion of which originate in business networks. E-mail and instant messaging have been embraced by corporations as a major communication and collaboration tool supporting interaction jobs.

Cell Phones and Smartphones

Chapter 1 has described the new mobile platforms that have emerged for coordinating and running the business, including cell phones and smartphones such as iPhones and BlackBerrys. Over 12 million BlackBerry subscribers use wireless devices made by Research in Motion for e-mail, text messaging, instant messaging, phone, and wireless Internet connections. Of the 300 million cell phone subscribers in the United States, one-third are business subscribers (Telecommunications Industry Association, 2008). Cell phones are today a basic part of a firm's telecommunications infrastructure for supporting professionals and other employees whose primary job is talk with one another, with customers and vendors, and with their managers. Cell phones, iPhones, and BlackBerrys are digital devices, and the data generated by their communications may be stored in large corporate systems for later review and use in legal proceedings.

Social Networking

We've all visited social networking sites such as MySpace and Facebook, which feature tools to help people share their interests and interact. Social networking sites such as LinkedIn.com provide networking services to business professionals, while other niche sites have sprung up to serve lawyers, doctors, engineers, and even dentists. IBM has built a Connections component into its Lotus collaboration software to add social networking features. Users are able to set up profiles, blog, tag documents of interest, and use online forums to communicate with other co-workers about their interests and projects. Social networking tools are quickly becoming a corporate tool for sharing ideas and collaborating among interaction-based jobs in the firm.

Wikis

Wikis are in reality a type of Web site that makes it easy for users to contribute and edit text content and graphics without any knowledge of Web page development or programming techniques. The most well-known wiki is Wikipedia, one of the largest collaboratively edited reference projects in the world. It relies on volunteers, makes no money, accepts no advertising, and is used by thirty-five million people in the United States alone. It has become the world's most successful online encyclopedia, with over 20 percent of the online reference market.

Wikis are ideal tools for storing and sharing company knowledge and insights. Enterprise software vendor SAP AG has a wiki that acts as a base of information for people outside the company, such as customers and software developers who build programs that interact with SAP software. In the past, those people asked and sometimes answered questions in an informal way on SAP online forums, but that was an inefficient system, with people asking and answering the same questions over and over.

At Intel Corporation, employees built their own internal wiki in 2006, and it has been edited about 100,000 times and viewed more than 27 million times by Intel employees. The most common search is for the meaning of Intel acronyms such as EASE for "employee access support environment" and POR for "plan of record." Other popular resources include a page about software-engineering processes at the company. Wikis are destined to become a major repository for unstructured corporate knowledge in part because they are so much less costly than formal knowledge management systems and they can be much more dynamic and current.

Virtual Worlds

The case study concluding Chapter 1 features a detailed description of Second Life, an online 3-D **virtual world** where 14 million "residents" have established lives by building graphical representations of themselves known as avatars. Organizations such as IBM and Insead, an international business school with campuses in France and Singapore, are using this virtual world to house online meetings, training sessions, and "lounges." Real-world people represented by avatars meet, interact, and exchange ideas at these virtual locations. Communication takes place in the form of text messages similar to instant messages.

E-BUSINESS, E-COMMERCE, AND E-GOVERNMENT

The systems and technologies we have just described are transforming firms' relationships with customers, employees, suppliers, and logistic partners into digital relationships using networks and the Internet. So much business is now enabled by or based upon digital networks that we use the terms *electronic business* and *electronic commerce* frequently throughout this text. **Electronic business**, or **e-business**, refers to the use of digital technology and the Internet to execute the major business processes in the enterprise. E-business includes activities for the internal management of the firm and for coordination with suppliers and other business partners. It also includes **electronic commerce**, or **e-commerce**. E-commerce is the part of e-business that deals with the buying and selling of goods and services over the Internet. It also encompasses activities supporting those market transactions, such as advertising, marketing, customer support, security, delivery, and payment.

The technologies associated with e-business have also brought about similar changes in the public sector. Governments on all levels are using Internet technology to deliver information and services to citizens, employees, and businesses with which they work. **E-government** refers to the application of the Internet and networking technologies to digitally enable government and public sector agencies' relationships with citizens, businesses, and other arms of government. In addition to improving delivery of government services, e-government can make government operations more efficient and also empower citizens by giving them easier access to information and the ability to network electronically with other citizens. For example, citizens in some states can renew their driver's licenses or apply for unemployment benefits online, and the Internet has become a powerful tool for instantly mobilizing interest groups for political action and fund-raising.

2.4 THE INFORMATION SYSTEMS FUNCTION IN BUSINESS

We've seen that businesses need information systems to operate today and that they use many different kinds of systems. But who is responsible for running these systems? Who is responsible for making sure the hardware, software, and other technologies used by these systems are running properly and are up to date? End users manage their systems from a business standpoint, but managing the technology requires a special information systems function.

In all but the smallest of firms, the **information systems department** is the formal organizational unit responsible for information technology services. The information systems department is responsible for maintaining the hardware, software, data storage, and networks that comprise the firm's IT infrastructure. We describe IT infrastructure in detail in Chapter 5.

THE INFORMATION SYSTEMS DEPARTMENT

The information systems department consists of specialists, such as programmers, systems analysts, project leaders, and information systems managers. **Programmers** are highly trained technical specialists who write the software instructions for computers. **Systems analysts** constitute the principal liaisons between the information systems groups and the rest of the organization. It is the systems analyst's job to translate business problems and requirements into information requirements and systems. **Information systems managers** are leaders of teams of programmers and analysts, project managers, physical facility managers, telecommunications managers, or database specialists. They are also managers of computer operations and data entry staff. In addition, external specialists, such as hardware vendors and manufacturers, software firms, and consultants, frequently participate in the day-to-day operations and long-term planning of information systems.

In many companies, the information systems department is headed by a **chief information officer (CIO)**. The CIO is a senior manager who oversees the use of information technology in the firm. Today's CIOs are expected to have a strong business background as well as information systems expertise and to play a leadership role in integrating technology into the firm's business strategy. Large firms today also have positions for a chief security officer, chief knowledge officer, and chief privacy officer all of whom work closely with the CIO.

The **chief security officer (CSO)** is in charge of information systems security for the firm and is responsible for enforcing the firm's information security policy (see Chapter 8). (Sometimes this position is called the chief information security officer (CISO) where information systems security is separated from physical security.) The CSO is responsible for educating and training users and information systems specialists about security, keeping management aware of security threats and breakdowns, and maintaining the tools and policies chosen to implement security.

Information systems security and the need to safeguard personal data have become so important that corporations collecting vast quantities of personal data have established positions for a **chief privacy officer (CPO)**. The CPO is responsible for ensuring that the company complies with existing data privacy laws.

The **chief knowledge officer (CKO)** is responsible for the firm's knowledge management program. The CKO helps design programs and systems to find new sources of knowledge or to make better use of existing knowledge in organizational and management processes.

End users are representatives of departments outside of the information systems group for whom applications are developed. These users are playing an increasingly large role in the design and development of information systems.

In the early years of computing, the information systems group was composed mostly of programmers who performed very highly specialized but limited technical functions. Today, a growing proportion of staff members are systems analysts and network specialists, with the information systems department acting as a powerful change agent in the organization. The information systems department suggests new business strategies and new information-based products and services, and coordinates both the development of the technology and the planned changes in the organization.

In the past, firms generally built their own software and managed their own computing facilities. Today, many firms are turning to external vendors to provide these services (see Chapters 5 and 13) and are using their information systems departments to manage these service providers.

ORGANIZING THE INFORMATION SYSTEMS FUNCTION

There are many types of business firms, and there are many ways in which the IT function is organized within the firm (see Figure 2-10). A very small company will not have a formal information systems group. It might have one employee who is responsible for keeping its networks and applications running, or it might use consultants for these services. Larger companies will have a separate information systems department, which may be organized along several different lines, depending on the nature and interests of the firm.

Sometimes you'll see a decentralized arrangement where each functional area of the business has its own information systems department and management that typically reports to a senior manager or chief information officer. In other words, the marketing department would have its own information systems group as would manufacturing and each of the other business functions. The job of the CIO is to review information technology investments and decisions in the functional areas. The advantage of this approach is that systems are built that directly address the business needs of the functional areas. However, central guidance is weak and the danger is high that many incompatible systems will be built, increasing costs as each group makes its own technology purchases.

In another arrangement, the information systems function operates as a separate department similar to the other functional departments with a large staff, a group of middle managers, and a senior management group that fights for its share of the company's resources. You'll see this approach in many large firms. This central information systems department makes technology decisions for the entire company, which is more likely to produce more compatible systems and more coherent long-term systems development plans.

FIGURE 2-10   ORGANIZATION OF THE INFORMATION SYSTEMS FUNCTION

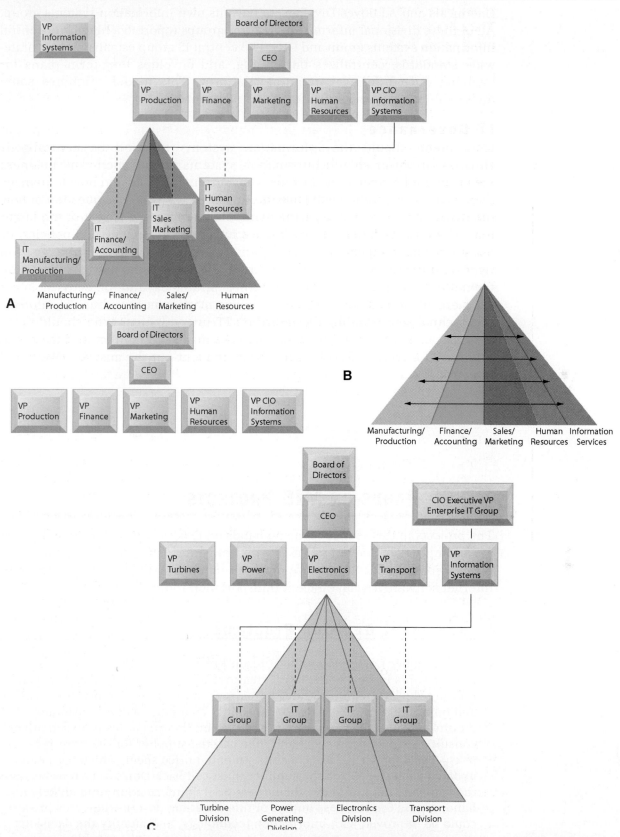

There are alternative ways of organizing the information systems function within the business: within each functional area (A), as a separate department under central control (B), or represented in each division of a large multidivisional company but under centralized control (C).

Very large "Fortune 1,000"-size firms with multiple divisions and product lines might allow each division (such as the Consumer Products Division or the Chemicals and Additives Division) to have its own information systems group. All of these divisional information systems groups report to a high-level central information systems group and CIO. The central IS group establishes corporate-wide standards, centralizes purchasing, and develops long-term plans for evolving the corporate computing platform. This model combines some divisional independence with some centralization.

IT Governance

How much should the information systems function be centralized? How much power should information systems management and business management be given to determine what systems to build and how to manage them? Each organization will have its own set of answers. The question of how the information systems department should be organized is part of the larger issue of **IT governance**. IT governance includes the strategy and policies for using information technology within an organization. It specifies the decision rights and framework for accountability to ensure that the use of information technology supports the organization's strategies and objectives. What decisions must be made to ensure effective management and use of information technology, including the return on IT invesetments? Who should make these decisions? How will these decisions be made and monitored? Firms with superior IT governance will have clearly thought out the answers (Weill and Ross, 2004).

2.5 | HANDS-ON MIS PROJECTS

The projects in this section give you hands-on experience analyzing opportunities to improve business processes with new information system applications, using a spreadsheet to improve decision making about suppliers, and using Internet software to plan efficient transportation routes.

Management Decision Problems

1. Don's Lumber Company on the Hudson River is one of the oldest retail lumber yards in New York State. It features a large selection of materials for flooring, decks, moldings, windows, siding, and roofing. The prices of lumber and other building materials are constantly changing. When a customer inquires about the price on pre-finished wood flooring, sales representatives consult a manual price sheet and then call the supplier for the most recent price. The supplier in turn consults a manual price sheet, which has been updated each day. Often the supplier must call back Don's sales reps because the company does not have the newest pricing information immediately on hand. Assess the business impact of this situation, describe how this process could be improved with information technology, and identify the decisions that would have to be made to implement a solution. Who would be making those decisions?

2. Henry's Hardware is a mom-and-pop business in Sacramento, California. Store space is limited and the rent has doubled over the past five years. The owners, Henry and Kathleen Nelson, are under pressure to use every square foot of space as profitably as possible. The Nelsons have never kept detailed records of stock in inventory or of their sales. As soon as a shipment of goods arrives, the items are immediately placed on store shelves to be sold. Invoices from suppliers are only kept for tax purposes. When an item is sold, the item number and price are rung up at the cash register. The Nelsons use their own judgment in identifying items that need to be reordered. Many times, however, they are caught short and lose a sale. What is the business impact of this situation? How could information systems help Henry and Kathleen run their business? What data should these systems capture? What reports should the systems produce? What decisions could the systems improve?

Improving Decision Making: Use a Spreadsheet to Select Suppliers

Software skills: Spreadsheet date functions, data filtering, DAVERAGE function
Business skills: Analyzing supplier performance and pricing

In this exercise, you will learn how to use spreadsheet software to improve management decisions about selecting suppliers. You will start with raw transactional data about suppliers organized as a large spreadsheet list. You will use the spreadsheet software to filter the data based on several different criteria to select the best supplies for your company.

You run a company that manufactures aircraft components. You have many competitors who are trying to offer lower prices and better service to customers, and you are trying to determine whether you can benefit from better supply chain management. At the Laudon Web site for Chapter 2, you will find a spreadsheet file that contains a list of all of the items that your firm has ordered from its suppliers during the past three months. A sample is shown on the next page, but the Web site may have a more recent version of this spreadsheet for this exercise. The fields in the spreadsheet file include vendor name, vendor identification number, purchaser's order number, item identification number and item description (for each item ordered from the vendor), cost per item, number of units of the item ordered (quantity), total cost of each order, vendor's accounts payable terms, order date, and actual arrival date for each order.

Prepare a recommendation of how you can use the data in this spreadsheet database to improve your decisions about selecting suppliers. Some criteria to consider for identifying preferred suppliers include the supplier's track record for on-time deliveries, suppliers offering the best accounts payable terms, and suppliers offering lower pricing when the same item can be provided by multiple suppliers. Use your spreadsheet software to prepare reports to support your recommendations.

Achieving Operational Excellence: Using Internet Software to Plan Efficient Transportation Routes

In this exercise, you will use the same online software tool that businesses use to map out their transportation routes and select the most efficient route. The MapQuest (www.mapquest.com)Web site includes interactive capabilities for planning a trip. The software on this Web site can calculate the distance between two points and provide itemized driving directions to any location.

You have just started working as a dispatcher for Cross-Country Transport, a new trucking and delivery service based in Cleveland, Ohio. Your first assignment is to plan a delivery of office equipment and furniture from Elkhart, Indiana (at the corner of E. Indiana Ave. and Prairie Street) to Hagerstown, Maryland (corner of Eastern Blvd. N. and Potomac Ave.). To guide your trucker, you need to know the most efficient route between the two cities. Use MapQuest to find the route that is the shortest distance between the two cities. Use MapQuest again to find the route that takes the least time. Compare the results. Which route should Cross-Country use?

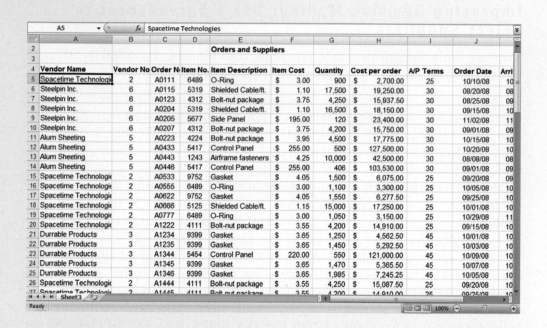

LEARNING TRACK MODULES

The following Learning Tracks provide content relevant to topics covered in this chapter.

1. Systems from a Functional Perspective
2. Challenges of Using Business Information Systems

Review Summary

1. *What are business processes? How are they related to information systems?*

A business process is a logically related set of activities that defines how specific business tasks are performed, and it represents a unique way in which an organization coordinates work, information, and knowledge. Managers need to pay attention to business processes because they determine how well the organization can execute its business, and they may be a source of strategic advantage. There are business processes specific to each of the major business functions, but many business processes are cross-functional. Information systems automate parts of business processes and they can help organizations redesign and streamline these processes.

2. *How do systems serve the various levels of management in a business?*

Systems serving operational management are transaction processing systems (TPS), such as payroll or order processing, that track the flow of the daily routine transactions necessary to conduct business. Management information systems (MIS) and decision-support systems (DSS) support middle management. Most MIS reports condense information from TPS and are not highly analytical. DSS support management decisions that are unique and rapidly changing using advanced analytical models and data analysis capabilities. Executive support systems (ESS) support senior management by providing data that are often in the form of graphs and charts delivered via portals using many sources of internal and external information.

3. *How do enterprise applications, collaboration and communication systems, and intranets improve organizational performance?*

Enterprise applications (enterprise systems, supply chain management systems, customer relationship management systems, and knowledge management systems) are designed to coordinate multiple functions and business processes. Enterprise systems integrate the key internal business processes of a firm into a single software system to improve coordination, efficiency, and decision making. Supply chain management systems help the firm manage its relationship with suppliers to optimize the planning, sourcing, manufacturing, and delivery of products and services. Customer relationship management uses information systems to coordinate all of the business processes surrounding the firm's interactions with its customers to optimize firm revenue and customer satisfaction. Knowledge management systems enable firms to optimize the creation, sharing, and distribution of knowledge. Jobs where interaction is the primary value-adding activity benefit from collaboration and communication systems. Intranets and extranets use Internet technology and standards to assemble information from disparate systems and present it to the user in a Web page format. Extranets make portions of private corporate intranets available to outsiders.

4. *What is the difference between e-business, e-commerce, and e-government?*

E-business (electronic business) refers to the use of digital technology and the Internet to execute a firm's business processes. It includes internal business processes and processes for coordination with suppliers and other external entities. E-commerce (electronic commerce) is the part of e-business dealing with the purchase and sale of goods and services over the Internet, including support activities such as marketing and customer support. E-government refers to the application of the Internet and networking technologies to digitally enable government and public sector agencies' relationships with citizens, businesses, and other governmental bodies.

5. *What is the role of the information systems function in a business?*

The information systems department is the formal organizational unit responsible for information technology services. It is responsible for maintaining the hardware, software, data storage, and networks that comprise the firm's IT infrastructure. The department consists of specialists, such as programmers, systems analysts, project leaders, and information systems managers, and is often headed by a CIO.

Key Terms

Chief information officer (CIO), 93
Chief knowledge officer (CKO), 94
Chief privacy officer (CPO), 94
Chief security officer (CSO), 93
Customer relationship management (CRM) systems, 87
Decision-support systems (DSS), 78
Digital dashboard, 82
Electronic business (e-business), 92
Electronic commerce (e-commerce), 92
E-government, 92
End users, 94
Enterprise applications, 82

Enterprise systems, 85
Executive support systems (ESS), 81
Information systems department, 93
Information systems managers, 93
Interorganizational system, 86
IT governance, 96
Knowledge management systems (KMS), 88
Management information systems (MIS), 77
Portal, 81
Programmers, 93
Supply chain management (SCM) systems, 86
Systems analysts, 93
Transaction processing systems (TPS), 75
Virtual world, 92

Review Questions

1. What are business processes? How are they related to information systems?

- Define business processes and describe their relationship to business performance.
- Describe the relationship between information systems and business processes.

2. How do systems serve the various levels of management in a business?

- Describe the characteristics of TPS and role they play in a business.
- Describe the characteristics of MIS and explain how MIS differ from TPS and from DSS.
- Describe the characteristics of DSS and explain how DSS differ from ESS.
- Describe the relationship between TPS, MIS, DSS, and ESS.

3. How do enterprise applications, collaboration and communication systems, and intranets improve organizational performance?

- Explain how enterprise applications improve organizational performance.
- Define enterprise systems and describe how they change the way an organization works.

- Define supply chain management systems and describe how they benefit businesses.
- Define customer relationship management systems and describe how they benefit businesses.
- Describe the role of knowledge management systems in the enterprise.
- List and describe the various types of collaboration and communication systems.
- Explain how intranets and extranets help firms integrate information and business processes.

4. What is the difference between e-business, e-commerce, and e-government?

- Distinguish between e-business and e-commerce.
- Define and describe e-government.

5. What is the role of the information systems function in a business?

- Describe how the information systems function supports a business.
- Compare the roles played by programmers, systems analysts, information systems managers, the CIO, CSO, and CKO.

Discussion Questions

1. How could information systems be used to support the order fulfillment process illustrated in Figure 2-1? What are the most important pieces of information these systems should capture? Explain your answer.

2. Adopting an enterprise application is a key business decision as well as a technology decision. Do you agree? Why or why not? Who should make this decision?

Video Cases

You will find video cases illustrating some of the concepts in this chapter on the Laudon Web site along with questions to help you analyze the cases.

Collaboration and Teamwork: Identifying Management Decisions and Systems

With a team of three or four other students, find a description of a manager in a corporation in *Business Week*, *Forbes*, *Fortune*, *The Wall Street Journal*, or another business publication or do your research on the Web. Gather information about what the manager does and the role he or she plays in the company. Identify the organizational level and business function where this manager works. Make a list of the kinds of decisions this manager has to make and the kind of information that manager would need for those decisions. Suggest how information systems could supply this information. If possible, use Google Sites to post links to Web pages, team communication announcements, and work assignments; to brainstorm; and to work collaboratively on project documents. Try to use Google Docs to develop a presentation of your findings for the class.

Modernization of NTUC Income
CASE STUDY

NTUC Income (Income), one of Singapore's largest insurers, has over 1.8 million policy holders with total assets of S$21.3 billion. The insurer employs about 3,400 insurance advisors and 1,200 office staff, with the majority located across an eight-branch network. On June 1, 2003, Income succeeded in the migration of its legacy insurance systems to a digital web-based system. The Herculean task required not only the upgrading of hardware and applications, it also required Income to streamline its decade-old business processes and IT practices.

Up until a few years ago, Income's insurance processes were very tedious and paper-based. The entire insurance process started with customers meeting an agent, filling in forms and submitting documents. The agent would then submit the forms at branches, from where they were sent by couriers to the Office Services department. The collection schedule could introduce delays of two to three days. Office Services would log documents, sort them, and then send them to departments for underwriting. Proposals were allocated to underwriting staff, mostly randomly. Accepted proposals were sent for printing at the Computer Services department and then redistributed. For storage, all original documents were packed and sent to warehouses where, over two to three days, a total of seven staff would log and store the documents. In all, paper policies comprising 45 million documents were stored in over 16,000 cartons at three warehouses. Whenever a document needed to be retrieved, it would take about two days to locate and ship it by courier. Refiling would again take about two days.

In 2002, despite periodic investments to upgrade the HP 3000 mainframe that hosted the core insurance applications as well as the accounting and management information systems, it still frequently broke down. According to James Kang, CIO at Income, "The system breakdowns were a real nightmare. Work would stop and the staff had to choose either data reconciliation, or backup. However, the HP 3000 backup system allowed restoration to only up to the previous day's backup data. If the daily backup was not completed at the end of the day, the affected day's data would be lost and costly and tedious reconciliation would be needed to bring the data up to date." In one of the hardware crashes, reconciliation took several months to restore the data loss. In all, the HP 3000 system experienced a total of three major hardware failures, resulting in a total of six days of complete downtime.

That was not enough. The COBOL programs that were developed in the early 1980s and maintained by Income's in-house IT team, also broke multiple times, halted the systems and caused temporary interruptions. In addition, the IT team found developing new products in COBOL to be quite cumbersome and the time taken to launch new products ranged from a few weeks to months.

At the same time, transaction processing for policy underwriting was still a batch process and information was not available to agents and advisors in real-time. As a result, when staff processed a new customer application for motor insurance, they did not know if the applicant was an existing customer of Income, which led to the loss of opportunities for cross-product sales. Commenting on the problems faced by the agents, Kang said, "When the agents tried to submit the documents using notebooks, they ran into a lot of problems. HP 3000 was a terrible machine to connect to such devices. And with more of the advisors telecommuting, availability became an issue too." In addition, various departments did not have up-to-date information and had to pass physical documents among each other.

All this changed in June 2003, when Income switched to the Java based eBao LifeSystem from eBao Technology. The software comprised three subsystems - Policy Administration, Sales Management and Supplementary Resources. Commenting on its features, Kang said, "It has everything we are looking for - a customer-centric design, seamless integration with imaging and barcode technology, a product definition module that supports new products, new channels and changes in business processes."

Implementation work started in September 2002 and the project was completed in nine months. By May 2003, all the customization, data migration of Income's individual and group life insurance businesses and training were completed.

The new system was immediately operational on high-availability platform. All applications resided on two or more servers, each connected by two or more communication lines, all of which were "load balanced." This robust architecture minimized downtime occurrence due to hardware or operating system failures.

As part of eBao implementation, Income decided to replace its entire IT infrastructure with a more robust, scalable architecture. For example, all servicing branches were equipped with scanners; monitors were changed to 20 inches; PC RAM size was upgraded to 128 MB; and new hardware and software for application servers, database servers, web servers, and disk storage systems were installed. Furthermore, the LAN cables were replaced with faster cables, a fiber-optic backbone, and wireless capability.

In addition, Income also revamped its business continuity and disaster-recovery plans. A real-time hot backup disaster-recovery center was implemented, where the machines were always running and fully operational. Data was transmitted immediately on the fly from the primary datacenter to the backup machines' data storage. In the event of the datacenter site becoming unavailable, the operations could be switched quickly to the disaster-recovery site without the need to rely on restoration of previous day data.

Moving to a paperless environment, however, was not easy. Income had to throw away all paper records, including legal paper documents. Under the new system, all documents were scanned and stored on "trusted" storage devices - secured, reliable digital vaults that enabled strict compliance with stringent statutory requirements. Income had to train employees who had been accustomed to working with paper to use the eBao system and change the way they worked.

As s result of adopting eBao Life System, about 500 office staff and 3,400 insurance advisors could access the system anytime, anywhere. Staff members who would telecommute enjoyed faster access to information, almost as fast as those who accessed the information in the office.

According to Kang, "We got a singular view of every customer - across products and channels and even better life and general insurance business lines. That allowed us opportunities to cross-sell and improve customer service. In addition, because of the straight through processing workflow capabilities, we had 50 percent savings on both the time and cost needed to process policies. We had also cut the time needed to design and launch new products which was reduced from weeks to just days using the table-driven rule-based product-definition module."

Commenting on the benefits of eBao system, the former CEO Tan Kin Lian remarked, "eBaoTech LifeSystem has the best straight through processing workflow and it is very flexible. It cuts our new product launch time from months to days. It also allows us to support agents, brokers, and customers to do online services easily. I got a fantastic deal: the best system with much lower cost and much shorter implementation time. I have to say that this is a revolution!"

Sources: Melanie Liew, Computerworld, July 2004; "NTUC Income of Singapore Successfully Implemented eBaoTech Lifesystem," ebaotech.com, accessed November 2008; Neerja Sethi & D G Allampallai, "NTUC Income of Singapore (A): Re-architecting Legacy Systems," asiacase.com, October 2005

CASE STUDY QUESTIONS

1. What were the problems faced by Income in this case? How were the problems resolved by the new digital system?

2. What types of information systems and business processes were used by Income before migrating to the fully digital system?

3. Describe the Information systems and IT infrastructure at Income after migrating to the fully digital system?

4. What benefits did Income reap from the new system?

5. How well is Income prepared for the future? Are the problems described in the case likely to be repeated?

• Case contributed by Neerja Sethi and Vijay Sethi, Nanyang Technological University.

Chapter 3

Information Systems, Organizations, and Strategy

LEARNING OBJECTIVES

After reading this chapter, you will be able to answer the following questions:

1. Which features of organizations do managers need to know about to build and use information systems successfully? What is the impact of information systems on organizations?

2. How does Porter's competitive forces model help companies develop competitive strategies using information systems?

3. How do the value chain and value web models help businesses identify opportunities for strategic information system applications?

4. How do information systems help businesses use synergies, core competencies, and network-based strategies to achieve competitive advantage?

5. What are the challenges posed by strategic information systems and how should they be addressed?

Interactive Sessions:

Can Technology Save Soldiers' Lives in Iraq?

Can Detroit Make the Cars Customers Want?

CHAPTER OUTLINE

EBAY FINE-TUNES ITS STRATEGY

EBay has been synonymous with Internet auctions. It started out as one of the first successful Internet auction businesses, mushrooming into a gigantic electronic marketplace hosting over 532,000 online storefronts all over the world. In 2007 eBay's marketplaces generated nearly 77 billion in revenue. Hundreds of thousands of people support themselves by selling on eBay and millions more use eBay to supplement their income. EBay now boasts 83 million active users.

EBay derives the bulk of its revenue from fees and commissions associated with its sales transactions. A portion of eBay's revenue comes from direct advertising on the site, and some comes from end-to-end service providers such as PayPal whose services increase the ease and speed of eBay transactions.

Not long ago, eBay's growth strategy focused on expansion in geography and scope and on continuing innovation to enhance the variety and appeal of products on its sites. EBay has been developing and acquiring new products and services that encompass all the activities people perform on the Internet. It has been fashioning a diversified portfolio of companies with a hand in each of the Internet's big cash pots: shopping, communicating, search, and entertainment.

PayPal, whose service enables the exchange of money between individuals over the Internet, brings additional transaction-based fee revenue. EBay is banking on PayPal becoming the standard payment method for online transactions. The service already receives 40 percent of its business from payment transactions that are not associated with eBay.

In 2005, eBay acquired Shopping.com, an online shopping comparison site, and Skype Technologies, which provides a service for free or low-cost voice calls over the Internet. Markets that eBay traditionally had trouble penetrating, such as real estate, travel, new-car sales, and expensive collectibles, require more communication among buyers and sellers than eBay currently offers, and Skype provides voice communication services to help.

EBay also acquired the ticket-reselling Web site StubHub, bought a 25-percent stake in classified ad site Craigslist, and purchased Kurant, now ProStores, whose technology helps users set up online stores. Some analysts report that while many of eBay's individual acquisitions appear successful, they haven't created the synergy that was intended, and diversification has detracted from eBay's core business, auctions.

But eBay's auction business is changing, too. EBay sells many items at a fixed price, and fixed sales already account for 40 percent of marketplace revenue. This side of the business is growing much more rapidly than online auctions. Amazon.com and other rivals are attracting more shoppers with fixed-price listings. To shift toward that model, eBay struck a deal with giant Web retailer Buy.com to sell millions of DVDs, electronics, books, and other items on eBay at lower fees than would be charged individual sellers. In August 2008, eBay lowered its

listing fees for all sellers offering fixed-priced items under its "Buy It Now" format.

Mom and pop dealers have objected vociferously, but eBay says that hosting fixed-price sales by reliable retailers makes shopping more customer-friendly and predictable. "We are challenging some of the core assumptions we have made about our business," observes Stephanie Tilenius, general manager of eBay North America. "Instead of focusing on being an auction business, we are looking at what it takes to create the best marketplace out there." Will bringing large sellers to its site dilute eBay's brand and reputation as a dynamic flea market? Or will it steer eBay toward the fastest part of e-commerce growth? The e-commerce world is watching.

Sources: Laurie J. Flynn, "EBay Is Planning to Emphasize Fixed-Price Sales Format Over Its Auction Model," *The New York Times*, August 20, 2008; Brad Stone, "Buy.com Deal with Ebay Angers Sellers," *The New York Times*, July 14, 2008, "Profit Climbs for eBay, but Auction Growth Is Slowing," *The New York Times*, July 17, 2008, and "EBay's Leader Moves Swiftly on a Revamping," *The New York Times*, January 24, 2008; Catherine Holahan, "eBay's Changing Identity," *Business Week*, April 23, 2007; and Associated Press, "eBay Rethinks Its Ways as It Enters Middle Age," accessed via CNN.com, June 18, 2007.

The story of eBay illustrates some of the ways that information systems help businesses compete, and the interdependence of business processes, information systems, and the organization's surrounding environment. It also illustrates the challenges of sustaining a competitive advantage.

The chapter-opening diagram calls attention to important points raised by this case and this chapter. EBay was able to take advantage of the opportunities created by the Internet. It pioneered in online auctions where individuals could sell to other individuals. This strategy catapulted eBay to become one of the first—and largest—Internet retailers. Today its name is still synonymous with Internet auctions.

But eBay operates in a very rapidly changing environment where customers can easily switch to other online retailers that offer more value and convenience. As time went on, eBay's original strategy was not enough to keep it profitable and growing. EBay started losing market share to Amazon and other online retailers who were able to offer the convenience of goods sold at a fixed-price and better service. EBay has had to continually fine-tune its strategy and business processes to remain competitive. EBay revised its strategy by acquiring other Internet businesses, and then by de-emphasizing online auctions in favor of fixed price sales by large companies such as Buy.com. Today it is a large but highly diversified online platform where many different types of businesses engage in e-commerce.

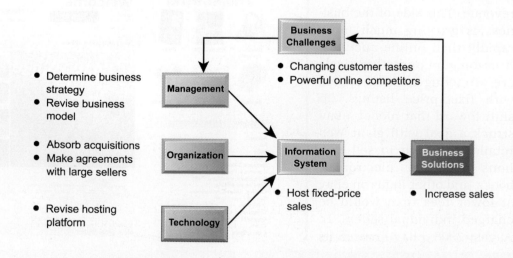

3.1 ORGANIZATIONS AND INFORMATION SYSTEMS

Information systems and organizations influence one another. Information systems are built by managers to serve the interests of the business firm. At the same time, the organization must be aware of and open to the influences of information systems to benefit from new technologies.

The interaction between information technology and organizations is complex and is influenced by many mediating factors, including the organization's structure, business processes, politics, culture, surrounding environment, and management decisions (see Figure 3-1). You will need to understand how information systems can change social and work life in your firm. You will not be able to design new systems successfully or understand existing systems without understanding your own business organization.

As a manager, you will be the one to decide which systems will be built, what they will do, and how they will be implemented. You may not be able to anticipate all of the consequences of these decisions. Some of the changes that occur in business firms because of new information technology (IT) investments cannot be foreseen and have results that may or may not meet your expectations. Who would have imagined ten years ago, for instance, that e-mail and instant messaging would become a dominant form of business communication and that many managers would be inundated with more than 200 e-mail messages each day?

WHAT IS AN ORGANIZATION?

An **organization** is a stable, formal social structure that takes resources from the environment and processes them to produce outputs. This technical definition focuses on three elements of an organization. Capital and labor are primary production factors provided by the environment. The organization

FIGURE 3-1   **THE TWO-WAY RELATIONSHIP BETWEEN ORGANIZATIONS AND INFORMATION TECHNOLOGY**

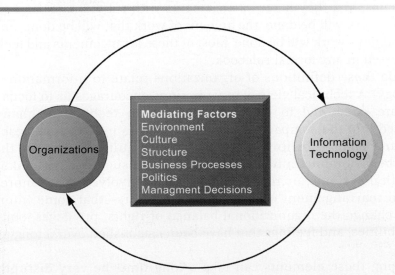

This complex two-way relationship is mediated by many factors, not the least of which are the decisions made—or not made—by managers. Other factors mediating the relationship include the organizational culture, structure, politics, business processes, and environment.

FIGURE 3-2 **THE TECHNICAL MICROECONOMIC DEFINITION OF THE ORGANIZATION**

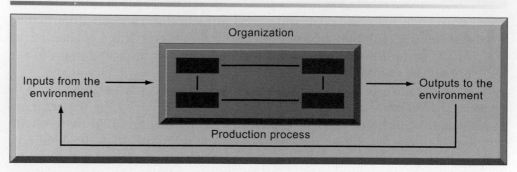

In the microeconomic definition of organizations, capital and labor (the primary production factors provided by the environment) are transformed by the firm through the production process into products and services (outputs to the environment). The products and services are consumed by the environment, which supplies additional capital and labor as inputs in the feedback loop.

(the firm) transforms these inputs into products and services in a production function. The products and services are consumed by environments in return for supply inputs (see Figure 3-2).

An organization is more stable than an informal group (such as a group of friends that meets every Friday for lunch) in terms of longevity and routineness. Organizations are formal legal entities with internal rules and procedures that must abide by laws. Organizations are also social structures because they are a collection of social elements, much as a machine has a structure—a particular arrangement of valves, cams, shafts, and other parts.

This definition of organizations is powerful and simple, but it is not very descriptive or even predictive of real-world organizations. A more realistic behavioral definition of an organization is that it is a collection of rights, privileges, obligations, and responsibilities that is delicately balanced over a period of time through conflict and conflict resolution (see Figure 3-3).

In this behavioral view of the firm, people who work in organizations develop customary ways of working; they gain attachments to existing relationships; and they make arrangements with subordinates and superiors about how work will be done, the amount of work that will be done, and under what conditions work will be done. Most of these arrangements and feelings are not discussed in any formal rulebook.

How do these definitions of organizations relate to information systems technology? A technical view of organizations encourages us to focus on how inputs are combined to create outputs when technology changes are introduced into the company. The firm is seen as infinitely malleable, with capital and labor substituting for each other quite easily. But the more realistic behavioral definition of an organization suggests that building new information systems, or rebuilding old ones, involves much more than a technical rearrangement of machines or workers—that some information systems change the organizational balance of rights, privileges, obligations, responsibilities, and feelings that have been established over a long period of time.

Changing these elements can take a long time, be very disruptive, and require more resources to support training and learning. For instance, the length of time required to implement effectively a new information system is

FIGURE 3-3   THE BEHAVIORAL VIEW OF ORGANIZATIONS

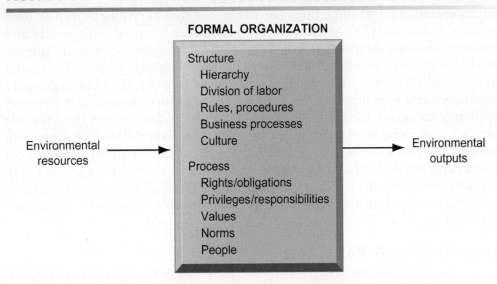

The behavioral view of organizations emphasizes group relationships, values, and structures.

much longer than usually anticipated simply because there is a lag between implementing a technical system and teaching employees and managers how to use the system.

Technological change requires changes in who owns and controls information, who has the right to access and update that information, and who makes decisions about whom, when, and how. This more complex view forces us to look at the way work is designed and the procedures used to achieve outputs.

The technical and behavioral definitions of organizations are not contradictory. Indeed, they complement each other: The technical definition tells us how thousands of firms in competitive markets combine capital, labor, and information technology, whereas the behavioral model takes us inside the individual firm to see how that technology affects the organization's inner workings. Section 3.2 describes how each of these definitions of organizations can help explain the relationships between information systems and organizations.

FEATURES OF ORGANIZATIONS

All modern organizations have certain characteristics. They are bureaucracies with clear-cut divisions of labor and specialization. Organizations arrange specialists in a hierarchy of authority in which everyone is accountable to someone and authority is limited to specific actions governed by abstract rules or procedures. These rules create a system of impartial and universal decision making. Organizations try to hire and promote employees on the basis of technical qualifications and professionalism (not personal connections). The organization is devoted to the principle of efficiency: maximizing output using limited inputs. Other features of organizations include their business processes, organizational culture, organizational politics, surrounding environments, structure, goals, constituencies, and leadership styles. All of these features affect the kinds of information systems used by organizations.

Routines and Business Processes

All organizations, including business firms, become very efficient over time because individuals in the firm develop **routines** for producing goods and services. Routines—sometimes called *standard operating procedures*—are precise rules, procedures, and practices that have been developed to cope with virtually all expected situations. As employees learn these routines, they become highly productive and efficient, and the firm is able to reduce its costs over time as efficiency increases. For instance, when you visit a doctor's office, receptionists have a well-developed set of routines for gathering basic information from you; nurses have a different set of routines for preparing you for an interview with a doctor; and the doctor has a well-developed set of routines for diagnosing you. *Business processes*, which we introduced in Chapters 1 and 2, are collections of such routines. A business firm in turn is a collection of business processes (Figure 3-4).

Organizational Politics

People in organizations occupy different positions with different specialties, concerns, and perspectives. As a result, they naturally have divergent viewpoints about how resources, rewards, and punishments should be

FIGURE 3-4   ROUTINES, BUSINESS PROCESSES, AND FIRMS

Routines, Business Processes, and Firms

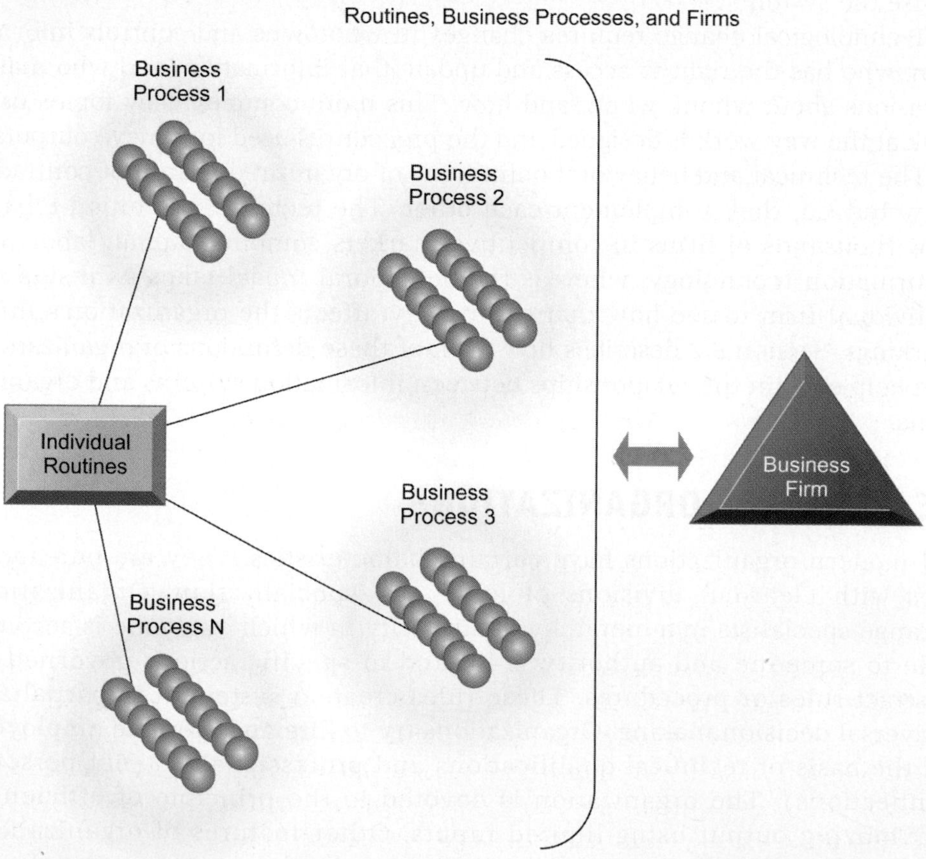

All organizations are composed of individual routines and behaviors, a collection of which make up a business process. A collection of business processes make up the business firm. New information system applications require that individual routines and business processes change to achieve high levels of organizational performance.

distributed. These differences matter to both managers and employees, and they result in political struggle for resources, competition, and conflict within every organization. Political resistance is one of the great difficulties of bringing about organizational change—especially the development of new information systems. Virtually all large information systems investments by a firm that bring about significant changes in strategy, business objectives, business processes, and procedures become politically charged events. Managers that know how to work with the politics of an organization will be more successful than less-skilled managers in implementing new information systems. Throughout this book you will find many examples of where internal politics defeated the best-laid plans for an information system.

Organizational Culture

All organizations have bedrock, unassailable, unquestioned (by the members) assumptions that define their goals and products. Organizational culture encompasses this set of assumptions about what products the organization should produce, how it should produce them, where, and for whom. Generally, these cultural assumptions are taken totally for granted and are rarely publicly announced or spoken about. Business processes—the actual way business firms produce value—are usually ensconced in the organization's culture.

You can see organizational culture at work by looking around your university or college. Some bedrock assumptions of university life are that professors know more than students, the reason students attend college is to learn, and classes follow a regular schedule. Organizational culture is a powerful unifying force that restrains political conflict and promotes common understanding, agreement on procedures, and common practices. If we all share the same basic cultural assumptions, agreement on other matters is more likely.

At the same time, organizational culture is a powerful restraint on change, especially technological change. Most organizations will do almost anything to avoid making changes in basic assumptions. Any technological change that threatens commonly held cultural assumptions usually meets a great deal of resistance. However, there are times when the only sensible way for a firm to move forward is to employ a new technology that directly opposes an existing organizational culture. When this occurs, the technology is often stalled while the culture slowly adjusts.

Organizational Environments

Organizations reside in environments from which they draw resources and to which they supply goods and services. Organizations and environments have a reciprocal relationship. On the one hand, organizations are open to, and dependent on, the social and physical environment that surrounds them. Without financial and human resources—people willing to work reliably and consistently for a set wage or revenue from customers—organizations could not exist. Organizations must respond to legislative and other requirements imposed by government, as well as the actions of customers and competitors. On the other hand, organizations can influence their environments. For example, business firms form alliances with other businesses to influence the political process; they advertise to influence customer acceptance of their products.

Figure 3-5 illustrates the role of information systems in helping organizations perceive changes in their environments and also in helping organizations act on their environments. Information systems are key instruments for *environmental scanning*, helping managers identify external changes that might require an organizational response.

Environments generally change much faster than organizations. New technologies, new products, and changing public tastes and values (many of which result in new government regulations) put strains on any organization's culture, politics, and people. Most organizations are unable to adapt to a rapidly changing environment. Inertia built into an organization's standard operating procedures, the political conflict raised by changes to the existing order, and the threat to closely held cultural values inhibit organizations from making significant changes. Young firms typically lack resources to sustain even short periods of troubled times. It is not surprising that only 10 percent of the Fortune 500 companies in 1919 still exist today.

Disruptive Technologies: Riding the Wave. Technology's impact on organizations is especially noteworthy because it has become such a disruptive force. Sometimes a new technology comes along like a tsunami and destroys everything in its path. Some firms are able to create these tsunamis and ride the wave to profits; others learn quickly and are able to swim with the current; still others are obliterated because their products, services and business models are obsolete. They may be very efficient at doing what no longer needs to be done! There are also cases where no firms benefit, and all the gains go to consumers (firms fail to capture any profits). Business history is filled with examples of **disruptive technologies**. Table 3-1 describes just a few disruptive technologies from the past and some from the likely near term future.

FIGURE 3-5 **ENVIRONMENTS AND ORGANIZATIONS HAVE A RECIPROCAL RELATIONSHIP**

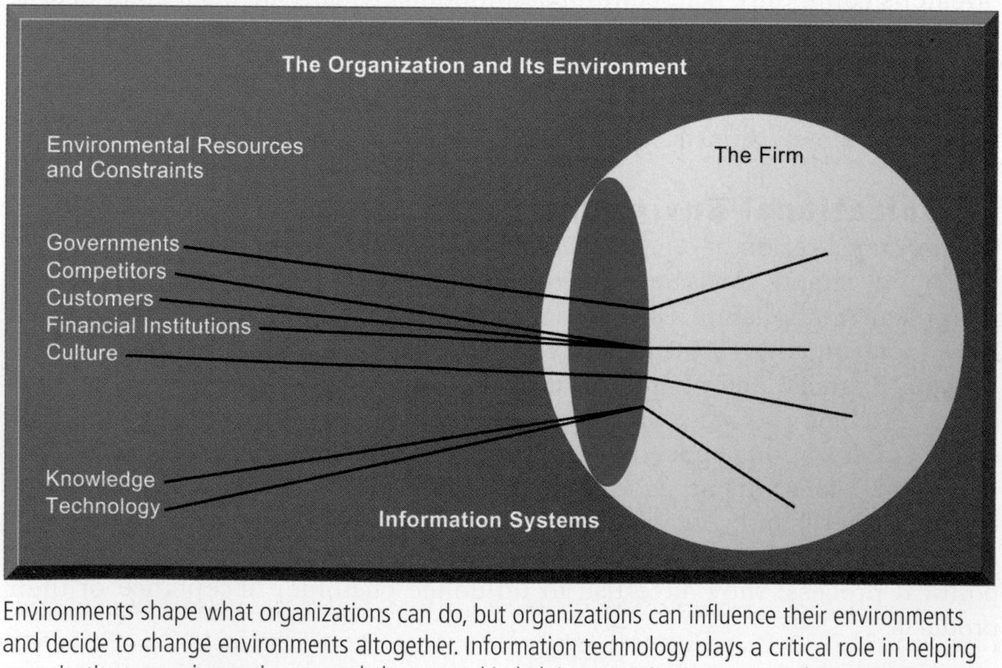

Environments shape what organizations can do, but organizations can influence their environments and decide to change environments altogether. Information technology plays a critical role in helping organizations perceive environmental change and in helping organizations act on their environment.

TABLE 3-1 DISRUPTIVE TECHNOLOGIES: WINNERS AND LOSERS

TECHNOLOGY	DESCRIPTION	WINNERS AND LOSERS
Microprocessor chips (1971)	Thousands and eventually millions of transistors on a silicon chip	Microprocessor firms win (Intel, Texas Instruments) while transistor firms (GE) decline.
Personal computers (1975)	Small, inexpensive, but fully functional desktop computers	PC manufacturers (HP, Apple, IBM), and chip manufacturers prosper (Intel), while mainframe (IBM) and minicomputer (DEC) firms lose.
PC word processing software (1979)	Inexpensive, limited but functional text editing and formatting for personal computers	PC and software manufacturers (Microsoft, HP, Apple) prosper while the typewriter industry disappears.
World Wide Web (1989)	A global database of digital files and "pages" instantly available	Owners of online content and news benefit, while traditional publishers (newspapers, magazines, and broadcast television) lose.
Internet music services (1998)	Repositories of downloadable music on the Web with acceptable fidelity	Owners of online music collections (MP3.com; iTunes), telecommunications providers who own Internet backbone (ATT, Verizon), local Internet service providers win, while record label firms and music retailers lose (Tower Records).
PageRank algorithm	A method for ranking Web pages in terms of their popularity to supplement Web search by key terms	Google is the winner (they own the patent), while traditional key word search engines (Alta Vista) lose.
Software as Web service	Using the Internet to provide remote access to online software	Online software services companies (Salesforce.com) win, while traditional "boxed" software companies (Microsoft, SAP, Oracle) lose.

Disruptive technologies are tricky. Firms that invent disruptive technologies as "first movers" do not always benefit if they lack the resources to really exploit the technology or fail to see the opportunity. The MITS Altair 8800 is widely considered the first PC, but its inventors did not take advantage of their first mover status. Second movers, so-called "fast followers" such as IBM and Microsoft, reaped the rewards. ATMs revolutionized retail banking, but the inventor, Citibank, was copied by other banks, and ultimately all banks used ATMs with the benefits going mostly to the consumers. Google was not a first mover in search, but an innovative follower that was able to maintain rights to a powerful new search algorithm called PageRank. So far it has been able to hold onto its lead while most other search engines have faded down to small market shares.

Organizational Structure

Organizations all have a structure or shape. Mintzberg's classification, described in Table 3-2, identifies five basic kinds of organizational structure (Mintzberg, 1979).

The kind of information systems you find in a business firm—and the nature of problems with these systems—often reflects the type of organizational structure. For instance, in a professional bureaucracy such as a hospital it is not unusual to find parallel patient record systems operated by the administration, another by doctors, and another by other professional staff such as nurses and social workers. In small entrepreneurial firms you will often find poorly designed systems developed in a rush that often outgrow their usefulness

TABLE 3-2 ORGANIZATIONAL STRUCTURES

ORGANIZATIONAL TYPE	DESCRIPTION	EXAMPLES
Entrepreneurial structure	Young, small firm in a fast-changing environment. It has a simple structure and is managed by an entrepreneur serving as its single chief executive officer.	Small start-up business
Machine bureaucracy	Large bureaucracy existing in a slowly changing environment, producing standard products. It is dominated by a centralized management team and centralized decision making.	Midsize manufacturing firm
Divisionalized bureaucracy	Combination of multiple machine bureaucracies, each producing a different product or service, all topped by one central headquarters.	Fortune 500 firms, such as General Motors
Professional bureaucracy	Knowledge-based organization where goods and services depend on the expertise and knowledge of professionals. Dominated by department heads with weak centralized authority.	Law firms, school systems, hospitals
Adhocracy	Task force organization that must respond to rapidly changing environments. Consists of large groups of specialists organized into short-lived multidisciplinary teams and has weak central management.	Consulting firms, such as the Rand Corporation

quickly. In huge multidivisional firms operating in hundreds of locations you will often find there is not a single integrating information system, but instead each locale or each division has its set of information systems.

Other Organizational Features

Organizations have goals and use different means to achieve them. Some organizations have coercive goals (e.g., prisons); others have utilitarian goals (e.g., businesses). Still others have normative goals (universities, religious groups). Organizations also serve different groups or have different constituencies, some primarily benefiting their members, others benefiting clients, stockholders, or the public. The nature of leadership differs greatly from one organization to another—some organizations may be more democratic or authoritarian than others. Another way organizations differ is by the tasks they perform and the technology they use. Some organizations perform primarily routine tasks that can be reduced to formal rules that require little judgment (such as manufacturing auto parts), whereas others (such as consulting firms) work primarily with nonroutine tasks.

3.2   How Information Systems Impact Organizations and Business Firms

Information systems have become integral, online, interactive tools deeply involved in the minute-to-minute operations and decision making of large organizations. Over the last decade, information systems have fundamentally altered the economics of organizations and greatly increased the possibilities for organizing work. Theories and concepts from economics and sociology help us understand the changes brought about by IT.

ECONOMIC IMPACTS

From the point of view of economics, IT changes both the relative costs of capital and the costs of information. Information systems technology can be viewed as a factor of production that can be substituted for traditional capital and labor. As the cost of information technology decreases, it is substituted for labor, which historically has been a rising cost. Hence, information technology should result in a decline in the number of middle managers and clerical workers as information technology substitutes for their labor (Laudon, 1990).

As the cost of information technology decreases, it also substitutes for other forms of capital such as buildings and machinery, which remain relatively expensive. Hence, over time we should expect managers to increase their investments in IT because of its declining cost relative to other capital investments.

IT also obviously affects the cost and quality of information and changes the economics of information. Information technology helps firms contract in size because it can reduce transaction costs—the costs incurred when a firm buys on the marketplace what it cannot make itself. According to **transaction cost theory**, firms and individuals seek to economize on transaction costs, much as they do on production costs. Using markets is expensive (Coase, 1937; Williamson, 1985) because of costs such as locating and communicating with distant suppliers, monitoring contract compliance, buying insurance, obtaining information on products, and so forth. Traditionally, firms have tried to reduce transaction costs through vertical integration, by getting bigger, hiring more employees, and buying their own suppliers and distributors, as both General Motors and Ford used to do.

Information technology, especially the use of networks, can help firms lower the cost of market participation (transaction costs), making it worthwhile for firms to contract with external suppliers instead of using internal sources. As a result, firms can shrink in size (numbers of employees) because it is far less expensive to outsource work to a competitive marketplace rather than hire employees.

For instance, by using computer links to external suppliers, the Chrysler Corporation can achieve economies by obtaining more than 70 percent of its parts from the outside. Information systems make it possible for companies such as Cisco Systems and Dell Inc. to outsource their production to contract manufacturers such as Flextronics instead of making their products themselves.

Figure 3-6 shows that as transaction costs decrease, firm size (the number of employees) should shrink because it becomes easier and cheaper for the firm to contract for the purchase of goods and services in the marketplace rather than to make the product or offer the service itself. Firm size can stay constant or contract even as the company increases its revenues. For example, when Eastman Chemical Company split off from Kodak in 1994, it had $3.3 billion in revenue and 24,000 full-time employees. In 2007, it generated $6.8 billion in revenue with only 11,000 employees.

Information technology also can reduce internal management costs. According to **agency theory**, the firm is viewed as a "nexus of contracts" among self-interested individuals rather than as a unified, profit-maximizing entity (Jensen and Meckling, 1976). A principal (owner) employs "agents" (employees) to perform work on his or her behalf. However, agents need constant supervision and management; otherwise, they will tend to pursue their own interests rather than those of the owners. As firms grow in size and scope, agency costs or coordination costs rise because owners must expend more and more effort supervising and managing employees.

FIGURE 3-6   **THE TRANSACTION COST THEORY OF THE IMPACT OF INFORMATION TECHNOLOGY ON THE ORGANIZATION**

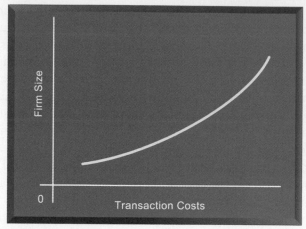

Firms traditionally grew in size to reduce transaction costs. IT potentially reduces the transaction costs for a given size, opening up the possibility of revenue growth without increasing size, or even revenue growth accompanied by shrinking size.

Information technology, by reducing the costs of acquiring and analyzing information, permits organizations to reduce agency costs because it becomes easier for managers to oversee a greater number of employees. Figure 3-7 shows that by reducing overall management costs, information technology enables firms to increase revenues while shrinking the number of middle managers and clerical workers. We have seen examples in earlier chapters where information technology expanded the power and scope of small organizations by enabling them to perform coordinating activities such as processing orders or keeping track of inventory with very few clerks and managers.

FIGURE 3-7   **THE AGENCY COST THEORY OF THE IMPACT OF INFORMATION TECHNOLOGY ON THE ORGANIZATION**

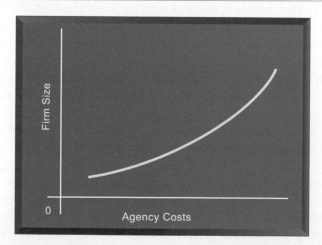

As firms grow in size and complexity, traditionally they experience rising agency costs. IT makes it possible to increase the number of employees who can be managed by a single manager, reducing the overall costs of management (agency costs). This creates the possibility that firms can shrink in managerial ranks and still increase revenues as management becomes more efficient.

Because IT reduces both agency and transaction costs for firms, we should expect firm size to shrink over time as more capital is invested in IT. Firms should have fewer managers, and we expect to see revenue per employee increase over time.

ORGANIZATIONAL AND BEHAVIORAL IMPACTS

Theories based in the sociology of complex organizations also provide some understanding about how and why firms change with the implementation of new IT applications.

IT Flattens Organizations

Large, bureaucratic organizations, which primarily developed before the computer age, are often inefficient, slow to change, and less competitive than newly created organizations. Some of these large organizations have downsized, reducing the number of employees and the number of levels in their organizational hierarchies.

Behavioral researchers have theorized that information technology facilitates flattening of hierarchies by broadening the distribution of information to empower lower-level employees and increase management efficiency (see Figure 3-8). IT pushes decision-making rights lower in the organization because lower-level employees receive the information they need to make decisions without supervision. (This empowerment is also possible because of higher educational levels among the workforce, which give employees the capabilities to make intelligent decisions.) Because managers now receive so much more accurate information on time, they become much faster at making decisions, so fewer managers are required. Management costs decline as a percentage of revenues, and the hierarchy becomes much more efficient.

FIGURE 3-8   FLATTENING ORGANIZATIONS

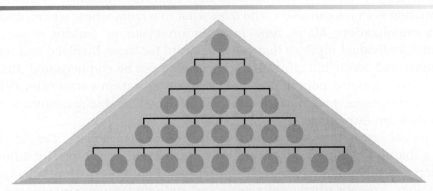

A traditional hierarchical organization with many levels of management

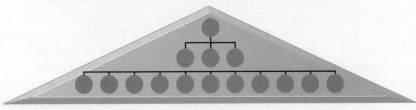

An organization that has been "flattened" by removing layers of management

Information systems can reduce the number of levels in an organization by providing managers with information to supervise larger numbers of workers and by giving lower-level employees more decision-making authority.

These changes mean that the management span of control has also been broadened, enabling high-level managers to manage and control more workers spread over greater distances. Many companies have eliminated thousands of middle managers as a result of these changes.

Postindustrial Organizations

Postindustrial theories based more on history and sociology than economics also support the notion that IT should flatten hierarchies. In postindustrial societies, authority increasingly relies on knowledge and competence, and not merely on formal positions. Hence, the shape of organizations flattens because professional workers tend to be self-managing, and decision making should become more decentralized as knowledge and information become more widespread throughout the firm (Drucker, 1988).

Information technology may encourage task force-networked organizations in which groups of professionals come together—face to face or electronically—for short periods of time to accomplish a specific task (e.g., designing a new automobile); once the task is accomplished, the individuals join other task forces. The global consulting service Accenture is an example. It has no operational headquarters and no formal branches. Many of its 186,000 employees move from location to location to work on projects at client locations in 49 different countries.

Who makes sure that self-managed teams do not head off in the wrong direction? Who decides which person works on which team and for how long? How can managers evaluate the performance of someone who is constantly rotating from team to team? How do people know where their careers are headed? New approaches for evaluating, organizing, and informing workers are required, and not all companies can make virtual work effective.

Understanding Organizational Resistance to Change

Information systems inevitably become bound up in organizational politics because they influence access to a key resource—namely, information. Information systems can affect who does what to whom, when, where, and how in an organization. Many new information systems require changes in personal, individual routines that can be painful for those involved and require retraining and additional effort that may or may not be compensated. Because information systems potentially change an organization's structure, culture, business processes, and strategy, there is often considerable resistance to them when they are introduced.

There are several ways to visualize organizational resistance. Leavitt (1965) used a diamond shape to illustrate the interrelated and mutually adjusting character of technology and organization (see Figure 3-9). Here, changes in technology are absorbed, deflected, and defeated by organizational task arrangements, structures, and people. In this model, the only way to bring about change is to change the technology, tasks, structure, and people simultaneously. Other authors have spoken about the need to "unfreeze" organizations before introducing an innovation, quickly implementing it, and "refreezing" or institutionalizing the change (Alter and Ginzberg, 1978; Kolb, 1970).

Because organizational resistance to change is so powerful, many information technology investments flounder and do not increase productivity. Indeed, research on project implementation failures demonstrates that the most common reason for failure of large projects to reach their objectives is not the failure of the technology, but organizational and political resistance to change. Chapter 14 treats this issue in detail. Therefore, as a manger involved in future

FIGURE 3-9   ORGANIZATIONAL RESISTANCE AND THE MUTUALLY ADJUSTING RELATIONSHIP BETWEEN TECHNOLOGY AND THE ORGANIZATION

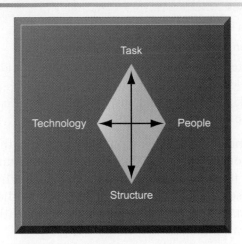

Implementing information systems has consequences for task arrangements, structures, and people. According to this model, to implement change, all four components must be changed simultaneously.
Source: Leavitt (1965).

IT investments, your ability to work with people and organizations is just as important as your technical awareness and knowledge.

THE INTERNET AND ORGANIZATIONS

The Internet, especially the World Wide Web, has an important impact on the relationships between many firms and external entities, and even on the organization of business processes inside a firm. The Internet increases the accessibility, storage, and distribution of information and knowledge for organizations. In essence, the Internet is capable of dramatically lowering the transaction and agency costs facing most organizations. For instance, brokerage firms and banks in New York can now deliver their internal operations procedures manuals to their employees at distant locations by posting them on the corporate Web site, saving millions of dollars in distribution costs. A global sales force can receive nearly instant price product information updates using the Web or instructions from management sent by e-mail. Vendors of some large retailers can access retailers' internal Web sites directly to find up-to-the-minute sales information and to initiate replenishment orders instantly.

Businesses are rapidly rebuilding some of their key business processes based on Internet technology and making this technology a key component of their IT infrastructures. If prior networking is any guide, one result will be simpler business processes, fewer employees, and much flatter organizations than in the past.

IMPLICATIONS FOR THE DESIGN AND UNDERSTANDING OF INFORMATION SYSTEMS

To deliver genuine benefits, information systems must be built with a clear understanding of the organization in which they will be used. In our experience, the central organizational factors to consider when planning a new system are the following:

- The environment in which the organization must function
- The structure of the organization: hierarchy, specialization, routines, and business processes
- The organization's culture and politics
- The type of organization and its style of leadership
- The principal interest groups affected by the system and the attitudes of workers who will be using the system
- The kinds of tasks, decisions, and business processes that the information system is designed to assist

As you read the Interactive Session on Management, think about what you have just learned about the relationship between information technology and organizations. What features of organizations explain why new technologies have not been as useful as envisioned in helping soldiers during combat? How did an understanding of this relationship make the Tactical Ground Reporting System more effective?

3.3 USING INFORMATION SYSTEMS TO ACHIEVE COMPETITIVE ADVANTAGE

In almost every industry you examine, you will find that some firms do better than most others. There's almost always a stand-out firm. In the automotive industry, Toyota is considered a superior performer. In pure online retail, Amazon is the leader, in off-line retail Wal-Mart, the largest retailer on earth, is the leader. In online music, Apple's iTunes is considered the leader with more than 75 percent of the downloaded music market, and in the related industry of digital music players, the iPod is the leader. In Web search, Google is considered the leader.

Firms that "do better" than others are said to have a competitive advantage over others: They either have access to special resources that others do not, or they are able to use commonly available resources more efficiently—usually because of superior knowledge and information assets. In any event, they do better in terms of revenue growth, profitability, or productivity growth (efficiency), all of which ultimately in the long run translate into higher stock market valuations than their competitors.

But why do some firms do better than others and how do they achieve competitive advantage? How can you analyze a business and identify its strategic advantages? How can you develop a strategic advantage for your own business? And how do information systems contribute to strategic advantages? One answer to that question is Michael Porter's competitive forces model.

PORTER'S COMPETITIVE FORCES MODEL

Arguably, the most widely used model for understanding competitive advantage is Michael Porter's **competitive forces model** (see Figure 3-10). This model provides a general view of the firm, its competitors, and the firm's environment. Earlier in this chapter, we described the importance of a firm's environment and the dependence of firms on environments. Porter's model is all about the firm's general business environment. In this model, five competitive forces shape the fate of the firm.

INTERACTIVE SESSION: MANAGEMENT

CAN TECHNOLOGY SAVE SOLDIERS' LIVES IN IRAQ?

Few areas demonstrate the need for effective information systems more than warfare. Poor communication and inefficient systems don't just waste money; they put soldiers in harm's way and increase their risk of being injured or killed. Though the U.S. Army has made great technological strides in recent years, many of those new technologies have not translated to better safety and more accurate flow of information in the combat zone. Some of the struggles of the U.S. counterinsurgency effort in Iraq illustrate these weaknesses.

The U.S. military went into the Iraq War with many technological advantages. These included data transmission capacity that was 42 times faster than what was available to U.S. forces during the Gulf War; a plethora of sensor technologies such as motion sensors, heat detectors, and reconnaissance eavesdroppers; and an advanced vehicle tracking system, Blue Force Tracker, which marks the location of U.S. units and enables e-mail communication. The technology available to the enemy forces pales in comparison.

But despite these significant advantages in information gathering, the methods used by the military to communicate that information suffered from critical flaws. Information about enemy movements and troop levels did not reach the officers on the ground in many cases, despite the wealth of technology available.

Why? First the technology itself was often less efficient than advertised. Units often outran the range of high-capacity communications relays, and mobile communications suffered from slow download speeds, buggy software, and lockups, some as long as 10 to 12 hours at a time. Communicating data required units to be stationary to send and receive the information, leaving the units vulnerable to attack.

The organization of U.S. military forces and the chain of command also played a role. Military experts point out that the networking of the Iraq War was inadequate because it was grafted onto old-fashioned processes for command and control, which were designed for directing forces on an enormous scale against conventional troops. Sensor information went up the chain of command. Commanders interpreted it, made decisions, and then transmitted commands and relevant data

down the chain. As a result, there were time delays and gaps in the flow of information to front-line officers.

The environment in Iraq did not suit this strategy. The Iraq War and subsequent U.S. occupation of Iraq consisted primarily of operations against small armed groups. The insurgents communicate information horizontally, without a hierarchical structure, which allows them to pass information quickly and efficiently. Peer-based information determines the insurgents' next move rather than information that must travel up and down long chains of command. These types of operations are better suited to a more decentralized type of military organization where small teams of networked soldiers in the front lines can freely exchange information with each other. Service members on the battlefield collect data, share the data, make decisions, and order strikes against the enemy. This same strategy was used to great effect by U.S. forces in Afghanistan.

To more effectively contend with their enemies in Iraq, the U.S. military has finally started using a similar strategy there. One of the most prominent new horizontal technologies is TIGR, or the Tactical Ground Reporting System, an application developed by the Defense Advanced Research Projects Agency (DARPA) and currently in use in Iraq.

TIGR can best be described as a cross between Google Maps and Wikipedia that helps soldiers access and distribute information about people, places, and activity in Iraq. The application revolves around maps that patrol leaders can review and edit. Clickable icons and lists display key locations and information associated with those locations, such as photos and backgrounds of local leaders, videos of hostile and safe places, and reports from previous patrols. The application supports a variety of media formats, including voice recordings, digital photos, and global positioning system (GPS) location information. DARPA describes the application as being able to effectively record and track people, places, and insurgent activity.

The two major challenges involved in the deployment of TIGR were to develop a method for synchronizing copies of the same data set located in many different areas, any one of which a returning patrol leader might modify, and giving soldiers a variety of multimedia information without overloading the system. The development of a network that carefully rations bandwidth helped to solve this problem.

DARPA's Web site lists the three major benefits of TIGR as follows. The system enhances local knowledge by collecting and organizing information on key infrastructure, landmarks, and terrain. Maps double as both the standard interface and navigational aids. Patrol officers can record events as specific as meetings with local leaders. TIGR accommodates the dynamic infrastructures of wartime environments and allows users to update information easily. Lastly, TIGR assists the unit rotation process. The system can be used to quickly brief new units on key historical and contextual information as they rotate into particular zones. The changeover to new groups in

the past required PowerPoint files, spreadsheets, and many bound volumes of data.

Patrol officers that have used the system praise it as life-saving. Implications for IEDs (improvised explosive devices) are enormous, as patrols are able to monitor which areas have experienced previous IED activity to warn future units and to avoid potential IED hot spots. TIGR should help the U.S. smoothly transform its force into one that shares information horizontally and one that can effectively combat insurgent groups with a new style of warfare.

Sources: David Talbot, "A Technology Surges," *Technology Review*, March/April 2008; Walter Pincus, "How Defense Research Is Making Troops More Effective in Wartime," *The Washington Post*, May 12, 2008; "Advanced Soldier Censor Information System and Technology (ASSIST)," DARPA, accessed June 1, 2008; David Talbot, "How Technology Failed in Iraq," *Technology Review*, November 2004.

CASE STUDY QUESTIONS

1. What features of organizations are relevant for explaining the performance of information systems during the Iraq War?

2. What difficulties did U.S. military forces in Iraq encounter with information systems? What management, organization, and technology factors contributed to these difficulties?

3. Describe TIGR and explain why it has been so beneficial to U.S. patrol groups in Iraq.

4. Why is TIGR an example of a horizontal technology?

5. How helpful will TIGR be in future military campaigns? Explain your answer.

MIS IN ACTION

Visit the DARPA Web site (www.darpa.gov) and then answer the following questions:

1. What is DARPA? What role does it play in developing U.S. military systems?

2. Pick out five different DARPA programs and write a brief description of how each would enhance the capabilities of the United States Armed Forces. If these projects are completed, what will be their impact on future U.S. military operations?

FIGURE 3-10   PORTER'S COMPETITIVE FORCES MODEL

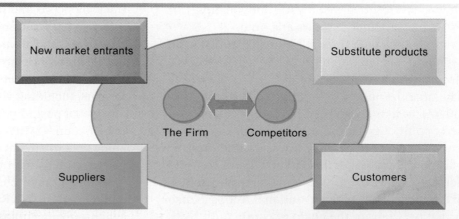

In Porter's competitive forces model, the strategic position of the firm and its strategies are determined not only by competition with its traditional direct competitors but also by four other forces in the industry's environment: new market entrants, substitute products, customers, and suppliers.

Traditional Competitors

All firms share market space with other competitors who are continuously devising new, more efficient ways to produce by introducing new products and services, and attempting to attract customers by developing their brands and imposing switching costs on their customers.

New Market Entrants

In a free economy with mobile labor and financial resources, new companies are always entering the marketplace. In some industries, there are very low barriers to entry, whereas in other industries, entry is very difficult. For instance, it is fairly easy to start a pizza business or just about any small retail business, but it is much more expensive and difficult to enter the computer chip business, which has very high capital costs and requires significant expertise and knowledge that is hard to obtain. New companies have several possible advantages: They are not locked into old plants and equipment, they often hire younger workers who are less expensive and perhaps more innovative, they are not encumbered by old worn-out brand names, and they are "more hungry" (more highly motivated) than traditional occupants of an industry. These advantages are also their weakness: They depend on outside financing for new plants and equipment, which can be expensive; they have a less-experienced workforce; and they have little brand recognition.

Substitute Products and Services

In just about every industry, there are substitutes that your customers might use if your prices become too high. New technologies create new substitutes all the time. Even oil has substitutes: Ethanol can substitute for gasoline in cars; vegetable oil for diesel fuel in trucks; and wind, solar, coal, and hydro power for industrial electricity generation. Likewise, the Internet telephone service can substitute for traditional telephone service, and fiber-optic telephone lines to the home can substitute for cable TV lines. And, of course, an Internet music service that allows you to download music tracks to an iPod is a substitute for CD-based music stores. The more substitute products and services in your industry, the less you can control pricing and the lower your profit margins.

Customers

A profitable company depends in large measure on its ability to attract and retain customers (while denying them to competitors), and charge high prices. The power of customers grows if they can easily switch to a competitor's products and services, or if they can force a business and its competitors to compete on price alone in a transparent marketplace where there is little **product differentiation**, and all prices are known instantly (such as on the Internet). For instance, in the used college textbook market on the Internet, students (customers) can find multiple suppliers of just about any current college textbook. In this case, online customers have extraordinary power over used-book firms.

Suppliers

The market power of suppliers can have a significant impact on firm profits, especially when the firm cannot raise prices as fast as can suppliers. The more different suppliers a firm has, the greater control it can exercise over suppliers in terms of price, quality, and delivery schedules. For instance, manufacturers of laptop PCs almost always have multiple competing suppliers of key components, such as keyboards, hard drives, and display screens.

INFORMATION SYSTEM STRATEGIES FOR DEALING WITH COMPETITIVE FORCES

What is a firm to do when it is faced with all these competitive forces? And how can the firm use information systems to counteract some of these forces? How do you prevent substitutes and inhibit new market entrants? There are four generic strategies, each of which often is enabled by using information technology and systems: low-cost leadership, product differentiation, focus on market niche, and strengthening customer and supplier intimacy.

Low-Cost Leadership

Use information systems to achieve the lowest operational costs and the lowest prices. The classic example is Wal-Mart. By keeping prices low and shelves well stocked using a legendary inventory replenishment system, Wal-Mart became the leading retail business in the United States. Wal-Mart's continuous replenishment system sends orders for new merchandise directly to suppliers as soon as consumers pay for their purchases at the cash register. Point-of-sale terminals record the bar code of each item passing the checkout counter and send a purchase transaction directly to a central computer at Wal-Mart headquarters. The computer collects the orders from all Wal-Mart stores and transmits them to suppliers. Suppliers can also access Wal-Mart's sales and inventory data using Web technology.

Because the system replenishes inventory with lightning speed, Wal-Mart does not need to spend much money on maintaining large inventories of goods in its own warehouses. The system also enables Wal-Mart to adjust purchases of store items to meet customer demands. Competitors, such as Sears, have been spending 24.9 percent of sales on overhead. But by using systems to keep operating costs low, Wal-Mart pays only 16.6 percent of sales revenue for overhead. (Operating costs average 20.7 percent of sales in the retail industry.)

Wal-Mart's continuous inventory replenishment system uses sales data captured at the checkout counter to transmit orders to restock merchandise directly to its suppliers. The system enables Wal-Mart to keep costs low while fine-tuning its merchandise to meet customer demands.

Wal-Mart's continuous replenishment system is also an example of an **efficient customer response system**. An efficient customer response system directly links consumer behavior to distribution and production and supply chains. Wal-Mart's continuous replenishment system provides such an efficient customer response. Dell Inc.'s assemble-to-order system, described in the following discussion, is another example of an efficient customer response system.

Product Differentiation

Use information systems to enable new products and services, or greatly change the customer convenience in using your existing products and services. For instance, Google continuously introduces new and unique search services on its Web site, such as Google Maps. By purchasing PayPal, an electronic payment system, in 2003, eBay made it much easier for customers to pay sellers and expanded use of its auction marketplace. Apple created the iPod, a unique portable digital music player, plus a unique online Web music service where songs can be purchased for 99 cents. Continuing to innovate, Apple introduced a portable iPod video player and a multimedia smartphone.

Manufacturers and retailers are using information systems to create products and services that are customized and personalized to fit the precise specifications of individual customers. Dell Inc. sells directly to customers using assemble-to-order manufacturing. Individuals, businesses, and government agencies can buy computers directly from Dell, customized with the exact features and components they need. They can place their orders directly using a toll-free telephone number or by accessing Dell's Web site. Once Dell's production control receives an order, it directs an assembly plant to assemble the computer using components from an on-site warehouse based on the configuration specified by the customer.

On the Dell Inc. Web site, customers can select the options they want and order their computer custom built to these specifications. Dell's assemble-to-order system is a major source of competitive advantage.

Lands' End customers can use its Web site to order jeans, dress pants, chino pants, and shirts custom-tailored to their own specifications. Customers enter their measurements into a form on the Web site, which then transmits each customer's specifications over a network to a computer that develops an electronic made-to-measure pattern for that customer. The individual patterns are then transmitted electronically to a manufacturing plant, where they are used to drive fabric-cutting equipment. There are almost no extra production costs because the process does not require additional warehousing, production overruns, and inventories, and the cost to the customer is only slightly higher than that of a mass-produced garment. Fourteen percent of Lands' End shirt and pants sales are now customized. This ability to offer individually tailored products or services using the same production resources as mass production is called **mass customization**.

Table 3-3 lists a number of companies that have developed IT-based products and services that other firms have found difficult to copy, or at least a long time to copy.

Focus on Market Niche

Use information systems to enable a specific market focus, and serve this narrow target market better than competitors. Information systems support this strategy by producing and analyzing data for finely tuned sales and marketing techniques. Information systems enable companies to analyze customer buying patterns, tastes, and preferences closely so that they efficiently pitch advertising and marketing campaigns to smaller and smaller target markets.

The data come from a range of sources—credit card transactions, demographic data, purchase data from checkout counter scanners at supermarkets and retail stores, and data collected when people access and interact with Web sites. Sophisticated software tools find patterns in these large pools of data and infer rules from them to guide decision making. Analysis of such data drives one-to-one marketing that creates personal messages based on individualized preferences. For example, Hilton Hotels' OnQ system analyzes detailed data collected on active guests in all of its properties to determine the preferences of each guest and each guest's profitability. Hilton uses this information to give its most profitable customers additional privileges, such as late check-outs.

TABLE 3-3 IT-ENABLED NEW PRODUCTS AND SERVICES PROVIDING COMPETITIVE ADVANTAGE

Amazon: One-click shopping	Amazon holds a patent on one-click shopping that it licenses to other online retailers
Online music: Apple iPod and iTunes	An integrated handheld player backed up with an online library of over 6 million songs
Golf club customization: Ping	Customers can select from more than one million different golf club options; a build-to-order system ships their customized clubs within 48 hours
Online bill payment: CheckFree.com	63 million households pay bills online, as of 2008
Online person-to-person payment: PayPal.com	Enables transfer of money between individual bank accounts and between bank accounts and credit card accounts

Contemporary customer relationship management (CRM) systems feature analytical capabilities for this type of intensive data analysis (see Chapters 2 and 9). The Interactive Session on Organizations describes how AutoNation is mining customer data to determine which models and options they are most likely to buy and then use that information to make better decisions about stocking inventory. Unfortunately, it has had trouble getting car manufacturers to use its findings from the data to drive production. What you have learned about the relationship between information systems and organizations will help you understand why.

Strengthen Customer and Supplier Intimacy

Use information systems to tighten linkages with suppliers and develop intimacy with customers. Chrysler Corporation uses information systems to facilitate direct access by suppliers to production schedules, and even permits suppliers to decide how and when to ship supplies to Chrysler factories. This allows suppliers more lead time in producing goods. On the customer side, Amazon.com keeps track of user preferences for book and CD purchases, and can recommend titles purchased by others to its customers. Strong linkages to customers and suppliers increase **switching costs** (the cost of switching from one product to a competing product), and loyalty to your firm.

Table 3-4 summarizes the competitive strategies we have just described. Some companies focus on one of these strategies, but you will often see companies pursuing several of them simultaneously. For example, Dell tries to emphasize low cost as well as the ability to customize its personal computers.

THE INTERNET'S IMPACT ON COMPETITIVE ADVANTAGE

The Internet has nearly destroyed some industries and has severely threatened more. The Internet has also created entirely new markets and formed the basis for thousands of new businesses. The first wave of e-commerce transformed the business world of books, music, and air travel. In the second wave, eight new industries are facing a similar transformation scenario: telephone services, movies, television, jewelry, real estate, hotels, bill payments, and software. The breadth of e-commerce offerings grows, especially in travel, information clearinghouses, entertainment, retail apparel, appliances, and home furnishings.

TABLE 3-4 FOUR BASIC COMPETITIVE STRATEGIES

STRATEGY	DESCRIPTION	EXAMPLE
Low-cost leadership	Use information systems to produce products and services at a lower price than competitors while enhancing quality and level of service	Wal-Mart
Product differentiation	Use information systems to differentiate products, and enable new services and products	Google, eBay, Apple, Lands' End
Focus on market niche	Use information systems to enable a focused strategy on a single market niche; specialize	Hilton Hotels, Harrah's
Customer and supplier intimacy	Use information systems to develop strong ties and loyalty with customers and suppliers	Chrysler Corporation Amazon.com

INTERACTIVE SESSION: ORGANIZATIONS

CAN DETROIT MAKE THE CARS CUSTOMERS WANT?

Burger King lets you "have it your way." Your local car dealer is usually not quite so customer friendly. A typical ready-to-buy car shopper may walk into the dealership with an idea of how much he or she wants to spend and which features the car should include for that price.

Many dealers will order a customized vehicle for a customer, but such an order usually adds six to eight weeks to the transaction. The customer who wants to buy on the spot must choose from cars on the lot that the manufacturer has already configured, priced, and shipped. Despite manufacturer incentives and rebates to entice customers to purchase, dealers often have a glut of new cars sitting in their lots for months at a time that no one wants to buy. The swollen inventory and slow turnaround hurt dealers because they must borrow money to pay for the cars the manufacturers ship.

AutoNation, the largest chain of car dealers in the United States, is no exception. With nearly $18 billion in annual revenue, AutoNation is the leading seller of automobiles in the country. The company has 244 dealerships in 16 states and sells four percent of all new cars sold in the United States. But it, too, has excessive inventory that it can't easily sell.

The upsurge in gasoline prices coupled with a weakened U.S. economy have made the problem even worse. U.S. dealers' lots are bulging with unsold gas-guzzling pickup trucks and SUVs. Detroit auto makers have lost even more market share to the Japanese and Koreans, who are adept at producing small fuel-efficient cars. U.S. auto manufacturers are scrambling to revamp their product lineups, but they cannot move quickly enough.

Why haven't auto manufacturers been able to produce the car models and options customers actually want? Why can't they just produce more small fuel-efficient vehicles? One reason is that their manufacturing processes are not set up to quickly change production models and have been geared toward optimizing the efficiency of the production plant. It has become imperative for the manufacturers to keep their plants running regardless of demand to pay for the rising costs of employee healthcare and pensions. Furthermore, auto workers must be paid most of their salaries regardless of whether they are working, so the manufacturers want them working all the time. Pushing out factory-friendly vehicles keeps revenue streams flowing because the automakers are paid as soon as the cars ship to the dealers. U.S. auto makers have to project their model lineups and manufacturing requirements about three years in advance, and experts say there are too many plants in the United States to keep busy all the time.

Historically, dealers have been independent or small chains selling a single brand of car and having little bargaining power. They had to accept whatever the auto manufacturers shipped them, even if it was bad for business. With the growth of chains like AutoNation, the dealers have gained more power in the relationship.

For years, AutoNation's CEO Michael J. Jackson has pressured the Big Three to cut back on production and focus on building cars that customers actually want. AutoNation already has experience working with data on the habits of car buyers and the most popular configurations of all makes of vehicles. The work started when the company put forth a major effort to consolidate the customer lists from its hundreds of dealerships.

AutoNation uses proprietary analytic software as well as assistance from DME, a marketing firm with expertise in creating customized direct mail campaigns. The chain has divided customers into 62 groups that receive mailings that have been customized for each group with relevant sales pitches and service specials. Service revenues in particular have received a boost from this sort of targeted marketing. AutoNation's goal for its data is to offer products and services that its customers want rather than sifting through its data to find customers that might want the products it already has.

AutoNation is trying to apply these principles of market intelligence to auto manufacturing. By mining consumer data, Jackson can not only determine the models that are in greatest demand, he can also pinpoint the configurations of each vehicle among thousands of possible variations that are most popular with buyers. That way, the manufacturers can focus on building these vehicles in the numbers that the data dictate.

Ford, GM, and Chrysler have all expressed their support for Jackson's attempts to integrate customer data with auto manufacturing processes, but have not done enough to bring production in line with consumer demand. Perhaps $4 per gallon gasoline and a future of sky-high fuel prices will push them toward demand-driven models of production. Until then, Jackson still has a lot of campaigning to do before market intelligence and auto manufacturing truly co-exist.

Sources: Jim Henry, "Can the Auto Industry Still Sell All Its Cars?" *Business Week*, July 16, 2008; Neal E. Boudette and Norihiko Shirouzu, "Car Makers' Boom Years Now Look Like a Bubble," *The Wall Street Journal*, May 20, 2008; Sarah A. Webster, "Detroit 3 Losing Buyers to Rivals," *Detroit Free Press*, July 15, 2008; Neal E. Boudette, "Big Dealer to Detroit: Fix How You Make Cars," *The Wall Street Journal*, February 9, 2007.

CASE STUDY QUESTIONS

1. Why is AutoNation having a problem with its inventory? Why is this also a problem for auto manufacturers such as GM, Ford, and Chrysler? How is this problem impacting the business performance of AutoNation and of the auto manufacturers?

2. What pieces of data do AutoNation need to determine what cars to stock in each of its dealerships? How can it obtain these data?

3. What is AutoNation's solution to its problem? What obstacles must AutoNation overcome to implement its solution? How effective will the solution be?

MIS IN ACTION

Explore autonation.com, examining all of its features and capabilities. Then answer the following questions:

1. How does this Web site help AutoNation forge closer ties with customers and potential customers?

2. What information could AutoNation collect from its Web site that would help it determine which makes and models of cars are of most interest to potential buyers?

For instance, the printed encyclopedia industry and the travel agency industry have been nearly decimated by the availability of substitutes over the Internet. Likewise, the Internet has had a significant impact on the retail, music, book, brokerage, and newspaper industries. At the same time, the Internet has enabled new products and services, new business models, and new industries to spring up every day from eBay and Amazon, to iTunes and Google. In this sense, the Internet is "transforming" entire industries, forcing firms to change how they do business.

Because of the Internet, the traditional competitive forces are still at work, but competitive rivalry has become much more intense (Porter, 2001). Internet technology is based on universal standards that any company can use, making it easy for rivals to compete on price alone and for new competitors to enter the market. Because information is available to everyone, the Internet raises the bargaining power of customers, who can quickly find the lowest-cost provider on the Web. Profits have been dampened. Some industries, such as the travel industry and the financial services industry, have been more impacted than others. Table 3-5 summarizes some of the potentially negative impacts of the Internet on business firms identified by Porter.

However, contrary to Porter's somewhat negative assessment, the Internet also creates new opportunities for building brands and building very large and loyal customer bases that are willing to pay a premium for the brand, for example, Yahoo!, eBay, BlueNile, RedEnvelope, Amazon, Google, and many others. In addition, as with all IT-enabled business initiatives, some firms are far better at using the Internet than other firms are, which creates new strategic opportunities for the successful firms.

TABLE 3-5 IMPACT OF THE INTERNET ON COMPETITIVE FORCES AND INDUSTRY STRUCTURE

COMPETITIVE FORCE	IMPACT OF THE INTERNET
Substitute products or services	Enables new substitutes to emerge with new approaches to meeting needs and performing functions
Customers' bargaining power	Availability of global price and product information shifts bargaining power to customers
Suppliers' bargaining power	Procurement over the Internet tends to raise bargaining power over suppliers; suppliers can also benefit from reduced barriers to entry and from the elimination of distributors and other intermediaries standing between them and their users
Threat of new entrants	The Internet reduces barriers to entry, such as the need for a sales force, access to channels, and physical assets; it provides a technology for driving business processes that makes other things easier to do
Positioning and rivalry among existing competitors	Widens the geographic market, increasing the number of competitors, and reducing differences among competitors; makes it more difficult to sustain operational advantages; puts pressure to compete on price

THE BUSINESS VALUE CHAIN MODEL

Although the Porter model is very helpful for identifying competitive forces and suggesting generic strategies, it is not very specific about what exactly to do, and it does not provide a methodology to follow for achieving competitive advantages. If your goal is to achieve operational excellence, where do you start? Here's where the business value chain model is helpful.

The **value chain model** highlights specific activities in the business where competitive strategies can best be applied (Porter, 1985) and where information systems are most likely to have a strategic impact. This model identifies specific, critical leverage points where a firm can use information technology most effectively to enhance its competitive position. The value chain model views the firm as a series or chain of basic activities that add a margin of value to a firm's products or services. These activities can be categorized as either primary activities or support activities (see Figure 3-11).

Primary activities are most directly related to the production and distribution of the firm's products and services, which create value for the customer. Primary activities include inbound logistics, operations, outbound logistics, sales and marketing, and service. Inbound logistics includes receiving and storing materials for distribution to production. Operations transforms inputs into finished products. Outbound logistics entails storing and distributing finished products. Sales and marketing includes promoting and selling the firm's products. The service activity includes maintenance and repair of the firm's goods and services.

Support activities make the delivery of the primary activities possible and consist of organization infrastructure (administration and management), human resources (employee recruiting, hiring, and training), technology (improving products and the production process), and procurement (purchasing input).

Now you can ask at each stage of the value chain, "How can we use information systems to improve operational efficiency, and improve customer and supplier intimacy?" This will force you to critically examine how you perform value-adding activities at each stage and how the business processes might be improved. You can also begin to ask how information systems can be used to improve the relationship with customers and with suppliers who lie outside the firms value chain but belong to the firm's extended value chain where they are

FIGURE 3-11   THE VALUE CHAIN MODEL

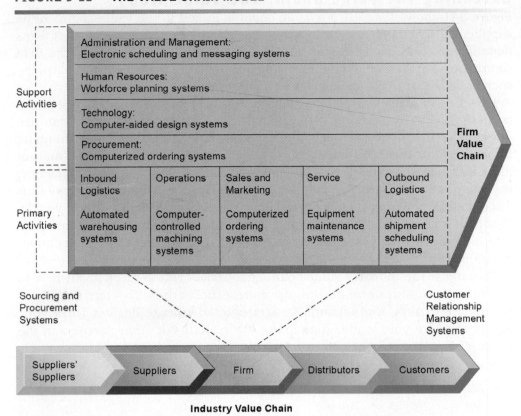

This figure provides examples of systems for both primary and support activities of a firm and of its value partners that can add a margin of value to a firm's products or services.

absolutely critical to your success. Here, supply chain management systems that coordinate the flow of resources into your firm, and customer relationship management systems that coordinate your sales and support employees with customers, are two of the most common system applications that result from a business value chain analysis. We discuss these enterprise applications in detail later in Chapter 9.

Using the business value chain model will also cause you to consider benchmarking your business processes against your competitors or others in related industries, and identifying industry best practices. **Benchmarking** involves comparing the efficiency and effectiveness of your business processes against strict standards and then measuring performance against those standards. Industry **best practices** are usually identified by consulting companies, research organizations, government agencies, and industry associations as the most successful solutions or problem-solving methods for consistently and effectively achieving a business objective.

Once you have analyzed the various stages in the value chain at your business, you can come up with candidate applications of information systems. Then, once you have a list of candidate applications, you can decide which to develop first. By making improvements in your own business value chain that your competitors might miss, you can achieve competitive advantage by attaining operational excellence, lowering costs, improving profit margins, and forging a closer relationship with customers and suppliers. If your competitors are making similar improvements, then at least you will not be at a competitive disadvantage—the worst of all cases!

Extending the Value Chain: The Value Web

Figure 3-11 shows that a firm's value chain is linked to the value chains of its suppliers, distributors, and customers. After all, the performance of most firms depends not only on what goes inside a firm but also on how well the firm coordinates with direct and indirect suppliers, delivery firms (logistics partners, such as FedEx or UPS), and, of course, customers.

How can information systems be used to achieve strategic advantage at the industry level? By working with other firms, industry participants can use information technology to develop industry-wide standards for exchanging information or business transactions electronically, which force all market participants to subscribe to similar standards. Such efforts increase efficiency, making product substitution less likely and perhaps raising entry costs—thus discouraging new entrants. Also, industry members can build industry-wide, IT-supported consortia, symposia, and communications networks to coordinate activities concerning government agencies, foreign competition, and competing industries.

Looking at the industry value chain encourages you to think about how to use information systems to link up more efficiently with your suppliers, strategic partners, and customers. Strategic advantage derives from your ability to relate your value chain to the value chains of other partners in the process. For instance, if you are Amazon.com, you want to build systems that:

- Make it easy for suppliers to display goods and open stores on the Amazon site
- Make it easy for customers to pay for goods
- Develop systems that coordinate the shipment of goods to customers
- Develop shipment tracking systems for customers

Internet technology has made it possible to create highly synchronized industry value chains called value webs. A **value web** is a collection of independent firms that use information technology to coordinate their value chains to produce a product or service for a market collectively. It is more customer driven and operates in a less linear fashion than the traditional value chain.

Figure 3-12 shows that this value web synchronizes the business processes of customers, suppliers, and trading partners among different companies in an industry or in related industries. These value webs are flexible and adaptive to changes in supply and demand. Relationships can be bundled or unbundled in response to changing market conditions. Firms will accelerate time to market and to customers by optimizing their value web relationships to make quick decisions on who can deliver the required products or services at the right price and location.

SYNERGIES, CORE COMPETENCIES, AND NETWORK-BASED STRATEGIES

A large corporation is typically a collection of businesses. Often, the firm is organized financially as a collection of strategic business units and the returns to the firm are directly tied to the performance of all the strategic business units. Information systems can improve the overall performance of these business units by promoting synergies and core competencies.

FIGURE 3-12   THE VALUE WEB

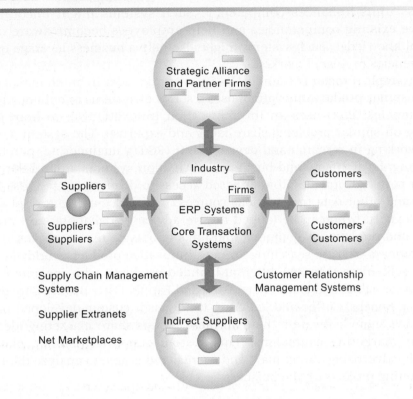

The value web is a networked system that can synchronize the value chains of business partners within an industry to respond rapidly to changes in supply and demand.

Synergies

The idea of synergies is that when the output of some units can be used as inputs to other units, or two organizations pool markets and expertise, these relationships lower costs and generate profits. Recent bank and financial firm mergers, such as the merger of JP Morgan Chase and Bank of New York as well as Bank of America and Countrywide Financial Corporation occurred precisely for this purpose.

One use of information technology in these synergy situations is to tie together the operations of disparate business units so that they can act as a whole. For example, merging with Bank of New York provided JP Morgan Chase with a massive network of retail branches in the Northeast United States. Information systems help the merged banks lower retailing costs and increase cross-marketing of financial products.

Enhancing Core Competencies

Yet another way to use information systems for competitive advantage is to think about ways that systems can enhance core competencies. The argument is that the performance of all business units will increase insofar as these business units develop, or create, a central core of competencies. A **core competency** is an activity for which a firm is a world-class leader. Core competencies may involve being the world's best miniature parts designer, the best package delivery service, or the best thin-film manufacturer. In general, a core competency relies on knowledge that is gained over many years of experience and a first-class research organization or simply key people who follow the literature and stay abreast of new external knowledge.

Any information system that encourages the sharing of knowledge across business units enhances competency. Such systems might encourage or enhance existing competencies and help employees become aware of new external knowledge; such systems might also help a business leverage existing competencies to related markets.

For example, Procter & Gamble (P&G), a world leader in brand management and consumer product innovation, uses a series of systems to enhance its core competencies. P&G uses an intranet called InnovationNet to help people working on similar problems share ideas and expertise. The system connects those working in research and development (R&D), engineering, purchasing, marketing, legal affairs, and business information systems around the world, using a portal to provide browser-based access to documents, reports, charts, videos, and other data from various sources. It includes a directory of subject matter experts who can be tapped to give advice or collaborate on problem solving and product development, and links to outside research scientists and entrepreneurs who are searching for new, innovative products worldwide.

P&G sells more than 300 different branded products, with separate lines of business for Fabric and Home Care, Baby and Family Care, Beauty Care, Health Care, and Snacks, Coffee and Pet Care. It now uses custom-developed marketing management software to help all these groups share marketing ideas and data for marketing campaigns. This system supports strategic planning, research, advertising, direct mail, and events, and is able to analyze the impact of marketing projects on the business.

Network-Based Strategies

The availability of Internet and networking technology have inspired strategies that take advantage of firms' abilities to create networks or network with each other. Network-based strategies include the use of network economics, a virtual company model, and business ecosystems.

Network Economics. Business models based on a network may help firms strategically by taking advantage of **network economics**. In traditional economics—the economics of factories and agriculture—production experiences diminishing returns. The more any given resource is applied to production, the lower the marginal gain in output, until a point is reached where the additional inputs produce no additional outputs. This is the law of diminishing returns, and it is the foundation for most of modern economics.

In some situations, the law of diminishing returns does not work. For instance, in a network, the marginal costs of adding another participant are about zero, whereas the marginal gain is much larger. The larger the number of subscribers in a telephone system or the Internet, the greater the value to all participants because each user can interact with more people. It is not much more expensive to operate a television station with 1,000 subscribers than with 10 million subscribers. The value of a community of people grows with size, whereas the cost of adding new members is inconsequential.

From this network economics perspective, information technology can be strategically useful. Internet sites can be used by firms to build communities of users—like-minded customers who want to share their experiences. This builds customer loyalty and enjoyment, and builds unique ties to customers. EBay, the giant online auction site, and iVillage, an online community for women, are examples. Both businesses are based on networks of millions of users, and both companies have used the Web and Internet communication tools to build communities. The more people offering products on eBay, the more valuable the eBay site is to everyone because more products are listed, and more competition among suppliers lowers prices. Network economics also provides strategic benefits to commercial software vendors. The value of their software and complementary software products increases as more people use them, and there is a larger installed base to justify continued use of the product and vendor support.

Virtual Company Model. Another network-based strategy uses the model of a virtual company to create a competitive business. A **virtual company**, also known as a virtual organization, uses networks to link people, assets, and ideas, enabling it to ally with other companies to create and distribute products and services without being limited by traditional organizational boundaries or physical locations. One company can use the capabilities of another company without being physically tied to that company. The virtual company model is useful when a company finds it cheaper to acquire products, services, or capabilities from an external vendor or when it needs to move quickly to exploit new market opportunities and lacks the time and resources to respond on its own.

Fashion companies, such as GUESS, Ann Taylor, Levi Strauss, and Reebok, enlist Hong Kong-based Li & Fung to manage production and shipment of their garments. Li & Fung handles product development, raw material sourcing, production planning, quality assurance, and shipping. Li & Fung does not own any fabric, factories, or machines, outsourcing all of its work to a network of more than 7,500 suppliers in 37 countries all over the world. Customers place orders to Li & Fung over its private extranet. Li & Fung then sends instructions to appropriate raw material suppliers and factories where the clothing is produced. The Li & Fung extranet tracks the entire production process for each order.

Working as a virtual company keeps Li & Fung flexible and adaptable so that it can design and produce the products ordered by its clients in short order to keep pace with rapidly changing fashion trends.

Business Ecosystems: Keystone and Niche Firms. The Internet and the emergence of digital firms call for some modification of the industry competitive forces model. The traditional Porter model assumes a relatively static industry environment; relatively clear-cut industry boundaries; and a relatively stable set of suppliers, substitutes, and customers, with the focus on industry players in a market environment. Instead of participating in a single industry, some of today's firms are much more aware that they participate in industry sets—collections of industries that provide related services and products (see Figure 3-13). **Business ecosystem** is another term for these loosely coupled but interdependent networks of suppliers, distributors, outsourcing firms, transportation service firms, and technology manufacturers (Iansiti and Levien 2004).

The concept of a business ecosystem builds on the idea of the value web described earlier, the main difference being that cooperation takes place across many industries rather than many firms. For instance, both Microsoft and Wal-Mart provide platforms composed of information systems, technologies, and services that thousands of other firms in different industries use to enhance their own capabilities. Microsoft has estimated that more than 40,000 firms use its Windows platform to deliver their own products, support Microsoft products, and extend the value of Microsoft's own firm. Wal-Mart's order entry and inventory management system is a platform used by thousands of suppliers to obtain real-time access to customer demand, track shipments, and control inventories.

Business ecosystems can be characterized as having one or a few keystone firms that dominate the ecosystem and create the platforms used by other niche firms. Keystone firms in the Microsoft ecosystem include Microsoft and technology producers such as Intel and IBM. Niche firms include thousands of software application firms, software developers, service firms, networking firms, and consulting firms that both support and rely on the Microsoft products.

Information technology plays a powerful role in establishing business ecosystems. Obviously, many firms use information systems to develop into keystone firms by building IT-based platforms that other firms can use. As the chapter-opening case notes, eBay has created a platform for auctions and online stores used by over 500,000 small businesses every day. In the digital firm era, we can expect greater emphasis on the use of IT to build industry ecosystems because the costs of participating in such ecosystems will fall and the benefits to all firms will increase rapidly as the platform grows.

Individual firms should consider how their information systems will enable them to become profitable niche players in larger ecosystems created by keystone firms. For instance, in making decisions about which products to build or which services to offer, a firm should consider the existing business ecosystems related to these products and how it might use IT to enable participation in these larger ecosystems.

A powerful, current example of a rapidly expanding ecosystem is the mobile Internet platform. In this ecosystem there are four industries: device makers (Apple iPhone, RIM BlackBerry, Motorola, LG, and others), wireless telecommunication firms (AT&T, Verizon, T-Mobile, Sprint, and others), independent software applications providers (generally small firms selling games, applications, and ring tones), and Internet service providers (who participate as providers of Internet service to the mobile platform).

FIGURE 3-13   AN ECOSYSTEM STRATEGIC MODEL

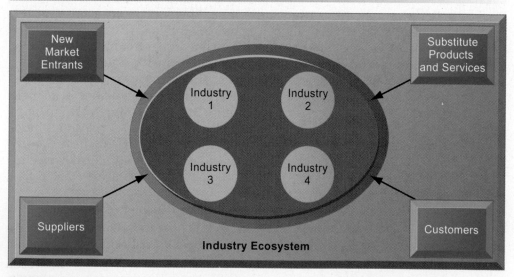

The digital firm era requires a more dynamic view of the boundaries among industries, firms, customers, and suppliers, with competition occurring among industry sets in a business ecosystem. In the ecosystem model, multiple industries work together to deliver value to the customer. IT plays an important role in enabling a dense network of interactions among the participating firms.

Each of these industries has its own history, interests, and driving forces. But these elements come together in a sometimes cooperative, and sometimes competitive, new industry we refer to as the mobile digital platform ecosystem. More than other firms, Apple has managed to combine these industries into a system. It is Apple's mission to sell physical devices (iPhones) which are nearly as powerful as today's personal computers. These devices work only with a high speed broadband network supplied by the wireless phone carriers. In order to attract a large customer base the iPhone had to be more than just a cell phone. Apple differentiated this product by making it a "smart phone," one capable of running thousands of different, useful applications. Apple could not develop all these applications itself. Instead it relies on generally small, independent software developers to provide these applications which can be purchased at the iTunes store. In the background is the Internet service provider industry which makes money whenever iPhone users connect to the Internet.

One of the most successful developers for the iPhone platform is Tapulous, a small start up company in Silicon Valley. Tapulous has developed and released two free applications, a game called Tap Tap Revenge, modeled after a popular arcade dance game, and Twinkle, an application that lets iPhone users send messages over Twitter or Tapulous's own system. The game has attracted 1.2 million downloads, while Twinkle has 100,000 users. Although the firm has not made a cent yet from its apps, it will someday charge for its premium services. Meanwhile, Apple plans to earn an additional $360 million in annual revenue as a result of the App Store. Apple keeps about 30% of the revenues.

3.4   USING SYSTEMS FOR COMPETITIVE ADVANTAGE: MANAGEMENT ISSUES

Strategic information systems often change the organization as well as its products, services, and operating procedures, driving the organization into new behavioral patterns. Successfully using information systems to achieve a competitive advantage is challenging and requires precise coordination of technology, organizations, and management.

SUSTAINING COMPETITIVE ADVANTAGE

The competitive advantages strategic systems confer do not necessarily last long enough to ensure long-term profitability. Because competitors can retaliate and copy strategic systems, competitive advantage is not always sustainable. Markets, customer expectations, and technology change; globalization has made these changes even more rapid and unpredictable. The Internet can make competitive advantage disappear very quickly because virtually all companies can use this technology. Classic strategic systems, such as American Airlines's SABRE computerized reservation system, Citibank's ATM system, and FedEx's package tracking system, benefited by being the first in their industries. Then rival systems emerged. Amazon.com, discussed earlier in this chapter, was an e-commerce leader but now faces competition from eBay, Yahoo!, and Google. Information systems alone cannot provide an enduring business advantage. Systems originally intended to be strategic frequently become tools for survival, required by every firm to stay in business, or they may inhibit organizations from making the strategic changes essential for future success.

ALIGNING IT WITH BUSINESS OBJECTIVES

The research on IT and business performance has found that (a) the more successfully a firm can align information technology with its business goals, the more profitable it will be, and (b) only one-quarter of firms achieve alignment of IT with the business. About half of a business firm's profits can be explained by alignment of IT with business (Luftman, 2003).

Most businesses get it wrong: Information technology takes on a life of its own and does not serve management and shareholder interests very well. Instead of business people taking an active role in shaping IT to the enterprise, they ignore it, claim not to understand IT, and tolerate failure in the IT area as just a nuisance to work around. Such firms pay a hefty price in poor performance. Successful firms and managers understand what IT can do and how it works, take an active role in shaping its use, and measure its impact on revenues and profits.

Performing a Strategic Systems Analysis

To align IT with the business and use information systems effectively for competitive advantage, managers need to perform a strategic systems analysis. To identify the types of systems that provide a strategic advantage to their firms, managers should ask the following questions:

1. What is the structure of the industry in which the firm is located?

- What are some of the competitive forces at work in the industry? Are there new entrants to the industry? What is the relative power of suppliers, customers, and substitute products and services over prices?
- Is the basis of competition quality, price, or brand?
- What are the direction and nature of change within the industry? From where are the momentum and change coming?
- How is the industry currently using information technology? Is the organization behind or ahead of the industry in its application of information systems?

2. What are the business, firm, and industry value chains for this particular firm?

- How is the company creating value for the customer—through lower prices and transaction costs or higher quality? Are there any places in the value chain where the business could create more value for the customer and additional profit for the company?
- Does the firm understand and manage its business processes using the best practices available? Is it taking maximum advantage of supply chain management, customer relationship management, and enterprise systems?
- Does the firm leverage its core competencies?
- Is the industry supply chain and customer base changing in ways that benefit or harm the firm?
- Can the firm benefit from strategic partnerships and value webs?
- Where in the value chain will information systems provide the greatest value to the firm?

3. Have we aligned IT with our business strategy and goals?

- Have we correctly articulated our business strategy and goals?
- Is IT improving the right business processes and activities to promote this strategy?
- Are we using the right metrics to measure progress toward those goals?

MANAGING STRATEGIC TRANSITIONS

Adopting the kinds of strategic systems described in this chapter generally requires changes in business goals, relationships with customers and suppliers, and business processes. These sociotechnical changes, affecting both social and technical elements of the organization, can be considered **strategic transitions**—a movement between levels of sociotechnical systems.

Such changes often entail blurring of organizational boundaries, both external and internal. Suppliers and customers must become intimately linked and may share each other's responsibilities. Managers will need to devise new business processes for coordinating their firms' activities with those of customers, suppliers, and other organizations. The organizational change requirements surrounding new information systems are so important that they merit attention throughout this text. Chapter 14 examines organizational change issues in more detail.

3.5   HANDS-ON MIS PROJECTS

The projects in this section give you hands-on experience identifying information systems to support a business strategy, analyzing organizational factors affecting the information systems of merging companies, using a database to improve decision making about business strategy, and using Web tools to configure and price an automobile.

Management Decision Problems

1. Macy's, Inc., through its subsidiaries, operates approximately 800 department stores in the United States. Its retail stores sell a range of merchandise, including men's, women's, and children's apparel, accessories, cosmetics, home furnishings, and housewares. Senior management has decided that Macy's needs to tailor merchandise more to local tastes, that the colors, sizes, brands, and styles of clothing and other merchandise should be based on the sales patterns in each individual Macy's store. For example, stores in Texas might stock clothing in larger sizes and brighter colors than those in New York, or the Macy's on Chicago's State Street might include a greater variety of makeup shades to attract trendier shoppers. How could information systems help Macy's management implement this new strategy? What pieces of data should these systems collect to help management make merchandising decisions that support this strategy?

2. Today's US Airways is the result of a merger between US Airways and America West Airlines. Before the merger, US Airways dated back to 1939 had very traditional business processes, a lumbering bureaucracy, and a rigid information systems function that had been outsourced to Electronic Data Systems. America West was formed in 1981 and had a younger workforce, a more freewheeling entrepreneurial culture, and managed its own information systems. The merger was designed to create synergies from US Airways' experience and strong network on the east coast of the United States with America West's low cost structure, information systems, and routes in the western United States. What features of organizations should management have considered as it merged the two companies and their information systems? What decisions need to be made to make sure the strategy works?

Improving Decision Making: Using a Database to Clarify Business Strategy

Software skills: Database querying and reporting; database design
Business skills: Reservation systems; customer analysis

In this exercise, you'll use database software to analyze the reservation transactions for a hotel and use that information to fine-tune the hotel's business strategy and marketing activities.

The Presidents' Inn is a small three-story hotel on the Atlantic Ocean in Cape May, New Jersey, a popular northeastern U.S. resort. Ten rooms overlook side streets, 10 rooms have bay windows that offer limited views of the ocean, and the remaining 10 rooms in the front of the hotel face the ocean. Room rates are based on room choice, length of stay, and number of guests per room. Room rates are the same for one to four guests. Fifth and sixth guests must pay an additional $20 charge each per day. Guests staying for seven days or more receive a 10-percent discount on their daily room rates.

Business has grown steadily during the past 10 years. Now totally renovated, the inn uses a romantic weekend package to attract couples, a vacation package to attract young families, and a weekday discount package to attract business travelers. The owners currently use a manual reservation and bookkeeping system, which has caused many problems. Sometimes two families have been booked in the same room at the same time. Management does not have immediate data about the hotel's daily operations and income.

At the Laudon Web site for Chapter 3, you will find a database for hotel reservation transactions developed in Microsoft Access. A sample is shown below, but the Web site may have a more recent version of this database for this exercise.

Develop some reports that provide information to help management make the business more competitive and profitable. Your reports should answer the following questions:

- What is the average length of stay per room type?
- What is the average number of visitors per room type?

I	Guest First Nam	Guest Last Nam	Room	Room Typ	Arrival Da	Departure Da	No of Gues	Daily
1	Barry	Lloyd	Hayes	Bay-window	12/1/2008	12/4/2008	2	$15
2	Michael	Lunsford	Cleveland	Ocean	12/1/2008	12/9/2008	3	$11
3	Kim	Kyuong	Coolidge	Bay-window	12/4/2008	12/7/2008	1	$15
4	Edward	Holt	Washington	Ocean	12/1/2008	12/3/2008	4	$32
5	Thomas	Collins	Lincoln	Ocean	12/9/2008	12/13/2008	2	$30
6	Paul	Bodkin	Coolidge	Bay-window	12/1/2008	12/3/2008	2	$15
7	Randall	Battenburg	Washington	Ocean	12/4/2008	12/12/2008	2	$29
8	Calvin	Nowotney	Lincoln	Ocean	12/2/2008	12/4/2008	1	$30
9	Homer	Gonzalez	Lincoln	Ocean	12/5/2008	12/7/2008	5	$32
10	David	Sanchez	Jefferson	Bay-window	12/5/2008	12/7/2008	2	$17
11	Buster	Whisler	Jackson	Ocean	12/5/2008	12/8/2008	2	$25
12	Julia	Martines	Reagan	Bay-window	12/10/2008	12/15/2008	1	$15
13	Samuel	Kim	Truman	Side	12/20/2008	12/30/2008	3	$11
14	Arthur	Gottfried	Garfield	Side	12/13/2008	12/15/2008	2	$12
15	Darlene	Shore	Arthur	Ocean	12/24/2008	12/31/2008	5	$15
16	Carlyle	Charleston	Quincy Adams	Bay-window	12/3/2008	12/6/2008	2	$15
17	Albert	Goldstone	Johnson	Ocean	12/5/2008	12/7/2008	3	$25
18	Charlene	Tilson	Van Buren	Bay-window	12/5/2008	12/7/2008	1	$15
19	Everett	Chad	Madison	Ocean	12/10/2008	12/14/2008	2	$27
20	Gerald	Pittsfield	Roosevelt	Ocean	12/5/2008	12/7/2008	2	$27

Record: 1 of 30 — No Filter — Search

- What is the base income per room (i.e., length of visit multiplied by the daily rate) during a specified period of time?
- What is the strongest customer base?

After answering these questions, write a brief report describing what the database information reveals about the current business situation. Which specific business strategies might be pursued to increase room occupancy and revenue? How could the database be improved to provide better information for strategic decisions?

Improving Decision Making: Using Web Tools to Configure and Price an Automobile

Software skills: Internet-based software
Business skills: Researching product information and pricing

In this exercise, you'll use software at Web sites for selling cars to find product information about a car of your choice and use that information to make an important purchase decision. You'll also evaluate two of these sites as selling tools.

You are interested in purchasing a new Ford Focus. (If you are personally interested in another car, domestic or foreign, investigate that one instead.) Go to the Web site of CarsDirect (www.carsdirect.com) and begin your investigation. Locate the Ford Focus. Research the various specific automobiles available in that model and determine which you prefer. Explore the full details about the specific car, including pricing, standard features, and options. Locate and read at least two reviews if possible. Investigate the safety of that model based on the U.S. government crash tests performed by the National Highway Traffic Safety Administration if those test results are available. Explore the features for locating a vehicle in inventory and purchasing directly. Finally, explore the other capabilities of the CarsDirect site for financing.

Having recorded or printed the information you need from CarsDirect for your purchase decision, surf the Web site of the manufacturer, in this case Ford (www.ford.com). Compare the information available on Ford's Web site with that of CarsDirect for the Ford Focus. Be sure to check the price and any incentives being offered (which may not agree with what you found at CarsDirect). Next, find a local dealer on the Ford site so that you can view the car before making your purchase decision. Explore the other features of Ford's Web site.

Try to locate the lowest price for the car you want in a local dealer's inventory. Which site would you use to purchase your car? Why? Suggest improvements for the sites of CarsDirect and Ford.

LEARNING TRACK MODULE

The following Learning Track provides content relevant to topics covered in this chapter.

1. The Changing Business Environment for Information Technology

Review Summary

1. *Which features of organizations do managers need to know about to build and use information systems successfully? What is the impact of information systems on organizations?*

   All modern organizations are hierarchical, specialized, and impartial, using explicit routines to maximize efficiency. All organizations have their own cultures and politics arising from differences in interest groups, and they are affected by their surrounding environment. Organizations differ in goals, groups served, social roles, leadership styles, incentives, types of tasks performed, and type of structure. These features help explain differences in organizations' use of information systems.

   Information systems and the organizations in which they are used interact with and influence each other. The introduction of a new information system will affect organizational structure, goals, work design, values, competition between interest groups, decision making, and day-to-day behavior. At the same time, information systems must be designed to serve the needs of important organizational groups and will be shaped by the organization's structure, business processes, goals, culture, politics, and management. Information technology can reduce transaction and agency costs, and such changes have been accentuated in organizations using the Internet. New systems disrupt established patterns of work and power relationships, so there is often considerable resistance to them when they are introduced.

2. *How does Porter's competitive forces model help companies develop competitive strategies using information systems?*

   In Porter's competitive forces model, the strategic position of the firm, and its strategies, are determined by competition with its traditional direct competitors, but they are also greatly affected by new market entrants, substitute products and services, suppliers, and customers. Information systems help companies compete by maintaining low costs, differentiating products or services, focusing on market niche, strengthening ties with customers and suppliers, and increasing barriers to market entry with high levels of operational excellence.

3. *How do the value chain and value web models help businesses identify opportunities for strategic information system applications?*

   The value chain model highlights specific activities in the business where competitive strategies and information systems will have the greatest impact. The model views the firm as a series of primary and support activities that add value to a firm's products or services. Primary activities are directly related to production and distribution, whereas support activities make the delivery of primary activities possible. A firm's value chain can be linked to the value chains of its suppliers, distributors, and customers. A value web consists of information systems that enhance competitiveness at the industry level by promoting the use of standards and industry-wide consortia, and by enabling businesses to work more efficiently with their value partners.

4. *How do information systems help businesses use synergies, core competencies, and network-based strategies to achieve competitive advantage?*

   Because firms consist of multiple business units, information systems achieve additional efficiencies or enhance services by tying together the operations of disparate business units. Information systems help businesses leverage their core competencies by promoting the sharing of knowledge across business units. Information systems facilitate business models based on large networks of users or subscribers that take advantage of network economics. A virtual company strategy uses networks to link to other firms so that a company can use the capabilities of other companies to build, market, and distribute products and services. In business ecosystems, multiple industries work together to deliver value to the customer. Information systems support a dense network of interactions among the participating firms.

5. *What are the challenges posed by strategic information systems and how should they be addressed?*

   Implementing strategic systems often requires extensive organizational change and a transition from one sociotechnical level to another. Such changes are called strategic transitions and are often difficult and painful to achieve. Moreover, not all strategic systems are profitable, and they can be expensive to build. Many strategic information systems are easily copied by other firms so that strategic advantage is not always sustainable.

Key Terms

Agency theory, 115
Benchmarking, 131
Best practices, 131
Business ecosystem, 135
Competitive forces model, 120
Core competency, 133
Disruptive technologies, 112
Efficient customer response system, 125
Mass customization, 126
Network economics, 134
Organization, 107

Primary activities, 130
Product differentiation, 123
Routines, 110
Strategic transitions, 139
Support activities, 130
Switching costs, 137
Transaction cost theory, 115
Value chain model, 130
Value web, 132
Virtual company, 135

Review Questions

1. Which features of organizations do managers need to know about to build and use information systems successfully? What is the impact of information systems on organizations?

   • Define an organization and compare the technical definition of organizations with the behavioral definition.

   • Identify and describe the features of organizations that help explain differences in organizations' use of information systems.

   • Describe the major economic theories that help explain how information systems affect organizations.

   • Describe the major behavioral theories that help explain how information systems affect organizations.

   • Explain why there is considerable organizational resistance to the introduction of information systems.

   • Describe the impact of the Internet and disruptive technologies on organizations.

2. How does Porter's competitive forces model help companies develop competitive strategies using information systems?

   • Define Porter's competitive forces model and explain how it works.

   • Describe what the competitive forces model explains about competitive advantage.

   • List and describe four competitive strategies enabled by information systems that firms can pursue.

   • Describe how information systems can support each of these competitive strategies and give examples.

   • Explain why aligning IT with business objectives is essential for strategic use of systems.

3. How do the value chain and value web models help businesses identify opportunities for strategic information system applications?

   • Define and describe the value chain model.

   • Explain how the value chain model can be used to identify opportunities for information systems.

   • Define the value web and show how it is related to the value chain.

   • Explain how the value web helps businesses identify opportunities for strategic information systems.

   • Describe how the Internet has changed competitive forces and competitive advantage.

4. How do information systems help businesses use synergies, core competences, and network-based strategies to achieve competitive advantage?

   • Explain how information systems promote synergies and core competencies.

   • Describe how promoting synergies and core competencies enhances competitive advantage.

   • Explain how businesses benefit by using network economics.

   • Define and describe a virtual company and the benefits of pursuing a virtual company strategy.

5. What are the challenges posed by strategic information systems and how should they be addressed?

   • List and describe the management challenges posed by strategic information systems.

   • Explain how to perform a strategic systems analysis.

Discussion Questions

1. It has been said that there is no such thing as a sustainable strategic advantage. Do you agree? Why or why not?

2. It has been said that the advantage that leading-edge retailers such as Dell and Wal-Mart have over their competition isn't technology; it's their management. Do you agree? Why or why not?

Video Cases

You will find video cases illustrating some of the concepts in this chapter on the Laudon Web site along with questions to help you analyze the cases.

Collaboration and Teamwork: Identifying Opportunities for Strategic Information Systems

With your team of three or four students, select a company described in *The Wall Street Journal, Fortune, Forbes,* or another business publication. Visit the company's Web site to find additional information about that company and to see how the firm is using the Web. On the basis of this information, analyze the business. Include a description of the organization's features, such as important business processes, culture, structure, and environment, as well as its business strategy. Suggest strategic information systems appropriate for that particular business, including those based on Internet technology, if appropriate. If possible, use Google Sites to post links to Web pages, team communication announcements, and work assignments; to brainstorm; and to work collaboratively on project documents. Try to use Google Docs to develop a presentation of your findings for the class.

Soundbuzz's Music Strategy for Asia-Pacific
CASE STUDY

Soundbuzz is Asia's largest online and mobile music company, providing downloadable music and videos, digit rights clearances, and acquisition of licenses from music publishers and recording companies. It operates in 13 markets under its own brand and in partnership with digital music player manufacturers, broadband providers, and telecommunications carriers. Its online music stores are distributed via soundbuzz.com, Creative Technology (bundled with Creative's MP3 players) and Windows Media Player 10. With its headquarters in Singapore, Soundbuzz has more than 750,000 tracks and 500,000 mobile music derivatives in its database, sourced from about 60 local and independent record labels. These include all major labels - SONY, BMG, Warner Music, EMI and Universal - as well as independents from the U.S., Europe, Australia, and Asia. Soundbuzz content is secured using digital rights management technologies and delivered from its back-end infrastructure in Singapore, consisting of Web servers, license servers, database servers and media servers.

A group of four professionals spanning the music, Internet and finance industries founded Soundbuzz in November 1999. Commenting on the launch of the portal, Shabnam Melwani, co-founder and Director said, "Soundbuzz.com will not only augment record company sales and promotion methods, but also provide a new platform for unsigned artists to showcase and sell their music....." At that time, the soundbuzz.com site featured an artist-upload interface site that allowed musicians and music producers to add their music and information about themselves to the soundbuzz.com music archives.

Soon after the launch, in February 2000, Soundbuzz signed a digital music deal with an Internet portal Lycos Asia to distribute its digital music on Lycos Asia's networks of localized portals in Singapore, Malaysia, China, Hong Kong, Taiwan and India. By March 2000, Soundbuzz had signed licensing agreements with 13 record labels across Asia including Synchronized, The Phiz & Psychic Scream from Malaysia, Viva records from the Philippines, and Music Studios etc. from Indonesia. These deals allowed their artists' music to be offered for downloading and sale on soundbuzz.com in encrypted MP3 format.

In October 2000, Soundbuzz signed the first major record label agreement with EMI Music Asia, a division of EMI Recorded Music. Commenting on the partnership, Sudhanshu Sarronwala, co-founder and CEO said, "This is a landmark moment for the Asian music industry as Soundbuzz becomes the only digital music retailer in Asia to partner with a global record label for the sale of secured, downloadable content for digital distribution...." Soon after, Soundbuzz signed a digital music distribution agreement with BMG Asia-Pacific. These deals made Soundbuzz the first and only digital music retailer in the Asia-Pacific region to sign digital distribution deals with two global major record labels. Licensing agreements with Sony, Warner Music and Universal followed shortly.

To provide its customers with multiple billing channels, Soundbuzz formed a partnership with Trivnet Ltd, a payment technology infrastructure provider, in early 2001. Using Trivnet's payment solution, Soundbuzz could offer multiple-billing channels through Internet Service Provider bills and mobile operator bills to its customers.

By late 2000, the crash of the technology bubble and the increasing use of peer-to-peer networks took a toll on the music industry, as well as Soundbuzz. Sales of CDs in retail music stores started declining, while MP3 songs, shared freely through sites encouraged by Napster and the like, started escalating. Though the traffic to Soundbuzz was in the millions of unique users, the customers were not buying the fee-based content. Their main attraction to the site was the free-download content. Despite all the effort by Soundbuzz, it was faced with becoming irrelevant due to its flawed business model.

In 2001, the Soundbuzz management decided to abandon the B2C model and instead focus back on a B2B model that was based on the deal they had closed with Lycos almost a year earlier. Aligned with the change in business model, a new B2B revenue model was also established. This model saw Soundbuzz aggregating record labels' music content and providing a technical platform and content management service to other portals. In November 2001, Soundbuzz provided an end-to-end digital music solution for Hewlett-Packard's (HP) digital music service that included developing a customized on-line music store, aggregation of digital music content and creation of unique promotions for HP with applications to its products. Soon after, Soundbuzz closed deals with other regional and local portals to provide them with digital music.

In early 2002, Soundbuzz decided to diversify in the wireless and device area. The company began developing software that integrated music entertainment as part of text and multimedia messaging, ring tones, and other digital services for mobile devices. Commenting on the technology focus of Soundbuzz, Sarronwala said, "Our skills are very much about music, licensing and music delivery. We have not dropped the idea of the music downloads/consumer model. I imagine we will get back to that at some point but I think it will take a few more years."

In July 2004, Soundbuzz decided to relaunch the B2C model and announced the rollout of its Asia Pacific digital music retail strategy with the launch of its digital music service in Singapore. Soundbuzz did not keep the entire margin in its B2B business and, with high sales volume, more was being distributed to clients. It was getting more difficult for "white label" services like Soundbuzz to acquire content, as the record companies were seeking to license their music catalogues to companies, which sell directly to consumers. In the face of this uncertainty, Soundbuzz decided to implement both B2B and B2C models.

Soundbuzz continued to form alliances with music device manufacturers to integrate Soundbuzz store in their devices. By August 2005, Soundbuzz had formed partnerships with Creative Technology and Reigncom, manufacturer of MP3 players, to deliver Soundbuzz music store through their digital music players. Alliances with ISPs were also forged to provide consumers with another option for making micro-payments. In Singapore, Soundbuzz formed partnerships with SingNet and Pacific Net as part of its retail strategy. With such partnerships, Soundbuzz was able to make use of their billing systems. The subscribers of these ISPs were able to download digital music from the Soundbuzz Web site and had the exclusive facility to charge their purchases to their monthly ISP billing statements.

In late 2005, Soundbuzz ventured into the U.S. In the same year, the company launched a new product segment - music video. Music video stores were launched in Singapore and Hong Kong in November 2005 and January 2006 respectively.

On January 6, 2008 Motorola signed an agreement to acquire Soundbuzz, with the aim to expand its MOTOMUSIC service beyond China, into India, SouthEast Asia, Australia and New Zealand. Commenting on the acquisition, Sudhanshu Sarronwala, CEO of Soundbuzz said, "Motorola's dedication to enhancing the digital music experience in Asia complements our own objectives and makes it the ideal partner."

Sources: "Soundbuzz.com - New Portal Launched to Pioneer Downloadable Music in Asia," soundbuzz.com, December 10, 1999; "Lycos Asia Signs Digital Music Deal with Soundbuzz," soundbuzz.com, February, 2000; "Soundbuzz Announces Strategic Partnership with EMI Recorded Music," soundbuzz.com, October 2000; "Soundbuzz Announces Asia-Pacific Digital Music Rollout," soundbuzz.com, July 2004; "Soundbuzz Blazes a Trail Through Hong Kong's Music World", soundbuzz.com, October 2005; "Motorola to Enhance Music Delivery Capabilities in Asia through Acquisition of Soundbuzz," motorola.com, accessed November 2008.

CASE STUDY QUESTIONS

1. Analyze Soundbuzz and its business strategy using the competitive forces models. What strategies did it develop for dealing with competitive forces?

2. What are the critical elements for an online music service? Using the value chain model, analyze Soundbuzz's business processes.

3. Why did Motorola acquire Soundbuzz? What synergies will be created through this partnership?

4. Explore the Soundbuzz Web site (www.soundbuzz.com). Briefly describe its products, technology platform, payment methods and revenue model.

5. Do you think Soundbuzz is successful? What are the things it can do to improve its business model? What can it learn from iTunes?

• Case provided by Neerja Sethi and Vijay Sethi, Nanyang Technological University

Chapter 4

Ethical and Social Issues in Information Systems

LEARNING OBJECTIVES

After reading this chapter, you will be able to answer the following questions:

1. What ethical, social, and political issues are raised by information systems?

2. What specific principles for conduct can be used to guide ethical decisions?

3. Why do contemporary information systems technology and the Internet pose challenges to the protection of individual privacy and intellectual property?

4. How have information systems affected everyday life?

Interactive Sessions:

Green IT at Wipro

Flexible Scheduling at Wal-Mart: Good or Bad for Employees?

CHAPTER OUTLINE

ETHICAL ISSUES FACING THE USE OF TECHNOLOGIES FOR THE AGED COMMUNITY

The Australian government takes a strong interest in the use of IT for the direct and indirect care of the aged community. Indirect care includes the administrative aspects of aged care in nursing and aged care communities. No doubt, IT has the potential to improve the quality of lifestyle for the aged. For example, access to the Internet makes the aged feel more in touch with the rest of the world and, in many cases, can assist with day-to-day living such as online grocery purchases, online bill payment and checking bank statements. However, this is conditional upon various factors such as their feeling comfortable with computers, having the computer knowledge and skill and, of course, a trust in online transactions.

Increasingly, new ideas are generated through research and development in an effort to enhanceet chronic illnesses like heart conditions, and diabetes. It is particularly the use of these technologies that poses a plethora of ethical issues of concern to healthcare providers and consumers. The 'Smart House' is a Sydney initiative, designed to allow future generations to remain in their own homes while ageing. It uses a range of 'telecare' sensor technology.

'This Smart House technology includes passive infrared detectors and a door-entry system, which will allow the resident to see who is at the door, via their TV, and open the door remotely. The technology also features emergency pendants and pull cords to trigger an emergency monitoring system, along with bed and chair sensors. Future incorporations into the Smart House will include central locking systems, electric windows and doors, electric curtain and blind openers and other devices.' (BCS, 2006)."

A recurring ethical issue in the use of such technology is invasion of the aged consumers' privacy. Many may not feel comfortable about being monitored in their own homes, 24-hours a day, even though they may see the benefits of such systems. There is also the question of awareness, consent, ownership, and access of any data collected from these aged consumers. Health-related data is particularly very sensitive and, thus, should not be given public access without prior privacy, security, and safety considerations. Socially and culturally, these systems may also not be acceptable as a replacement for traditional human carers (most often close family members) who can produce a much more personalised level of care. In Australia, a number of aged care providers focus on

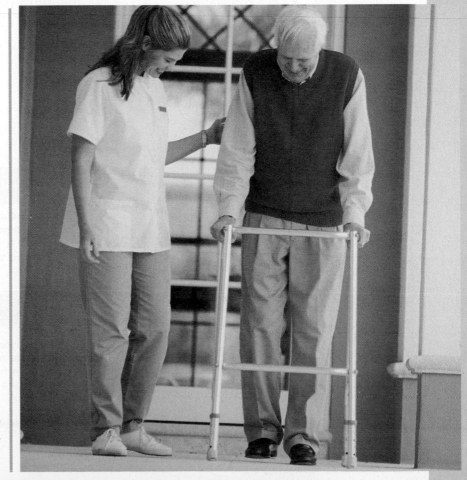

different minority groups (for example Chinese and Koreans) and there is increasing awareness that the technology adopted for them must be socially acceptable and culturally competent, with the facility to adapt to the social and cultural needs of these minority groups (for example, use of appropriate language - voice or textual - interface, or exhibiting understanding of the living habits and preferences in the design of the technology).

Sources: BCS (2006). Smart House holds key to future aged care needs, Baptist Community Services NSW & ACT, Media Release, 1st May 2006, http://www.bcs.org.au/resource/R0058Corp.pdf.

The opening case highlights a number of ethical issues that are specific to healthcare for the ageing population. However, some of these are recurring issues in other healthcare domains, or in organizations in general (such as privacy and security). For example, the data collected from the monitoring and tracking of consumers can be both beneficial from a business viewpoint (in the opening case, it can improve the quality of life, and/or the clinical care of the aged), but at the same time, it also creates opportunities for ethical abuse by invading the privacy of consumers. Such ethical dilemmas arise in the building of new information systems that potentially promise increased efficiency and effectiveness in business processes. In this chapter, we wish to highlight the need to be aware of the negative impact of information systems, alongside the positive benefits. In many cases, management needs to create an acceptable trade-off through the creation of appropriate policies and standards, as agreed upon by all stakeholders, prior to system implementation.

• Case contributed by Dr. Lesley Land, University of New South Wales

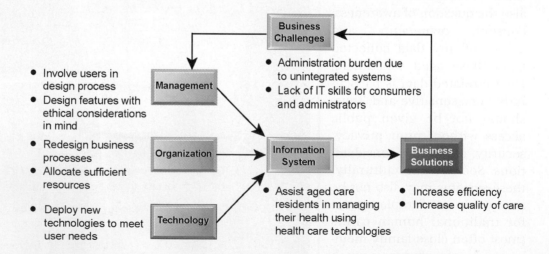

4.1 UNDERSTANDING ETHICAL AND SOCIAL ISSUES RELATED TO SYSTEMS

In the past ten years we have witnessed, arguably, one of the most ethically challenging periods for U.S. and global business. Table 4-1 provides a small sample of recent cases demonstrating failed ethical judgment by senior and middle managers. These lapses in management ethical and business judgment occurred across a broad spectrum of industries.

In today's new legal environment, managers who violate the law and are convicted will most likely spend time in prison. U.S. Federal Sentencing Guidelines adopted in 1987 mandate that federal judges impose stiff sentences on business executives based on the monetary value of the crime, the presence of a conspiracy to prevent discovery of the crime, the use of structured financial transactions to hide the crime, and failure to cooperate with prosecutors (U.S. Sentencing Commission, 2004).

Although in the past business firms would often pay for the legal defense of their employees enmeshed in civil charges and criminal investigations, now firms are encouraged to cooperate with prosecutors to reduce charges against the entire firm for obstructing investigations. These developments mean that, more than ever, as a manager or an employee, you will have to decide for yourself what constitutes proper legal and ethical conduct.

Although these major instances of failed ethical and legal judgment were not masterminded by information systems departments, information systems were instrumental in many of these frauds. In many cases, the perpetrators of these crimes artfully used financial reporting information systems to bury their decisions from public scrutiny in the vain hope they would never be caught. We deal with the issue of control in information systems in Chapter 8. In this chapter, we talk about the ethical dimensions of these and other actions based on the use of information systems.

Ethics refers to the principles of right and wrong that individuals, acting as free moral agents, use to make choices to guide their behaviors. Information systems raise new ethical questions for both individuals and societies because they create opportunities for intense social change, and thus threaten existing distributions of power, money, rights, and obligations. Like other technologies, such as steam engines, electricity, the telephone, and the radio, information technology can be used to achieve social progress, but it can also be used to

TABLE 4-1 RECENT EXAMPLES OF FAILED ETHICAL JUDGMENT BY MANAGERS

Enron	Top three executives convicted for misstating earnings using illegal accounting schemes and making false representations to shareholders. Bankruptcy declared in 2001.
WorldCom	Second-largest U.S. telecommunications firm. Chief executive convicted for improperly inflating revenue by billions using illegal accounting methods. Bankruptcy declared in July 2002 with $41 billion in debts.
Brocade Communications	CEO convicted for backdating stock options and concealing millions of dollars of compensation expenses from shareholders.
Parmalat	Ten executives in Italy's eighth-largest industrial group convicted for misstating more than $5 billion in revenues, earnings, and assets over several years.
Bristol-Myers Squibb	Pharmaceutical firm agreed to pay a fine of $150 million for misstating its revenues by $1.5 billion, and inflating its stock value.

commit crimes and threaten cherished social values. The development of information technology will produce benefits for many and costs for others.

Ethical issues in information systems have been given new urgency by the rise of the Internet and electronic commerce. Internet and digital firm technologies make it easier than ever to assemble, integrate, and distribute information, unleashing new concerns about the appropriate use of customer information, the protection of personal privacy, and the protection of intellectual property.

Other pressing ethical issues raised by information systems include establishing accountability for the consequences of information systems, setting standards to safeguard system quality that protects the safety of the individual and society, and preserving values and institutions considered essential to the quality of life in an information society. When using information systems, it is essential to ask, "What is the ethical and socially responsible course of action?"

A MODEL FOR THINKING ABOUT ETHICAL, SOCIAL, AND POLITICAL ISSUES

Ethical, social, and political issues are closely linked. The ethical dilemma you may face as a manager of information systems typically is reflected in social and political debate. One way to think about these relationships is given in Figure 4-1. Imagine society as a more or less calm pond on a summer day, a delicate ecosystem in partial equilibrium with individuals and with social and political institutions. Individuals know how to act in this pond because social institutions (family, education, organizations) have developed well-honed rules of behavior, and these are supported by laws developed in the political sector that prescribe behavior and promise sanctions for violations. Now toss a rock into the center of the pond. But imagine instead of a rock that the disturbing force is a powerful shock of new information technology and systems hitting a society more or less at rest. What happens? Ripples, of course.

Suddenly, individual actors are confronted with new situations often not covered by the old rules. Social institutions cannot respond overnight to these ripples—it may take years to develop etiquette, expectations, social responsibility, politically correct attitudes, or approved rules. Political institutions also require time before developing new laws and often require the demonstration of real harm before they act. In the meantime, you may have to act. You may be forced to act in a legal gray area.

We can use this model to illustrate the dynamics that connect ethical, social, and political issues. This model is also useful for identifying the main moral dimensions of the information society, which cut across various levels of action—individual, social, and political.

FIVE MORAL DIMENSIONS OF THE INFORMATION AGE

The major ethical, social, and political issues raised by information systems include the following moral dimensions:

Information rights and obligations. What **information rights** do individuals and organizations possess with respect to themselves? What can they protect? What obligations do individuals and organizations have concerning this information?

FIGURE 4-1   THE RELATIONSHIP BETWEEN ETHICAL, SOCIAL, AND POLITICAL ISSUES IN AN INFORMATION SOCIETY

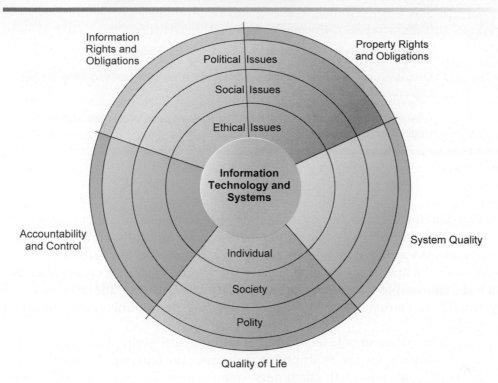

The introduction of new information technology has a ripple effect, raising new ethical, social, and political issues that must be dealt with on the individual, social, and political levels. These issues have five moral dimensions: information rights and obligations, property rights and obligations, system quality, quality of life, and accountability and control.

Property rights and obligations. How will traditional intellectual property rights be protected in a digital society in which tracing and accounting for ownership are difficult and ignoring such property rights is so easy?

Accountability and control. Who can and will be held accountable and liable for the harm done to individual and collective information and property rights?

System quality. What standards of data and system quality should we demand to protect individual rights and the safety of society?

Quality of life. What values should be preserved in an information- and knowledge-based society? Which institutions should we protect from violation? Which cultural values and practices are supported by the new information technology?

We explore these moral dimensions in detail in Section 4.3.

KEY TECHNOLOGY TRENDS THAT RAISE ETHICAL ISSUES

Ethical issues long preceded information technology. Nevertheless, information technology has heightened ethical concerns, taxed existing social arrangements, and made some laws obsolete or severely crippled. There are four key technological trends responsible for these ethical stresses and they are summarized in Table 4-2.

TABLE 4-2 TECHNOLOGY TRENDS THAT RAISE ETHICAL ISSUES

TREND	IMPACT
Computing power doubles every 18 months	More organizations depend on computer systems for critical operations
Data storage costs rapidly declining	Organizations can easily maintain detailed databases on individuals
Data analysis advances	Companies can analyze vast quantities of data gathered on individuals to develop detailed profiles of individual behavior
Networking advances and the Internet	Copying data from one location to another and accessing personal data from remote locations are much easier

The doubling of computing power every 18 months has made it possible for most organizations to use information systems for their core production processes. As a result, our dependence on systems and our vulnerability to system errors and poor data quality have increased. Social rules and laws have not yet adjusted to this dependence. Standards for ensuring the accuracy and reliability of information systems (see Chapter 8) are not universally accepted or enforced.

Advances in data storage techniques and rapidly declining storage costs have been responsible for the multiplying databases on individuals—employees, customers, and potential customers—maintained by private and public organizations. These advances in data storage have made the routine violation of individual privacy both cheap and effective. Already massive data storage systems are cheap enough for regional and even local retailing firms to use in identifying customers.

Advances in data analysis techniques for large pools of data are another technological trend that heightens ethical concerns because companies and government agencies are able to find out much detailed personal information about individuals. With contemporary data management tools (see Chapter 6), companies can assemble and combine the myriad pieces of information about you stored on computers much more easily than in the past.

Think of all the ways you generate computer information about yourself—credit card purchases; telephone calls; magazine subscriptions; video rentals; mail-order purchases; banking records; local, state, and federal government records (including court and police records); and visits to Web sites. Put together and mined properly, this information could reveal not only your credit information but also your driving habits, your tastes, your associations, and your political interests.

Companies with products to sell purchase relevant information from these sources to help them more finely target their marketing campaigns. Chapters 3 and 6 describe how companies can analyze large pools of data from multiple sources to rapidly identify buying patterns of customers and suggest individual responses. The use of computers to combine data from multiple sources and create electronic dossiers of detailed information on individuals is called **profiling**.

For example, hundreds of Web sites allow DoubleClick (www.doubleclick.net), an Internet advertising broker, to track the activities of their visitors in exchange for revenue from advertisements based on visitor information DoubleClick gathers. DoubleClick uses this information to create a profile of each online

Credit card purchases can make personal information available to market researchers, telemarketers, and direct-mail companies. Advances in information technology facilitate the invasion of privacy.

visitor, adding more detail to the profile as the visitor accesses an associated DoubleClick site. Over time, DoubleClick can create a detailed dossier of a person's spending and computing habits on the Web that is sold to companies to help them target their Web ads more precisely.

ChoicePoint gathers data from police, criminal, and motor vehicle records; credit and employment histories; current and previous addresses; professional licenses; and insurance claims to assemble and maintain electronic dossiers on almost every adult in the United Sates. The company sells this personal information to businesses and government agencies. Demand for personal data is so enormous that data broker businesses such as ChoicePoint are flourishing.

A new data analysis technology called **nonobvious relationship awareness (NORA)** has given both the government and the private sector even more powerful profiling capabilities. NORA can take information about people from many disparate sources, such as employment applications, telephone records, customer listings, and "wanted" lists, and correlate relationships to find obscure hidden connections that might help identify criminals or terrorists (see Figure 4-2).

NORA technology scans data and extracts information as the data are being generated so that it could, for example, instantly discover a man at an airline ticket counter who shares a phone number with a known terrorist before that person boards an airplane. The technology is considered a valuable tool for homeland security but does have privacy implications because it can provide such a detailed picture of the activities and associations of a single individual.

Finally, advances in networking, including the Internet, promise to reduce greatly the costs of moving and accessing large quantities of data and open the possibility of mining large pools of data remotely using small desktop machines, permitting an invasion of privacy on a scale and with a precision heretofore unimaginable.

FIGURE 4-2   NONOBVIOUS RELATIONSHIP AWARENESS (NORA)

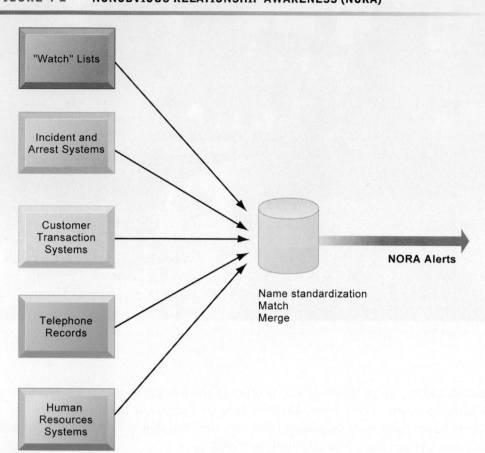

NORA technology can take information about people from disparate sources and find obscure, nonobvious relationships. It might discover, for example, that an applicant for a job at a casino shares a telephone number with a known criminal and issue an alert to the hiring manager.

The development of global digital superhighway communication networks widely available to individuals and businesses poses many ethical and social concerns. Who will account for the flow of information over these networks? Will you be able to trace information collected about you? What will these networks do to the traditional relationships between family, work, and leisure? How will traditional job designs be altered when millions of "employees" become subcontractors using mobile offices for which they themselves must pay? In the next section, we consider some ethical principles and analytical techniques for dealing with these kinds of ethical and social concerns.

4.2   ETHICS IN AN INFORMATION SOCIETY

Ethics is a concern of humans who have freedom of choice. Ethics is about individual choice: When faced with alternative courses of action, what is the correct moral choice? What are the main features of ethical choice?

BASIC CONCEPTS: RESPONSIBILITY, ACCOUNTABILITY, AND LIABILITY

Ethical choices are decisions made by individuals who are responsible for the consequences of their actions. **Responsibility** is a key element of ethical action. Responsibility means that you accept the potential costs, duties, and obligations for the decisions you make. **Accountability** is a feature of systems and social institutions: It means that mechanisms are in place to determine who took responsible action, who is responsible. Systems and institutions in which it is impossible to find out who took what action are inherently incapable of ethical analysis or ethical action. Liability extends the concept of responsibility further to the area of laws. **Liability** is a feature of political systems in which a body of laws is in place that permits individuals to recover the damages done to them by other actors, systems, or organizations. **Due process** is a related feature of law-governed societies and is a process in which laws are known and understood and there is an ability to appeal to higher authorities to ensure that the laws are applied correctly.

These basic concepts form the underpinning of an ethical analysis of information systems and those who manage them. First, information technologies are filtered through social institutions, organizations, and individuals. Systems do not have impacts by themselves. Whatever information system impacts exist are products of institutional, organizational, and individual actions and behaviors. Second, responsibility for the consequences of technology falls clearly on the institutions, organizations, and individual managers who choose to use the technology. Using information technology in a socially responsible manner means that you can and will be held accountable for the consequences of your actions. Third, in an ethical, political society, individuals and others can recover damages done to them through a set of laws characterized by due process.

ETHICAL ANALYSIS

When confronted with a situation that seems to present ethical issues, how should you analyze it? The following five-step process should help.

1. *Identify and describe clearly the facts.* Find out who did what to whom, and where, when, and how. In many instances, you will be surprised at the errors in the initially reported facts, and often you will find that simply getting the facts straight helps define the solution. It also helps to get the opposing parties involved in an ethical dilemma to agree on the facts.

2. *Define the conflict or dilemma and identify the higher-order values involved.* Ethical, social, and political issues always reference higher values. The parties to a dispute all claim to be pursuing higher values (e.g., freedom, privacy, protection of property, and the free enterprise system). Typically, an ethical issue involves a dilemma: two diametrically opposed courses of action that support worthwhile values. For example, the chapter-ending case study illustrates two competing values: the need to improve health care record keeping and the need to protect individual privacy.

3. *Identify the stakeholders.* Every ethical, social, and political issue has stakeholders: players in the game who have an interest in the outcome, who have invested in the situation, and usually who have vocal opinions. Find out the identity of these groups and what they want. This will be useful later when designing a solution.

4. *Identify the options that you can reasonably take.* You may find that none of the options satisfy all the interests involved, but that some options do a better job than others. Sometimes arriving at a good or ethical solution may not always be a balancing of consequences to stakeholders.

5. *Identify the potential consequences of your options.* Some options may be ethically correct but disastrous from other points of view. Other options may work in one instance but not in other similar instances. Always ask yourself, "What if I choose this option consistently over time?"

CANDIDATE ETHICAL PRINCIPLES

Once your analysis is complete, what ethical principles or rules should you use to make a decision? What higher-order values should inform your judgment? Although you are the only one who can decide which among many ethical principles you will follow, and how you will prioritize them, it is helpful to consider some ethical principles with deep roots in many cultures that have survived throughout recorded history.

1. Do unto others as you would have them do unto you (the **Golden Rule**). Putting yourself into the place of others, and thinking of yourself as the object of the decision, can help you think about fairness in decision making.

2. If an action is not right for everyone to take, it is not right for anyone **(Immanuel Kant's Categorical Imperative)**. Ask yourself, "If everyone did this, could the organization, or society, survive?"

3. If an action cannot be taken repeatedly, it is not right to take at all **(Descartes' rule of change)**. This is the slippery-slope rule: An action may bring about a small change now that is acceptable, but if it is repeated, it would bring unacceptable changes in the long run. In the vernacular, it might be stated as "once started down a slippery path, you may not be able to stop."

4. Take the action that achieves the higher or greater value **(Utilitarian Principle)**. This rule assumes you can prioritize values in a rank order and understand the consequences of various courses of action.

5. Take the action that produces the least harm or the least potential cost **(Risk Aversion Principle)**. Some actions have extremely high failure costs of very low probability (e.g., building a nuclear generating facility in an urban area) or extremely high failure costs of moderate probability (speeding and automobile accidents). Avoid these high-failure-cost actions, paying greater attention to high-failure-cost potential of moderate to high probability.

6. Assume that virtually all tangible and intangible objects are owned by someone else unless there is a specific declaration otherwise. (This is the **ethical "no free lunch" rule**.) If something someone else has created is useful to you, it has value, and you should assume the creator wants compensation for this work.

Although these ethical rules cannot be guides to action, actions that do not easily pass these rules deserve some very close attention and a great deal of caution. The appearance of unethical behavior may do as much harm to you and your company as actual unethical behavior.

PROFESSIONAL CODES OF CONDUCT

When groups of people claim to be professionals, they take on special rights and obligations because of their special claims to knowledge, wisdom, and respect. Professional codes of conduct are promulgated by associations of professionals, such as the American Medical Association (AMA), the American Bar Association (ABA), the Association of Information Technology Professionals (AITP), and the Association of Computing Machinery (ACM). These professional groups take responsibility for the partial regulation of their professions by determining entrance qualifications and competence. Codes of ethics are promises by professions to regulate themselves in the general interest of society. For example, avoiding harm to others, honoring property rights (including intellectual property), and respecting privacy are among the General Moral Imperatives of the ACM's Code of Ethics and Professional Conduct.

SOME REAL-WORLD ETHICAL DILEMMAS

Information systems have created new ethical dilemmas in which one set of interests is pitted against another. For example, many of the large telephone companies in the United States are using information technology to reduce the sizes of their workforces. Voice recognition software reduces the need for human operators by enabling computers to recognize a customer's responses to a series of computerized questions. Many companies monitor what their employees are doing on the Internet to prevent them from wasting company resources on non-business activities (see the Chapter 7 Interactive Session on Management).

In each instance, you can find competing values at work, with groups lined up on either side of a debate. A company may argue, for example, that it has a right to use information systems to increase productivity and reduce the size of its workforce to lower costs and stay in business. Employees displaced by information systems may argue that employers have some responsibility for their welfare. Business owners might feel obligated to monitor employee e-mail and Internet use to minimize drains on productivity. Employees might believe they should be able to use the Internet for short personal tasks in place of the telephone. A close analysis of the facts can sometimes produce compromised solutions that give each side "half a loaf." Try to apply some of the principles of ethical analysis described to each of these cases. What is the right thing to do?

4.3 THE MORAL DIMENSIONS OF INFORMATION SYSTEMS

In this section, we take a closer look at the five moral dimensions of information systems first described in Figure 4-1. In each dimension we identify the ethical, social, and political levels of analysis and use real-world examples to illustrate the values involved, the stakeholders, and the options chosen.

INFORMATION RIGHTS: PRIVACY AND FREEDOM IN THE INTERNET AGE

Privacy is the claim of individuals to be left alone, free from surveillance or interference from other individuals or organizations, including the state. Claims to privacy are also involved at the workplace: Millions of employees are subject to electronic and other forms of high-tech surveillance (Ball, 2001). Information technology and systems threaten individual claims to privacy by making the invasion of privacy cheap, profitable, and effective.

The claim to privacy is protected in the U.S., Canadian, and German constitutions in a variety of different ways and in other countries through various statutes. In the United States, the claim to privacy is protected primarily by the First Amendment guarantees of freedom of speech and association, the Fourth Amendment protections against unreasonable search and seizure of one's personal documents or home, and the guarantee of due process.

Table 4-3 describes the major U.S. federal statutes that set forth the conditions for handling information about individuals in such areas as credit reporting, education, financial records, newspaper records, and electronic communications. The Privacy Act of 1974 has been the most important of these laws, regulating the federal government's collection, use, and disclosure of information. At present, most U.S. federal privacy laws apply only to the federal government and regulate very few areas of the private sector.

Most American and European privacy law is based on a regime called **Fair Information Practices (FIP)** first set forth in a report written in 1973 by a federal government advisory committee (U.S. Department of Health, Education, and Welfare, 1973). FIP is a set of principles governing the collection and use of information about individuals. FIP principles are based on the notion of a mutuality of interest between the record holder and the individual. The individual has an interest in engaging in a transaction, and the record keeper—usually a business or government agency—requires information about the individual to support the transaction. Once information is gathered, the individual maintains an interest in the record, and the record may not be used to support other activities without the individual's consent. In 1998, the Federal Trade Commission (FTC) restated and extended the original FIP to provide guidelines for protecting online privacy. Table 4-4 describes the FTC's Fair Information Practice principles.

The FTC's FIP are being used as guidelines to drive changes in privacy legislation. In July 1998, the U.S. Congress passed the Children's Online Privacy Protection Act (COPPA), requiring Web sites to obtain parental permission before collecting information on children under the age of 13. (This law is in danger of being overturned.) The FTC has recommended additional legislation to protect online consumer privacy in advertising networks that collect

TABLE 4-3 FEDERAL PRIVACY LAWS IN THE UNITED STATES

GENERAL FEDERAL PRIVACY LAWS	PRIVACY LAWS AFFECTING PRIVATE INSTITUTIONST
Freedom of Information Act of 1966 as Amended (5 USC 552)	Fair Credit Reporting Act of 1970
Privacy Act of 1974 as Amended (5 USC 552a)	Family Educational Rights and Privacy Act of 1974
Electronic Communications Privacy Act of 1986	Right to Financial Privacy Act of 1978
Computer Matching and Privacy Protection Act of 1988	Privacy Protection Act of 1980
Computer Security Act of 1987	Cable Communications Policy Act of 1984
Federal Managers Financial Integrity Act of 1982	Electronic Communications Privacy Act of 1986
Driver's Privacy Protection Act of 1994	Video Privacy Protection Act of 1988
E-Government Act of 2002	The Health Insurance Portability and Accountability Act of 1996 (HIPAA)
	Children's Online Privacy Protection Act of 1998 (COPPA)
	Financial Modernization Act (Gramm–Leach-Bliley Act) of 1999

TABLE 4-4 FEDERAL TRADE COMMISSION FAIR INFORMATION PRACTICE PRINCIPLES

1. Notice/awareness (core principle). Web sites must disclose their information practices before collecting data. Includes identification of collector; uses of data; other recipients of data; nature of collection (active/inactive); voluntary or required status; consequences of refusal; and steps taken to protect confidentiality, integrity, and quality of the data.

2. Choice/consent (core principle). There must be a choice regime in place allowing consumers to choose how their information will be used for secondary purposes other than supporting the transaction, including internal use and transfer to third parties.

3. Access/participation. Consumers should be able to review and contest the accuracy and completeness of data collected about them in a timely, inexpensive process.

4. Security. Data collectors must take responsible steps to assure that consumer information is accurate and secure from unauthorized use.

5. Enforcement. There must be in place a mechanism to enforce FIP principles. This can involve self-regulation, legislation giving consumers legal remedies for violations, or federal statutes and regulations.

records of consumer Web activity to develop detailed profiles, which are then used by other companies to target online ads. Other proposed Internet privacy legislation focuses on protecting the online use of personal identification numbers, such as Social Security numbers; protecting personal information collected on the Internet that deals with individuals not covered by the Children's Online Privacy Protection Act of 1998; and limiting the use of data mining for homeland security.

Privacy protections have also been added to recent laws deregulating financial services and safeguarding the maintenance and transmission of health information about individuals. The Gramm-Leach-Bliley Act of 1999, which repeals earlier restrictions on affiliations among banks, securities firms, and insurance companies, includes some privacy protection for consumers of financial services. All financial institutions are required to disclose their policies and practices for protecting the privacy of nonpublic personal information and to allow customers to opt out of information-sharing arrangements with nonaffiliated third parties.

The Health Insurance Portability and Accountability Act of 1996 (HIPAA), which took effect on April 14, 2003, includes privacy protection for medical records. The law gives patients access to their personal medical records maintained by healthcare providers, hospitals, and health insurers and the right to authorize how protected information about themselves can be used or disclosed. Doctors, hospitals, and other healthcare providers must limit the disclosure of personal information about patients to the minimum amount necessary to achieve a given purpose.

The European Directive on Data Protection

In Europe, privacy protection is much more stringent than in the United States. Unlike the United States, European countries do not allow businesses to use personally identifiable information without consumers' prior consent. On October 25, 1998, the European Commission's Directive on Data Protection went into effect, broadening privacy protection in the European Union (EU) nations. The directive requires companies to inform people when they collect information about them and disclose how it will be stored and used. Customers must provide their informed consent before any company can legally use data about them, and they have the right to access that information, correct it, and request that no further data be collected. **Informed consent** can be defined as consent given with knowledge of all the facts needed to make a rational decision. EU member nations must translate these principles into their own laws and cannot transfer personal data to countries, such as the United States, that do not have similar privacy protection regulations.

Working with the European Commission, the U.S. Department of Commerce developed a safe harbor framework for U.S. firms. A **safe harbor** is a private, self-regulating policy and enforcement mechanism that meets the objectives of government regulators and legislation but does not involve government regulation or enforcement. U.S. businesses would be allowed to use personal data from EU countries if they develop privacy protection policies that meet EU standards. Enforcement would occur in the United States using self-policing, regulation, and government enforcement of fair trade statutes.

Internet Challenges to Privacy

Internet technology has posed new challenges for the protection of individual privacy. Information sent over this vast network of networks may pass through many different computer systems before it reaches its final destination. Each of these systems is capable of monitoring, capturing, and storing communications that pass through it.

It is possible to record many online activities, including what searches have been conducted, which Web sites and Web pages have been visited, the online content a person has accessed, and what items that person has inspected or purchased over the Web. Much of this monitoring and tracking of Web site visitors occurs in the background without the visitor's knowledge. It is conducted not just by individual Web sites but by advertising networks such as DoubleClick that are capable of tracking all browsing behavior at thousands of Web sites. Tools to monitor visits to the World Wide Web have become popular because they help businesses determine who is visiting their Web sites and how to better target their offerings. (Some firms also monitor the Internet usage of their employees to see how they are using company network resources.) The commercial demand for this personal information is virtually insatiable.

Web sites can learn the identities of their visitors if the visitors voluntarily register at the site to purchase a product or service or to obtain a free service, such as information. Web sites can also capture information about visitors without their knowledge using cookie technology.

Cookies are tiny files deposited on a computer hard drive when a user visits certain Web sites. Cookies identify the visitor's Web browser software and track visits to the Web site. When the visitor returns to a site that has stored a cookie, the Web site software will search the visitor's computer, find the cookie, and know what that person has done in the past. It may also update the cookie, depending on the activity during the visit. In this way, the site can customize its contents for each visitor's interests. For example, if you purchase a book on the Amazon.com Web site and return later from the same browser, the site will welcome you by name and recommend other books of interest based on your past purchases. DoubleClick, described earlier in this chapter, uses cookies to build its dossiers with details of online purchases and to examine the behavior of Web site visitors. Figure 4-3 illustrates how cookies work.

Web sites using cookie technology cannot directly obtain visitors' names and addresses. However, if a person has registered at a site, that information can be combined with cookie data to identify the visitor. Web site owners can also combine the data they have gathered from cookies and other Web site monitoring tools with personal data from other sources, such as offline data collected from surveys or paper catalog purchases, to develop very detailed profiles of their visitors.

FIGURE 4-3   HOW COOKIES IDENTIFY WEB VISITORS

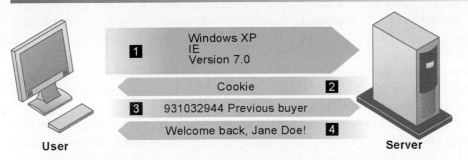

1. The Web server reads the user's Web browser and determines the operating system, browser name, version number, Internet address, and other information.
2. The server transmits a tiny text file with user identification information called a cookie, which the user's browser receives and stores on the user's computer hard drive.
3. When the user returns to the Web site, the server requests the contents of any cookie it deposited previously in the user's computer.
4. The Web server reads the cookie, identifies the visitor, and calls up data on the user.

Cookies are written by a Web site on a visitor's hard drive. When the visitor returns to that Web site, the Web server requests the ID number from the cookie and uses it to access the data stored by that server on that visitor. The Web site can then use these data to display personalized information.

There are now even more subtle and surreptitious tools for surveillance of Internet users. Marketers use Web bugs as another tool to monitor online behavior. **Web bugs** are tiny graphic files embedded in e-mail messages and Web pages that are designed to monitor who is reading the e-mail message or Web page and transmit that information to another computer. Other **spyware** can secretly install itself on an Internet user's computer by piggybacking on larger applications. Once installed, the spyware calls out to Web sites to send banner ads and other unsolicited material to the user, and it can also report the user's movements on the Internet to other computers. More information is available about Web bugs, spyware, and other intrusive software in Chapter 8.

Google has started using behavioral targeting to help it display more relevant ads based on users' search activities. One of its programs enables advertisers to target ads based on the search histories of Google users, along with any other information the user submits to Google or Google can obtain, such as age, demographics, region, and other Web activities (such as blogging). An additional program allows Google to help advertisers select keywords and design ads for various market segments based on search histories, such as helping a clothing Web site create and test ads targeted at teenage females.

Google has also been scanning the contents of messages received by users of its free Web-based e-mail service called Gmail. Ads that users see when they read their e-mail are related to the subjects of these messages. Profiles are developed on individual users based on the content in their e-mail. Google's Chrome Web browser, introduced in 2008, has a Suggest feature which automatically suggests related queries and Web sites as the user enters a search. Critics pointed out this was a key-logger device that would record every keystroke of users forever. Google subsequently announced it would anonymize the data in twenty-four hours.

The United States has allowed businesses to gather transaction information generated in the marketplace and then use that information for other marketing purposes without obtaining the informed consent of the individual whose information is being used. U.S. e-commerce sites are largely content to publish statements on their Web sites informing visitors about how their information will be used. Some have added opt-out selection boxes to these information policy statements. An **opt-out** model of informed consent permits the collection of personal information until the consumer specifically requests that the data not be collected. Privacy advocates would like to see wider use of an **opt-in** model of informed consent in which a business is prohibited from collecting any personal information unless the consumer specifically takes action to approve information collection and use.

The online industry has preferred self-regulation to privacy legislation for protecting consumers. In 1998, the online industry formed the Online Privacy Alliance to encourage self-regulation to develop a set of privacy guidelines for its members. The group promotes the use of online seals, such as that of TRUSTe, certifying Web sites adhering to certain privacy principles. Members of the advertising network industry, including DoubleClick, have created an additional industry association called the Network Advertising Initiative (NAI) to develop its own privacy policies to help consumers opt out of advertising network programs and provide consumers redress from abuses.

Individual firms like AOL, Yahoo!, and Google have recently adopted policies on their own in an effort to address public concern about tracking people online. AOL established an opt-out policy that allows users of its site to not be tracked. Yahoo follows NAI guidelines and also allows opt out for tracking and Web beacons (Web bugs). Google has reduced retention time for tracking data.

In general, most Internet businesses do little to protect the privacy of their customers, and consumers do not do as much as they should to protect themselves. Many companies with Web sites do not have privacy policies. Of the companies that do post privacy polices on their Web sites, about half do not monitor their sites to ensure they adhere to these policies. The vast majority of online customers claim they are concerned about online privacy, but less than half read the privacy statements on Web sites (Laudon and Traver, 2009).

Web sites are posting their privacy policies for visitors to review. The TRUSTe seal designates Web sites that have agreed to adhere to TRUSTe's established privacy principles of disclosure, choice, access, and security.

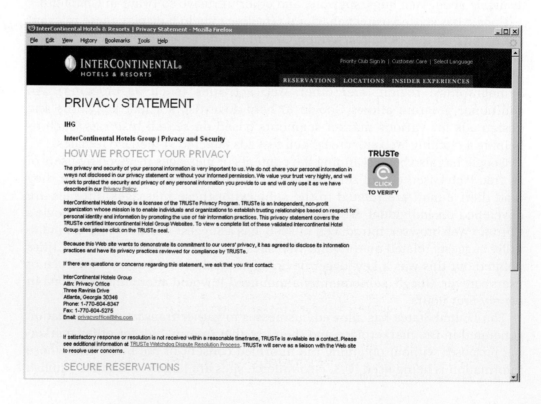

Technical Solutions

In addition to legislation, new technologies are available to protect user privacy during interactions with Web sites. Many of these tools are used for encrypting e-mail, for making e-mail or surfing activities appear anonymous, for preventing client computers from accepting cookies, or for detecting and eliminating spyware.

There are now tools to help users determine the kind of personal data that can be extracted by Web sites. The Platform for Privacy Preferences, known as P3P, enables automatic communication of privacy policies between an e-commerce site and its visitors. **P3P** provides a standard for communicating a Web site's privacy policy to Internet users and for comparing that policy to the user's preferences or to other standards, such as the FTC's new FIP guidelines or the European Directive on Data Protection. Users can use P3P to select the level of privacy they wish to maintain when interacting with the Web site.

The P3P standard allows Web sites to publish privacy policies in a form that computers can understand. Once it is codified according to P3P rules, the privacy policy becomes part of the software for individual Web pages (see Figure 4-4). Users of Microsoft Internet Explorer Web browsing software can access and read the P3P site's privacy policy and a list of all cookies coming from the site. Internet Explorer enables users to adjust their computers to screen out all cookies or let in selected cookies based on specific levels of privacy. For example, the "medium" level accepts cookies from first-party host sites that have opt-in or opt-out policies but rejects third-party cookies that use personally identifiable information without an opt-in policy.

However, P3P only works with Web sites of members of the World Wide Web Consortium who have translated their Web site privacy policies into P3P format. The technology will display cookies from Web sites that are not part of the consortium, but users will not be able to obtain sender information or privacy statements. Many users may also need to be educated about interpreting company privacy statements and P3P levels of privacy.

FIGURE 4-4   THE P3P STANDARD

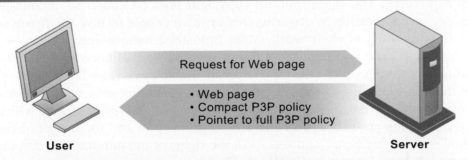

1. The user with P3P Web browsing software requests a Web page.
2. The Web server returns the Web page along with a compact version of the Web site's policy and a pointer to the full P3P policy. If the Web site is not P3P compliant, no P3P data are returned.
3. The user's Web browsing software compares the response from the Web site with the user's privacy preferences. If the Web site does not have a P3P policy or the policy does not match the privacy levels established by the user, it warns the user or rejects the cookies from the Web site. Otherwise, the Web page loads normally.

P3P enables Web sites to translate their privacy policies into a standard format that can be read by the user's Web browser software. The browser software evaluates the Web site's privacy policy to determine whether it is compatible with the user's privacy preferences.

PROPERTY RIGHTS: INTELLECTUAL PROPERTY

Contemporary information systems have severely challenged existing law and social practices that protect private intellectual property. **Intellectual property** is considered to be intangible property created by individuals or corporations. Information technology has made it difficult to protect intellectual property because computerized information can be so easily copied or distributed on networks. Intellectual property is subject to a variety of protections under three different legal traditions: trade secrets, copyright, and patent law.

Trade Secrets

Any intellectual work product—a formula, device, pattern, or compilation of data—used for a business purpose can be classified as a **trade secret**, provided it is not based on information in the public domain. Protections for trade secrets vary from state to state. In general, trade secret laws grant a monopoly on the ideas behind a work product, but it can be a very tenuous monopoly.

Software that contains novel or unique elements, procedures, or compilations can be included as a trade secret. Trade secret law protects the actual ideas in a work product, not only their manifestation. To make this claim, the creator or owner must take care to bind employees and customers with nondisclosure agreements and to prevent the secret from falling into the public domain.

The limitation of trade secret protection is that, although virtually all software programs of any complexity contain unique elements of some sort, it is difficult to prevent the ideas in the work from falling into the public domain when the software is widely distributed.

Copyright

Copyright is a statutory grant that protects creators of intellectual property from having their work copied by others for any purpose during the life of the author plus an additional 70 years after the author's death. For corporate-owned works, copyright protection lasts for 95 years after their initial creation. Congress has extended copyright protection to books, periodicals, lectures, dramas, musical compositions, maps, drawings, artwork of any kind, and motion pictures. The intent behind copyright laws has been to encourage creativity and authorship by ensuring that creative people receive the financial and other benefits of their work. Most industrial nations have their own copyright laws, and there are several international conventions and bilateral agreements through which nations coordinate and enforce their laws.

In the mid-1960s, the Copyright Office began registering software programs, and in 1980 Congress passed the Computer Software Copyright Act, which clearly provides protection for software program code and for copies of the original sold in commerce, and sets forth the rights of the purchaser to use the software while the creator retains legal title.

Copyright protects against copying of entire programs or their parts. Damages and relief are readily obtained for infringement. The drawback to copyright protection is that the underlying ideas behind a work are not protected, only their manifestation in a work. A competitor can use your software, understand how it works, and build new software that follows the same concepts without infringing on a copyright.

"Look and feel" copyright infringement lawsuits are precisely about the distinction between an idea and its expression. For instance, in the early 1990s, Apple Computer sued Microsoft Corporation and Hewlett-Packard for infringement of the expression of Apple's Macintosh interface, claiming that the defendants copied the expression of overlapping windows. The defendants countered that the idea of overlapping windows can be expressed only in a single way and, therefore, was not protectable under the merger doctrine of copyright law. When ideas and their expression merge, the expression cannot be copyrighted.

In general, courts appear to be following the reasoning of a 1989 case—*Brown Bag Software vs. Symantec Corp.*—in which the court dissected the elements of software alleged to be infringing. The court found that similar concept, function, general functional features (e.g., drop-down menus), and colors are not protectable by copyright law (*Brown Bag Software vs. Symantec Corp.*, 1992).

Patents

A **patent** grants the owner an exclusive monopoly on the ideas behind an invention for 20 years. The congressional intent behind patent law was to ensure that inventors of new machines, devices, or methods receive the full financial and other rewards of their labor and yet make widespread use of the invention possible by providing detailed diagrams for those wishing to use the idea under license from the patent's owner. The granting of a patent is determined by the United States Patent and Trademark Office and relies on court rulings.

The key concepts in patent law are originality, novelty, and invention. The Patent Office did not accept applications for software patents routinely until a 1981 Supreme Court decision that held that computer programs could be a part of a patentable process. Since that time, hundreds of patents have been granted and thousands await consideration.

The strength of patent protection is that it grants a monopoly on the underlying concepts and ideas of software. The difficulty is passing stringent criteria of nonobviousness (e.g., the work must reflect some special understanding and contribution), originality, and novelty, as well as years of waiting to receive protection.

Challenges to Intellectual Property Rights

Contemporary information technologies, especially software, pose severe challenges to existing intellectual property regimes and, therefore, create significant ethical, social, and political issues. Digital media differ from books, periodicals, and other media in terms of ease of replication; ease of transmission; ease of alteration; difficulty in classifying a software work as a program, book, or even music; compactness—making theft easy; and difficulties in establishing uniqueness.

The proliferation of electronic networks, including the Internet, has made it even more difficult to protect intellectual property. Before widespread use of networks, copies of software, books, magazine articles, or films had to be stored on physical media, such as paper, computer disks, or videotape, creating some hurdles to distribution. Using networks, information can be more widely reproduced and distributed. The Fifth Annual Global Software Piracy Study conducted by the International Data Corporation and the Business Software Alliance found that 38 percent of the software installed in 2007 on PCs worldwide was obtained illegally, representing $48 billion in global losses from software piracy. Worldwide, for every two dollars of software purchased legitimately, one dollar's worth was obtained illegally (Business Software Alliance, 2008).

The Internet was designed to transmit information freely around the world, including copyrighted information. With the World Wide Web in particular, you can easily copy and distribute virtually anything to thousands and even millions of people around the world, even if they are using different types of computer systems. Information can be illicitly copied from one place and distributed through other systems and networks even though these parties do not willingly participate in the infringement.

Individuals have been illegally copying and distributing digitized MP3 music files on the Internet for a number of years. File sharing services such as Napster, and later Grokster, Kazaa, and Morpheus, sprung up to help users locate and swap digital music files, including those protected by copyright. Illegal file-sharing became so widespread that it threatened the viability of the music recording industry. The recording industry won some legal battles for shutting these services down, but has not been able to halt illegal file sharing entirely. As more and more homes adopt high-speed Internet access, illegal file sharing of videos will pose similar threats to the motion picture industry (see the case study concluding Chapter 3).

Mechanisms are being developed to sell and distribute books, articles, and other intellectual property legally on the Internet, and the **Digital Millennium Copyright Act (DMCA)** of 1998 is providing some copyright protection. The DMCA implemented a World Intellectual Property Organization Treaty that makes it illegal to circumvent technology-based protections of copyrighted materials. Internet service providers (ISPs) are required to take down sites of copyright infringers that they are hosting once they are notified of the problem.

Microsoft and other major software and information content firms are represented by the Software and Information Industry Association (SIIA), which lobbies for new laws and enforcement of existing laws to protect intellectual property around the world. The SIIA runs an antipiracy hotline for individuals to report piracy activities and educational programs to help organizations combat software piracy and has published guidelines for employee use of software.

ACCOUNTABILITY, LIABILITY, AND CONTROL

Along with privacy and property laws, new information technologies are challenging existing liability law and social practices for holding individuals and institutions accountable. If a person is injured by a machine controlled, in part, by software, who should be held accountable and, therefore, held liable? Should a public bulletin board or an electronic service, such as America Online, permit the transmission of pornographic or offensive material (as broadcasters), or should they be held harmless against any liability for what users transmit (as is true of common carriers, such as the telephone system)? What about the Internet? If you outsource your information processing, can you hold the external vendor liable for injuries done to your customers? Some real-world examples may shed light on these questions.

Computer-Related Liability Problems

During the weekend of March 15, 2002, tens of thousands of Bank of America customers in California, Arizona, and Nevada were unable to use their paychecks and Social Security payments that had just been deposited electronically. Checks bounced. Withdrawals were blocked because of insufficient funds. Because of an operating error at the bank's computer center in Nevada, a batch of direct deposit transactions was not processed. The bank lost track of money that should have been credited to customers' accounts, and it took days to rectify the problem (Carr and Gallagher, 2002). Who is liable for any economic harm caused to individuals or businesses that could not access their full account balances in this period?

This case reveals the difficulties faced by information systems executives who ultimately are responsible for any harm done by systems developed by their staffs. In general, insofar as computer software is part of a machine, and the machine injures someone physically or economically, the producer of the software and the operator can be held liable for damages. Insofar as the software acts like a book, storing and displaying information, courts have been reluctant to hold authors, publishers, and booksellers liable for contents (the exception being instances of fraud or defamation), and hence courts have been wary of holding software authors liable for booklike software.

In general, it is very difficult (if not impossible) to hold software producers liable for their software products that are considered to be like books, regardless of the physical or economic harm that results. Historically, print publishers, books, and periodicals have not been held liable because of fears that liability claims would interfere with First Amendment rights guaranteeing freedom of expression.

What about software as a service? ATM machines are a service provided to bank customers. Should this service fail, customers will be inconvenienced and perhaps harmed economically if they cannot access their funds in a timely manner. Should liability protections be extended to software publishers and operators of defective financial, accounting, simulation, or marketing systems?

Software is very different from books. Software users may develop expectations of infallibility about software; software is less easily inspected than a book, and it is more difficult to compare with other software products for quality; software claims actually to perform a task rather than describe a task, as a book does; and people come to depend on services essentially based on software. Given the centrality of software to everyday life, the chances are excellent that liability law will extend its reach to include software even when the software merely provides an information service.

Telephone systems have not been held liable for the messages transmitted because they are regulated common carriers. In return for their right to provide telephone service, they must provide access to all, at reasonable rates, and achieve acceptable reliability. But broadcasters and cable television systems are subject to a wide variety of federal and local constraints on content and facilities. Organizations can be held liable for offensive content on their Web sites; and online services, such as America Online, might be held liable for postings by their users. Although U.S. courts have increasingly exonerated Web sites and ISPs for posting material by third parties, the threat of legal action still has a chilling effect on small companies or individuals who cannot afford to take their cases to trial.

SYSTEM QUALITY: DATA QUALITY AND SYSTEM ERRORS

The debate over liability and accountability for unintentional consequences of system use raises a related but independent moral dimension: What is an acceptable, technologically feasible level of system quality? At what point should system managers say, "Stop testing, we've done all we can to perfect this software. Ship it!" Individuals and organizations may be held responsible for avoidable and foreseeable consequences, which they have a duty to perceive and correct. And the gray area is that some system errors are foreseeable and correctable only at very great expense, an expense so great that pursuing this level of perfection is not feasible economically—no one could afford the product.

For example, although software companies try to debug their products before releasing them to the marketplace, they knowingly ship buggy products because the time and cost of fixing all minor errors would prevent these products from ever being released. What if the product was not offered on the marketplace, would social welfare as a whole not advance and perhaps even decline? Carrying this further, just what is the responsibility of a producer of computer services—should it withdraw the product that can never be perfect, warn the user, or forget about the risk (let the buyer beware)?

Three principal sources of poor system performance are (1) software bugs and errors, (2) hardware or facility failures caused by natural or other causes, and (3) poor input data quality. A Chapter 8 Learning Track discusses why zero defects in software code of any complexity cannot be achieved and why the seriousness of remaining bugs cannot be estimated. Hence, there is a technological barrier to perfect software, and users must be aware of the potential for catastrophic failure. The software industry has not yet arrived at testing standards for producing software of acceptable but not perfect performance.

Although software bugs and facility catastrophes are likely to be widely reported in the press, by far the most common source of business system failure is data quality. Few companies routinely measure the quality of their data, but individual organizations report data error rates ranging from 0.5 to 30 percent.

QUALITY OF LIFE: EQUITY, ACCESS, AND BOUNDARIES

The negative social costs of introducing information technologies and systems are beginning to mount along with the power of the technology. Many of these negative social consequences are not violations of individual rights or property crimes. Nevertheless, these negative consequences can be extremely harmful to individuals, societies, and political institutions. Computers and information technologies potentially can destroy valuable elements of our culture and society even while they bring us benefits. If there is a balance of good and bad consequences of using information systems, who do we hold responsible for the bad consequences? Next, we briefly examine some of the negative social consequences of systems, considering individual, social, and political responses.

Balancing Power: Center Versus Periphery

An early fear of the computer age was that huge, centralized mainframe computers would centralize power at corporate headquarters and in the nation's capital, resulting in a Big Brother society, as was suggested in George Orwell's novel *1984*. The shift toward highly decentralized computing, coupled with an ideology of empowerment of thousands of workers, and the decentralization of decision making to lower organizational levels have reduced the fears of power centralization in institutions. Yet much of the empowerment described in popular business magazines is trivial. Lower-level employees may be empowered to make minor decisions, but the key policy decisions may be as centralized as in the past.

Rapidity of Change: Reduced Response Time to Competition

Information systems have helped to create much more efficient national and international markets. The now-more-efficient global marketplace has reduced the normal social buffers that permitted businesses many years to adjust to competition. Time-based competition has an ugly side: The business you work for may not have enough time to respond to global competitors and may be wiped out in a year, along with your job. We stand the risk of developing a "just-in-time society" with "just-in-time jobs" and "just-in-time" workplaces, families, and vacations.

Maintaining Boundaries: Family, Work, and Leisure

Parts of this book were produced on trains and planes, as well as on vacations and during what otherwise might have been "family" time. The danger to ubiquitous computing, telecommuting, nomad computing, and the "do anything anywhere" computing environment is that it might actually come true. If so, the traditional boundaries that separate work from family and just plain leisure will be weakened.

Although authors have traditionally worked just about anywhere (typewriters have been portable for nearly a century), the advent of information systems, coupled with the growth of knowledge-work occupations, means that more and more people will be working when traditionally they would have been playing or communicating with family and friends. The work umbrella now extends far beyond the eight-hour day.

Even leisure time spent on the computer threatens these close social relationships. Extensive Internet use, even for entertainment or recreational purposes, takes people away from their family and friends. Among middle school and teenage children, it can lead to harmful anti-social behavior. Weakening these institutions poses clear-cut risks. Family and friends historically have provided powerful support mechanisms for individuals, and they act as balance points in a society by preserving private life, providing a place for people to collect their thoughts, allowing people to think in ways contrary to their employer, and dream.

Although some people enjoy the convenience of working at home, the "do anything anywhere" computing environment can blur the traditional boundaries between work and family time.

INTERACTIVE SESSION: MANAGEMENT

GREEN I.T. AT WIPRO

Wipro Technologies (Wipro), a division of Wipro Limited, provides integrated business, technology and process solutions. In the Indian market, Wipro is a leader in providing IT solutions and services for the corporate segment in India, offering system integration, software solutions and IT services. It is a global U.S. $ 10 billion company that has won numerous awards for its leadership, social responsibility, and customer care.

Wipro started its green journey with consolidation and virtualization to scale down the energy consumption in its own datacenter. The exponential growth of Wipro's server use was becoming a major problem and created an impact on energy costs. The IT team decided to tackle the problem with blade servers and virtualization. Commenting on the decision, CIO Laxman Badiga said, "... The amount of space we used in the datacenter was optimized by consolidating our servers for different applications. This helped open space and optimize our cooling needs."

The move to convert a non-green datacenter into a green one, however, was not easy. There was a lot of financial strain associated with the move. For example, the initial investment to virtualize the infrastructure was Rs. 6 million, which needed to be augmented by 5 to 10 percent with the increase in business needs. Furthermore, the entire datacenter blueprint - which maintained data like how the organization laid out its racks, how much cooling and power were needed per rack - had to undergo review; and the power and cooling requirements had to be re-architected for the new datacenter. Commenting on the challenges, Jethin Chandran GM-IT Planning, said, "Retrofitting can create a lot of impact. Then there are challenges in downtime."

In August 2005, the company embarked on tackling the e-waste problem by getting its manufacturing facility certified under ISO 14001. A year later, the company announced an e-waste disposal program for its customers, whereby it collected discarded systems from customers and sent them to vendors certified by the Pollution Control Board to dispose of the parts. The e-waste management initiative dubbed - Green Computing - enabled end-to-end e-waste management in its product lifecycle, spanning designing, manufacturing and up to the final disposal of the product.

In June 2007, Wipro became the first Indian company to introduce an eco-friendly range of desktops and laptops aimed at reducing e-waste in the environment. The new ranges of products, named GreenWare, were compliant with the European Restriction of Hazardous Substances (RoHS) directive. The RoHS directive, adopted in 2003 by the European Union, restricts the use of six hazardous materials in the manufacture of various types of electronic and electrical equipment. The new PCs would be free of hazardous materials such as brominated flame retardants (BFR), Polyvinyl chloride (PVC) and heavy metals like lead, cadmium and mercury that had been regularly used in the manufacture of computers.

In June 2008, Wipro joined the Green Grid, a global consortium dedicated to advancing energy efficiency in datacenters and business computing ecosystems. In the same month, Wipro commenced the EcoEye initiative, a comprehensive program for increasing ecological sustainability in all its operations and engaging its shareholders.

Commenting on this initiative, Chandran said, "... It is a collaborative effort between our customers, suppliers and employees. We are also working on establishing supply chain social environment responsibility guidelines and work with suppliers to identify materials that will reduce the environmental impact of their products."

All this would not have been possible without the commitment from the top. Azim Premji, chairman and CEO, made it his personal mission to drive the change.

He had been closely involved with EcoEye from its inception and monitored its progress on a regular basis. The governing council comprised the senior most leaders including the CIO, CFO, CTO, Head of HR, and Chief Strategy Officer. At the lower level, business units were responsible for driving green initiatives to the 95,000 plus Wipro employees. All projects were looked at from an ecological, as well as financial, perspective and were signed off by the governing council.

As a result of adopting green IT practices, Wipro reduced its servers from 400 to 100 and saved about 1 million KWh of power annually. The power consumption reduced by 26 percent as a result of rolling out power management tools. With virtualization and consolidation, the company is targeting a reduction in its server footprint by 3 percent.

Sources: John Riberiro, "Wipro Goes Green as India's E-Waste Mounts," www.cio.com, June 2007; "Expanding Green IT," www.cio.in, November 2008; "Wipro Launches EcoEye Initiative," www.thehindubusinessline.com, June 2008; Tim Gray, "Wipro Joins the Green Grid," green.tmcnet.com, June 2008.

CASE STUDY QUESTIONS   MIS IN ACTION

1. What were the various green initiatives undertaken by Wipro?

2. What were some of the challenges faced by Wipro? What benefits did Wipro reap from green computing?

3. What lessons can other organizations learn from Wipro's experience?

4. Should green-computing be driven by IT vendors, or should it be driven by corporate customers? Discuss.

Visit the Web site at www.wipro.com and also search the Internet to answer the following questions:

1. How is IT contributing to increased carbon emissions? What are some estimates of the extent of the problem? Which IT practices are some of the biggest culprits?

2. What is Wipro's carbon accounting tool? How can it help companies?

3. What are carbon credits? How can they be used by Wipro?

4. What are the green initiatives undertaken by other major IT vendors, specifically IBM, Microsoft, and HP?

• Case contributed by Neerja Sethi and Vijay Sethi, Nanyang Technological University

Dependence and Vulnerability

Today, our businesses, governments, schools, and private associations, such as churches, are incredibly dependent on information systems and are, therefore, highly vulnerable if these systems fail. With systems now as ubiquitous as the telephone system, it is startling to remember that there are no regulatory or standard-setting forces in place that are similar to telephone, electrical, radio, television, or other public utility technologies. The absence of standards and the criticality of some system applications will probably call forth demands for national standards and perhaps regulatory oversight.

Computer Crime and Abuse

New technologies, including computers, create new opportunities for committing crime by creating new valuable items to steal, new ways to steal them, and new ways to harm others. **Computer crime** is the commission of illegal acts through the use of a computer or against a computer system. Computers or computer systems can be the object of the crime (destroying a company's computer center or a company's computer files), as well as the instrument of a crime (stealing computer lists by illegally gaining access to a computer system using a home computer). Simply accessing a computer system without authorization or with intent to do harm, even by accident, is now a federal crime.

Computer abuse is the commission of acts involving a computer that may not be illegal but that are considered unethical. The popularity of the Internet and e-mail has turned one form of computer abuse—spamming—into a serious problem for both individuals and businesses. **Spam** is junk e-mail sent by an organization or individual to a mass audience of Internet users who have expressed no interest in the product or service being marketed. Spammers tend to market pornography, fraudulent deals and services, outright scams, and other products not widely approved in most civilized societies. Some countries have passed laws to outlaw spamming or to restrict its use. In the United States, it is still legal if it does not involve fraud and the sender and subject of the e-mail are properly identified.

Spamming has mushroomed because it only costs a few cents to send thousands of messages advertising wares to Internet users. According to Sophos, a leading vendor of security software, spam accounted for 92.3 percent of all e-mail traffic during the first quarter of 2008 (Sophos, 2008). Spam costs for businesses are very high (an estimated $50 billion per year) because of the computing and network resources consumed by billions of unwanted e-mail messages and the time required to deal with them.

Internet service providers and individuals can combat spam by using spam filtering software to block suspicious e-mail before it enters a recipient's e-mail inbox. However, spam filters may block legitimate messages. Spammers know how to skirt around filters by continually changing their e-mail accounts, by incorporating spam messages in images, by embedding spam in e-mail attachments and electronic greeting cards, and by using other people's computers that have been hijacked by botnets (see Chapter 8). Many spam messages are sent from one country while another country hosts the spam Web site.

Spamming is more tightly regulated in Europe than in the United States. On May 30, 2002, the European Parliament passed a ban on unsolicited commercial messaging. Electronic marketing can be targeted only to people who have given prior consent.

The U.S. CAN-SPAM Act of 2003, which went into effect on January 1, 2004, does not outlaw spamming but does ban deceptive e-mail practices by requiring commercial e-mail messages to display accurate subject lines, identify the true senders, and offer recipients an easy way to remove their names from e-mail lists. It also prohibits the use of fake return addresses. A few people have been prosecuted under the law, but it has had a negligible impact on spamming.

Employment: Trickle-Down Technology and Reengineering Job Loss

Reengineering work is typically hailed in the information systems community as a major benefit of new information technology. It is much less frequently noted that redesigning business processes could potentially cause millions of middle-level managers and clerical workers to lose their jobs. One economist has raised the possibility that we will create a society run by a small "high tech elite of corporate professionals . . . in a nation of the permanently unemployed" (Rifkin, 1993).

Other economists are much more sanguine about the potential job losses. They believe relieving bright, educated workers from reengineered jobs will result in these workers moving to better jobs in fast-growth industries. Missing from this equation are unskilled, blue-collar workers and older, less well-educated middle managers. It is not clear that these groups can be retrained easily for high-quality (high-paying) jobs. Careful planning and sensitivity to employee needs can help companies redesign work to minimize job losses.

The Interactive Session on Management explores another consequence of reengineered jobs. In this case, Wal-Mart's changes in job scheduling for more efficient use of its employees did not cause employees to lose their jobs directly. But it did impact their personal lives and forced them to accept more irregular part-time work. As you read this case, try to identify the problem this company is facing, what alternative solutions are available to management, and whether the chosen solution was the best way to address this problem.

Equity and Access: Increasing Racial and Social Class Cleavages

Does everyone have an equal opportunity to participate in the digital age? Will the social, economic, and cultural gaps that exist in the United States and other societies be reduced by information systems technology? Or will the cleavages be increased, permitting the better off to become even more better off relative to others?

These questions have not yet been fully answered because the impact of systems technology on various groups in society has not been thoroughly studied. What is known is that information, knowledge, computers, and access to these resources through educational institutions and public libraries are inequitably distributed along ethnic and social class lines, as are many other information resources. Several studies have found that certain ethnic and income groups in the United States are less likely to have computers or online Internet access even though computer ownership and Internet access have soared in the past five years. Although the gap is narrowing, higher-income families in each ethnic group are still more likely to have home computers and Internet access than lower-income families in the same group.

A similar **digital divide** exists in U.S. schools, with schools in high-poverty areas less likely to have computers, high-quality educational technology programs, or Internet access availability for their students. Left uncorrected, the digital divide could lead to a society of information haves, computer literate and skilled, versus a large group of information have-nots, computer illiterate and unskilled. Public interest groups want to narrow this digital divide by making digital information services—including the Internet— available to virtually everyone, just as basic telephone service is now.

Health Risks: RSI, CVS, and Technostress

The most common occupational disease today is **repetitive stress injury (RSI)**. RSI occurs when muscle groups are forced through repetitive actions often with high-impact loads (such as tennis) or tens of thousands of repetitions under low-impact loads (such as working at a computer keyboard).

INTERACTIVE SESSION: MANAGEMENT

FLEXIBLE SCHEDULING AT WAL-MART: GOOD OR BAD FOR EMPLOYEES?

With nearly 1.4 million workers domestically, Wal-Mart is the largest private employer in the United States. Wal-Mart is also the nation's number one retailer in terms of sales, registering nearly $379 billion in sales revenue for the fiscal year ending January 31, 2008. Wal-Mart achieved its lofty status through a combination of low prices and low operational costs, enabled by a superb continuous inventory replenishment system.

Now Wal-Mart is trying to lower costs further by changing its methods for scheduling the work shifts of its employees. In early 2007, Wal-Mart revealed that it was adopting a computerized scheduling system, a move that has been roundly criticized by workers' rights advocates for the impact it may have on employees' lives.

Traditionally, scheduling employee shifts at big box stores such as Wal-Mart was the domain of store managers who arranged schedules manually. They based their decisions in part on current store promotions as well as on weekly sales data from the previous year. Typically, the process required a full day of effort for a store manager. Multiply that labor intensity by the number of stores in a chain and you have an expensive task with results that are marginally beneficial to the company.

By using a computerized scheduling system, such as the system from Kronos that Wal-Mart adopted, a retail enterprise can produce work schedules for every store in its chain in a matter of hours. Meanwhile, store managers can devote their time to running their individual stores more effectively.

The Kronos scheduling system tracks individual store sales, transactions, units sold, and customer traffic. The system logs these metrics over 15-minute increments for seven weeks at a time, and then measures them against the same data from the previous year. It can also integrate data such as the number of in-store customers at certain hours or the average time required to sell a television set or unload a truck and predict the number of workers needed at any given hour.

A typical result of this type of scheduling might call for a sparse staff early in the day, a significant increase for the midday rush, scaling back toward the end of the afternoon, and then fortifying the staff once again for an evening crowd. However, for a chain like Wal-Mart, which operates thousands of 24-hour stores and has also run into trouble previously for its labor practices, the transition to a computerized scheduling system has resulted in controversy.

For Wal-Mart, using Kronos translates to improved productivity and customer satisfaction. Management reported a 12-percent gain in labor productivity in the quarter ending January 31, 2008.

For Wal-Mart employees, known to the company as associates, the change may decrease the stability of their jobs and, possibly, create financial hardship. The scheduling generated by Kronos can be unpredictable, requiring associates to be more flexible with their work hours. Stores may ask them to be on call in case of a rush, or to go home during a slow spell. Irregular hours, and inconsistent paychecks, make it more difficult for employees to organize their lives, from scheduling babysitters to paying bills. Alerts from the system may also enable store managers to avoid paying overtime or full-time wages by cutting back the hours of associates who are approaching the thresholds that cause extra benefits to kick in. Associates are almost always people who need all the work they can get.

According to Paul Blank of the Web site WakeUpWalMart.com, which is supported by the United Food and Commercial Workers union, "What the computer is trying to optimize is the most number of part-time and least number of full-time workers at lower labor costs, with no regard for the effect that it has on workers' lives." Sarah Clark, speaking on behalf of Wal-Mart, insists the system's goal is simply to improve customer service by shortening checkout lines and better meeting the needs of shoppers.

To assist in the deployment of its computerized scheduling system in all of its stores, Wal-Mart requests that its associates submit "personal availability" forms. Language on the form instructs associates that "Limiting your personal availability may restrict the number of hours you are scheduled." Anecdotal evidence suggests that some workers have indeed seen their hours cut and their shifts bounced around. Experienced associates with high pay rates have expressed concern that the system enables managers to pressure them into quitting. If they are unwilling to work nights and weekends, managers have a justification for replacing them with new workers who will make much less per hour. Sarah Clark denies that the system is used in this manner.

Critics of the system can cite the Clayton Antitrust Act of 1914, which states, "The labor of a human being is not a commodity or article of commerce." No legal battles over computerized scheduling appear imminent, so interpreting whether Wal-Mart's strategy equals treating its labor force as a commodity will have to wait.

In the meantime, Wal-Mart is once again at the forefront of technology trends in its industry. Ann Taylor Stores, Limited Brands, Gap, Williams-Sonoma, and GameStop have all installed similar workforce scheduling systems.

Sources: Vanessa O'Connell, "Retailers Reprogram Workers in Efficiency Push," *The Wall Street Journal*, September 10, 2008; Kris Maher, "Wal-Mart Seeks New Flexibility in Worker Shifts," *The Wall Street Journal*, January 3, 2007; www.kronos.com, accessed July 15, 2008; Bob Evans, "Wal-Mart's Latest 'Orwellian' Technology Move: Get Over It," *InformationWeek*, April 6, 2007 and "More Opinions on Wal-Mart's Flexible Scheduling," *InformationWeek*, April 17, 2007.

CASE STUDY QUESTIONS

1. What is the ethical dilemma facing Wal-Mart in this case? Do Wal-Mart's associates also face an ethical dilemma? If so, what is it?
2. What ethical principles apply to this case? How do they apply?
3. What are the potential effects of computerized scheduling on employee morale? What are the consequences of these effects for Wal-Mart?

MIS IN ACTION

Visit the Web site at www.WakeUpWalMart.com and then answer the following questions:

1. What are this group's major points of contention with Wal-Mart?
2. How well does the Web site serve their cause? Does the site help their cause or hurt it?
3. What other approach could the organization take to bring about change?

Using Wal-Mart's Web site and Google for research, answer the following questions:

4. How does Wal-Mart address the issues raised by organizations such as WakeUpWalMart.com?
5. Are the company's methods effective?
6. If you were a public relations expert advising Wal-Mart, what suggestions would you make for handling criticism?

Repetitive stress injury (RSI) is the leading occupational disease today. The single largest cause of RSI is computer keyboard work.

The single largest source of RSI is computer keyboards. The most common kind of computer-related RSI is **carpal tunnel syndrome (CTS)**, in which pressure on the median nerve through the wrist's bony structure, called a carpal tunnel, produces pain. The pressure is caused by constant repetition of keystrokes: In a single shift, a word processor may perform 23,000 keystrokes. Symptoms of carpal tunnel syndrome include numbness, shooting pain, inability to grasp objects, and tingling. Millions of workers have been diagnosed with carpal tunnel syndrome.

RSI is avoidable. Designing workstations for a neutral wrist position (using a wrist rest to support the wrist), proper monitor stands, and footrests all contribute to proper posture and reduced RSI. New, ergonomically correct keyboards are also an option. These measures should be supported by frequent rest breaks and rotation of employees to different jobs.

RSI is not the only occupational illness computers cause. Back and neck pain, leg stress, and foot pain also result from poor ergonomic designs of workstations. **Computer vision syndrome (CVS)** refers to any eyestrain condition related to computer display screen use. Its symptoms, which are usually temporary, include headaches, blurred vision, and dry and irritated eyes.

The newest computer-related malady is **technostress**, which is stress induced by computer use. Its symptoms include aggravation, hostility toward humans, impatience, and fatigue. According to experts, humans working continuously with computers come to expect other humans and human institutions to behave like computers, providing instant responses, attentiveness, and an absence of emotion. Technostress is thought to be related to high levels of job turnover in the computer industry, high levels of early retirement from computer-intense occupations, and elevated levels of drug and alcohol abuse.

The incidence of technostress is not known but is thought to be in the millions and growing rapidly in the United States. Computer-related jobs now top the list of stressful occupations based on health statistics in several industrialized countries.

To date, the role of radiation from computer display screens in occupational disease has not been proved. Video display terminals (VDTs) emit nonionizing electric and magnetic fields at low frequencies. These rays enter the body and have unknown effects on enzymes, molecules, chromosomes, and cell membranes. Long-term studies are investigating low-level electromagnetic fields and birth defects, stress, low birth weight, and other diseases. All manufacturers have reduced display screen emissions since the early 1980s, and European countries, such as Sweden, have adopted stiff radiation emission standards.

The computer has become a part of our lives—personally as well as socially, culturally, and politically. It is unlikely that the issues and our choices will become easier as information technology continues to transform our world. The growth of the Internet and the information economy suggests that all the ethical and social issues we have described will be heightened further as we move into the first digital century.

4.4   HANDS-ON MIS PROJECTS

The projects in this section give you hands-on experience in analyzing the privacy implications of using online data brokers, developing a corporate policy for employee Web usage, using blog creation tools to create a simple blog, and using Internet newsgroups for market research.

Management Decision Problems

1. USAData's Web site is linked to massive databases that consolidate personal data on millions of people. Anyone with a credit card can purchase marketing lists of consumers broken down by location, age, income level, and interests. If you click on Consumer Leads to order a consumer mailing list, you can find the names, addresses, and sometimes phone numbers of potential sales leads residing in a specific location and purchase the list of those names. One could use this capability to obtain a list, for example, of everyone in Peekskill, New York, making $150,000 or more per year. Do data brokers such as USAData raise privacy issues? Why or why not? If your name and other personal information were in this database, what limitations on access would you want in order to preserve your privacy? Consider the following data users: government agencies, your employer, private business firms, other individuals.

2. As the head of a small insurance company with six employees, you are concerned about how effectively your company is using its networking and human resources. Budgets are tight, and you are struggling to meet payrolls because employees are reporting many overtime hours. You do not believe that the employees have a sufficiently heavy work load to warrant working longer hours and are looking into the amount of time they spend on the Internet. Each employee uses a computer with Internet access on the job. You requested the following weekly report of employee Web usage from your information systems department.

WEB USAGE REPORT FOR THE WEEK ENDING JANUARY 9, 2009:

USER NAME	MINUTES ONLINE	WEB SITE VISITED
Kelleher, Claire	45	www.doubleclick.net
Kelleher, Claire	107	www.yahoo.com
Kelleher, Claire	96	www.insweb.com
McMahon, Patricia	83	www.itunes.com
McMahon, Patricia	44	www.insweb.com
Milligan, Robert	112	www.youtube.com
Milligan, Robert	43	www.travelocity.com
Olivera, Ernesto	40	www.CNN.com
Talbot, Helen	125	www.etrade.com
Talbot, Helen	27	www.nordstrom.com
Talbot, Helen	35	www.yahoo.com
Talbot, Helen	73	www.ebay.com
Wright, Steven	23	www.facebook.com
Wright, Steven	15	www.autobytel.com

- Calculate the total amount of time each employee spent on the Web for the week and the total amount of time that company computers were used for this purpose. Rank the employees in the order of the amount of time each spent on-line.

- Do your findings and the contents of the report indicate any ethical problems employees are creating? Is the company creating an ethical problem by monitoring its employees' use of the Internet?

- Use the guidelines for ethical analysis presented in this chapter to develop a solution to the problems you have identified.

Achieving Operational Excellence: Creating a Simple Blog

Software skills: Blog creation
Business skills: Blog and Web page design

In this project, you'll learn how to build a simple blog of your own design using the online blog creation software available at Blogger.com. Pick a sport, hobby, or topic of interest as the theme for your blog. Name the blog, give it a title, and choose a template for the blog. Post at least four entries to the blog, adding a label for each posting. Edit your posts, if necessary. Upload an image, such as a photo from your hard drive or the Web to your blog. (Google recommends Open Photo, Flickr: Creative Commons, or Creative Commons Search as sources for photos. Be sure to credit the source for your image.) Add capabilities for other registered users, such as team members, to comment on your blog. Briefly describe how your blog could be useful to a company selling products or services related to the theme of your blog. List the tools available to Blogger (including Gadgets) that would make your blog more useful for business and describe the business uses of each. Save your blog and show it to your instructor.

Improving Decision Making: Using Internet Newsgroups for Online Market Research

Software Skills: Web browser software and Internet newsgroups
Business Skills: Using Internet newsgroups to identify potential customers

This project will help develop your Internet skills in using newsgroups for marketing. It will also ask you to think about the ethical implications of using information in online discussion groups for business purposes.

You are producing hiking boots that you sell through a few stores at this time. You think your boots are more comfortable than those of your competition. You believe you can undersell many of your competitors if you can significantly increase your production and sales. You would like to use Internet discussion groups interested in hiking, climbing, and camping both to sell your boots and to make them well known. Visit groups.google.com, which stores discussion postings from many thousands of newsgroups. Through this site you can locate all relevant newsgroups and search them by keyword, author's name, forum, date, and subject. Choose a message and examine it carefully, noting all the information you can obtain, including information about the author.

- How could you use these newsgroups to market your boots?
- What ethical principles might you be violating if you use these messages to sell your boots? Do you think there are ethical problems in using newsgroups this way? Explain your answer.

- Next use Google or Yahoo.com to search the hiking boots industry and locate sites that will help you develop other new ideas for contacting potential customers.
- Given what you have learned in this and previous chapters, prepare a plan to use newsgroups and other alternative methods to begin attracting visitors to your site.

LEARNING TRACK MODULES

The following Learning Tracks provide content relevant to the topics covered in this chapter:

1. Developing a Corporate Code of Ethics for Information Systems
2. Creating a Web Page

Review Summary

1. **What ethical, social, and political issues are raised by information systems?**

    Information technology is introducing changes for which laws and rules of acceptable conduct have not yet been developed. Increasing computing power, storage, and networking capabilities—including the Internet—expand the reach of individual and organizational actions and magnify their impacts. The ease and anonymity with which information is now communicated, copied, and manipulated in online environments pose new challenges to the protection of privacy and intellectual property. The main ethical, social, and political issues raised by information systems center around information rights and obligations, property rights and obligations, accountability and control, system quality, and quality of life.

2. **What specific principles for conduct can be used to guide ethical decisions?**

    Six ethical principles for judging conduct include the Golden Rule, Immanuel Kant's Categorical Imperative, Descartes' rule of change, the Utilitarian Principle, the Risk Aversion Principle, and the ethical "no free lunch" rule. These principles should be used in conjunction with an ethical analysis.

3. **Why do contemporary information systems technology and the Internet pose challenges to the protection of individual privacy and intellectual property?**

    Contemporary data storage and data analysis technology enables companies to easily gather personal data about individuals from many different sources and analyze these data to create detailed electronic profiles about individuals and their behaviors. Data flowing over the Internet can be monitored at many points. Cookies and other Web monitoring tools closely track the activities of Web site visitors. Not all Web sites have strong privacy protection policies, and they do not always allow for informed consent regarding the use of personal information. Traditional copyright laws are insufficient to protect against software piracy because digital material can be copied so easily and transmitted to many different locations simultaneously over the Internet.

4. **How have information systems affected everyday life?**

    Although computer systems have been sources of efficiency and wealth, they have some negative impacts. Computer errors can cause serious harm to individuals and organizations. Poor data quality is also responsible for disruptions and losses for businesses. Jobs can be lost when computers replace workers or tasks become unnecessary in reengineered business processes. The ability to own and use a computer may be exacerbating socioeconomic disparities among different racial groups and social classes. Widespread use of computers increases opportunities for computer crime and computer abuse. Computers can also create health problems, such as RSI, computer vision syndrome, and technostress.

Key Terms

Review Questions

1. What ethical, social, and political issues are raised by information systems?

   - Explain how ethical, social, and political issues are connected and give some examples.

   - List and describe the key technological trends that heighten ethical concerns.

   - Differentiate between responsibility, accountability, and liability?

2. What specific principles for conduct can be used to guide ethical decisions?

   - List and describe the five steps in an ethical analysis.

   - Identify and describe six ethical principles.

3. Why do contemporary information systems technology and the Internet pose challenges to the protection of individual privacy and intellectual property?

   - Define privacy and fair information practices.

   - Explain how the Internet challenges the protection of individual privacy and intellectual property.

   - Explain how informed consent, legislation, industry self-regulation, and technology tools help protect the individual privacy of Internet users.

   - List and define are the three different regimes that protect intellectual property rights.

4. How have information systems have affected everyday life?

   - Explain why it is so difficult to hold software services liable for failure or injury.

   - List and describe the principal causes of system quality problems.

   - Name and describe four quality of life impacts of computers and information systems.

   - Define and describe technostress and RSI and explain their relationship to information technology.

Discussion Questions

1. Should producers of software-based services, such as ATMs, be held liable for economic injuries suffered when their systems fail?

2. Should companies be responsible for unemployment caused by their information systems? Why or why not?

Video Cases

You will find video cases illustrating some of the concepts in this chapter on the Laudon Web site along with questions to help you analyze the cases.

Collaboration and Teamwork: Developing a Corporate Ethics Code

With three or four of your classmates, develop a corporate ethics code on privacy that addresses both employee privacy and the privacy of customers and users of the corporate Web site. Be sure to consider e-mail privacy and employer monitoring of worksites, as well as corporate use of information about employees concerning their off-the-job behavior (e.g., lifestyle, marital arrangements, and so forth). If possible, use Google Sites to post links to Web pages, team communication announcements, and work assignments; to brainstorm; and to work collaboratively on project documents. Try to use Google Docs to develop your solution and presentation for the class.

Should Google Organize Your Medical Records?
CASE STUDY

During a typical trip to the doctor, you will see shelves full of folders and papers devoted to the storage of medical records. Every time you visit, your records are created or modified, and often duplicate copies are generated throughout the course of a visit to the doctor or a hospital. The majority of medical records are currently paper-based, making effective communication and access to the records difficult. Americans made well over a billion visits to doctors and hospitals over the past year, with each American making approximately four visits on average. As a result, there are millions of paper medical records lining the corridors of thousands of local medical practices, and for the most part, they cannot be systematically examined, and they are difficult to share. Though the challenge of updating this antiquated system is enormous, companies such as Google appear to be taking up the task.

In March 2008, Google announced an application that it hopes will alleviate the inefficiency of the current medical record storage system: Google Health. Google Health will allow consumers to enter their basic medical data into an online respository and invite doctors to send relevant information to Google electronically. The service is free to users. Features will include a 'health profile' for medications, conditions, and allergies, reminder messages for prescription refills or doctor visits, directories for nearby doctors, and personalized health advice. The application will also be able to accept information from many different recordkeeping technologies currently in use by hospitals and other institutions. The intent of the system is to make patients' records easily accessible and more complete and to streamline recordkeeping.

Google's mission is "to organize the world's information and make it universally accessible and useful." It's hard to disagree with the worthiness of this goal, and as the undisputed leader in Web search, Google has proven that it is very good at what it does. But what if Google were seeking personal information about you? You might not feel as good about Google's quest to organize the world's information when you consider that some of that information is information that you'd prefer remain private.

Google's development of its Google Health application illustrates the conflict between its self-avowed mission and the individual's right to privacy. As with similar cases such as government surveillance and data aggregation, the question is whether or not the privacy risks posed by information systems are significant enough to abandon or curtail the collection of useful information. If information gathering should be curtailed—but not eliminated—how will this be decided and who should decide? Google is no stranger to this conflict of values; this is merely one example of many where Google has clashed with privacy advocates regarding its information collection practices and handling of that information.

With the launch of Google Health, Google aims to be the catalyst for the process of digitizing and standardizing the nation's medical records in an easy-to-use format. Currently only a small fraction, under 15%, of American medical practices keep their medical records online, making it difficult for patients and other doctors to quickly and easily access them. When a patient changes doctors, begins seeing a new doctor, or moves, the absence of online medical records can be a source of needless hassle and effort on the part of both patient and practice. Sometimes, access to medical records can even be a life or death matter in the rare cases when power failure prevents access to local data storage systems.

But the added convenience of easily accessible medical records is just one potential benefit of going electronic. As the healthcare industry continues to face budget pressures from Medicare cutbacks and reductions in managed-care fees, digitizing patient records has become increasingly attractive as a cost-cutting measure. Although many practices consider the costs of implementing new software to be prohibitive, the potential benefits for the industry as a whole are significant. One survey found that 26 percent of healthcare technology professionals cited lack of financial support as the most important factor preventing them from digitizing their recordkeeping. But once practices make the initial investment in new technology, the increase in efficiency is likely to reduce future costs by an estimated $80 to $240 billion dollars, more than enough to make the switch worthwhile.

Google Health and other efforts to convert to electronic health records stand to provide much-needed organization and efficiency to the healthcare industry, the single largest segment of America's gross domestic product (GDP). But concerned individuals and privacy advocates argue that electronic health records will be stored in such a way that increases the likelihood of privacy invasions. Some potential users of the system are concerned that Google will make their medical information accessible to advertisers in a manner similar to the targeted advertisements Gmail users currently see based on the content of their e-mail.

These privacy concerns are far from unfounded. HIPAA—the Health insurance Portability and Accountability Act of 1996—provides very limited protections for personal medical records. (It primarily covers information flowing between healthcare providers, health insurers, and clearing-houses for payment processing.) There are currently no federal privacy protections for patients who set up personal health records online. Even hospitals and practices that currently use electronic storage formats report a high incidence of security breaches, with a quarter of healthcare technology professionals reporting at least one security breach in the past year. According to a 2006 Federal Trade Commission study, about 249,000 Americans had their personal information misused for the purpose of obtaining medical treatment, supplies, or services. But breaches and other forms of medical identity theft are not the biggest concern surrounding electronic health records.

Most people are more worried that sensitive information legitimately accessible via electronic health records might lead to their losing health insurance or job opportunities. For instance, if employers knew that you had a chronic heart condition, would they want to hire you?

Though the healthcare industry argues that these privacy concerns are for the most part misplaced, there is evidence that these fears are justified. Horror stories like those of Patricia Galvin reinforce the worries many people have about the privacy of their medical records. Galvin's attempts to acquire disability benefits for her chronic back pain were turned down on the basis of her psychologist's notes, which were supposed to be confidential. The number of monthly medical-privacy complaints received by the Department of Health and Human Services has been steadily approaching 750 per month over the past several years, up from 150 in 2003. People fear that a switch to electronic medical records could be even more vulnerable to security breaches and privacy violations.

Proponents of electronic health records argue that computer technology, once fully implemented, would enhance security rather than threaten it. They also believe that it is more important to first get the system up and running than to worry about privacy matters. Congressional Representative Joe Barton of Texas, an advocate of legislation that would speed the development of such records, said that "(p)rivacy is an important issue, but more important is that we get a health information system in place." Lawmakers like Barton feel that the benefits of systems like Google Health outweigh the privacy risks, and that further legislation to impose privacy controls can be added after the fact.

Some experts disagree with that stance, saying that unless an electronic system has sufficient privacy controls from the outset, it is less likely to become universally used. Even if the system's security controls are sufficient, it is important that consumers are aware of those controls and confident that they can use the system without fear of their records being accessed by unauthorized parties. Creating an electronic health system without the proper security controls would not only be an unacceptable privacy risk, but would be doomed to failure because potential users would be unwilling to cooperate with the information requirements of the system.

Google has tried to reassure the public that its security is iron-tight and that businesses and individuals should have confidence in its ability to store and protect their data. According to Google senior security manager Eran Feigenbaum, "We've taken an in-depth approach to security, with lots of different layers that build on each other." However, Google has not provided much detail about its security practices—where its computer centers are located, how many people it employs in its security department, and how it protects its army of servers against attack—for fear of opening itself up to attacks.

"Businesses are hoping Google will pick the right tools to secure the infrastructure, but they have no assurances and no say in what it will pick," notes Randall Gamby, security analyst for Burton Group, a Midvale, Utah, research and advisory firm. Feigenbaum adds that Google relies on its own security system and applications for its day-to-day business operations, and that should be proof that its security works.

Google is not the only company to set its sights on online medical records. Microsoft and Revolution Health Group LLC, founded by AOL co-founder Steve Case, among others, are also launching similar sites where users can maintain online health profiles. As of yet it is too early to tell whether any of these ventures will be successful in the long term, but Revolution Health Group was forced to fire a quarter of its employees in the face of lower-than-expected earnings in 2007. Microsoft's venture, HealthVault, is still in its infancy along with Google Health. The federal office in charge of creating a national network of electronic health records, the Office of the Coordinator of Health Information Technology, announced in March of 2008 that it plans to integrate its system with both Google and Microsoft's healthcare databases, among others. The office did not provide details or a timetable on how the integration would occur. Privacy concerns are not likely to halt the shift towards digitizing our records entirely, but will continue to be arguably the most significant obstacle for these ventures as they work towards creating a standardized, digital system for medical recordkeeping.

Sources: Ericka Chickowski, "Are Google's Security Practices Up to Snuff?" Baselinemag.com, May 23, 2008; Chris Gonsalves, "Google, Microsoft Take Health Care IT Pulse," Baselinemag.com, March 31, 2008 and "Securing, Digitizing Medical Records Remain Priorities in Healthcare IT," Baselinemag.com, February 26, 2008; Bob Brewin, "National Health Records Network to Hook Up With Google, Microsoft," govexec.com, March 27, 2008; Kristen Gerencher, "As More of Our Health Records Move Online, Privacy Concerns Grow," FoxBusiness.com, March 26, 2008; "Preying on Patients," *MarketWatch*, June 19, 2008; and "To Trust or Not to Trust Personal Health Records?" MarketWatch, March 26, 2008; Christopher Lawton and Ben Worthen, "Google to Offer Health Records On The Web," *The Wall Street Journal*, February 28, 2008; and Lissa Harris, "Google Health Heads to the Hospital," *Technology Review*, May 28, 2008.

CASE STUDY QUESTIONS

1. What concepts in the chapter are illustrated in this case? Who are the stakeholders in this case?

2. What are the problems with America's current medical recordkeeping system? How would electronic medical records alleviate these problems?

3. What management, organization, and technology factors are most critical to the creation and development of electronic medical records?

4. What are the pros and cons of electronic patient records? Do you think the concerns over digitizing our medical records are valid? Why or why not?

5. Should people entrust Google with their electronic medical records? Why or why not?

6. If you were in charge of designing an electronic medical recordkeeping system, what are some features you would include? What are features you would avoid?

Information Technology Infrastructure

Part Two provides the technical foundation for understanding information systems by examining hardware, software, database, and networking technologies along with tools and techniques for security and control. This part answers questions such as: What technologies do businesses today need to accomplish their work? What do I need to know about these technologies to make sure they enhance the performance of the firm? How are these technologies likely to change in the future? What technologies and procedures are required to ensure that systems are reliable and secure?

Chapter 5

IT Infrastructure and Emerging Technologies

LEARNING OBJECTIVES

After reading this chapter, you will be able to answer the following questions:

1. What is IT infrastructure and what are its components?

2. What are the stages and technology drivers of IT infrastructure evolution?

3. What are the current trends in computer hardware platforms?

4. What are the current trends in software platforms?

5. What are the challenges of managing IT infrastructure and management solutions?

Interactive Sessions:

Computing Goes Green

Salesforce.com: Software As A Service Goes Mainstream

CARS.COM'S IT INFRASTRUCTURE DRIVES RAPID BUSINESS GROWTH

I f you've ever tried to research or buy a car online, you may have used Cars.com. It's the number one destination for online car shoppers. With comprehensive pricing information, photo galleries, side-by-side comparison tools, videos, and a huge selection of new- and used-car inventory, Cars.com gives millions of car buyers the information they need to make confident buying decisions.

No wonder, then, that the company has experienced explosive growth. In 2008, Cars.com experienced record traffic and dealer leads. Unfortunately, its information systems were unable to keep pace with its aggressive business strategy and expansion. Cars.com was saddled with a haphazard collection of technologies that had evolved over ten years that made it difficult to get much work done. It used multiple versions of the Linux operating system, including AGT Linux, which is no longer supported, as well as aging Hewlett-Packard and Sun Microsystems servers running BEA Java. According to the company's Chief Technology Officer Manny Montejano, "Not only did we have multiple pieces of technology from multiple vendors and multiple sources, but we had multiple versions within those. "As a result, Cars.com's information systems staff was spending more time trying to integrate legacy software and systems rather than developing applications to meet new business demands.

Working with Perficient information technology consultants, Cars.com management decided that it would have to replace the firm's entire IT infrastructure in order to achieve its business goals. The project began in January 2007. Cars.com standardized on an IBM platform and a service-oriented architecture (SOA). IBM's WebSphere application server runs on four IBM Power series servers with the P5 chip set using AIX, IBM's version of the Unix operating system. The IBM servers have significantly reduced Cars.com's data center costs because they have lower power, cooling, and space requirements.

The Cars.com application on the application server is written in Java. The IBM Information Server combines data from both end users and dealers so it can be integrated with the company's applications. With over millions of vehicles in Cars.com's inventory, customers are able to precisely locate what they are looking for. IBM Rational software helps Cars.com programmers rapidly design, develop, and test Java applications. The SOA environment allows the company to build new applications and services more rapidly using plug-and-play technologies.

So far Cars.com's investment in a new IT infrastructure has delivered strong returns. The company can develop new systems much more rapidly, and the information systems department now has the time and resources to take on projects that will help grow the business. For example, the new infrastructure allowed the company to participate in Super Bowl commercials, because its systems were now capable of handling large spikes in traffic when its two 30-second ads appeared on TV. The infrastructure also allowed

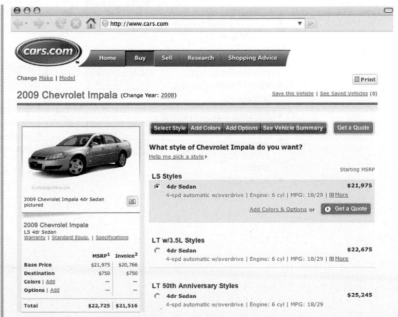

Cars.com to become the exclusive provider of used car listings and exclusive listing service for private party sellers on Yahoo Autos. Dealer leads have increased 40 percent over 2007. Handling inventory of 2.7 million vehicles, thousands of dealers, and millions of unique Web site visitors each month, Cars.com's new IT infrastructure is clearly up to the task.

Sources: Karen D. Schwartz, "Cars.com Firing on All Cylinders," *eWeek,* June 9 2008; IBM, "Cars.com Turns to IBM Software and SOA Expertise to Drive Rapid Business Growth," April 18, 2008.

Cars.com has an enviable track record as a successful online retail business. Unfortunately, its aggressive growth plans and daily operations were hampered by unmanageable and outdated technology. Cars.com's management felt the best solution was to replace its antiquated old IT infrastructure with new computer hardware and software technologies and to standardize on the technology of a single vendor—IBM. This case highlights the critical role that hardware and software investments can play in improving business performance.

The chapter-opening diagram calls attention to important points raised by this case and this chapter. Management decided that the best way to make technology promote business objectives was to overhaul and standardize IT infrastructure. Cars.com now uses more powerful and efficient servers and a series of IBM software tools along with a service-oriented architecture (SOA) that makes it much easier to develop new applications and services. The entire infrastructure is easier to manage and capable of scaling to accomodate spikes in Web site traffic, growing transaction loads, and new business opportunities.

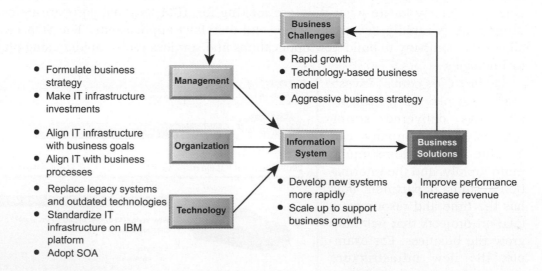

5.1 IT INFRASTRUCTURE

I n Chapter 1, we defined *information technology (IT)* infrastructure as the shared technology resources that provide the platform for the firm's specific information system applications. IT infrastructure includes investment in hardware, software, and services—such as consulting, education, and training—that are shared across the entire firm or across entire business units in the firm. A firm's IT infrastructure provides the foundation for serving customers, working with vendors, and managing internal firm business processes (see Figure 5-1).

Supplying U.S. firms with IT infrastructure is a $1.8 trillion industry when telecommunications, networking equipment and telecommunications services (Internet, telephone, and data transmission) are included. Investments in infrastructure account for between 25 and 35 percent of information technology expenditures in large firms (Weill et al. 2002).

DEFINING IT INFRASTRUCTURE

IT infrastructure consists of a set of physical devices and software applications that are required to operate the entire enterprise. But IT infrastructure is also a set of firmwide services budgeted by management and comprising both human and technical capabilities. These services include the following:

- Computing platforms used to provide computing services that connect employees, customers, and suppliers into a coherent digital environment, including large mainframes, desktop and laptop computers, and personal digital assistants (PDAs) and Internet appliances.

FIGURE 5-1   CONNECTION BETWEEN THE FIRM, IT INFRASTRUCTURE, AND BUSINESS CAPABILITIES

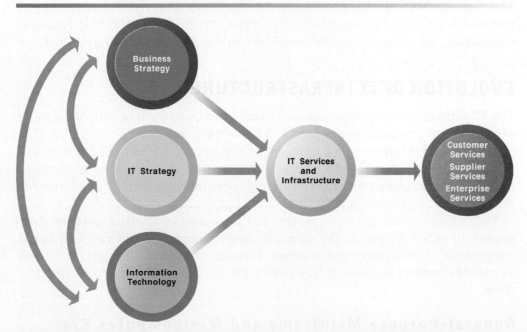

The services a firm is capable of providing to its customers, suppliers, and employees are a direct function of its IT infrastructure. Ideally, this infrastructure should support the firm's business and information systems strategy. New information technologies have a powerful impact on business and IT strategies, as well as the services that can be provided to customers.

- Telecommunications services that provide data, voice, and video connectivity to employees, customers, and suppliers.
- Data management services that store and manage corporate data and provide capabilities for analyzing the data.
- Application software services that provide enterprise-wide capabilities such as enterprise resource planning, customer relationship management, supply chain management, and knowledge management systems that are shared by all business units.
- Physical facilities management services that develop and manage the physical installations required for computing, telecommunications, and data management services.
- IT management services that plan and develop the infrastructure, coordinate with the business units for IT services, manage accounting for the IT expenditure, and provide project management services.
- IT standards services that provide the firm and its business units with policies that determine which information technology will be used, when, and how.
- IT education services that provide training in system use to employees and offer managers training in how to plan for and manage IT investments.
- IT research and development services that provide the firm with research on potential future IT projects and investments that could help the firm differentiate itself in the marketplace.

This "service platform" perspective makes it easier to understand the business value provided by infrastructure investments. For instance, the real business value of a fully loaded personal computer operating at 3 gigahertz that costs about $1,000 or a high-speed Internet connection is hard to understand without knowing who will use it and how it will be used. When we look at the services provided by these tools, however, their value becomes more apparent: The new PC makes it possible for a high-cost employee making $100,000 a year to connect to all the company's major systems and the public Internet. The high-speed Internet service saves this employee about one hour per day in reduced wait time for Internet information. Without this PC and Internet connection, the value of this one employee to the firm might be cut in half.

EVOLUTION OF IT INFRASTRUCTURE

The IT infrastructure in organizations today is an outgrowth of over 50 years of evolution in computing platforms. There have been five stages in this evolution, each representing a different configuration of computing power and infrastructure elements (see Figure 5-2). The five eras are general-purpose mainframe and minicomputer computing, personal computers, client/server networks, enterprise computing, and cloud computing.

Technologies that characterize one era may also be used in another time period for other purposes. For example, some companies still run traditional mainframe or minicomputer systems. Mainframe computers today are used as massive servers supporting large Web sites and corporate enterprise applications.

General-Purpose Mainframe and Minicomputer Era: (1959 to Present)

The introduction of the IBM 1401 and 7090 transistorized machines in 1959 marked the beginning of widespread commercial use of **mainframe** computers.

FIGURE 5-2   **ERAS IN IT INFRASTRUCTURE EVOLUTION**

Stages in IT Infrastructure Evolution

Mainframe/
Minicomputer
(1959–present)

Personal
Computer
(1981–present)

Client Server
(1983–present)

Enterprise
Internet
(1992–present)

Enterprise
Server

Internet

Cloud
Computing
(2000–present)

THE INTERNET

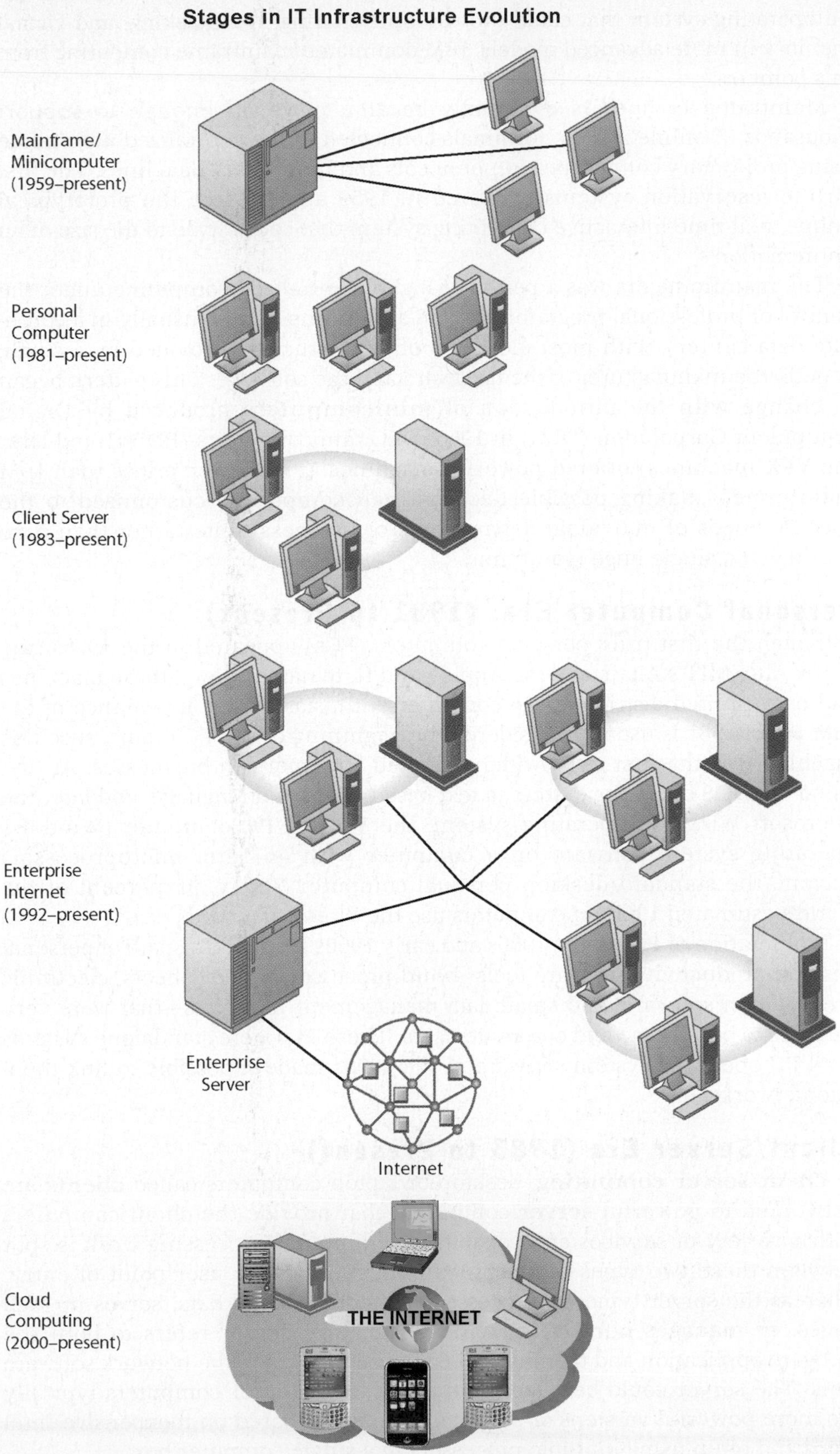

Illustrated here are the typical computing configurations characterizing each of the five eras of IT infrastructure evolution.

In 1965 the mainframe computer truly came into its own with the introduction of the IBM 360 series. The 360 was the first commercial computer with a powerful operating system that could provide time sharing, multitasking, and virtual memory in more advanced models. IBM dominated mainframe computing from this point on.

Mainframe computers eventually became powerful enough to support thousands of online remote terminals connected to the centralized mainframe using proprietary communication protocols and proprietary data lines. The first airline reservation systems appeared in 1959 and became the prototypical online, real-time interactive computing system that could scale to the size of an entire nation.

The mainframe era was a period of highly centralized computing under the control of professional programmers and systems operators (usually in a corporate data center), with most elements of infrastructure provided by a single vendor, the manufacturer of the hardware and the software. This pattern began to change with the introduction of **minicomputers** produced by Digital Equipment Corporation (DEC) in 1965. DEC minicomputers (PDP-11 and later the VAX machines) offered powerful machines at far lower prices than IBM mainframes, making possible decentralized computing, customized to the specific needs of individual departments or business units rather than time sharing on a single huge mainframe.

Personal Computer Era: (1981 to Present)

Although the first truly personal computers (PCs) appeared in the 1970s (the Xerox Alto, MIT's Altair, and the Apple I and II, to name a few), these machines had only limited distribution to computer enthusiasts. The appearance of the IBM PC in 1981 is usually considered the beginning of the PC era because this machine was the first to be widely adopted by American businesses. At first using the DOS operating system, a text-based command language, and later the Microsoft Windows operating system, the **Wintel PC** computer (Windows operating system software on a computer with an Intel microprocessor) became the standard desktop personal computer. Today, 95 percent of the world's estimated 1 billion computers use the Wintel standard.

Proliferation of PCs in the 1980s and early 1990s launched a spate of personal desktop productivity software tools—word processors, spreadsheets, electronic presentation software, and small data management programs—that were very valuable to both home and corporate users. These PCs were standalone systems until PC operating system software in the 1990s made it possible to link them into networks.

Client/Server Era (1983 to Present)

In **client/server computing**, desktop or laptop computers called **clients** are networked to powerful **server** computers that provide the client computers with a variety of services and capabilities. Computer processing work is split between these two types of machines. The client is the user point of entry, whereas the server typically processes and stores shared data, serves up Web pages, or manages network activities. The term server refers to both the software application and the physical computer on which the network software runs. The server could be a mainframe, but today server computers typically are more powerful versions of personal computers, based on inexpensive Intel chips and often using multiple processors in a single computer box.

The simplest client/server network consists of a client computer networked to a server computer, with processing split between the two types of machines.

This is called a *two-tiered client/server architecture*. Whereas simple client/server networks can be found in small businesses, most corporations have more complex, **multitiered** (often called **N-tier**) **client/server architectures** in which the work of the entire network is balanced over several different levels of servers, depending on the kind of service being requested (see Figure 5-3).

For instance, at the first level a **Web server** will serve a Web page to client in response for a request for service. Web server software is responsible for locating and managing stored Web pages. If the client requests access to a corporate system (a product list or price information, for instance), the request is passed along to an **application server**. Application server software handles all application operations between a user and an organization's back-end business systems. The application server may reside on the same computer as the Web server or on its own dedicated computer. Chapters 6 and 7 provide more detail on other pieces of software that are used in multitiered client/server architectures for e-commerce and e-business.

Client/server computing enables businesses to distribute computing work across a series of smaller, inexpensive machines that cost much less than minicomputers or centralized mainframe systems. The result is an explosion in computing power and applications throughout the firm.

Novell Netware was the leading technology for client/server networking at the beginning of the client/server era. Today Microsoft is the market leader with its **Windows** operating systems (Windows Server, Windows Vista, Windows XP).

Enterprise Computing Era (1992 to Present)

In the early 1990s, firms turned to networking standards and software tools that could integrate disparate networks and applications throughout the firm into an enterprise-wide infrastructure. As the Internet developed into a trusted communications environment after 1995, business firms began seriously using the *Transmission Control Protocol/Internet Protocol (TCP/IP)* networking standard to tie their disparate networks together. We discuss TCP/IP in detail in Chapter 7.

FIGURE 5-3   **A MULTITIERED CLIENT/SERVER NETWORK (N-TIER)**

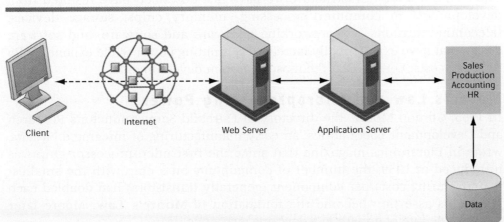

In a multitiered client/server network, client requests for service are handled by different levels of servers.

The resulting IT infrastructure links different pieces of computer hardware and smaller networks into an enterprise-wide network so that information can flow freely across the organization and between the firm and other organizations. It can link different types of computer hardware, including mainframes, servers, PCs, mobile phones, and other handheld devices, and it includes public infrastructures such as the telephone system, the Internet, and public network services. The enterprise infrastructure also requires software to link disparate applications and enable data to flow freely among different parts of the business, such as enterprise applications (see Chapters 2 and 9) and Web services (discussed in section 5.4).

Cloud Computing Era (2000 to Present)

The growing bandwidth power of the Internet has pushed the client/server model one step further, towards what is called the "Cloud Computing Model." **Cloud computing** refers to a model of computing where firms and individuals obtain computing power and software applications over the Internet, rather than purchasing their own hardware and software. Currently, cloud computing is the fastest growing form of computing, with an estimated market size in 2009 of $8 billion, and a projected size of $160 billion in 2012 (Gartner, 2008; Merrill Lynch, 2008).

Hardware firms IBM, HP, and Dell are building huge, scalable cloud computing centers which provide computing power, data storage, and high speed Internet connections to firms who rely on the Internet for business software applications. Software firms such as Google, Microsoft, SAP, Oracle, and Salesforce.com sell software applications as services delivered over the Internet. For instance, over 500,000 firms in 2009 will use Google Apps, a suite of Internet-based desktop software applications such as word processing, spreadsheets, and calendars. (Hamm, 2008; King, 2008). In 2009, more than 43,000 firms worldwide will be using Salesforce.com's customer relationship management software, some on their iPhones (see this chapter's Interactive Session on Organizations).

Table 5-1 compares each era on the infrastructure dimensions introduced.

TECHNOLOGY DRIVERS OF INFRASTRUCTURE EVOLUTION

The changes in IT infrastructure we have just described have resulted from developments in computer processing, memory chips, storage devices, telecommunications and networking hardware and software, and software design that have exponentially increased computing power while exponentially reducing costs. Let's look at the most important developments.

Moore's Law and Microprocessing Power

In 1965, Gordon Moore, the directory of Fairchild Semiconductor's Research and Development Laboratories, an early manufacturing of integrated circuits, wrote in Electronics magazine that since the first microprocessor chip was introduced in 1959, the number of components on a chip with the smallest manufacturing costs per component (generally transistors) had doubled each year. This assertion became the foundation of **Moore's Law**. Moore later reduced the rate of growth to a doubling every two years.

This law would later be interpreted in multiple ways. There are at least three variations of Moore's Law, none of which Moore ever stated: (1) the power of

TABLE 5-1 STAGES IN IT INFRASTRUCTURE EVOLUTION

INFRASTRUCTURE DIMENSION	MAINFRAME ERA (1959 TO PRESENT)	PC ERA (1981 TO PRESENT)	CLIENT/SERVER ERA (1983 TO PRESENT)	ENTERPRISE ERA (1992 TO PRESENT)	CLOUD COMPUTING ERA (PRESENT)
Signature Firm(s)	IBM	Microsoft/Intel Dell HP IBM	Novell Microsoft	SAP Oracle PeopleSoft	Google Salesforce.com IBM
Hardware Platform	Centralized mainframe	Wintel computers	Wintel computers	Multiple: • Mainframe • Server • Client	Remote servers Clients (PCs, netbooks, cell phones, smartphones)
Operating System	IBM 360 IBM 370 Unix	DOS/Windows Linux IBM 390	Windows 3.1 Windows Server Linux	Multiple: • Unix/Linux • OS 390 • Windows Server	Linux Windows Mac OS X
Application and Enterprise Software	Few enterprise-wide applications; departmental applications created by in-house programmers	No enterprise connectivity; boxed software	Few enterprise-wide applications; boxed software applications for workgroups and departments	Enterprise-wide applications linked to desktop and departmental applications: • mySAP • Oracle E-Business Suite • PeopleSoft Enterprise One	Google Apps Salesforce.com
Networking/ Telecommunications	Vendor-provided: • Systems Network Architecture (IBM) • DECNET (Digital) • AT&T voice	None or limited	Novell NetWare Windows Server Linux AT&T voice	LAN Enterprise-wide area network (WAN) TCP/IP Internet standards-enabled	Internet Wi-Fi Wireless broadband cellular networks
System Integration	Vendor-provided	None	Accounting and consulting firms Service firms	Software manufacturer Accounting and consulting firms System integration firms Service firms	SaaS firms
Data Storage and Database Management	Magnetic storage Flat files Relational databases	DBase II and III Access	Multiple database servers with optical and magnetic storage	Enterprise database servers	Remote enterprise database servers
Internet Platforms	Poor to none	None at first Later browser-enabled clients	None at first Later: • Apache server • Microsoft IIS	None in the early years Later: • Intranet- and Internet-delivered enterprise services • Large server farms	Large server farms

microprocessors doubles every 18 months; (2) computing power doubles every 18 months; and (3) the price of computing falls by half every 18 months.

Figure 5-4 illustrates the relationship between number of transistors on a microprocessor and millions of instructions per second (MIPS), a common measure of processor power. Figure 5-5 shows the exponential decline in the cost of transistors and rise in computing power.

FIGURE 5-4   MOORE'S LAW AND MICROPROCESSOR PERFORMANCE

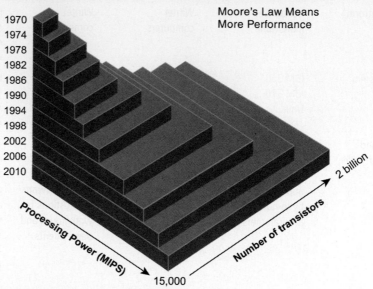

Packing more transistors into a tiny microprocessor has exponentially increased processing power.
Source: Intel, 2004, updated by the authors.

FIGURE 5-5   FALLING COST OF CHIPS

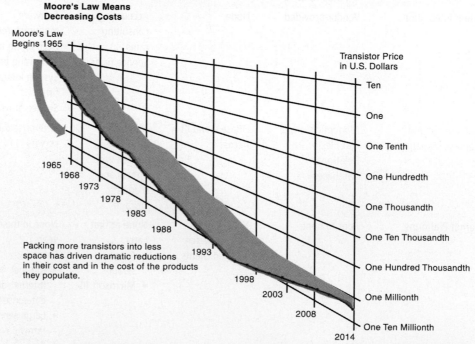

An Intel ® processor today can contain as many as one billion transistors, deliver over 10,000 MIPS, at a cost of less than 1/10,000th of a cent. That's a little less than the cost of one printed character in this book.
Source: © Intel 2004, updated by the authors.

Exponential growth in the number of transistors and the power of processors coupled with an exponential decline in computing costs is likely to continue. Chip manufacturers continue to miniaturize components. Today's transistors should no longer be compared to the size of a human hair but rather to the size a virus, the smallest form of organic life.

By using nanotechnology, chip manufacturers can even shrink the size of transistors down to the width of several atoms. **Nanotechnology** uses individual atoms and molecules to create computer chips and other devices that are thousands of times smaller than current technologies permit. Chip manufacturers are trying to develop a manufacturing process that could produce nanotube processors economically (Figure 5-6). IBM has just started making microprocessors in a production setting using this technology.

As processor speeds increase, heat is generated that cannot be dissipated with air fans. Consumers are pressing for low power consumption for longer battery life and low weight to increase laptop and handheld computer portability. For this reason, Intel and other firms are designing the next generation of chips to be less power hungry and lower in weight. Other options include putting multiple processors on a single chip (see Section 5-3).

FIGURE 5-6   EXAMPLES OF NANOTUBES

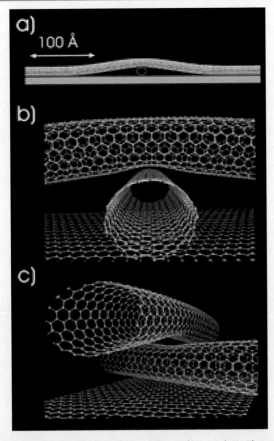

Nanotubes are tiny tubes about 10,000 times thinner than a human hair. They consist of rolled up sheets of carbon hexagons. Discovered in 1991 by researchers at NEC, they have the potential uses as minuscule wires or in ultrasmall electronic devices and are very powerful conductors of electrical current.

The Law of Mass Digital Storage

A second technology driver of IT infrastructure change is the Law of Mass Digital Storage. The world produces as much as 5 exabytes of unique information per year (an exabyte is a billion gigabytes, or 10^{18} bytes). The amount of digital information is roughly doubling every year (Lyman and Varian 2003). Almost all of this information growth involves magnetic storage of digital data, and printed documents account for only 0.003 percent of the annual growth.

Fortunately, the cost of storing digital information is falling at an exponential rate of 100 percent a year. Figure 5-7 shows that PC hard drive capacity has experienced a compound annual growth rate of 25 percent in the early years to over 60 percent a year since 1990. Today's PC hard drives have storage densities approaching 1 gigabyte per square inch and total capacities of over 600 gigabytes.

Figure 5-8 shows that the number of kilobytes that can be stored on magnetic disks for one dollar from 1950 to the present roughly doubled every 15 months.

Metcalfe's Law and Network Economics

Moore's Law and the Law of Mass Storage help us understand why computing resources are now so readily available. But why do people want more computing and storage power? The economics of networks and the growth of the Internet provide some answers.

Robert Metcalfe—inventor of Ethernet local area network technology— claimed in 1970 that the value or power of a network grows exponentially as a function of the number of network members. Metcalfe and others point to the *increasing returns to scale* that network members receive as more and more people join the network. As the number of members in a network grows linearly, the value of the entire system grows exponentially and continues to grow forever as members increase. Demand for information technology has been driven by the social and business value of digital networks, which rapidly multiply the number of actual and potential links among network members.

Declining Communications Costs and the Internet

A fourth technology driver transforming IT infrastructure is the rapid decline in the costs of communication and the exponential growth in the size of the

FIGURE 5-7   **THE CAPACITY OF HARD DISK DRIVES GROWS EXPONTENTIALLY 1980-2008**

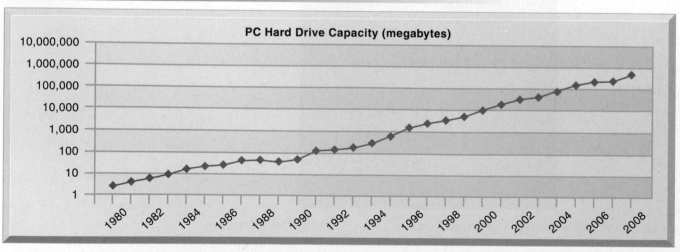

From 1980 to 1990, hard disk drive capacities for PCs experienced a rate of 25 percent annual compound growth, but after 1990 growth accelerated to more than 65 percent each year.

Source: Kurzweil 2003 updated by authors.

FIGURE 5-8   **THE COST OF STORING DATA DECLINES EXPONENTIALLY, 1950-2010**

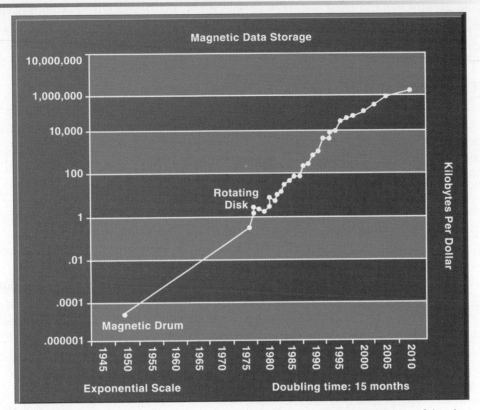

Since the first magnetic storage device was used in 1955, the cost of storing a kilobyte of data has fallen exponentially, doubling the amount of digital storage for each dollar expended every 15 months on average.
Source: Kurzweil 2003 and authors.

Internet. An estimated 1.5 billion people worldwide now have Internet access. Figure 5-9 illustrates the exponentially declining cost of communication both over the Internet and over telephone networks (which increasingly are based on the Internet). As communication costs fall toward a very small number and approach 0, utilization of communication and computing facilities explodes.

FIGURE 5-9   **EXPONENTIAL DECLINES IN INTERNET COMMUNICATION COSTS**

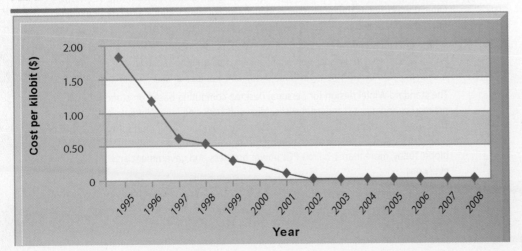

One reason for the growth in the Internet population is the rapid decline in Internet connection and overall communication costs. The cost per kilobit of Internet access has fallen exponentially since 1995. Digital Subscriber Line (DSL) and cable modems now deliver a kilobit of communication for a retail price of around 2 cents.

To take advantage of the business value associated with the Internet, firms must greatly expand their Internet connections, including wireless connectivity, and greatly expand the power of their client/server networks, desktop clients, and mobile computing devices. There is every reason to believe these trends will continue.

Standards and Network Effects

Today's enterprise infrastructure and Internet computing would be impossible—both now and in the future—without agreements among manufacturers and widespread consumer acceptance of **technology standards**. Technology standards are specifications that establish the compatibility of products and the ability to communicate in a network (Stango 2004).

Technology standards unleash powerful economies of scale and result in price declines as manufacturers focus on the products built to a single standard. Without these economies of scale, computing of any sort would be far more expensive than is currently the case. Table 5-2 describes important standards that have shaped IT infrastructure.

Beginning in the 1990s, corporations started moving toward standard computing and communications platforms. The Wintel PC with the Windows operating system and Microsoft Office desktop productivity applications became the standard desktop and mobile client computing platform. Widespread adoption of Unix as the enterprise server operating system of choice made possible the replace-

TABLE 5-2 SOME IMPORTANT STANDARDS IN COMPUTING

STANDARD	SIGNIFICANCE
American Standard Code for Information Interchange (ASCII)(1958)	Made it possible for computer machines from different manufacturers to exchange data; later used as the universal language linking input and output devices such as keyboards and mice to computers. Adopted by the American National Standards Institute in 1963.
Common Business Oriented Language (COBOL) (1959)	An easy-to-use software language that greatly expanded the ability of programmers to write business-related programs and reduced the cost of software. Sponsored by the Defense Department in 1959.
Unix (1969–1975)	A powerful multitasking, multiuser, portable operating system initially developed at Bell Labs (1969) and later released for use by others (1975). It operates on a wide variety of computers from different manufacturers. Adopted by Sun, IBM, HP, and others in the 1980s and became the most widely used enterprise-level operating system.
Transmission Control Protocol/Internet Protocol (TCP/IP) (1974)	Suite of communications protocols and a common addressing scheme that enables millions of computers to connect together in one giant global network (the Internet). Later, it was used as the default networking protocol suite for local area networks and intranets. Developed in the early 1970s for the U.S. Department of Defense.
Ethernet (1973)	A network standard for connecting desktop computers into local area networks that enabled the widespread adoption of client/server computing and local area networks and further stimulated the adoption of personal computers.
IBM/Microsoft/Intel Personal Computer (1981)	The standard Wintel design for personal desktop computing based on standard Intel processors and other standard devices, Microsoft DOS, and later Windows software. The emergence of this standard, low-cost product laid the foundation for a 25-year period of explosive growth in computing throughout all organizations around the globe. Today, more than 1 billion PCs power business and government activities every day.
World Wide Web (1989–1993)	Standards for storing, retrieving, formatting, and displaying information as a worldwide web of electronic pages incorporating text, graphics, audio, and video enables the creation of a global repository of billions of Web pages by 2004.

ment of proprietary and expensive mainframe infrastructure. In telecommunications, the Ethernet standard enabled PCs to connect together in small local area networks (LANs; see Chapter 7), and the TCP/IP standard enabled these LANs to be connected into firm-wide networks, and ultimately, to the Internet.

5.2 INFRASTRUCTURE COMPONENTS

IT infrastructure today is composed of seven major components. Figure 5-10 illustrates these infrastructure components and the major vendors within each component category. These components constitute investments that must be coordinated with one another to provide the firm with a coherent infrastructure.

In the past, technology vendors supplying these components were often in competition with one another, offering purchasing firms a mixture of incompatible, proprietary, partial solutions. But increasingly the vendor firms have been forced by large customers to cooperate in strategic partnerships with one another. For instance, a hardware and services provider such as IBM cooperates with all the major enterprise software providers, has strategic relationships with system integrators (often accounting firms), and promises to work with whichever database products its client firms wish to use (even though it sells its

FIGURE 5-10　　THE IT INFRASTRUCTURE ECOSYSTEM

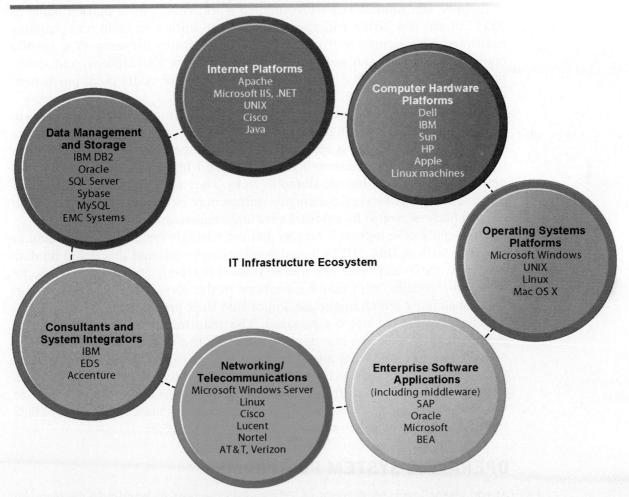

There are seven major components that must be coordinated to provide the firm with a coherent IT infrastructure. Listed here are major technologies and suppliers for each component.

A blade server is a thin, modular processing device that is intended for a single dedicated application (such as serving Web pages). It can be easily inserted into a space-saving rack with many similar servers.

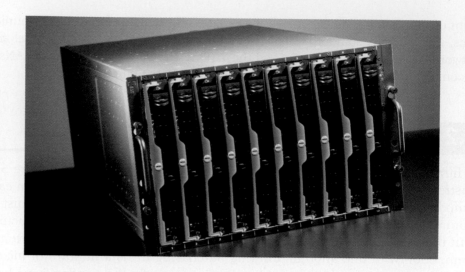

own database management software called DB2). Let's examine the size and dynamics of each these infrastructure components and their markets.

COMPUTER HARDWARE PLATFORMS

In 2008, 285 million PCs were shipped worldwide, with a market value of $253 billion. U.S. firms will spend about $150 billion in 2008 on computer hardware. This component includes client machines (desktop PCs, mobile computing devices such as iPhones and Blackberrys, and laptops) and server machines. The client machines use primarily Intel or AMD microprocessors. Gartner, 2008; Metrics 2.0, 2008).

The server market is more complex, using mostly Intel or AMD processors in the form of blade servers in racks, but also includes Sun SPARC microprocessors and IBM PowerPC chips specially designed for server use. **Blade servers** are ultrathin computers consisting of a circuit board with processors, memory, and network connections that are stored in racks. They take up less space than traditional box-based servers. Secondary storage may be provided by a hard drive in each blade server or by external very large mass-storage drives.

The supply of computer hardware has increasingly become concentrated in top firms such as IBM, HP, Dell, and Sun Microsystems, and three chip producers, Intel, AMD, and IBM. The industry has collectively settled on Intel as the standard processor, with major exceptions in the server market for Unix and Linux machines, which might use Sun or IBM Unix processors.

Mainframes have not disappeared. The mainframe market has actually grown steadily over the last decade, although the number of providers has dwindled to one: IBM. IBM has also repurposed its mainframe systems so they can be used as giant servers for massive enterprise networks and corporate Web sites. A single IBM mainframe can run up to 17,000 instances of Linux or Windows server software and is capable of replacing thousands of smaller blade servers (see the discussion of virtualization in section 5.3).

OPERATING SYSTEM PLATFORMS

At the client level, 95 percent of PCs and 45 percent of handheld devices use some form of Microsoft Windows **operating system** (such as Windows Vista,

Windows XP, or Windows Mobile) to manage the resources and activities of the computer. Windows comprises 70 percent of the server operating market, with 30 of corporate servers using some form of the **Unix** operating system or **Linux**, an inexpensive and robust open source relative of Unix. Microsoft Windows Server 2008 is capable of providing enterprise-wide operating system and network services, and appeals to organizations seeking Windows-based IT infrastructures.

Unix and Linux are scalable, reliable, and much less expensive than mainframe operating systems. They can also run on many different types of processors. The major providers of Unix operating systems are IBM, HP, and Sun, each with slightly different and partially incompatible versions.

ENTERPRISE SOFTWARE APPLICATIONS

In addition to software for applications used by specific groups or business units, U.S. firms will spend about $250 billion in 2008 on software for enterprise applications that are treated as components of IT infrastructure. The largest providers of enterprise application software are SAP and Oracle (which acquired PeopleSoft). Also included in this category is middleware software supplied by vendors such as BEA (also acquired by Oracle in 2008) for achieving firmwide integration by linking the firm's existing application systems.

Microsoft is attempting to move into the lower ends of this market by focusing on small and medium-sized businesses that have not yet implemented enterprise applications. In general, most large firms already use enterprise applications and have developed long-term relationships with their providers. Once a firm decides to work with an enterprise vendor, switching can be difficult and costly, though not impossible.

DATA MANAGEMENT AND STORAGE

There are few choices for enterprise database management software, which is responsible for organizing and managing the firm's data so that it can be efficiently accessed and used. Chapter 6 describes this software in detail. The leading database software providers are IBM (DB2), Oracle, Microsoft (SQL Server), and Sybase (Adaptive Server Enterprise), which supply more than 90 percent of the U.S. database software marketplace. A growing new entrant is MySQL, a Linux open source relational database product available for free on the Internet and increasingly supported by HP and others.

The physical data storage market is dominated by EMC Corporation for large-scale systems, and a small number of PC hard disk manufacturers led by Seagate, Maxtor, and Western Digital. In addition to traditional disk arrays and tape libraries, large firms are turning to network-based storage technologies. **Storage area networks (SANs)** connect multiple storage devices on a separate high-speed network dedicated to storage. The SAN creates a large central pool of storage that can be rapidly accessed and shared by multiple servers.

The amount of new digital information in the world is doubling every three years, driven in part by e-commerce and e-business and by statutes and regulations requiring firms to invest in extensive data storage and management facilities. Consequently, the market for digital data storage devices has been growing at more than 15 percent annually over the last five years.

NETWORKING/TELECOMMUNICATIONS PLATFORMS

U.S. firms in 2008 will spend $210 billon a year on networking and telecommunications hardware and a huge $850 billion on networking services (consisting mainly of telecommunications and telephone company charges for voice lines and Internet access; these are not included in this discussion). Chapter 7 is devoted to an in-depth description of the enterprise networking environment, including the Internet. Windows Server is predominantly used as local area network operating system, followed by Linux and Unix. Large enterprise wide area networks primarily use some variant of Unix. Many local area networks, as well as wide area enterprise networks, use the TCP/IP protocol suite as a standard (see Chapter 7).

The leading networking hardware providers are Cisco, Lucent, Nortel, and Juniper Networks. Telecommunications platforms are typically provided by telecommunications/telephone services companies that offer voice and data connectivity, wide area networking, and Internet access. Leading telecommunications service vendors include AT&T and Verizon. As noted in Chapter 7, this market is exploding with new providers of cellular wireless, Wi-Fi, and Internet telephone services.

INTERNET PLATFORMS

Internet platforms overlap with, and must relate to, the firm's general networking infrastructure and hardware and software platforms. U.S. firms will spend in 2008 an estimated $52 billion on Internet-related infrastructure. These expenditures were for hardware, software, and management services to support a firm's Web site, including Web hosting services, and for intranets and extranets. A **Web hosting service** maintains a large Web server, or series of servers, and provides fee-paying subscribers with space to maintain their Web sites.

The Internet revolution of the late 1990s led to a veritable explosion in server computers, with many firms collecting thousands of small servers to run their Internet operations. Since then there has been a steady push toward server consolidation, reducing the number of server computers by increasing the size and power of each. The Internet hardware server market has become increasingly concentrated in the hands of Dell, HP/Compaq, and IBM as prices have fallen dramatically.

The major Web software application development tools and suites are supplied by Microsoft (the Microsoft .NET family of development tools used to create Web sites using Active Server Pages for dynamic content), Sun (Sun's Java is the most widely used tool for developing interactive Web applications on both the server and client sides), and a host of independent software developers, including Macromedia (Flash), media software (Real Media), and text tools (Adobe Acrobat). Chapter 7 describes the components of the firm's Internet platform in greater detail.

CONSULTING AND SYSTEM INTEGRATION SERVICES

Although 20 years ago it might have been possible for a large firm to implement all its own IT infrastructure, today this is far less common. Even large firms do not have the staff, the skills, the budget, or the necessary experience to do so. Implementing new infrastructure requires (as noted in Chapters 13 and 14) significant changes in business processes and procedures, training and education, and software integration. Leading consulting firms providing this expertise include Accenture, IBM Global Services, Electronic Data Systems, HP Technology Solutions, Infosys, and Wipro Technologies.

Software integration means ensuring the new infrastructure works with the firm's older, so-called legacy systems and ensuring the new elements of the infrastructure work with one another. **Legacy systems** are generally older transaction processing systems created for mainframe computers that continue to be used to avoid the high cost of replacing or redesigning them. Replacing these systems is cost prohibitive and generally not necessary if these older systems can be integrated into a contemporary infrastructure.

5.3 CONTEMPORARY HARDWARE PLATFORM TRENDS

Although the cost of computing has fallen exponentially, the cost of the IT infrastructure has actually expanded as a percentage of corporate budgets. Why? The costs of computing services (consulting, systems integration) and software are high, and the intensity of computing and communicating has increased as other costs have declined. For instance, employees now use much more sophisticated applications, requiring more powerful and expensive hardware of many different types (laptop, desktop, mobile handheld computers).

Firms face a number of other challenges. They need to integrate information stored in different applications, on different platforms (telephone, legacy systems, intranet, Internet sites, desktop, and mobile devices). Firms also need to build resilient infrastructures that can withstand huge increases in peak loads and routine assaults from hackers and viruses while conserving electrical power. Firms need to increase their service levels to respond to growing customer and employee expectations for service. The trends in hardware and software platforms we now describe address some or all of these challenges.

THE EMERGING MOBILE DIGITAL PLATFORM

As computing increasingly takes place over the network, new mobile digital computing platforms have emerged. Communication devices such as cell phones and smartphones such as the BlackBerry and iPhone have taken on many functions of handheld computers, including transmission of data, surfing the Web, transmitting e-mail and instant messages, displaying digital content, and exchanging data with internal corporate systems. The new mobile platform also includes small low-cost lightweight subnotebooks called **netbooks** optimized for wireless communication and Internet access, with core computing functions such as word processing, and digital e-book readers such as Amazon's Kindle with some Web access capabilities. More and more business computing is moving from PCs and desktop machines to these mobile devices; managers are increasingly using these devices to coordinate work and communicate with employees.

GRID COMPUTING

Grid computing involves connecting geographically remote computers into a single network to create a virtual supercomputer by combining the computational power of all computers on the grid. Grid computing takes advantage of

The Eee PC netbook designed by ASUS weighs only two pounds and uses a Linux-based operating system to provide wireless Internet access and a series of open-source desktop productivity tools. Portability, ease of use, and low cost have made netbooks increasingly popular computing platforms.

the fact that most computers in the United States use their central processing units on average only 25 percent of the time for the work they have been assigned, leaving these idle resources available for other processing tasks. Grid computing was impossible until high-speed Internet connections enabled firms to connect remote machines economically and move enormous quantities of data.

Grid computing requires software programs to control and allocate resources on the grid. Client software communicates with a server software application. The server software breaks data and application code into chunks that are then parceled out to the grid's machines. The client machines can perform their traditional tasks while running grid applications in the background.

The business case for using grid computing involves cost savings, speed of computation, and agility. For example, Royal Dutch/Shell Group is using a scalable grid computing platform that improves the accuracy and speed of its scientific modeling applications to find the best oil reservoirs. This platform, which links 1,024 IBM servers running Linux, in effect creates one of the largest commercial Linux supercomputers in the world. The grid adjusts to accommodate the fluctuating data volumes that are typical in this seasonal business. Royal Dutch/Shell Group claims the grid has enabled the company to cut processing time for seismic data, while improving output quality and helping its scientists pinpoint problems in finding new oil supplies.

CLOUD COMPUTING AND THE COMPUTING UTILITY

Earlier in this chapter, we introduced cloud computing, in which hardware and software capabilities are provided as services over the Internet (also referred to as "the cloud"). Data are permanently stored in remote servers in massive data centers and accessed and updated over the Internet using clients that include desktops, notebooks, netbooks, entertainment centers, and mobile devices. For example, Google Apps provides common business applications online that are accessed from a Web browser, while the software and user data are stored on the servers.

Since organizations using cloud computing generally do not own the infrastructure, they do not have to make large investments in their own hardware and software. Instead, they purchase their computing services from remote providers and pay only for the amount of computing power they actually use (or are billed on a subscription basis). You'll hear the terms **on-demand computing** or **utility computing** used to describe these services. The Interactive Session on Salesforce.com and the chapter-ending case on Amazon.com describe examples of cloud computing hardware and software services providers.

Some analysts believe that cloud computing represents a sea change in the way computing will be performed by corporations as business computing shifts out of private data centers into "the cloud." (Carr, 2008).) This remains a matter of debate. Cloud computing is more immediately appealing to small and medium-size businesses that lack resources to purchase and own their own hardware and software. However, large corporations have huge investments in complex proprietary systems supporting unique business processes, some of which give them strategic advantages. The most likely scenario is a hybrid computing model where firms will use their own infrastructure for their most essential core activities and adopt cloud computing for less critical systems. Cloud computing will gradually shift firms from having a fixed infrastructure capacity toward a more flexible infrastructure, some of it owned by the firm, and some of it rented from giant computer centers owned by computer hardware vendors.

AUTONOMIC COMPUTING

Computer systems have become so complex today that some experts believe they may not be manageable in the future. With operating systems, enterprise, and database software weighing in at millions of lines of code, and large systems encompassing many thousands of networked devices, the problem of managing these systems looms very large.

It is estimated that one-third to one-half of a company's total IT budget is spent preventing or recovering from system crashes. About 40 percent of these crashes are caused by operator error. The reason is not because operators are not well trained or do not have the right capabilities. Rather, it is because the complexities of today's computer systems are too difficult to understand, and IT operators and managers are under pressure to make decisions about problems in seconds.

One approach to dealing with this problem from a computer hardware perspective is to employ autonomic computing. **Autonomic computing** is an industry-wide effort to develop systems that can configure themselves, optimize and tune themselves, heal themselves when broken, and protect themselves from outside intruders and self-destruction. Imagine, for instance, a desktop PC that could know it was invaded by a computer virus. Instead of blindly allowing the virus to invade, the PC would identify and eradicate the virus or, alternatively, turn its workload over to another processor and shut itself down before the virus destroyed any files.

A few of these capabilities are present in desktop operating systems. For instance, virus and firewall protection software can detect viruses on PCs, automatically defeat the viruses, and alert operators. These programs can be updated automatically as the need arises by connecting to an online virus

INTERACTIVE SESSION: TECHNOLOGY

COMPUTING GOES GREEN

Computer rooms are becoming too hot to handle. Data-hungry tasks such as video on demand, music downloads, exchanging photos, and maintaining Web sites require more and more power-hungry machines. Between 2000 and 2007 the number of severs in corporate data center servers increased from 5.6 million to an estimated 12 million in the United States, and 29 million worldwide. During the same period, the total annual cost of electricity for data center servers jumped from $1.3 billion to $2.7 billion in the United States and from $3.2 billion to $7.2 billion across the world.

What's more, the heat generated from all of these severs is causing equipment to fail. Firms are forced to spend even more on cooling their data centers or to find other solutions. Some organizations spend more money to keep their data centers cool than they spend to lease the property itself. Cooling costs have helped raise the average annual utility bill of a 100,000-square-foot data center to $5.9 million. It's a vicious cycle, as companies must pay to power their servers, and then pay again to keep them cool and operational. Cooling a server requires roughly the same number of kilowatts of energy as running one. All this additional power consumption has a negative impact on the environment and as well as corporate operating costs.

At Pomona Valley Hospital Medical Center in Pomona, California, a 6,000-square-foot data center housed so many servers that the room temperature skyrocketed to nearly 100 degrees. IT managers aim to keep such rooms in the 60s. The elevated temperature caused server malfunctions and one case of outright failure. The hospital resolved the issue by investing $500,000 in a network of overhead air conditioners. Temperatures now hover at 64 degrees.

Emerson Network Power of St. Louis offers a cooling solution called Liebert XD that sits directly on top of server racks and conditions the air with pipes containing waterless refrigerant. US Internet Corp., a regional ISP in Minneapolis, installed the Liebert XD product to combat the 90-degree temperatures in one of its data centers. Without the system, US Internet was suffering from daily breakdowns of servers and storage drives.

Another cooling solution comes from Degree Controls Inc., based in Milford, New Hampshire. Degree Controls installs floor tiles equipped with powerful fans that blow cool air directly onto servers. The tiles cost $1,800 each.

Some of the world's most prominent firms are tackling their power consumption issues with one eye toward saving the environment and the other toward saving dollars. Google, Microsoft, and HSBC are all building data centers that will take advantage of hydroelectric power. Salesforce.com plans to offset its carbon footprint by investing in renewable energy projects and alternative energy sources.

Hewlett Packard is working on a series of technologies to reduce the carbon footprint of data centers by 75 percent, replace the copper wiring on microprocessors with light pulses, and develop new software and services to measure energy use and carbon emissions. It reduced its power costs by 20 to 25 percent through a consolidation of servers and data centers. None of these companies claim that their efforts will save the world, but they do demonstrate recognition of a growing problem and the commencement of the green computing era.

IT managers also have hardware and software options that conserve power. Some organizations are choosing to use thin client computers, which are very basic terminal machines that connect directly to servers and consume significantly less power than normal desktop clients. A call center operated by Verizon Wireless in Chandler, Arizona replaced 1,700 PCs with thin clients from Sun Microsystems and saw its power consumption go down by one-third. Sun states that on average its thin clients use less than half of the electricity that PCs require.

Two years ago, City University of New York adopted software called Surveyor made by Verdiem Corp. for its 20,000 PCs. The software enables IT managers to have the computers turn themselves off when they are inactive at night. Surveyor has trimmed 10 percent from CUNY's power bills, creating an annual savings of around $320,000. Quad Graphics Inc., of Sussex, Wisconsin, also deployed Surveyor after tests indicated savings on power of 35 to 50 percent, or up to $70,000 annually, were possible.

Microsoft's Windows Vista operating system has enhanced sleep features that reduce power consumption by much greater margins than the standby modes in previous versions of Windows. In sleep mode, computers may draw as little as 3 to 4 watts of power versus 100 watts for an idle computer that is not asleep. Businesses also have the options of using more efficient chips in their servers.

Virtualization is a highly effective tool for more cost-effective greener computing because it reduces the number of servers required to run a firm's applications. The University of Pittsburgh Medical Center and Swinerton Construction in San Francisco are among many firms that have benefited from this technology. Swinerton saved $140,000 in one year

alone by using virtualization, which included a $50,000 savings power and cooling cost reductions as well as reductions in its server purchases.

Sources: Scott Ferguson, "Cooling the Data Center," *eWeek*, June 9, 2008; Rob Bernard, "Microsoft's Green Growth," *eWeek*, April 7, 2008; Eric Chabrow, "The Wild, Wild Cost of Data Centers," *CIO Insight*, May 2008; Jim Carlton, "IT Managers Make a Power Play," *The Wall Street Journal*, March 27, 2007, and "IT Managers Find Novel Ways to Cool Powerful Servers," *The Wall Street Journal*, April 10, 2007; and Marianne Kolbasuk McGee, "Data Center Electricity Bills Double," *Information Week*, February 17, 2007.

CASE STUDY QUESTIONS

1. What business and social problems does data center power consumption cause?

2. What solutions are available for these problems? Which are the most environment-friendly?

3. What are the business benefits and costs of these solutions?

4. Should all firms move toward green computing? Why or why not?

MIS IN ACTION

Perform an Internet search on the phrase "green computing" and then answer the following questions:

1. How would you define green computing?

2. Who are some of the leaders of the green computing movement? Which corporations are leading the way? Which environmental organizations are playing an important role?

3. What are the latest trends in green computing? What kind of impact are they having?

4. What can individuals do to contribute to the green computing movement? Is the movement worthwhile?

protection service such as McAfee. IBM and other vendors are starting to build autonomic features into products for large systems.

VIRTUALIZATION AND MULTICORE PROCESSORS

As companies deploy hundreds or thousands of servers, many have discovered that they are spending almost as much on electricity to power and cool their systems as they did on purchasing the hardware. Energy consumed by data centers more than doubled between 2000 and 2008, and the U.S. Environmental Protection Agency estimated that data centers will use more than 2 percent of all U.S. electrical power by 2011. Cutting power consumption in data centers is now a major business challenge. The Interactive Session on Technology examines this problem. As you read this case, try to identify the alternative solutions for this problem and the advantages and disadvantages of each.

This Interactive Session described organizations curbing hardware proliferation and power consumption by using virtualization to reduce the number of computers required for processing. **Virtualization** is the process of presenting a set of computing resources (such as computing power or data storage) so that they can all be accessed in ways that are not restricted by physical configuration or geographic location. Server virtualization enables companies to run more than one operating system at the same time on a single machine.

Most servers run at just 10 to 15 percent of capacity, and virtualization can boost utilization server utilization rates to 70 percent or higher. Higher utilization rates translate into fewer computers required to process the same amount of work.

For example, the Christus Health network of hospitals and health care facilities in the southern and Western United States and in Mexico was formerly managing more than 2000 servers in 8 data centers, with 70 percent in the San Antonio data center. In that location, 97 percent of the systems were using 20 percent or less of their processing power and only 29 percent of available memory. The health care organization used virtualization to consolidate the work of 824 servers onto 83 blade servers, saving $1.8 million, including reductions in electrical power (Conklin et. al., 2008).

Server virtualization software runs between the operating system and the hardware, masking server resources, including the number and identity of physical servers, processors, and operating systems, from server users. VMware is the leading server virtualization software vendor for Windows and Linux systems. Microsoft offers its own Virtual Server product and has built virtualization capabilities into the newest version of Windows Server.

In addition to reducing hardware and power expenditures, virtualization allows businesses to run their legacy applications on older versions of an operating system on the same server as newer applications. Virtualization also facilitates centralization of hardware administration.

Multicore Processors

Another way to reduce power requirements and hardware sprawl is to use multicore processors. A **multicore processor** is an integrated circuit to which two or more processors have been attached for enhanced performance, reduced power consumption and more efficient simultaneous processing of multiple tasks. This technology enables two processing engines with reduced power requirements and heat dissipation to perform tasks faster than a resource-hungry chip with a single processing core. Today you'll find dual-core processors in PCs and quad-core processors in servers. Sun Microsystems' UltraSparc T2 chip for managing Web applications has 8 processors, and will soon be followed by a 16-core processor.

5.4 CONTEMPORARY SOFTWARE PLATFORM TRENDS

There are five major themes in contemporary software platform evolution:

- Linux and open source software
- Java and Ajax
- Web services and service-oriented architecture
- Software mashups and Web 2.0 applications
- Software outsourcing

LINUX AND OPEN SOURCE SOFTWARE

Open source software is software produced by a community of several hundred thousand programmers around the world. According to the leading open source professional association, OpenSource.org, open source software is free and can be modified by users. Works derived from the original code must also be free, and the software can be redistributed by the user without additional licensing. Open source software is by definition not restricted to any specific operating system or hardware technology, although most open source software is currently based on a Linux or Unix operating system.

Open source software is based on the premise that it is superior to commercially produced proprietary software because thousands of programmers around the world working for no pay can read, perfect, distribute, and modify the source code much faster, and with more reliable results, than small teams of programmers working for a single software company. The open source movement has been evolving for more than 30 years and has demonstrated after many years of effort that it can produce commercially acceptable, high-quality software.

Now many thousands of open source programs are available from hundreds of Web sites. Popular open source software tools include the Linux operating system, the Apache HTTP Web server, the Mozilla Firefox Web browser, and the OpenOffice desktop productivity suite. Open source tools are being used on netbooks as inexpensive alternatives to Microsoft Office. Major hardware and software vendors, including IBM, Hewlett-Packard, Dell, Oracle, and SAP, now offer Linux-compatible versions of their products. You can find out more out more about the Open Source Definition from the Open Source Initiative and the history of open source software at the Learning Tracks for this chapter.

Linux

Perhaps the most well known open source software is Linux, an operating system related to Unix. Linux was created by the Finnish programmer Linus Torvalds and first posted on the Internet in August 1991. Linux applications are embedded in cell phones, smartphones, netbooks, and other handheld devices. Linux is available in free versions downloadable from the Internet or in low cost commercial versions that include tools and support from vendors such as Red Hat.

Linux is currently a small but rapidly growing presence on the desktop, especially as an operating system for Internet-enabled netbooks. It plays a major role in the back office running local area networks, Web servers, and high-performance computing work, with 20 percent of the server operating system market. IBM, HP, Intel, Dell, and Sun have made Linux a central part of their offerings to corporations. More than two dozen countries in Asia, Europe, and Latin America have adopted open source software and Linux.

The rise of open source software, particularly Linux and the applications it supports, has profound implications for corporate software platforms: cost reduction, reliability and resilience, and integration, because Linux works on all the major hardware platforms from mainframes to servers to clients.

SOFTWARE FOR THE WEB: JAVA AND AJAX

Java is an operating system-independent, processor-independent, object-oriented programming language that has become the leading interactive programming environment for the Web. Java was created by James Gosling and the Green Team at Sun Microsystems in 1992.

Nearly all Web browsers come with a Java platform built in. More recently, the Java platform has migrated into cellular phones, smartphones, automobiles, music players, game machines, and finally, into set-top cable television systems serving interactive content and pay-per-view services. Java software is designed to run on any computer or computing device, regardless of the specific microprocessor or operating system the device uses. For each of the computing environments in which Java is used, Sun has created a Java Virtual Machine that interprets Java programming code for that machine. In this manner, the code is written once and can be used on any machine for which there exists a Java Virtual Machine.

Java is a very robust language that can handle text, data, graphics, sound, and video, all within one program if needed. Java enables PC users to manipulate data on networked systems using Web browsers, reducing the need to write specialized software. A **Web browser** is an easy-to-use software tool with a graphical user interface for displaying Web pages and for accessing the Web and other Internet resources. Microsoft's Internet Explorer, Mozilla Firefox, and Netscape Browser are examples. At the enterprise level, Java is being used for more complex e-commerce and e-business applications that require communication with an organization's back-end transaction processing systems.

The rapid deployment of Java was hindered in the past because of disagreements between Sun Microsystems and Microsoft over Java standards. In April 2004, under pressure from major customers such as General Motors, Microsoft agreed to stop distributing the Microsoft Java Virtual Machine (MSJVM) it had developed for its proprietary version of Java and to cooperate with Sun in the development of new technologies, including Java.

Ajax

Have you ever filled out a Web order form, made a mistake, and then had to start all over again after a long wait for a new order form page to appear on your computer screen? Or visited a map site, clicked the North arrow once, and waited some time for an entire new page to load? **Ajax** (Asynchronous JavaScript and XML) is another Web development technique for creating interactive Web applications that prevents all of this inconvenience.

Ajax allows a client and server to exchange small pieces of data behind the scene so that an entire Web page does not have to be reloaded each time the user requests a change. So if you click North on a map site, such as Google Maps, the server downloads just that part of the application that changes with no wait for an entirely new map. You can also grab maps in map applications and move the map in any direction without forcing a reload of the entire page. Ajax uses JavaScript programs downloaded to your client to maintain a near-continuous conversation with the server you are using, making the user experience more seamless.

WEB SERVICES AND SERVICE-ORIENTED ARCHITECTURE

Web services refer to a set of loosely coupled software components that exchange information with each other using universal Web communication standards and languages. They can exchange information between two different systems regardless of the operating systems or programming languages on which the systems are based. They can be fused to build open standard Web-based applications linking systems of two different organizations, and they can also be used to create applications that link disparate systems within a single company. Web services are not tied to any one operating system or programming language, and different applications can use them to communicate with each other in a standard way without time-consuming custom coding.

The foundation technology for Web services is **XML**, which stands for **Extensible Markup Language**. This language was developed in 1996 by the World Wide Web Consortium (W3C, the international body that oversees the development of the Web) as a more powerful and flexible markup language than hypertext markup language (HTML) for Web pages. **Hypertext markup language (HTML)** is a page description language for specifying how text, graphics, video, and sound are placed on a Web page document. Whereas HTML is limited to describing how data should be presented in the form of Web pages, XML can perform presentation, communication, and storage of data. In XML, a number is not simply a number; the XML tag specifies whether the number represents a price, a date, or a ZIP code. Table 5-3 illustrates some sample XML statements.

By tagging selected elements of the content of documents for their meanings, XML makes it possible for computers to manipulate and interpret their data automatically and perform operations on the data without human intervention. Web browsers and computer programs, such as order processing or enterprise resource planning (ERP) software, can follow programmed rules for applying and displaying the data. XML provides a standard format for data exchange, enabling Web services to pass data from one process to another.

Web services communicate through XML messages over standard Web protocols. *SOAP*, which stands for *Simple Object Access Protocol*, is a set of rules for structuring messages that enables applications to pass data and instructions to one another. *WSDL* stands for *Web Services Description Language*; it is a common framework for describing the tasks performed by a Web service and the commands and data it will accept so that it can be used by other applications. *UDDI*, which stands for *Universal Description, Discovery,* and *Integration*, enables a Web service to be listed in a directory of Web services so that it can be easily located. Companies discover and locate Web services through this directory much as they would locate services in the yellow pages of a telephone book. Using these protocols, a software application can connect freely to other applications without custom programming for each different application with which it wants to communicate. Everyone shares the same standards.

The collection of Web services that are used to build a firm's software systems constitutes what is known as a service-oriented architecture. A **service-oriented architecture (SOA)** is set of self-contained services that communicate with each other to create a working software application. Business tasks are accomplished by executing a series of these services. Software developers reuse these services in other combinations to assemble other applications as needed.

Virtually all major software vendors provide tools and entire platforms for building and integrating software applications using Web services. IBM includes

TABLE 5-3 EXAMPLES OF XML

PLAIN ENGLISH	XML
Subcompact	<AUTOMOBILETYPE="Subcompact">
4 passenger	<PASSENGERUNIT="PASS">4</PASSENGER>
$16,800	<PRICE CURRENCY="USD">$16,800</PRICE>

Web service tools in its WebSphere e-business software platform, and Microsoft has incorporated Web services tools in its Microsoft .NET platform.

Dollar Rent A Car's systems use Web services for its online booking system with Southwest Airlines' Web site. Although both companies' systems are based on different technology platforms, a person booking a flight on SouthwestAir.com can reserve a car from Dollar without leaving the airline's Web site. Instead of struggling to get Dollar's reservation system to share data with Southwest's information systems, Dollar used Microsoft .NET Web services technology as an intermediary. Reservations from Southwest are translated into Web services protocols, which are then translated into formats that can be understood by Dollar's computers.

Other car rental companies have linked their information systems to airline companies' Web sites before. But without Web services, these connections had to be built one at a time. Web services provide a standard way for Dollar's computers to "talk" to other companies' information systems without having to build special links to each one. Dollar is now expanding its use of Web services to link directly to the systems of a small tour operator and a large travel reservation system as well as a Wireless Web site for mobile phones and PDAs. It does not have to write new software code for each new partner's information systems or each new wireless device (see Figure 5-11).

MASHUPS AND WIDGETS

In the past, software such as Microsoft Word or Adobe Illustrator came in a box and was designed to operate on a single machine. Increasingly, software is

FIGURE 5-11   HOW DOLLAR RENT A CAR USES WEB SERVICES

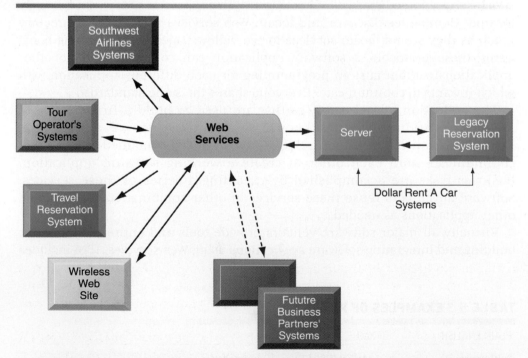

Dollar Rent A Car uses Web services to provide a standard intermediate layer of software to "talk" to other companies' information systems. Dollar Rent A Car can use this set of Web services to link to other companies' information systems without having to build a separate link to each firm's systems.

downloadable from the Internet and composed of interchangeable components that integrate freely with other applications on the Internet. Individual users and entire companies mix and match these software components to create their own customized applications and to share information with others and the resulting software applications are called **mashups**. The idea is to take software from different sources and combine it in order to produce a application that is "greater than" the sum of its parts.

Part of the movement called Web 2.0 (see Chapter 7), and in the spirit of musical mashups, Web mashups combine the capabilities of two or more online applications to create a kind of hybrid that provides more customer value than the original sources alone. One area of great innovation is the mashup of mapping and satellite image software with local content. For instance, ChicagoCrime.org combines Google Maps with crime data for the city of Chicago. Users can search by location, police beat, or type of crime, and the results are displayed as color-coded map points on a Google Map. Google, Yahoo!, and Microsoft now offer tools to allow other applications to pull in information from their map and satellite images with relatively little programming.

You have performed a mashup if you've ever personalized your Facebook profile or your blog with a capability to display videos or slide shows. The small pieces of software code which enable users to embed content from one site into a Web page or another Web site are called widgets. **Widgets** are small software programs that can be added to Web pages or placed on the desktop to provide additional functionality. For example, the Flixter widget on Facebook profiles transports users to a place where they can list the films they've seen along with their ratings and reviews, view their friends' ratings and reviews, and what's playing in theaters.

Web widgets run inside a Web page or blog. Desktop widgets integrate content from an external source into the user's desktop to provide services such as a calculator, dictionary, or display of current weather conditions. The Apple Dashboard, Microsoft Windows Vista Sidebar, and Google Desktop Gadgets are examples of desktop widgets.

Widgets also provide storefront windows for advertising and selling products and services. Random House Inc. has a widget that enables visitors to its Web site to click through to purchase new book releases from its online store. Amazon.com and Wal-Mart have toolbar widgets that enable surfers to search their Web stores while staying on their social network or another personal page. Widgets have become so powerful and useful that Facebook and Google launched programs to attract developers of widgets for their Web sites.

SOFTWARE OUTSOURCING

Today most business firms continue to operate their legacy systems that continue to meet a business need and that would be extremely costly to replace. But they will purchase most of their new software applications from external sources. Figure 5-12 illustrates the rapid growth in external sources of software for U.S. firms.

There are three external sources for software: software packages from a commercial software vendor, software services from an online service provider, and outsourcing custom application development to an outside software firm, often offshore firms in low-wage areas of the world.

FIGURE 5-12   CHANGING SOURCES OF FIRM SOFTWARE

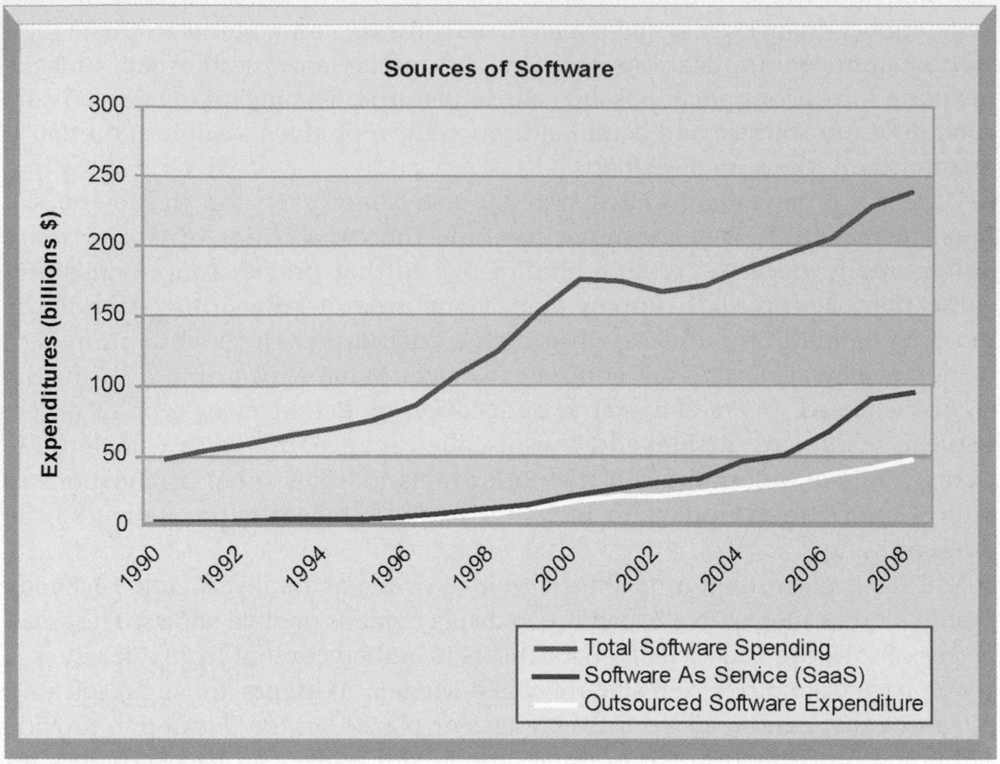

U.S. firms currently spend about $250 billion each year on software. In 2008, about 40 percent of that software will originate outside the firm, either from enterprise software vendors selling firmwide applications or individual application service providers selling software modules.

Sources: BEA National Income and Product Accounts, 2008; Gartner Research, 2008; and author estimates.

Software Packages and Enterprise Software

We have already described software packages for enterprise applications as one of the major types of software components in contemporary IT infrastructures. A **software package** is a prewritten commercially available set of software programs that eliminates the need for a firm to write its own software programs for certain functions, such as payroll processing or order handling.

Enterprise application software vendors such as SAP and Oracle-PeopleSoft have developed powerful software packages that can support the primary business processes of a firm worldwide from warehousing, customer relationship management, supply chain management, and finance to human resources. These large-scale enterprise software systems provide a single, integrated, worldwide software system for firms at a cost much less than they would pay if they developed it themselves. Chapter 9 discusses enterprise systems in detail.

Software as a Service (SaaS)

It is clear that software will be increasingly be delivered and used over networks as a service. Earlier in this chapter, we described cloud computing, in which software is delivered as a service over the Internet. In addition to free or low-cost tools for individuals and small businesses provided by Google or Yahoo!, enterprise software and other complex business functions are available as services from the major commercial software vendors. Instead of buying and installing software programs, subscribing companies rent the same functions from these services, with users paying either on a subscription or per transaction basis. Services for delivering and providing access to software remotely as a Web-based service are now referred to as **Software as a Service (SaaS)**.

A leading example is Salesforce.com, which provides on-demand software services for customer relationship management, including salesforce automation, partner relationship management, marketing, and customer service. It includes tools for customization, integrating its software with other corporate applications, and integrating new applications to run other parts of the business. The Interactive Session on Organizations provides more detail on these capabilities.

Companies considering the SaaS model need to carefully assess the costs and benefits of the service, weighing all people, organizational, and technology issues, including the ability to integrate with existing systems and deliver a level of service and performance that is acceptable for the business. In some cases, the cost of renting software will add up to more than purchasing and maintaining the application in-house. Yet there may be benefits to paying more for software as a service if this decision allows the company to focus on core business issues instead of technology challenges.

Software Outsourcing

A third external source of software is **outsourcing**, in which a firm contracts custom software development or maintenance of existing legacy programs to outside firms, frequently firms that operate offshore in low-wage areas of the world. According to the Gartner Group, worldwide outsourcing totalled over $441 billion in 2008, and it is growing at about 8% a year (Gartner, 2008). The largest expenditure here is paid to domestic U.S. firms providing middleware, integration services, and other software support that are often required to operate larger enterprise systems. IBM has the largest share of this global market (8%) followed by EDS (5%) and ADP (3%). About 50% of all global outsourcing originates in the financial services sector.

For example, in March 2008 Royal Dutch Shell PLC, the world's third largest oil producer, signed a five-year, $4 billion outsourcing deal with T-Systems International GmbH, AT&T, and Electronic Data Systems (EDS). The agreement assigned AT&T responsibility for networking and telecommunications, T-Systems for hosting and storage, and EDS for end-user computing services and for integration of the infrastructure services. Outsourcing this work will help Shell cut costs and focus on systems that improve its competitive position in the oil and gas market.

Offshore outsourcing firms have primarily provided lower-level maintenance, data entry, and call center operations. However with the growing sophistication and experience of offshore firms, particularly in India, more and more new-program development is taking place offshore. Chapter 13 discusses offshore software outsourcing in greater detail.

In order to manage their relationship with an outsourcer or technology service provider, firms will need a contract that includes a **service level agreement (SLA)**. The SLA is a formal contract between customers and their service providers that defines the specific responsibilities of the service provider and the level of service expected by the customer. SLAs typically specify the nature and level of services provided, criteria for performance measurement, support options, provisions for security and disaster recovery, hardware and software ownership and upgrades, customer support, billing, and conditions for terminating the agreement. The Companion Web site features a Learning Track on this topic.

INTERACTIVE SESSION: ORGANIZATIONS

SALESFORCE.COM: SOFTWARE-AS-A-SERVICE GOES MAINSTREAM

Salesforce.com has been considered one of the most disruptive technology companies of the past few years and is credited with single-handedly shaking up the software industry with its innovative business model and resounding success. This company provides CRM solutions in the form of 'software-as-a-service' leased over the Internet, as opposed to software bought and installed on machines locally. It was founded in 1999 by former Oracle executive Marc Benioff, and has since grown to 2,600 employees and earned $748 million in revenue in 2007.

Salesforce.com has over 43,000 corporate customers and well over 1 million subscribers.

Salesforce.com attributes its success to the many benefits of its on-demand model of software distribution. The on-demand model eliminates the need for large up-front capital investments in systems and lengthy implementations on corporate computers. Subscriptions start as low as $9 per month per user for the pared-down Group version for small sales and marketing teams, with monthly subscriptions for more advanced versions for large enterprises starting around $65 per user.

Salesforce.com implementations take 0-3 months. There is no hardware for subscribers to purchase, scale, and maintain, no operating systems, database servers, or application servers to install, no consultants and staff, and no expensive licensing and maintenance fees. The system is accessible via a standard Web browser, and Salesforce.com continually updates its software behind the scenes. There are tools for customizing some features of the software to support a company's unique business processes. Salesforce.com's solutions offer better scalability than those provided by large enterprise software vendors because they eliminate the cost and complexity of managing multiple layers of hardware and software.

Benioff believes that all of these advantages will inevitably lead to 'the end of software', or, more appropriately, a new future of software in which the software-as-a-service model will supplant the current model and become the new paradigm. However, it's still too soon to tell whether this prediction will turn out to be true. Salesforce faces significant challenges as it continues to grow and refine its business.

The first challenge comes from increased competition, both from traditional industry leaders and

new challengers hoping to replicate Salesforce's success. Microsoft, SAP, and Oracle have rolled out subscription-based versions of their CRM products in response to Salesforce. Smaller competitors like NetSuite also have made some inroads against Salesforce's market share.

Analysts predict that Microsoft has a chance to compete with Salesforce by developing merely an acceptable on-demand CRM product, because of the average customer's already-established familiarity with Microsoft applications. Also, Microsoft plans to offer their product at half the price of Salesforce.com, using a tactic they have employed with great effect in other marketplaces to pressure their competitors. Salesforce.com still has plenty of catching up to do to reach the size and market share of their larger competitors. As of 2007, SAP's CRM market share was 25.7 percent, compared to only 7 percent for Salesforce.com. IBM's customer base includes 9,000 software companies that run their applications on their software and that are likelier to choose a solution offered by IBM over Salesforce.com.

Another challenge for Salesforce.com is to expand its business model into other areas. Salesforce is currently used mostly by sales staff needing to keep track of leads and customer lists. One way the company is trying to provide additional functionality is through a partnership with Google and more specifically Google Apps. Salesforce.com is combining its services with Gmail, Google Docs, Google Talk, and Google Calendar to allow its customers to accomplish more tasks via the Web.

The partnership between Salesforce.com and Google represents a united front against Microsoft intended to cut into the popularity of Microsoft Office. Currently, Salesforce.com describes the partnership as "primarily a distribution deal", but it could grow stronger based on the idea that businesses prefer to manage CRM in one place. Salesforce.com and Google both hope that their Salesforce.com for Google Apps initiative will galvanize further growth in on-demand software.

Salesforce opened up its Force.com application development platform to other independent software developers and listed their programs on its AppExchange. Using AppExchange, small businesses can go online and easily download over 800 software applications, some add-ons to Salesforce.com and others that are unrelated. 24 Hour Fitness, the world's largest privately owned and operated fitness chain, uses App Exchange along with Salesforce.com's Enterprise edition for company-wide salesforce automation and customer service. One of its App Exchange applications integrates Hoover's database of up to 21 million companies and 28 million executives with Salesforce and another allow users to easily create and distribute on-demand surveys and response forms.

The question is whether the audience for the App Exchange application platform will prove large enough to deliver the level of growth Salesforce wants. Some analysts believe the platform may not be attractive to larger companies for their application needs.

A third challenge-availability. Salesforce.com subscribers depend on the service being available 24/7.

But occasional outages have occurred (see the Chapter 8 Interactive Session on Technology), making some companies rethink their dependency on software as a service. Salesforce.com provides tools to assure customers about its system reliability and also offers PC applications that tie into their services so users can work offline.

Sources: J. Nicholas Hoover, "Service Outages Force Cloud Adopters to Rethink Tactics," *Information Week*, August 18/25, 2008; Jay Greene, "Google and Salesforce: A Tighter Bond," *Business Week*, April 15, 2008; Mary Hayes Weier, "Salesforce, Google Show Fruits of Their Collaboration," *Information Week*, April 21, 2008; John Pallatto and Clint Boulton, "An On-Demand Partnership," *eWeek*, April 21, 2008; Gary Rivlin, "Software for Rent," *The New York Times*, November 13, 2007; Steve Hamm, " A Big Sales Job for Salesforce.com," *Business Week*, September 24, 2007; Mary Hayes Weier, "Salesforce.com" and Marianne Kolbasuk McGee, "Salesforce as B-to-B Broker," *Information Week*, December 10, 2007; Salesforce.com, Report on Form 10-K for the fiscal year ended January 31, 2008, filed with the SEC on 2/29/08.

CASE STUDY QUESTIONS

1. What are the advantages and disadvantages of the software-as-a-service model?
2. What are some of the challenges facing Salesforce as it continues its growth? How well will it be able to meet those challenges?
3. What kinds of businesses could benefit from switching to Salesforce and why?
4. What factors would you take into account in deciding whether to use Saleforce.com for your business?

MIS IN ACTION

Explore the Salesforce.com Web site. Go to the App Exchange portion of the site, and examine the applications available for each of the categories listed. Then answer the following questions:

1. What are the most popular applications on App Exchange? What kinds of processes do they support?
2. Could a company run its entire business using Salesforce.com and App Exchange? Explain your answer.
3. What kinds of companies are most likely to use App Exchange? What does this tell you about how Salesforce.com is being used?

5.5 MANAGEMENT ISSUES

Creating and managing a coherent IT infrastructure raises multiple challenges: dealing with platform and technology change, management and governance, and making wise infrastructure investments.

DEALING WITH PLATFORM AND INFRASTRUCTURE CHANGE

As firms grow, they can quickly outgrow their infrastructure. As firms shrink, they can get stuck with excessive infrastructure purchased in better times. How can a firm remain flexible when most of the investments in IT infrastructure are fixed cost purchases and licenses? How well does the infrastructure scale? **Scalability** refers to the ability of a computer, product, or system to expand to serve a large number of users without breaking down. New applications, mergers and acquisitions, and changes in business volume all impact computer workload and must be considered when planning hardware capacity.

Firms using mobile computing and cloud computing platforms will require new policies and procedures for managing these new platforms. They will need to inventory all of their mobile devices in business use and develop policies and tools for tracking, updating, and securing them and for controlling the data and applications that run on them. Firms using cloud computing and SaaS will need to fashion new contractual arrangements with remote vendors to make sure that the hardware and software for critical applications are always available when needed. It is up to business management to determine acceptable levels of computer response time and availability for the firm's mission-critical systems to maintain the level of business performance they expect.

MANAGEMENT AND GOVERNANCE

A long-standing issue among information system managers and CEOs has been the question of who will control and manage the firm's IT infrastructure. Chapter 2 introduced the concept of IT governance and described some issues it addresses. Other important questions about IT governance are: Should departments and divisions have the responsibility of making their own information technology decisions or should IT infrastructure be centrally controlled and managed? What is the relationship between central information systems management and business unit information systems management? How will infrastructure costs be allocated among business units? Each organization will need to arrive at answers based on its own needs.

MAKING WISE INFRASTRUCTURE INVESTMENTS

IT infrastructure is a major investment for the firm. If too much is spent on infrastructure, it lies idle and constitutes a drag on firm financial performance. If too little is spent, important business services cannot be delivered and the firm's competitors (who spent just the right amount) will outperform the under-investing firm. How much should the firm spend on infrastructure? This question is not easy to answer.

A related question is whether a firm should purchase its own IT infrastructure components or rent them from external suppliers. As we discussed earlier, a major trend in computing platforms—both hardware and software—is to outsource to external providers. The decision either to purchase your own IT assets or rent them from external providers is typically called the *rent versus buy* decision.

Competitive Forces Model for IT Infrastructure Investment

Figure 5-13 illustrates a competitive forces model you can use to address the question of how much your firm should spend on IT infrastructure.

Market demand for your firm's services. Make an inventory of the services you currently provide to customers, suppliers, and employees. Survey each group, or hold focus groups to find out if the services you currently offer are meeting the needs of each group. For example, are customers

FIGURE 5-13   COMPETITIVE FORCES MODEL FOR IT INFRASTRUCTURE

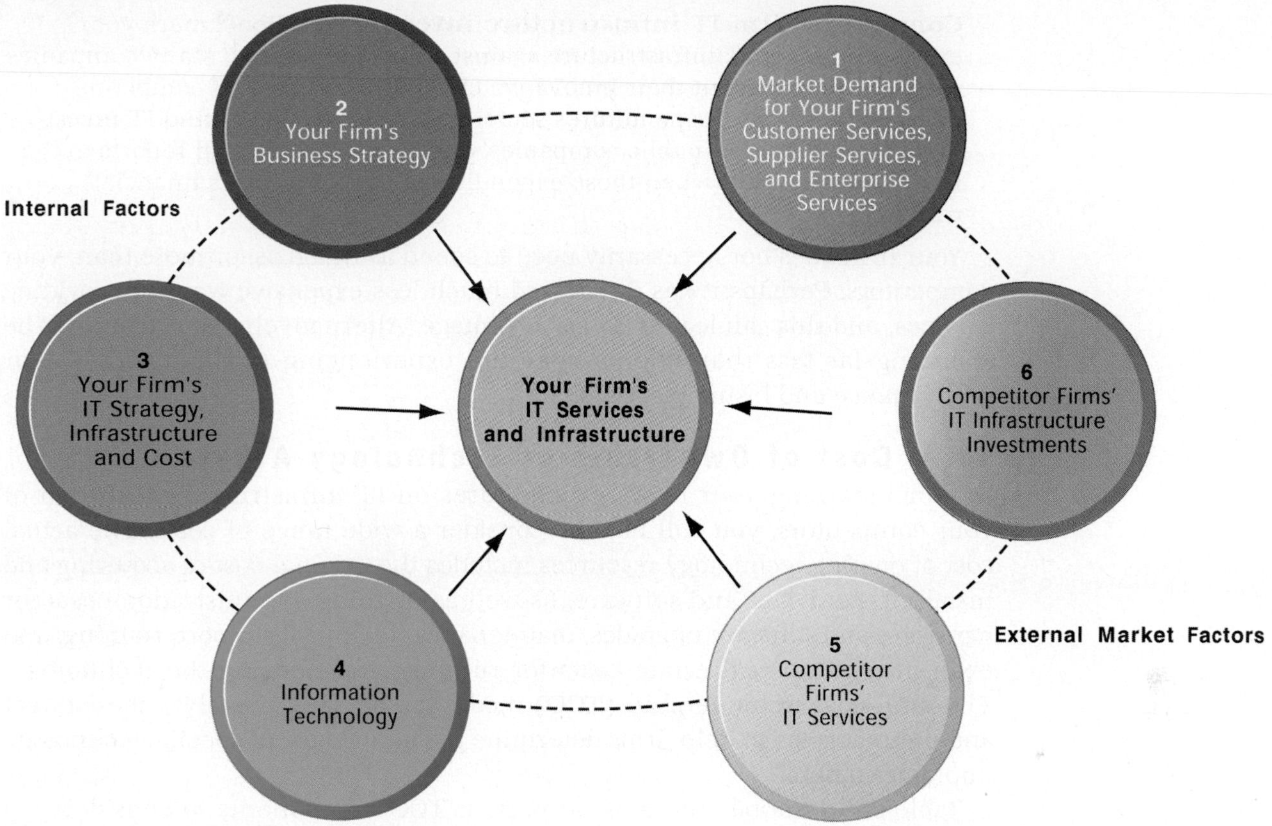

There are six factors you can use to answer the question, "How much should our firm spend on IT infrastructure?"

complaining of slow responses to their queries about price and availability? Are employees complaining about the difficulty of finding the right information for their jobs? Are suppliers complaining about the difficulties of discovering your production requirements?

Your firm's business strategy. Analyze your firm's five-year business strategy and try to assess what new services and capabilities will be required to achieve strategic goals.

Your firm's information technology (IT) strategy, infrastructure, and cost. Examine your firm's information technology plans for the next five years and assess its alignment with the firm's business plans. Determine total IT infrastructure costs. You will want to perform a total cost of ownership analysis (see the discussion later). If your firm has no IT strategy, you will need to devise one that takes into account the firm's five-year strategic plan.

Information technology assessment. Is your firm behind the technology curve or at the bleeding edge of information technology? Both situations are to be avoided. It is usually not desirable to spend resources on advanced technologies that are still experimental, often expensive, and sometimes unreliable. You want to spend on technologies for which standards have been established and IT vendors are competing on cost, not design, and where there are multiple suppliers. However, you do not want to put off investment in new technologies or allow competitors to develop new business models and capabilities based on the new technologies.

Competitor firm services. Try to assess what technology services competitors offer to customers, suppliers, and employees. Establish quantitative and qualitative measures to compare them to those of your firm. If your firm's service levels fall short, your company is at a competitive disadvantage. Look for ways your firm can excel at service levels.

Competitor firm IT infrastructure investments. Benchmark your expenditures for IT infrastructure against your competitors. Many companies are quite public about their innovative expenditures on IT. If competing firms try to keep IT expenditures secret, you may be able to find IT investment information in public companies' SEC Form 10-K annual reports to the federal government when those expenditures impact a firm's financial results.

Your firm does not necessarily need to spend as much as, or more than, your competitors. Perhaps it has discovered much less expensive ways of providing services, and this can lead to a cost advantage. Alternatively, your firm may be spending far less than competitors and experiencing commensurate poor performance and losing market share.

Total Cost of Ownership of Technology Assets

In benchmarking your firm's expenditures on IT infrastructure with that of your competitors, you will need to consider a wide range of costs. The actual cost of owning technology resources includes the original cost of acquiring and installing hardware and software, as well as ongoing administration costs for hardware and software upgrades, maintenance, technical support, training, and even utility and real estate costs for running and housing the technology. The **total cost of ownership (TCO)** model can be used to analyze these direct and indirect costs to help firms determine the actual cost of specific technology implementations.

Table 5-4 describes the most important TCO components to consider in a TCO analysis.

When all these cost components are considered, the TCO for a PC might run up to three times the original purchase price of the equipment. Hidden costs for support staff, downtime, and additional network management can make distributed client/server architectures—especially those incorporating mobile wireless devices—more expensive than centralized mainframe architectures.

Hardware and software acquisition costs account for only about 20 percent of TCO, so managers must pay close attention to administration costs to understand the full cost of the firm's hardware and software. It is possible to reduce

TABLE 5-4 TOTAL COST OF OWNERSHIP (TCO) COST COMPONENTS

INFRASTRUCTURE COMPONENT	COST COMPONENTS
Hardware acquisition	Purchase price of computer hardware equipment, including computers, terminals, storage, and printers
Software acquisition	Purchase or license of software for each user
Installation	Cost to install computers and software
Training	Cost to provide training for information systems specialists and end users
Support	Cost to provide ongoing technical support, help desks, and so forth
Maintenance	Cost to upgrade the hardware and software
Infrastructure	Cost to acquire, maintain, and support related infrastructure, such as networks and specialized equipment (including storage backup units)
Downtime	Cost of lost productivity if hardware or software failures cause the system to be unavailable for processing and user tasks
Space and energy	Real estate and utility costs for housing and providing power for the technology

some of these administration costs through better management. Many large firms are saddled with redundant, incompatible hardware and software because their departments and divisions have been allowed to make their own technology purchases.

These firms could reduce their TCO through greater centralization and standardization of their hardware and software resources, as did Cars.com, described in the chapter-opening case. Companies could reduce the size of the information systems staff required to support their infrastructure if the firm minimizes the number of different computer models and pieces of software that employees are allowed to use. In a centralized infrastructure, systems can be administered from a central location and troubleshooting can be performed from that location.

5.6   HANDS-ON MIS PROJECTS

The projects in this section give you hands-on experience in developing solutions for managing IT infrastructures and IT outsourcing, using spreadsheet software to evaluate alternative desktop systems, and using Web research to budget for a sales conference.

Management Decision Problems

1. The University of Pittsburgh Medical Center (UPMC) relies on information systems to operate 19 hospitals, a network of other care sites, and international and commercial ventures. Demand for additional servers and storage technology was growing by 20 percent each year. UPMC was setting up a separate server for every application, and its servers and other computers were running a number of different operating systems, including several versions of Unix and Windows. UPMC had to manage technologies from many different vendors, including Hewlett-Packard (HP), Sun Microsystems, Microsoft, and IBM. Assess the impact of this situation on business performance. What factors and management decisions must be considered when developing a solution to this problem?

2. Qantas Airways, Australia's leading airline, faces cost pressures from high fuel prices and lower levels of global airline traffic. To remain competitive, the airline must find ways to keep costs low while providing a high level of customer service. Qantas had a 30 year old data center. Management had to decide whether to replace its IT infrastructure with newer technology or outsource it. What factors should be considered by Qantas management when deciding whether to outsource? If Qantas decides to outsource, list and describe points that should be addressed in a service level agreement.

Improving Decision Making: Using a Spreadsheet to Evaluate Hardware and Software Options

Software skills: Spreadsheet formulas
Business skills: Technology pricing

In this exercise, you will use spreadsheet software to calculate the cost of alternative desktop systems.

You have been asked to obtain pricing information on hardware and software for an office of 30 people. Using the Internet, get pricing for 30 PC desktop systems (monitors, computers, and keyboards) manufactured by Lenovo, Dell, and HP/Compaq as listed at their respective corporate Web sites. (For the purposes of this exercise, ignore the fact that desktop systems usually come with preloaded software packages.) Also obtain pricing on 15 desktop printers manufactured by Hewlett-Packard, Canon, and Dell. Each desktop system must satisfy the minimum specifications shown in the following table:

MINIMUM DESKTOP SPECIFICATIONS

Processor speed	Dual core 2 GHz
Hard drive	250 GB
RAM	3 GB
DVD-ROM drive	16 x
Monitor (diagonal measurement)	17 inches

Each desktop printer must satisfy the minimum specifications shown in the following table:

MINIMUM MONOCHROME PRINTER SPECIFICATIONS

Print speed (black and white)	20 pages per minute
Print resolution	600 × 600
Network ready?	Yes
Maximum price/unit	$700

After pricing the desktop systems and printers, obtain pricing on 30 copies of the most recent versions of Microsoft Office, Lotus SmartSuite, and Sun StarOffice desktop productivity packages, and on 30 copies of Microsoft Windows Vista Business. The application software suite packages come in various versions, so be sure that each package contains programs for word processing, spreadsheet analysis, database analysis, graphics preparation, and e-mail.

Prepare a spreadsheet showing your research results for the desktop systems, for the printers, and for the software. Use your spreadsheet software to determine the desktop system, printer, and software combination that will offer both the best performance and pricing per worker. Because every two workers will share one printer (15 printers/30 systems), assume only half a printer cost per worker in the spreadsheet. Assume that your company will take the standard warranty and service contract offered by each product's manufacturer.

Improving Decision Making: Using Web Research to Budget for a Sales Conference

Software skills: Internet-based software
Business skills: Researching transportation and lodging costs

In this exercise, you'll use software at various online travel sites to arrange transportation and lodging for a large sales force to attend a sales conference at two alternative locations. You'll use that information to calculate total travel and lodging costs and decide where to hold the conference.

The Foremost Composite Materials Company is planning a two-day sales conference for October 15-16, starting with a reception on the evening of October 14. The conference consists of all-day meetings that the entire sales force, numbering 125 sales representatives and their 16 managers, must attend. Each sales representative requires his or her own room, and the company needs two common meeting rooms, one large enough to hold the entire sales force plus a few visitors (200) and the other able to hold half the force. Management has set a budget of $105,000 for the representatives' room rentals.

The hotel must also have such services as overhead and computer projectors as well as business center and banquet facilities. It also should have facilities for the company reps to be able to work in their rooms and to enjoy themselves in a swimming pool or gym facility. The company would like to hold the conference in either Miami or Marco Island, Florida.

Foremost usually likes to hold such meetings in Hilton- or Marriott-owned hotels. Use the Hilton and Marriott Web sites to select a hotel in whichever of these cities that would enable the company to hold its sales conference within its budget.

Link to the two sites' homepages, and search them to find a hotel that meets Foremost's sales conference requirements. Once you have selected the hotel, locate flights arriving the afternoon prior to the conference because the attendees will need to check in the day before and attend your reception the evening prior to the conference. Your attendees will be coming from Los Angeles (54), San Francisco (32), Seattle (22), Chicago (19), and Pittsburgh (14). Determine costs of each airline ticket from these cities. When you are finished, create a budget for the conference. The budget will include the cost of each airline ticket, the room cost, and $60 per attendee per day for food.

- What was your final budget?
- Which did you select as the best hotel for the sales conference and why?

LEARNING TRACK MODULES

The following Learning Tracks provide content relevant to topics covered in this chapter:

1. How Computer Hardware and Software Work
2. Service Level Agreements

Review Summary

1. **What is IT infrastructure and what are its components?**

    IT infrastructure is the shared technology resources that provide the platform for the firm's specific information system applications. IT infrastructure includes hardware, software, and services that are shared across the entire firm. Major IT infrastructure components include computer hardware platforms, operating system platforms, enterprise software platforms, networking and telecommunications platforms, database management software, Internet platforms, and consulting services and systems integrators.

2. **What are the stages and technology drivers of IT infrastructure evolution?**

    The five stages of IT infrastructure evolution are: the mainframe era, the personal computer era, the client/server era, the enterprise computing era, and the cloud computing era. Moore's Law deals with the exponential increase in processing power and decline in the cost of computer technology, stating that every 18 months the power of microprocessors doubles and the price of computing falls in half. The Law of Mass Digital Storage deals with the exponential decrease in the cost of storing data, stating that the number of kilobytes of data that can be stored on magnetic media for $1 roughly doubles every 15 months. Metcalfe's Law helps shows that a network's value to participants grows exponentially as the network takes on more members. Also driving exploding computer use is the rapid decline in costs of communication and growing agreement in the technology industry to use computing and communications standards.

3. *What are the current trends in computer hardware platforms?*

The emerging mobile digital computing platform, grid computing, and on-demand cloud computing demonstrate that, increasingly, computing is taking place over a network. Grid computing involves connecting geographically remote computers into a single network to create a computational grid that combines the computing power of all the computers on the network with which to attack large computing problems. Cloud computing is a model of computing where firms and individuals obtain computing power and software applications over the Internet, rather than purchasing and installing the hardware and software on their own computers. In autonomic computing, computer systems have capabilities for automatically configuring and repairing themselves.

Virtualization organizes computing resources so that their use is not restricted by physical configuration or geographic location. Server virtualization enables companies to run more than one operating system at the same time on the same computer. A multicore processor is a microprocessor to which two or more processors have been attached for enhanced performance, reduced power consumption and more efficient simultaneous processing of multiple tasks.

4. *What are the current trends in software platforms?*

Contemporary software platform trends include the growing use of Linux, open source software, Java and Ajax, Web services, mashups and widgets, and software outsourcing. Open source software is produced and maintained by a global community of programmers and is downloadable for free. Linux is a powerful, resilient open source operating system that can run on multiple hardware platforms and is used widely to run Web servers. Java is an operating-system- and hardware-independent programming language that is the leading interactive programming environment for the Web.

Web services are loosely coupled software components based on open Web standards that are not product-specific and can work with any application software and operating system. They can be used as components of Web-based applications linking the systems of two different organizations or to link disparate systems of a single company. Mashups and widgets are the building blocks of new software applications and services based on the cloud computing model. Companies are purchasing their new software applications from outside sources, including software packages, by outsourcing custom application development to an external vendor (that may be offshore), or by renting software services (SaaS).

5. *What are the challenges of managing IT infrastructure and management solutions?*

Major challenges include dealing with platform and infrastructure change, infrastructure management and governance, and making wise infrastructure investments. Solution guidelines include using a competitive forces model to determine how much to spend on IT infrastructure and where to make strategic infrastructure investments, and establishing the total cost of ownership (TCO) of information technology assets. The total cost of owning technology resources includes not only the original cost of computer hardware and software but also costs for hardware and software upgrades, maintenance, technical support, and training.

Key Terms

Ajax, 214

Application server, 195

Autonomic computing, 209

Blade servers, 204

Clients, 194

Client/server computing, 194

Cloud computing, 196

Extensible Markup Language (XML), 215

Grid computing, 207

Hypertext Markup Language (HTML), 215

Java, 213

Legacy systems, 207

Linux, 205

Mainframe, 194

Mashup, 217

Minicomputers, 196

Moore's Law, 196

Multicore processor, 212

Multitiered (N-tier) client/server architecture, 195

Nanotechnology, 199

Netbook, 207

On-demand computing, 209

Open source software, 212

Operating system, 204

Outsourcing, 219

SaaS (Software as a Service), 219

Scalability, 222

Service level agreement (SLA), 219

Server, 194

Service-oriented architecture (SOA), 215

Software package, 218

Storage area network (SAN), 205

Technology standards, 202

Total cost of ownership (TCO), 224

Review Questions

1. What is IT infrastructure and what are its components?
   - Define IT infrastructure from both a technology and a services perspective.
   - List and describe the components of IT infrastructure that firms need to manage.

2. What are the stages and technology drivers of IT infrastructure evolution?
   - List each of the eras in IT infrastructure evolution and describe its distinguishing characteristics.
   - Define and describe the following: Web server, application server, multitiered client/server architecture.
   - Describe Moore's Law and the Law of Mass Digital Storage
   - Describe how network economics, declining communications costs, and technology standards affect IT infrastructure.

3. What are the current trends in computer hardware platforms?
   - Describe the evolving mobile platform, grid computing, and cloud computing.

   - Explain how businesses can benefit from autonomic computing, virtualization, and multicore processors.

4. What are the current trends in software platforms?
   - Define and describe open source software and Linux and explain their business benefits.
   - Define Java and Ajax and explain why they are important.
   - Define and describe Web services and the role played by XML.
   - Define and describe software mashups and widgets.
   - Name and describe the three external sources for software.

5. What are the challenges of managing IT infrastructure and management solutions?
   - Name and describe the management challenges posed by IT infrastructure.
   - Explain how using a competitive forces model and calculating the total cost of ownership (TCO) of technology assets help firms make good infrastructure investments.

Discussion Questions

1. Why is selecting computer hardware and software for the organization an important management decision? What management, organization, and technology issues should be considered when selecting computer hardware and software?

2. Should organizations use software service providers for all their software needs? Why or why not? What management, organization, and technology factors should be considered when making this decision?

Video Cases

You will find video cases illustrating some of the concepts in this chapter on the Laudon Web site along with questions to help you analyze the cases.

Collaboration and Teamwork: Evaluating Server Operating Systems

Form a group with three or four of your classmates. One group should research and compare the capabilities and costs of Linux versus the most recent version of the Windows operating system for servers. Another group should research and compare the capabilities and costs of Linux versus Unix. If possible, use Google

Sites to post links to Web pages, team communication announcements, and work assignments; to brainstorm; and to work collaboratively on project documents. Try to use Google Docs to develop a presentation of your findings for the class.

Amazon's New Store: Utility Computing
CASE STUDY

Looking for a good deal on that DVD box set of The West Wing or the last Harry Potter book? Since opening as an online bookstore in 1995, Amazon.com has morphed into a virtual superstore with product offerings in 36 categories, including furniture, jewelry, clothing, and groceries. But what if what you really need is a place to store several terabytes of data? Or the computing power of 100 Linux servers? Now you can get those from Amazon too.

Over its first twelve years, Amazon.com committed $2 billion to refine the information technology infrastructure that was largely responsible for making it the top online retailer in the world. Following the burst of the dot com bubble in 2001, Amazon focused heavily on modernizing its data centers and software so that it could add new features to its product pages such as discussion forums and software for audio and video.

In March 2006, Amazon introduced the first of several new services that founder Jeff Bezos hoped would transform its future business. With Simple Storage Service (S3) and later Elastic Compute Cloud (EC2), Amazon entered the cloud utility computing market. The company had realized that the benefits of its $2 billion investment in technology could also be valuable to other companies.

Amazon had tremendous computing capacity, but like most companies, only used a small portion of it at any one time. Moreover, the Amazon infrastructure was considered by many to be among the most robust in the world. So, the one-time bookseller exposed the guts of its entire system over the Internet to any developer who could make use of them. Amazon began to sell its computing power on a per usage basis, just like a power company sells electricity.

S3 is a data storage service that is designed to make Web-scale computing easier and more affordable for developers. Customers pay 15 cents per gigabyte of data stored per month on Amazon's network of disk drives. There is also a charge of 20 cents per gigabyte of data transferred. The service has neither a minimum fee nor a start-up charge. Customers pay for exactly what they use and no more. Data may be stored as objects ranging in size from 1 byte to 5 gigabytes, with an unlimited number of objects permitted. Using S3 does not require any client software,

nor does it require the user to set up any hardware. Amazon designed S3 to provide a fast, simple, and inexpensive method for businesses to store data on a system that is scalable and reliable. S3 promises 99.99 percent availability through a mechanism of fault tolerance that fixes failures without any downtime.

Working in conjunction with S3, EC2 enables businesses to utilize Amazon's servers for computing tasks, such as testing software. Using EC2 incurs charges of 10 cents per instance-hour consumed. An instance supplies the user with the equivalent of a 1.7 GHz x86 processor with 1.75 GB of RAM, a 160 GB hard drive, and 250 megabits per second of bandwidth on the network. The service also includes 20 cents per GB of data traffic inbound and outbound per month, as well as the standard S3 pricing for storing an Amazon Machine Image (AMI), which contains the applications, libraries, data and configuration settings that a business uses to run its processes.

According to Adam Selipsky, vice president of product management and developer relations for Amazon Web Services (AWS), Amazon is really a technology company that can bring a wealth of engineering prowess and experience to independent developers and corporations by allowing them to run their processes on Amazon's computer systems. Selipsky also emphasizes that AWS is not simply about providing great amounts of storage capacity and server time. AWS creates the opportunity for others to work at Web scale without making the mistakes that Amazon has already made and learned from. Simplicity and ease-of-use are not generally terms that go along with building a Web-scale application, but they are major selling points for AWS. Users build on the services through Application Programming Interfaces (APIs) made available by Amazon.

From the very beginning, customers have responded strongly to S3 and EC2. Bezos targeted micro-sized businesses and Web startups as customers for AWS, but the services have also attracted some mid-size businesses and potential big players in e-business.

MileMeter Inc. is a Dallas-based startup that plans to sell auto insurance by the mile. It initially ran its own server in a data center but moved most of its applications onto "virtual" computers in Amazon's EC2. CEO Chris Gay said, "I don't need to have a systems administrator or a network administrator. I don't have to worry about hardware becoming irrelevant."

Webmail.us provides e-mail management services for thousands of companies around the world from its Blacksburg, Virginia, headquarters. When the company needed to increase its short-term storage capacity and the redundancy of its primary data backups, it selected S3 as its storage provider. Webmail.us sends more than a terabyte of data to Amazon to store with S3 every week. Bill Boebel, cofounder and chief technology officer of Webmail.us, was very pleased that his company was able to create a simple interface with which Amazon can accept the abundant small files that his company manages. Other backup systems have had difficulty handling the typical Webmail.us backup load and most hosting companies would require a custom application to handle such data. Webmail.us even used EC2 to develop its storage interface. According to CEO Pat Matthews, Amazon immediately reduced his company's data backup costs by 75 percent.

Powerset is an up-and-coming search engine company based in San Francisco that wants to focus its time, and the $12.5 million it has raised, on its core business, natural language search technology. By using S3 and EC2, Powerset saves upfront cash expenditure, and eliminates the risk that building an infrastructure will take longer than expected. Many of the traditional utility computing suppliers charge around one dollar per CPU hour, or ten times what Amazon charges.

Powerset's CEO Barney Pell says that the pay-as-you go model is very important because his company does not know how fast it will grow. What he does know is that the demand for Powerset's service will come in bursts, and trying to predict hardware needs is a dangerous game. If Powerset overestimates its peak usage capacity, the company will waste money on unnecessary hardware. If the company underestimates peak usage, it could fail to meet its users' expectations and damage its business. With AWS in place, Powerset never has to worry about being unable to add computing power when a spike in usage occurs.

SmugMug Inc., an online photo-sharing startup, was immediately drawn to the ease with which it could back up photos on Amazon's S3. Storing its users' photos on Amazon's devices prevents SmugMug from having to purchase its own additional storage and saved the company $1 million during the first year it used Amazon's services.

As with any large business initiative, there are issues for Amazon to confront before anyone can declare AWS to be a successful venture Larger businesses may be more inclined to use a more established company, especially one with more experience hosting core applications and data. Currently, Amazon's flexible, pay-as-you-go model gives the company a competitive advantage over companies that require service contracts.

However, according to Daniel Golding, vice president of Tier 1 Research, the established companies, such as IBM, Hewlett-Packard, and Sun Microsystems, may follow Amazon's lead and offer utility computing without service-level agreements (SLAs). Complicating the matter is that some companies are wary of using a supplier that does not offer SLAs, which guarantee the availability of services in terms of time. Golding suggests that Amazon may have launched a major shift in the industry, but others will reap the rewards while Amazon may suffer for it.

One more challenge for Amazon is the viability of AWS itself. Will the services actually function as planned? The company's track record with new technology projects is mixed. Amazon launched its A9.com search site with much fanfare, but the site never really caught on with users. Moreover, the growth of AWS could be harmful to Amazon's Web services line as well as to its retail line if Amazon does not position itself to handle a dramatic increase in demand on its infrastructure. AWS customers could drop the service, and Amazon.com could falter.

In January 2007, February 2008, and July 2008, Amazon's S3 servers experienced significant outages, with service lost for 8 hours in July. The January 2007 problem was caused by faulty hardware installed during an upgrade, and it was resolved quickly. The July 2008 outage was more problematic. Amazon reported that components were unable to interact properly due to a problem with "internal system communications." Amazon promised to provide a fuller explanation once it determined the root cause. Some users were critical and questioned whether Amazon was capable of being their solution for hosted storage going forward.

AWS has charmed some high-profile clients. Microsoft uses S3 to increases software download speeds for its users. Linden Lab, creator of the online virtual world Second Life, uses the service to alleviate the pounding its servers take when the company releases its frequent software upgrades.

The Nasdaq stock exchange uses S3 to host data for Nasdaq Market Replay, an application that lets companies play back historical market data in real time. However, Nasdaq is reluctant to use an online service for transactional or highly secure data.

To better support large accounts, Amazon started round-the-clock phone support and credits if S3 availability falls below 99.99 percent in a single month. For now, the potential of AWS is being converted into performance mostly by tech savvy developers with financial backing. More than 370,000 developers, ranging from individuals to large companies, have signed up. As more developers contribute and the services evolve, Amazon hopes one day to make it possible for anyone with an idea and an Internet connection to begin to put together the next Amazon.com.

Sources: Thomas Claburn, "Amazon's S3 Cloud Service Turns into a Puff of Smoke," *Information Week*, July 28, 2008; Chris Preimesberger, "Perils in the Cloud," *eWeek*, August 4, 2008; Jessica Mintz, "Amazon's Hot New Item: Its Data Center,"Associated Press, February 1, 2008; J. Nicholas Hoover, "Ahead in the Cloud: Google, Others Expand Online Services," *Information Week*, April 14, 2008; J. Nicholas Hoover and Richard Martin, "Demystifying the Cloud," *Information Week*, June 23, 2008; Edward Cone, "Amazon at Your Service," *CIO Insight*, January 7, 2007; Robert D. Hof, "So You Wanna Be a Web Tycoon? Amazon Can Help," www.webworker-daily.com, January 24, 2007; and Thomas Claburn, "Open Source Developers Build on Amazon Web Services," TechWeb.com, January 12, 2007.

CASE STUDY QUESTIONS

1. What technology services does Amazon provide? What are the business advantages to Amazon and to subscribers of these services? What are the disadvantages to each? What kinds of businesses are likely to benefit from these services?

2. How do the concepts of capacity planning, scalability, and TCO apply to this case? Apply these concepts both to Amazon and to subscribers of its services.

3. Search the Internet for companies that supply utility computing. Select two or three such companies and compare them to Amazon. What services do these companies provide? What promises do they make about availability? What is their payment model? Who is their target client? If you were launching a Web startup business, would you choose one of these companies over Amazon for Web services? Why or why not? Would your answer change if you were working for a larger company and had to make a recommendation to the CTO?

4. Think of an idea for a Web-based startup business. Explain how this business could utilize Amazon's S3 and EC2 services.

Chapter 6

Foundations of Business Intelligence: Databases and Information Management

LEARNING OBJECTIVES

After reading this chapter, you will be able to answer the following questions:

1. What are the problems of managing data resources in a traditional file environment and how are they solved by a database management system?

2. What are the major capabilities of database management systems (DBMS) and why is a relational DBMS so powerful?

3. What are some important principles of database design?

4. What are the principal tools and technologies for accessing information from databases to improve business performance and decision making?

5. Why are information policy, data administration, and data quality assurance essential for managing the firm's data resources?

Interactive Sessions:

The Internal Revenue Service Uncovers Tax Fraud with a Data Warehouse

The Databases Behind MySpace

CHAPTER OUTLINE

6.1 **ORGANIZING DATA IN A TRADITIONAL FILE ENVIRONMENT**
File Organization Terms and Concepts
Problems with the Traditional File Environment

6.2 **THE DATABASE APPROACH TO DATA MANAGEMENT**
Database Management Systems
Capabilities of Database Management Systems
Designing Databases

6.3 **USING DATABASES TO IMPROVE BUSINESS PERFORMANCE AND DECISION MAKING**
Data Warehouses
Business Intelligence, Multidimensional Data Analysis, and Data Mining
Databases and the Web

6.4 **MANAGING DATA RESOURCES**
Establishing an Information Policy
Ensuring Data Quality

6.5 **HANDS-ON MIS PROJECTS**
Management Decision Problems
Achieving Operational Excellence: Building a Relational Database for Inventory Management
Improving Decision Making: Searching Online Databases for Overseas Business Resources

LEARNING TRACK MODULES
Database Design, Normalization, and Entity-Relationship Diagramming
Introduction to SQL
Hierarchical and Network Data Models

CAN HP MINE SUCCESS FROM AN ENTERPRISE DATA WAREHOUSE?

Hewlett-Packard (HP) is one of the world's largest vendors of information technology, including personal computers, server computers, printers, and consulting services. Although the company had considerable systems expertise to sell to other companies, it was bedeviled by information technology problems of its own. HP had plenty of data, but they were stored in multiple applications and data repositories across departments, business units, and geographic locations. HP's numerous systems and applications were unable to deliver the information the company needed for a complete and consistent picture of its business operations.

CEO Mark Hurd had difficulty collecting and analyzing "consistent, timely data spanning different parts of the business." Some systems tracked sales and pricing by product, while others tracked sales information geographically. Commonly used financial information such as gross margins to measure profitability were calculated differently from business unit to business unit. Corporate management was obtaining information from more than 750 separate sources of data throughout the company.

Lack of data consistency dragged down sales and profits. Compiling information about the business from various systems could take up to a week, so managers had to make decisions based on relatively stale data. Seemingly simple questions, such as how much the company was spending on marketing across its different businesses, were difficult to answer. Without a consistent view of the enterprise, senior executives struggled with decisions on matters such as the size of sales and service teams assigned to particular systems. Management clearly needed better information.

HP management decided the solution was to build a data warehouse with a single global enterprise-wide database of shareable information that delivers a unified, accurate vision of the business. The data warehouse replaces 17 different database technologies and unites 14,000 databases currently in use, giving HP's workforce access to data in real time with no departmental or geographic boundaries.

In November 2005, HP CIO Randy Mott created a team to model the enterprise-wide database that would be the foundation of the data warehouse. They developed a way of modeling data across the entire company and ensuring that the data would always be up to date, consistent for the entire enterprise, and complete. HP developed its own proprietary platform for the warehouse, consisting of an integrated set of servers, storage, operating system, database management system (DBMS) and software for querying and reporting, all optimized for data warehousing. HP's data warehouse platform proved so successful that the company decided to sell it to other companies as a "data warehouse appliance" product called Neoview. Upon completion, HP's data warehouse contained over 400 terabytes of data and was being

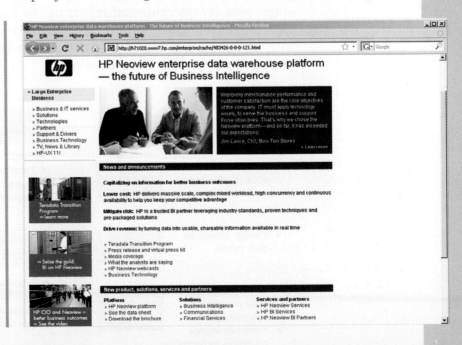

235

utilized by 50,000 HP workers. All of HP's financial data are accessible via the data warehouse.

HP's efforts appear to be paying off. The company is now able to perform 12 times the number of data queries, updates, and other transactions in its financial database over a three-month period than before it implemented the data warehouse. (One month's transactions peaked at nearly 50 billion.) HP can track how much it spends on marketing across all of its business units, spending by media sector and customer segment, worldwide, or by country. The company was unable to do these things before. The information helps HP management make better decisions about where to spend to get the biggest bang.

Sources: Doug Henschen,"HP Upgrades Neoview Data Warehouse Appliance," *Intelligent Enterprise*, June 2008; "HP Neoview Enterprise Data Warehouse," www.hp.com, accessed June 8, 2008; Christopher Lawton, "Data, Data Everywhere," *The Wall Street Journal*, September 24, 2007; and John Foley, "Inside Hewlett-Packard's Data Warehouse Gamble," *InformationWeek*, January 6, 2007.

HP's experience illustrates the importance of data management and database systems for business. The company was unable to fully understand how it was performing as a company or make timely decisions because its data were redundant, inconsistent, and fragmented among many different systems and applications. How businesses store, organize, and manage their data has a tremendous impact on organizational effectiveness.

The chapter-opening diagram calls attention to important points raised by this case and this chapter. HP's corporate data had been stored in a number of different databases where they could not be easily retrieved and analyzed. Management determined that profitability and efficiency were curtailed because it could not obtain consistent, company-wide information for measuring business performance. It authorized a team to develop a company-wide model of its data using company-wide standards and business rules for defining, organizing, and accessing the data. It chose to develop its own data warehousing technology for integrating the data from all of its disparate sources into a single comprehensive database, storing the data, organizing the data, and providing tools for making the data easily accessible to large numbers of employees for querying and reporting. By creating a data model for a single view of the company and a database reflecting this model for company-wide querying and reporting, HP has become much more efficient and its managers are making better decisions.

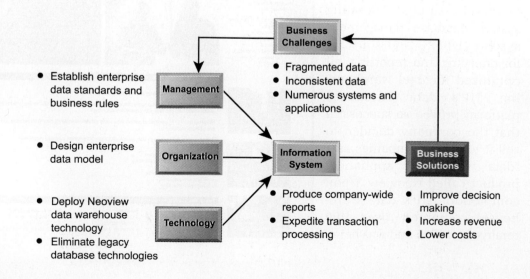

6.1 ORGANIZING DATA IN A TRADITIONAL FILE ENVIRONMENT

An effective information system provides users with accurate, timely, and relevant information. Accurate information is free of errors. Information is timely when it is available to decision makers when it is needed. Information is relevant when it is useful and appropriate for the types of work and decisions that require it.

You might be surprised to learn that many businesses don't have timely, accurate, or relevant information because the data in their information systems have been poorly organized and maintained. That's why data management is so essential. To understand the problem, let's look how information systems arrange data in computer files and traditional methods of file management.

FILE ORGANIZATION TERMS AND CONCEPTS

A computer system organizes data in a hierarchy that starts with bits and bytes and progresses to fields, records, files, and databases (see Figure 6-1). A bit represents the smallest unit of data a computer can handle. A group of bits, called a byte, represents a single character, which can be a letter, a

FIGURE 6-1   THE DATA HIERARCHY

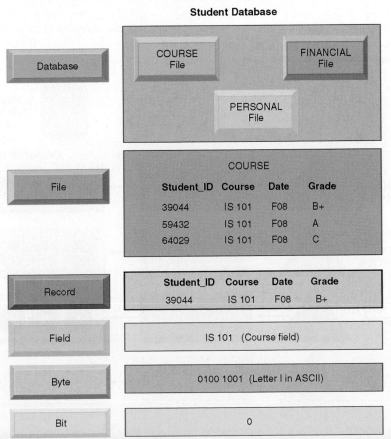

A computer system organizes data in a hierarchy that starts with the bit, which represents either a 0 or a 1. Bits can be grouped to form a byte to represent one character, number, or symbol. Bytes can be grouped to form a field, and related fields can be grouped to form a record. Related records can be collected to form a file, and related files can be organized into a database.

number, or another symbol. A grouping of characters into a word, a group of words, or a complete number (such as a person's name or age) is called a **field**. A group of related fields, such as the student's name, the course taken, the date, and the grade, comprises a **record**; a group of records of the same type is called a **file**.

For example, the records in Figure 6-1 could constitute a student course file. A group of related files makes up a **database**. The student course file illustrated in Figure 6-1 could be grouped with files on students' personal histories and financial backgrounds to create a student database.

A record describes an entity. An **entity** is a person, place, thing, or event on which we store and maintain information. Each characteristic or quality describing a particular entity is called an **attribute**. For example, Student_ID, Course, Date, and Grade are attributes of the entity COURSE. The specific values that these attributes can have are found in the fields of the record describing the entity COURSE.

PROBLEMS WITH THE TRADITIONAL FILE ENVIRONMENT

In most organizations, systems tended to grow independently without a company-wide plan. Accounting, finance, manufacturing, human resources, and sales and marketing all developed their own systems and data files. Figure 6-2 illustrates the traditional approach to information processing.

FIGURE 6-2   **TRADITIONAL FILE PROCESSING**

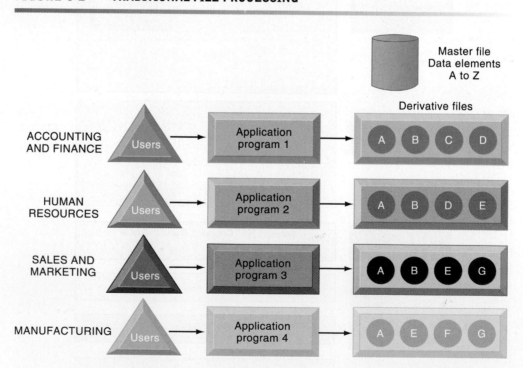

The use of a traditional approach to file processing encourages each functional area in a corporation to develop specialized applications. Each application requires a unique data file that is likely to be a subset of the master file. These subsets of the master file lead to data redundancy and inconsistency, processing inflexibility, and wasted storage resources.

Each application, of course, required its own files and its own computer program to operate. For example, the human resources functional area might have a personnel master file, a payroll file, a medical insurance file, a pension file, a mailing list file, and so forth until tens, perhaps hundreds, of files and programs existed. In the company as a whole, this process led to multiple master files created, maintained, and operated by separate divisions or departments. As this process goes on for 5 or 10 years, the organization is saddled with hundreds of programs and applications that are very difficult to maintain and manage. The resulting problems are data redundancy and inconsistency, program-data dependence, inflexibility, poor data security, and an inability to share data among applications.

Data Redundancy and Inconsistency

Data redundancy is the presence of duplicate data in multiple data files so that the same data are stored in more than place or location. Data redundancy occurs when different groups in an organization independently collect the same piece of data and store it independently of each other. Data redundancy wastes storage resources and also leads to **data inconsistency**, where the same attribute may have different values. For example, in instances of the entity COURSE illustrated in Figure 6-1, the Date may be updated in some systems but not in others. The same attribute, Student_ID, may also have different names in different systems throughout the organization. Some systems might use Student_ID and others might use ID, for example.

Additional confusion might result from using different coding systems to represent values for an attribute. For instance, the sales, inventory, and manufacturing systems of a clothing retailer might use different codes to represent clothing size. One system might represent clothing size as "extra large," whereas another might use the code "XL" for the same purpose. The resulting confusion would make it difficult for companies to create customer relationship management, supply chain management, or enterprise systems that integrate data from different sources.

Program-Data Dependence

Program-data dependence refers to the coupling of data stored in files and the specific programs required to update and maintain those files such that changes in programs require changes to the data. Every traditional computer program has to describe the location and nature of the data with which it works. In a traditional file environment, any change in a software program could require a change in the data accessed by that program. One program might be modified from a five-digit to a nine-digit ZIP code. If the original data file were changed from five-digit to nine-digit ZIP codes, then other programs that required the five-digit ZIP code would no longer work properly. Such changes could cost millions of dollars to implement properly.

Lack of Flexibility

A traditional file system can deliver routine scheduled reports after extensive programming efforts, but it cannot deliver ad hoc reports or respond to unanticipated information requirements in a timely fashion. The information required by ad hoc requests is somewhere in the system but may be too expensive to retrieve. Several programmers might have to work for weeks to put together the required data items in a new file.

Poor Security

Because there is little control or management of data, access to and dissemination of information may be out of control. Management may have no way of knowing who is accessing or even making changes to the organization's data.

Lack of Data Sharing and Availability

Because pieces of information in different files and different parts of the organization cannot be related to one another, it is virtually impossible for information to be shared or accessed in a timely manner. Information cannot flow freely across different functional areas or different parts of the organization. If users find different values of the same piece of information in two different systems, they may not want to use these systems because they cannot trust the accuracy of their data.

6.2 THE DATABASE APPROACH TO DATA MANAGEMENT

Database technology cuts through many of the problems of traditional file organization. A more rigorous definition of a **database** is a collection of data organized to serve many applications efficiently by centralizing the data and controlling redundant data. Rather than storing data in separate files for each application, data are stored so as to appear to users as being stored in only one location. A single database services multiple applications. For example, instead of a corporation storing employee data in separate information systems and separate files for personnel, payroll, and benefits, the corporation could create a single common human resources database.

DATABASE MANAGEMENT SYSTEMS

A **database management system (DBMS)** is software that permits an organization to centralize data, manage them efficiently, and provide access to the stored data by application programs. The DBMS acts as an interface between application programs and the physical data files. When the application program calls for a data item, such as gross pay, the DBMS finds this item in the database and presents it to the application program. Using traditional data files, the programmer would have to specify the size and format of each data element used in the program and then tell the computer where they were located.

The DBMS relieves the programmer or end user from the task of understanding where and how the data are actually stored by separating the logical and physical views of the data. The *logical view* presents data as they would be perceived by end users or business specialists, whereas the *physical view* shows how data are actually organized and structured on physical storage media.

The database management software makes the physical database available for different logical views required by users. For example, for the human resources database illustrated in Figure 6-3, a benefits specialist might require a view consisting of the employee's name, Social Security number, and health insurance coverage. A payroll department member might need data such as the employee's name, Social Security number, gross pay, and net pay. The data for

FIGURE 6-3   **HUMAN RESOURCES DATABASE WITH MULTIPLE VIEWS**

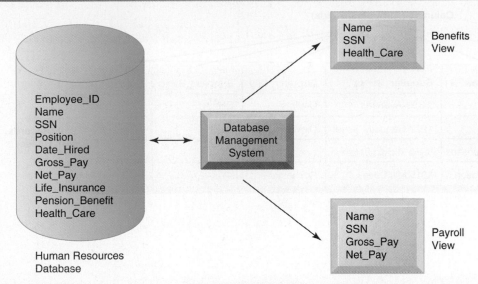

A single human resources database provides many different views of data, depending on the information requirements of the user. Illustrated here are two possible views, one of interest to a benefits specialist and one of interest to a member of the company's payroll department.

all these views are stored in a single database, where they can be more easily managed by the organization.

How a DBMS Solves the Problems of the Traditional File Environment

A DBMS reduces data redundancy and inconsistency by minimizing isolated files in which the same data are repeated. The DBMS may not enable the organization to eliminate data redundancy entirely, but it can help control redundancy. Even if the organization maintains some redundant data, using a DBMS eliminates data inconsistency because the DBMS can help the organization ensure that every occurrence of redundant data has the same values. The DBMS uncouples programs and data, enabling data to stand on their own. Access and availability of information will be increased and program development and maintenance costs reduced because users and programmers can perform ad hoc queries of data in the database. The DBMS enables the organization to centrally manage data, their use, and security.

Relational DBMS

Contemporary DBMS use different database models to keep track of entities, attributes, and relationships. The most popular type of DBMS today for PCs as well as for larger computers and mainframes is the **relational DBMS**. Relational databases represent data as two-dimensional tables (called relations). Tables may be referred to as files. Each table contains data on an entity and its attributes. Microsoft Access is a relational DBMS for desktop systems, whereas DB2, Oracle Database, and Microsoft SQL Server are relational DBMS for large mainframes and midrange computers. MySQL is a popular open-source DBMS, and Oracle Database Lite is a DBMS for small handheld computing devices.

FIGURE 6-4   **RELATIONAL DATABASE TABLES**

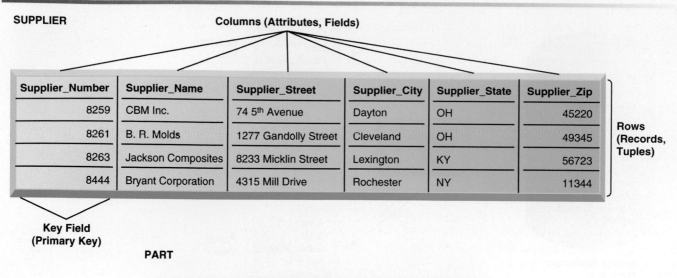

A relational database organizes data in the form of two-dimensional tables. Illustrated here are tables for the entities SUPPLIER and PART showing how they represent each entity and its attributes. Supplier_Number is a primary key for the SUPPLIER table and a foreign key for the PART table.

Let's look at how a relational database organizes data about suppliers and parts (see Figure 6-4). The database has a separate table for the entity SUPPLIER and a table for the entity PART. Each table consists of a grid of columns and rows of data. Each individual element of data for each entity is stored as a separate field, and each field represents an attribute for that entity. Fields in a relational database are also called columns. For the entity SUPPLIER, the supplier identification number, name, street, city, state, and ZIP code are stored as a separate fields within the SUPPLIER table and each field represents an attribute for the entity SUPPLIER.

The actual information about a single supplier that resides in a table is called a row. Rows are commonly referred to as **records**, or in very technical terms, as **tuples**. Data for the entity PART have their own separate table.

The field for Supplier_Number in the SUPPLIER table uniquely identifies each record so that so that the record can be retrieved, updated, or sorted and it is called a **key field**. Each table in a relational database has one field that is designated as its **primary key**. This key field is the unique identifier for all the information in any row of the table and this primary key cannot be duplicated.

Supplier_Number is the primary key for the SUPPLIER table and Part_Number is the primary key for the PART table. Note that Supplier_Number appears in both the SUPPLIER and PART tables. In the SUPPLIER table, Supplier_Number is the primary key. When the field Supplier_Number appears in the PART table it is called a **foreign key** and is essentially a lookup field to look up data about the supplier of a specific part.

Operations of a Relational DBMS

Relational database tables can be combined easily to deliver data required by users, provided that any two tables share a common data element. Suppose we wanted to find in this database the names of suppliers who could provide us with part number 137 or part number 150. We would need information from two tables: the SUPPLIER table and the PART table. Note that these two files have a shared data element: Supplier_Number.

In a relational database, three basic operations, as shown in Figure 6-5, are used to develop useful sets of data: select, join, and project. The *select* operation creates a subset consisting of all records in the file that meet stated criteria. Select creates, in other words, a subset of rows that meet certain criteria. In our example, we want to select records (rows) from the PART table where the Part_Number equals 137 or 150. The *join* operation combines relational tables to provide the user with more information than is available in individual tables. In our example, we want to join the now-shortened PART table (only parts 137 or 150 will be presented) and the SUPPLIER table into a single new table.

The *project* operation creates a subset consisting of columns in a table, permitting the user to create new tables that contain only the information required. In our example, we want to extract from the new table only the following columns: Part_Number, Part_Name, Supplier_Number, and Supplier_Name.

Object-Oriented DBMS

Many applications today and in the future require databases that can store and retrieve not only structured numbers and characters but also drawings, images, photographs, voice, and full-motion video. DBMS designed for organizing structured data into rows and columns are not well suited to handling graphics-based or multimedia applications. Object-oriented databases are better suited for this purpose.

An **object-oriented DBMS** stores the data and procedures that act on those data as objects that can be automatically retrieved and shared. Object-oriented database management systems (OODBMS) are becoming popular because they can be used to manage the various multimedia components or Java applets used in Web applications, which typically integrate pieces of information from a variety of sources.

Although object-oriented databases can store more complex types of information than relational DBMS, they are relatively slow compared with relational DBMS for processing large numbers of transactions. Hybrid **object-relational DBMS** systems are now available to provide capabilities of both object-oriented and relational DBMS.

CAPABILITIES OF DATABASE MANAGEMENT SYSTEMS

A DBMS includes capabilities and tools for organizing, managing, and accessing the data in the database. The most important are its data definition language, data dictionary, and data manipulation language.

FIGURE 6-5 **THE THREE BASIC OPERATIONS OF A RELATIONAL DBMS**

PART

Part_Number	Part_Name	Unit_Price	Supplier_Number
137	Door latch	22.00	8259
145	Side mirror	12.00	8444
150	Door molding	6.00	8263
152	Door lock	31.00	8259
155	Compressor	54.00	8261
178	Door handle	10.00	8259

Select Part_Number = 137 or 150

SUPPLIER

Supplier_Number	Supplier_Name	Supplier_Street	Supplier_City	Supplier_State	Supplier_Zip
8259	CBM Inc.	74 5th Avenue	Dayton	OH	45220
8261	B. R. Molds	1277 Gandolly Street	Cleveland	OH	49345
8263	Jackson Components	8233 Micklin Street	Lexington	KY	56723
8444	Bryant Corporation	4315 Mill Drive	Rochester	NY	11344

Join by Supplier_Number

Part_Number	Part_Name	Supplier_Number	Supplier_Name
137	Door latch	8259	CBM Inc.
150	Door molding	8263	Jackson Components

Project selected columns

The select, join, and project operations enable data from two different tables to be combined and only selected attributes to be displayed.

DBMS have a **data definition** capability to specify the structure of the content of the database. It would be used to create database tables and to define the characteristics of the fields in each table. This information about the database would be documented in a data dictionary. A **data dictionary** is an automated or manual file that stores definitions of data elements and their characteristics.

Microsoft Access has a rudimentary data dictionary capability that displays information about the name, description, size, type, format, and other properties of each field in a table (see Figure 6-6). Data dictionaries for large corporate databases may capture additional information, such as usage, ownership (who in the organization is responsible for maintaining the data); authorization; security; and the individuals, business functions, programs, and reports that use each data element.

Querying and Reporting

DBMS includes tools for accessing and manipulating information in databases. Most DBMS have a specialized language called a **data manipulation language** that is used to add, change, delete, and retrieve the data in the database. This language contains commands that permit end users and programming specialists to extract data from the database to satisfy information requests and develop applications. The most prominent data manipulation language today is **Structured Query Language**, or **SQL**. Figure 6-7 illustrates the SQL query that would produce the new resultant table in Figure 6-5. You can find out more about how to perform SQL queries in our Learning Tracks for this chapter, which can be found on the Laudon Web site.

FIGURE 6-6   MICROSOFT ACCESS DATA DICTIONARY FEATURES

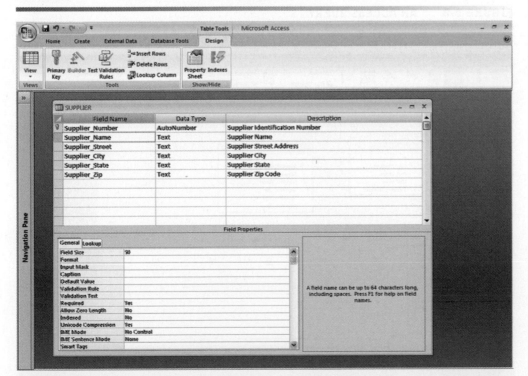

Microsoft Access has a rudimentary data dictionary capability that displays information about the size, format, and other characteristics of each field in a database. Displayed here is the information maintained in the SUPPLIER table. The small key icon to the left of Supplier_Number indicates that it is a key field.

FIGURE 6-7   EXAMPLE OF AN SQL QUERY

SELECT PART.Part_Number, PART.Part_Name, SUPPLIER.Supplier_Number,
SUPPLIER.Supplier_Name
FROM PART, SUPPLIER
WHERE PART.Supplier_Number = SUPPLIER.Supplier_Number AND
Part_Number = 137 OR Part_Number = 150;

Illustrated here are the SQL statements for a query to select suppliers for parts 137 or 150.
They produce a list with the same results as Figure 6-5.

Users of DBMS for large and midrange computers, such as DB2, Oracle, or SQL Server, would employ SQL to retrieve information they needed from the database. Microsoft Access also uses SQL, but it provides its own set of user-friendly tools for querying databases and for organizing data from databases into more polished reports.

In Microsoft Access, you will find features that enable users to create queries by identifying the tables and fields they want and the results, and then selecting the rows from the database that meet particular criteria. These actions in turn are translated into SQL commands. Figure 6-8 illustrates how the same query as the SQL query to select parts and suppliers would be constructed using the Microsoft query-building tools.

FIGURE 6-8   AN ACCESS QUERY

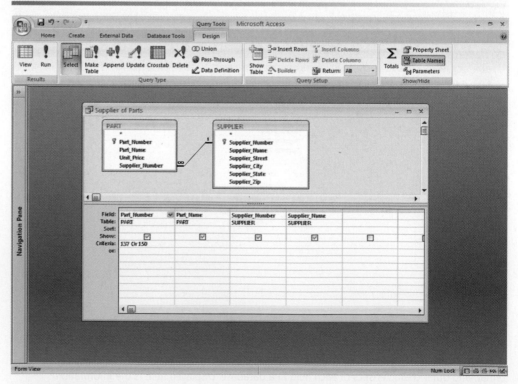

Illustrated here is how the query in Figure 6-7 would be constructed using Microsoft Access query-building tools. It shows the tables, fields, and selection criteria used for the query.

Microsoft Access and other DBMS include capabilities for report generation so that the data of interest can be displayed in a more structured and polished format than would be possible just by querying. Crystal Reports is a popular report generator for large corporate DBMS, although it can also be used with Access. Access also has capabilities for developing desktop system applications. These include tools for creating data entry screens, reports, and developing the logic for processing transactions.

DESIGNING DATABASES

To create a database, you must understand the relationships among the data, the type of data that will be maintained in the database, how the data will be used, and how the organization will need to change to manage data from a company-wide perspective. The database requires both a conceptual design and a physical design. The conceptual, or logical, design of a database is an abstract model of the database from a business perspective, whereas the physical design shows how the database is actually arranged on direct-access storage devices.

Normalization and Entity-Relationship Diagrams

The conceptual database design describes how the data elements in the database are to be grouped. The design process identifies relationships among data elements and the most efficient way of grouping data elements together to meet business information requirements. The process also identifies redundant data elements and the groupings of data elements required for specific application programs. Groups of data are organized, refined, and streamlined until an overall logical view of the relationships among all the data in the database emerges.

To use a relational database model effectively, complex groupings of data must be streamlined to minimize redundant data elements and awkward many-to-many relationships. The process of creating small, stable, yet flexible and adaptive data structures from complex groups of data is called **normalization**. Figures 6-9 and 6-10 illustrate this process.

In the particular business modeled here, an order can have more than one part but each part is provided by only one supplier. If we build a relation called ORDER with all the fields included here, we would have to repeat the name and address of the supplier for every part on the order, even though the order is for parts from a single supplier. This relationship contains what are called repeating data groups because there can be many parts on a single order to a given supplier. A more efficient way to arrange the data is to break down ORDER into smaller relations, each of which describes a single entity. If we go step by step and normalize the relation ORDER, we emerge with the relations illustrated in Figure 6-10. You can find out more about normalization, entity-relationship diagramming, and database design in the Learning Tracks for this chapter.

FIGURE 6-9   AN UNNORMALIZED RELATION FOR ORDER

ORDER (Before Normalization)

Order_ Number	Order_ Date	Part_ Number	Part_ Name	Unit_ Price	Part_ Quantity	Supplier_ Number	Supplier_ Name	Supplier_ Street	Supplier_ City	Supplier_ State	Supplier_ Zip

An unnormalized relation contains repeating groups. For example, there can be many parts and suppliers for each order. There is only a one-to-one correspondence between Order_Number and Order_Date.

FIGURE 6-10   NORMALIZED TABLES CREATED FROM ORDER

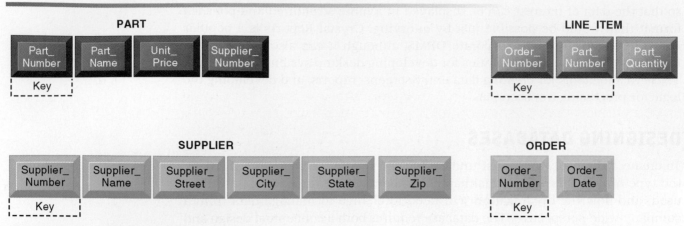

After normalization, the original relation ORDER has been broken down into four smaller relations. The relation ORDER is left with only two attributes and the relation LINE_ITEM has a combined, or concatenated, key consisting of Order_Number and Part_Number.

Relational database systems try to enforce **referential integrity** rules to ensure that relationships between coupled tables remain consistent. When one table has a foreign key that points to another table, you may not add a record to the table with the foreign key unless there is a corresponding record in the linked table. In the database we examined earlier in this chapter, the foreign key Supplier_Number links the PART table to the SUPPLIER table. We may not add a new record to the PART table for a part with Supplier_Number 8266 unless there is corresponding record in the SUPPLIER table for Supplier_Number 8266. We must also delete the corresponding record in the PART table if we delete the record in the SUPPLIER table for Supplier_Number 8266. In other words, we shouldn't have parts from nonexistent suppliers!

Database designers document their data model with an **entity-relationship diagram**, illustrated in Figure 6-11. This diagram illustrates the relationship between the entities ORDER, PART, LINE_ITEM, and SUPPLIER. The boxes represent entities. The lines connecting the boxes represent relationships. A line connecting two entities that ends in two short marks designates a one-to-one relationship. A line connecting two entities that ends with a crow's foot topped by a short mark indicates a one-to-many relationship. Figure 6-11 shows that one ORDER can contain many LINE_ITEMs. (A PART can be ordered many times and appear many times as a line item in a single order.) Each PART can have only one SUPPLIER, but many PARTs can be provided by the same SUPPLIER.

FIGURE 6-11   AN ENTITY-RELATIONSHIP DIAGRAM

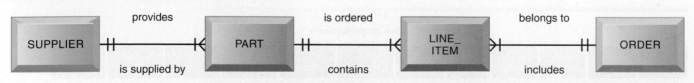

This diagram shows the relationships between the entities ORDER, PART, LINE_ITEM, and SUPPLIER that might be used to model the database in Figure 6-10.

It can't be emphasized enough: If the business doesn't get its data model right, the system won't be able to serve the business well. The company's systems will not be as effective as they could be because they'll have to work with data that may be inaccurate, incomplete, or difficult to retrieve. Understanding the organization's data and how they should be represented in a database is perhaps the most important lesson you can learn from this course.

For example, Famous Footwear, a shoe store chain with more than 800 locations in 49 states, could not achieve its goal of having "the right style of shoe in the right store for sale at the right price" because its database was not properly designed for rapidly adjusting store inventory. The company had an Oracle relational database running on an IBM AS/400 midrange computer, but the database was designed primarily for producing standard reports for management rather than for reacting to marketplace changes. Management could not obtain precise data on specific items in inventory in each of its stores. The company had to work around this problem by building a new database where the sales and inventory data could be better organized for analysis and inventory management.

Distributing Databases

Database design also considers how the data are to be distributed. Information systems can be designed with a centralized database that is used by a single central processor or by multiple processors in a client/server network. Alternatively, the database can be distributed. A **distributed database** is one that is stored in more than one physical location.

There are two main methods of distributing a database (see Figure 6-12). In a *partitioned* database, parts of the database are stored and maintained physically in one location and other parts are stored and maintained in other locations (see Figure 6-12a) so that each remote processor has the necessary data to serve its local area. Changes in local files can be justified with the central database on a batch basis, often at night. Another strategy is to *replicate* (that is, duplicate in its entirety) the central database (Figure 6-12b) at all remote locations.

FIGURE 6-12   DISTRIBUTED DATABASES

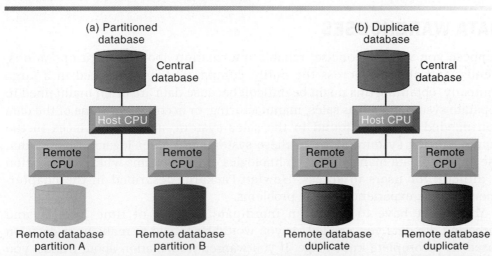

There are alternative ways of distributing a database. The central database can be partitioned (a) so that each remote processor has the necessary data to serve its own local needs. The central database also can be replicated (b) at all remote locations.

For example, Lufthansa Airlines replaced its centralized mainframe database with a replicated database to make information more immediately available to flight dispatchers. Any change made to Lufthansa's Frankfort DBMS is automatically replicated in New York and Hong Kong. This strategy also requires updating the central database during off-hours.

Distributed systems reduce the vulnerability of a single, massive central site. They increase service and responsiveness to local users and often can run on smaller, less expensive computers. However, local databases can sometimes depart from central data standards and definitions, and they pose security problems by widely distributing access to sensitive data. Database designers need to weigh these factors in their decisions.

6.3   USING DATABASES TO IMPROVE BUSINESS PERFORMANCE AND DECISION MAKING

Businesses use their databases to keep track of basic transactions, such as paying suppliers, processing orders, keeping track of customers, and paying employees. But they also need databases to provide information that will help the company run the business more efficiently, and help managers and employees make better decisions. If a company wants to know which product is the most popular or who is its most profitable customer, the answer lies in the data.

For example, by analyzing data from customer credit card purchases, Louise's Trattoria, a Los Angeles restaurant chain, learned that quality was more important than price for most of its customers, who were college-educated and liked fine wine. Acting on this information, the chain introduced vegetarian dishes, more seafood selections, and more expensive wines, raising sales by more than 10 percent.

In a large company, with large databases or large systems for separate functions, such as manufacturing, sales, and accounting, special capabilities and tools are required for analyzing vast quantities of data and for accessing data from multiple systems. These capabilities include data warehousing, data mining, and tools for accessing internal databases through the Web.

DATA WAREHOUSES

Suppose you wanted concise, reliable information about current operations, trends, and changes across the entire company? If you worked in a large company, obtaining this might be difficult because data are often maintained in separate systems, such as sales, manufacturing, or accounting. Some of the data you needed might be found in the sales system, and other pieces in the manufacturing system. Many of these systems are older legacy systems that use outdated data management technologies or file systems where information is difficult for users to access. Hewlett-Packard, described in the chapter-opening case, experienced these problems.

You might have to spend an inordinate amount of time locating and gathering the data you needed, or you would be forced to make your decision based on incomplete knowledge. If you wanted information about trends, you might also have trouble finding data about past events because most firms only make their current data immediately available. Data warehousing addresses these problems.

What Is a Data Warehouse?

A **data warehouse** is a database that stores current and historical data of potential interest to decision makers throughout the company. The data originate in many core operational transaction systems, such as systems for sales, customer accounts, and manufacturing, and may include data from Web site transactions. The data warehouse consolidates and standardizes information from different operational databases so that the information can be used across the enterprise for management analysis and decision making.

Figure 6-13 illustrates how a data warehouse works. The data warehouse makes the data available for anyone to access as needed, but it cannot be altered. A data warehouse system also provides a range of ad hoc and standardized query tools, analytical tools, and graphical reporting facilities. Many firms use intranet portals to make the data warehouse information widely available throughout the firm.

The Interactive Session on Organizations illustrates how the Internal Revenue Service (IRS) Compliance Data Warehouse can serve as a powerful tool to enhance decision making and operational efficiency. Because taxpayer data were fragmented among many different systems that had been created over the years, the IRS was unable to piece together a complete and comprehensive picture of taxpayers, nor could it easily analyze taxpayer data to identify people most likely to be cheating on their income tax payments. A data warehouse enabled the IRS to integrate and centralize taxpayer data so that it could perform this task and respond more rapidly to taxpayer queries. As you read this case, try to identify the problem the IRS was facing, what alternative solutions were available to management; and the management, organization, and technology issues that had to be addressed when developing the solution.

FIGURE 6-13   COMPONENTS OF A DATA WAREHOUSE

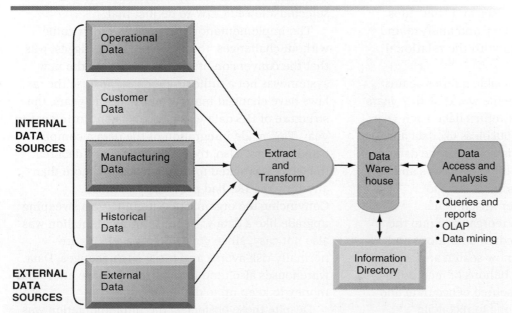

The data warehouse extracts current and historical data from multiple operational systems inside the organization. These data are combined with data from external sources and reorganized into a central database designed for management reporting and analysis. The information directory provides users with information about the data available in the warehouse.

INTERACTIVE SESSION: ORGANIZATIONS

THE INTERNAL REVENUE SERVICE UNCOVERS TAX FRAUD WITH A DATA WAREHOUSE

The Internal Revenue Service (IRS) is the U.S. government agency that collects taxes and enforces tax law. Since its creation in the 1860s, the IRS has grown by orders of magnitude along with the American population. In 2006, the IRS processed nearly 134 million individual tax returns that pulled in revenue amounting to $1.2 trillion. It's no surprise that any inefficiency in their information systems could result in a great deal of lost revenue for the federal government. Fortunately for the IRS and perhaps unfortunately for some unscrupulous Americans, the IRS and Sybase have teamed up to implement a data warehouse, known as the Compliance Data Warehouse (CDW), that has drastically improved efficiency and increased the amount of money that the IRS collects from delinquent taxpayers.

The IRS needed a data warehouse to organize its accumulated information, which includes personal information of taxpayers and archived tax returns. The data were stored in legacy systems designed to process tax return forms efficiently and organized in many different formats, including hierarchical mainframe databases, Oracle relational databases, and non-database "flat" files. The data in the older style hierarchical databases and "flat" files were nearly impossible to query and analyze and could not easily be combined with the relational data.

The CDW enables highly flexible queries against one of the largest databases in the world, with 7 years of individual and business tax return data. Each year 4 terabytes of individual and business tax data are loaded into the system. The database for the data warehouse is relational, with billions of rows and over 200 columns, all with complex links to associated schedules and other attachments. Once the data arrive they are reorganized into the relational structure using standard definitions and formats. IRS researchers can now search and analyze hundreds of millions or even billions of records at one time using a centralized source of accurate and consistent data instead of having to reconcile information from multiple inconsistent sources.

Implementation of the CDW has vastly improved the IRS' ability to manage and make use of the data

it had collected. As a result, it allowed the agency to recoup many billions of dollars in tax revenue that was lost under the old system. For example, in 2006 the IRS collected $59.2 billion in additional revenue via 1.4 million audits of taxpayers questioned for underreporting taxes.

The CDW has grown in capacity from three terabytes at its creation in the late 1990s to approximately 150 terabytes of data today. It allows users to search through the data with a variety of tools. The CDW initially consisted of Sybase Adaptive Server IQ (relational database software for data warehouses, now called Sybase IQ), Sybase PowerBuilder (application development tools for user reporting and accessing database content), Sybase Open Client (interface between client systems and Sybase servers), Open Database Connectivity application programming interfaces, Dual Sun Enterprise 6000 servers running Solaris 2.6 (Sun's version of Unix), and EMC disk arrays. The most important feature of the data warehouse was that it be sufficiently large to accommodate multiple terabytes of data, but also accessible enough to allow queries of its data using many different tools. The components that the IRS selected allowed CDW to do just that.

The implementation of the CDW didn't come without challenges, though. One of the biggest was that the conversion of the legacy data to the new system was not a uniform process. Because the tax laws have changed many times over the years, the structure of IRS data was not consistent from year to year. This made integration of the data a complicated process. Also, the sheer amount of data that the CDW was slated to manage was far more than anything the IRS had previously handled. Convincing the organization to undergo a sweeping upgrade like a data warehouse implementation was also not easy, since government agencies are normally risk-averse and resist such changes. Data warehouses also tend to require extensive effort and money to keep up to date.

Despite those obstacles, the implementation was a resounding success. The IRS reports that it achieved a 200-1 return on investment ratio very shortly after the implementation of the CDW, which cost only $2 million to complete. Much of the savings from the CDW came from the speed and ease with which the system detected mistakes in tax returns. Using the data warehouse, analysts are able to determine patterns in groups of people most likely to cheat on their taxes, such as divorced couples each claiming their children on their tax forms during the same year, people abusing the earned income tax credit or small business tax shelters, or recent college graduates burdened with student loans who might be more likely to fall behind on tax payments. The data warehouse reduced the time it takes to trace mistakes in claims and analyze data from six to eight months to a only few hours.

More recently, the IRS upgraded the way it transports data to its central warehouse. In the early stages of the warehouse's development, the agency transported its data using tapes that each held just 2 gigabytes. In 2006, they replaced the tapes with 2-terabyte network-attached storage appliances, which are of comparable size to tapes, but hold data equivalent to the amount stored by 1,500 tapes. Also, the storage devices are encrypted, ensuring that the data are safe when being transported, whereas the tapes were not secure and left taxpayer information unprotected while in transit. This change is estimated to save the agency millions of dollars over the course of a five-year period.

The number of audits performed by the IRS suggests that the CDW is working well, resulting in more audits of tax cheats and fewer audits of honest taxpayers. The chances of being audited rose to 1 in 140 in 2006, up from 1 in 377 in 2000. Taxpayers who earned a million dollars or more annually had a 1-in-11 chance of being audited in 2006. In 2003, the chances were 1 in 20 for that same income bracket. But the IRS has been able to reduce the number of audits performed on innocent taxpayers, so the increased number of audits has primarily affected those who are actually at fault.

CASE STUDY QUESTIONS

1. Why was it so difficult for the IRS to analyze the taxpayer data it had collected?

2. What kind of challenges did the IRS encounter when implementing its CDW? What management, organization, and technology issues had to be addressed?

3. How did the CDW improve decision making and operations at the IRS? Are there benefits to taxpayers?

4. Do you think data warehouses could be useful in other areas of the federal sector? Which ones? Why or why not?

MIS IN ACTION

1. Go to www.irs.gov and download a 1040 tax return form. What are some of the fields from that form that would most likely be included in the CDW?

2. How could IRS researchers use these data to determine whether someone was underreporting (cheating on) taxes?

Data Marts

Companies often build enterprise-wide data warehouses, where a central data warehouse serves the entire organization, or they create smaller, decentralized warehouses called data marts. A **data mart** is a subset of a data warehouse in which a summarized or highly focused portion of the organization's data is placed in a separate database for a specific population of users. For example, a company might develop marketing and sales data marts to deal with customer information. A data mart typically focuses on a single subject area or line of business, so it usually can be constructed more rapidly and at lower cost than an enterprise-wide data warehouse.

BUSINESS INTELLIGENCE, MULTIDIMENSIONAL DATA ANALYSIS, AND DATA MINING

Once data have been captured and organized in data warehouses and data marts, they are available for further analysis. A series of tools enables users to analyze these data to see new patterns, relationships, and insights that are useful for guiding decision making. These tools for consolidating, analyzing, and providing access to vast amounts of data to help users make better business decisions are often referred to **business intelligence (BI)**. Principal tools for business intelligence include software for database query and reporting, tools for multidimensional data analysis (online analytical processing), and data mining.

When we think of *intelligence* as applied to humans, we typically think of people's ability to combine learned knowledge with new information and change behaviors in such a way that they succeed at their task or adapt to a new situation. Likewise, business intelligence provides firms with the capability to amass information; develop knowledge about customers, competitors, and internal operations; and change decision-making behavior to achieve higher profitability and other business goals.

For instance, Harrah's Entertainment, the second-largest gambling company in its industry, continually analyzes data about its customers gathered when people play its slot machines or use Harrah's casinos and hotels. Harrah's marketing department uses this information to build a detailed gambling profile, based on a particular customer's ongoing value to the company. This information guides management decisions about how to cultivate the most profitable customers, encourage those customers to spend more, and attract more customers with high revenue-generating potential. Business intelligence has improved Harrah's profits so much that it has become the centerpiece of the firm's business strategy.

Figure 6-14 illustrates how business intelligence works. The firm's operational databases keep track of the transactions generated by running the business. These databases feed data to the data warehouse. Managers use business intelligence tools to find patterns and meanings in the data. Managers then act on what they have learned from analyzing the data by making more informed and intelligent business decisions.

This section will introduce you to the most important business intelligence technologies and tools. We'll provide more detail about business intelligence applications in Chapter 12.

Online Analytical Processing (OLAP)

Suppose your company sells four different products—nuts, bolts, washers, and screws—in the East, West, and Central regions. If you wanted to ask a fairly straightforward question, such as how many washers sold during the past quarter, you could easily find the answer by querying your sales database. But what if you wanted to know how many washers sold in each of your sales regions and compare actual results with projected sales?

To obtain the answer, you would need **online analytical processing (OLAP)**. OLAP supports multidimensional data analysis, enabling users to view the same data in different ways using multiple dimensions. Each aspect of information—product, pricing, cost, region, or time period—represents a different dimension. So, a product manager could use a multidimensional data analysis tool to learn how many washers were sold in the East in June, how that compares with the previous month and the previous June, and how it compares with the sales forecast. OLAP enables users to obtain online answers to ad hoc

FIGURE 6-14 **BUSINESS INTELLIGENCE**

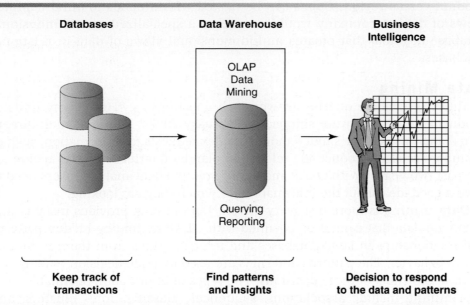

A series of analytical tools works with data stored in databases to find patterns and insights for helping managers and employees make better decisions to improve organizational performance.

questions such as these in a fairly rapid amount of time, even when the data are stored in very large databases, such as sales figures for multiple years.

Figure 6-15 shows a multidimensional model that could be created to represent products, regions, actual sales, and projected sales. A matrix of actual sales can be stacked on top of a matrix of projected sales to form a cube with six faces. If you rotate the cube 90 degrees one way, the face showing will be product versus actual and projected sales. If you rotate the cube 90 degrees again, you will see region versus actual and projected sales. If you

FIGURE 6-15 **MULTIDIMENSIONAL DATA MODEL**

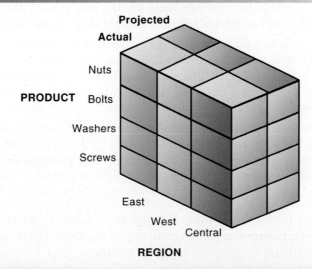

The view that is showing is product versus region. If you rotate the cube 90 degrees, the face that will show product versus actual and projected sales. If you rotate the cube 90 degrees again, you will see region versus actual and projected sales. Other views are possible.

rotate 180 degrees from the original view, you will see projected sales and product versus region. Cubes can be nested within cubes to build complex views of data. A company would use either a specialized multidimensional database or a tool that creates multidimensional views of data in relational databases.

Data Mining

Traditional database queries answer such questions as, "How many units of product number 403 were shipped in February 2007?" OLAP, or multidimensional analysis, supports much more complex requests for information, such as "Compare sales of product 403 relative to plan by quarter and sales region for the past two years." With OLAP and query-oriented data analysis, users need to have a good idea about the information for which they are looking.

Data mining is more discovery-driven. Data mining provides insights into corporate data that cannot be obtained with OLAP by finding hidden patterns and relationships in large databases and inferring rules from them to predict future behavior. The patterns and rules are used to guide decision making and forecast the effect of those decisions. The types of information obtainable from data mining include associations, sequences, classifications, clusters, and forecasts.

- *Associations* are occurrences linked to a single event. For instance, a study of supermarket purchasing patterns might reveal that, when corn chips are purchased, a cola drink is purchased 65 percent of the time, but when there is a promotion, cola is purchased 85 percent of the time. This information helps managers make better decisions because they have learned the profitability of a promotion.

- In *sequences*, events are linked over time. We might find, for example, that if a house is purchased, a new refrigerator will be purchased within two weeks 65 percent of the time, and an oven will be bought within one month of the home purchase 45 percent of the time.

- *Classification* recognizes patterns that describe the group to which an item belongs by examining existing items that have been classified and by inferring a set of rules. For example, businesses such as credit card or telephone companies worry about the loss of steady customers. Classification helps discover the characteristics of customers who are likely to leave and can provide a model to help managers predict who those customers are so that the managers can devise special campaigns to retain such customers.

- *Clustering* works in a manner similar to classification when no groups have yet been defined. A data mining tool can discover different groupings within data, such as finding affinity groups for bank cards or partitioning a database into groups of customers based on demographics and types of personal investments.

- Although these applications involve predictions, *forecasting* uses predictions in a different way. It uses a series of existing values to forecast what other values will be. For example, forecasting might find patterns in data to help managers estimate the future value of continuous variables, such as sales figures.

These systems perform high-level analyses of patterns or trends, but they can also drill down to provide more detail when needed. There are data mining applications for all the functional areas of business, and for government and scientific work. One popular use for data mining is to provide detailed analyses of patterns in customer data for one-to-one marketing campaigns or for identifying profitable customers.

For example, Virgin Mobile Australia uses a data warehouse and data mining to increase customer loyalty and roll out new services. The data warehouse consolidates data from its enterprise system, customer relationship management system, and customer billing systems in a massive database. Data mining has enabled management to determine the demographic profile of new customers and relate it to the handsets they purchased as well as the performance of each store and point-of-sale campaigns, consumer reactions to new products and services, customer attrition rates, and the revenue generated by each customer.

Predictive analysis uses data mining techniques, historical data, and assumptions about future conditions to predict outcomes of events, such as the probability a customer will respond to an offer or purchase a specific product. For example, the U.S. division of The Body Shop International plc used predictive analysis with its database of catalog, Web, and retail store customers to identify customers who were more likely to make catalog purchases. That information helped the company build a more precise and targeted mailing list for its catalogs, improving the response rate for catalog mailings and catalog revenues.

Text Mining and Web Mining

Business intelligence tools deal primarily with data that have been structured in databases and files. However, unstructured data, most in the form of text files, is believed to account for over 80 percent of an organization's useful information. E-mail, memos, call center transcripts, survey responses, legal cases, patent descriptions, and service reports are all valuable for finding patterns and trends that will help employees make better business decisions. **Text mining** tools are now available to help businesses analyze these data. These tools are able to extract key elements from large unstructured data sets, discover patterns and relationships, and summarize the information. Businesses might turn to text mining to analyze transcripts of calls to customer service centers to identify major service and repair issues.

Air Products and Chemicals in Allentown, Pennsylvania, is using text mining to help identify documents that require special record retention procedures to comply with the Sarbanes-Oxley Act. The company has over 9 terabytes of unstructured data (not including e-mail.). SmartDiscovery software from Inxight Software classifies and organizes these data so that the company can apply business rules to a category of documents rather than individual documents. If a document is found to deal with operations covered by Sarbanes-Oxley, the company will make sure the document meets the law's data retention requirements.

The Web is another rich source of valuable information, some of which can now be mined for patterns, trends, and insights into customer behavior. The discovery and analysis of useful patterns and information from the World Wide Web is called **Web mining**. Businesses might turn to Web mining to help them understand customer behavior, evaluate the effectiveness of a particular Web site, or quantify the success of a marketing campaign. For instance, marketers use Google Trends and Google Insights for Search services, which track the popularity of various words and phrases used in Google search queries, to learn what people are interested in and what they are interested in buying.

Web mining looks for patterns in data through content mining, structure mining, and usage mining. Web content mining is the process of extracting knowledge from the content of Web pages, which may include text, image, audio, and video data. Web structure mining examines data related to the structure of a particular Web site. For example, links pointing to a document indicate the popularity of the document, while links coming out of a document indicate the richness or perhaps the variety of topics covered in the document. Web usage mining examines user interaction data recorded by a Web server whenever requests for a Web site's resources are received. The usage data records the user's behavior when the user browses or makes transactions on the Web site and collects the data in a server log. Analyzing such data can help companies determine the value of particular customers, cross marketing strategies across products, and the effectiveness of promotional campaigns, etc.

DATABASES AND THE WEB

Have you ever tried to use the Web to place an order or view a product catalog? If so, you were probably using a Web site linked to an internal corporate database. Many companies now use the Web to make some of the information in their internal databases available to customers and business partners.

Suppose, for example, a customer with a Web browser wants to search an online retailer's database for pricing information. Figure 6-16 illustrates how that customer might access the retailer's internal database over the Web. The user accesses the retailer's Web site over the Internet using Web browser software on his or her client PC. The user's Web browser software requests data from the organization's database, using HTML commands to communicate with the Web server.

Because many "back-end" databases cannot interpret commands written in HTML, the Web server passes these requests for data to software that translates HTML commands into SQL so that they can be processed by the DBMS working with the database. In a client/server environment, the DBMS resides on a dedicated computer called a **database server**. The DBMS receives the SQL requests and provides the required data. The middleware transfers information from the organization's internal database back to the Web server for delivery in the form of a Web page to the user.

Figure 6-16 shows that the middleware working between the Web server and the DBMS is an application server running on its own dedicated computer (see Chapter 5). The application server software handles all application operations, including transaction processing and data access, between browser-based computers and a company's back-end business applications or databases. The application server takes requests from the Web server, runs the business logic to process transactions based on those requests, and provides connectivity to the organization's back-end systems or databases. Alternatively, the software for

FIGURE 6-16   LINKING INTERNAL DATABASES TO THE WEB

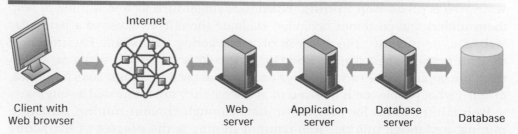

Users access an organization's internal database through the Web using their desktop PCs and Web browser software.

handling these operations could be a custom program or a CGI script. A CGI script is a compact program using the *Common Gateway Interface (CGI)* specification for processing data on a Web server.

There are a number of advantages to using the Web to access an organization's internal databases. First, Web browser software is much easier to use than proprietary query tools. Second, the Web interface requires few or no changes to the internal database. It costs much less to add a Web interface in front of a legacy system than to redesign and rebuild the system to improve user access.

Accessing corporate databases through the Web is creating new efficiencies, opportunities, and business models. ThomasNet.com provides an up-to-date online directory of more than 600,000 suppliers of industrial products, such as chemicals, metals, plastics, rubber, and automotive equipment. Formerly called Thomas Register, the company used to send out huge paper catalogs with this information. Now it provides this information to users online via its Web site and has become a smaller, leaner company.

Other companies have created entirely new businesses based on access to large databases through the Web. One is the social networking site MySpace, which helps users stay connected with each other or meet new people. MySpace features music, comedy, videos, and "profiles" with information supplied by 175 million users about their age, hometown, dating preferences, marital status, and interests. It maintains a massive database to house and manage all of this content. Because the site grew so rapidly, it had to make a series of changes to its underlying database technology. The Interactive Session on Technology explores this topic. As you read this case, try to identify the problem MySpace is facing; what alternative solutions are available to management; and the management, organization, and technology issues that have to be addressed when developing the solution.

6.4 MANAGING DATA RESOURCES

Setting up a database is only a start. In order to make sure that the data for your business remain accurate, reliable, and readily available to those who need it, your business will need special policies and procedures for data management.

ESTABLISHING AN INFORMATION POLICY

Every business, large and small, needs an information policy. Your firm's data are an important resource, and you don't want people doing whatever they want with them. You need to have rules on how the data are to be organized and maintained, and who is allowed to view the data or change them.

An **information policy** specifies the organization's rules for sharing, disseminating, acquiring, standardizing, classifying, and inventorying information. Information policy lays out specific procedures and accountabilities, identifying which users and organizational units can share information, where information can be distributed, and who is responsible for updating and maintaining the information. For example, a typical information policy would specify that only selected members of the payroll and human resources department would have the right to change and view sensitive employee data, such as an employee's salary or social security number, and that these departments are responsible for making sure that such employee data are accurate.

INTERACTIVE SESSION: TECHNOLOGY

THE DATABASES BEHIND MYSPACE

MySpace.com, the popular social networking site, has experienced one of the greatest growth spurts in the history of the Internet. The site launched in November 2003 and by May 2007, it had 175 million member accounts. The challenge for MySpace has been to avoid technological letdowns that degrade Web site performance and frustrate its rapidly expanding network of users.

The technical requirements of a site like MySpace are vastly different from other heavily trafficked Web sites. Generally, a small number of people change the content on a news site a few times a day. The site may retrieve thousands of read-only requests from its underlying database without having to update the database. On MySpace, tens of millions of users are constantly updating their content, resulting in an elevated percentage of database interactions that require updates to the underlying database. Each time a user views a profile on MySpace, the resulting page is stitched together from database lookups that organize information from multiple tables stored in multiple databases residing on multiple servers.

In its initial phases, MySpace operated with two Web servers communicating with one database server and a Microsoft SQL Server database. Such a setup is ideal for small to medium-size sites because of its simplicity. At MySpace, the setup showed signs of stress as more users came aboard. At first, MySpace reduced the load by adding Web servers to handle the increased user requests. But when the number of accounts stretched to 500,000 in 2004, one database server was not sufficient. Deploying additional database servers is more complicated than adding Web servers because the data must be divided among multiple databases without any loss in accessibility or performance. MySpace deployed three SQL Server databases. One served as a master database, which received all new data and copied them to the other two databases. These databases focused on retrieving data for user page requests.

As MySpace approached 2 million accounts, the database servers approached their input/output capacity, which refers to the speed at which they could read and write data. This caused the site to lag behind in content updates. MySpace switched to a vertical partitioning model in which separate databases supported distinct functions of the Web site, such as the log-in screen, user profiles, and blogs.

However, the distinct functions also had occasion to share data, and this became problematic when the site reached 3 million accounts. Furthermore, some functions of the site grew too large to be served by only one database server. After considering a scale-up strategy of investing in more powerful and expensive servers, MySpace instead scaled out by adding many cheaper servers to share the database workload.

The more economical solution of a distributed architecture required a new design in which all of the servers combined to work as one logical computer. Under this design, the workload still needed to be spread out, which was accomplished by dividing the user accounts into groups of 1 million, and putting all the data related to those accounts in a separate instance of SQL Server.

Despite these gains in efficiency, the workload was not distributed evenly, which would sometimes cause an overload in the storage area for a particular database. MySpace tried to correct this issue manually, but the work was demanding and not an effective use of resources. So, MySpace switched to a virtualized storage architecture, which ended the practice of attaching disks dedicated to specific applications in favor of a single pool of storage space available to all applications. Under this arrangement, databases could write data to any available disk, thus eliminating the possibility of an application's dedicated disk becoming overloaded.

In 2005, MySpace also fortified its infrastructure by installing a layer of servers between the database servers and the Web servers to store and serve copies of frequently accessed data objects so that the site's Web servers wouldn't have to query the database servers with lookups as frequently.

Despite all these measures, MySpace still overloads more frequently than other major Web sites. Users have expressed frustration at not being able to log in or view certain pages. Log-in errors occur at a rate of 20 to 40 percent some days. Site activity continues to challenge the limitations of the technology. So far, the site's continued growth suggests that users are willing to put up with periodic "Unexpected Error" screens. MySpace developers continue to redesign the Web site's database, software, and storage systems, to keep pace with its exploding growth, but their job is never done.

Sources: Joel Martinez, "Deconstructing MySpace.com Part 1-Social Networking Database," www.communitymx.com, accessed June 2, 2008; David F. Carr, "Inside MySpace.com," *Baseline Magazine*, January 16, 2007; Mark Brunelli, "Oracle Database 10g Powers Growing MySpace.com Competitor," SearchOracle.com, January 31, 2007.

CASE STUDY QUESTIONS

1. What kind of databases and database servers does MySpace use?
2. Why is database technology so important for a business such as MySpace?
3. How effectively does MySpace organize and store the data on its site?
4. What data management problems have arisen? How has MySpace solved, or attempted to solve, these problems?

MIS IN ACTION

Explore MySpace.com, examining the features and tools that are not restricted to registered members. Then answer the following questions:

1. Based on what you can view without registering, what are the entities in MySpace's database?
2. Which of these entities have some relationship to individual members?
3. Select one of these entities and describe the attributes for that entity.

If you are in a small business, the information policy would be established and implemented by the owners or managers. In a large organization, managing and planning for information as a corporate resource often requires a formal data administration function. **Data administration** is responsible for the specific policies and procedures through which data can be managed as an organizational resource. These responsibilities include developing information policy, planning for data, overseeing logical database design and data dictionary development, and monitoring how information systems specialists and end-user groups use data.

You may hear the term **data governance** used to describe many of these activities. Promoted by IBM, data governance deals with the policies and processes for managing the availability, usability, integrity, and security of the data employed in an enterprise, with special emphasis on promoting privacy, security, data quality, and compliance with government regulations.

A large organization will also have a database design and management group within the corporate information systems division that is responsible for defining and organizing the structure and content of the database, and maintaining the database. In close cooperation with users, the design group establishes the physical database, the logical relations among elements, and the access rules and security procedures. The functions it performs are called **database administration**.

ENSURING DATA QUALITY

A well-designed database and information policy will go a long way toward ensuring that the business has the information it needs. However, additional steps must be taken to ensure that the data in organizational databases are accurate and remain reliable.

What would happen if a customer's telephone number or account balance were incorrect? What would be the impact if the database had the wrong price for the product you sold or your sales system and inventory system showed different prices for the same product? Data that are inaccurate, untimely, or inconsistent with other sources of information lead to incorrect decisions, product recalls, and financial losses. Inaccurate data in criminal justice and national security databases might even subject you to unnecessarily surveillance or detention, as described in the chapter-ending case study.

According to Forrester Research, 20 percent of U.S. mail and commercial package deliveries were returned because of incorrect names or addresses. Gartner Inc. reported that more than 25 percent of the critical data in large Fortune 1000 companies' databases is inaccurate or incomplete, including bad product codes and product descriptions, faulty inventory descriptions, erroneous financial data, incorrect supplier information, and incorrect employee data. (Gartner, 2007).

Think of all the times you've received several pieces of the same direct mail advertising on the same day. This is very likely the result of having your name maintained multiple times in a database. Your name may have been misspelled or you used your middle initial on one occasion and not on another or the information was initially entered onto a paper form and not scanned properly into the system. Because of these inconsistencies, the database would treat you as different people! We often receive redundant mail addressed to Laudon, Lavdon, Lauden, or Landon.

If a database is properly designed and enterprise-wide data standards established, duplicate or inconsistent data elements should be minimal. Most data quality problems, however, such as misspelled names, transposed numbers, or incorrect or missing codes, stem from errors during data input. The incidence of such errors is rising as companies move their businesses to the Web and allow customers and suppliers to enter data into their Web sites that directly update internal systems.

Before a new database is in place, organizations need to identify and correct their faulty data and establish better routines for editing data once their database is in operation. Analysis of data quality often begins with a **data quality audit**, which is a structured survey of the accuracy and level of completeness of the data in an information system. Data quality audits can be performed by surveying entire data files, surveying samples from data files, or surveying end users for their perceptions of data quality.

Data cleansing, also known as *data scrubbing*, consists of activities for detecting and correcting data in a database that are incorrect, incomplete, improperly formatted, or redundant. Data cleansing not only corrects errors but also enforces consistency among different sets of data that originated in separate information systems. Specialized data-cleansing software is available to automatically survey data files, correct errors in the data, and integrate the data in a consistent company-wide format.

6.5 HANDS-ON MIS PROJECTS

The projects in this section give you hands-on experience in analyzing data quality problems, establishing company-wide data standards, creating a database for inventory management, and using the Web to search online databases for overseas business resources.

Management Decision Problems

1. Emerson Process Management, a global supplier of measurement, analytical, and monitoring instruments and services based in Austin, Texas, had a new data warehouse designed for analyzing customer activity to improve service and marketing that was full of inaccurate and redundant data. The data in the warehouse came from numerous transaction processing systems in Europe, Asia, and other locations around the world. The team that designed the warehouse had assumed that sales groups in all these areas would enter customer names and addresses the same way, regardless of their location. In fact, cultural differences combined with complications from absorbing companies that Emerson had acquired led to multiple ways of entering quote, billing, shipping, and other data. Assess the potential business impact of these data quality problems. What decisions have to be made and steps taken to reach a solution?

2. Your industrial supply company wants to create a data warehouse where management can obtain a single corporate-wide view of critical sales information to identify best-selling products in specific geographic areas, key customers, and sales trends. Your sales and product information are stored in several different systems: a divisional sales system running on a UNIX server and a corporate sales system running on an IBM mainframe. You would like to create a single standard format that consolidates these data from both systems. The following format has been proposed.

PRODUCT_ID	PRODUCT_DESCRIPTION	COST_PER_UNIT	UNITS_SOLD	SALES_REGION	DIVISION	CUSTOMER_ID

The following are sample files from the two systems that would supply the data for the data warehouse:

CORPORATE SALES SYSTEM

PRODUCT_ID	PRODUCT_DESCRIPTION	UNIT_COST	UNITS_SOLD	SALES_TERRITORY	DIVISION
60231	Bearing, 4"	5.28	900,245	Northeast	Parts
85773	SS assembly unit	12.45	992,111	Midwest	Parts

MECHANICAL PARTS DIVISION SALES SYSTEM

PROD_NO	PRODUCT_DESCRIPTION	COST_PER_UNIT	UNITS_SOLD	SALES_REGION	CUSTOMER_ID
60231	4" Steel bearing	5.28	900,245	N.E.	Anderson
85773	SS assembly unit	12.45	992,111	M.W.	Kelly Industries

- What business problems are created by not having these data in a single standard format?

- How easy would it be to create a database with a single standard format that could store the data from both systems? Identify the problems that would have to be addressed.

- Should the problems be solved by database specialists or general business managers? Explain.

- Who should have the authority to finalize a single company-wide format for this information in the data warehouse?

Achieving Operational Excellence: Building a Relational Database for Inventory Management

Software skills: Database design, querying and reporting
Business skills: Inventory management

Businesses today depend on databases to provide reliable information about items in inventory, items that need restocking, and inventory costs. In this exercise, you'll use database software to design a database for managing inventory for a small business.

Sylvester's Bike Shop, located in San Francisco, California, sells road, mountain, hybrid, leisure, and children's bicycles. Currently, Sylvester's purchases bikes from three suppliers but plans to add new suppliers in the near future. This rapidly growing business needs a database system to manage this information.

Initially, the database should house information about suppliers and products. The database will contain two tables: a supplier table and a product table. The reorder level refers to the number of items in inventory that triggers a decision to order more items to prevent a stockout. (In other words, if the number of units of a particular item in inventory falls below the reorder level, the item should be reordered.) The user should be able to perform several queries and produce several managerial reports based on the data contained in the two tables.

Using the information found in the tables on the Laudon Web site for Chapter 6, build a simple relational database for Sylvester's. Once you have built the database, perform the following activities:

- Prepare a report that identifies the five most expensive bicycles. The report should list the bicycles in descending order from most expensive to least expensive, the quantity on hand for each, and the markup percentage for each.

- Prepare a report that lists each supplier, its products, the quantities on hand, and associated reorder levels. The report should be sorted alphabetically by supplier. Within each supplier category, the products should be sorted alphabetically.

- Prepare a report listing only the bicycles that are low in stock and need to be reordered. The report should provide supplier information for the items identified.

- Write a brief description of how the database could be enhanced to further improve management of the business. What tables or fields should be added? What additional reports would be useful?

Improving Decision Making: Searching Online Databases for Overseas Business Resources

Software skills: Online databases
Business skills: Researching services for overseas operations

Internet users have access to many thousands of Web-enabled databases with information on services and products in faraway locations. This project develops skills in searching these online databases.

Your company is located in Greensboro, North Carolina, and manufactures office furniture of various types. You have recently acquired several new customers in Australia, and a study you commissioned indicates that, with a presence there, you could greatly increase your sales. Moreover, your study indicates that you could do even better if you actually manufactured many of your products locally (in Australia). First, you need to set up an office in Melbourne to establish a presence, and then you need to begin importing from the United States. You then can plan to start producing locally.

You will soon be traveling to the area to make plans to actually set up an office, and you want to meet with organizations that can help you with your operation. You will need to engage people or organizations that offer many services necessary for you to open your office, including lawyers, accountants, import-export experts, telecommunications equipment and support, and even trainers who can help you to prepare your future employees to work for you. Start by searching for U.S. Department of Commerce advice on doing business in Australia. Then try the following online databases to locate companies that you would like to meet with during your coming trip: Australian Business Register (abr.business.gov.au/), Australia Trade Now (australiatradenow.com/), and the Nationwide Business Directory of Australia (www.nationwide.com.au). If necessary, you could also try search engines such as Yahoo! and Google. Then perform the following activities:

- List the companies you would contact to interview on your trip to determine whether they can help you with these and any other functions you think vital to establishing your office.

- Rate the databases you used for accuracy of name, completeness, ease of use, and general helpfulness.

- What does this exercise tell you about the design of databases?

LEARNING TRACK MODULES

The following Learning Tracks provide content relevant to topics covered in this chapter:

1. Database Design, Normalization, and Entity-Relationship Diagramming
2. Introduction to SQL
3. Hierarchical and Network Data Models

Review Summary

1. **What are the problems of managing data resources in a traditional file environment and how are they solved by a database management system?**

    Traditional file management techniques make it difficult for organizations to keep track of all of the pieces of data they use in a systematic way and to organize these data so that they can be easily accessed. Different functional areas and groups were allowed to develop their own files independently. Over time, this traditional file management environment creates problems such as data redundancy and inconsistency, program-data dependence, inflexibility, poor security, and lack of data sharing and availability. A database management system (DBMS) solves these problems with software that permits centralization of data and data management so that businesses have a single consistent source for all their data needs. Using a DBMS minimizes redundant and inconsistent files.

2. **What are the major capabilities of DBMS and why is a relational DBMS so powerful?**

    The principal capabilities of a DBMS includes a data definition capability, a data dictionary capability, and a data manipulation language. The data definition capability specifies the structure and content of the database. The data dictionary is an automated or manual file that stores information about the data in the database, including names, definitions, formats, and descriptions of data elements. The data manipulation language, such as SQL, is a specialized language for accessing and manipulating the data in the database.

    The relational database is the primary method for organizing and maintaining data today in information system because it is so flexible and accessible. It organizes data in two-dimensional tables called relations with rows and columns. Each table contains data about an entity and its attributes. Each row represents a record and each column represents an attribute or field. Each table also contains a key field to uniquely identify each record for retrieval or manipulation. Relational database tables can be combined easily to deliver data required by users, provided that any two tables share a common data element.

3. **What are some important database design principles?**

    Designing a database requires both a logical design and a physical design. The logical design models the database from a business perspective. The organization's data model should reflect its key business processes and decision-making requirements. The process of creating small, stable, flexible, and adaptive data structures from complex groups of data when designing a relational database is termed normalization. A well-designed relational database will not have many-to-many relationships, and all attributes for a specific entity will only apply to that entity. It will try to enforce referential integrity rules to ensure that relationships between coupled tables remain consistent. An entity-relationship diagram graphically depicts the relationship between entities (tables) in a relational database. Database design also considers whether a complete database or portions of the database can be distributed to more than one location to increase responsiveness and reduce vulnerability and costs. There are two major types of distributed databases: replicated databases and partitioned databases.

4. **What are the principal tools and technologies for accessing information from databases to improve business performance and decision making?**

    Powerful tools are available to analyze and access the information in databases. A data warehouse consolidates current and historical data from many different operational systems in a central database designed for reporting and analysis. Data warehouses support multidimensional data analysis, also known as online analytical processing (OLAP). OLAP represents relationships among data as a multidimensional structure, which can be visualized as cubes of data and cubes within cubes of data, enabling more sophisticated data analysis. Data mining analyzes large pools of data, including the contents of data warehouses, to find patterns and rules that can be used to predict future behavior and guide decision making. Text mining tools help businesses analyze large unstructured data sets consisting of text.Web mining tools focus on analysis of useful patterns and information from the World Wide Web, examining the structure of Web sites and activities of Web site users as well as the contents of Web pages. Conventional databases can be linked via middleware to the Web or a Web interface to facilitate user access to an organization's internal data.

5. *Why are information policy, data administration, and data quality assurance essential for managing the firm's data resources?*

Developing a database environment requires policies and procedures for managing organizational data as well as a good data model and database technology. A formal information policy governs the maintenance, distribution, and use of information in the organization. In large corporations, a formal data administration function is responsible for information policy, as well as for data planning, data dictionary development, and monitoring data usage in the firm.

Data that are inaccurate, incomplete, or inconsistent create serious operational and financial problems for businesses because they may create inaccuracies in product pricing, customer accounts, and inventory data, and lead to inaccurate decisions about the actions that should be taken by the firm. Firms must take special steps to make sure they have a high level of data quality. These include using enterprise-wide data standards, databases designed to minimize inconsistent and redundant data, data quality audits, and data cleansing software.

Key Terms

Attribute, 238

Business intelligence, 254

Data administration, 261

Data cleansing, 262

Data definition, 255

Data dictionary, 245

Data governance, 261

Data inconsistency, 239

Data manipulation language, 245

Data mart, 253

Data mining, 256

Data quality audit, 262

Data redundancy, 239

Data warehouse, 251

Database, 240

Database (rigorous definition), 240

Database administration, 261

Database management system (DBMS), 240

Database server, 258

Distributed database, 249

Entity, 238

Entity-relationship diagram, 248

Field, 238

File, 238

Foreign key, 243

Information policy, 259

Key field, 242

Normalization, 247

Object-oriented DBMS, 243

Object-relational DBMS, 243

Online analytical processing (OLAP), 254

Predictive analysis, 257

Primary key, 242

Program-data dependence, 239

Record, 242

Referential integrity, 248

Relational DBMS, 241

Structured Query Language (SQL), 245

Text mining, 257

Tuple, 242

Web mining, 257

Review Questions

1. What are the problems of managing data resources in a traditional file environment and how are they solved by a database management system?

- List and describe each of the components in the data hierarchy.

- Define and explain the significance of entities, attributes, and key fields.

- List and describe the problems of the traditional file environment.

- Define a database and a database management system and describe how it solves the problems of a traditional file environment.

2. What are the major capabilities of DBMS and why is a relational DBMS so powerful?

- Name and briefly describe the capabilities of a DBMS.

- Define a relational DBMS and explain how it organizes data.

- List and describe the three operations of a relational DBMS.

3. What are some important database design principles?

- Define and describe normalization and referential integrity and explain how they contribute to a well-designed relational database.

- Define a distributed database and describe the two main ways of distributing data.

4. What are the principal tools and technologies for accessing information from databases to improve business performance and decision making?

- Define a data warehouse, explaining how it works and how it benefits organizations.

- Define business intelligence and explain how it is related to database technology.

- Describe the capabilities of online analytical processing (OLAP).

- Define data mining, describing how it differs from OLAP and the types of information it provides.

- Explain how text mining and Web mining differ from conventional data mining.

- Describe how users can access information from a company's internal databases through the Web.

5. Why are information policy, data administration, and data quality assurance essential for managing the firm's data resources?

- Describe the roles of information policy and data administration in information management.

- Explain why data quality audits and data cleansing are essential.

Discussion Questions

1. It has been said that you do not need database management software to create a database environment. Discuss.

2. To what extent should end users be involved in the selection of a database management system and database design?

Video Cases

You will find video cases illustrating some of the concepts in this chapter on the Laudon Web site along with questions to help you analyze the cases.

Collaboration and Teamwork: Identifying Entities and Attributes in an Online Database

With your team of three or four students, select an online database to explore, such as AOL Music, iGo.com, or the Internet Movie Database. Explore one of these Web sites to see what information it provides. Then list the entities and attributes that the company running the Web site must keep track of in its databases. Diagram the relationship between the entities you have identified. If possible, use Google Sites to post links to Web pages, team communication announcements, and work assignments; to brainstorm; and to work collaboratively on project documents. Try to use Google Docs to develop a presentation of your findings for the class.

Trouble with the Terrorist Watch List Database
CASE STUDY

In the aftermath of the 9-11 attacks, both critics and defenders of the information systems employed by the U.S. intelligence community united to help analyze where things went wrong and how to prevent future terrorist incidents. The FBI's Terrorist Screening Center, or TSC, was established to organize and standardize information about suspected terrorists between multiple government agencies into a single list to enhance communication between agencies. A database of suspected terrorists known as the terrorist watch list was born from these efforts in 2003 in response to criticisms that multiple agencies were maintaining separate lists and that these agencies lacked a consistent process to share relevant information concerning the individuals on each agency's list.

Records in the TSC database contain sensitive but unclassified information on terrorist identities, such as name and date of birth, that can be shared with other screening agencies. Classified information about the people in the watch list is maintained in other law enforcement and intelligence agency databases. Records for the watch list database are provided by two sources: the National Counterterrorism Center (NCTC) managed by the Office of the Director of National Intelligence provides identifying information on individuals with ties to international terrorism. The FBI provides identifying information on individuals with ties to purely domestic terrorism. These agencies collect and maintain terrorist information and nominate individuals for inclusion in the TSC's consolidated watch list. They are required to follow strict procedures established by the head of the agency concerned and approved by the U.S. Attorney General. TSC staff must review each record submitted before it is added to the database. An individual will remain on the watch list until the respective department or agency that nominated that person to the list determines that the person should be removed from the list and deleted from its database.

The watch list database is updated daily with new nominations, modifications to existing records, and deletions. The list has grown to over 750,000 records since its creation and is continuing to grow at a rate of 200,000 records each year since 2004. Information on the list is distributed to a wide range of govern-ment agency systems for use in efforts to deter or detect the movements of known or suspected terrorists, including the FBI, CIA, National Security Agency (NSA), Transportation Security Administration (TSA), U.S. Department of Homeland Security, State Department, U.S. Customs and Border Protection, Secret Service, U.S. Marshals Service, and the White House, among others. Airlines use data supplied by the TSA system in their NoFly and Selectee lists for prescreening passengers, while the U.S. Customs and Border Protection system uses the watch list data to help screen travelers entering the United States. The State Department system screens applicants for visas to enter the United States and U.S. residents applying for passports, while state and local law enforcement agencies use the FBI system to help with arrests, detentions, and other criminal justice activities.

Each of these agencies receives the subset of data in the watch list that pertains to its specific mission. For example, records on U.S. citizens and lawful permanent residents are not exported to the State Department system for screening visa applicants because these individuals would not apply for a U.S. visa. All of these databases require certain minimum biographic or identifying data to accept records from the consolidated watch list.

When an individual makes an airline reservation, arrives at a U.S. port of entry, applies for a U.S. visa, or is stopped by state or local police within the United States, the frontline screening agency or airline conducts a name-based search of the individual against the records in the terrorist watch list database. When the computerized name-matching system generates a "hit" (a potential name match) against a watch list record, the airline or agency will review each potential match. The agency or airline is supposed to resolve any obvious mismatches that crop up. Matches that are clearly positive or exact matches that are inconclusive (uncertain or difficult to verify) are referred to the applicable screening agency's intelligence or operations center and to the TSC for closer examination. In turn, TSC checks its databases and other sources, including classified databases maintained by the NCTC and FBI, to confirm whether the individual is a positive, negative, or inconclusive match to the watch list record. TSC creates a daily report summarizing all positive matches to the watch list and distributes them to numerous federal agencies.

While the unification of various terrorism watch lists has been a positive step towards streamlining the process of locating and apprehending terrorists, the project has been a slow and painstaking one, requiring the integration of at least 12 different databases. Two years after the process of integration took place, 10 of the 12 databases had been processed. The remaining two databases (the U.S. Immigration and Customs Enforcement's Automatic Biometric Identification System and the FBI's Integrated Fingerprint Identification System) are both fingerprint databases, and not technically watch lists. There is still more work to be done to optimize the list's usefulness.

The TSC's list has introduced new issues and concerns regarding the adequacy of the information systems involved in the maintenance and usage of terrorism-related data. Reports from both the Government Accountability Office (GAO) and the Office of the Inspector General confirm that the list contains inaccuracies and that policies for nomination and removal from the lists are not uniform between governmental departments.

There has also been public outcry resulting from the size of the list and well-publicized incidents of obvious non-terrorists finding that they are included on the list.

Information about the process for inclusion on the list must necessarily be carefully protected if the list is to be effective against terrorists; if the algorithms behind the list were public knowledge, terrorists could more easily avoid detection, defeating the list's purpose. On the other hand, for innocent people who are unnecessarily inconvenienced, the inability to ascertain how they came to be on the list is upsetting. Given the list's large size and constant growth rate, one major criticism is that the criteria for inclusion on the list may be too minimal.

While the specific criteria for inclusion on the list are not public knowledge, government agencies populate their watch lists by performing wide sweeps of information gathered on travelers, using many misspellings and alternate variations of the names of suspected terrorists. This often leads to the inclusion of people that do not belong on watch lists, known as 'false positives'. It also results in some people being listed multiple times under different spellings of their names, so the 750,000 'records' do not correspond to 750,000 different individuals. Reports indicate that certain individuals may have as many

as 50 different records on the list due to various aliases and alternate spellings of their names. From December 2003 through May 2007, individuals were positively matched to watch lists 53,000 times. Many individuals were matched multiple times.

While these selection criteria may be effective for tracking as many potential terrorists as possible, they also lead to many more erroneous entries on the list than if the process required more finely-tuned information to add new entries. Notable examples of 'false positives' include U.S. Marine Daniel Brown, who was stopped at the airport for additional screening after an 8-month tour in Iraq; senator Ted Kennedy, who has been repeatedly delayed in the past because his name resembles an alias once used by a suspected terrorist; and John Anderson, a 6-year old boy who was stopped at an airport for additional investigation despite his young age. Like Kennedy, Anderson may have been added because his name is the same or similar to a different suspected terrorist.

These incidents call attention to the quality and accuracy of the data in the TSC consolidated watch list. In June 2005, a report by the Department of Justice (DOJ) Office of the Inspector General found inconsistent record counts, duplicate records, and records that lacked data fields or had unclear sources for their data. Although TSC subsequently enhanced its efforts to identify and correct incomplete or inaccurate watch list records, the Inspector General noted in September 2007 that TSC management of the watch list still showed some weaknesses.

Critics of the list question whether or not a list that will soon grow to over a million entries could have any real usefulness or significance in apprehending terrorists. The American Civil Liberties Union (ACLU) has been a vocal critic of the size of the list, claiming that it harasses and needlessly violates the privacy of thousands of people in an effort to monitor the movements of a decidedly smaller group of suspects. Senator Joe Lieberman, the Chairman of the Homeland Security Committee, said of the list that "serious hurdles remain if it is to be as effective as we need it to be. Some of the concerns stem from its rapid growth, which could call into question the quality of the list itself."

Given the option between a list that tracks every potential terrorist at the cost of unnecessarily tracking some innocents, and a list that fails to track many terrorists in an effort to avoid tracking innocents, many would choose the list that tracked every terrorist despite the drawbacks. But to make matters worse for those already inconvenienced by wrongful inclusion on the list, there is currently no simple and quick redress process for innocents that hope to remove themselves from it.

The number of requests for removal from the watch list continues to mount, with over 24,000 requests recorded (about 2,000 each month) and only 54% of them resolved. The average time to process a request in 2008 is 40 days, which, although a mild improvement from 44 days in November 2007, is not fast enough to keep pace with the number of requests for removal coming in. As a result, law-abiding travelers that inexplicably find themselves on the watch list are left with no easy way to remove themselves from it.

In February 2007, the Department of Homeland Security instituted its Traveler Redress Inquiry Program (TRIP) to help people that have been erroneously added to terrorist watch lists remove themselves and avoid extra screening and questioning. John Anderson's mother claimed that despite her best efforts, she was unable to remove her son from the watch lists. Senator Kennedy reportedly was only able to remove himself from the list by personally bringing up the matter to Tom Ridge, then the Director of the Department of Homeland Security.

Security officials say that mistakes such as the one that led to Anderson and Kennedy's inclusion on no-fly and consolidated watch lists occur due to the matching of imperfect data in airline reservation systems with imperfect data on the watch lists. Many airlines don't include gender, middle name, or date of birth in their reservations records, which increases the likelihood of false matches. While government agencies have been able to synchronize their data into a single list, there is still more work to be done to integrate that list with those maintained by airlines, individual states, and other localities using more information to differentiate individuals. The TSA is continuing to update their screening process so that the government, not individual airlines, is responsible for matching travelers to watch lists.

Privacy is yet another concern surrounding the watch list. One way to improve screening and help reduce the number of people erroneously marked for additional investigation would be to use a more sophisticated system involving more personal data about individuals on the list. The TSA is developing just such a system, called "Secure Flight," but it has been continually delayed due to privacy concerns regarding the sensitivity and safety of the data it would collect. Other similar surveillance

programs and watch lists, such as the NSA's attempts to gather information about suspected terrorists, have drawn criticism for potential privacy violations.

Additionally, the watch list has drawn criticism because of its potential to promote racial profiling and discrimination. Some allege that they were included by virtue of their race and ethnic descent, such as David Fathi, an attorney for the ACLU of Iranian descent, and Asif Iqbal, a U.S. citizen of Pakistani decent with the same name as a Guantanamo detainee. Outspoken critics of U.S. foreign policy, such as some elected officials and university professors, have also found themselves on the list.

A report issued in March 2008 by DOJ Inspector General Glenn A. Fine and reports from the GAO also indicated that the FBI lacked standard and consistent procedures for nominating individuals to the list, performing modifications to information, and relaying those changes to other governmental offices. The FBI sometimes delayed updating the list with new information or removing people from the list who were no longer deemed a threat. Nominations from FBI field offices were sometimes inaccurate or incomplete. FBI field offices submitted names of people who were not subjects of terrorism investigations directly to the NCTC, bypassing the required headquarters review that could catch errors. FBI officials claim that the bureau has made improvements, and now requires field office supervisors to review watch-list nominations for accuracy and completeness.

Some non-FBI offices, including the Drug Enforcement Administration; the Bureau of Alcohol, Tobacco, Firearms, and Explosives (ATF); and others reported that they did not believe themselves to be a part of the watch list information process, or that they disagreed with the FBI over what constituted terrorist activity. Many DOJ offices acquire terrorism-related information that would help the FBI in populating the watch list, but share that information in an informal way and sometimes not at all. Improved coordination between the FBI and other intelligence agencies would go a long way towards improving the quality and efficacy of the terror watch list.

The TSC is taking actions to improve watch list data and procedures for managing these data. The sooner, the better—in early 2008 it was revealed that 20 known terrorists were not correctly listed on the consolidated watch list (whether these individuals were able to enter the U.S. as a result is unclear).

Sources: Bob Egelko, "Watch-list Name Confusion Causes Hardship," *San Francisco Chronicle*, March 20, 2008; Siobhan Gorman, "NSA's Domestic Spying Grows as Agency Sweeps Up Data," *The Wall Street Journal*, March 10, 2008; Ellen Nakashima, "Reports Cite Lack of Uniform Policy for Terrorist Watch List," *The Washington Post*, March 18, 2008; Scott McCartney, "When Your Name is Mud at the Airport," *The Wall Street Journal*, January 29, 2008; Audrey Hudson, "Airport Watch List Now Reviewed Often," *The Washington Times*, April 11, 2008; Mimi Hall, "15,000 Want Off the U.S. Terror Watch List", *USA Today*, November 8, 2007 and "Terror Watch List Swells to More Than 755,000," *USA Today*, October 23, 2007; "Justice Department Report Tells of Flaws in Terrorist Watch List," CNN.com, September 7, 2007; Burt Helm, "The Terror Watch List's Tangle", Businessweek.com, May 11, 2005, Paul Rosenzweig and Jeff Jonas, "Correcting False Positives: Redress and the Watch List Conundrum," The Heritage Foundation, June 17, 2005.

CASE STUDY QUESTIONS

1. What concepts in this chapter are illustrated in this case?

2. Why was the consolidated terror watch list created? What are the benefits of the list?

3. Describe some of the weaknesses of the watch list. What management, organization, and technology factors are responsible for these weaknesses?

4. If you were responsible for the management of the TSC watch list database, what steps would you take to correct some of these weaknesses?

5. Do you believe that the watch list represents a significant threat to individuals' privacy or Constitutional rights? Why or why not?

Chapter 7

Telecommunications, the Internet, and Wireless Technology

LEARNING OBJECTIVES

After reading this chapter, you will be able to answer the following questions:

1. What are the principal components of telecommunications networks and key networking technologies?

2. What are the main telecommunications transmission media and types of networks?

3. How do the Internet and Internet technology work, and how do they support communication and e-business?

4. What are the principal technologies and standards for wireless networking, communication, and Internet access?

5. Why are radio frequency identification (RFID) and wireless sensor networks valuable for business?

Interactive Sessions:

Should Network Neutrality Continue?

Monitoring Employees on Networks: Unethical or Good Business?

CHAPTER OUTLINE

VIRGIN MEGASTORES KEEPS SPINNING WITH UNIFIED COMMUNICATIONS

Have you ever been in a Virgin Megastore? Inside you'll find racks and racks of CDs, DVDs, books, video games, and clothing, with videos playing on overhead screens. You can use Virgin Vault digital kiosks to preview music, videos, and games. You might also see a DJ sitting in a booth overlooking the sales floor and spinning the latest hits or tracks from undiscovered artists. Virgin Megastores are very media- and technology-intensive.

These stores are a carefully orchestrated response to an intensely competitive environment, because the company must compete with "big box" discount chains such as Wal-Mart and online music download services. The business must be able to react instantly to sales trends and operate efficiently to keep prices down. A new CD or DVD release might achieve half of its total sales within the first couple of weeks after its release. Too much or too little of a CD in stores at a specific time can translate into large losses. Although Virgin Megastores' inventory data warehouse based on Microsoft SQL Server database software provides up-to-the-minute information on sales and current stock levels, acting on a rapidly changing picture of supply and demand requires human communication.

Virgin Megastores USA has 1,400 employees in 11 retail locations throughout the United States. Its Los Angeles-based home office shares information with the retail stores via voice mail, e-mail, and audio weekly conference calls, which are used to discuss upcoming promotions and events, product inventory issues, and current market trends. People shied away from conference calling because of its costs, choosing a less expensive but also less immediate way of communicating, such as sending out a mass e-mail message. Recipients of that message might not respond right away.

To speed up interaction, Virgin Megastores chose unified communications technology that integrated its voice mail, e-mail, conference calling, and instant messaging into a single solution that would be a natural and seamless way of working. In the fall of 2007 it deployed Microsoft's Office Communication Server, Office Communicator, and RoundTable conferencing and collaboration tools. The technology has presence awareness capabilities that display other people's availability and status (such as whether the person is already using the phone, in a Web conference, or working remotely) within the Microsoft productivity software they use in the course of their work.

Users can see the people they work with in one window of Office Communicator and switch from one type of messaging to another as naturally and easy as picking up a telephone.

Calls integrating audio and video are helping employees resolve issues more quickly. The company is saving $50,000 annually in conferencing costs, and now has in-house video and Web conferencing as well as audio conferencing.

Sources: Lauren McKay, "All Talk," *Customer Relationship Management Magazine*, June 2008; John Edwards, "How to Get the Most from Unified Communications," *CIO*, February 8, 2008; and "Virgin Megastores USA Turns Up the Volume with Unified Communications," www.microsoft.com, accessed June 19, 2008.

Virgin Megastores USA's experience illustrates some of the powerful new capabilities—and opportunities—provided by contemporary networking technology. The company used unified communications technology to provide managers and employees with integrated voice, e-mail, and conferencing capabilities, with the ability to switch seamlessly from one type of messaging to another. Using the technology accelerated information sharing and decision making, enabling the company to manage its inventory more precisely.

The chapter-opening diagram calls attention to important points raised by this case and this chapter. The retail music industry is exceptionally competitive and time-sensitive. To stay in the game, Virgn Megastores must be able to respond very rapidly to sales trends. The company's outdated networking and voice technology made it difficult to do this. Management decided that new technology could provide a solution and selected a new unified communications technology platform. Switching to unified communications technology saved time and facilitated information sharing between managers and employees and between retail outlets and corporate headquarters. With more fresh information, the company is able to respond more rapidly to sales trends and adjust inventory accordingly. These improvements save time and reduce inventory costs. Virgin Megastores had to make some changes in employee job functions and work flow to take advantage of the new technology.

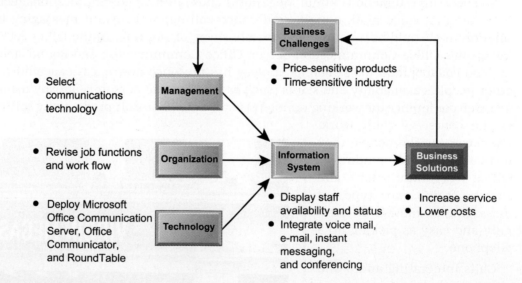

7.1   TELECOMMUNICATIONS AND NETWORKING IN TODAY'S BUSINESS WORLD

If you run or work in a business, you can't do without networks. You need to communicate rapidly with your customers, suppliers, and employees. Until about 1990, you would have used the postal system or telephone system with voice or fax for business communication. Today, however, you and your employees use computers and e-mail, the Internet, cell phones, and mobile computers connected to wireless networks for this purpose. Networking and the Internet are now nearly synonymous with doing business.

NETWORKING AND COMMUNICATION TRENDS

Firms in the past used two fundamentally different types of networks: telephone networks and computer networks. Telephone networks historically handled voice communication, and computer networks handled data traffic. Telephone networks were built by telephone companies throughout the twentieth century using voice transmission technologies (hardware and software), and these companies almost always operated as regulated monopolies throughout the world. Computer networks were originally built by computer companies seeking to transmit data between computers in different locations.

Thanks to continuing telecommunications deregulation and information technology innovation, telephone and computer networks are slowly converging into a single digital network using shared Internet-based standards and equipment. Telecommunications providers, such as AT&T and Verizon, today offer data transmission, Internet access, wireless telephone service, and television programming as well as voice service. Cable companies, such as Cablevision and Comcast, now offer voice service and Internet access. Computer networks have expanded to include Internet telephone and limited video services. Increasingly, all of these voice, video, and data communications are based on Internet technology.

Both voice and data communication networks have also become more powerful (faster), more portable (smaller and mobile), and less expensive. For instance, the typical Internet connection speed in 2000 was 56 kilobits per second, but today more than 60 percent of U.S. Internet users have high-speed **broadband** connections provided by telephone and cable TV companies running at one million bits per second. The cost for this service has fallen exponentially, from 25 cents per kilobit in 2000, to less than 1 cent today.

Increasingly, voice and data communication as well as Internet access are taking place over broadband wireless platforms, such as cell phones, handheld digital devices, and PCs in wireless networks. In fact, mobile wireless broadband Internet access (2.5G and 3G cellular, which we describe in Section 7.4) was the fastest-growing form of Internet access in 2008, growing at a 96-percent compound annual growth rate. Fixed wireless broadband (Wi-Fi) is growing at a 28-percent compound annual growth rate, the second fastest growing form of Internet access.

WHAT IS A COMPUTER NETWORK?

If you had to connect the computers for two or more employees together in the same office, you would need a computer network. Exactly what is a network? In its simplest form, a network consists of two or more connected computers.

Figure 7-1 illustrates the major hardware, software, and transmission components used in a simple network: a client computer and a dedicated server computer, network interfaces, a connection medium, network operating system software, and either a hub or a switch.

Each computer on the network contains a network interface device called a **network interface card (NIC)**. Most personal computers today have this card built into the motherboard. The connection medium for linking network components can be a telephone wire, coaxial cable, or radio signal in the case of cell phone and wireless local-area networks (Wi-Fi networks).

The **network operating system (NOS)** routes and manages communications on the network and coordinates network resources. It can reside on every computer in the network, or it can reside primarily on a dedicated server computer for all the applications on the network. A server computer is a computer on a network that performs important network functions for client computers, such as serving up Web pages, storing data, and storing the network operating system (and hence controlling the network). Server software, such as Microsoft Windows Server, Linux, and Novell NetWare, are the most widely used network operating systems.

Most networks also contain a switch or a hub acting as a connection point between the computers. **Hubs** are very simple devices that connect network components, sending a packet of data to all other connected devices. A **switch** has more intelligence than a hub and can filter and forward data to a specified destination on the network.

What if you want to communicate with another network, such as the Internet? You would need a router. A **router** is a communications processor

FIGURE 7-1   COMPONENTS OF A SIMPLE COMPUTER NETWORK

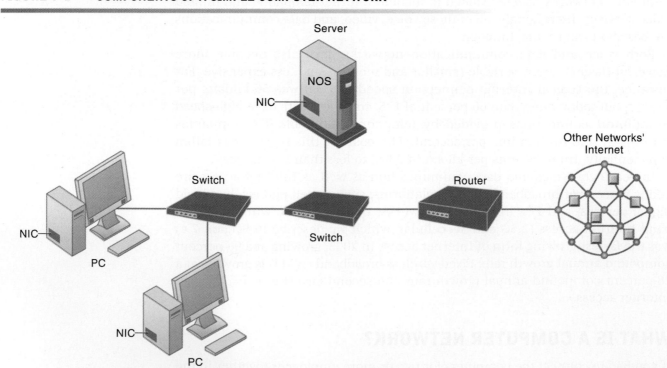

Illustrated here is a very simple computer network, consisting of computers, a network operating system residing on a dedicated server computer, cable (wiring) connecting the devices, network interface cards (NIC), switches, and a router.

used to route packets of data through different networks, ensuring that the data sent gets to the correct address.

Networks in Large Companies

The network we've just described might be suitable for a small business. But what about large companies with many different locations and thousands of employees? As a firm grows, and collects hundreds of small local-area networks (LANs), these networks can be tied together into a corporate-wide networking infrastructure. The network infrastructure for a large corporation consists of a large number of these small local-area networks linked to other local-area networks and to firmwide corporate networks. A number of powerful servers support a corporate Web site, a corporate intranet, and perhaps an extranet. Some of these servers link to other large computers supporting backend systems.

Figure 7-2 provides an illustration of these more complex, larger scale corporate-wide networks. Here you can see that the corporate network infrastructure supports a mobile sales force using cell phones; mobile employees linking to the company Web site, or internal company networks using mobile wireless local-area networks (Wi-Fi networks); and a videoconferencing system to support managers across the world. In addition to these computer networks, the firm's infrastructure usually includes a separate telephone network that handles most voice data. Many firms are dispensing with their traditional telephone networks and using Internet telephones that run on their existing data networks (described later).

FIGURE 7-2   CORPORATE NETWORK INFRASTRUCTURE

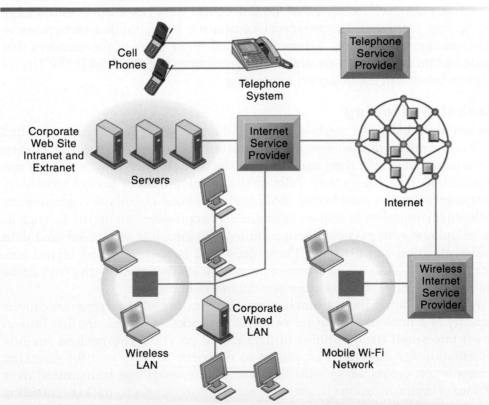

Today's corporate network infrastructure is a collection of many different networks from the public switched telephone network; to the Internet; to corporate local-area networks linking workgroups, departments, or office floors.

As you can see from this figure, a large corporate network infrastructure uses a wide variety of technologies—everything from ordinary telephone service and corporate data networks to Internet service, wireless Internet, and wireless cell phones. One of the major problems facing corporations today is how to integrate all the different communication networks and channels into a coherent system that enables information to flow from one part of the corporation to another, from one system to another. As more and more communication networks become digital, and based on Internet technologies, it will become easier to integrate them.

KEY DIGITAL NETWORKING TECHNOLOGIES

Contemporary digital networks and the Internet are based on three key technologies: client/server computing, the use of packet switching, and the development of widely used communications standards (the most important of which is Transmission Control Protocol/Internet Protocol, or TCP/IP) for linking disparate networks and computers.

Client/Server Computing

We introduced client/server computing in Chapter 5. Client/server computing is a distributed computing model in which some of the processing power is located within small, inexpensive client computers, and resides literally on desktops, laptops, or in handheld devices. These powerful clients are linked to one another through a network that is controlled by a network server computer. The server sets the rules of communication for the network and provides every client with an address so others can find it on the network.

Client/server computing has largely replaced centralized mainframe computing in which nearly all of the processing takes place on a central large mainframe computer. Client/server computing has extended computing to departments, workgroups, factory floors, and other parts of the business that could not be served by a centralized architecture. The Internet is the largest implementation of client/server computing.

Packet Switching

Packet switching is a method of slicing digital messages into parcels called packets, sending the packets along different communication paths as they become available, and then reassembling the packets once they arrive at their destinations (see Figure 7-3). Prior to the development of packet switching, computer networks used leased, dedicated telephone circuits to communicate with other computers in remote locations. In circuit-switched networks, such as the telephone system, a complete point-to-point circuit is assembled, and then communication can proceed. These dedicated circuit-switching techniques were expensive and wasted available communications capacity—the circuit was maintained regardless of whether any data were being sent.

Packet switching makes much more efficient use of the communications capacity of a network. In packet-switched networks, messages are first broken down into small fixed bundles of data called packets. The packets include information for directing the packet to the right address and for checking transmission errors along with the data. The packets are transmitted over various communications channels using routers, each packet traveling independently. Packets of data originating at one source will be routed through many different paths and networks before being reassembled into the original message when they reach their destinations.

FIGURE 7-3 **PACKED-SWITCHED NETWORKS AND PACKET COMMUNICATIONS**

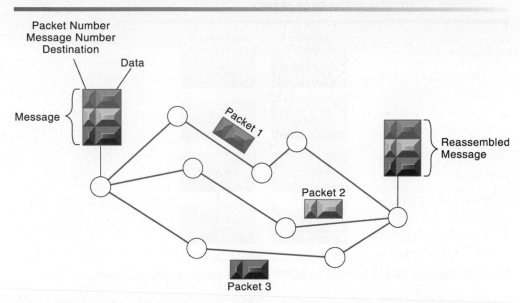

Data are grouped into small packets, which are transmitted independently over various communications channels and reassembled at their final destination.

TCP/IP and Connectivity

In a typical telecommunications network, diverse hardware and software components need to work together to transmit information. Different components in a network communicate with each other only by adhering to a common set of rules called protocols. A **protocol** is a set of rules and procedures governing transmission of information between two points in a network.

In the past, many diverse proprietary and incompatible protocols often forced business firms to purchase computing and communications equipment from a single vendor. But today corporate networks are increasingly using a single, common, worldwide standard called **Transmission Control Protocol/ Internet Protocol (TCP/IP)**. TCP/IP was developed during the early 1970s to support U.S. Department of Defense Advanced Research Projects Agency (DARPA) efforts to help scientists transmit data among different types of computers over long distances.

TCP/IP uses a suite of protocols, the main ones being TCP and IP. *TCP* refers to the Transmission Control Protocol (TCP), which handles the movement of data between computers. TCP establishes a connection between the computers, sequences the transfer of packets, and acknowledges the packets sent. *IP* refers to the Internet Protocol (IP), which is responsible for the delivery of packets and includes the disassembling and reassembling of packets during transmission. Figure 7-4 illustrates the four-layered Department of Defense reference model for TCP/IP.

1. Application layer. The application layer enables client application programs to access the other layers and defines the protocols that applications use to exchange data. One of these application protocols is the Hypertext Transfer Protocol (HTTP), which is used to transfer Web page files.

2. Transport layer. The transport layer is responsible for providing the application layer with communication and packet services. This layer includes TCP and other protocols.

FIGURE 7-4 **THE TRANSMISSION CONTROL PROTOCOL/INTERNET PROTOCOL (TCP/IP) REFERENCE MODEL**

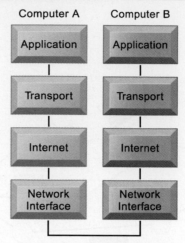

This figure illustrates the four layers of the TCP/IP reference model for communications.

3. Internet layer. The Internet layer is responsible for addressing, routing, and packaging data packets called IP datagrams. The Internet Protocol is one of the protocols used in this layer.

4. Network interface layer. At the bottom of the reference model, the network interface layer is responsible for placing packets on and receiving them from the network medium, which could be any networking technology.

Two computers using TCP/IP are able to communicate even if they are based on different hardware and software platforms. Data sent from one computer to the other passes downward through all four layers, starting with the sending computer's application layer and passing through the network interface layer. After the data reach the recipient host computer, they travel up the layers and are reassembled into a format the receiving computer can use. If the receiving computer finds a damaged packet, it asks the sending computer to retransmit it. This process is reversed when the receiving computer responds.

7.2 COMMUNICATIONS NETWORKS

Let's look more closely at alternative networking technologies available to businesses.

SIGNALS: DIGITAL VS. ANALOG

There are two ways to communicate a message in a network: either an analog signal or a digital signal. An *analog signal* is represented by a continuous waveform that passes through a communications medium and has been used for voice communication. The most common analog devices are the telephone handset, the speaker on your computer, or your iPod earphone, all of which create analog wave forms that your ear can hear.

A *digital signal* is a discrete, binary waveform, rather than a continuous waveform. Digital signals communicate information as strings of two discrete states: one bit and zero bits, which are represented as on—off electrical pulses.

FIGURE 7-5   FUNCTIONS OF THE MODEM

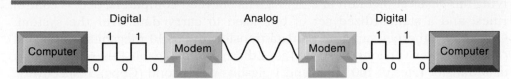

A modem is a device that translates digital signals from a computer into analog form so that they can be transmitted over analog telephone lines. The modem also translates analog signals back into digital form for the receiving computer.

Computers use digital signals, so if you want to use the analog telephone system to send digital data, you'll need a device called a **modem** to translate digital signals into analog form (see Figure 7-5). *Modem* stands for modulator-demodulator.

TYPES OF NETWORKS

There are many different kinds of networks and ways of classifying them. One way of looking at networks is in terms of their geographic scope (see Table 7-1).

Local-Area Networks

If you work in a business that uses networking, you are probably connecting to other employees and groups via a local-area network. A **local-area network (LAN)** is designed to connect personal computers and other digital devices within a half-mile or 500-meter radius. LANs typically connect a few computers in a small office, all the computers in one building, or all the computers in several buildings in close proximity. LANs can link to long-distance wide-area networks (WANs, described later in this section) and other networks around the world using the Internet.

Review Figure 7-1, which could serve as a model for a small LAN that might be used in an office. One computer is a dedicated network file server, providing users with access to shared computing resources in the network, including software programs and data files. The server determines who gets access to what and in which sequence. The router connects the LAN to other networks, which could be the Internet or another corporate network, so that the LAN can exchange information with networks external to it. The most common LAN operating systems are Windows, Linux, and Novell. Each of these network operating systems supports TCP/IP as their default networking protocol.

TABLE 7-1 TYPES OF NETWORKS

TYPE	AREA
Local-area network (LAN)	Up to 500 meters (half a mile); an office or floor of a building
Campus-area network (CAN)	Up to 1,000 meters (a mile); a college campus or corporate facility
Metropolitan-area network (MAN)	A city or metropolitan area
Wide-area network (WAN)	A transcontinental or global area

Ethernet is the dominant LAN standard at the physical network level, specifying the physical medium to carry signals between computers; access control rules; and a standardized set of bits used to carry data over the system. Originally, Ethernet supported a data transfer rate of 10 megabits per second (Mbps). Newer versions, such as Fast Ethernet and Gigabit Ethernet, support data transfer rates of 100 Mbps and 1 gigabits per second (Gbps), respectively, and are used in network backbones.

The LAN illustrated in Figure 7-1 uses a client/server architecture where the network operating system resides primarily on a single file server, and the server provides much of the control and resources for the network. Alternatively, LANs may use a **peer-to-peer** architecture. A peer-to-peer network treats all processors equally and is used primarily in small networks with 10 or fewer users. The various computers on the network can exchange data by direct access and can share peripheral devices without going through a separate server.

In LANs using the Windows Server family of operating systems, the peer-to-peer architecture is called the *workgroup network model* in which a small group of computers can share resources, such as files, folders, and printers, over the network without a dedicated server. The Windows *domain network model*, in contrast, uses a dedicated server to manage the computers in the network.

Larger LANs have many clients and multiple servers, with separate servers for specific services, such as storing and managing files and databases (file servers or database servers), managing printers (print servers), storing and managing e-mail (mail servers), or storing and managing Web pages (Web servers).

Sometimes LANs are described in terms of the way their components are connected together, or their **topology**. There are three major LAN topologies: star, bus, and ring (see Figure 7-6).

In a **star topology**, all devices on the network connect to a single hub. Figure 7-6 illustrates a simple star topology in which all network traffic flows through the hub. In an *extended star network*, multiple layers or hubs are organized into a hierarchy.

In a **bus topology**, one station transmits signals, which travel in both directions along a single transmission segment. All of the signals are broadcast in both directions to the entire network. All machines on the network receive the same signals, and software installed on the client's enables each client to listen for messages addressed specifically to it. The bus topology is the most common Ethernet topology.

A **ring topology** connects network components in a closed loop. Messages pass from computer to computer in only one direction around the loop, and only one station at a time may transmit. The ring topology is primarily found in older LANs using Token Ring networking software.

Metropolitan- and Wide-Area Networks

Wide-area networks (WANs) span broad geographical distances—entire regions, states, continents, or the entire globe. The most universal and powerful WAN is the Internet. Computers connect to a WAN through public networks, such as the telephone system or private cable systems, or through leased lines or satellites. A **metropolitan-area network (MAN)** is a network that spans a metropolitan area, usually a city and its major suburbs. Its geographic scope falls between a WAN and a LAN.

FIGURE 7-6   NETWORK TOPOLOGIES

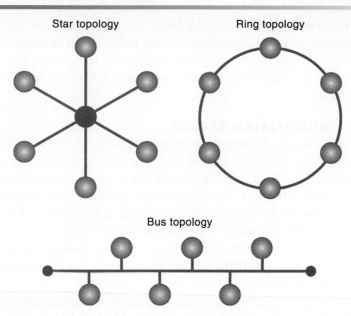

The three basic network topologies are the bus, star, and ring.

PHYSICAL TRANSMISSION MEDIA

Networks use different kinds of physical transmission media, including twisted wire, coaxial cable, fiber optics, and media for wireless transmission. Each has advantages and limitations. A wide range of speeds is possible for any given medium depending on the software and hardware configuration.

Twisted Wire

Twisted wire consists of strands of copper wire twisted in pairs and is an older type of transmission medium. Many of the telephone systems in buildings had twisted wires installed for analog communication, but they can be used for digital communication as well. Although an older physical transmission medium, the twisted wires used in today's LANs, such as CAT5, can obtain speeds up to 1 Gbps. Twisted-pair cabling is limited to a maximum recommended run of 100 meters (328 feet).

Coaxial Cable

Coaxial cable, similar to that used for cable television, consists of thickly insulated copper wire, which can transmit a larger volume of data than twisted wire. Cable was used in early LANs and is still used today for longer (more than 100 meters) runs in large buildings. Coaxial has speeds up to 1 Gbps.

Fiber Optics and Optical Networks

Fiber-optic cable consists of bound strands of clear glass fiber, each the thickness of a human hair. Data are transformed into pulses of light, which are sent through the fiber-optic cable by a laser device at rates varying from 500 kilobits to several trillion bits per second in experimental settings. Fiber-optic cable is considerably faster, lighter, and more durable than wire media, and is well suited to systems requiring transfers of large volumes of data. However, fiber-optic cable is more expensive than other physical transmission media and harder to install.

Until recently, fiber-optic cable had been used primarily for the high-speed network backbone, which handles the major traffic. Now telecommunications companies are starting to bring fiber lines into the home for new types of services, such as ultra high-speed Internet access (5 to 50 Mbps) and on-demand video.

Wireless Transmission Media

Wireless transmission is based on radio signals of various frequencies. **Microwave** systems, both terrestrial and celestial, transmit high-frequency radio signals through the atmosphere and are widely used for high-volume, long-distance, point-to-point communication. Microwave signals follow a straight line and do not bend with the curvature of the earth. Therefore, long-distance terrestrial transmission systems require that transmission stations be positioned about 37 miles apart. Long-distance transmission is also possible by using communication satellites as relay stations for microwave signals transmitted from terrestrial stations.

Communication satellites are typically used for transmission in large, geographically dispersed organizations that would be difficult to network using cabling media or terrestrial microwave. For instance, the global energy company BP p.l.c. uses satellites for real-time data transfer of oil field exploration data gathered from searches of the ocean floor. Using geosynchronous satellites, exploration ships transfer these data to central computing centers in the United States for use by researchers in Houston, Tulsa, and suburban Chicago. Figure 7-7 illustrates how this system works.

Cellular systems use radio waves to communicate with radio antennas (towers) placed within adjacent geographic areas called cells. Communications transmitted from a **cell phone** to a local cell pass from antenna to antenna—cell to cell—until they reach their final destination.

FIGURE 7-7 **BP'S SATELLITE TRANSMISSION SYSTEM**

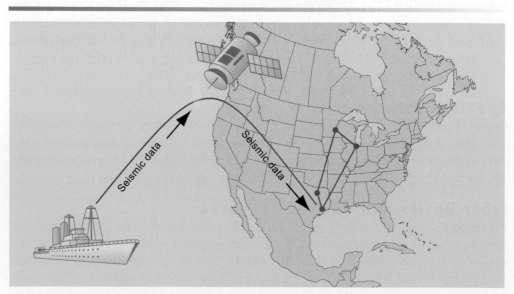

Communication satellites help BP transfer seismic data between oil exploration ships and research centers in the United States.

Wireless networks are supplanting traditional wired networks for many applications and creating new applications, services, and business models. In Section 7.4 we provide a detailed description of the applications and technology standards driving the "wireless revolution."

Transmission Speed

The total amount of digital information that can be transmitted through any telecommunications medium is measured in bits per second (bps). One signal change, or cycle, is required to transmit one or several bits; therefore, the transmission capacity of each type of telecommunications medium is a function of its frequency. The number of cycles per second that can be sent through that medium is measured in **hertz**—one hertz is equal to one cycle of the medium.

The range of frequencies that can be accommodated on a particular telecommunications channel is called its **bandwidth**. The bandwidth is the difference between the highest and lowest frequencies that can be accommodated on a single channel. The greater the range of frequencies, the greater the bandwidth and the greater the channel's transmission capacity. Table 7-2 compares the transmission speeds of the major types of media.

7.3 THE GLOBAL INTERNET

We all use the Internet, and many of us can't do without it. It's become an indispensable personal and business tool. But what exactly is the Internet? How does it work, and what does Internet technology have to offer for business? Let's look at the most important Internet features.

WHAT IS THE INTERNET?

The Internet has become the world's most extensive, public communication system that now rivals the global telephone system in reach and range. It's also the world's largest implementation of client/server computing and internetworking, linking millions of individual networks all over the world. This gigantic network of networks began in the early 1970s as a U.S. Department of Defense network to link scientists and university professors around the world.

TABLE 7-2 TYPICAL SPEEDS OF TELECOMMUNICATIONS TRANSMISSION MEDIA

MEDIUM	SPEED
Twisted wire	Up to 1 Gbps
Microwave	Up to 600 + Mbps
Satellite	Up to 600 + Mbps
Coaxial cable	Up to 1 Gbps
Fiber-optic cable	Up to 6 + Tbps

Mbps = megabits per second
Gbps = gigabits per second
Tbps = terabits per second

Most homes and small businesses connect to the Internet by subscribing to an Internet service provider. An **Internet service provider (ISP)** is a commercial organization with a permanent connection to the Internet that sells temporary connections to retail subscribers. EarthLink, NetZero, AT&T, and Microsoft Network (MSN) are ISPs. Individuals also connect to the Internet through their business firms, universities, or research centers that have designated Internet domains.

There are a variety of services for ISP Internet connections. Connecting via a traditional telephone line and modem, at a speed of 56.6 kilobits per second (Kbps) used to be the most common form of connection worldwide, but it is quickly being replaced by broadband connections. Digital subscriber line (DSL), cable, and satellite Internet connections, and T lines provide these broadband services.

Digital subscriber line (DSL) technologies operate over existing telephone lines to carry voice, data, and video at transmission rates ranging from 385 Kbps all the way up to 9 Mbps. **Cable Internet connections** provided by cable television vendors use digital cable coaxial lines to deliver high-speed Internet access to homes and businesses. They can provide high-speed access to the Internet of up to 10 Mbps. In areas where DSL and cable services are unavailable, it is possible to access the Internet via satellite, although some satellite Internet connections have slower upload speeds than these other broadband services.

T1 and T3 are international telephone standards for digital communication. They are leased, dedicated lines suitable for businesses or government agencies requiring high-speed guaranteed service levels. **T1 lines** offer guaranteed delivery at 1.54 Mbps, and T3 lines offer delivery at 45 Mbps.

INTERNET ADDRESSING AND ARCHITECTURE

The Internet is based on the TCP/IP networking protocol suite described earlier in this chapter. Every computer on the Internet is assigned a unique **Internet Protocol (IP) address**, which currently is a 32-bit number represented by four strings of numbers ranging from 0 to 255 separated by periods. For instance, the IP address of www.microsoft.com is 207.46.250.119.

When a user sends a message to another user on the Internet, the message is first decomposed into packets using the TCP protocol. Each packet contains its destination address. The packets are then sent from the client to the network server and from there on to as many other servers as necessary to arrive at a specific computer with a known address. At the destination address, the packets are reassembled into the original message.

The Domain Name System

Because it would be incredibly difficult for Internet users to remember strings of 12 numbers, a **Domain Name System (DNS)** converts IP addresses to domain names. The **domain name** is the English-like name that corresponds to the unique 32-bit numeric IP address for each computer connected to the Internet. DNS servers maintain a database containing IP addresses mapped to their corresponding domain names. To access a computer on the Internet, users need only specify its domain name.

DNS has a hierarchical structure (see Figure 7-8). At the top of the DNS hierarchy is the root domain. The child domain of the root is called a top-level domain, and the child domain of a top-level domain is called is a second-level domain. Top-level domains are two-and three-character names you are familiar with from surfing the Web, for example, .com, .edu, .gov, and the various

FIGURE 7-8   THE DOMAIN NAME SYSTEM

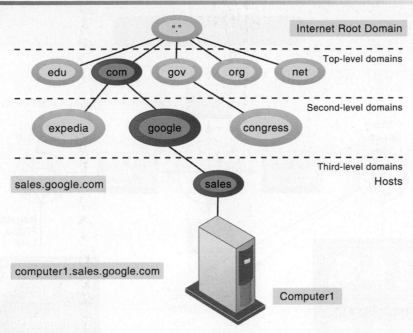

Domain Name System is a hierarchical system with a root domain, top-level domains, second-level domains, and host computers at the third level.

country codes such as .ca for Canada or .it for Italy. Second-level domains have two parts, designating a top-level name and a second-level name—such as buy.com, nyu.edu, or amazon.ca. A host name at the bottom of the hierarchy designates a specific computer on either the Internet or a private network.

The most common domain extensions currently available and officially approved are shown in the following list. Countries also have domain names such as .uk, .au, and .fr (United Kingdom, Australia, and France, respectively). In the future, this list will expand to include many more types of organizations and industries.

.com   Commercial organizations/businesses

.edu   Educational institutions

.gov   U.S. government agencies

.mil   U.S. military

.net   Network computers

.org   Nonprofit organizations and foundations

.biz   Business firms

.info   Information providers

Internet Architecture and Governance

Internet data traffic is carried over transcontinental high-speed backbone networks that generally operate today in the range of 45 Mbps to 2.5 Gbps (see Figure 7-9). These trunk lines are typically owned by long-distance telephone companies (called *network service providers*) or by national governments. Local connection lines are owned by regional telephone and cable television companies in the United States that connect retail users in homes and businesses to the Internet. The regional networks lease access to ISPs, private companies, and government institutions.

FIGURE 7-9 INTERNET NETWORK ARCHITECTURE

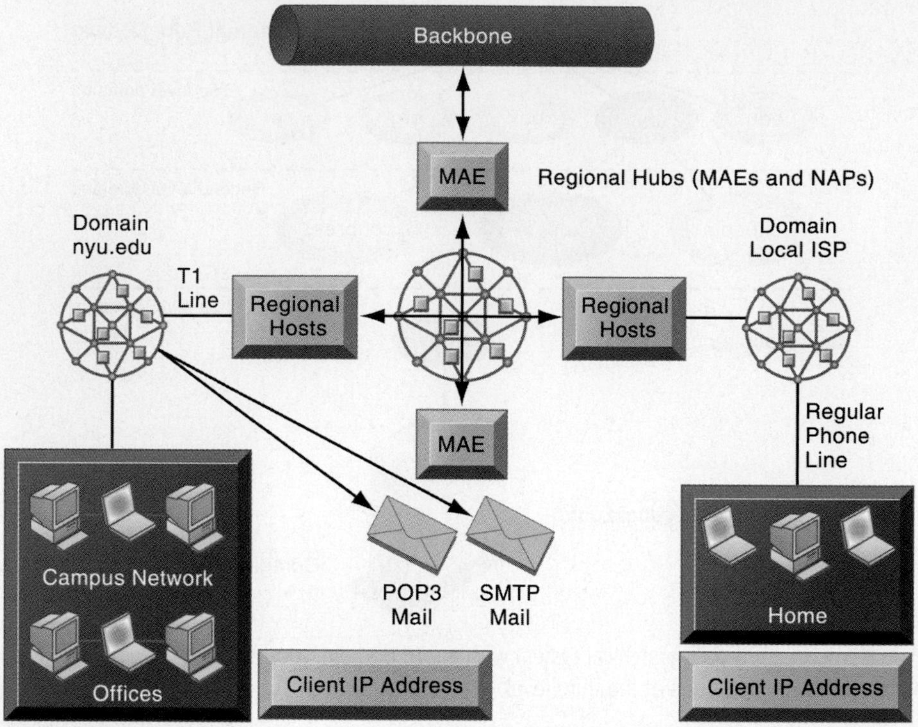

The Internet backbone connects to regional networks, which in turn provide access to Internet service providers, large firms, and government institutions. Network access points (NAPs) and metropolitan area exchanges (MAEs) are hubs where the backbone intersects regional and local networks and where backbone owners connect with one another.

Each organization pays for its own networks and its own local Internet connection services, a part of which is paid to the long-distance trunk line owners. Individual Internet users pay ISPs for using their service, and they generally pay a flat subscription fee, no matter how much or how little they use the Internet. A debate is now raging on whether this arrangement should continue or whether heavy Internet users who download large video and music files should pay more for the bandwidth they consume. The Interactive Session on Organizations explores this topic, as it examines the pros and cons of network neutrality.

No one "owns" the Internet, and it has no formal management. However, worldwide Internet policies are established by a number of professional organizations and government bodies, including the Internet Architecture Board (IAB), which helps define the overall structure of the Internet; the Internet Corporation for Assigned Names and Numbers (ICANN), which assigns IP addresses; and the World Wide Web Consortium (W3C), which sets Hypertext Markup Language (HTML) and other programming standards for the Web.

These organizations influence government agencies, network owners, ISPs and software developers with the goal of keeping the Internet operating as efficiently as possible. The Internet must also conform to the laws of the sovereign nation-states in which it operates, as well as the technical infrastructures that exist within the nation-states. Although in the early years of the

INTERACTIVE SESSION: ORGANIZATIONS

SHOULD NETWORK NEUTRALITY CONTINUE?

What kind of Internet user are you? Do you primarily use the Net to do a little e-mail and look up phone numbers? Or are you online all day, watching YouTube videos, downloading music files, or playing massively multiplayer online games? If you're the latter, you are consuming a great deal of bandwidth, and hundreds of millions of people like you might start to slow the Internet down. YouTube consumed as much bandwidth in 2007 as the entire Internet did in 2000. That's one of the arguments being made today for charging Internet users based on the amount of transmission capacity they use.

According to one November 2007 report, a research firm projected that user demand for the Internet could outpace network capacity by 2011. If this happens, the Internet might not come to a screeching halt, but users would be faced with sluggish download speeds and slow performance of YouTube, Facebook, and other data-heavy services. Other researchers believe that as digital traffic on the Internet grows, even at a rate of 50 percent per year, the technology for handling all this traffic is advancing at an equally rapid pace.

In addition to these technical issues, the debate about metering Internet use centers around the concept of network neutrality. Network neutrality is the idea that Internet service providers must allow customers equal access to content and applications, regardless of the source or nature of the content. Presently, the Internet is indeed neutral: all Internet traffic is treated equally on a first-come, first-serve basis by Internet backbone owners. The Internet is neutral because it was built on phone lines, which are subject to 'common carriage' laws. These laws require phone companies to treat all calls and customers equally. They cannot offer extra benefits to customers willing to pay higher premiums for faster or clearer calls, a model known as tiered service.

Now telecommunications and cable companies want to be able to charge differentiated prices based on the amount of bandwidth consumed by content being delivered over the Internet. In June 2008, Time Warner Cable started testing metered pricing for its Internet access service in the city of Beaumont, Texas. Under the pilot program, Time Warner charged customers an additional $1 per month for each gigabyte of content they downloaded or sent over the bandwidth limit of their monthly plan. The company reported that 5 percent of its customers had been using half the capacity on its local lines without paying any more than low-usage customers, and that metered pricing was "the fairest way" to finance necessary investments in its network infrastructure.

This is not how Internet service has worked traditionally and contradicts the goals of network neutrality. Advocates of net neutrality are pushing Congress to regulate the industry, requiring network providers to refrain from these types of practices. The strange alliance of net neutrality advocates includes MoveOn.org, the Christian Coalition, the American Library Association, every major consumer group, many bloggers and small businesses, and some large Internet companies like Google and Amazon. Representative Ed Markey and Senators Byron Dorgan and Olympia Snowe have responded to these concerns by drafting the Internet Freedom Preservation Act and the Net Neutrality Act, which would ban discriminatory methods of managing Internet traffic. However, any legislation regarding net neutrality is considered unlikely to be passed quickly because of significant resistance by Internet service providers.

Internet service providers point to the upsurge in piracy of copyrighted materials over the Internet. Comcast, the second largest Internet service provider in the United States, reported that illegal file sharing of copyrighted material was consuming 50 percent of its network capacity. At one point Comcast slowed down transmission of BitTorrent files, used extensively for piracy and illegal sharing of copyrighted materials, including video. Comcast drew fierce criticism for its handling of BitTorrent packets, and later switched to a "plaform-agnostic" approach. It currently slows down the connection of any customer who uses too much bandwidth during congested periods without singling out the specific services the customer is using. In controlling piracy and prioritizing bandwidth usage on the Internet, Comcast claims to be providing better service for its customers who are using the Web legally.

Net neutrality advocates argue that the risk of censorship increases when network operators can selectively block or slow access to certain content. There are already many examples of Internet providers restricting access to sensitive materials (such as anti-Bush comments from an online Pearl Jam concert, a text-messaging program from pro-choice group NARAL, or access to competitors like Vonage). Pakistan's government blocked access to anti-Muslim sites and YouTube as a whole in response to content they deemed defamatory to Islam.

Proponents of net neutrality also argue that a neutral Internet encourages everyone to innovate without permission from the phone and cable companies or other authorities, and this level playing field has spawned countless new businesses. Allowing unrestricted information flow becomes essential to free markets and democracy as commerce and society increasingly move online.

Network owners believe regulation like the bills proposed by net neutrality advocates will impede U.S. competitiveness by stifling innovation and hurt customers who will benefit from 'discriminatory' network practices. U.S. Internet service lags behind other many other nations in overall speed, cost, and quality of service, adding credibility to the providers' arguments.

Network neutrality advocates counter that U.S. carriers already have too much power due to lack of options for service. Without sufficient competition, the carriers have more freedom to set prices and policies, and customers cannot seek recourse via other options. Carriers can discriminate in favor of their own content. Even broadband users in large metropolitan areas lack many options for service. With enough options for Internet access, net neutrality would not be such a pressing issue. Dissatisfied consumers could simply switch to providers who enforce net neutrality and allow unlimited Internet use.

The issue is a long way from resolution. Even notable Internet personalities disagree, such as the co-inventors of the Internet Protocol, Vint Cerf and Bob Kahn. Cerf favors net neutrality, saying that variable access to content would detract from the Internet's continued ability to thrive ("allowing broadband carriers to control what people see and do online would fundamentally undermine the principles that have made the Internet such a success"). Kahn is more cautious, saying that net neutrality removes the incentive for network providers to innovate, provide new capabilities, and upgrade to new technology. Who's right, who's wrong? The debate continues.

Sources: Andy Dornan, "Is Your Network Neutral?" *Information Week*, May 18, 2008; Rob Preston, "Meter is Starting to Tick on Internet Access Pricing," *Information Week*, June 9, 2008; Damian Kulash, Jr. "Beware of the New New Thing," *The New York Times*, April 5, 2008; Steve Lohr, "Video Road Hogs Stir Fear of Internet Traffic Jam," *The New York Times*, March 13, 2008; Peter Burrows, "The FCC, Comcast, and Net Neutrality," *Business Week*, February 26, 2008; S. Derek Turner, "Give Net Neutrality a Chance," *Business Week*, July 12, 2008; K.C. Jones, "Piracy Becomes Focus of Net Neutrality Debate," *Information Week*, May 6, 2008; Jane Spencer, "How a System Error in Pakistan Shut YouTube," *The Wall Street Journal*, February 26, 2008.

CASE STUDY QUESTIONS

1. What is network neutrality? Why has the Internet operated under net neutrality up to this point in time?

2. Who's in favor of network neutrality? Who's opposed? Why?

3. What would be the impact on individual users, businesses, and government if Internet providers switched to a tiered service model?

4. Are you in favor of legislation enforcing network neutrality? Why or why not?

MIS IN ACTION

1. Visit the Web site of the Open Internet Coalition and select five member organizations. Then visit the Web site of each of these organizations or surf the Web to find out more information about each. Write a short essay explaining why each organization is in favor of network neutrality.

2. Calculate how much bandwidth you consume when using the Internet every day. How many e-mails do you send daily and what is the size of each? (Your e-mail program may have e-mail file size information.) How many music and video clips do you download daily and what is the size of each? If you view YouTube often, surf the Web to find out the size of a typical YouTube file. Add up the number of e-mail, audio, and video files you transmit or receive on a typical day.

Internet and the Web there was very little legislative or executive interference, this situation is changing as the Internet plays a growing role in the distribution of information and knowledge, including content that some find objectionable.

The Future Internet: IPv6 and Internet2

The Internet was not originally designed to handle the transmission of massive quantities of data and billions of users. Because many corporations and governments have been given large blocks of millions of IP addresses to accommodate current and future workforces, and because of sheer Internet population growth, the world will run out of available IP addresses using the existing addressing convention by 2012 or 2013. Under development is a new version of the IP addressing schema called *Internet Protocol version 6* (*IPv6*), which contains 128-bit addresses (2 to the power of 128), or more than a quadrillion possible unique addresses.

Internet2 and Next-Generation Internet (NGI) are consortia representing 200 universities, private businesses, and government agencies in the United States that are working on a new, robust, high-bandwidth version of the Internet. They have established several new high-performance backbone networks with bandwidths ranging from 2.5 Gbps to 9.6 Gbps. Internet2 research groups are developing and implementing new technologies for more effective routing practices; different levels of service, depending on the type and importance of the data being transmitted; and advanced applications for distributed computation, virtual laboratories, digital libraries, distributed learning, and tele-immersion. These networks do not replace the public Internet, but they do provide test beds for leading-edge technology that may eventually migrate to the public Internet.

INTERNET SERVICES AND COMMUNICATION TOOLS

The Internet is based on client/server technology. Individuals using the Internet control what they do through client applications on their computers, such as Web browser software. The data, including e-mail messages and Web pages, are stored on servers. A client uses the Internet to request information from a particular Web server on a distant computer, and the server sends the requested information back to the client over the Internet. Chapters 5 and 6 describe how Web servers work with application servers and database servers to access information from an organization's internal information systems applications and their associated databases. Client platforms today include not only PCs and other computers but also cell phones, small handheld digital devices, and other information appliances.

Internet Services

A client computer connecting to the Internet has access to a variety of services. These services include e-mail, electronic discussion groups, chatting and instant messaging, **Telnet**, **File Transfer Protocol (FTP)**, and the World Wide Web. Table 7-3 provides a brief description of these services.

Each Internet service is implemented by one or more software programs. All of the services may run on a single server computer, or different services may be allocated to different machines. Figure 7-10 illustrates one way that these services can be arranged in a multitiered client/server architecture.

TABLE 7-3 MAJOR INTERNET SERVICES

CAPABILITY	FUNCTIONS SUPPORTED
E-mail	Person-to-person messaging; document sharing
Chatting and instant messaging	Interactive conversations
Newsgroups	Discussion groups on electronic bulletin boards
Telnet	Logging on to one computer system and doing work on another
File Transfer Protocol (FTP)	Transferring files from computer to computer
World Wide Web	Retrieving, formatting, and displaying information (including text, audio, graphics, and video) using hypertext links

FIGURE 7-10   CLIENT/SERVER COMPUTING ON THE INTERNET

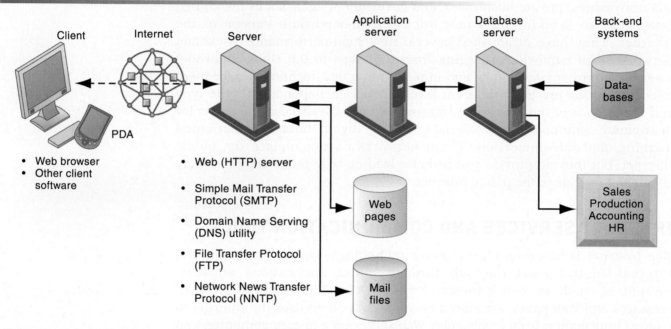

Client computers running Web browser and other software can access an array of services on servers over the Internet. These services may all run on a single server or on multiple specialized servers.

E-mail enables messages to be exchanged from computer to computer, with capabilities for routing messages to multiple recipients, forwarding messages, and attaching text documents or multimedia files to messages. Although some organizations operate their own internal electronic mail systems, most e-mail today is sent through the Internet. The costs of e-mail is far lower than equivalent voice, postal, or overnight delivery costs, making the Internet a very inexpensive and rapid communications medium. Most e-mail messages arrive anywhere in the world in a matter of seconds.

Nearly 90 percent of U.S. workplaces have employees communicating interactively using **chat** or instant messaging tools. Chatting enables two or more people who are simultaneously connected to the Internet to hold live, interactive conversations. Chat systems now support voice and video chat as well as written conversations. Many online retail businesses offer chat services on their Web sites to attract visitors, to encourage repeat purchases, and to improve customer service.

Instant messaging is a type of chat service that enables participants to create their own private chat channels. The instant messaging system alerts the user whenever someone on his or her private list is online so that the user can initiate a chat session with other individuals. Instant messaging systems for consumers include Yahoo! Messenger and AOL Instant Messenger. Companies concerned with security use proprietary instant messaging systems such as Lotus Sametime.

Newsgroups are worldwide discussion groups posted on Internet electronic bulletin boards on which people share information and ideas on a defined topic, such as radiology or rock bands. Anyone can post messages on these bulletin boards for others to read. Many thousands of groups exist that discuss almost all conceivable topics.

Employee use of e-mail, instant messaging, and the Internet is supposed to increase worker productivity, but the accompanying Interactive Session on Management shows that this may not always be the case. Many company managers now believe they need to monitor and even regulate their employees' online activity. But is this ethical? Although there are some strong business reasons why companies may need to monitor their employees' e-mail and Web activities, what does this mean for employee privacy?

Voice over IP

The Internet has also become a popular platform for voice transmission and corporate networking. **Voice over IP (VoIP)** technology delivers voice information in digital form using packet switching, avoiding the tolls charged by local and long-distance telephone networks (see Figure 7-11). Calls that would ordinarily be transmitted over public telephone networks would travel over the corporate network based on the Internet Protocol, or the public Internet. Voice calls can be made and received with a desktop computer equipped with a microphone and speakers or with a VoIP-enabled telephone.

FIGURE 7-11   HOW VOICE OVER IP WORKS

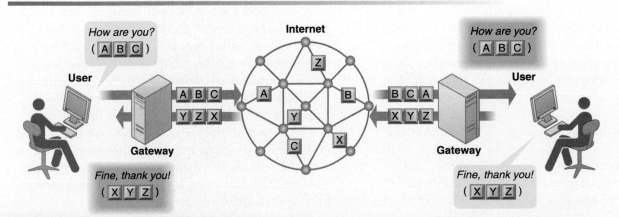

An VoIP phone call digitizes and breaks up a voice message into data packets that may travel along different routes before being reassembled at the final destination. A processor nearest the call's destination, called a *gateway*, arranges packets in the proper order and directs them to the telephone number of the receiver or the IP address of the receiving computer.

INTERACTIVE SESSION: MANAGEMENT

MONITORING EMPLOYEES ON NETWORKS: UNETHICAL OR GOOD BUSINESS?

As Internet use has exploded worldwide, so have the use of e-mail and the Web for personal business at the workplace. Several management problems have emerged: First, checking e-mail, responding to instant messages, or sneaking in a brief YouTube or MySpace video create a series of nonstop interruptions that divert employee attention from the job tasks they are supposed to be performing. According to Basex, a New York City business research company, these distractions take up as much as 28 percent of the average U.S. worker's day and result in $650 billion in lost productivity each year.

Second, these interruptions are not necessarily work-related. A number of studies have concluded that at least 25 percent of employee online time is spent on non-work-related Web surfing, and perhaps as many as 90 percent of employees receive or send personal e-mail at work.

Many companies have begun monitoring their employee use of e-mail, blogs, and the Internet, sometimes without their knowledge. A recent American Management Association (AMA) survey of 304 U.S. companies of all sizes found that 66 percent of these companies monitor employee e-mail messages and Web connections. Although U.S. companies have the legal right to monitor employee Internet and e-mail activity while they are at work, is such monitoring unethical, or is it simply good business?

Managers worry about the loss of time and employee productivity when employees are focusing on personal rather than company business. Too much time on personal business, on the Internet or not, can mean lost revenue or overbilled clients. Some employees may be charging time they spend trading their personal stocks online or pursuing other personal business to clients, thus overcharging the clients.

If personal traffic on company networks is too high, it can also clog the company's network so that legitimate business work cannot be performed. Schemmer Associates, an architecture firm in Omaha, Nebraska, and Potomac Hospital in Woodridge, Virginia, found their computing resources were limited by a lack of bandwidth caused by employees using corporate Internet connections to watch and download video files.

When employees use e-mail or the Web at employer facilities or with employer equipment, anything they do, including anything illegal, carries the company's name. Therefore, the employer can be traced and held liable. Management in many firms fear that racist, sexually explicit, or other potentially offensive material accessed or traded by their employees could result in adverse publicity and even lawsuits for the firm. Even if the company is found not to be liable, responding to lawsuits could cost the company tens of thousands of dollars.

Companies also fear leakage of confidential information and trade secrets through e-mail or blogs. Ajax Boiler, based in Santa Ana, California, learned that one of its senior managers was able to access the network of a former employer and read the e-mail of that company's human resources manager. The Ajax employee was trying to gather information for a lawsuit against the former employer.

Companies that allow employees to use personal e-mail accounts at work face legal and regulatory trouble if they do not retain those messages. E-mail today is an important source of evidence for lawsuits, and companies are now required to retain all of their e-mail messages for longer periods than in the past. Courts do not discriminate about whether e-mails involved in lawsuits were sent via personal or business e-mail accounts. Not producing those e-mails could result in a five-to six-figure fine.

U.S. companies have the legal right to monitor what employees are doing with company equipment during business hours. The question is whether electronic surveillance is an appropriate tool for maintaining an efficient and positive workplace. Some companies try to ban all personal activities on corporate networks—zero tolerance. Others block employee access to specific Web sites or limit personal time on the Web using software that enables IT departments to track the Web sites employees visit, the amount of time employees spend at these sites, and the files they download. Ajax uses software from SpectorSoft Corporation that records all the Web sites employees visit, time spent at each site, and all e-mails sent. Schemmer Associates uses OpenDNS to categorize and filter Web content and block unwanted video.

Some firms have fired employees who have stepped out of bounds. One-third of the companies surveyed in the AMA study had fired workers for misusing the Internet on the job. Among managers who fired employees for Internet misuse, 64 percent did so because the employees' e-mail contained inappropriate or offensive language, and more than 25 percent fired workers for excessive personal use of e-mail.

No solution is problem free, but many consultants believe companies should write corporate policies on employee e-mail and Internet use. The policies should include explicit ground rules that state, by position or level, under what circumstances employees can use company facilities for e-mail, blogging, or Web surfing. The policies should also inform employees whether these activities are monitored and explain why.

The rules should be tailored to specific business needs and organizational cultures. For example, although some companies may exclude all employees from visiting sites that have explicit sexual material, law firm or hospital employees may require access to these sites. Investment firms will need to allow many of their employees access to other investment sites. A company dependent on widespread information sharing, innovation, and independence could very well find that monitoring creates more problems than it solves.

Sources: Nancy Gohring, "Over 50 Percent of Companies Fire Workers for E-Mail, Net Abuse," *InfoWorld*, February 28, 2008; Bobby White, "The New Workplace Rules: No Video-Watching," *The Wall Street Journal*, March 4, 2008; Maggie Jackson, "May We Have Your Attention, Please?" *Business Week*, June 23, 2008; Katherine Wegert, "Workers Can Breach Security Knowingly Or Not," Dow Jones News Service, June 24, 2007; Andrew Blackman, "Foul Sents," *The Wall Street Journal*, March 26, 2007.

CASE STUDY QUESTIONS

1. Should managers monitor employee e-mail and Internet usage? Why or why not?
2. Describe an effective e-mail and Web use policy for a company.

MIS IN ACTION

Explore the Web site of online employee monitoring software such as SpectorSoft or SpyTech NetVizor and answer the following questions.

1. What employee activities does this software track? What can an employer learn about an employee by using this software?
2. How can businesses benefit from using this software?
3. How would you feel if your employer used this software where you work to monitor what you are doing on the job? Explain your response.

Telecommunications service providers (such as Verizon) and cable firms (such as Time Warner and Cablevision) provide VoIP services. Skype, acquired by eBay, offers free VoIP worldwide using a peer-to-peer network, and Google has its own free VoIP service.

Although there are up-front investments required for an IP phone system, VoIP can reduce communication and network management costs by 20 to 30 percent. For example, VoIP saves Virgin Entertainment Group $700,000 per year in long-distance bills. In addition to lowering long-distance costs and eliminating monthly fees for private lines, an IP network provides a single voice-data infrastructure for both telecommunications and computing services. Companies no longer have to maintain separate networks or provide support services and personnel for each different type of network.

Another advantage of VoIP is its flexibility. Unlike the traditional telephone network, phones can be added or moved to different offices without rewiring or reconfiguring the network. With VoIP, a conference call is arranged by a simple click-and-drag operation on the computer screen to select the names of the conferees. Voice mail and e-mail can be combined into a single directory.

Unified Communications

In the past, each of the firm's networks for wired and wireless data, voice communications, and videoconferencing operated independently of each other and had to be managed separately by the information systems department. Now, however, firms are able to merge disparate communications modes into a single universally accessible service using **unified communications** technology. As the chapter-opening case on Virgin Megastores points out, unified communications integrates disparate channels for voice communications, data communications, instant messaging, e-mail, and electronic conferencing into a single experience where users can seamlessly switch back and forth between different communication modes. Presence technology shows whether a person is available to receive a call. Companies will need to examine how work flows and business processes will be altered by this technology in order to gauge its value.

Virtual Private Networks

What if you had a marketing group charged with developing new products and services for your firm with members spread across the United States? You would want to be able to e-mail each other and communicate with the home office without any chance that outsiders could intercept the communications. In the past, one answer to this problem was to work with large private networking firms who offered secure, private, dedicated networks to customers. But this was an expensive solution. A much less-expensive solution is to create a virtual private network within the public Internet.

A **virtual private network (VPN)** is a secure, encrypted, private network that has been configured within a public network to take advantage of the economies of scale and management facilities of large networks, such as the Internet (see Figure 7-12). A VPN provides your firm with secure, encrypted communications at a much lower cost than the same capabilities offered by traditional non-Internet providers who use their private networks to secure communications. VPNs also provide a network infrastructure for combining voice and data networks.

Several competing protocols are used to protect data transmitted over the public Internet, including *Point-to-Point Tunneling Protocol (PPTP)*. In a process called tunneling, packets of data are encrypted and wrapped inside IP packets. By adding this wrapper around a network message to hide its content, business firms create a private connection that travels through the public Internet.

THE WORLD WIDE WEB

You've probably used the World Wide Web to download music, to find information for a term paper, or to obtain news and weather reports. The Web is the most popular Internet service. It's a system with universally accepted standards for storing, retrieving, formatting, and displaying information using a client/server architecture. Web pages are formatted using hypertext with embedded links that connect documents to one another and that also link pages to other objects, such as sound, video, or animation files. When you click a graphic and a video clip plays, you have clicked a hyperlink. A typical **Web site** is a collection of Web pages linked to a home page.

FIGURE 7-12   A VIRTUAL PRIVATE NETWORK USING THE INTERNET

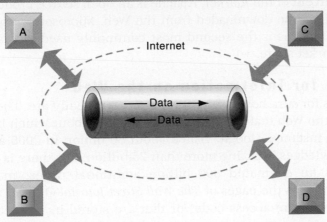

This VPN is a private network of computers linked using a secure "tunnel" connection over the Internet. It protects data transmitted over the public Internet by encoding the data and "wrapping" them within the Internet Protocol (IP). By adding a wrapper around a network message to hide its content, organizations can create a private connection that travels through the public Internet.

Hypertext

Web pages are based on a standard Hypertext Markup Language (HTML), which formats documents and incorporates dynamic links to other documents and pictures stored in the same or remote computers (see Chapter 5). Web pages are accessible through the Internet because Web browser software operating your computer can request Web pages stored on an Internet host server using the **Hypertext Transfer Protocol (HTTP)**. HTTP is the communications standard used to transfer pages on the Web. For example, when you type a Web address in your browser, such as www.sec.gov, your browser sends an HTTP request to the sec.gov server requesting the home page of sec.gov.

HTTP is the first set of letters at the start of every Web address, followed by the domain name, which specifies the organization's server computer that is storing the document. Most companies have a domain name that is the same as or closely related to their official corporate name. The directory path and document name are two more pieces of information within the Web address that help the browser track down the requested page. Together, the address is called a **uniform resource locator (URL)**. When typed into a browser, a URL tells the browser software exactly where to look for the information. For example, in the URL http://www.megacorp.com/content/features/082602.html, *http* names the protocol used to display Web pages, *www.megacorp.com* is the domain name, *content/features* is the directory path that identifies where on the domain Web server the page is stored, and *082602.html* is the document name and the name of the format it is in (it is an HTML page).

Web Servers

A Web server is software for locating and managing stored Web pages. It locates the Web pages requested by a user on the computer where they are stored and delivers the Web pages to the user's computer. Server applications usually run on dedicated computers, although they can all reside on a single computer in small organizations.

The most common Web server in use today is Apache HTTP Server, which controls 60 percent of the market. Apache is an open source product that is free of charge and can be downloaded from the Web. Microsoft's product Internet Information Services is the second most commonly used Web server, with a 40-percent market share.

Searching for Information on the Web

No one knows for sure how many Web pages there really are. The surface Web is the part of the Web that search engines visit and about which information is recorded. For instance, Google visited about 50 billion in 2008 although publicly it acknowledges indexing more than 25 billion. But there is a "deep Web" that contains an estimated 800 billion additional pages, many of them proprietary (such as the pages of *The Wall Street Journal* Online, which cannot be visited without an access code) or that are stored in protected corporate databases.

Search Engines Obviously, with so many Web pages, finding specific Web pages that can help you or your business, nearly instantly, is an important problem. The question is, how can you find the one or two pages you really want and need out of billions of indexed Web pages? **Search engines** attempt to solve the problem of finding useful information on the Web nearly instantly, and, arguably, they are the "killer app" of the Internet era. Today's search engines can sift through HTML files, files of Microsoft Office applications, and PDF files, with developing capabilities for searching audio, video, and image files. There are hundreds of different search engines in the world, but the vast majority of search results are supplied by three top providers: Google, Yahoo!, and Microsoft.

Web search engines started out in the early 1990s as relatively simple software programs that roamed the nascent Web, visiting pages and gathering information about the content of each page. The first search engines were simple keyword indexes of all the pages they visited, leaving the user with lists of pages that may not have been truly relevant to their search.

In 1994, Stanford University computer science students David Filo and Jerry Yang created a hand-selected list of their favorite Web pages and called it "Yet Another Hierarchical Officious Oracle," or Yahoo!. Yahoo! was not initially a search engine but rather an edited selection of Web sites organized by categories the editors found useful, but it has since developed its own search engine capabilities.

In 1998, Larry Page and Sergey Brin, two other Stanford computer science students, released their first version of Google. This search engine was different: Not only did it index each Web page's words but it also ranked search results based on the relevance of each page. Page patented the idea of a page ranking system (PageRank System), which essentially measures the popularity of a Web page by calculating the number of sites that link to that page. Brin contributed a unique Web crawler program that indexed not only keywords on a page but also combinations of words (such as authors and the titles of their articles). These two ideas became the foundation for the Google search engine. Figure 7-13 illustrates how Google works.

Web sites for locating information such as Yahoo!, Google, and MSN have become so popular and easy to use that they also serve as major portals for the Internet (see Chapter 10). Their search engines have become major shopping tools by offering what is now called **search engine marketing**. When users

FIGURE 7-13   HOW GOOGLE WORKS

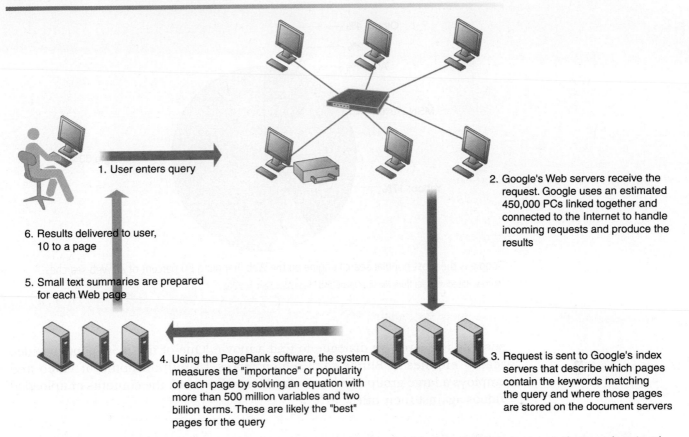

1. User enters query

6. Results delivered to user, 10 to a page

5. Small text summaries are prepared for each Web page

2. Google's Web servers receive the request. Google uses an estimated 450,000 PCs linked together and connected to the Internet to handle incoming requests and produce the results

4. Using the PageRank software, the system measures the "importance" or popularity of each page by solving an equation with more than 500 million variables and two billion terms. These are likely the "best" pages for the query

3. Request is sent to Google's index servers that describe which pages contain the keywords matching the query and where those pages are stored on the document servers

The Google search engine is continuously crawling the Web, indexing the content of each page, calculating its popularity, and storing the pages so that it can respond quickly to user requests to see a page. The entire process takes about one-half second.

enter a search term at Google, MSN, Yahoo!, or any of the other sites serviced by these search engines, they receive two types of listings: sponsored links, for which advertisers have paid to be listed (usually at the top of the search results page), and unsponsored "organic" search results. In addition, advertisers can purchase tiny text boxes on the side of the Google and MSN search results page. The paid, sponsored advertisements are the fastest-growing form of Internet advertising and are powerful new marketing tools that precisely match consumer interests with advertising messages at the right moment (see the chapter-ending case study). Search engine marketing monetizes the value of the search process.

In 2008, 71 million people each day in the United States alone used a search engine, producing over 10 billion searches a month. There are hundreds of search engines but the top three (Google, Yahoo!, and MSN) account for 90 percent of all searches (see Figure 7-14).

Although search engines were originally built to search text documents, the explosion in online video and images has created a demand for search engines that can quickly find specific videos. The words "dance," "love," "music," and "girl" are all exceedingly popular in titles of YouTube videos, and searching on these keywords produces a flood of responses even though the actual contents of the video may have nothing to do with the search term. Searching videos is challenging because computers are not very good or quick at recognizing digital images. Some search engines have started indexing movies scripts so it will be

FIGURE 7-14   TOP U.S. WEB SEARCH ENGINES

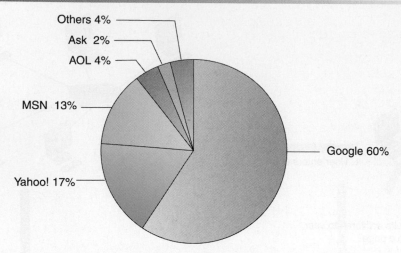

Google is the most popular search engine on the Web, handling 60 percent of all Web searches.

Sources: Based on data from Nielsen Online and MegaView Search, 2008.

possible to search on dialogue to find a movie. One of the most popular video search engines is Blinkx.com, which stores 18 million hours of video and employs a large group of human classifiers who check the contents of uploaded videos against their titles.

Intelligent Agent Shopping Bots Chapter 11 describes the capabilities of software agents with built-in intelligence that can gather or filter information and perform other tasks to assist users. **Shopping bots** use intelligent agent software for searching the Internet for shopping information. Shopping bots such as MySimon or Froogle can help people interested in making a purchase filter and retrieve information about products of interest, evaluate competing products according to criteria the users have established, and negotiate with vendors for price and delivery terms. Many of these shopping agents search the Web for pricing and availability of products specified by the user and return a list of sitcs that sell the item along with pricing information and a purchase link.

Web 2.0

If you've shared photos over the Internet at Flickr or another photo site, blogged, looked up a word on Wikipedia, or contributed information yourself, you've used services that are part of **Web 2.0**. Today's Web sites don't just contain static content—they enable people to collaborate, share information, and create new services online. Web 2.0 refers to these second-generation interactive Internet-based services.

The technologies and services that distinguish Web 2.0 include cloud computing, software mashups and widgets, blogs, RSS, and wikis. Mashups and widgets, which we introduced in Chapter 5, are software services that enable users and system developers to mix and match content or software components to create something entirely new. For example, Yahoo's photo storage and sharing site Flickr combines photos with other information about the images provided by users and tools to make it usable within other programming environments.

These software applications run on the Web itself instead of the desktop and bring the vision of Web-based computing closer to realization. With Web 2.0, the Web is not just a collection of destination sites, but a source of data and services that can be combined to create applications users need. Web 2.0 tools and services have fueled the creation of social networks and other online communities where people can interact with one another in the manner of their choosing.

A **blog**, the popular term for a Weblog, is an informal yet structured Web site where subscribing individuals can publish stories, opinions, and links to other Web sites of interest. Blogs have become popular personal publishing tools, but they also have business uses (see Chapters 10 and 11). For example, Wells Fargo uses blogs to help executives communicate with employees and customers. One of these blogs is dedicated to student loans.

If you're an avid blog reader, you might use RSS to keep up with your favorite blogs without constantly checking them for updates. **RSS**, which stands for Rich Site Summary or Really Simple Syndication, syndicates Web site content so that it can be used in another setting. RSS technology pulls specified content from Web sites and feeds it automatically to users' computers, where it can be stored for later viewing.

To receive an RSS information feed, you need to install aggregator or news reader software that can be downloaded from the Web. (Microsoft Internet Explorer 7 includes RSS reading capabilities.) Alternatively, you can establish an account with an aggregator Web site. You tell the aggregator to collect all updates from a given Web page, or list of pages, or gather information on a given subject by conducting Web searches at regular intervals. Once subscribed, you automatically receive new content as it is posted to the specified Web site. A number of businesses use RSS internally to distribute updated corporate information. Wells Fargo uses RSS to deliver news feeds that employees can customize to see the business news of greatest relevance to their jobs.

Blogs allow visitors to add comments to the original content, but they do not allow visitors to change the original posted material. **Wikis**, in contrast, are collaborative Web sites where visitors can add, delete, or modify content on the site, including the work of previous authors. Wiki comes from the Hawaiian word for "quick." Probably the best-known wiki site is Wikipedia, the massive online open-source encyclopedia to which anyone can contribute. But wikis are also used for business. For example, Motorola sales representatives use wikis for sharing sales information. Instead of developing a different pitch for every client, reps reuse the information posted on the wiki.

Web 3.0: The Future Web

Every day about 75 million Americans enter 330 million queries to search engines. How many of these 330 million queries produce a meaningful result (a useful answer in the first three listings)? Arguably, fewer than half. Google, Yahoo!, Microsoft, and Amazon are all trying to increase the odds of people finding meaningful answers to search engine queries. But with over 50 billion Web pages indexed, the means available for finding the information you really want are quite primitive, based on the words used on the pages, and the relative popularity of the page among people who use those same search terms. In other words, it's hit and miss.

To a large extent, the future of the Web involves developing techniques to make searching the 50 billion Web pages more productive and meaningful for ordinary people. Web 1.0 solved the problem of obtaining access to information. Web 2.0 solved the problem of sharing that information with others, and building new Web experiences. **Web 3.0** is the promise of a future Web where all this digital information, all these contacts, can be woven together into a single meaningful experience.

Sometimes this is referred to as the **Semantic Web**. "Semantic" refers to meaning. Most of the Web's content today is designed for humans to read and for computers to display, not for computer programs to analyze and manipulate. Search engines can discover when a particular term or keyword appears in a Web document, but they do not really understand its meaning or how it relates to other information on the Web. You can check this out on Google by entering two searches. First, enter "Paris Hilton". Next, enter "Hilton in Paris". Because Google does not understand ordinary English, it has no idea that you are interested in the Hilton Hotel in Paris in the second search. Because it cannot understand the meaning of pages it has indexed, Google's search engine returns the most popular pages for those queries where 'Hilton' and 'Paris' appear on the pages.

First described in a 2001 *Scientific American* article, the Semantic Web is a collaborative effort led by the World Wide Web Consortium to add a layer of meaning atop the existing Web to reduce the amount of human involvement in searching for and processing Web information (Berners-Lee et al., 2001).

Views on the future of the Web vary, but they generally focus on ways to make the Web more "intelligent," with machine-facilitated understanding of information promoting a more intuitive and effective user experience. For instance, let's say you want to set up a party with your tennis buddies at a local restaurant Friday night after work. One problem is that you had earlier scheduled to go to a movie with another friend. In a Semantic Web 3.0 environment, you would be able to coordinate this change in plans with the schedules of your tennis buddies, the schedule of your movie friend, and make a reservation at the restaurant all with a single set of commands issued as text or voice to your handheld smartphone. Right now, this capability is beyond our grasp.

Work proceeds slowly on making the Web a more intelligent experience, in large part because it is difficult to make machines, including software programs, that are truly intelligent like humans. But there are other views of the future Web. Some see a 3D Web where you can walk through pages in a 3D environment. Others point to the idea of a pervasive Web that controls everything from the lights in your living room, to your car's rear view mirror, not to mention managing your calendar and appointments.

Other complementary trends leading toward a future Web 3.0 include more widespread use of cloud computing and SaaS business models, ubiquitous connectivity among mobile platforms and Internet access devices, and the transformation of the Web from a network of separate siloed applications and content into a more seamless and interoperable whole. These more modest visions of the future Web 3.0 are more likely to be realized in the near term.

INTRANETS AND EXTRANETS

Organizations use Internet networking standards and Web technology to create private networks called *intranets*. We introduced intranets in Chapter 1, explaining that an intranet is an internal organizational network that provides access to data across the enterprise. It uses the existing company network infrastructure along with Internet connectivity standards and software developed for the World Wide Web. Intranets create networked applications that can run on many different kinds of computers throughout the organization, including mobile handheld computers and wireless remote access devices.

Whereas the Web is available to anyone, an intranet is private and is protected from public visits by **firewalls**—security systems with specialized software to prevent outsiders from entering private networks. Intranet software technology is the same as that of the World Wide Web. A simple intranet can be created by linking a client computer with a Web browser to a computer with Web server software using a TCP/IP network and a firewall.

Extranets

A firm creates an extranet to allow authorized vendors and customers to have limited access to its internal intranet. For example, authorized buyers could link to a portion of a company's intranet from the public Internet to obtain information about the costs and features of the company's products. The company uses firewalls to ensure that access to its internal data is limited and remains secure; firewalls also authenticate users, making sure that only authorized users access the site.

Both intranets and extranets reduce operational costs by providing the connectivity to coordinate disparate business processes within the firm and to link electronically to customers and suppliers. Extranets often are employed for collaborating with other companies for supply chain management, product design and development, and training efforts.

7.4   THE WIRELESS REVOLUTION

If you have a cell phone, do you use it for taking and sending photos, sending text messages, or downloading music clips? Do you take your laptop to class or to the library to link up to the Internet? If so, you're part of the wireless revolution! Cell phones, laptops, and small handheld devices have morphed into portable computing platforms that let you perform some of the computing tasks you used to do at your desk.

Wireless communication helps businesses more easily stay in touch with customers, suppliers, and employees and provides more flexible arrangements for organizing work. Wireless technology has also created new products, services, and sales channels, which we discuss in Chapter 10.

If you require mobile communication and computing power or remote access to corporate systems, you can work with an array of wireless devices: cell phones, personal digital assistants, and smartphones. Personal computers are also starting to be used in wireless transmission.

Personal digital assistants (PDAs) are small, handheld computers featuring applications such as electronic schedulers, address books, memo pads, and expense trackers. Models with digital cell phone capabilities such as e-mail messaging, wireless access to the Internet, voice communication, and digital cameras are called **smartphones**.

CELLULAR SYSTEMS

Cell phones and smartphones have become all-purpose devices for digital data transmission. In addition to voice communication, mobile phones are now used for transmitting text and e-mail messages, instant messaging, digital photos, and short video clips; for playing music and games; for surfing the Web; and even for transmitting and receiving corporate data. For example, Aflac, the giant insurance company, has an application that delivers information on policy servicing questions, the status of claims payments, and customers' existing or past policies to the smartphones of its entire field force (Sacco, 2008).

Within a few years, a new generation of mobile processors and faster mobile networks will enable these devices to function as digital computing platforms performing many of the tasks of today's PCs. Smartphones will have the storage and processing power of a PC and be able to run all of your key applications and access all of your digital content.

Cellular Network Standards and Generations

Digital cellular service uses several competing standards. In Europe and much of the rest of the world outside the United Sates, the standard is Global System for Mobile Communications (GSM). GSM's strength is its international roaming capability. There are GSM cell phone systems in the United States, including T-Mobile and AT&T.

The major standard in the United States is Code Division Multiple Access (CDMA), which is the system used by Verizon and Sprint. CDMA was developed by the military during World War II. It transmits over several frequencies, occupies the entire spectrum, and randomly assigns users to a range of frequencies over time. In general, CDMA is cheaper to implement, is more efficient in its use of spectrum, and provides higher quality throughput of voice and data than GSM.

Earlier generations of cellular systems were designed primarily for voice and limited data transmission in the form of short text messages. Wireless carriers are now rolling out more powerful cellular networks called **third-generation** or **3G networks**, with transmission speeds ranging from 144 Kbps for mobile users in, say, a car, to more than 2 Mbps for stationary users. This is sufficient transmission capacity for video, graphics, and other rich media, in addition to voice, making 3G networks suitable for wireless broadband Internet access. Many of the cellular handsets available today are 3G-enabled, including the newest version of Apple's iPhone.

3G networks are widely used in Japan, South Korea, Taiwan, Hong Kong, Singapore, and parts of northern Europe, but such services are not yet available in many U.S. locations. To compensate, U.S. cellular carriers have upgraded their networks to support higher-speed transmission. These interim 2.5G networks provide data transmission rates ranging from 60 to 354 Kbps, enabling cell phones to be used for Web access, music downloads, and other broadband services. AT&T's EDGE network used by the first-generation iPhone is an example. PCs equipped with a special card can use these broadband cellular services for ubiquitous wireless Internet access.

The next complete evolution in wireless communication, termed 4G, will be entirely packet-switched and capable of providing between 1 Mbps and 1 Gbps speeds, with premium quality and high security. Voice, data, and high-quality streaming video will be available to users anywhere, anytime. International telecommunications regulatory and standardization bodies are working for commercial deployment of 4G networks between 2012 and 2015.

WIRELESS COMPUTER NETWORKS AND INTERNET ACCESS

If you have a laptop computer, you might be able to use it to access the Internet as you move from room to room in your dorm, or table to table in your university library. An array of technologies provide high-speed wireless access to the

Internet for PCs and other wireless handheld devices as well as for cell phones. These new high-speed services have extended Internet access to numerous locations that could not be covered by traditional wired Internet services.

Bluetooth

Bluetooth is the popular name for the 802.15 wireless networking standard, which is useful for creating small **personal-area networks (PANs)**. It links up to eight devices within a 10-meter area using low-power, radio-based communication and can transmit up to 722 Kbps in the 2.4-GHz band.

Wireless phones, pagers, computers, printers, and computing devices using Bluetooth communicate with each other and even operate each other without direct user intervention (see Figure 7-15). For example, a person could direct a notebook computer to send a document file wirelessly to a printer. Bluetooth connects wireless keyboards and mice to PCs or cell phones to earpieces without wires. Bluetooth has low-power requirements, making it appropriate for battery-powered handheld computers, cell phones, or PDAs.

Although Bluetooth lends itself to personal networking, it has uses in large corporations. For example, FedEx drivers use Bluetooth to transmit the delivery data captured by their handheld PowerPad computers to cellular transmitters, which forward the data to corporate computers. Drivers no longer need to spend time docking their handheld units physically in the transmitters, and Bluetooth has saved FedEx $20 million per year.

Wi-Fi

The 802.11 set of standards for wireless LANs is also known as **Wi-Fi** . There are three standards in this family: 802.11a, 802.11b, and 802.11g. 802.11n is an

FIGURE 7-15   A BLUETOOTH NETWORK (PAN)

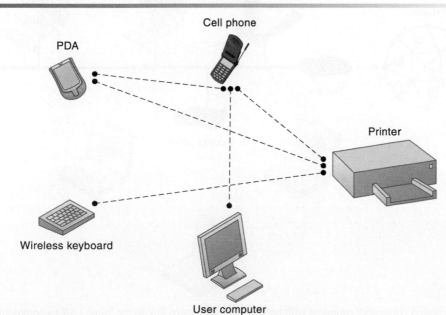

Bluetooth enables a variety of devices, including cell phones, PDAs, wireless keyboards and mice, PCs, and printers, to interact wirelessly with each other within a small 30-foot (10-meter) area. In addition to the links shown, Bluetooth can be used to network similar devices to send data from one PC to another, for example.

emerging standard for increasing the speed and capacity of wireless networking.

The 802.11a standard can transmit up to 54 Mbps in the unlicensed 5-GHz frequency range and has an effective distance of 10 to 30 meters. The 802.11b standard can transmit up to 11 Mbps in the unlicensed 2.4-GHz band and has an effective distance of 30 to 50 meters, although this range can be extended outdoors by using tower-mounted antennas. The 802.11g standard can transmit up to 54 Mbps in the 2.4-GHz range. 802.11n will transmit at more than 100 Mbps.

802.11b was the first wireless standard to be widely adopted for wireless LANs and wireless Internet access. 802.11g is increasingly used for this purpose, and dual-band systems capable of handling 802.11b and 802.11g are available.

In most Wi-Fi communications, wireless devices communicate with a wired LAN using access points. An access point is a box consisting of a radio receiver/transmitter and antennas that links to a wired network, router, or hub.

Figure 7-16 illustrates an 802.11 wireless LAN operating in infrastructure mode that connects a small number of mobile devices to a larger wired LAN. Most wireless devices are client machines. The servers that the mobile client stations need to use are on the wired LAN. The access point controls the wireless stations and acts as a bridge between the main wired LAN and the wireless LAN. (A bridge connects two LANs based on different technologies.) The access point also controls the wireless stations.

Laptop PCs now come equipped with chips to receive Wi-Fi signals. Older models may need an add-in wireless network interface card.

FIGURE 7-16   AN 802.11 WIRELESS LAN

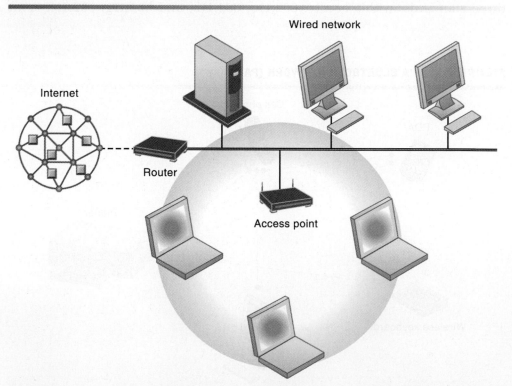

Mobile laptop computers equipped with network interface cards link to the wired LAN by communicating with the access point. The access point uses radio waves to transmit network signals from the wired network to the client adapters, which convert them into data that the mobile device can understand. The client adapter then transmits the data from the mobile device back to the access point, which forwards the data to the wired network.

Wi-Fi and Wireless Internet Access

The 802.11 standard also provides wireless access to the Internet using a broadband connection. In this instance, an access point plugs into an Internet connection, which could come from a cable TV line or DSL telephone service. Computers within range of the access point use it to link wirelessly to the Internet.

Businesses of all sizes are using Wi-Fi networks to provide low-cost wireless LANs and Internet access. Wi-Fi hotspots are springing up in hotels, airport lounges, libraries, cafes, and college campuses to provide mobile access to the Internet. Dartmouth College is one of many campuses where students now use Wi-Fi for research, course work, and entertainment.

Hotspots typically consist of one or more access points positioned on a ceiling, wall, or other strategic spot in a public place to provide maximum wireless coverage for a specific area. Users in range of a hotspot are able to access the Internet from laptops, handhelds, or cell phones that are Wi-Fi enabled, such as Apple's iPhone. Some hotspots are free or do not require any additional software to use; others may require activation and the establishment of a user account by providing a credit card number over the Web.

Wi-Fi technology poses several challenges, however. Right now, users cannot freely roam from hotspot to hotspot if these hotspots use different Wi-Fi network services. Unless the service is free, users would need to log on to separate accounts for each service, each with its own fees.

One major drawback of Wi-Fi is its weak security features, which make these wireless networks vulnerable to intruders. We provide more detail about Wi-Fi security issues in Chapter 8.

Another drawback of Wi-Fi networks is susceptibility to interference from nearby systems operating in the same spectrum, such as wireless phones, microwave ovens, or other wireless LANs. Wireless networks based on the 802.11n specification will solve this problem by using multiple wireless antennas in tandem to transmit and receive data and technology to coordinate multiple simultaneous radio signals. This technology is called *MIMO (multiple input multiple output)*.

WiMax

A surprisingly large number of areas in the United States and throughout the world do not have access to Wi-Fi or fixed broadband connectivity. The range of Wi-Fi systems is no more than 300 feet from the base station, making it difficult for rural groups that don't have cable or DSL service to find wireless access to the Internet.

The IEEE developed a new family of standards known as WiMax to deal with these problems. **WiMax**, which stands for Worldwide Interoperability for Microwave Access, is the popular term for IEEE Standard 802.16, known as the "Air Interface for Fixed Broadband Wireless Access Systems." WiMax has a wireless access range of up to 31 miles, compared to 300 feet for Wi-Fi and 30 feet for Bluetooth, and a data transfer rate of up to 75 Mbps. The 802.16 specification has robust security and quality-of-service features to support voice and video.

WiMax antennas are powerful enough to beam high-speed Internet connections to rooftop antennas of homes and businesses that are miles away. Sprint Nextel is building a national WiMax network to support video, video calling, and other data-intensive wireless services, and Intel has a special chips that facilitate WiMax access from mobile computers.

RFID AND WIRELESS SENSOR NETWORKS

Mobile technologies are creating new efficiencies and ways of working throughout the enterprise. In addition to the wireless systems we have just described, radio frequency identification systems and wireless sensor networks are having a major impact.

Radio Frequency Identification (RFID)

Radio frequency identification (RFID) systems provide a powerful technology for tracking the movement of goods throughout the supply chain. RFID systems use tiny tags with embedded microchips containing data about an item and its location to transmit radio signals over a short distance to RFID readers. The RFID readers then pass the data over a network to a computer for processing. Unlike bar codes, RFID tags do not need line-of-sight contact to be read.

The RFID tag is electronically programmed with information that can uniquely identify an item plus other information about the item, such as its location, where and when it was made, or its status during production. Embedded in the tag is a microchip for storing the data. The rest of the tag is an antenna that transmits data to the reader.

The reader unit consists of an antenna and radio transmitter with a decoding capability attached to a stationary or handheld device. The reader emits radio waves in ranges anywhere from 1 inch to 100 feet, depending on its power output, the radio frequency employed, and surrounding environmental conditions. When an RFID tag comes within the range of the reader, the tag is activated and starts sending data. The reader captures these data, decodes them, and sends them back over a wired or wireless network to a host computer for further processing (see Figure 7-17). Both RFID tags and antennas come in a variety of shapes and sizes.

Active RFID tags are powered by an internal battery and typically enable data to be rewritten and modified. Active tags can transmit for hundreds of feet

FIGURE 7-17   HOW RFID WORKS

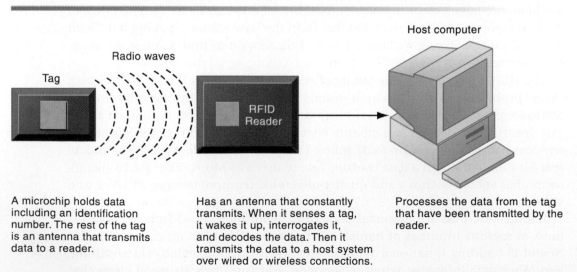

A microchip holds data including an identification number. The rest of the tag is an antenna that transmits data to a reader.

Has an antenna that constantly transmits. When it senses a tag, it wakes it up, interrogates it, and decodes the data. Then it transmits the data to a host system over wired or wireless connections.

Processes the data from the tag that have been transmitted by the reader.

RFID uses low-powered radio transmitters to read data stored in a tag at distances ranging from 1 inch to 100 feet. The reader captures the data from the tag and sends them over a network to a host computer for processing.

but cost $5 and upward per tag. Automated toll-collection systems such as New York's E-ZPass use active RFID tags.

Passive RFID tags do not have their own power source and obtain their operating power from the radio frequency energy transmitted by the RFID reader. They are smaller, lighter, and less expensive than active tags, but only have a range of several feet.

In inventory control and supply chain management, RFID systems capture and manage more detailed information about items in warehouses or in production than bar coding systems. If a large number of items are shipped together, RFID systems track each pallet, lot, or even unit item in the shipment. This technology may help companies such as Wal-Mart improve receiving and storage operations by improving their ability to "see" exactly what stock is stored in warehouses or on retail store shelves.

Wal-Mart has installed RFID readers at store receiving docks to record the arrival of pallets and cases of goods shipped with RFID tags. The RFID reader reads the tags a second time just as the cases are brought onto the sales floor from backroom storage areas. Software combines sales data from Wal-Mart's point-of-sale systems and the RFID data regarding the number of cases brought out to the sales floor. The program determines which items will soon be depleted and automatically generates a list of items to pick in the warehouse to replenish store shelves before they run out. This information helps Wal-Mart reduce out-of-stock items, increase sales, and further shrink its costs.

The cost of RFID tags used to be too high for widespread use, but now it is approaching 10 cents per passive tag in the United States. As the price decreases, RFID is starting to become cost-effective for some applications.

In addition to installing RFID readers and tagging systems, companies may need to upgrade their hardware and software to process the massive amounts of data produced by RFID systems—transactions that could add up to tens or hundreds of terabytes.

Special software is required to filter, aggregate, and prevent RFID data from overloading business networks and system applications. Applications will need to be redesigned to accept massive volumes of frequently generated RFID data and to share those data with other applications. Major enterprise software vendors, including SAP and Oracle-PeopleSoft, now offer RFID-ready versions of their supply chain management applications.

Wireless Sensor Networks

If your company wanted state-of-the art technology to monitor building security or detect hazardous substances in the air, it might deploy a wireless sensor network. **Wireless sensor networks (WSNs)** are networks of interconnected wireless devices that are embedded into the physical environment to provide measurements of many points over large spaces. These devices have built-in processing, storage, and radio frequency sensors and antennas. They are linked into an interconnected network that routes the data they capture to a computer for analysis.

These networks range from hundreds to thousands of nodes. Because wireless sensor devices are placed in the field for years at a time without any maintenance or human intervention, they must have very low power requirements and batteries capable of lasting for years.

Figure 7-18 illustrates one type of wireless sensor network, with data from individual nodes flowing across the network to a server with greater processing power. The server acts as a gateway to a network based on Internet technology.

FIGURE 7-18   A WIRELESS SENSOR NETWORK

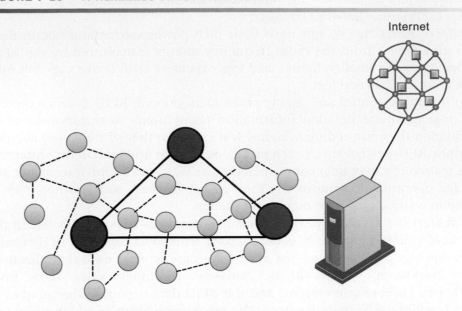

Internet

The small circles represent lower-level nodes and the larger circles represent high-end nodes. Lower-level nodes forward data to each other or to higher-level nodes, which transmit data more rapidly and speed up network performance.

Wireless sensor networks are valuable in areas such as monitoring environmental changes; monitoring traffic or military activity; protecting property; efficiently operating and managing machinery and vehicles; establishing security perimeters; monitoring supply chain management; or detecting chemical, biological, or radiological material.

7.5   HANDS-ON MIS PROJECTS

The projects in this section give you hands-on experience evaluating and selecting communications technology, using spreadsheet software to improve selection of telecommunications services, and using Web search engines for business research.

Management Decision Problems

1. Your company supplies ceramic floor tiles to Home Depot, Lowe's, and other home improvement stores. You have been asked to start using radio frequency identification tags on each case of the tiles you ship to help your customers improve the management of your products and those of other suppliers in their warehouses. Use the Web to identify the cost of hardware, software, and networking components for an RFID system for your company. What factors should be considered? What are the key decisions that have to be made in determining whether your firm should adopt this technology?

2. BestMed Medical Supplies Corporation sells medical and surgical products and equipment from over 700 different manufacturers to hospitals, health clinics, and medical offices. The company employs 500 people at seven different

locations in western and midwestern states, including account managers, customer service and support representatives, and warehouse staff. Employees communicate via traditional telephone voice services, e-mail, instant messaging, and cell phones. Management is inquiring about whether the company should adopt a system for unified communications. What factors should be considered? What are the key decisions that have to be made in determining whether to adopt this technology? Use the Web, if necessary to find out more about unified communications and its costs.

Improving Decision Making: Using Spreadsheet Software to Evaluate Wireless Services

Software skills: Spreadsheet formulas, formatting
Business skills: Analyzing telecommunications services and costs

In this project, you'll use the Web to research alternative wireless services and use spreadsheet software to calculate wireless service costs for a sales force.

You would like to equip your sales force of 35 based in Cincinnati, Ohio, with mobile phones that have capabilities for voice transmission, text messaging, and taking and sending photos. Use the Web to select a wireless service provider that provides nationwide service as well as good service in your home area. Examine the features of the mobile handsets offered by each of these vendors. Assume that each of the 35 salespeople will need to spend three hours per day during business hours (8 A.M. to 6 P.M.) on mobile voice communication, send 30 text messages per day, and five photos per week. Use your spreadsheet software to determine the wireless service and handset that will offer the best pricing per user over a two-year period. For the purposes of this exercise, you do not need to consider corporate discounts.

Achieving Operational Excellence: Using Web Search Engines for Business Research

Software skills: Web search tools
Business skills: Researching new technologies

This project will help develop your Internet skills in using Web search engines for business research.

You want to learn more about ethanol as an alternative fuel for motor vehicles. Use the following search engines to obtain that information: Yahoo!, Google, and MSN. If you wish, try some other search engines as well. Compare the volume and quality of information you find with each search tool. Which tool is the easiest to use? Which produced the best results for your research? Why?

LEARNING TRACK MODULES

The following Learning Tracks provide content relevant to topics covered in this chapter:

1. Computing and Communications Services Provided by Commercial Communications Vendors
2. Broadband Network Services and Technologies
3. Cellular System Generations
4. Wireless Applications for Customer Relationship Management, Supply Chain Management, and Healthcare
5. Web 2.0

Review Summary

1. *What are the principal components of telecommunications networks and key networking technologies?*

   A simple network consists of two or more connected computers. Basic network components include computers, network interfaces, a connection medium, network operating system software, and either a hub or a switch. The networking infrastructure for a large company includes the traditional telephone system, mobile cellular communication, wireless local-area networks, video-conferencing systems, a corporate Web site, intranets, extranets, and an array of local and wide-area networks, including the Internet.

   Contemporary networks have been shaped by the rise of client/server computing, the use of packet switching, and the adoption of Transmission Control Protocol/Internet Protocol (TCP/IP) as a universal communications standard for linking disparate networks and computers, including the Internet. Protocols provide a common set of rules that enable communication among diverse components in a telecommunications network.

2. *What are the main telecommunications transmission media and types of networks?*

   The principal physical transmission media are twisted copper telephone wire, coaxial copper cable, fiber-optic cable, and wireless transmission. Twisted wire enables companies to use existing wiring for telephone systems for digital communication, although it is relatively slow. Fiber-optic and coaxial cable are used for high-volume transmission but are expensive to install. Microwave and communications satellites are used for wireless communication over long distances.

   Local-area networks (LANs) connect PCs and other digital devices together within a 500-meter radius and are used today for many corporate computing tasks. Network components may be connected together using a star, bus, or ring topology. Wide-area networks (WANs) span broad geographical distances, ranging from several miles to continents, and are private networks that are independently managed. Metropolitan-area networks (MANs) span a single urban area.

   Digital subscriber line (DSL) technologies, cable Internet connections, and T1 lines are often used for high-capacity Internet connections.

   Cable Internet connections provide high-speed access to the Web or corporate intranets at speeds of up to 10 Mbps. A T1 line supports a data transmission rate of 1.544 Mbps.

3. *How do the Internet and Internet technology work and how do they support communication and e-business?*

   The Internet is a worldwide network of networks that uses the client/server model of computing and the TCP/IP network reference model. Every computer on the Internet is assigned a unique numeric IP address. The Domain Name System (DNS) converts IP addresses to more user-friendly domain names. Worldwide Internet policies are established by organizations and government bodies, such as the Internet Architecture Board and the World Wide Web Consortium.

   Major Internet services include e-mail, newgroups, chatting, instant messaging, Telnet, FTP, and the World Wide Web. Web pages are based on Hypertext Markup Language (HTML) and can display text, graphics, video, and audio. Web site directories, search engines, and RSS technology help users locate the information they need on the Web. RSS, blogs, and wikis are features of Web 2.0. Web technology and Internet networking standards provide the connectivity and interfaces for internal private intranets and private extranets that be accessed by many different kinds of computers inside and outside the organization.

   Firms are also starting to realize economies by using Internet VoIP technology for voice transmission and by using virtual private networks (VPNs) as low-cost alternatives to private WANs.

4. *What are the principal technologies and standards for wireless networking, communication and Internet access?*

   Cellular networks are evolving toward high-speed, high-bandwidth, digital packet-switched transmission. Broadband 3G networks are capable of transmitting data at speeds ranging from 144 Kbps to more than 2 Mbps. However, 3G services are still not available in most U.S. locations, so U.S. cellular carriers have upgraded their networks to support higher-speed transmission. These interim

2.5G networks provide data transmission rates ranging from 60 to 354 Kbps, enabling cell phones to be used for Web access, music downloads, and other broadband services.

Major cellular standards include Code Division Multiple Access (CDMA), which is used primarily in the United States, and Global System for Mobile Communications (GSM), which is the standard in Europe and much of the rest of the world.

Standards for wireless computer networks include Bluetooth (802.15) for small personal-area networks (PANs), Wi-Fi (802.11) for local-area networks (LANs), and WiMax (802.16) for metropolitan-area networks (MANs).

5. *Why are radio frequency identification (RFID) and wireless sensor networks valuable for business?*

Radio frequency identification (RFID) systems provide a powerful technology for tracking the movement of goods by using tiny tags with embedded data about an item and its location. RFID readers read the radio signals transmitted by these tags and pass the data over a network to a computer for processing. Wireless sensor networks (WSNs) are networks of interconnected wireless sensing and transmitting devices that are embedded into the physical environment to provide measurements of many points over large spaces.

Key Terms

3G networks, 306
Bandwidth, 287
Blog, 303
Bluetooth, 307
Broadband, 277
Bus topology, 284
Cable Internet connections, 288
Cell phone, 286
Chat, 294
Coaxial cable, 285
Digital subscriber line (DSL), 288
Domain name, 288
Domain Name System (DNS), 288
E-mail, 294
Fiber-optic cable, 285
File Transfer Protocol (FTP), 293
Firewalls, 305
Hertz, 287
Hotspots, 309
Hubs, 278
Hypertext Transfer Protocol (HTTP), 299
Instant messaging, 295
Internet Protocol (IP) address, 288
Internet service provider (ISP), 288
Internet2, 293
Local area network (LAN), 283
Metropolitan-area network (MAN), 284
Microwave, 286
Modem, 283
Network interface card (NIC), 288
Network operating system (NOS), 288
Packet switching, 280
Peer-to-peer, 284

Personal-area networks (PANs), 307
Personal digital assistants (PDAs), 305
Protocol, 281
Radio frequency identification (RFID), 310
Ring topology, 284
Router, 278
RSS, 304
Search engines, 300
Search engine marketing, 300
Semantic Web, 304
Shopping bots, 302
Smartphones, 305
Star topology, 284
Switch, 278
T1 lines, 288
Telnet, 293
Topology, 284
Transmission Control Protocol/Internet Protocol (TCP/IP), 281
Twisted wire, 285
Unified communications, 298
Uniform resource locator (URL), 299
Virtual private network (VPN), 298
Voice over IP (VoIP), 295
Web 2.0, 302
Web 3.0, 304
Web site, 298
Wide area networks (WANs), 284
Wi-Fi, 307
Wiki, 303
WiMax, 309
Wireless sensor networks (WSNs), 311

Review Questions

1. What are the principal components of telecommunications networks and key networking technologies?

   - Describe the features of a simple network and the network infrastructure for a large company.

   - Name and describe the principal technologies and trends that have shaped contemporary telecommunications systems.

2. What are the main telecommunications transmission media and types of networks?

   - Name the different types of physical transmission media and compare them in terms of speed and cost.

   - Define a LAN, and describe its components and the functions of each component.

   - Name and describe the principal network topologies.

3. How do the Internet and Internet technology work and how do they support communication and e-business?

   - Define the Internet, describe how it works, and explain how it provides business value.

   - Explain how the Domain Name System (DNS) and IP addressing system work.

   - List and describe the principal Internet services.

   - Define and describe VoIP and virtual private networks, and explain how they provide value to businesses.

   - List and describe alternative ways of locating information on the Web.

   - Compare Web 2.0 and Web 3.0.

   - Define and explain the difference between intranets and extranets. Explain how they provide value to businesses.

4. What are the principal technologies and standards for wireless networking, communications, and Internet access?

   - Define Bluetooth, Wi-Fi, WiMax, and 3G networks.

   - Describe the capabilities of each and for which types of applications each is best suited.

5. Why are RFID and wireless sensor networks (WSNs) valuable for business?

   - Define RFID, explain how it works and how it provides value to businesses.

   - Define WSNs, explain how they work, and describe the kinds of applications that use them.

Discussion Questions

1. It has been said that within the next few years, smartphones will become the single most important digital device we own. Discuss the implications of this statement.

2. Should all major retailing and manufacturing companies switch to RFID? Why or why not?

Video Cases

You will find video cases illustrating some of the concepts in this chapter on the Laudon Web site along with questions to help you analyze the cases.

Collaboration and Teamwork: Evaluating Smartphones

Form a group with three or four of your classmates. Compare the capabilities of Apple's iPhone with a smartphone handset from another vendor with similar features. Your analysis should consider the purchase cost of each device, the wireless networks where each device can operate, service plan and handset costs, and the services available for each device. You should also consider other capabilities of each device, including the ability to integrate with existing corporate or PC applications. Which device would you select? What criteria would you use to guide your selection? If possible, use Google Sites to post links to Web pages, team communication announcements, and work assignments; to brainstorm; and to work collaboratively on project documents. Try to use Google Docs to develop a presentation of your findings for the class.

Google Versus Microsoft: Clash of the Technology Titans
CASE STUDY

Google and Microsoft, two of the most prominent technology companies to arise in the past several decades, are poised to square off for dominance of the workplace, the Internet, and the technological world. In fact, the battle is already well underway. Both companies have already achieved dominance in their areas of expertise. Google has dominated the Internet, while Microsoft has dominated the desktop. But both are increasingly seeking to grow into the other's core businesses. The competition between the companies promises to be fierce.

The differences in the strategies and business models of the two companies illustrate why this conflict will shape our technological future. Google began as one search company among many. But the effectiveness of its PageRank search algorithm and online advertising services, along with its ability to attract the best and brightest minds in the industry, have helped Google become one of the most prominent companies in the world. The company's extensive infrastructure allows it to offer the fastest search speeds and a variety of Web-based products.

Microsoft grew to its giant stature on the strength of its Windows operating system and Office desktop productivity applications, which are used by 500 million people worldwide. Sometimes vilified for its anti-competitive practices, the company and its products are nevertheless staples for businesses and consumers looking to improve their productivity with computer-based tasks.

Today, the two companies have very different visions for the future, influenced by the continued development of the Internet and increased availability of broadband Internet connections. Google believes that the maturation of the Internet will allow more and more computing tasks to be performed via the Web, on computers sitting in data centers rather than on your desktop. This idea is known as cloud computing, and it is central to Google's business model going forward. Microsoft, on the other hand, has built its success around the model of desktop computing. Microsoft's goal is to embrace the Internet while persuading consumers to retain the desktop as the focal point for computing tasks.

Only a small handful of companies have the cash flow and manpower to manage and maintain a cloud, and Google and Microsoft are among them. With a vast array of Internet-based products and tools for online search, online advertising, digital mapping, digital photo management, digital radio broadcasting, and online video viewing, Google has pioneered cloud computing. It is obviously banking that Internet-based computing will supplant desktop computing as the way most people work with their computers. Users would use various connectivity devices to access applications from remote servers stored in data centers, as opposed to working locally from their machine.

One advantage to the cloud computing model is that users would not be tied to a particular machine to access information or do work. Another is that Google would be responsible for most of the maintenance of the data centers that house these applications. But the disadvantages of the model are the requirement of an Internet connection to use the applications, as well as the security concerns surrounding Google's handling of your information. Google is banking on the increasing ubiquity of the Internet and availability of broadband and Wi-Fi connections to offset these drawbacks.

Microsoft already has several significant advantages to help remain relevant even if cloud computing is as good as Google advertises. The company has a well-established and popular set of applications that many consumers and businesses feel comfortable using. When Microsoft launches a new product, users of Office products and Windows can be sure that they will know how to use the product and that it will work with their system.

And Google itself claims that it isn't out to supplant Microsoft, but rather provide products and services that will be used in tandem with Microsoft applications. Dave Girouard, president of Google's Enterprise division, says that "people are just using both [Google products and Office] and they use what makes sense for a particular task."

But cloud computing nevertheless represents a threat to Microsoft's core business model, which revolves around the desktop as the center for all computing tasks. If, rather than buying software from Microsoft, consumers can instead buy access to applications stored on remote servers for a much cheaper cost, the desktop suddenly no longer occupies that central position. In the past, Microsoft used the popularity of its Windows operating system (found on 95 percent of the world's personal computers) and Office to destroy competing products such as Netscape Navigator, Lotus 1-2-3, and WordPerfect. But Google's offerings are Web-based, and thus not reliant on Windows or Office. Google believes that the vast majority of computing tasks, around 90 percent, can be done in the cloud. Microsoft disputes this claim, calling it grossly overstated.

Microsoft clearly wants to bolster its Internet presence in the event that Google is correct. Their recent attempts to acquire Internet portal Yahoo! indicate this desire. No other company would give Microsoft more Internet search market share than Yahoo!. Google controls over 60 percent of the Internet search market, with Yahoo! a distant second at just over 20 percent, and Microsoft third at under 10 percent. While Microsoft-Yahoo! would still trail Google by a wide margin, the merger would at least increase the possibility of dethroning Google. Microsoft's initial buyout attempts were met with heavy resistance from Yahoo!.

With its attempted acquisition of Yahoo!, Microsoft wanted not only to bolster its Internet presence but also to end the threat of an advertising deal between Google and Yahoo!. In June 2008, those chances diminished further due to a partnership between Google and Yahoo! under which Yahoo! will outsource a portion of its advertising to Google. Google plans to deliver some of its ads alongside some of the less profitable areas of Yahoo!'s search, since Google's technology is far more sophisticated and generates more revenue per search than any competitor. Yahoo! recently introduced a comprehensive severance package that critics dismissed as a 'poison pill' intended to make them less appealing for acquisition to Microsoft. In response to this and other moves he considered to be incompetent, billionaire investor Carl Icahn has built up a large stake in the company and has agitated for change in Yahoo! leadership and reopening of negotiations with Microsoft, but the advertising deal between the two companies casts doubt over whether Microsoft can actually pull off a buyout.

With or without Yahoo!, the company's online presence will need a great deal of improvement. Microsoft's online services division's performance has worsened while Google's has improved. Microsoft lost $732 million in 2007 and was on track for an even worse year in 2008. Google gained $4.2 billion in profits over the same 2007 span.

Microsoft's goals are to "innovate and disrupt in search, win in display ads, and reinvent portal and social media experiences." Its pursuit of Yahoo! suggests skepticism even on Microsoft's own part that the company can do all of this on its own. Developing scale internally is far more difficult than simply buying it outright. In attempting to grow into this new area, Microsoft faces considerable challenges. The industry changes too quickly for one company to be dominant for very long, and Microsoft has had difficulty sustaining its growth rates since the Internet's inception. Even well-managed companies encounter difficulties when faced with disruptive new technologies, and Microsoft may be no exception.

Google faces difficulties of its own in its attempts to encroach on Microsoft's turf. The centerpiece of their efforts is their Google Apps suite. These are a series of Web-based applications that include Gmail, instant messaging, calendar, word processing, presentation, and spreadsheet applications (Google Docs), and tools for creating collaborative Web sites. These applications are simpler versions of Microsoft Office applications, and Google is offering basic versions of them for free, and 'Premier' editions for a fraction of the price. Subscribing to the Premier edition of Google Apps costs $50 per year per person, as opposed to approximately $500 per year per person for Microsoft Office.

Google believes that most Office users don't need the advanced features of Word, Excel, and other Office applications, and have a great deal to gain by switching to Google Apps. Small businesses, for example, might prefer cheaper, simpler versions of word processing, spreadsheet, and electronic presentation applications because they don't require the complex features of Microsoft Office. Microsoft disputes this, saying that Office is a result of many years and dollars of research indicating what consumers want, and that consumers are very satisfied with their products. Many businesses agree, saying that they are reluctant to move away from Office because it is the 'safe choice'. These firms are often concerned that their data is not stored on-site and that they may be in violation of laws like Sarbanes-Oxley as a result, which requires that companies maintain and report their data to the government upon request.

Microsoft is also offering more software features and Web-based services to bolster its online presence. These include SharePoint, a Web-based collaboration and document management platform, and Microsoft Office Live, providing Web-based services for e-mail, project management, and organizing information, and online extensions to Office.

The battle between Google and Microsoft isn't just being waged in the area of office productivity tools. The two companies are trading blows in a multitude of other fields, including Web browsers, Web maps, online video, cell phone software, and online health recordkeeping tools. Salesforce.com (see the Interactive Session in Chapter 5) represents the site of another conflict between the two giants. Microsoft has attempted to move in on the software-as-a-service model popularized by Salesforce.com, offering a competing CRM product for a fraction of the cost. Google has gone the opposite route, partnering with Salesforce to integrate their CRM applications with Google Apps and creating a new sales channel to market Google Apps to businesses that have already adopted Salesforce CRM software.

Additionally, both companies are attempting to open themselves up as platforms to developers. Google has already launched its Google App Engine, which allows outside programmers to develop and launch their own applications for minimal cost. In a move that represented a drastic change from their previous policy, Microsoft announced that they would reveal many key details of its software that they had previously kept secret. Programmers will have an easier time building services that work with Microsoft programs. Microsoft's secrecy once helped them control the marketplace by forcing other companies to use Windows rather than develop alternatives, but if they can't do the same to Google Apps, it makes sense to try a different approach to attract developers.

Time will tell whether or not Microsoft is able to fend off Google's challenge to its dominance in the tech industry. Many other prominent companies have fallen victim to paradigm shifts, such as mainframes to personal computers, traditional print media to Internet distribution, and, if Google has its way, personal computers to cloud computing.

Sources: Clint Boulton, "Microsoft Marks the Spot," *eWeek*, May 5, 2008; Andy Kessler, "The War for the Web," *The Wall Street Journal*, May 6, 2008; John Pallatto and Clint Boulton, "An On-Demand Partnership" and Clint Boulton, "Google Apps Go to School," *eWeek*, April 21, 2008; Miguel Helft, "Ad Accord for Yahoo! and Google," *The New York Times*, June 13, 2008 and "Google and Salesforce Join to Fight Microsoft," *The New York Times*, April 14, 2008; Clint Boulton, "Google Tucks Jotspot into Apps," *eWeek*, March 3, 2008; Robert A. Guth, Ben Worthen, and Charles Forelle, "Microsoft to Allow Software Secrets on Internet," *The Wall Street Journal*, February 22, 2008; J. Nicholas Hoover, "Microsoft-Yahoo! Combo Would Involve Overlap—and Choices," *Information Week*, February 18, 2008; Steve Lohr, "Yahoo! Offer is Strategy Shift for Microsoft," *The New York Times*, February 2, 2008; and John Markoff, "Competing as Software Goes to Web," *The New York Times*, June 5, 2007.

CASE STUDY QUESTIONS

1. Define and compare the business strategies and business models of Google and Microsoft.

2. Has the Internet taken over the PC desktop as the center of the action? Why or why not?

3. Why did Microsoft attempt to acquire Yahoo!? How did it affect its business model? Do you believe this was a good move?

4. What is the significance of Google Apps to Google's future success?

5. Would you use Google Apps instead of Microsoft Office applications for computing tasks? Why or why not?

6. Which company and business model do you believe will prevail in this epic struggle? Justify your answer.

Chapter 8

Securing Information Systems

Interactive Sessions:

The Worst Data Theft Ever?

Security at ICICI Bank

BOSTON CELTICS SCORE BIG POINTS AGAINST SPYWARE

While the Boston Celtics were fighting for a spot in the playoffs several years ago, another fierce battle was being waged by its information systems. Jay Wessel, the team's vice president of technology, was trying to score points against computer spyware. Wessel and his IT staff manage about 100 laptops issued to coaches and scouts, and sales, marketing, and finance employees, and these machines were being overwhelmed by malware (malicious software).

Like any sports franchise, the Celtics are on the road a great deal of time during the playing season. Coaches, recruiters, and other staff members are at away games 40 or more times each season, using their mobile laptop computers to review plays and update the status of players. They continually sign onto the Internet and connect to the Celtics' internal network from airports, hotels, and other public places. According to Wessel, "Hotel Internet connections are a hotbed for spyware activity." People would bring laptops that had been infected on the road back to team headquarters in Boston and clog up the network. Moreover, the spyware was affecting the accessibility and performance of the Celtics' proprietary statistical database created with Microsoft SQL Server, which the coaches use to prepare for each game. Wessel and his staff were overwhelmed spending too much time trying to rid the machines and the network of infections.

During one playoff battle, a torrent of spyware poured into the laptops via a bad Internet connection in an Indiana hotel. At that point, Wessel decided to take a more aggressive stance toward spyware. His options were limited because his staff is small and the company does not have many resources for dealing with security. The security software solutions that the Celtics had been using (Aladdin eSafe Security Gateway and Webroot Spy Sweeper) were too unwieldy. The only way the Celtics could run a video-editing suite used for scouting new players was to temporarily remove these products.

Wessel decided to use Mi5 Networks' Webgate security appliance as a solution. The tool sits between the Celtics' corporate firewall and network, where it stops spyware from entering the Celtics' corporate network and prevents machines that have already been infected from connecting to the network. Webgate also prevents machines infected with spyware from transmitting data back to the source of the spyware.

Infected machines are quarantined and cleaned up by Wessel's staff. Webgate provides an executive summary screen for Wessel to review a list of infected machines, internal botnet activity, remote attacks, and spyware attempts to surreptitiously communicate with its authors. To supplement Webgate, the Celtics use SurfControl (now part of Websense) to filter e-mail and Web surfing activity, Trend Micro antivirus software, SonicWALL firewall and intrusion detection technology, and Aladdin eSafe for additional malware detection.

Since installing Webgate and these other tools, the Celtics' network has been spyware-free. Laptop performance, which used to be slowed down by malicious software, has improved, the corporate network runs much faster, and calls are down to the Celtics' IT help desk. Wessel is quick to point out that this security system would not work without user education. Employees are required to sign an acceptable use policy that states what they are allowed to do on their work machines, and they are explicitly discouraged from visiting Web sites that could transmit more malware to the Celtics' network.

Sources: Doug Bartholomew, "The Boston Celtics' New Malware Point Guard," *Baseline Magazine*, January 2008 and Bill Brenner, "Boston Celtics Face Off Against Spyware," SearchSecurity.com, accessed June 23, 2008.

The problems created by spyware for the Boston Celtics illustrate some of the reasons why businesses need to pay special attention to information system security. Malicious spyware that had infected coaches' and employees' laptops when they were on the road impaired performance of the company's internal systems, making it difficult for employees to obtain the information they needed to perform their jobs.

The chapter-opening diagram calls attention to important points raised by this case and this chapter. The Boston Celtics coaches and other staff members need to use their laptops to connect to the company's internal systems while they are traveling with the team. Linking to public Wi-Fi networks at hotels and airports exposed the laptops to malicious spyware, which the laptops then transmitted to corporate systems. The company was spending too much time and money ridding its systems of malware. Management decided to invest in new security technology to provide additional layers of protection. It also revised security procedures requiring infected laptops to be quarantined so they could not infect corporate systems. The chosen solution has kept the Celtics' systems free of spyware and speeded up system performance.

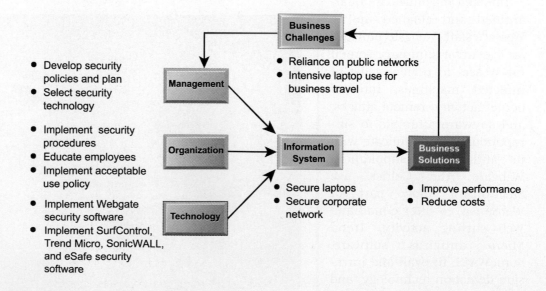

8.1 SYSTEM VULNERABILITY AND ABUSE

C an you imagine what would happen if you tried to link to the Internet without a firewall or antivirus software? Your computer would be disabled in a few seconds, and it might take you many days to recover. If you used the computer to run your business, you might not be able to sell to your customers or place orders with your suppliers while it was down. And you might find that your computer system had been penetrated by outsiders, who perhaps stole or destroyed valuable data, including confidential payment data from your customers. If too much data were destroyed or divulged, your business might never be able to operate!

In short, if you operate a business today, you need to make security and control a top priority. **Security** refers to the policies, procedures, and technical measures used to prevent unauthorized access, alteration, theft, or physical damage to information systems. **Controls** are methods, policies, and organizational procedures that ensure the safety of the organization's assets; the accuracy and reliability of its records; and operational adherence to management standards.

WHY SYSTEMS ARE VULNERABLE

When large amounts of data are stored in electronic form, they are vulnerable to many more kinds of threats than when they existed in manual form. Through communications networks, information systems in different locations are interconnected. The potential for unauthorized access, abuse, or fraud is not limited to a single location but can occur at any access point in the network. Figure 8-1 illustrates the most common threats against contemporary information systems. They can stem from technical, organizational, and environmental factors compounded by poor management decisions. In the multi-tier client/server computing environment illustrated here, vulnerabilities exist at each layer and in the communications between the layers. Users at the client

FIGURE 8-1   CONTEMPORARY SECURITY CHALLENGES AND VULNERABILITIES

Client (User)	Communications Lines	Corporate Servers	Corporate Systems

Hardware
Operating Systems
Software

- Unauthorized access
- Errors

- Tapping
- Sniffing
- Message alteration
- Theft and fraud
- Radiation

- Hacking
- Viruses and worms
- Theft and fraud
- Vandalism
- Denial-of-service attacks

- Theft of data
- Copying data
- Alteration of data
- Hardware failure
- Software failure

The architecture of a Web-based application typically includes a Web client, a server, and corporate information systems linked to databases. Each of these components presents security challenges and vulnerabilities. Floods, fires, power failures, and other electrical problems can cause disruptions at any point in the network.

layer can cause harm by introducing errors or by accessing systems without authorization. It is possible to access data flowing over networks, steal valuable data during transmission, or alter messages without authorization. Radiation may disrupt a network at various points as well. Intruders can launch denial-of-service attacks or malicious software to disrupt the operation of Web sites. Those capable of penetrating corporate systems can destroy or alter corporate data stored in databases or files.

Systems malfunction if computer hardware breaks down, is not configured properly, or is damaged by improper use or criminal acts. Errors in programming, improper installation, or unauthorized changes cause computer software to fail. Power failures, floods, fires, or other natural disasters can also disrupt computer systems.

Domestic or offshore partnering with another company adds to system vulnerability if valuable information resides on networks and computers outside the organization's control. Without strong safeguards, valuable data could be lost, destroyed, or could fall into the wrong hands, revealing important trade secrets or information that violates personal privacy.

The growing use of mobile devices for business computing adds to these woes. Portability makes cell phones and smartphones easy to lose or steal, and their networks are vulnerable to access by outsiders. Smartphones used by corporate executives may contain sensitive data such as sales figures, customer names, phone numbers, and e-mail addresses. Intruders may be able to access internal corporate networks through these devices. Unauthorized downloads may introduce disabling software.

Internet Vulnerabilities

Large public networks, such as the Internet, are more vulnerable than internal networks because they are virtually open to anyone. The Internet is so huge that when abuses do occur, they can have an enormously widespread impact. When the Internet becomes part of the corporate network, the organization's information systems are even more vulnerable to actions from outsiders.

Computers that are constantly connected to the Internet by cable modems or digital subscriber line (DSL) lines are more open to penetration by outsiders because they use fixed Internet addresses where they can be easily identified. (With dial-up service, a temporary Internet address is assigned for each session.) A fixed Internet address creates a fixed target for hackers.

Telephone service based on Internet technology (see Chapter 7) is more vulnerable than the switched voice network if it does not run over a secure private network. Most voice over IP (VoIP) traffic over the public Internet is not encrypted, so anyone with a network can listen in on conversations. Hackers can intercept conversations or shut down voice service by flooding servers supporting VoIP with bogus traffic.

Vulnerability has also increased from widespread use of e-mail, instant messaging (IM), and peer-to-peer file-sharing programs. E-mail may contain attachments that serve as springboards for malicious software or unauthorized access to internal corporate systems. Employees may use e-mail messages to transmit valuable trade secrets, financial data, or confidential customer information to unauthorized recipients. Popular instant messaging applications for consumers do not use a secure layer for text messages, so they can be intercepted and read by outsiders during transmission over the public Internet. IM activity over the Internet can in some cases be used as a back door to an otherwise secure network. Sharing files over peer-to-peer (P2P) networks, such as those for illegal music sharing, may also transmit malicious software or expose information on either individual or corporate computers to outsiders.

Wireless Security Challenges

Is it safe to log onto a wireless network at an airport, library, or other public location? It depends on how vigilant you are. Even the wireless network in your home is vulnerable because radio frequency bands are easy to scan. Both Bluetooth and Wi-Fi networks are susceptible to hacking by eavesdroppers. Although the range of Wi-Fi networks is only several hundred feet, it can be extended up to one-fourth of a mile using external antennae. Local-area networks (LANs) using the 802.11 standard can be easily penetrated by outsiders armed with laptops, wireless cards, external antennae, and hacking software. Hackers use these tools to detect unprotected networks, monitor network traffic, and, in some cases, gain access to the Internet or to corporate networks. The Interactive Session on Organizations describes how poor wireless security may have enabled criminals to break into the corporate systems of TJX Companies and other major retailers and steal credit card and personal data on over 41 million people.

Wi-Fi transmission technology was designed to make it easy for stations to find and hear one another. The *service set identifiers (SSIDs)* identifying the access points in a Wi-Fi network are broadcast multiple times and can be picked up fairly easily by intruders' sniffer programs (see Figure 8-2). Wireless networks in many locations do not have basic protections against **war driving**, in which eavesdroppers drive by buildings or park outside and try to intercept wireless network traffic.

FIGURE 8-2   WI-FI SECURITY CHALLENGES

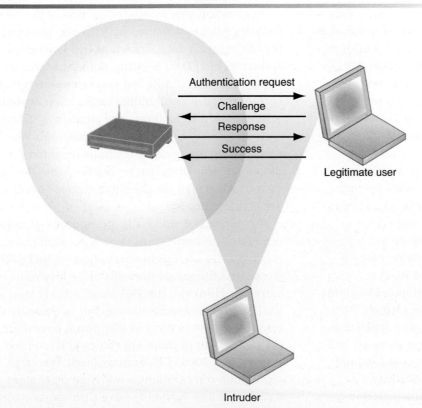

Many Wi-Fi networks can be penetrated easily by intruders using sniffer programs to obtain an address to access the resources of a network without authorization.

INTERACTIVE SESSION: ORGANIZATIONS

THE WORST DATA THEFT EVER?

In early August 2008, U.S. federal prosecutors charged 11 men in five countries, including the United States, Ukraine, and China, with stealing more than 41 million credit and debit card numbers. This is now the biggest known theft of credit card numbers in history. The thieves focused on major retail chains such as OfficeMax, Barnes & Noble, BJ's Wholesale Club, the Sports Authority, and T.J. Maxx.

The thieves drove around and scanned the wireless networks of these retailers to identify network vulnerabilities and then installed sniffer programs obtained from overseas collaborators. The sniffer programs tapped into the retailers' networks for processing credit cards, intercepting customers' debit and credit card numbers and PINs (personal identification numbers). The thieves then sent that information to computers in the Ukraine, Latvia, and the United States. They sold the credit card numbers online and imprinted other stolen numbers on the magnetic stripes of blank cards so they could withdraw thousands of dollars from ATM machines. Albert Gonzalez of Miami was identified as a principal organizer of the ring.

The conspirators began their largest theft in July 2005, when they identified a vulnerable network at a Marshall's department store in Miami and used it to install a sniffer program on the computers of the chain's parent company, TJX. They were able to access the central TJX database, which stored customer transactions for T.J. Maxx, Marshalls, HomeGoods, and A.J. Wright stores in the United States and Puerto Rico, and for Winners and HomeSense stores in Canada. Fifteen months later, TJX reported that the intruders had stolen records with up to 45 million credit and debit card numbers.

TJX was still using the old Wired Equivalent Privacy (WEP) encryption system, which is relatively easy for hackers to crack. Other companies had switched to the more secure Wi-Fi Protected Access (WPA) standard with more complex encryption, but TJX did not make the change. An auditor later found that TJX had also neglected to install firewalls and data encryption on many of the computers using the wireless network, and did not properly install another layer of security software it had purchased. TJX acknowledged in a Securities and Exchange Commission filing that it transmitted credit card data to banks without encryption, violating credit card company guidelines.

Incidents of credit card fraud tied to TJX stores started surfacing in the United States and abroad. Customers at Fidelity Homestead, the Louisiana savings bank, began seeing strange transactions on their credit card bills in November 2005—unauthorized purchases in Wal-Mart stores in Mexico and in supermarkets and other stores in southern California.

In March 2007, the Gainesville Police Department and the Florida Department of Law Enforcement arrested six people using fake credit cards with the stolen TJX data. They had purchased $8 million in gift cards from Wal-Mart and Sam's Club stores in 50 Florida counties, and used them to buy flat-screen TVs, computers, and other electronics.

The following July, the U.S. Secret Service arrested four more people in south Florida who had been using the stolen TJX customer data. The arrests recovered about 200,000 stolen credit card numbers used in fraud losses calculated to be more than $75 million.

In question was whether TJX was adhering to the security rules established by Visa and MasterCard for storing such data, known as the Payment Card Industry (PCI) Data Security Standard. According to these rules, merchants are not supposed to maintain certain types of cardholder data in their systems because the data facilitate the creation of fraudulent card accounts. Communications between Visa and card-issuing financial institutions revealed that TJX did violate this principle by holding onto data for years, rather than for the short amount of time they are actually needed.

On paper, PCI standards are rigorous. It requires merchants to implement twelve account-protection mechanisms, including encryption, vulnerability scans, and the use of firewalls and antivirus software. However, the PCI standards are not well enforced. Merchants who fail to abide by them remain eligible to process electronic payments, and only a fraction of them are thoroughly audited.

In March 2008, TJX management agreed to strengthen the company's information system security. It also agreed to have third-party auditors review security measures every 2 years for the next 20 years.

A few months earlier, TJX had reached an agreement with Visa U.S.A. to establish a $40.9 million fund to compensate banks that were affected by its security breach. Banks that issued the credit and debit cards might have to spend $300 million just to replace the stolen cards, in addition to covering fraudulent purchases.

TJX reported having already spent $202 million to deal with its data theft, including legal settlements, and that it expected to spend $23 million more in fiscal 2009. Forrester Research estimates that the cost to TJX for the data breach could surpass $1 billion over five years, including costs for consultants, security upgrades, attorney fees, and additional marketing to reassure customers. TJX declined to comment on those numbers.

A report from Javelin Strategy & Research revealed that more than 75% of the consumers it surveyed would not continue to shop at stores that had been victimized by data theft. The same study showed that consumers trust credit card companies to protect their data far more than retailers.

Sources: Brad Stone, "11 Charged in Theft of 41 Million Card Numbers," *The New York Times*, August 6, 2008; Andrew Conry-Murray, "PCI and the Circle of Blame," *Information Week*, February 25, 2008; Dan Berthiaume, "Data Breaches Cause Concern," *eWeek*, April 7, 2008; Joseph Pereira, Jennifer Levitz, and Jeremy Singer-Vine, "Some Stores Quiet Over Card Breach," *The Wall Street Journal*, August 11, 2008; Robin Sidel, "Giant Retailer Reveals Customer Data Breach," *The Wall Street Journal*, January 18, 2007; "Hack Attack Means Headaches for TJ Maxx," *Information Week*, February 3, 2007, and T.J. Maxx Probe Reveals Data Breach Worse Than Originally Thought," *Information Week*, February 21, 2007.

CASE STUDY QUESTIONS

1. List and describe the security control weaknesses at TJX Companies.
2. What management, organization, and technology factors contributed to these weaknesses?
3. What was the business impact of TJX's data loss on TJX, consumers, and banks?
4. How effectively did TJX deal with these problems?
5. Who should be held liable for the losses caused by the use of fraudulent credit cards in this case? TJX? The banks issuing the credit cards? The consumers? Justify your answer.
6. What solutions would you suggest to prevent the problems?

MIS IN ACTION

Explore the Web site of the PCI Security Standards Council (www.pcisecuritystandards.org) and review the PCI Data Security Standard (PCI DSS).

1. Based on the details in this case study, how well was TJX complying with the PCI DSS. What requirements did it fail to meet?
2. Would complying with this standard have prevented the theft of credit card data from TJX?

A hacker can employ an 802.11 analysis tool to identify the SSID. (Windows XP and Vista have capabilities for detecting the SSID used in a network and automatically configuring the radio NIC within the user's device.) An intruder that has associated with an access point by using the correct SSID is capable of accessing other resources on the network, using the Windows operating system to determine which other users are connected to the network, access their computer hard drives, and open or copy their files.

Intruders also use the information they have gleaned to set up rogue access points on a different radio channel in physical locations close to users to force a user's radio NIC to associate with the rogue access point. Once this association occurs, hackers using the rogue access point can capture the names and passwords of unsuspecting users.

The initial security standard developed for Wi-Fi, called *Wired Equivalent Privacy (WEP)*, is not very effective. WEP is built into all standard 802.11 products, but its use is optional. Many users neglect to use WEP security features, leaving them unprotected. The basic WEP specification calls for an access point and all of its users to share the same 40-bit encrypted password, which can be easily decrypted by hackers from a small amount of traffic. Stronger encryption and authentication systems are now available, but users must be willing to install them.

MALICIOUS SOFTWARE: VIRUSES, WORMS, TROJAN HORSES, AND SPYWARE

Malicious software programs are referred to as **malware** and include a variety of threats, such as computer viruses, worms, and Trojan horses. (A **computer virus** is a rogue software program that attaches itself to other software programs or data files in order to be executed, usually without user knowledge or permission. Most computer viruses deliver a "payload." The payload may be relatively benign, such as the instructions to display a message or image, or it may be highly destructive—destroying programs or data, clogging computer memory, reformatting a computer's hard drive, or causing programs to run improperly. Viruses typically spread from computer to computer when humans take an action, such as sending an e-mail attachment or copying an infected file.

Most recent attacks have come from **worms**, which are independent computer programs that copy themselves from one computer to other computers over a network. (Unlike viruses, they can operate on their own without attaching to other computer program files and rely less on human behavior in order to spread from computer to computer. This explains why computer worms spread much more rapidly than computer viruses.) Worms destroy data and programs as well as disrupt or even halt the operation of computer networks.

Worms and viruses are often spread over the Internet from files of downloaded software, from files attached to e-mail transmissions, or from compromised e-mail messages or instant messaging. Viruses have also invaded computerized information systems from "infected" disks or infected machines. E-mail worms are currently the most problematic.

There are now more than 200 viruses and worms targeting mobile phones, such as CABIR, Comwarrior, and Frontal A. Frontal A, for example, installs a corrupted file that causes phone failure and prevents the user from rebooting. Mobile device viruses could pose serious threats to enterprise computing because so many wireless devices are now linked to corporate information systems.

Web 2.0 applications, such as blogs, wikis, and social networking sites such as Facebook and MySpace, have emerged as new conduits for malware or spyware. These applications allow users to post software code as part of the permissible content, and such code can be launched automatically as soon as a Web page is viewed. For example, in August 2008, malicious hackers targeted unsuspecting Facebook users via postings on the site's Wall feature, which is used by members to leave each other messages. Impersonating members' friends, malicious hackers posted messages urging users to click on a link to view a video that transported them to a rogue Web page where they were told to download a new version of Adobe's Flash player in order to view the video. If users authorized the download, the site would install a Trojan horse, Troj/Dloadr-BPL, that funneled other malicious code to their PCs (Perez, 2008).

Table 8-1 describes the characteristics of some of the most harmful worms and viruses that have appeared to date.

Over the past decade, worms and viruses have cause billions of dollars of damage to corporate networks, e-mail systems, and data. According to Consumer Reports' State of the Net 2008 survey, U.S. consumers lost $8.5 billion because of malware and online scams, and the majority of these losses came from malware (Consumer Reports, 2008).

A **Trojan horse** is a software program that appears to be benign but then does something other than expected. The Trojan horse is not itself a virus because it does not replicate but is often a way for viruses or other malicious code to be introduced into a computer system. The term *Trojan horse* is based on the huge wooden horse used by the Greeks to trick the Trojans into opening the gates to their fortified city during the Trojan War. Once inside the city walls, Greek soldiers hidden in the horse revealed themselves and captured the city.

An example of a modern-day Trojan horse is Pushdo Trojan, which uses electronic greeting-card lures in e-mail to trick Windows users into launching an executable program. Once the Trojan is executed, it pretends to be an Apache Web server and tries to deliver executable malware programs to the infected Windows machines.

TABLE 8-1 EXAMPLES OF MALICIOUS CODE

NAME	TYPE	DESCRIPTION
Storm	Worm/ Trojan horse	First identified in January 2007. Spreads via e-mail spam with a fake attachment. Infected up to 10 million computers, causing them to join its zombie network of computers engaged in criminal activity.
Sasser.ftp	Worm	First appeared in May 2004. Spread over the Internet by attacking random IP addresses. Causes computers to continually crash and reboot, and infected computers to search for more victims. Affected millions of computers worldwide, disrupting British Airways flight check-ins, operations of British coast guard stations, Hong Kong hospitals, Taiwan post office branches, and Australia's Westpac Bank. Sasser and its variants caused an estimated $14.8 billion to $18.6 billion in damages worldwide.
MyDoom.A	Worm	First appeared on January 26, 2004. Spreads as an e-mail attachment. Sends e-mail to addresses harvested from infected machines, forging the sender's address. At its peak this worm lowered global Internet performance by 10 percent and Web page loading times by as much as 50 percent. Was programmed to stop spreading after February 12, 2004.
Sobig.F	Worm	First detected on August 19, 2003. Spreads via e-mail attachments and sends massive amounts of mail with forged sender information. Deactivated itself on September 10, 2003, after infecting more than 1 million PCs and doing $5 to $10 billion in damage.
ILOVEYOU	Virus	First detected on May 3, 2000. Script virus written in Visual Basic script and transmitted as an attachment to e-mail with the subject line ILOVEYOU. Overwrites music, image, and other files with a copy of itself and did an estimated $10 billion to $15 billion in damage.
Melissa	Macro virus/ worm	First appeared in March 1999. Word macro script mailing infected Word file to first 50 entries in user's Microsoft Outlook address book. Infected 15 to 29 percent of all business PCs, causing $300 million to $600 million in damage.

Some types of **spyware** also act as malicious software. These small programs install themselves surreptitiously on computers to monitor user Web surfing activity and serve up advertising. Thousands of forms of spyware have been documented. Harris Interactive found that 92 percent of the companies surveyed in its Web@Work study reported detecting spyware on their networks (Mitchell, 2006).

Many users find such spyware annoying and some critics worry about its infringement on computer users' privacy. Some forms of spyware are especially nefarious. **Keyloggers** record every keystroke made on a computer to steal serial numbers for software, to launch Internet attacks, to gain access to e-mail accounts, to obtain passwords to protected computer systems, or to pick up personal information such as credit card numbers. Other spyware programs reset Web browser home pages, redirect search requests, or slow computer performance by taking up too much memory.

HACKERS AND COMPUTER CRIME

A **hacker** is an individual who intends to gain unauthorized access to a computer system. Within the hacking community, the term *cracker* is typically used to denote a hacker with criminal intent, although in the public press, the terms hacker and cracker are used interchangeably. Hackers and crackers gain unauthorized access by finding weaknesses in the security protections employed by Web sites and computer systems, often taking advantage of various features of the Internet that make it an open system that is easy to use.

Hacker activities have broadened beyond mere system intrusion to include theft of goods and information, as well as system damage and **cybervandalism**, the intentional disruption, defacement, or even destruction of a Web site or corporate information system. For example, cybervandals have turned many of the MySpace "group" sites, which are dedicated to interests such as home beer brewing or animal welfare, into cyber-graffiti walls, filled with offensive comments and photographs (Kirk, 2008).

Spoofing and Sniffing

Hackers attempting to hide their true identities often spoof, or misrepresent, themselves by using fake e-mail addresses or masquerading as someone else. **Spoofing** also may involve redirecting a Web link to an address different from the intended one, with the site masquerading as the intended destination. For example, if hackers redirect customers to a fake Web site that looks almost exactly like the true site, they can then collect and process orders, effectively stealing business as well as sensitive customer information from the true site. We provide more detail on other forms of spoofing in our discussion of computer crime.

A **sniffer** is a type of eavesdropping program that monitors information traveling over a network. When used legitimately, sniffers help identify potential network trouble spots or criminal activity on networks, but when used for criminal purposes, they can be damaging and very difficult to detect. Sniffers enable hackers to steal proprietary information from anywhere on a network, including e-mail messages, company files, and confidential reports.

Denial-of-Service Attacks

In a **denial-of-service (DoS) attack**, hackers flood a network server or Web server with many thousands of false communications or requests for services to crash the network. The network receives so many queries that it cannot keep up with them and is thus unavailable to service legitimate requests. A **distributed denial-of-service (DDoS)** attack uses numerous computers to inundate and overwhelm the network from numerous launch points. For example, Bill O'Reilly's official Web site was bombarded by data that overloaded the system's firewalls for two days in early March 2007, forcing the site to be taken down to protect it (Schmidt, 2007).

Although DoS attacks do not destroy information or access restricted areas of a company's information systems, they often cause a Web site to shut down, making it impossible for legitimate users to access the site. For busy e-commerce sites, these attacks are costly; while the site is shut down, customers cannot make purchases. Especially vulnerable are small and midsize businesses whose networks tend to be less protected than those of large corporations.

Perpetrators of DoS attacks often use thousands of "zombie" PCs infected with malicious software without their owners' knowledge and organized into a **botnet**. Hackers create these botnets by infecting other people's computers with bot malware that opens a back door through which an attacker can give instructions. The infected computer then becomes a slave, or zombie, serving a master computer belonging to someone else. Once a hacker infects enough computers, her or she can use the amassed resources of the botnet to launch DDos attacks, phishing campaigns, or unsolicited "spam" e-mail.

In the first six months of 2007, security product provider Symantec observed over 5 million distinct bot-infected computers. Bots and botnets are an extremely serious threat because they can be used to launch very large attacks using many different techniques. For example, the Storm worm, which was responsible for one of the largest e-mail attacks in the past few years, was propagated via a massive botnet of nearly 2 million computers. Botnet attacks thought to have originated in Russia were responsible for crippling the Web sites of the Estonian government in April 2007 and the Georgian government in July 2008.

Computer Crime

Most hacker activities are criminal offenses, and the vulnerabilities of systems we have just described make them targets for other types of computer crime as well. For example, Yung-Sun Lin was charged in January 2007 with installing a "logic bomb" program on the computers of his employer, Medco Health Solutions of Franklin Lakes, New Jersey. Lin's program could have erased critical prescription information for 60 million Americans (Gaudin, 2007). **Computer crime** is defined by the U.S. Department of Justice as "any violations of criminal law that involve a knowledge of computer technology for their perpetration, investigation, or prosecution." Table 8-2 provides examples of the computer as a target of crime and as an instrument of crime.

No one knows the magnitude of the computer crime problem—how many systems are invaded, how many people engage in the practice, or the total economic damage. According to the 2007 CSI Computer Crime and Security Survey of nearly 500 companies, participants' average annual loss from computer crime and security attacks was $350,424 (Richardson, 2007). Many companies are reluctant to report computer crimes because the crimes may involve employees, or the company fears that publicizing its vulnerability will hurt its reputation. The most economically damaging kinds of computer crime are DoS attacks, introducing viruses, theft of services, and disruption of computer systems.

TABLE 8-2 EXAMPLES OF COMPUTER CRIME

COMPUTERS AS TARGETS OF CRIME

Breaching the confidentiality of protected computerized data

Accessing a computer system without authority

Knowingly accessing a protected computer to commit fraud

Intentionally accessing a protected computer and causing damage, negligently or deliberately

Knowingly transmitting a program, program code, or command that intentionally causes damage to a protected computer

Threatening to cause damage to a protected computer

COMPUTERS AS INSTRUMENTS OF CRIME

Theft of trade secrets

Unauthorized copying of software or copyrighted intellectual property, such as articles, books, music, and video

Schemes to defraud

Using e-mail for threats or harassment

Intentionally attempting to intercept electronic communication

Illegally accessing stored electronic communications, including e-mail and voice mail

Transmitting or possessing child pornography using a computer

Identity Theft

With the growth of the Internet and electronic commerce, identity theft has become especially troubling. **Identity theft** is a crime in which an imposter obtains key pieces of personal information, such as Social Security identification numbers, driver's license numbers, or credit card numbers, to impersonate someone else. The information may be used to obtain credit, merchandise, or services in the name of the victim or to provide the thief with false credentials. According to Javelin Strategy and Research, 8.4 million Americans were victims of identity theft in 2007 and they suffered losses totaling $49.3 billion (Stempel, 2007).

Identify theft has flourished on the Internet, with credit card files a major target of Web site hackers. Moreover, e-commerce sites are wonderful sources of customer personal information—name, address, and phone number. Armed with this information, criminals are able to assume new identities and establish new credit for their own purposes.

One increasingly popular tactic is a form of spoofing called **phishing**. Phishing involves setting up fake Web sites or sending e-mail messages that look like those of legitimate businesses to ask users for confidential personal data. The e-mail message instructs recipients to update or confirm records by providing social security numbers, bank and credit card information, and other confidential data either by responding to the e-mail message, by entering the information at a bogus Web site, or by calling a telephone number. EBay, PayPal, Amazon.com, Wal-Mart, and a variety of banks, are among the top spoofed companies.

New phishing techniques called evil twins and pharming are harder to detect. **Evil twins** are wireless networks that pretend to offer trustworthy Wi-Fi connections to the Internet, such as those in airport lounges, hotels, or coffee shops. The bogus network looks identical to a legitimate public network. Fraudsters try to capture passwords or credit card numbers of unwitting users who log on to the network.

Pharming redirects users to a bogus Web page, even when the individual types the correct Web page address into his or her browser. This is possible if pharming perpetrators gain access to the Internet address information stored by Internet service providers to speed up Web browsing and the ISP companies have flawed software on their servers that allows the fraudsters to hack in and change those addresses.

The U.S. Congress addressed the threat of computer crime in 1986 with the Computer Fraud and Abuse Act. This act makes it illegal to access a computer system without authorization. Most states have similar laws, and nations in Europe have comparable legislation. Congress also passed the National Information Infrastructure Protection Act in 1996 to make virus distribution and hacker attacks to disable Web sites federal crimes. U.S. legislation, such as the Wiretap Act, Wire Fraud Act, Economic Espionage Act, Electronic Communications Privacy Act, E-Mail Threats and Harassment Act, and Child Pornography Act, covers computer crimes involving intercepting electronic communication, using electronic communication to defraud, stealing trade secrets, illegally accessing stored electronic communications, using e-mail for threats or harassment, and transmitting or possessing child pornography.

Click Fraud

When you click on an ad displayed by a search engine, the advertiser typically pays a fee for each click, which is supposed to direct potential buyers to its products. **Click fraud** occurs when an individual or computer program fraudulently clicks on an online ad without any intention of learning more about the advertiser or making a purchase. Click fraud has become a serious problem at Google and other Web sites that feature pay-per-click online advertising.

Some companies hire third parties (typically from low-wage countries) to fraudulently click on a competitor's ads to weaken them by driving up their marketing costs. Click fraud can also be perpetrated with software programs doing the clicking, and botnets are often used for this purpose. Search engines such as Google attempt to monitor click fraud but have been reluctant to publicize their efforts to deal with the problem.

Global Threats: Cyberterrorism and Cyberwarfare

The cybercriminal activities we have described—launching malware, denial-of-service attacks, and phishing probes—are borderless. Computer security firm Sophos reported that 42 percent of the malware it identified in early 2008 originated in the United States, while 30.1 percent came from China, and 10.3 percent from Russia (Sophos, 2008). The global nature of the Internet makes it possible for cybercriminals to operate—and to do harm—anywhere in the world.

Concern is mounting that the vulnerabilities of the Internet or other networks make digital networks easy targets for digital attacks by terrorists, foreign intelligence services, or other groups seeking to create widespread disruption and harm. Such cyberattacks might target the software that runs electrical power grids, air traffic control systems, or networks of major banks and financial institutions. At least 20 countries, including China, are believed to be developing offensive and defensive cyberwarfare capabilities. In 2007, there were 12,986 reported attacks on U.S. government agencies, with incursions on U.S. military networks up 55 percent from a year earlier. Companies that are defense department contractors have also come under siege (Grow et al., 2008).

Malware is active throughout the globe. These three charts show the regional distribution of worms and computer viruses worldwide reported by online security provider Trend Micro over periods of 24 hours, 7 days, and 30 days. The virus count represents the number of infected files, and the percentage shows the relative prevalence in each region compared to worldwide statistics for each measuring period.

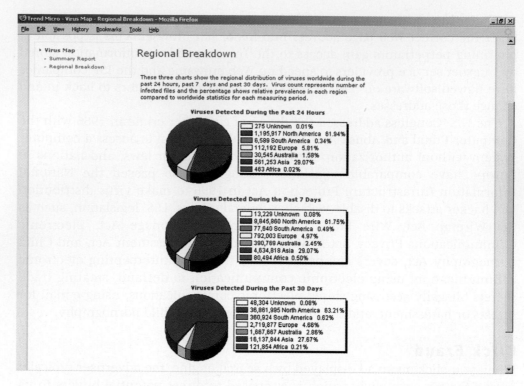

To deal with this threat, President George W. Bush signed a Cyber Initiative directive on January 8, 2008, authorizing the National Security Agency to monitor the computer networks of all federal agencies and identify the source of cyber-attacks. The U.S. Department of Homeland Security will work to protect the systems, and the Pentagon will devise strategies for counterattacks against intruders. All government agencies were ordered to cut the number of ports, or communication channels, through which their networks connect to the Internet from more than 4,000 to less than 100.

INTERNAL THREATS: EMPLOYEES

We tend to think the security threats to a business originate outside the organization. In fact, company insiders pose serious security problems. Employees have access to privileged information, and in the presence of sloppy internal security procedures, they are often able to roam throughout an organization's systems without leaving a trace.

Studies have found that user lack of knowledge is the single greatest cause of network security breaches. Many employees forget their passwords to access computer systems or allow co-workers to use them, which compromises the system. Malicious intruders seeking system access sometimes trick employees into revealing their passwords by pretending to be legitimate members of the company in need of information. This practice is called **social engineering**.

Both end users and information systems specialists are also a major source of errors introduced into information systems. End users introduce errors by entering faulty data or by not following the proper instructions for processing data and using computer equipment. Information systems specialists may create software errors as they design and develop new software or maintain existing programs.

SOFTWARE VULNERABILITY

Software errors pose a constant threat to information systems, causing untold losses in productivity. Growing complexity and size of software programs, coupled with demands for timely delivery to markets, have contributed to an increase in software flaws or vulnerabilities For example, a flawed software upgrade shut down the BlackBerry e-mail service throughout North America for about 12 hours between April 17 and April 18, 2007. Millions of business users who depended on BlackBerry were unable to work, and BlackBerry's reputation for reliability was tarnished (Martin, 2007). The U.S. Department of Commerce National Institute of Standards and Technology (NIST) reported that software flaws (including vulnerabilities to hackers and malware) cost the U.S. economy $59.6 billion each year (NIST, 2005).

A major problem with software is the presence of hidden **bugs** or program code defects. Studies have shown that it is virtually impossible to eliminate all bugs from large programs. The main source of bugs is the complexity of decision-making code. A relatively small program of several hundred lines will contain tens of decisions leading to hundreds or even thousands of different paths. Important programs within most corporations are usually much larger, containing tens of thousands or even millions of lines of code, each with many times the choices and paths of the smaller programs.

Zero defects cannot be achieved in larger programs. Complete testing simply is not possible. Fully testing programs that contain thousands of choices and millions of paths would require thousands of years. Even with rigorous testing, you would not know for sure that a piece of software was dependable until the product proved itself after much operational use.

Flaws in commercial software not only impede performance but also create security vulnerabilities that open networks to intruders. Each year security firms identify about 5,000 software vulnerabilities in Internet and PC software. For instance, in 2007 Symantec identified 39 vulnerabilities in Microsoft Internet Explorer, 34 in Mozilla browsers, 25 in Apple Safari, and 7 in Opera. Some of these vulnerabilities are critical (Symantec, 2007).

To correct software flaws once they are identified, the software vendor creates small pieces of software called **patches** to repair the flaws without disturbing the proper operation of the software. An example is Microsoft's Windows Vista Service Pack 1, released in February 2008, which includes some security enhancements to counter malware and hackers. It is up to users of the software to track these vulnerabilities, test, and apply all patches. This process is called *patch management*.

Because a company's IT infrastructure is typically laden with multiple business applications, operating system installations, and other system services, maintaining patches on all devices and services used by a company is often time-consuming and costly. Malware is being created so rapidly that companies have very little time to respond between the time a vulnerability and a patch are announced and the time malicious software appears to exploit the vulnerability.

8.2 BUSINESS VALUE OF SECURITY AND CONTROL

Many firms are reluctant to spend heavily on security because it is not directly related to sales revenue. However, protecting information systems is so critical to the operation of the business that it deserves a second look.

Companies have very valuable information assets to protect. Systems often house confidential information about individuals' taxes, financial assets, medical records, and job performance reviews. They also can contain information on corporate operations, including trade secrets, new product development plans, and marketing strategies. Government systems may store information on weapons systems, intelligence operations, and military targets. These information assets have tremendous value, and the repercussions can be devastating if they are lost, destroyed, or placed in the wrong hands. One study estimated that when the security of a large firm is compromised, the company loses approximately 2.1 percent of its market value within two days of the security breach, which translates into an average loss of $1.65 billion in stock market value per incident (Cavusoglu, Mishra, and Raghunathan, 2004).

Inadequate security and control may result in serious legal liability. Businesses must protect not only their own information assets but also those of customers, employees, and business partners. Failure to do so may open the firm to costly litigation for data exposure or theft. An organization can be held liable for needless risk and harm created if the organization fails to take appropriate protective action to prevent loss of confidential information, data corruption, or breach of privacy (see the Interactive Session on Organizations). For example, BJ's Wholesale Club was sued by the U.S. Federal Trade Commission for allowing hackers to access its systems and steal credit and debit card data for fraudulent purchases. Banks that issued the cards with the stolen data sought $13 million from BJ's to compensate them for reimbursing card holders for the fraudulent purchases (McDougall, 2006). A sound security and control framework that protects business information assets can thus produce a high return on investment.

Strong security and control also increase employee productivity and lower operational costs. For example, Axia NextMedia Corp., a Calgary, Alberta firm that builds and manages open-access broadband networks, saw employee productivity go up and costs go down after it installed an information systems configuration and control system in 2004. Before then, Axia had lost valuable employee work time because of security or other network incidents that caused system outages. Between 2004 and 2007, the new configuration and control system saved the company $590,000 by minimizing system outages (Bartholomew, 2007).

LEGAL AND REGULATORY REQUIREMENTS FOR ELECTRONIC RECORDS MANAGEMENT

Recent U.S. government regulations are forcing companies to take security and control more seriously by mandating the protection of data from abuse, exposure, and unauthorized access. Firms face new legal obligations for the retention and storage of electronic records as well as for privacy protection.

If you work in the healthcare industry, your firm will need to comply with the Health Insurance Portability and Accountability Act (HIPAA) of 1996. **HIPAA** outlines medical security and privacy rules and procedures for simplifying the administration of healthcare billing and automating the transfer of healthcare data between healthcare providers, payers, and plans. It requires members of the healthcare industry to retain patient information for six years and ensure the confidentiality of those records. It specifies privacy, security, and electronic transaction standards for healthcare providers handling patient information, providing penalties for breaches of medical privacy, disclosure of patient records by e-mail, or unauthorized network access.

If you work in a firm providing financial services, your firm will need to comply with the Financial Services Modernization Act of 1999, better known as the **Gramm-Leach-Bliley Act** after its congressional sponsors. This act requires financial institutions to ensure the security and confidentiality of customer data. Data must be stored on a secure medium, and special security measures must be enforced to protect such data on storage media and during transmittal.

If you work in a publicly traded company, your company will need to comply with the Public Company Accounting Reform and Investor Protection Act of 2002, better known as the **Sarbanes-Oxley Act** after its sponsors Senator Paul Sarbanes of Maryland and Representative Michael Oxley of Ohio. This Act was designed to protect investors after the financial scandals at Enron, WorldCom, and other public companies. It imposes responsibility on companies and their management to safeguard the accuracy and integrity of financial information that is used internally and released externally. One of the Learning Tracks for this chapter discusses Sarbanes-Oxley in detail.

Sarbanes-Oxley is fundamentally about ensuring that internal controls are in place to govern the creation and documentation of information in financial statements. Because information systems are used to generate, store, and transport such data, the legislation requires firms to consider information systems security and other controls required to ensure the integrity, confidentiality, and accuracy of their data. Each system application that deals with critical financial reporting data requires controls to make sure the data are accurate. Controls to secure the corporate network, prevent unauthorized access to systems and data, and ensure data integrity and availability in the event of disaster or other disruption of service are essential as well.

ELECTRONIC EVIDENCE AND COMPUTER FORENSICS

Security, control, and electronic records management have become essential for responding to legal actions. Much of the evidence today for stock fraud, embezzlement, theft of company trade secrets, computer crime, and many civil cases is in digital form. In addition to information from printed or typewritten pages, legal cases today increasingly rely on evidence represented as digital data stored on portable floppy disks, CDs, and computer hard disk drives, as well as in e-mail, instant messages, and e-commerce transactions over the Internet. E-mail is currently the most common type of electronic evidence.

In a legal action, a firm is obligated to respond to a discovery request for access to information that may be used as evidence, and the company is required by law to produce those data. The cost of responding to a discovery request can be enormous if the company has trouble assembling the required data or the data have been corrupted or destroyed. Courts now impose severe financial and even criminal penalties for improper destruction of electronic documents.

An effective electronic document retention policy ensures that electronic documents, e-mail, and other records are well organized, accessible, and neither retained too long nor discarded too soon. It also reflects an awareness of how to preserve potential evidence for computer forensics. **Computer forensics** is the scientific collection, examination, authentication, preservation, and analysis of data held on or retrieved from computer storage media in such a way that the information can be used as evidence in a court of law. It deals with the following problems:

- Recovering data from computers while preserving evidential integrity
- Securely storing and handling recovered electronic data
- Finding significant information in a large volume of electronic data
- Presenting the information to a court of law

Electronic evidence may reside on computer storage media in the form of computer files and as *ambient data*, which are not visible to the average user. An example might be a file that has been deleted on a PC hard drive. Data that a computer user may have deleted on computer storage media can be recovered through various techniques. Computer forensics experts try to recover such hidden data for presentation as evidence.

An awareness of computer forensics should be incorporated into a firm's contingency planning process. The CIO, security specialists, information systems staff, and corporate legal counsel should all work together to have a plan in place that can be executed if a legal need arises. You can find out more about computer forensics in the Learning Tracks for this chapter.

8.3 ESTABLISHING A FRAMEWORK FOR SECURITY AND CONTROL

Even with the best security tools, your information systems won't be reliable and secure unless you know how and where to deploy them. You'll need to know where your company is at risk and what controls you must have in place to protect your information systems. You'll also need to develop a security policy and plans for keeping your business running if your information systems aren't operational.

INFORMATION SYSTEMS CONTROLS

Information systems controls are both manual and automated and consist of both general controls and application controls. **General controls** govern the design, security, and use of computer programs and the security of data files in general throughout the organization's information technology infrastructure. On the whole, general controls apply to all computerized applications and consist of a combination of hardware, software, and manual procedures that create an overall control environment.

General controls include software controls, physical hardware controls, computer operations controls, data security controls, controls over implementation of system processes, and administrative controls. Table 8-3 describes the functions of each of these controls.

Application controls are specific controls unique to each computerized application, such as payroll or order processing. They include both automated and manual procedures that ensure that only authorized data are completely and accurately processed by that application. Application controls can be classified as (1) input controls, (2) processing controls, and (3) output controls.

Input controls check data for accuracy and completeness when they enter the system. There are specific input controls for input authorization, data conversion, data editing, and error handling. *Processing controls* establish that data are

TABLE 8-3 GENERAL CONTROLS

TYPE OF GENERAL CONTROL	DESCRIPTION
Software controls	Monitor the use of system software and prevent unauthorized access of software programs, system software, and computer programs.
Hardware controls	Ensure that computer hardware is physically secure, and check for equipment malfunction. Organizations that are critically dependent on their computers also must make provisions for backup or continued operation to maintain constant service.
Computer operations controls	Oversee the work of the computer department to ensure that programmed procedures are consistently and correctly applied to the storage and processing of data. They include controls over the setup of computer processing jobs and backup and recovery procedures for processing that ends abnormally.
Data security controls	Ensure that valuable business data files on either disk or tape are not subject to unauthorized access, change, or destruction while they are in use or in storage.
Implementation controls	Audit the systems development process at various points to ensure that the process is properly controlled and managed.
Administrative controls	Formalize standards, rules, procedures, and control disciplines to ensure that the organization's general and application controls are properly executed and enforced.

complete and accurate during updating. *Output controls* ensure that the results of computer processing are accurate, complete, and properly distributed. You can find more detail about application and general controls in our Learning Tracks.

RISK ASSESSMENT

Before your company commits resources to security and information systems controls, it must know which assets require protection and the extent to which these assets are vulnerable. A risk assessment helps answer these questions and determine the most cost-effective set of controls for protecting assets.

A **risk assessment** determines the level of risk to the firm if a specific activity or process is not properly controlled. Not all risks can be anticipated and measured, but most businesses will be able to acquire some understanding of the risks they face. Business managers working with information systems specialists should try to determine the value of information assets, points of vulnerability, the likely frequency of a problem, and the potential for damage. For example, if an event is likely to occur no more than once a year, with a maximum of a $1,000 loss to the organization, it is not be wise to spend $20,000 on the design and maintenance of a control to protect against that event. However, if that same event could occur at least once a day, with a potential loss of more than $300,000 a year, $100,000 spent on a control might be entirely appropriate.

Table 8-4 illustrates sample results of a risk assessment for an online order processing system that processes 30,000 orders per day. The likelihood of each exposure occurring over a one-year period is expressed as a percentage. The next column shows the highest and lowest possible loss that could be expected each time the exposure occurred and an average loss calculated by adding the highest and lowest figures together and dividing by two. The expected annual loss for each exposure can be determined by multiplying the average loss by its probability of occurrence.

TABLE 8-4 ONLINE ORDER PROCESSING RISK ASSESSMENT

EXPOSURE	PROBABILITY OF OCCURRENCE (%)	LOSS RANGE/ AVERAGE ($)	EXPECTED ANNUAL LOSS ($)
Power failure	30%	$5,000–$200,000 ($102,500)	$30,750
Embezzlement	5%	$1,000–$50,000 ($25,500)	$1,275
User error	98%	$200–$40,000 ($20,100)	$19,698

This risk assessment shows that the probability of a power failure occurring in a one-year period is 30 percent. Loss of order transactions while power is down could range from $5,000 to $200,000 (averaging $102,500) for each occurrence, depending on how long processing is halted. The probability of embezzlement occurring over a yearly period is about 5 percent, with potential losses ranging from $1,000 to $50,000 (and averaging $25,500) for each occurrence. User errors have a 98 percent chance of occurring over a yearly period, with losses ranging from $200 to $40,000 (and averaging $20,100) for each occurrence.

Once the risks have been assessed, system builders will concentrate on the control points with the greatest vulnerability and potential for loss. In this case, controls should focus on ways to minimize the risk of power failures and user errors because anticipated annual losses are highest for these areas.

SECURITY POLICY

Once you've identified the main risks to your systems, your company will need to develop a security policy for protecting the company's assets. A **security policy** consists of statements ranking information risks, identifying acceptable security goals, and identifying the mechanisms for achieving these goals. What are the firm's most important information assets? Who generates and controls this information in the firm? What existing security policies are in place to protect the information? What level of risk is management willing to accept for each of these assets? Is it willing, for instance, to lose customer credit data once every 10 years? Or will it build a security system for credit card data that can withstand the once-in-a-hundred-year disaster? Management must estimate how much it will cost to achieve this level of acceptable risk.

The security policy drives policies determining acceptable use of the firm's information resources and which members of the company have access to its information assets. An **acceptable use policy (AUP)** defines acceptable uses of the firm's information resources and computing equipment, including desktop and laptop computers, wireless devices, telephones, and the Internet. The policy should clarify company policy regarding privacy, user responsibility, and personal use of company equipment and networks. A good AUP defines unacceptable and acceptable actions for every user and specifies consequences for noncompliance. For example, security policy at Unilever, the giant multinational consumer goods company, requires every employee equipped with a laptop mobile handheld device to use a company-specified device and employ a password or other method of identification when logging onto the corporate network.

Authorization policies determine differing levels of access to information assets for different levels of users. **Authorization management systems** establish where and when a user is permitted to access certain parts of a Web site or a corporate database. Such systems allow each user access only to those portions of a system that person is permitted to enter, based on information established by a set of access rules.

The authorization management system knows exactly what information each user is permitted to access as shown in Figure 8-3. This figure illustrates the security allowed for two sets of users of an online personnel database containing sensitive information, such as employees' salaries, benefits, and medical histories. One set of users consists of all employees who perform clerical functions, such as inputting employee data into the system. All individuals with this type of profile can update the system but can neither read nor update sensitive fields, such as salary, medical history, or earnings data. Another profile applies to a divisional manager, who cannot update the system but who can read all employee data fields for his or her division, including medical history and salary. These profiles are based on access rules supplied by business groups. The system illustrated in Figure 8-3 provides very fine-grained security restrictions, such as allowing authorized personnel users to inquire about all employee information except that in confidential fields, such as salary or medical history.

FIGURE 8-3   SECURITY PROFILES FOR A PERSONNEL SYSTEM

SECURITY PROFILE 1

User: Personnel Dept. Clerk

Location: Division 1

Employee Identification
Codes with This Profile: 00753, 27834, 37665, 44116

Data Field Restrictions	Type of Access
All employee data for Division 1 only	Read and Update
• Medical history data	None
• Salary	None
• Pensionable earnings	None

SECURITY PROFILE 2

User: Divisional Personnel Manager

Location: Division 1

Employee Identification
Codes with This Profile: 27321

Data Field Restrictions	Type of Access
All employee data for Division 1 only	Read Only

These two examples represent two security profiles or data security patterns that might be found in a personnel system. Depending on the security profile, a user would have certain restrictions on access to various systems, locations, or data in an organization.

DISASTER RECOVERY PLANNING AND BUSINESS CONTINUITY PLANNING

If you run a business, you need to plan for events, such as power outages, floods, earthquakes, or terrorist attacks that will prevent your information systems and your business from operating. **Disaster recovery planning** devises plans for the restoration of computing and communications services after they have been disrupted. Disaster recovery plans focus primarily on the technical issues involved in keeping systems up and running, such as which files to back up and the maintenance of backup computer systems or disaster recovery services.

For example, MasterCard maintains a duplicate computer center in Kansas City, Missouri, to serve as an emergency backup to its primary computer center in St. Louis. Rather than build their own backup facilities, many firms contract with disaster recovery firms, such as Comdisco Disaster Recovery Services in Rosemont, Illinois, and SunGard Availability Services, headquartered in Wayne, Pennsylvania. These disaster recovery firms provide hot sites housing spare computers at locations around the country where subscribing firms can run their critical applications in an emergency. For example, Champion Technologies, which supplies chemicals used in oil and gas operations, is able to switch its enterprise systems from Houston to a SunGard hot site in Scottsdale, Arizona in two hours (Duvall, 2007).

Business continuity planning focuses on how the company can restore business operations after a disaster strikes. The business continuity plan identifies critical business processes and determines action plans for handling mission-critical functions if systems go down. For example, Deutsche Bank, which provides investment banking and asset management services in 74 different countries, has a well-developed business continuity plan that it continually updates and refines. It maintains full-time teams in Singapore, Hong Kong, Japan, India, and Australia to coordinate plans addressing loss of facilities, personnel, or critical systems so that the company can continue to operate when a catastrophic event occurs. Deutsche Bank's plan distinguishes between processes critical for business survival and those critical to crisis support and is coordinated with the company's disaster recovery planning for its computer centers.

Business managers and information technology specialists need to work together on both types of plans to determine which systems and business processes are most critical to the company. They must conduct a business impact analysis to identify the firm's most critical systems and the impact a systems outage would have on the business. Management must determine the maximum amount of time the business can survive with its systems down and which parts of the business must be restored first.

THE ROLE OF AUDITING

How does management know that information systems security and controls are effective? To answer this question, organizations must conduct comprehensive and systematic audits. An **MIS audit** examines the firm's overall security environment as well as controls governing individual information systems. The auditor should trace the flow of sample transactions through the system and perform tests, using, if appropriate, automated audit software. The MIS audit may also examine data quality, as described in Chapter 6.

FIGURE 8-4   SAMPLE AUDITOR'S LIST OF CONTROL WEAKNESSES

Function: Loans Location: Peoria, IL	Prepared by: J. Ericson Date: June 16, 2009		Received by: T. Benson Review date: June 28, 2009	
Nature of Weakness and Impact	Chance for Error/Abuse		Notification to Management	
	Yes/ No	Justification	Report date	Management response
User accounts with missing passwords	Yes	Leaves system open to unauthorized outsiders or attackers	5/10/09	Eliminate accounts without passwords
Network configured to allow some sharing of system files	Yes	Exposes critical system files to hostile parties connected to the network	5/10/09	Ensure only required directories are shared and that they are protected with strong passwords
Software patches can update production programs without final approval from Standards and Controls group	No	All production programs require management approval; Standards and Controls group assigns such cases to a temporary production status		

This chart is a sample page from a list of control weaknesses that an auditor might find in a loan system in a local commercial bank. This form helps auditors record and evaluate control weaknesses and shows the results of discussing those weaknesses with management, as well as any corrective actions taken by management.

Security audits review technologies, procedures, documentation, training, and personnel. A thorough audit will even simulate an attack or disaster to test the response of the technology, information systems staff, and business employees.

The audit lists and ranks all control weaknesses and estimates the probability of their occurrence. It then assesses the financial and organizational impact of each threat. Figure 8-4 is a sample auditor's listing of control weaknesses for a loan system. It includes a section for notifying management of such weaknesses and for management's response. Management is expected to devise a plan for countering significant weaknesses in controls.

8.4   TECHNOLOGIES AND TOOLS FOR PROTECTING INFORMATION RESOURCES

Businesses have an array of tools and technologies for protecting their information resources. They include tools and technologies for securing systems and data, ensuring system availability, and ensuring software quality.

ACCESS CONTROL

Access control consists of all the policies and procedures a company uses to prevent improper access to systems by unauthorized insiders and outsiders.

To gain access a user must be authorized and authenticated. **Authentication** refers to the ability to know that a person is who he or she claims to be. Access control software is designed to allow only authorized users to use systems or to access data using some method for authentication.

Authentication is often established by using passwords known only to authorized users. An end user uses a password to log on to a computer system and may also use passwords for accessing specific systems and files. However, users often forget passwords, share them, or choose poor passwords that are easy to guess, which compromises security. Password systems that are too rigorous hinder employee productivity. When employees must change complex passwords frequently, they often take shortcuts, such as choosing passwords that are easy to guess or writing down their passwords at their workstations in plain view. Passwords can also be "sniffed" if transmitted over a network or stolen through social engineering.

New authentication technologies, such as tokens, smart cards, and biometric authentication, overcome some of these problems. A **token** is a physical device, similar to an identification card, that is designed to prove the identity of a single user. Tokens are small gadgets that typically fit on key rings and display passcodes that change frequently. A **smart card** is a device about the size of a credit card that contains a chip formatted with access permission and other data. (Smart cards are also used in electronic payment systems.) A reader device interprets the data on the smart card and allows or denies access.

Biometric authentication uses systems that read and interpret individual human traits, such as fingerprints, irises, and voices, in order to grant or deny access. Biometric authentication is based on the measurement of a physical or behavioral trait that makes each individual unique. It compares a person's unique characteristics, such as the fingerprints, face, or retinal image, against a stored profile of these characteristics to determine whether there are any differences between these characteristics and the stored profile. If the two profiles match, access is granted. Fingerprint and facial recognition technologies are

This NEC PC has a biometric fingerprint reader for fast yet secure access to files and networks. New models of PCs are starting to use biometric identification to authenticate users.

just beginning to be used for security applications. PC laptops are starting to be equipped with fingerprint identification devices.

FIREWALLS, INTRUSION DETECTION SYSTEMS, AND ANTIVIRUS SOFTWARE

Without protection against malware and intruders, connecting to the Internet would be very dangerous. Firewalls, intrusion detection systems, and antivirus software have become essential business tools.

Firewalls

Chapter 7 describes the use of *firewalls* to prevent unauthorized users from accessing private networks. A firewall is a combination of hardware and software that controls the flow of incoming and outgoing network traffic. It is generally placed between the organization's private internal networks and distrusted external networks, such as the Internet, although firewalls can also be used to protect one part of a company's network from the rest of the network (see Figure 8-5).

The firewall acts like a gatekeeper who examines each user's credentials before access is granted to a network. The firewall identifies names, IP addresses, applications, and other characteristics of incoming traffic. It checks this information against the access rules that have been programmed into the system by the network administrator. The firewall prevents unauthorized communication into and out of the network.

FIGURE 8-5   A CORPORATE FIREWALL

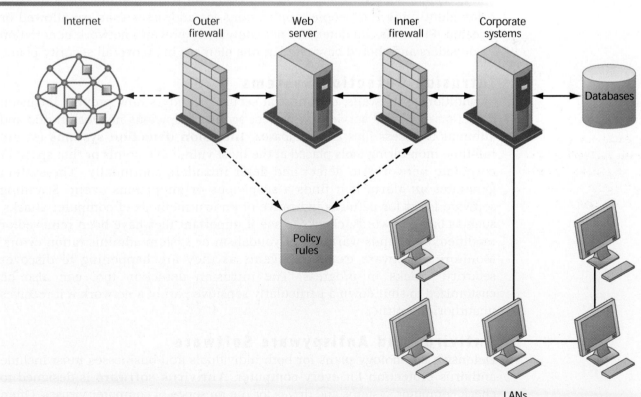

The firewall is placed between the firm's private network and the public Internet or another distrusted network to protect against unauthorized traffic.

In large organizations, the firewall often resides on a specially designated computer separate from the rest of the network, so no incoming request directly accesses private network resources. There are a number of firewall screening technologies, including static packet filtering, stateful inspection, Network Address Translation, and application proxy filtering. They are frequently used in combination to provide firewall protection.

Packet filtering examines selected fields in the headers of data packets flowing back and forth between the trusted network and the Internet, examining individual packets in isolation. This filtering technology can miss many types of attacks. *Stateful inspection* provides additional security by determining whether packets are part of an ongoing dialogue between a sender and a receiver. It sets up state tables to track information over multiple packets. Packets are accepted or rejected based on whether they are part of an approved conversation or whether they are attempting to establish a legitimate connection.

Network Address Translation (NAT) can provide another layer of protection when static packet filtering and stateful inspection are employed. NAT conceals the IP addresses of the organization's internal host computer(s) to prevent sniffer programs outside the firewall from ascertaining them and using that information to penetrate internal systems.

Application proxy filtering examines the application content of packets. A proxy server stops data packets originating outside the organization, inspects them, and passes a proxy to the other side of the firewall. If a user outside the company wants to communicate with a user inside the organization, the outside user first "talks" to the proxy application and the proxy application communicates with the firm's internal computer. Likewise, a computer user inside the organization goes through the proxy to talk with computers on the outside.

To create a good firewall, an administrator must maintain detailed internal rules identifying the people, applications, or addresses that are allowed or rejected. Firewalls can deter, but not completely prevent, network penetration by outsiders and should be viewed as one element in an overall security plan.

Intrusion Detection Systems

In addition to firewalls, commercial security vendors now provide intrusion detection tools and services to protect against suspicious network traffic and attempts to access files and databases. **Intrusion detection systems** feature full-time monitoring tools placed at the most vulnerable points or "hot spots" of corporate networks to detect and deter intruders continually. The system generates an alarm if it finds a suspicious or anomalous event. Scanning software looks for patterns indicative of known methods of computer attacks, such as bad passwords, checks to see if important files have been removed or modified, and sends warnings of vandalism or system administration errors. Monitoring software examines events as they are happening to discover security attacks in progress. The intrusion detection tool can also be customized to shut down a particularly sensitive part of a network if it receives unauthorized traffic.

Antivirus and Antispyware Software

Defensive technology plans for both individuals and businesses must include antivirus protection for every computer. **Antivirus software** is designed to check computer systems and drives for the presence of computer viruses. Often the software eliminates the virus from the infected area. However, most antivirus software is effective only against viruses already known when the software was written. To remain effective, the antivirus software must be continually updated. Antivirus products are available for many different types of mobile and handheld devices in addition to servers, workstations, and desktop PCs.

Leading antivirus software vendors, such as McAfee, Symantec, and Trend Micro, have enhanced their products to include protection against spyware. Antispyware software tools such as Ad-Aware, Spybot S&D, and Spyware Doctor are also very helpful.

Unified Threat Management Systems

To help businesses reduce costs and improve manageability, security vendors have combined into a single appliance various security tools, including firewalls, virtual private networks, intrusion detection systems, and Web content filtering and antispam software. These comprehensive security management products are called **unified threat management (UTM)** systems. Although initially aimed at small and medium-sized businesss, UTM products are available for all sizes of networks. Leading UTM vendors include Crossbeam, Fortinent, and Secure Computing, and networking vendors such as Cisco Systems and Juniper Networks provide some UTM capabilities in their equipment.

SECURING WIRELESS NETWORKS

Despite its flaws, WEP provides some margin of security if Wi-Fi users remember to activate it. A simple first step to thwart hackers is to assign a unique name to your network's SSID and instruct your router not to broadcast it. Corporations can further improve Wi-Fi security by using it in conjunction with virtual private network (VPN) technology when accessing internal corporate data.

In June 2004 the Wi-Fi Alliance industry trade group finalized the 802.11i specification (also referred to as Wi-Fi Protected Access 2 or WPA2) that replaces WEP with stronger security standards. Instead of the static encryption keys used in WEP, the new standard uses much longer keys that continually change, making them harder to crack. It also employs an encrypted authentication system with a central authentication server to ensure that only authorized users access the network.

ENCRYPTION AND PUBLIC KEY INFRASTRUCTURE

Many businesses use encryption to protect digital information that they store, physically transfer, or send over the Internet. **Encryption** is the process of transforming plain text or data into cipher text that cannot be read by anyone other than the sender and the intended receiver. Data are encrypted by using a secret numerical code, called an encryption key, that transforms plain data into cipher text. The message must be decrypted by the receiver.

Two methods for encrypting network traffic on the Web are SSL and S-HTTP. **Secure Sockets Layer (SSL)** and its successor Transport Layer Security (TLS) enable client and server computers to manage encryption and decryption activities as they communicate with each other during a secure Web session. **Secure Hypertext Transfer Protocol (S-HTTP)** is another protocol used for encrypting data flowing over the Internet, but it is limited to individual messages, whereas SSL and TLS are designed to establish a secure connection between two computers.

The capability to generate secure sessions is built into Internet client browser software and servers. The client and the server negotiate what key and what level of security to use. Once a secure session is established between the client and the server, all messages in that session are encrypted.

There are two alternative methods of encryption: symmetric key encryption and public key encryption. In symmetric key encryption, the sender and receiver establish a secure Internet session by creating a single encryption key and sending it to the receiver so both the sender and receiver share the same key. The strength of the encryption key is measured by its bit length. Today, a typical key will be 128 bits long (a string of 128 binary digits).

The problem with all symmetric encryption schemes is that the key itself must be shared somehow among the senders and receivers, which exposes the key to outsiders who might just be able to intercept and decrypt the key. A more secure form of encryption called **public key encryption** uses two keys: one shared (or public) and one totally private as shown in Figure 8-6. The keys are mathematically related so that data encrypted with one key can be decrypted using only the other key. To send and receive messages, communicators first create separate pairs of private and public keys. The public key is kept in a directory and the private key must be kept secret. The sender encrypts a message with the recipient's public key. On receiving the message, the recipient uses his or her private key to decrypt it.

Digital certificates are data files used to establish the identity of users and electronic assets for protection of online transactions (see Figure 8-7). A digital certificate system uses a trusted third party, known as a certificate authority (CA), to validate a user's identity. There are many CAs in the United States and around the world, including VeriSign, IdenTrust, and Australia's KeyPost.

The CA verifies a digital certificate user's identity offline. This information is put into a CA server, which generates an encrypted digital certificate containing owner identification information and a copy of the owner's public key. The certificate authenticates that the public key belongs to the designated owner. The CA makes its own public key available publicly either in print or perhaps on the Internet. The recipient of an encrypted message uses the CA's public key to decode the digital certificate attached to the message, verifies it was issued by the CA, and then obtains the sender's public key and identification information contained in the certificate. Using this information, the recipi-

FIGURE 8-6 PUBLIC KEY ENCRYPTION

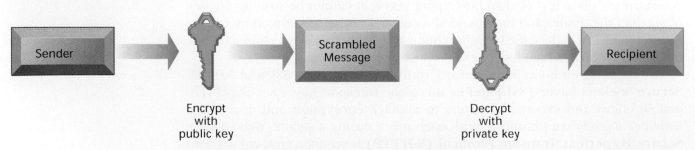

A public key encryption system can be viewed as a series of public and private keys that lock data when they are transmitted and unlock the data when they are received. The sender locates the recipient's public key in a directory and uses it to encrypt a message. The message is sent in encrypted form over the Internet or a private network. When the encrypted message arrives, the recipient uses his or her private key to decrypt the data and read the message.

ent can send an encrypted reply. The digital certificate system would enable, for example, a credit card user and a merchant to validate that their digital certificates were issued by an authorized and trusted third party before they exchange data. **Public key infrastructure (PKI)**, the use of public key cryptography working with a certificate authority, is now widely used in e-commerce.

ENSURING SYSTEM AVAILABILITY

As companies increasingly rely on digital networks for revenue and operations, they need to take additional steps to ensure that their systems and applications are always available. Firms such as those in the airline and financial services industries with critical applications requiring online transaction processing have traditionally used fault-tolerant computer systems for many years to ensure 100-percent availability. In **online transaction processing**, transactions entered online are immediately processed by the computer. Multitudinous changes to databases, reporting, and requests for information occur each instant.

Fault-tolerant computer systems contain redundant hardware, software, and power supply components that create an environment that provides continuous, uninterrupted service. Fault-tolerant computers use special software routines or self-checking logic built into their circuitry to detect hardware failures and automatically switch to a backup device. Parts from these computers can be removed and repaired without disruption to the computer system.

Fault tolerance should be distinguished from **high-availability computing**. Both fault tolerance and high-availability computing try to minimize downtime. **Downtime** refers to periods of time in which a system is not operational.

FIGURE 8-7   DIGITAL CERTIFICATES

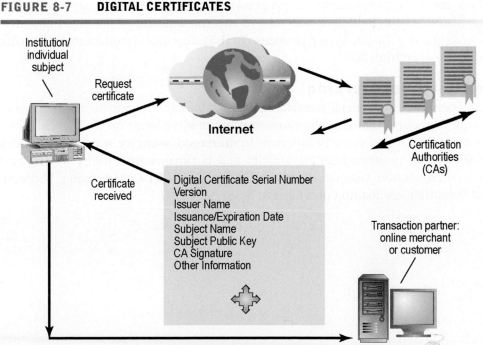

Digital certificates help establish the identity of people or electronic assets. They protect online transactions by providing secure, encrypted, online communication.

However, high-availability computing helps firms recover quickly from a system crash, whereas fault tolerance promises continuous availability and the elimination of recovery time altogether.

High-availability computing environments are a minimum requirement for firms with heavy e-commerce processing or for firms that depend on digital networks for their internal operations. High-availability computing requires backup servers, distribution of processing across multiple servers, high-capacity storage, and good disaster recovery and business continuity plans. The firm's computing platform must be extremely robust with scalable processing power, storage, and bandwidth.

Researchers are exploring ways to make computing systems recover even more rapidly when mishaps occur, an approach called **recovery-oriented computing**. This work includes designing systems that recover quickly, and implementing capabilities and tools to help operators pinpoint the sources of faults in multi-component systems and easily correct their mistakes.

Controlling Network Traffic: Deep Packet Inspection

Have you ever tried to use your campus network and found it was very slow? It may be because your fellow students are using the network to download music or watch YouTube. Bandwith-consuming applications such as file-sharing programs, Internet phone service, and online video are able to clog and slow down corporate networks, degrading performance. For example, Ball Sate University in Muncie, Indiana, found its network had slowed because a small minority of students were using peer-to-peer file sharing programs to download movies and music.

A technology called **deep packet inspection (DPI)** helps solve this problem. DPI examines data files and sorts out low-priority online material while assigning higher priority to business-critical files. Based on the priorities established by a network's operators, it decides whether a specific data packet can continue to its destination or should be blocked or delayed while more important traffic proceeds. Using a DPI system from Allot Communications, Ball State was able to cap the amount of file-sharing traffic and assign it a much lower priority. Ball State's preferred network traffic speeded up (White, 2007).

Security Outsourcing

Many companies, especially small businesses, lack the resources or expertise to provide a secure high-availability computing environment on their own. They can outsource many security functions to **managed security service providers (MSSPs)** that monitor network activity and perform vulnerability testing and intrusion detection. Guardent (acquired by VeriSign), BT Counterpane, VeriSign, and Symantec are leading providers of MSSP services.

INTERACTIVE SESSION: TECHNOLOGY

SECURITY AT ICICI BANK

ICICI Bank Limited (ICICI Bank) is India's second largest bank, with total assets of U.S. $ 79.00 billion at March 31, 2007. It provides a wide range of products and services related to consumer/retail banking, and corporate banking. It has a network of about 950 branches, 3,300 ATMs in India and presence in 17 countries.

Started in 1994, ICICI Bank's systems were built up from a point at which nothing had been done, as there was no old legacy system in place. It adopted a flexible IT structure instead of a traditional mainframe-based system. It had centralized its back office operations, leaving branches to focus on the customers for better service. Information security was also managed with central control.

By June 2003, the bank already had a security infrastructure in place. To perfect its security strategies, it hired Murli Nambiar as Head of the Information Security Group in 2005. The first thing on Nambiar's agenda was to identify the vulnerable areas to determine security gaps. For example, perimeter security, internal networks and wireless networks were some of the areas that were identified. Securing these different domains, one at a time, coupled with the stress on security awareness for users and regular policy compliance audits, helped the bank to have a well-rounded security strategy.

In 2007, a risk management framework was developed to assess every application for risk before it was deployed at the bank's datacenter. To avoid internal risk, the bank developed stringent policies to lock down devices, and facilities were provided on a need-to-use basis. Only a few employees were allowed to use external storage devices such as pen drives and CD-Rs.

A security operations center for monitoring the security 24/ 7 was also set up. The group normally resolved the issues and escalated matters to the security officers - comprising domain experts for LAN, WAN, Web and database security - for second level support. The security officers further escalated the issues to the management for any corporate decisions.

An alternate disaster-recovery site, with the equipment identical at both the primary and secondary site, was also created. The BCP plan included the recovery time objective for each system.

Several security systems were used to protect the assets from internal and external threats. Firewalls, intrusion detection systems, anti-virus, as well as routers, were use to secure the perimeter. Encryption software was loaded on desktops, servers and laptops. The bank also developed in-house messenger software to provide secure instant messaging for users. The wireless LAN was secured with encryption and unnecessary protocols were disabled on the network printers.

In order to make sure that each device on the network was always updated with the latest patches, the bank's Information Security team decided to centralize and automate the process of updating and rolling out patches. This was accomplished by customizing LANDesk Manager from Allied Digital, in order to inhibit selected applications from launching and protect data leakages through centralized port control.

The bank also conducted training programs for the IT administrators, system and application owners and Web developers. While the Web developers were trained annually on secure coding practices, code reviews were done to determine the efficacy of the process. E-mails were sent regularly to end users and administrators to make them aware of the security threats.

In May 2008, the bank developed the Logical Access Management (LAM) system as a centralized control application for users accessing the bank's Web site. In the past, the bank had used paper/mail based approval for identity and access management, which involved retaining the record for audit and compliance. The centralized repository of user database across applications was not available and manual review of user access rights in various applications was time-consuming. LAM had helped the bank in reducing turnaround time for requests, strengthening access controls and reducing cost in servicing customers.

In September 2008, the bank was awarded the Symantec Visionary Award for innovative use of Symantec's products for secure and better management of systems and information. The bank implemented an array of new systems including Symantec Endpoint Protection for endpoint security; Symantec Security Information Manager for centralized security management; and Symantec DeepSight Threat management System for real-time threat reports.

Sources: Anil Patrick R., "Step by Step," networkmagazineindia.com, accessed November 2008; Vinita Gupta, "ICICI Bank," networkmagazineindia.com, accessed November 2008; "ICICI Bank - Security and Patch Management," www.ciol.com, accessed November 2008; Fakir Balaji, "ICICI Bank, TVS Motor Bag Symantec Awards," sify.com, September 2008; "ICICI Bank: Logical Access Management," pcquest.ciol.com, May 2008.

CASE STUDY QUESTIONS   MIS IN ACTION

1. List and describe the security measures at ICICI bank.
2. For each security measure, describe the threats that it is effective for.
3. Do you think these measures are adequate? What should the bank do to safeguard its systems in future?
4. How do the measures at ICICI bank compare with those mentioned in sections 8.3 and 8.4 of the chapter? Are there any gaps?

Visit the ICICI Web site at www.icicibank.com and then answer the following questions related to Internet security:

1. What assurances, if any, does the bank provide on its Web site to indicate to its customers that its banking systems are safe and secure? For example, look under Internet Banking (and customer care).
2. Look at the information present at the link below. http://www.icicibank.com/Pfsuser/temp/onlinesecurity.htm
3. What types of IT breaches are mentioned and what recommendations does the bank have for its customers? Compare them with the guidelines mentioned in the chapter.

• Case contributed by Neerja Sethi and Vijay Sethi, Nanyang Technological University

ENSURING SOFTWARE QUALITY

In addition to implementing effective security and controls, organizations can improve system quality and reliability by employing software metrics and rigorous software testing. Software metrics are objective assessments of the system in the form of quantified measurements. Ongoing use of metrics allows the information systems department and end users to jointly measure the performance of the system and identify problems as they occur. Examples of software metrics include the number of transactions that can be processed in a specified unit of time, online response time, the number of payroll checks printed per hour, and the number of known bugs per hundred lines of program code. For metrics to be successful, they must be carefully designed, formal, objective, and used consistently.

Early, regular, and thorough testing will contribute significantly to system quality. Many view testing as a way to prove the correctness of work they have done. In fact, we know that all sizable software is riddled with errors, and we must test to uncover these errors.

Good testing begins before a software program is even written by using a *walkthrough*—a review of a specification or design document by a small group of people carefully selected based on the skills needed for the particular objectives being tested. Once developers start writing software programs, coding walkthroughs also can be used to review program code. However, code must be tested by computer runs. When errors are discovered, the source is found and eliminated through a process called *debugging*. You can find out more about the various stages of testing required to put an information system into operation in Chapter 11. Our Learning Tracks also contain descriptions of methodologies for developing software programs that also contribute to software quality.

8.5 HANDS-ON MIS PROJECTS

The projects in this section give you hands-on experience analyzing security vulnerabilities, using spreadsheet software for risk analysis, and using Web tools to research security outsourcing services.

Management Decision Problems

1. K2 Network operates online game sites used by about 16 million people in over 100 countries. Players are allowed to enter a game for free, but must buy digital "assets" from K2, such as swords to fight dragons, if they want to be deeply involved. The games can accomodate millions of players at once and are played simultaneously by people all over the world. Prepare a security analysis for this Internet-based business. What kinds of threats should it anticipate? What would be their impact on the business? What steps can it take to prevent damage to its Web sites and continuing operations?

2. A survey of your firm's information technology infrastructure has produced the following security analysis statistics:

SECURITY VULNERABILITIES BY TYPE OF COMPUTING PLATFORM

PLATFORM	NUMBER OF COMPUTERS	HIGH RISK	MEDIUM RISK	LOW RISK	TOTAL VULNERABILITIES
Windows Server (corporate applications)	1	11	37	19	
Windows Vista Ultimate (high-level administrators)	3	56	242	87	
Linux (e-mail and printing services)	1	3	154	98	
Sun Solaris (UNIX) (E-commerce and Web servers)	2	12	299	78	
Windows Vista Ultimate user desktops and laptops with office productivity tools that can also be linked to the corporate network running corporate applications and intranet	195	14	16	1,237	

High risk vulnerabilities include non-authorized users accessing applications, guessable passwords, user names matching the password, active user accounts with missing passwords, and the existence of unauthorized programs in application systems.

Medium risk vulnerabilities include the ability of users to shut down the system without being logged on, passwords and screen saver settings that were not established for PCs, and outdated versions of software still being stored on hard drives.

Low risk vulnerabilities include the inability of users to change their passwords, user passwords that have not been changed periodically, and passwords that were smaller than the minimum size specified by the company.

- Calculate the total number of vulnerabilities for each platform. What is the potential impact of the security problems for each computing platform on the organization?

- If you only have one information systems specialist in charge of security, which platforms should you address first in trying to eliminate these vulnerabilities? Second? Third? Last? Why?

- Identify the types of control problems illustrated by these vulnerabilities and explain the measures that should be taken to solve them.

- What does your firm risk by ignoring the security vulnerabilities identified?

Improving Decision Making: Using Spreadsheet Software to Perform a Security Risk Assessment

Software skills: Spreadsheet formulas and charts
Business skills: Risk assessment

This project uses spreadsheet software to calculate anticipated annual losses from various security threats identified for a small company.

Mercer Paints is a small but highly regarded paint manufacturing company located in Alabama. The company has a network in place linking many of its business operations. Although the firm believes that its security is adequate, the recent addition of a Web site has become an open invitation to hackers. Management requested a risk assessment. The risk assessment identified a number of potential exposures. These exposures, their associated probabilities, and average losses are summarized in the following table.

MERCER PAINTS RISK ASSESSMENT

EXPOSURE	PROBABILITY OF OCCURRENCE (%)	AVERAGE LOSS ($)
Malware attack	60%	$75,000
Data loss	12%	$70,000
Embezzlement	3%	$30,000
User errors	95%	$25,000
Threats from hackers	95%	$90,000
Improper use by employees	5%	$5,000
Power failure	15%	$300,000

- In addition to the potential exposures listed, you should identify at least three other potential threats to Mercer Paints, assign probabilities, and estimate a loss range.
- Use spreadsheet software and the risk assessment data to calculate the expected annual loss for each exposure.
- Present your findings in the form of a chart. Which control points have the greatest vulnerability? What recommendations would you make to Mercer Paints? Prepare a written report that summarizes your findings and recommendations.

Improving Decision Making: Evaluating Security Outsourcing Services

Software skills: Web browser and presentation software
Business skills: Evaluating business outsourcing services

Businesses today have a choice of whether to outsource the security function or maintain their own internal staff for this purpose. This project will help develop your Internet skills in using the Web to research and evaluate security outsourcing services.

As an information systems expert in your firm, you have been asked to help management decide whether to outsource security or keep the security function within the firm. Search the Web to find information to help you decide whether to outsource security and to locate security outsourcing services.

- Present a brief summary of the arguments for and against outsourcing computer security for your company.
- Select two firms that offer computer security outsourcing services, and compare them and their services.
- Prepare an electronic presentation for management summarizing your findings. Your presentation should make the case on whether or not your company should outsource computer security. If you believe your company should outsource, the presentation should identify which security outsourcing service should be selected and justify your selection.

LEARNING TRACK MODULES

The following Learning Tracks provide content relevant to topics covered in this chapter:

1. The Booming Job Market in IT Security
2. The Sarbanes-Oxley Act
3. Computer Forensics
4. General and Application Controls for Information Systems
5. Software Vulnerability and Reliability
6. Management Challenges of Security and Control

Review Summary

1. **Why are information systems vulnerable to destruction, error, and abuse?**

   Digital data are vulnerable to destruction, misuse, error, fraud, and hardware or software failures. The Internet is designed to be an open system and makes internal corporate systems more vulnerable to actions from outsiders. Hackers can unleash denial-of-service (DoS) attacks or penetrate corporate networks, causing serious system disruptions. Wi-Fi networks can easily be penetrated by intruders using sniffer programs to obtain an address to access the resources of the network. Computer viruses and worms can disable systems and Web sites. Software presents problems because software bugs may be impossible to eliminate and because software vulnerabilities can be exploited by hackers and malicious software. End users often introduce errors.

2. **What is the business value of security and control?**

   Lack of sound security and control can cause firms relying on computer systems for their core business functions to lose sales and productivity. Information assets, such as confidential employee records, trade secrets, or business plans, lose much of their value if they are revealed to outsiders or if they expose the firm to legal liability. New laws, such as HIPAA, the Sarbanes-Oxley Act, and the Gramm-Leach-Bliley Act, require companies to practice stringent electronic records management and adhere to strict standards for security, privacy, and control. Legal actions requiring electronic evidence and computer forensics also require firms to pay more attention to security and electronic records management.

3. **What are the components of an organizational framework for security and control?**

   Firms need to establish a good set of both general and application controls for their information systems. A risk assessment evaluates information assets, identifies control points and control weaknesses, and determines the most cost-effective set of controls. Firms must also develop a coherent corporate security policy and plans for continuing business operations in the event of disaster or disruption. The security policy includes policies for acceptable use and authorization. Comprehensive and systematic MIS auditing helps organizations determine the effectiveness of security and controls for their information systems.

4. **What are the most important tools and technologies for safeguarding information resources?**

   Firewalls prevent unauthorized users from accessing a private network when it is linked to the Internet. Intrusion detection systems monitor private networks from suspicious network traffic and attempts to access corporate systems. Passwords, tokens, smart cards, and biometric authentication are used to authenticate system users. Antivirus software checks computer systems for infections by viruses and worms and often eliminates the malicious software, while antispyware software combats intrusive and harmful spyware programs. Encryption, the coding and scrambling of messages, is a widely used technology for securing electronic transmissions over unprotected networks. Digital certificates combined with public key encryption provide further protection of electronic transactions by authenticating a user's identity. Companies can use fault-tolerant computer systems or create high-availability computing environments to make sure that their information systems are always available. Use of software metrics and rigorous software testing help improve software quality and reliability.

Key Terms

Acceptable use policy (AUP), 340

Access control, 343

Antivirus software, 346

Application controls, 338

Authentication, 344

Authorization management systems, 340

Authorization policies, 340

Biometric authentication, 344

Botnet, 331

Bugs, 335

Business continuity planning, 342

Click fraud, 333

Computer crime, 331

Computer forensics, 337

Computer virus, 328

Controls, 323

Cybervandalism, 330

Deep packet inspection (DPI), 350

Denial-of-service (DoS) attack, 330

Digital certificates, 348

Review Questions

1. Why are information systems vulnerable to destruction, error, and abuse?

   - List and describe the most common threats against contemporary information systems.
   - Define malware and distinguish among a virus, a worm, and a Trojan horse.
   - Define a hacker and explain how hackers create security problems and damage systems.
   - Define computer crime. Provide two examples of crime in which computers are targets and two examples in which computers are used as instruments of crime.
   - Define identity theft and phishing and explain why identity theft is such a big problem today.
   - Describe the security and system reliability problems created by employees.
   - Explain how software defects affect system reliability and security.

2. What is the business value of security and control?
   - Explain how security and control provide value for businesses.
   - Describe the relationship between security and control and recent U.S. government regulatory requirements and computer forensics.

3. What are the components of an organizational framework for security and control?

   - Define general controls and describe each type of general control.
   - Define application controls and describe each type of application control.
   - Describe the function of risk assessment and explain how it is conducted for information systems.
   - Define and describe the following: security policy, acceptable use policy, authorization policy.
   - Explain how MIS auditing promotes security and control.

4. What are the most important tools and technologies for safeguarding information resources?
   - Name and describe three authentication methods.
   - Describe the roles of firewalls, intrusion detection systems, and antivirus software in promoting security.
   - Explain how encryption protects information.
   - Describe the role of encryption and digital certificates in a public key infrastructure.
   - Distinguish between fault-tolerant and high-availability computing, and between disaster recovery planning and business continuity planning.
   - Describe measures for improving software quality and reliability

Discussion Questions

1. Security isn't simply a technology issue, it's a business issue. Discuss.

2. If you were developing a business continuity plan for your company, where would you start? What aspects of the business would the plan address?

Video Cases

You will find video cases illustrating some of the concepts in this chapter on the Laudon Web site along with questions to help you analyze the cases.

Collaboration and Teamwork: Evaluating Security Software Tools

With a group of three or four students, use the Web to research and evaluate security products from two competing vendors, such as antivirus software, firewalls, or antispyware software. For each product, describe its capabilities, for what types of businesses it is best suited, and its cost to purchase and install.

Which is the best product? Why? If possible, use Google Sites to post links to Web pages, team communication announcements, and work assignments; to brainstorm; and to work collaboratively on project documents. Try to use Google Docs to develop a presentation of your findings for the class.

A Rogue Trader at Societe Generale Roils the World Financial System
CASE STUDY

Societe Generale is one of the world's most respected corporate and investment banks and one of France's oldest and most highly regarded financial institutions. Founded in 1864 by Napoleon III, the company has over 130,000 employees and 22.5 million customers worldwide. The three core businesses of the company include corporate and investment banking, retail banking and financial services, and global investment management services. Known within the financial services industry as SocGen, the company's reputation was badly tarnished in early 2008 by the revelation that a rogue trader was responsible for losses totaling approximately 5 billion euros ($7.2 billion).

In January 2008, SocGen discovered that one of its traders, 31-year-old Jerome Kerviel, had been making unauthorized trades over the course of the previous year that somehow went unnoticed by the bank's security and risk management systems. The losses represented the largest fraud in investment banking history at a time when world markets were already under pressure due to the U.S. subprime mortgage crisis. Kerviel was so successful in evading SocGen's internal controls that he was able to amass over $73 billion in uncovered positions, well over the bank's total market capitalization of approximately $53 billion, en route to the $7.2 billion loss.

Kerviel himself was a quiet and unassuming trader with an unimpressive pedigree compared to many of his SocGen co-workers. He earned an advanced degree in trading from the University of Lyon before joining the company in 2000. By contrast, many of the bank's top officials and traders attended top French universities such as Polytechnique and Ecole Nationale d'Administration. He initially worked in the company's risk management office, which was scornfully nicknamed 'the mine' by the higher-level trading units. There, he gained familiarity with many of the company's security procedures and back-office systems. He was eventually promoted to a lower-level trading desk known as Delta One. Kerviel's desire to impress his fellow traders, who generally had more prestigious educational backgrounds, may have motivated him to abuse his knowledge of the company's trading transaction systems in his new role.

Kerviel's task at the Delta One desk was to trade index futures. He was entrusted to purchase one portfolio of European stock index futures and at the same time sell a similar mixture of index futures of different value as a hedge. The goal was to produce a small, low-risk profit stream as a result of performing a large volume of these transactions over time. Kerviel was able to bypass nearly every control for the company's information systems to accomplish something quite different—amassing uncovered and unauthorized positions with the potential to either make or lose billions based on the market activity of that day. He accomplished this by performing legitimate transactions in one direction, but falsifying the hedges that were supposed to 'offset' the legitimate ones. Kerviel made his first fictitious transactions in late 2005, but took increasingly larger positions in 2006 and 2007 en route to his eventual $73 billion in accumulated positions. How could Kerviel have possibly gotten away with this?

Kerviel's first task was to enter fictitious trades so that they would be undetectable against his real trades. To do this, he entered the false transactions in a separate portfolio, distinct from the one containing his real trades, and did so in such a way that no actual cash was required to exchange hands. When his books were checked together, the real portfolio and fake portfolio offset one another and appeared to be well within Kerviel's limit for acceptable risk. These actions made it possible for Kerviel's supervisors to see a balanced book when in fact he was exposing the bank to substantial risk. The limit for the entire Delta One desk where Kerviel worked was 125 million euros; using this method, Kerviel was able to place single positions worth over 600 million euros.

Kerviel still had to evade SocGen's more thorough internal checks on each trader's books, which would have revealed his fictitious portfolio. Because he knew the schedule of SocGen's internal controls, he was able to eliminate his fake trades from the system just minutes prior to the scheduled checks and re-enter them soon after. The temporary imbalance did not trigger an alert. He also used this tactic to cancel and enter new trades before confirmations of the trades were ever sent to other banks. Kerviel allegedly used other employees' access codes and user information to accomplish this, leading to reports that Kerviel had 'hacked' SocGen's systems to commit fraud. But it is as of yet unclear whether or not Kerviel performed any complicated computer operations to get around SocGen's controls.

Finally, Kerviel had to somehow keep his schemes from co-workers and supervisors. A common practice among investment bankers is to take scheduled vacation days so that their portfolios can be scrutinized by other bankers while they are away. This increases the chances of uncovering the kinds of fraud Kerviel committed. Kerviel reportedly worked late into the night long after other traders had gone home and took only four vacation days over the course of 2007 to prevent this from occurring. And while his supervisors did spot mistakes in his books, Kerviel was able to cover his tracks enough to quickly 'fix' errors and then continue his fraudulent activities.

The extent to which Kerviel's co-workers and superiors had knowledge of his fraudulent activities while he was committing them is still unclear. SocGen maintains that Kerviel was acting alone, but Kerviel has expressed skepticism that his superiors could have been unaware of his actions. Some reports claim that Kerviel used the computer of his manager, Eric Cordelle, to execute several of his fraudulent trades with Cordelle looking on. Several other brokers supposedly responsible for entering some of Kerviel's authentic trades in full knowledge of his schemes have undergone questioning by police. Kerviel's defense lawyers argue that he acted with the tacit approval of his superiors during his more successful initial period of fraudulent activity, when he accumulated over $2 billion in gains for SocGen that were never realized. Also, the bank ignored many warning signs that Kerviel was capable of this level of fraud. In 2005, Kerviel was reprimanded for exceeding his trading limits with bets on Allianz SE securities and was told he would be fired for doing so in the future. The bank also reportedly failed to follow up on 75 warnings on Kerviel's positions over the course of the past several years. SocGen dismissed the warnings, claiming that all traders amass similar amounts of warnings over time.

Two striking aspects of Kerviel's fraudulent activity are how simplistic his methods were, as well as how little Kerviel stood to gain personally from his trades. SocGen's controls were capable of detecting more complicated errors and fraudulent transactions than those committed by Kerviel, but in the end Kerviel's simple strategies were more than sufficient to bypass them. The manager of SocGen's investment banking division said of the fraud that "Societe Generale got caught just like

someone who would have installed a highly sophisticated alarm...and gets robbed because he forgot to shut the window." And while Kerviel may have been hoping to secure a larger bonus for himself through his fraudulent trading activity, it does appear that he was motivated primarily by "earning money for my bank."

If SocGen had performed random checks on the trading history of its traders, Kerviel would likely have been caught well before his losses spiraled out of control. Likewise, if SocGen had a system to track deleted or altered trades, Kerviel's methods would have been uncovered quickly and without incident. And if Kerviel's supervisors had bothered to investigate how a trader whose job was supposed to amass modest profits based on careful bets could have racked up billions in gains and eventually in losses, they could perhaps have lessened the damage done to a large degree. Kerviel himself has stated that his supervisors must have known that he was resorting to unusual tactics to earn such large sums of money, but that "as long as you earn money and it isn't too obvious, and it's convenient, nobody says anything."

Instead, SocGen was left with a mess on their hands and may have made things much worse with their handling of it. SocGen decided to unload Kerviel's positions soon after discovering the fraud, despite the fact that the market conditions at the time were decidedly unfavorable. When SocGen dumped Kerviel's positions into the weak world markets, it hastened an even larger plunge in late January 2008. On the Monday after the fraud was revealed, the DAX, FTSE, and CAC-40 indexes fell 7.2, 5.5, and 6.8 percent, respectively, with the DAX continuing to fall in the ensuing days. Their abrupt drop was believed to be a major reason for the Federal Reserve cutting interest rates in the U.S. soon afterwards. Soon after, the SEC launched an investigation into whether or not SocGen violated U.S. securities laws by unwinding Kerviel's positions covertly after the fraud was revealed as well as whether or not insider information played a role in the selling of SocGen stock prior to the announcement of the scandal. Some estimates indicate that the losses incurred by Kerviel amounted to closer to 2 billion euros, and the bank's handling of Kerviel's positions resulted in the remainder of the 4.9 billion euro loss.

The incident was the most glaring example among many of the failures of risk management controls at a prominent international financial institution. Together, these failures contributed heavily to the subprime mortgage crisis and resulting credit crunch that victimized other investment banks.

So what does SocGen plan to do to prevent future fraudulent trades? The answer remains to be seen. Even if Kerviel is the malevolent genius that SocGen claims, his ability to accumulate positions larger than the bank's net worth indicates severe failings in the company's control systems. One former SocGen risk auditor, Maxime Legrand, called the control procedures used to monitor the activity of its traders a sham and that the management "pretend(s) to have an inspection to please the banking commission." In the wake of SocGen's fraud and other investment banking failures like the collapse of Bear Stearns, financial institutions will be under a great deal of pressure to improve their risk management systems and internal controls.

Sources: Natasha de Teran, "Market Targets Loopholes in Equity Derivatives," Financialnews-US.com, March 28, 2008; Brian Cleary, "Employee Role Changes and SocGen: Good Lessons From a Bad Example," SCMagazineUS.com, April 1, 2008; Nicola Clark and David Jolly, "French Bank Says Rogue Trader Lost $7 Billion", *The New York Times*, January 25, 2008; Nicolas Parasie, "SocGen Discloses More Detail, Chronology of Alleged Fraud," MarketWatch.com, January 27, 2008; Andrew Hurst and Thierry Leveque, "SocGen Under Pressure as Rogue Trader Released," Yahoo! News, January 28, 2008; David Gauthier-Villars and Carrick Mollenkamp, "The Loss Where No One Looked," *The Wall Street Journal*, January 28, 2008; Randall Smith and Kate Kelly, "Once Again, the Risk Protection Fails," *The Wall Street Journal*, January 25, 2008; Adam Sage, "Ex-SocGen Risk Auditor Calls Systems a Sham," *The Times*, February 7, 2008; "Trader Says SocGen Bosses Had To Know," *The New York Times*, January 29, 2008; David Gauthier-Villars, Carrick Mollenkamp, and Alistair Macdonald, "French Bank Rocked by Rogue Trader," *The Wall Street Journal*, January 25, 2008; David Gauthier-Villars and Stacy Meichtry, "Kerviel Felt Out of His League," *The Wall Street Journal*, January 31, 2008; Heather Smith and Gregory Viscusi, "SocGen Threatened to Fire Kerviel in 2005, Court Document Says," Bloomberg.com, March 25, 2008.

CASE STUDY QUESTIONS

1. What concepts in this chapter are illustrated in this case?

2. Describe the control weaknesses at SocGen. What management, organization, and technology factors contributed to those weaknesses?

3. Who should be held responsible for Kerviel's trading losses? What role did SocGen's systems play? What role did management play?

4. What are some ways SocGen could have prevented Kerviel's fraud?

5. If you were responsible for redesigning SocGen's systems, what would you do to address their control problems?

PART THREE

Key System Applications for the Digital Age

Part Three examines the core information system applications businesses are using today to improve operational excellence and decision making. These applications include enterprise systems; systems for supply chain management, customer relationship management, collaboration, and knowledge management; e-commerce applications; and decision-support systems. This part answers questions such as: How can enterprise applications improve business performance? How do firms use e-commerce to extend the reach of their businesses? How can systems improve collaboration and decision making and help companies make better use of their knowledge assets?

Chapter 9

Achieving Operational Excellence and Customer Intimacy: Enterprise Applications

LEARNING OBJECTIVES

After reading this chapter, you will be able to answer the following questions:

1. How do enterprise systems help businesses achieve operational excellence?

2. How do supply chain management systems coordinate planning, production, and logistics with suppliers?

3. How do customer relationship management systems help firms achieve customer intimacy?

4. What are the challenges posed by enterprise applications?

5. How are enterprise applications used in platforms for new cross-functional services?

Interactive Sessions:

Procter & Gamble Tries to Optimize Inventory

Customer Relationship Management Helps Chase Card Services Manage Customer Calls

CHAPTER OUTLINE

TASTY BAKING COMPANY: AN ENTERPRISE SYSTEM TRANSFORMS AN OLD FAVORITE

Tasty Baking Company's name says it all. It is known for its Tastykake single-portion cupcakes, snack pies, cookies, and donuts, which are pre-wrapped fresh at its bakery and sold through approximately 15,500 convenience stores and supermarkets in the eastern United States. The Philadelphia-based company, which sold $28 in cakes its first day of business in 1914, rang up nearly $170 million in sales in 2007.

Although Tasty Baking Company made customers smile, management and stockholders were frowning. Tasty is a fairly small enterprise in a maturing business, and saw its market share and sales dropping in the mid-1990s. In 2002, profitability levels were at an all-time low, with a –4.9 percent operating margin. To turn the company around, Tasty's new president and CEO Charles Pizzi introduced a new management team and strategic transformation plan.

The strategy required new manufacturing methods and new information systems. Tasty's existing systems were technically challenged, inflexible, and posed serious compliance and other business risks. Many key processes were traditional and heavily manual, and the company did not have timely information for tracking manufacturing outputs and warehouse shipments. Tasty had to physically count all the items in its warehouses every day. Even so, inventory information was still inaccurate and out of date. Shipments were missed, and excess inventory had to be sold at a discount at bakery thrift stores. Tasty's market share and sales dropped while operating costs rose.

Much of Tasty's information about sales and products comes from its network of sales distributors. Tasty needed to create better connections with its sales operation to receive this information as soon as it was available.

Tasty's new management team decided to implement a new enterprise system using software from SAP designed specifically for the food and beverage industry. Consultants from SAP and Deloitte helped the company identify its business processes and figure out how to make them work with the SAP software. By limiting changes to the software and enforcing rigorous project management standards, the company was able to implement the new enterprise system on time and on budget in nine months. Tasty's SAP enterprise system uses a Microsoft SQL Server database and Windows operating system running on an Intel server.

Tasty was willing to make many changes in its business processes to take maximum advantage of the enterprise software's capabilities. It adopted Deloitte's template of best practices for the food and beverage industry. Tasty implemented the SAP modules for financials, order entry, manufacturing resource planning (MRP), and scheduling. The system integrates information that was previously maintained manually or in separate systems, and provides real-time information for inventory and warehouse management, financial activities, and centralized procurement. It provides more precise information about customer demand and inventory that helps managers make better decisions.

365

Since implementing SAP's enterprise system, Tasty's financial condition has become much healthier. The company has reduced inventory write-downs by 60 percent and price markdowns by 40 percent. Customer satisfaction has increased, as reflected in lower return rates and higher order fill rates. Tasty increased sales 11 percent without having to hire more staff.

Sources: "Tasty Baking Company," and "Tasty Baking," www.mysap.com, accessed July 5, 2007 and Tasty Baking Company 10-K Annual Report filed March 12, 2008.

Tasty Banking Company's problems with its inventory and work processes illustrate the critical role of enterprise applications. The company's costs were too high because it did not have accurate and timely information to manage its inventory. Tasty also lost sales from missed shipments.

The chapter-opening diagram calls attention to important points raised by this case and this chapter. Tasty's fresh-baked products have a fairly short shelf life. Key business processes were manual, preventing the company from knowing exactly what items had shipped and what items were in inventory. Management couldn't access the data rapidly enough for daily decision making and planning.

Management could have chosen to add more employees or automate its existing business processes with newer technology. Instead, it decided to change many of its business processes to conform to industry-wide best practices and to implement an enterprise system. The enterprise system integrated financial, order entry, scheduling, and manufacturing information and made it more widely available throughout the company. Data on manufacturing output and warehouse shipments are captured as soon as they are created. Instant availability of more timely and accurate information helps employees work more efficiently and helps managers make better decisions.

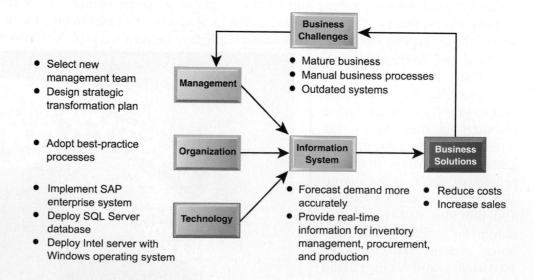

9.1 ENTERPRISE SYSTEMS

Around the globe, companies are increasingly becoming more connected, both internally and with other companies. If you run a business, you'll want to be able to react instantaneously when a customer places a large order or when a shipment from a supplier is delayed. You may also want to know the impact of these events on every part of the business and how the business is performing at any point in time, especially if you're running a large company. Enterprise systems provide the integration to make this possible. Let's look at how they work and what they can do for the firm.

WHAT ARE ENTERPRISE SYSTEMS?

Imagine that you had to run a business based on information from tens or even hundreds of different databases and systems, none of which could speak to one another? Imagine your company had 10 different major product lines, each produced in separate factories, and each with separate and incompatible sets of systems controlling production, warehousing, and distribution.

For example, Alcoa, the world's leading producer of aluminum and aluminum products with operations spanning 41 countries and 500 locations, had initially been organized around lines of business, each of which had its own set of information systems. Many of these systems were redundant and inefficient. Alcoa's costs for executing requisition-to-pay and financial processes were much higher and its cycle times were longer than those of other companies in its industry. (Cycle time refers to the total elapsed time from the beginning to the end of a process.) The company could not operate as a single worldwide entity.

At the very least, your decision making would often be based on manual hard copy reports, often out of date, and it would be difficult to really understand what is happening in the business as whole. You now have a good idea of why firms need a special enterprise system to integrate information.

Chapter 2 introduced enterprise systems, also known as enterprise resource planning (ERP) systems, which are based on a suite of integrated software modules and a common central database. The database collects data from many different divisions and departments in a firm, and from a large number of key business processes in manufacturing and production, finance and accounting, sales and marketing, and human resources, making the data available for applications that support nearly all of an organization's internal business activities. When new information is entered by one process, the information is made immediately available to other business processes (see Figure 9-1).

If a sales representative places an order for tire rims, for example, the system verifies the customer's credit limit, schedules the shipment, identifies the best shipping route, and reserves the necessary items from inventory. If inventory stock were insufficient to fill the order, the system schedules the manufacture of more rims, ordering the needed materials and components from suppliers. Sales and production forecasts are immediately updated. General ledger and corporate cash levels are automatically updated with the revenue and cost information from the order. Users could tap into the system and find out where that particular order was at any minute. Management could obtain information at any point in time about how the business was operating. The system could also generate enterprise-wide data for management analyses of product cost and profitability.

FIGURE 9-1   HOW ENTERPRISE SYSTEMS WORK

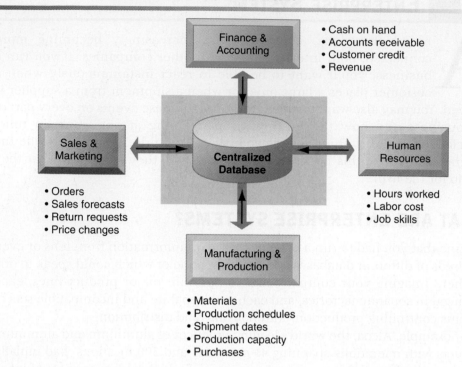

Enterprise systems feature a set of integrated software modules and a central database that enables data to be shared by many different business processes and functional areas throughout the enterprise.

ENTERPRISE SOFTWARE

Enterprise software is built around thousands of predefined business processes that reflect best practices. Table 9-1 describes some of the major business processes supported by enterprise software.

Companies implementing this software must first select the functions of the system they wish to use and then map their business processes to the prc-defined business processes in the software. (One of our Learning Tracks shows how SAP enterprise software handles the procurement process for a new piece of equipment.) Tasty Baking Company, described in the chapter-opening case, identified its existing business processes and then translated

TABLE 9-1 BUSINESS PROCESSES SUPPORTED BY ENTERPRISE SYSTEMS

Financial and accounting processes, including general ledger, accounts payable, accounts receivable, fixed assets, cash management and forecasting, product-cost accounting, cost-center accounting, asset accounting, tax accounting, credit management, and financial reporting

Human resources processes, including personnel administration, time accounting, payroll, personnel planning and development, benefits accounting, applicant tracking, time management, compensation, workforce planning, performance management, and travel expense reporting

Manufacturing and production processes, including procurement, inventory management, purchasing, shipping, production planning, production scheduling, material requirements planning, quality control, distribution, transportation execution, and plant and equipment maintenance

Sales and marketing processes, including order processing, quotations, contracts, product configuration, pricing, billing, credit checking, incentive and commission management, and sales planning

them into the business processes built into the SAP ERP software it had selected. A firm would use configuration tables provided by the software to tailor a particular aspect of the system to the way it does business. For example, the firm could use these tables to select whether it wants to track revenue by product line, geographical unit, or distribution channel.

If the enterprise software does not support the way the organization does business, companies can rewrite some of the software to support the way their business processes work. However, enterprise software is unusually complex, and extensive customization may degrade system performance, compromising the information and process integration that are the main benefits of the system. If companies want to reap the maximum benefits from enterprise software, they must change the way they work to conform to the business processes in the software. To ensure it obtained these benefits, Tasty Baking Company deliberately planned for customizing less than 5 percent of the system and made very few changes to the SAP software itself. It used as many tools and features that were already built into the SAP software as it could. SAP has more than 3000 configuration tables for its enterprise software. Identifying the organization's business processes to be included in the system and then mapping them to the processes in the enterprise software is often a major effort.

Major enterprise software vendors include SAP, Oracle (with its acquisition of PeopleSoft), and SSA Global. There are versions of enterprise software packages designed for small businesses and versions obtained through software service providers over the Web. Although initially designed to automate the firm's internal "back-office" business processes, enterprise systems have become more externally oriented and capable of communicating with customers, suppliers, and other organizations.

BUSINESS VALUE OF ENTERPRISE SYSTEMS

Enterprise systems provide value both by increasing operational efficiency and by providing firm-wide information to help managers make better decisions. Large companies with many operating units in different locations have used enterprise systems to enforce standard practices and data so that everyone does business the same way worldwide.

Coca Cola, for instance, implemented a SAP enterprise system to standardize and coordinate important business processes in 200 countries. Lack of standard, company-wide business processes prevented the company from leveraging its worldwide buying power to obtain lower prices for raw materials and from reacting rapidly to market changes. Nestle SA installed a SAP enterprise system to standardize business processes in 500 facilities in 80 countries for the same reason.

Enterprise systems help firms respond rapidly to customer requests for information or products. Because the system integrates order, manufacturing, and delivery data, manufacturing is better informed about producing only what customers have ordered, procuring exactly the right amount of components or raw materials to fill actual orders, staging production, and minimizing the time that components or finished products are in inventory.

After implementing enterprise software from Oracle, Alcoa eliminated many redundant processes and systems. The enterprise system helped Alcoa reduce requisition-to-pay cycle time (the total elapsed time from the time a purchase requisition is generated to the time the payment for the purchase is made) by verifying receipt of goods and automatically generating receipts for payment.

Alcoa's accounts payable transaction processing dropped 89 percent. Alcoa was able to centralize financial and procurement activities, which helped the company reduce nearly 20 percent of its worldwide costs.

Enterprise systems provide much valuable information for improving management decision making. Corporate headquarters has access to up-to-the-minute data on sales, inventory, and production and uses this information to create more accurate sales and production forecasts. Enterprise software includes analytical tools for using data captured by the system to evaluate overall organizational performance. Enterprise system data have common standardized definitions and formats that are accepted by the entire organization. Performance figures mean the same thing across the company. Enterprise systems allow senior management to easily find out at any moment how a particular organizational unit is performing, determine which products are most or least profitable, or calculate costs for the company as a whole.

For example, Alcoa's enterprise system includes functionality for global human resources management that shows correlations between investment in employee training and quality; measures the company-wide costs of delivering services to employees; and measures the effectiveness of employee recruitment, compensation, and training.

9.2 SUPPLY CHAIN MANAGEMENT SYSTEMS

If you manage a small firm that makes a few products or sells a few services, chances are you will have a small number of suppliers. You could coordinate your supplier orders and deliveries using a telephone and fax machine. But if you manage a firm that produces more complex products and services, then you will have hundreds of suppliers, and your suppliers will each have their own set of suppliers. Suddenly, you are in a situation where you will need to coordinate the activities of hundreds or even thousands of other firms in order to produce your products and services. Supply chain management systems, which we introduced in Chapter 2, are an answer to these problems of supply chain complexity and scale.

THE SUPPLY CHAIN

A firm's **supply chain** is a network of organizations and business processes for procuring raw materials, transforming these materials into intermediate and finished products, and distributing the finished products to customers. It links suppliers, manufacturing plants, distribution centers, retail outlets, and customers to supply goods and services from source through consumption. Materials, information, and payments flow through the supply chain in both directions.

Goods start out as raw materials and, as they move through the supply chain, are transformed into intermediate products (also referred to as components or parts), and finally, into finished products. The finished products are shipped to distribution centers and from there to retailers and customers. Returned items flow in the reverse direction from the buyer back to the seller.

Let's look at the supply chain for Nike sneakers as an example. Nike designs, markets, and sells sneakers, socks, athletic clothing, and accessories throughout the world. Its primary suppliers are contract manufacturers with factories in China, Thailand, Indonesia, Brazil, and other countries. These companies fashion Nike's finished products.

Nike's contract suppliers do not manufacture sneakers from scratch. They obtain components for the sneakers—the laces, eyelets, uppers, and soles—from other suppliers and then assemble them into finished sneakers. These suppliers in turn have their own suppliers. For example, the suppliers of soles have suppliers for synthetic rubber, suppliers for chemicals used to melt the rubber for molding, and suppliers for the molds into which to pour the rubber. Suppliers of laces would have suppliers for their thread, for dyes, and for the plastic lace tips.

Figure 9-2 provides a simplified illustration of Nike's supply chain for sneakers; it shows the flow of information and materials among suppliers, Nike, Nike's distributors, retailers, and customers. Nike's contract manufacturers are its primary suppliers. The suppliers of soles, eyelets, uppers, and laces are the secondary (Tier 2) suppliers. Suppliers to these suppliers are the tertiary (Tier 3) suppliers.

The *upstream* portion of the supply chain includes the company's suppliers, the suppliers' suppliers, and the processes for managing relationships with them. The *downstream* portion consists of the organizations and processes for distributing and delivering products to the final customers. Companies doing manufacturing, such as Nike's contract suppliers of sneakers, also manage their own *internal supply chain* processes for transforming materials, components, and services furnished by their suppliers into finished products or intermediate products (components or parts) for their customers and for managing materials and inventory.

FIGURE 9-2   NIKE'S SUPPLY CHAIN

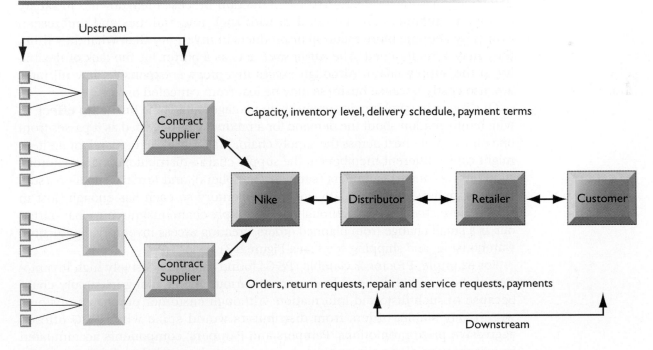

This figure illustrates the major entities in Nike's supply chain and the flow of information upstream and downstream to coordinate the activities involved in buying, making, and moving a product. Shown here is a simplified supply chain, with the upstream portion focusing only on the suppliers for sneakers and sneaker soles.

The supply chain illustrated in Figure 9-2 has been simplified. It only shows two contract manufacturers for sneakers and only the upstream supply chain for sneaker soles. Nike has hundreds of contract manufacturers turning out finished sneakers, socks, and athletic clothing, each with its own set of suppliers. The upstream portion of Nike's supply chain would actually comprise thousands of entities. Nike also has numerous distributors and many thousands of retail stores where its shoes are sold, so the downstream portion of its supply chain is also large and complex.

INFORMATION SYSTEMS AND SUPPLY CHAIN MANAGEMENT

Inefficiencies in the supply chain, such as parts shortages, underutilized plant capacity, excessive finished goods inventory, or high transportation costs, are caused by inaccurate or untimely information. For example, manufacturers may keep too many parts in inventory because they do not know exactly when they will receive their next shipments from their suppliers. Suppliers may order too few raw materials because they do not have precise information on demand. These supply chain inefficiencies waste as much as 25 percent of a company's operating costs.

If a manufacturer had perfect information about exactly how many units of product customers wanted, when they wanted them, and when they could be produced, it would be possible to implement a highly efficient **just-in-time strategy**. Components would arrive exactly at the moment they were needed and finished goods would be shipped as they left the assembly line.

In a supply chain, however, uncertainties arise because many events cannot be foreseen—uncertain product demand, late shipments from suppliers, defective parts or raw materials, or production process breakdowns. To satisfy customers, manufacturers often deal with such uncertainties and unforeseen events by keeping more material or products in inventory than what they think they may actually need. The *safety stock* acts as a buffer for the lack of flexibility in the supply chain. Although excess inventory is expensive, low fill rates are also costly because business may be lost from canceled orders.

One recurring problem in supply chain management is the **bullwhip effect**, in which information about the demand for a product gets distorted as it passes from one entity to the next across the supply chain. A slight rise in demand for an item might cause different members in the supply chain—distributors, manufacturers, suppliers, secondary suppliers (suppliers' suppliers), and tertiary suppliers (suppliers' suppliers' suppliers)—to stockpile inventory so each has enough "just in case." These changes ripple throughout the supply chain, magnifying what started out as a small change from planned orders, creating excess inventory, production, warehousing, and shipping costs (see Figure 9-3).

For example, Procter & Gamble (P&G) found it had excessively high inventories of its Pampers disposable diapers at various points along its supply chain because of such distorted information. Although customer purchases in stores were fairly stable, orders from distributors would spike when P&G offered aggressive price promotions. Pampers and Pampers' components accumulated in warehouses along the supply chain to meet demand that did not actually exist. To eliminate this problem, P&G revised its marketing, sales, and supply chain processes and used more accurate demand forecasting (Lee, Padmanabhan, and Wang, 1997).

The bullwhip is tamed by reducing uncertainties about demand and supply when all members of the supply chain have accurate and up-to-date informa-

FIGURE 9-3   THE BULLWHIP EFFECT

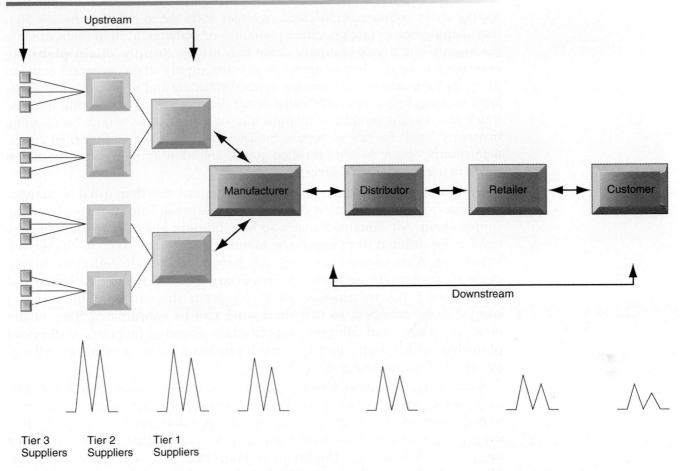

Inaccurate information can cause minor fluctuations in demand for a product to be amplified as one moves further back in the supply chain. Minor fluctuations in retail sales for a product can create excess inventory for distributors, manufacturers, and suppliers.

tion. If all supply chain members share dynamic information about inventory levels, schedules, forecasts, and shipments, they have more precise knowledge about how to adjust their sourcing, manufacturing, and distribution plans. Supply chain management systems provide the kind of information that helps members of the supply chain make better purchasing and scheduling decisions. Table 9-2 describes how firms benefit from these systems.

TABLE 9-2 HOW INFORMATION SYSTEMS FACILITATE SUPPLY CHAIN MANAGEMENT

INFORMATION FROM SUPPLY CHAIN MANAGEMENT SYSTEMS HELPS FIRMS
Decide when and what to produce, store, and move
Rapidly communicate orders
Track the status of orders
Check inventory availability and monitor inventory levels
Reduce inventory, transportation, and warehousing costs
Track shipments
Plan production based on actual customer demand
Rapidly communicate changes in product design

SUPPLY CHAIN MANAGEMENT SOFTWARE

Supply chain software is classified as either software to help businesses plan their supply chains (supply chain planning) or software to help them execute the supply chain steps (supply chain execution). **Supply chain planning systems** enable the firm to model its existing supply chain, generate demand forecasts for products, and develop optimal sourcing and manufacturing plans. Such systems help companies make better decisions such as determining how much of a specific product to manufacture in a given time period; establishing inventory levels for raw materials, intermediate products, and finished goods; determining where to store finished goods; and identifying the transportation mode to use for product delivery.

For example, if a large customer places a larger order than usual or changes that order on short notice, it can have a widespread impact throughout the supply chain. Additional raw materials or a different mix of raw materials may need to be ordered from suppliers. Manufacturing may have to change job scheduling. A transportation carrier may have to reschedule deliveries. Supply chain planning software makes the necessary adjustments to production and distribution plans. Information about changes is shared among the relevant supply chain members so that their work can be coordinated. One of the most important—and complex—supply chain planning functions is **demand planning**, which determines how much product a business needs to make to satisfy all of its customers' demands.

Whirlpool Corporation, which produces washing; machines, dryers, refrigerators, ovens, and other home appliances, uses supply chain planning systems to make sure what it produces matches customer demand. The company uses supply chain planning software from i2 Technologies, that includes modules for Master Scheduling, Deployment Planning, and Inventory Planning. Whirlpool also installed i2's Web-based tool for Collaborative Planning, Forecasting, and Replenishment (CPFR) for sharing and combining its sales forecasts with those of its major sales partners. Improvements in supply chain planning helped Whirlpool increase availability of products in stock when customers needed them to 97 percent, while reducing the number of excess finished goods in inventory by 20 percent and forecasting errors by 50 percent (i2, 2007).

Supply chain execution systems manage the flow of products through distribution centers and warehouses to ensure that products are delivered to the right locations in the most efficient manner. They track the physical status of goods, the management of materials, warehouse and transportation operations, and financial information involving all parties. Haworth Incorporated's Transportation Management System and Warehouse Management System described in Chapter 2 are examples of such systems. Manugistics and i2 Technologies (both acquired by JDA Software) are major supply chain management software vendors, and enterprise software vendors SAP and Oracle-PeopleSoft offer supply chain management modules.

The Interactive Session on Technology describes how supply chain management software improves operational performance and decision making at Procter & Gamble. This multinational giant manages global supply chains for more than 300 brands, each of which has many different configurations. Its supply chains are numerous and complex. P&G has many supply chain management applications. The one described here is for inventory optimization.

INTERACTIVE SESSION: TECHNOLOGY

PROCTER & GAMBLE TRIES TO OPTIMIZE INVENTORY

The shampoo and lipstick aisles at Target and Wal-Mart hardly seem like battlegrounds, but they are actually sites for an unending struggle among consumer products companies for retail shelf space. No company knows this better than Procter & Gamble, one of the world's largest consumer goods companies, with annual revenue surpassing $76 billion and 138,000 employees in 80 countries. The company sells more than 300 brands worldwide, including Cover Girl cosmetics, Olay skin care, Crest, Charmin, Tide, Pringles, and Pampers.

Demand variability for P&G's products from its Beauty division is very high. A popular eye shadow or lipstick color may quickly fall out of favor, while fashion trends call for new products continually to come on stream. Major retail outlets such as Wal-Mart and Target compete by offering brand-name products at the lowest price possible.

In response to these pressures, P&G is constantly searching for ways to reduce supply chain costs and improve efficiency throughout its entire manufacturing and distribution network. It recently implemented a multi-echelon inventory optimization system to manage its supply chain more efficiently.

The supply chains of a company as large as P&G are extremely complicated, featuring thousands of suppliers, manufacturing facilities, and markets. Even the slightest of changes at any part of the supply chain has significant effects on all of the other participants. What's more, because P&G's supply chains are so extensive, the chance for any errors or inefficiencies to occur are greater than with smaller, more compact supply chains. Inventory optimization for a company as large as P&G is therefore critical to cutting costs and increasing revenues. P&G was already renowned for its supply chain management, successfully reducing its surplus inventory with sales and operations planning, better forecasting, just-in-time delivery strategies, and vendor-managed inventory activity. But multi-echelon inventory optimization has provided the company with a new means to achieve even higher levels of efficiency.

Multi-echelon networks are networks in which products are located in a variety of locations along their path to distribution, some of which are in different 'echelons', or tiers, of the enterprise's distribution network. For example, large retailers' distribution networks often consist of a regional distribution center and a larger number of forward distribution centers. The presence of multiple echelons in a distribution network makes inventory management more difficult because each echelon is isolated from other echelons, so changes in inventory made by one echelon may have unpredictable consequences on the others.

Multi-echelon inventory optimization seeks to minimize the total inventory in all of the echelons of a company's supply chain. This is more complicated than traditional inventory optimization because of the additional lead times between each echelon, the bullwhip effect, and the need to synchronize orders and control costs between echelons. Companies with this level of complexity in their supply chains must replenish and divide their inventories at each distribution point along the supply chain, as opposed to just one distribution point or even just the inventory of the initial supplier. Each point in the supply chain is also unaware of the inventory levels of points beyond those that they have immediate contact with, which creates a lack of visibility up and down the supply chain.

The multi-echelon approach to inventory management consists of the following factors: multiple independent forecast updates in each echelon; accounting for all lead times and variations in lead times; management of the bullwhip effect; creation of visibility up and down the demand chain; synchronized order strategies; and appropriate modeling of the effects of different echelons' replenishment strategies on one another.

P&G prefers to develop its own analytical tools, but in this case turned to Optiant for its PowerChain Suite multi-echelon inventory optimization solution. Gillette, which P&G was preparing to acquire at the time, had already begun using Optiant software with strong results.

PowerChain Suite determines appropriate inventory configurations that can adapt smoothly to quickly changing demand. The solution uses mathematical models, based on award-winning research from MIT, which balance costs, resources, and customer service to arrive at these configurations. PowerChain tools pool inventory to minimize risk across products, components, and customers and also coordinate inventory policy across different items. (When inventory is available at the same time, this helps reduce early stock). PowerChain enables companies to design new supply chains and to model their end-to-end supply chain. They then can quickly evaluate the cost and performance of alternate supply chain structures and sourcing options to make better decisions. Optiant has provided supply chain management for other leading manufacturers such as Black & Decker, HP, IKEA, Imation, Intel, Kraft, Microsoft, and Sonoco.

P&G's beauty division served as the pilot project for the adoption of the Optiant software. Beauty is one of the company's largest, most complicated, and most profitable divisions. P&G believed that if multi-echelon inventory strategies could increase profitability at this division, it would work at any unit of the company.

The Optiant software first configured P&G's existing cosmetics supply chain, pulling in the previous 18 months of demand data and using the previous three months' demand variability. It then optimized the inventory strategy within that supply chain, aiming for target service levels above 99%. A third step identified alternate supply chain designs, and the final step created an optimal redesign of the supply network.

Results have been impressive. P&G's beauty division trimmed its total inventory by 3 to 7 percent and maintained service levels above 99%. In the first fiscal year after implementation of the new software, the division's earnings rose 13% and sales rose 7%. Inventory days on hand were down by eight days compared to the previous fiscal year. The results were so successful that P&G began rolling out multi-echelon inventory strategies across all of its various manufacturing branches.

Sources: John Kerr, "Procter & Gamble Takes Inventory Up a Notch," *Supply Chain Management Review,* February 13, 2008. Optiant, "Optiant Announces Multi-Echelon Inventory Optimization Enterprise Agreement with P&G," October 17, 2007; and www. optiant.com accessed July 17, 2008.

CASE STUDY QUESTIONS

1. Why are larger supply chains more difficult to manage? List several reasons.

2. Why is supply chain management so important at a company such as P&G?

3. How did inventory optimization impact operations and decision making at P&G?

4. Why wouldn't a small company derive much benefit from multi-echelon inventory optimization as a large company? Explain your answer.

MIS IN ACTION

1. Surf the Web for the ingredients of a Procter & Gamble product such as Crest toothpaste or Cover Girl lipstick or look for the list of ingredients on the packaging for these products in a retail store. Make a list of the ingredients for the product you selected.

2. Use the Web to find the major suppliers for each of these ingredients and their locations.

3. What did you learn from your investigation about P&G's supply chains for these products? What factors would determine price and availability of these products?

GLOBAL SUPPLY CHAINS AND THE INTERNET

Before the Internet, supply chain coordination was hampered by the difficulties of making information flow smoothly among disparate internal supply chain systems for purchasing, materials management, manufacturing, and distribution. It was also difficult to share information with external supply chain partners because the systems of suppliers, distributors, or logistics providers were based on incompatible technology platforms and standards. Enterprise systems supply some integration of internal supply chain processes but they are not designed to deal with external supply chain processes.

FIGURE 9-4   INTRANETS AND EXTRANETS FOR SUPPLY CHAIN MANAGEMENT

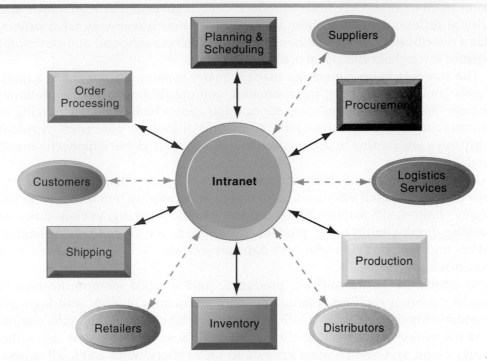

Intranets integrate information from isolated business processes within the firm to help manage its internal supply chain. Access to these private intranets can also be extended to authorized suppliers, distributors, logistics services, and, sometimes, to retail customers to improve coordination of external supply chain processes.

Some supply chain integration is supplied inexpensively using Internet technology. Firms use intranets to improve coordination among their internal supply chain processes, and they use extranets to coordinate supply chain processes shared with their business partners (see Figure 9-4).

Using intranets and extranets, all members of the supply chain are instantly able to communicate with each other, using up-to-date information to adjust purchasing, logistics, manufacturing, packaging, and schedules. A manager will use a Web interface to tap into suppliers' systems to determine whether inventory and production capabilities match demand for the firm's products. Business partners will use Web-based supply chain management tools to collaborate online on forecasts. Sales representatives will access suppliers' production schedules and logistics information to monitor customers' order status.

Global Supply Chain Issues

More and more companies are entering international markets, outsourcing manufacturing operations and obtaining supplies from other countries as well as selling abroad. Their supply chains extend across multiple countries and regions. There are additional complexities and challenges to managing a global supply chain.

Global supply chains typically span greater geographic distances and time differences than domestic supply chains and have participants from a number of different countries. Although the purchase price of many goods might be lower abroad, there are often additional costs for transportation, inventory (the need for a larger buffer of safety stock), and local taxes or fees. Performance standards may vary from region to region or from nation to nation. Supply chain management may need to reflect foreign government regulations and cultural differences. All of these factors impact how a company takes orders, plans distribution, sizes warehousing, and manages inbound and outbound logistics throughout the global markets it services.

The Internet helps companies manage many aspects of their global supply chains, including sourcing, transportation, communications, and international finance. Today's apparel industry, for example, relies heavily on outsourcing to contract manufacturers in China and other low-wage countries. Apparel companies are starting to use the Web to manage their global supply chain and production issues.

For example, Koret of California, a subsidiary of apparel maker Kellwood Co., uses e-SPS Web-based software to gain end-to-end visibility into its entire global supply chain. E-SPS features Web-based software for sourcing, work-in-progress tracking, production routing, product-development tracking, problem identification and collaboration, delivery-date projections, and production-related inquiries and reports.

As goods are being sourced, produced, and shipped, communication is required among retailers, manufacturers, contractors, agents, and logistics providers. Many, especially smaller companies still share product information over the phone, via e-mail, or through faxes. These methods slow down the supply chain and also increase errors and uncertainty. With e-SPS, all supply chain members communicate through a Web-based system. If one of Koret's vendors makes a change in the status of a product, everyone in the supply chain sees the change.

In addition to contract manufacturing, globalization has encouraged outsourcing warehouse management, transportation management, and related operations to third-party logistics providers, such as UPS Supply Chain Services and American Port Services. These logistics services offer Web-based software to give their customers a better view of their global supply chains. American Port Services invested in software to synchronize processes with freight forwarders, logistics hubs, and warehouses around the world that it uses for managing its clients' shipments and inventory. Customers are able to check a secure Web site to monitor inventory and shipments, helping them run their global supply chains more efficiently.

Demand-Driven Supply Chains: From Push to Pull Manufacturing and Efficient Customer Response

In addition to reducing costs, supply chain management systems facilitate efficient customer response, enabling the workings of the business to be driven more by customer demand. (We introduced efficient customer response systems in Chapter 3.)

Earlier supply chain management systems were driven by a push-based model (also known as build-to-stock). In a **push-based model**, production master schedules are based on forecasts or best guesses of demand for products, and products are "pushed" to customers. With new flows of information made possible by Web-based tools, supply chain management more easily follows a **pull-based model**. In a pull-based model, also known as a demand-driven model or build-to-order, actual customer orders or purchases trigger events in the supply chain. Transactions to produce and deliver only what customers have ordered move up the supply chain from retailers to distributors to manufacturers and eventually to suppliers. Only products to fulfill these orders move back down the supply chain to the retailer. Manufacturers use only

FIGURE 9-5   PUSH- VERSUS PULL-BASED SUPPLY CHAIN MODELS

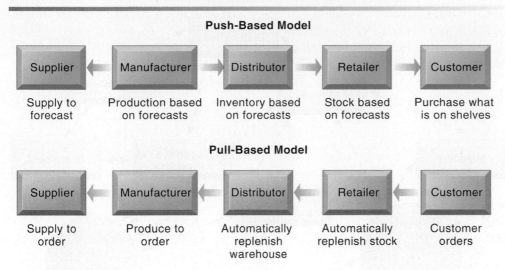

The difference between push- and pull-based models is summarized by the slogan "Make what we sell, not sell what we make."

actual order demand information to drive their production schedules and the procurement of components or raw materials, as illustrated in Figure 9-5. Wal-Mart's continuous replenishment system and Dell Computer's build-to-order system, both described in Chapter 3, are examples of the pull-based model.

The Internet and Internet technology make it possible to move from sequential supply chains, where information and materials flow sequentially from company to company, to concurrent supply chains, where information flows in many directions simultaneously among members of a supply chain network. Members of the network immediately adjust to changes in schedules or orders. Ultimately, the Internet could create a "digital logistics nervous system" throughout the supply chain (see Figure 9-6).

BUSINESS VALUE OF SUPPLY CHAIN MANAGEMENT SYSTEMS

You have just seen how supply chain management systems enable firms to streamline both their internal and external supply chain processes and provide management with more accurate information about what to produce, store, and move. By implementing a networked and integrated supply chain management system, companies match supply to demand, reduce inventory levels, improve delivery service, speed product time to market, and use assets more effectively.

Total supply chain costs represent the majority of operating expenses for many businesses and in some industries approach 75 percent of the total operating budget. Reducing supply chain costs may have a major impact on firm profitability.

In addition to reducing costs, supply chain management systems help increase sales. If a product is not available when a customer wants it, customers often try to purchase it from someone else. More precise control of the supply chain enhances the firm's ability to have the right product available for customer purchases at the right time.

FIGURE 9-6   THE FUTURE INTERNET-DRIVEN SUPPLY CHAIN

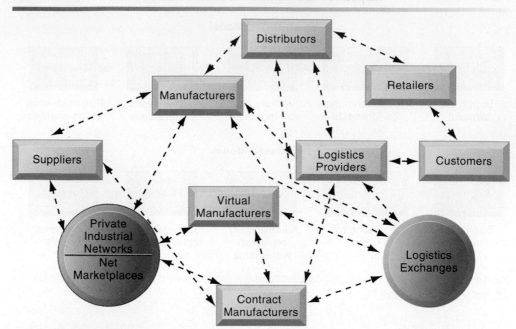

The future Internet-driven supply chain operates like a digital logistics nervous system. It provides multidirectional communication among firms, networks of firms, and e-marketplaces so that entire networks of supply chain partners can immediately adjust inventories, orders, and capacities.

9.3 CUSTOMER RELATIONSHIP MANAGEMENT SYSTEMS

You've probably heard phrases such as "the customer is always right" or "the customer comes first." Today these words ring more true than ever. Because competitive advantage based on an innovative new product or service is often very short lived, companies are realizing that their only enduring competitive strength may be their relationships with their customers. Some say that the basis of competition has switched from who sells the most products and services to who "owns" the customer, and that customer relationships represent a firm's most valuable asset.

WHAT IS CUSTOMER RELATIONSHIP MANAGEMENT?

What kinds of information would you need to build and nurture strong, long-lasting relationships with customers? You'd want to know exactly who your customers are, how to contact them, whether they are costly to service and sell to, what kinds of products and services they are interested in, and how much money they spend on your company. If you could, you'd want to make sure you knew each of your customers well, as if you were running a small-town store. And you'd want to make your good customers feel special.

In a small business operating in a neighborhood, it is possible for business owners and managers to really know their customers on a personal, face-to-face basis. But in a large business operating on a metropolitan, regional, national, or even global basis, it is impossible to "know your customer" in this intimate way. In these kinds of businesses there are too many customers and too many different ways that customers interact with the firm (over the Web, the phone, fax, and face-to-face). It becomes especially difficult to integrate information from all theses sources and to deal with the large numbers of customers.

A large business's processes for sales, service, and marketing tend to be highly compartmentalized, and these departments do not share much essential customer information. Some information on a specific customer might be stored and organized in terms of that person's account with the company. Other pieces of information about the same customer might be organized by products that were purchased. There is no way to consolidate all of this information to provide a unified view of a customer across the company.

This is where customer relationship management systems help. Customer relationship management (CRM) systems, which we introduced in Chapter 2, capture and integrate customer data from all over the organization, consolidate the data, analyze the data, and then distribute the results to various systems and customer touch points across the enterprise. A **touch point** (also known as a contact point) is a method of interaction with the customer, such as telephone, e-mail, customer service desk, conventional mail, Web site, wireless device, or retail store.

Well-designed CRM systems provide a single enterprise view of customers that is useful for improving both sales and customer service. Such systems likewise provide customers with a single view of the company regardless of what touch point the customer uses (see Figure 9-7).

Good CRM systems provide data and analytical tools for answering questions such as these: "What is the value of a particular customer to the firm over his or her lifetime?" "Who are our most loyal customers?" (It can cost six times more to sell to a new customer than to an existing customer.) "Who are our most profitable customers?" and "What do these profitable customers want to buy?" Firms use the answers to these questions to acquire new customers, provide better service and support to existing customers, customize their offerings more precisely to customer preferences, and provide ongoing value to retain profitable customers.

FIGURE 9-7   CUSTOMER RELATIONSHIP MANAGEMENT (CRM)

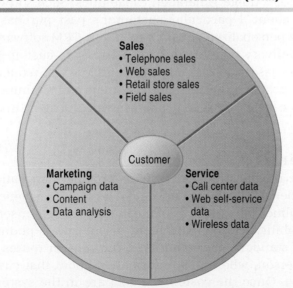

CRM systems examine customers from a multifaceted perspective. These systems use a set of integrated applications to address all aspects of the customer relationship, including customer service, sales, and marketing.

CRM SOFTWARE

Commercial CRM software packages range from niche tools that perform limited functions, such as personalizing Web sites for specific customers, to large-scale enterprise applications that capture myriad interactions with customers, analyze them with sophisticated reporting tools, and link to other major enterprise applications, such as supply chain management and enterprise systems. The more comprehensive CRM packages contain modules for **partner relationship management (PRM)** and **employee relationship management (ERM)**.

PRM uses many of the same data, tools, and systems as customer relationship management to enhance collaboration between a company and its selling partners. If a company does not sell directly to customers but rather works through distributors or retailers, PRM helps these channels sell to customers directly. It provides a company and its selling partners with the ability to trade information and distribute leads and data about customers, integrating lead generation, pricing, promotions, order configurations, and availability. It also provides a firm with tools to assess its partners' performances so it can make sure its best partners receive the support they need to close more business.

ERM software deals with employee issues that are closely related to CRM, such as setting objectives, employee performance management, performance-based compensation, and employee training. Major CRM application software vendors include Oracle-owned Siebel Systems and PeopleSoft, SAP, Salesforce.com, and Microsoft Dynamics CRM.

Customer relationship management systems typically provide software and online tools for sales, customer service, and marketing. We briefly describe some of these capabilities.

Sales Force Automation (SFA)

Sales force automation modules in CRM systems help sales staff increase their productivity by focusing sales efforts on the most profitable customers, those who are good candidates for sales and services. CRM systems provide sales prospect and contact information, product information, product configuration capabilities, and sales quote generation capabilities. Such software can assemble information about a particular customer's past purchases to help the salesperson make personalized recommendations. CRM software enables sales, marketing, and delivery departments to easily share customer and prospect information. It increases each salesperson's efficiency in reducing the cost per sale as well as the cost of acquiring new customers and retaining old ones. CRM software also has capabilities for sales forecasting, territory management, and team selling.

Customer Service

Customer service modules in CRM systems provide information and tools to increase the efficiency of call centers, help desks, and customer support staff. They have capabilities for assigning and managing customer service requests.

One such capability is an appointment or advice telephone line: When a customer calls a standard phone number, the system routes the call to the correct service person, who inputs information about that customer into the system only once. Once the customer's data are in the system, any service representative can handle the customer relationship. Improved access to consistent and accurate customer information help call centers handle more calls per day and decrease the duration of each call. Thus, call centers and customer service groups achieve greater productivity, reduced transaction time, and higher quality of service at lower cost. The customer is happier because he or she spends less time on the phone restating his or her problem to customer service representatives.

The Interactive Session on Organizations describes another CRM capability for improving customer service and operational efficiency. Implementation of Enkata software helped JP Morgan Chase increase its rate of first call resolution, which takes place when a call center agent is able resolve a customer service issue during the first call.

CRM systems may also include Web-based self-service capabilities: The company Web site can be set up to provide inquiring customers personalized support information as well as the option to contact customer service staff by phone for additional assistance.

Marketing

CRM systems support direct-marketing campaigns by providing capabilities for capturing prospect and customer data, for providing product and service information, for qualifying leads for targeted marketing, and for scheduling and tracking direct-marketing mailings or e-mail (see Figure 9-8). Marketing modules also include tools for analyzing marketing and customer data, identifying profitable and unprofitable customers, designing products and services to satisfy specific customer needs and interests, and identifying opportunities for cross-selling.

Cross-selling is the marketing of complementary products to customers. (For example, in financial services, a customer with a checking account might be sold a money market account or a home improvement loan.) CRM tools also help firms manage and execute marketing campaigns at all stages, from planning to determining the rate of success for each campaign.

FIGURE 9-8   HOW CRM SYSTEMS SUPPORT MARKETING

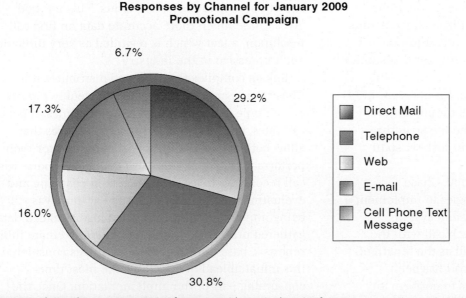

Customer relationship management software provides a single point for users to manage and evaluate marketing campaigns across multiple channels, including e-mail, direct mail, telephone, the Web, and wireless messages.

INTERACTIVE SESSION: ORGANIZATIONS

CUSTOMER RELATIONSHIP MANAGEMENT HELPS CHASE CARD SERVICES MANAGE CUSTOMER CALLS

If you have a credit card, there's a good chance that it is from Chase. Chase Card Services is the division of JP Morgan Chase which specializes in credit cards, offering a vast array of credit card products such as the Chase Rewards Platinum Visa card. As one of the largest credit card issuers in the United States, the company fields a correspondingly large amount of calls from people seeking customer service for their credit card accounts. Each of Chase's 6,000 call center agents worldwide at the company's 11 call centers fields field up to 120 calls per day. The company handles slightly less than 200 million calls each year from a customer base of 100 million.

Even a small reduction of 1% to the amount of calls received results in savings of millions of dollars and improved customer service for Chase. Achieving such a reduction is easier said than done, however. In 2006, Chase Card Services attempted to accomplish this by improving first-call resolution. First-call resolution is when a call center agent is able to resolve a customer's issues during the initial call to customer service without requiring additional calls.

The problem was that the company's record keeping did not give an accurate account of current rates of first-call resolution. Chase had previously tried tracking first-call resolution rates by having agents log the content and results of each call they received. But this task was time-consuming and was not standardized, since agents tended to record results subjectively and not in a uniform way. Company policies for some customer requests were also far from ideal for increasing first-call resolution. For example, agents were only able to process balance transfers for customers calling from their homes, and the fee structure underwent multiple changes over a short span, prompting repeat calls.

To improve call center efficiency, Chase contracted with Enkata Technologies to implement a performance and talent management system. The system monitors and tags each call with the topic and length of the call as well as the length of time the agent that handled the call has been working. It doesn't require agents to perform any action to acquire this information; it tracks calls automatically by keeping track of the keyboard strokes of each agent.

As soon as an agent clicks on the feature of the account that the customer is calling about, the Enkata system automatically identifies the reason for the call. Proprietery algorithms match the reason and caller identification to the amount of time predetermined for each type of call.

The system then monitors discrepancies in call time, depending on the reason for the call. For example, a call from a customer requiring card activation should be a quick call, so the system will pinpoint card activation calls that take longer than normal, or fee dispute calls that are shorter than normal. But sometimes customers have multiple reasons for calling, which would have been very difficult to track prior to the implementation of Enkata's system. Now Enkata separates each individual reason for calling and organizes them into a sequence, so that a call with multiple issues to resolve is analyzed using the appropriate time frame.

By separating and organizing reasons for calling into distinct categories, Chase is able to determine criteria for declaring particular calls 'resolved.' For example, a card activation call will be considered resolved after only a few days without a follow-up call, but a disputed fee call won't be considered resolved until the customer received another statement without any complaints. This method gives Chase much more accurate data on first-call resolution, a feat which is regarded as very difficult and impressive in the industry.

Enkata compiles this data and distributes it to Chase Card Services in the form of weekly reports on call type and length, call handling times, repeat call rates, and other performance measures that allow both agents and supervisors to monitor their performance. The system also connects reports with call recordings to assist managers in coaching and evaluating their agents. When the system was still being implemented, Enkata used historical call data gathered prior to the implementation to create initial reports. Chase Card Services executives considered this initial upload of data to be the most time-consuming part of the implementation. Once the implementation was complete, the company hoped that improvements in the interpretation and management of this information would lead to improvements in agent performance, customer satisfaction, and customer retention.

The results speak for themselves. Chase Card Services improved its first-call resolution rate to 91%, an increase of 3%, in its first year after the implementation of the Enkata system. That represented a total savings of $8 million. Approximately $2.5 million of that total savings was a direct result of the average call time decreasing by two seconds. The company hopes to reach its goal of 95% within the next few years. A perfect rate of 100% first-call resolution is not feasible because some additional calls after the first are acceptable under certain circumstances, such as a customer remembering a charge that he or she had initially disputed.

Within three months time, 30% of agents that had scored below the acceptable rate for first-call resolution improved to an acceptable rate. And although the number of active customer accounts grew by 5.2% in the six months after implementation of the system, call volume decreased 8.3% over that same span.

Encouraged by these successes, Chase Card Services is now looking to expand the capabilities of the system to classify calls into even more categories, and to link their collected data to marketing programs to foster cross-selling and upselling.

Sources: Marshall Lager, "Credit Where Due," *Customer Relationship Management*, April 2008; Michele Heller, "How Chase Got Control of Call-Center Expenses," *American Banker*, February 26, 2008.

CASE STUDY QUESTIONS

1. What functions of customer relationship management systems are illustrated in this case?

2. Why is the call center so important for Chase Card Services? How could Chase's call centers help it improve relationships with customers?

3. Describe the problem at Chase call centers. What management, organization, or technology factors contributed to the problem?

3. How did using Enkata improve operational performance and decision making? Give examples.

4. What management, organization, or technology factors would have to be considered in implementing the Enkata solution?

MIS IN ACTION

Visit the Enkata Web site and explore the features of its products, then answer the following questions:

1. How could Enkata's system be used for analyzing customer service at another type of business (such as a cell phone provider or clothing retailer with catalog and Web ordering, for example)?

2. What kinds of questions might customers call in to ask? What kinds of problems might call center agents encounter in answering these questions? How could Enkata software help?

Figure 9-9 illustrates the most important capabilities for sales, service, and marketing processes that would be found in major CRM software products. Like enterprise software, this software is business-process driven, incorporating hundreds of business processes thought to represent best practices in each of these areas. To achieve maximum benefit, companies need to revise and model their business processes to conform to the best-practice business processes in the CRM software.

Figure 9-10 illustrates how a best practice for increasing customer loyalty through customer service might be modeled by CRM software. Directly servicing customers provides firms with opportunities to increase customer retention by singling out profitable long-term customers for preferential treatment. CRM software can assign each customer a score based on that person's value and loyalty to the company and provide that information to help call centers route each customer's service request to agents who can best handle that customer's needs. The system would automatically provide the service agent with a detailed profile of that customer that included his or her

FIGURE 9-9 **CRM SOFTWARE CAPABILITIES**

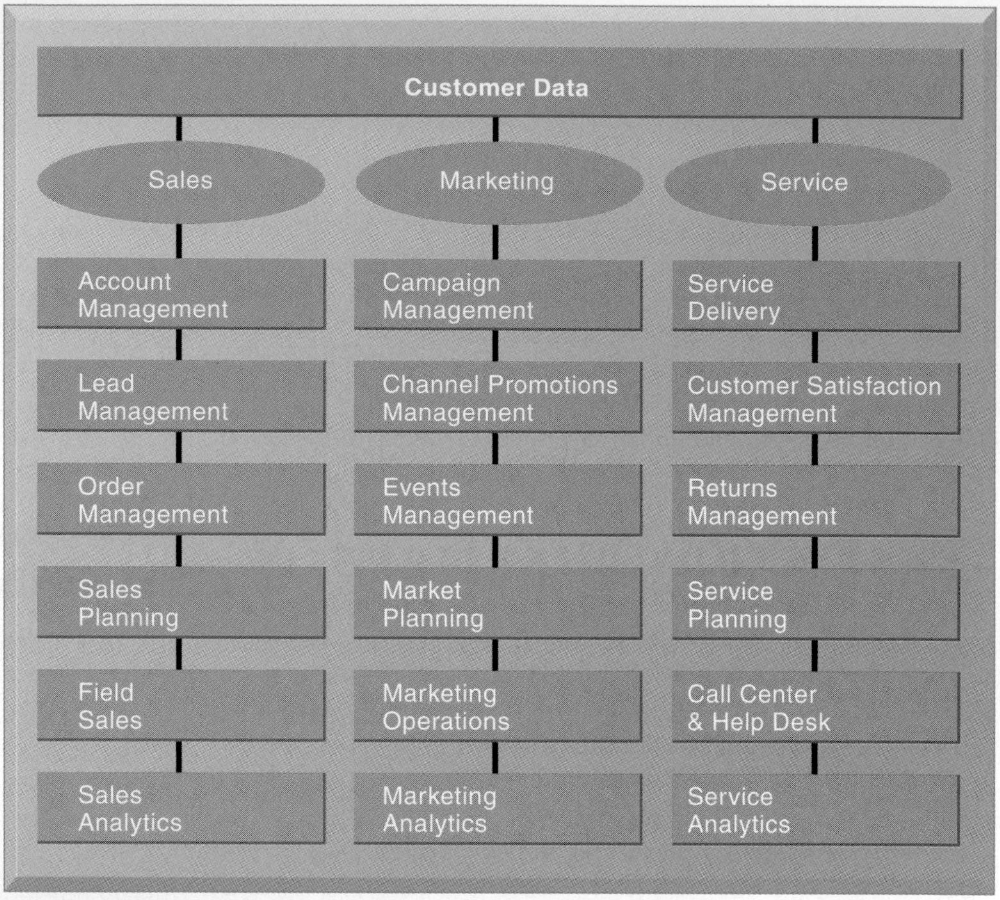

Customer Data		
Sales	Marketing	Service
Account Management	Campaign Management	Service Delivery
Lead Management	Channel Promotions Management	Customer Satisfaction Management
Order Management	Events Management	Returns Management
Sales Planning	Market Planning	Service Planning
Field Sales	Marketing Operations	Call Center & Help Desk
Sales Analytics	Marketing Analytics	Service Analytics

The major CRM software products support business processes in sales, service, and marketing, integrating customer information from many different sources. Included are support for both the operational and analytical aspects of CRM.

FIGURE 9-10 **CUSTOMER LOYALTY MANAGEMENT PROCESS MAP**

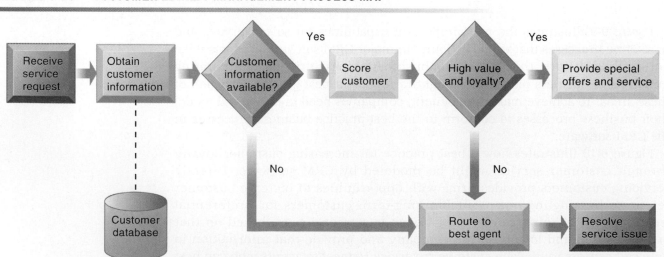

This process map shows how a best practice for promoting customer loyalty through customer service would be modeled by customer relationship management software. The CRM software helps firms identify high-value customers for preferential treatment.

score for value and loyalty. The service agent would use this information to present special offers or additional service to the customer to encourage the customer to keep transacting business with the company. You will find more information on other best-practice business processes in CRM systems in our Learning Tracks.

OPERATIONAL AND ANALYTICAL CRM

All of the applications we have just described support either the operational or analytical aspects of customer relationship management. **Operational CRM** includes customer-facing applications, such as tools for sales force automation, call center and customer service support, and marketing automation. **Analytical CRM** includes applications that analyze customer data generated by operational CRM applications to provide information for improving business performance.

Analytical CRM applications are based on data warehouses that consolidate the data from operational CRM systems and customer touch points for use with online analytical processing (OLAP), data mining, and other data analysis techniques (see Chapter 6). Customer data collected by the organization might be combined with data from other sources, such as customer lists for direct-marketing campaigns purchased from other companies or demographic data. Such data are analyzed to identify buying patterns, to create segments for targeted marketing, and to pinpoint profitable and unprofitable customers (see Figure 9-11).

Another important output of analytical CRM is the customer's lifetime value to the firm. **Customer lifetime value (CLTV)** is based on the relationship between the revenue produced by a specific customer, the expenses incurred in acquiring and servicing that customer, and the expected life of the relationship between the customer and the company.

FIGURE 9-11   ANALYTICAL CRM DATA WAREHOUSE

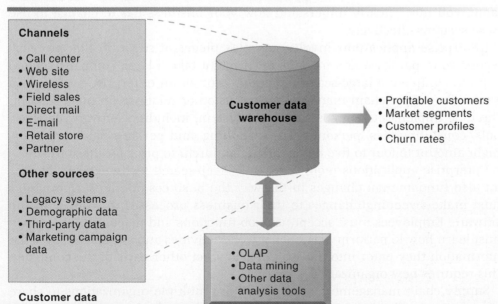

Analytical CRM uses a customer data warehouse and tools to analyze customer data collected from the firm's customer touch points and from other sources.

BUSINESS VALUE OF CUSTOMER RELATIONSHIP MANAGEMENT SYSTEMS

Companies with effective customer relationship management systems realize many benefits, including increased customer satisfaction, reduced direct-marketing costs, more effective marketing, and lower costs for customer acquisition and retention. Information from CRM systems increases sales revenue by identifying the most profitable customers and segments for focused marketing and cross-selling.

Customer churn is reduced as sales, service, and marketing better respond to customer needs. The **churn rate** measures the number of customers who stop using or purchasing products or services from a company. It is an important indicator of the growth or decline of a firm's customer base.

9.4 ENTERPRISE APPLICATIONS: NEW OPPORTUNITIES AND CHALLENGES

Many firms have implemented enterprise systems and systems for supply chain management and customer relationship because they are such powerful instruments for achieving operational excellence and enhancing decision making. But precisely because they are so powerful in changing the way the organization works, they are challenging to implement. Let's briefly examine some of these challenges, as well as new ways of obtaining value from these systems.

ENTERPRISE APPLICATION CHALLENGES

Promises of dramatic reductions in inventory costs, order-to-delivery time, as well as more efficient customer response and higher product and customer profitability make enterprise systems and systems for supply chain management and customer relationship management very alluring. But to obtain this value, you must clearly understand how your business has to change to use these systems effectively.

Enterprise applications involve complex pieces of software that are very expensive to purchase and implement. It might take a large company several years to complete a large-scale implementation of an enterprise system or a system for supply chain management or customer relationship management. The total implementation cost of a large system, including software, database tools, consulting fees, personnel costs, training, and perhaps hardware costs, might amount to four to five times the initial purchase price for the software.

Enterprise applications require not only deep-seated technological changes but also fundamental changes in the way the business operates. Companies must make sweeping changes to their business processes to work with the software. Employees must accept new job functions and responsibilities. They must learn how to perform a new set of work activities and understand how the information they enter into the system can affect other parts of the company. This requires new organizational learning.

Supply chain management systems require multiple organizations to share information and business processes. Each participant in the system may have to change some of its processes and the way it uses information to create a system that best serves the supply chain as a whole.

Some firms experienced enormous operating problems and losses when they first implemented enterprise applications because they did not understand how much organizational change was required.

- Kmart had trouble getting products to store shelves when it implemented supply chain management software from i2 Technologies in July 2000. The i2 software did not work well with Kmart's promotion-driven business model, which creates sharp spikes and drops in demand for products, and it was not designed to handle the massive number of products stocked in Kmart stores.

- Hershey Foods' profitability dropped when it tried to implement SAP enterprise software, Manugistics SCM software, and Siebel Systems CRM software on a crash schedule in 1999 without thorough testing and employee training. Shipments ran two weeks late and many customers did not receive enough candy to stock shelves during the busy Halloween selling period. Hershey lost sales and customers during that period, although the new systems eventually improved operational efficiency.

Enterprise applications also introduce "switching costs." Once you adopt an enterprise application from a single vendor, such as SAP, Oracle, or others, it is very costly to switch vendors, and your firm becomes dependent on the vendor to upgrade its product and maintain your installation.

Enterprise applications are based on organization-wide definitions of data. You'll need to understand exactly how your business uses its data and how the data would be organized in a customer relationship management, supply chain management, or enterprise system. CRM systems typically require some data cleansing work.

In a nutshell, it takes a lot of work to get enterprise applications to work properly. Everyone in the organization must be involved. Of course, for those companies that have successfully implemented CRM, SCM, and enterprise systems, the results have justified the effort.

NEXT-GENERATION ENTERPRISE APPLICATIONS

Today, enterprise application vendors are delivering more value by becoming more flexible, Web-enabled, and capable of integration with other systems. Standalone enterprise systems, customer relationship systems, and supply chain management systems are becoming a thing of the past.

The major enterprise software vendors have created what they call *enterprise solutions*, *enterprise suites*, or *e-business suites* to make their customer relationship management, supply chain management, and enterprise systems work closely with each other, and link to systems of customers and suppliers. SAP Business Suite, Oracle's e-Business Suite, and Microsoft's Dynamics suite (aimed at mid-sized companies) are examples, and they now utilize Web services and service-oriented architecture (SOA, see Chapter 5).

SAP's next generation enterprise applications are based on its enterprise service-oriented architecture. It incorporates service-oriented architecture (SOA) standards and uses its NetWeaver tool as an integration platform linking SAP's own applications and also Web services developed by independent software vendors. The goal is to make enterprise applications easier to implement and manage

For example, the current version of SAP enterprise software combines key applications in finance, logistics and procurement, and human resources administration into a core ERP component. Businesses then extend these applications by linking to function-specific Web services such as employee recruiting or collections management provided by SAP and other vendors. SAP provides over 500 Web services through its Web site.

Oracle also has included SOA and business process management capabilities into its Fusion middleware products. Businesses can use Oracle tools to customize Oracle's applications without breaking the entire application.

Next-generation enterprise applications also include open source and on-demand solutions. Compared to commercial enterprise application software, open-source products such as Compiere, Open for Business, and Openbravo are not as mature, nor do they include as much support. However, companies such as small manufacturers are choosing this option because there are no software licensing fees. (Support and customization for open-source products cost extra.)

The most explosive growth in SaaS (software as a service) offerings has been for customer relationship management. Salesforce.com (see Chapters 5 and 8) and Oracle's Siebel Systems have been the leaders in hosted CRM solutions, and Microsoft Dynamics CRM has an online on-demand version. SaaS versions of enterprise systems are much less popular, and not yet available from the major enterprise vendors.

Salesforce.com and Oracle now include some Web 2.0 capabilities that enable organizations to identify new ideas more rapidly, improve team productivity, and deepen interactions with customers. For example, Salesforce Ideas allows employees, customers, and business partners to suggest and then vote on new ideas. Dell Computer deployed this technology as Dell IdeaStorm (dellideastorm.com) to enable custommers to suggest and vote on new concepts and feature changes in Dell products. Ideas contributed on the service encouraged Dell to add higher-resolution screens to the Dell 1530 laptop (Greenfield, 2008).

Service Platforms

Another way of extending enterprise applications is to use them to create service platforms for new or improved business processes that integrate information from multiple functional areas. These enterprise-wide service platforms provide a greater degree of cross-functional integration than the traditional enterprise applications. A **service platform** integrates multiple applications from multiple business functions, business units, or business partners to deliver a seamless experience for the customer, employee, manager, or business partner.

For instance, the order-to-cash process involves receiving an order and seeing it all the way through obtaining payment for the order. This process begins with lead generation, marketing campaigns, and order entry, which are typically supported by CRM systems. Once the order is received, manufacturing is scheduled and parts availability is verified—processes that are usually supported by enterprise software. The order then is handled by processes for distribution planning, warehousing, order fulfillment, and shipping, which are usually supported by supply chain management systems. Finally, the order is billed to the customer, which is handled by either enterprise financial applications or accounts receivable. If the purchase at some point required customer service, customer relationship management systems would again be invoked.

A service such as order-to-cash requires data from enterprise applications and financial systems to be further integrated into an enterprise-wide composite process. To accomplish this, firms need software tools that use existing applications as building blocks for new cross-enterprise processes (see Figure 9-12). Enterprise application vendors provide middleware and tools that use XML and Web services for integrating enterprise applications with older legacy applications and systems from other vendors.

FIGURE 9-12   ORDER-TO-CASH SERVICE

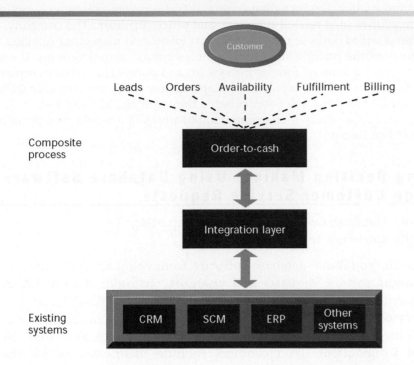

Composite process

Existing systems

Order-to-cash is a composite process that integrates data from individual enterprise systems and legacy financial applications. The process must be modeled and translated into a software system using application integration tools.

Increasingly, these new services will be delivered through portals. Portal software can integrate information from enterprise applications and disparate in-house legacy systems, presenting it to users through a Web interface so that the information appears to be coming from a single source. For example, Valero Energy, North America's largest refiner, used SAP NetWeaver Portal to create a service for wholesale clients to view their account information all at once. SAP NetWeaver Portal provides an interface to clients' invoice, price, electronic funds, and credit card transaction data stored in SAP's customer relationship management system data warehouse as well as in non-SAP systems (Zaino, 2007).

9.5   HANDS-ON MIS PROJECTS

The projects in this section give you hands-on experience analyzing business process integration, suggesting supply chain management and customer relationship management applications, using database software to manage customer service requests, and evaluating supply chain management business services.

Management Decision Problems

1. Toronto-based Mercedes-Benz Canada, with a network of 55 dealers, did not know enough about its customers. Dealers provided customer data to the company on an ad hoc basis. Mercedes did not force dealers to report this information, and its process for tracking dealers that failed to report was cumbersome. There was no real incentive for dealers to share information with the company. How could customer relationship management (CRM) and partner relationship management (PRM) systems help solve this problem?

2. Office Depot sells a wide range of office products and services in the United States and internationally, including general office supplies, computer supplies, business machines (and related supplies), and office furniture. The company tries to offer a wider range of office supplies at lower cost than other retailers by using just-in-time replenishment and tight inventory control systems. It uses information from a demand forecasting system and point-of-sale data to replenish its inventory in its 1,600 retail stores. Explain how these systems help Office Depot minimize costs and any other benefits they provide. Identify and describe other supply chain management applications that would be especially helpful to Office Depot.

Improving Decision Making: Using Database Software to Manage Customer Service Requests

Software skills: Database design; querying and reporting
Business skills: Customer service analysis

In this exercise, you'll use database software to develop an application that tracks customer service requests and analyzes customer data to identify customers meriting priority treatment.

Prime Service is a large service company that provides maintenance and repair services for close to 1,200 commercial businesses in New York, New Jersey, and Connecticut. Its customers include businesses of all sizes. Customers with service needs call into its customer service department with requests for repairing heating ducts, broken windows, leaky roofs, broken water pipes, and other problems. The company assigns each request a number and writes down the service request number, identification number of the customer account, the date of the request, the type of equipment requiring repair, and a brief description of the problem. The service requests are handled on a first-come-first-served basis. After the service work has been completed, Prime calculates the cost of the work, enters the price on the service request form, and bills the client.

Management is not happy with this arrangement because the most important and profitable clients—those with accounts of more than $70,000—are treated no differently from its clients with small accounts. It would like to find a way to provide its best customers with better service. Management would also like to know which types of service problems occur the most frequently so that it can make sure it has adequate resources to address them.

Prime Service has a small database with client account information, which can be found on the Laudon Web site for Chapter 9. A sample is shown on the next page, but the Web site may have a more recent version of this database for this exercise. The database table includes fields for the account ID, company (account) name, street address, city, state, ZIP code, account size (in dollars), contact last name, contact first name, and contact telephone number. The contact is the name of the person in each company who is responsible for contacting Prime about maintenance and repair work. Use your database software to design a solution that would enable Prime's customer service representatives to identify the most important customers so that they could receive priority service. Your solution will require more than one table. Populate your database with at least 15 service requests. Create several reports that would be of interest to management, such as a list of the highest- and lowest-priority accounts or a report showing the most frequently occurring service problems. Create a report showing customer service representatives which service calls they should respond to first on a specific date.

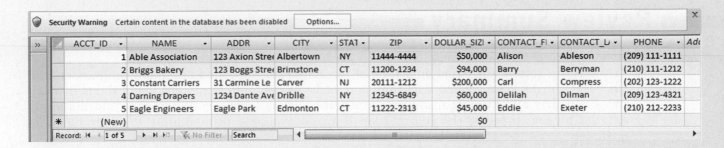

	ACCT_ID	NAME	ADDR	CITY	STAT	ZIP	DOLLAR_SIZI	CONTACT_FI	CONTACT_L	PHONE	Ad
	1	Able Association	123 Axion Stree	Albertown	NY	11444-4444	$50,000	Alison	Ableson	(209) 111-1111	
	2	Briggs Bakery	123 Boggs Stree	Brimstone	CT	11200-1234	$94,000	Barry	Berryman	(210) 111-1212	
	3	Constant Carriers	31 Carmine Le	Carver	NJ	20111-1212	$200,000	Carl	Compress	(202) 123-1222	
	4	Darning Drapers	1234 Dante Ave	Driblle	NY	12345-6849	$60,000	Delilah	Dilman	(209) 123-4321	
	5	Eagle Engineers	Eagle Park	Edmonton	CT	11222-2313	$45,000	Eddie	Exeter	(210) 212-2233	
*	(New)						$0				

Achieving Operational Excellence: Evaluating Supply Chain Management Services

Software skills: Web browser and presentation software
Business skills: Evaluating supply chain management services

Trucking companies no longer merely carry goods from one place to another. Some also provide supply chain management services to their customers and help them manage their information. In this project, you'll use the Web to research and evaluate two of these business services.

Investigate the Web sites of two companies, J.B. Hunt and Schneider Logistics, to see how these companies' services can be used for supply chain management. Then respond to the following questions:

- What supply chain processes can each of these companies support for their clients?
- How can customers use the Web sites of each company to help them with supply chain management?
- Compare the supply chain management services provided by these companies. Which company would you select to help your firm manage its supply chain? Why?

LEARNING TRACK MODULES

The following Learning Tracks provide content relevant to topics covered in this chapter:

1. SAP Business Process Map
2. Business Processes in Supply Chain Management and Supply Chain Metrics
3. Best-Practice Business Processes in CRM Software

■ Review Summary ■

1. *How do enterprise systems help businesses achieve operational excellence?*

    Enterprise software is based on a suite of integrated software modules and a common central database. The database collects data from and feeds the data into numerous applications that can support nearly all of an organization's internal business activities. When new information is entered by one process, the information is made available immediately to other business processes.

    Enterprise systems support organizational centralization by enforcing uniform data standards and business processes throughout the company and a single unified technology platform. The firmwide data generated by enterprise systems helps managers evaluate organizational performance.

2. *How do supply chain management systems coordinate planning, production, and logistics with suppliers?*

    Supply chain management systems automate the flow of information among members of the supply chain so they can use it to make better decisions about when and how much to purchase, produce, or ship. More accurate information from supply chain management systems reduces uncertainty and the impact of the bullwhip effect.

    Supply chain management software includes software for supply chain planning and for supply chain execution. Internet technology facilitates the management of global supply chains by providing the connectivity for organizations in different countries to share supply chain information. Improved communication among supply chain members also facilitates efficient customer response and movement toward a demand-driven model.

3. *How do customer relationship management systems help firms achieve customer intimacy?*

    Customer relationship management (CRM) systems integrate and automate customer-facing processes in sales, marketing, and customer service, providing an enterprise-wide view of customers. Companies can use this customer knowledge when they interact with customers to provide them with better service or to sell new products and services. These systems also identify profitable or nonprofitable customers or opportunities to reduce the churn rate.

    The major customer relationship management software packages provide capabilities for both operational CRM and analytical CRM. They often include modules for managing relationships with selling partners (partner relationship management) and for employee relationship management.

4. *What are the challenges posed by enterprise applications?*

    Enterprise applications are difficult to implement. They require extensive organizational change, large new software investments, and careful assessment of how these systems will enhance organizational performance. Enterprise applications cannot provide value if they are implemented atop flawed processes or if firms do not know how to use these systems to measure performance improvements. Employees require training to prepare for new procedures and roles. Attention to data management is essential.

5. *How are enterprise applications used in platforms for new cross-functional services?*

    Service platforms integrate data and processes from the various enterprise applications (customer relationship management, supply chain management, and enterprise systems), as well as from disparate legacy applications to create new composite business processes. Web services tie various systems together. The new services are delivered through enterprise portals, which can integrate disparate applications so that information appears to be coming from a single source.

Key Terms

Review Questions

1. How do enterprise systems help businesses achieve operational excellence?
   - Define an enterprise system and explain how enterprise software works.
   - Describe how enterprise systems provide value for a business.

2. How do supply chain management systems coordinate planning, production, and logistics with suppliers?
   - Define a supply chain and identify each of its components.
   - Explain how supply chain management systems help reduce the bullwhip effect and how they provide value for a business.
   - Define and compare supply chain planning systems and supply chain execution systems.
   - Describe the challenges of global supply chains and how Internet technology can help companies manage them better.
   - Distinguish between a push-based and pull-based model of supply chain management and explain how contemporary supply chain management systems facilitate a pull-based model.

3. How do customer relationship management systems help firms achieve customer intimacy?
   - Define customer relationship management and explain why customer relationships are so important today.
   - Describe how partner relationship management (PRM) and employee relationship management (ERM) are related to customer relationship management (CRM).
   - Describe the tools and capabilities of customer relationship management software for sales, marketing, and customer service.
   - Distinguish between operational and analytical CRM.

4. What are the challenges posed by enterprise applications?
   - List and describe the challenges posed by enterprise applications
   - Explain how these challenges can be addressed.

5. How are enterprise applications used in platforms for new cross-functional services?
   - Define a service platform and describe the tools for integrating data from enterprise applications.

Discussion Questions

1. Supply chain management is less about managing the physical movement of goods and more about managing information. Discuss the implications of this statement.

2. If a company wants to implement an enterprise application, it had better do its homework. Discuss the implications of this statement.

Video Cases

You will find video cases illustrating some of the concepts in this chapter on the Laudon Web site along with questions to help you analyze the cases.

Collaboration and Teamwork: Analyzing Enterprise Application Vendors

With a group of three or four students, use the Web to research and evaluate the products of two vendors of enterprise application software. You could compare, for example, the SAP and Oracle enterprise systems, the supply chain management systems from i2 and SAP, or the customer relationship management systems of Oracle's Siebel Systems and Salesforce.com. Use what you have learned from these companies' Web sites to compare the software packages you have selected in terms of business functions supported, technology platforms, cost, and ease of use. Which vendor would you select? Why? Would you select the same vendor for a small business as well as a large one? If possible, use Google Sites to post links to Web pages, team communication announcements, and work assignments; to brainstorm; and to work collaboratively on project documents. Try to use Google Docs to develop a presentation of your findings for the class.

Symantec's ERP Turmoil
CASE STUDY

Symantec Corporation is a leading software vendor specializing in security and information management. The company is well known for its Norton brand of security products in addition to a variety of other security and storage software. Symantec has operations in more than 40 countries and over 17,500 employees. A major source of Symantec's growth since the company's creation in the 1980s has been the acquisition of other companies, including Norton, Brightmail, Altiris, and many smaller software developers. In 2005, the company made its largest acquisition to date, acquiring Veritas Software for approximately $13.5 billion in what was the largest software industry merger ever at that time.

While Symantec's focus was security and information management for consumers, Veritas specialized in storage management software geared toward large-scale licensing. Because the two companies were of similar size and specialized in different types of software, many industry pundits questioned whether or not they were ideal candidates for a merger. Today, those questions appear to have been well-founded, in large part because of the difficulties incurred by Symantec's attempts to complete an overhaul of their enterprise resource planning systems.

Shortly after acquiring Veritas in late 2005, Symantec began an ERP rollout, referred to internally as 'Project Oasis,' intended to standardize and unify the Symantec and Veritas information systems. The goal of the rollout was to create a single ERP system, within which all of the company's extensive network of resellers, integrators, distributors, and customers could place orders for over 250,000 different products Symantec offered in the same way. The two companies had each used Oracle E-Business Suite 11d prior to the merger, but both used highly customized versions of the systems that made integration a daunting task.

An overhaul of the combined company's enterprise systems was needed to combine Symantec and Veritas's data from key business processes. A common enterprise system would also reduce the cost of maintaining Symantec's IT infrastructure and licensing fees for the enterprise software.

For their new system, Symantec opted to upgrade to Oracle's E-Business Suite 11i, running it on Sun Solaris servers. The system used an Oracle Fusion middleware portal on the front end, providing a single contact point for all of Symantec's partners and customers. Both Symantec's security applications and Veritas's backup and storage applications are available via the same portal. On the front end, the new Oracle system was linked to Salesforce.com's on-demand customer relationship management system and on the back end, the system linked to Symantec's Oracle PeopleSoft Enterprise human resources applications.

The initial reaction to the launch of the new system was decidedly negative. While the system itself was technically sound and working exactly as intended, users struggled to process the large amount of information provided to them and were overwhelmed by the increased number of steps, all of them new, required to place orders. Unhappy with the new system, customers began calling Symantec's support team in record numbers, but the company was unprepared to meet the increased demand for customer support. Wait times ballooned from an average of 2 minutes to an average of 25 minutes for a typical customer support call. Once customers reached a Symantec employee, they could spend up to 20 more minutes troubleshooting the problems, and were often told that there was nothing that could be done.

Symantec also neglected to coordinate the development of its new ERP system with the launch of other products from different divisions within the company, compounding the issues with customer support and response times. For example, the new system's launch coincided with the launch of the newest version of Symantec Backup Exec 10d, one of the company's flagship products. There was simply too much change occurring all at once for typical customers to handle. Even longtime partners expressed displeasure at the steep drop in the quality of Symantec's customer service.

Customers were also unhappy with Symantec's changes to its stock-keeping unit product system, or SKU system. Symantec improved the system by creating a single set of codes for all of its applications. Although reducing the number of codes made ordering products simpler and easier, it also caught many smaller partners of Symantec off guard. Some smaller distributors and partners didn't update their systems to handle the new SKUs and were unable to submit purchase orders electronically, forcing Symantec to process orders manually. Although Symantec extended the deadline for its partners to switch to the new purchasing system to accommodate these customers, the overhaul still represented an annoyance for many who had been satisfied with the previous system.

Symantec's changes to the software licensing process were another irritant to customers. Prior to the ERP rollout, the software licensing program worked well. Customers could put in an order and receive a license certificate promptly, usually within a couple of days. After the rollout, licensing became much more difficult for Symantec's customers and partners, forcing them to wait multiple weeks before receiving their licenses. When licenses didn't show up, unhappy customers called Symantec for support, further burdening their already overworked customer service department. The changes to the licensing system were also not coordinated with the rest of Project Oasis, creating unnecessary confusion.

Symantec had designed the new enterprise system to show customers their existing licenses. However, one company could have multiple accounts with variations in corporate names when divisions and branch offices purchased their own licenses separately from the central office.

Channel partners reported that buying Symantec products through distribution via companies like Ingram Micro became unusually difficult. One Symantec channel partner commented that "the multiplication of cryptically described part numbers has rendered it impossible to purchase Symantec licenses from Ingram Micro without assistance from the licensing help desk. This makes the process much more time-consuming." For its part, Ingram Micro said they were working with Symantec to fix these issues, but many partners were unhappy with Symantec's slow response.

As a result of these many missteps, Symantec was in danger of losing many loyal customers. Most of the issues were due to the company's shortsightedness in implementing Project Oasis. Although the ERP rollout cost 7.75% less than budgeted, Symantec reported lower-than-expected earnings in the third quarter of 2007 and blamed these results on their ERP woes. Management said the company would need to cut $200 million in annual costs through layoffs or restructuring activities. Symantec CEO John Thompson said of the botched upgrade, "Systems changes such as these certainly don't come without issues. And we may have had more than our fair share of them with this set of changes, where we incurred higher expenses than planned and lost some revenue opportunities during the quarter."

Almost immediately, the company set about undoing mistakes with a follow-up project, named Project Nero. The goal of Project Nero was to recapture the loyalty of customers who were disenchanted by the changes brought about by Oasis, both by reaching out to those customers and by fixing the problems with their information systems to improve response times and streamline operations. Symantec had overlooked the needs of many customers while designing a technically sound but user-unfriendly ERP system. Project Nero's purpose was to assure those customers that Symantec still had their best interests in mind.

The company began by adding over 150 new customer representatives to handle the increased volume of calls, reducing wait times and increasing customer satisfaction. Symantec's executives traveled the country in order to improve relations with angered customers and partners. To correct the issue of product updates being released at the same time as the ERP overhaul, the company introduced a master list of product releases readily available and standardized its communication methods between departments regarding new projects and change management.

Symantec also used Net Promoter methodology to measure and increase customer loyalty. Developed shortly before the acquisition of Veritas, Net Promoter was an initiative in which the company periodically surveyed customers to gauge their satisfaction with Symantec. The results from Net Promoter identified specific criticisms and problems of customers and dramatically aided Symantec in correcting those problems. One such example is the master list of product releases, which was a direct result of customer suggestions received via Net Promoter.

Symantec's customer satisfaction levels were at all-time lows after the launch of Project Oasis, but Project Nero has helped the company to weather the worst of the crisis. Symantec reports that it now enjoys satisfaction levels on par with the rest of its industry and averted a potential disaster. However, the company does not release the results of its Net Promoter surveys to the public, so the extent to which it has repaired its reputation is unclear. Smaller value-added resellers and distributors report that they are receiving more attention from their regional representatives at Symantec than ever before, with some reporting that CEO Thompson routinely calls to check up on the quality of customer service. Although Symantec has done well to recover from the fallout after its initial ERP implementation, Project Oasis serves as a cautionary tale for businesses undertaking ERP overhauls. Even the most careful planning and well-designed systems can quickly go awry if customers are unable to make use of the new system.

Sources: Lawrence Walsh, "Symantec's Midnight at the Oasis," *Baseline Magazine*, March 31, 2008; *Kevin McLaughlin*, "Partners Still Hung Over from Symantec ERP Upgrade," ChannelWeb, March 2, 2007; Marc L. Songini, "ERP Rollout Whacks Symantec's Bottom Line," *Computerworld*, January 31, 2007, "ERP Rollout Continues to Weigh Down Symantec," *Computerworld*, February 5, 2007, and "ERP Rollout Weighs Symantec Down," *Computerworld*, February 12, 2007.

CASE STUDY QUESTIONS

1. What concepts in this chapter are illustrated in this case?

2. What management, organization, and technology factors were responsible for Symantec's difficulties in overhauling its ERP systems?

3. Was Symantec's response to the problem adequate? Explain your reasoning.

4. What would you have done differently to prevent the implementation problems that arose at Symantec?

5. If you were a partner or customer of Symantec, would you have switched vendors in response to the ERP overhaul issues? Why or why not?

Chapter 10

E-Commerce: Digital Markets, Digital Goods

LEARNING OBJECTIVES

After reading this chapter, you will be able to answer the following questions:

1. What are the unique features of e-commerce, digital markets, and digital goods?

2. How has Internet technology changed business models?

3. What are the various types of e-commerce and how has e-commerce changed consumer retailing and business-to-business transactions?

4. What is the role of m-commerce in business and what are the most important m-commerce applications?

5. What are the principal payment systems for electronic commerce?

Interactive Sessions:

Turner Sports New Media Marries TV and the Internet

Can J&R Electronics Grow with E-commerce?

CHAPTER OUTLINE

10.1 ELECTRONIC COMMERCE AND THE INTERNET
E-Commerce Today
Why E-Commerce is Different
Key Concepts in E-Commerce: Digital Markets and Digital Goods in a Global Marketplace
Internet Business Models

10.2 ELECTRONIC COMMERCE
Types of Electronic Commerce
Achieving Customer Intimacy: Interactive Marketing, Personalization, and Self-Service
Business-to-Business E-Commerce: New Efficiencies and Relationships

10.3 M-COMMERCE
M-Commerce Services and Applications
Accessing Information from the Wireless Web

10.4 ELECTRONIC COMMERCE PAYMENT SYSTEMS
Types of Electronic Payment Systems
Digital Payment Systems for M-Commerce

10.5 HANDS-ON MIS PROJECTS
Management Decision Problems
Improving Decision Making: Using Spreadsheet Software to Analyze a Dot-Com Business
Achieving Operational Excellence: Evaluating E-Commerce Hosting Services

LEARNING TRACK MODULES
E-Commerce Challenges: The Story of Online Groceries
Build an E-Commerce Business Plan
Hot New Careers in E-Commerce

NEXON GAMES: E-COMMERCE GOES SOCIAL

If you like to play online games, you may already be familiar with MapleStory. It an online role-playing game in which players assume the identities of warriors, magicians, and thieves to collectively fight monsters. You can play the game for free, but if you want your avatar to have a new outfit, wacky hairstyle, or funny pet, you'll need to pay for these extras. And if you want your MapleStory characters to marry each other in an elaborate Las Vegas ceremony attended by other in-game buddies, it will cost $20 to $29.

MapleStory is a recent creation of Nexon Holdings Inc., the world leader in massively multiplayer online role playing games. Nexon is headquartered in South Korea, with branch offices in China, Japan, and the United States. Nexon pioneered in the "item" (microtransactions) business model, where users can access the full game for free but later opt to pay for game enhancements (items). Nexon charges players anywhere from 30 cents to $30 each for virtual "items" to enhance their game experiences. MapleStory has 85 million users globally, with 5.9 million registered in the United States. In 2007, players worldwide purchased more than 1.3 million articles of clothing and over 1 million hair makeovers for their MapleStory characters.

One source of Nexon's popularity is the ability to socialize with other users. According to Min Kim, vice president of marketing at Nexon's U.S. division, "we sell social experiences, not packaged product." During much of the last decade, most games were played alone. As the Internet and PCs developed more capabilities for rich-media experiences, solitary gaming has given way to social gaming. Whether it's integrated instant messaging, voice-over IP, or text messaging, there are now multiple mechanisms for players to communicate with their friends. Video games now attract a whole new type of consumer—people who want to have a social experience.

Other popular Nexon games include Sugar Rush, Mabinogi, and Kart Rider. Kart Rider is an anime-style online racing game that allows player to customize their vehicles and chat with friends. Sugar Rush players are able to fight each other while collecting virtual coins. Inspired by Celtic mythology, Mabinogi allows players to participate in mundane tasks such as farming, writing music, and marrying as well as fighting. The game continuously evolves through the release of patches (termed "Generations" and "Chapters") that intro- duce new areas to explore and advance the story line. All Nexon games feature Forums where players are invited to socialize with friends, share hints, or just "hang out."

Nexon looks like it has a winning formula for success online. In the United States alone, 2007 revenue tripled to $29.3 million from $8.5 million the previous year. Prepaid cards used to purchase Nexon game items are now the second best-selling entertainment gift card (after Apple's iTunes Store) at Target Stores.

Sources: Nick Wingfield, "Korea's Nexon Bets on Sales of Virtual Gear for Free Online Games," *The Wall Street Journal*, May 23, 2008; Kara Swisher, "Playing with Others," *The Wall Street Journal*, June 9, 2008; and www.nexon.com, accessed May 25, 2008.

Nexon's online games exemplify the new face of e-commerce. Selling physical goods on the Internet is still important, but much of the excitement and interest now centers around services and social experiences—social networking, photo sharing, sharing music, sharing ideas, and multiplayer online games where users communicate and interact with other users. The ability to link with other users and with other Web sites has spawned a huge wave of new businesses built around linking and sharing.

The chapter-opening diagram calls attention to important points raised by this case and this chapter. Nexon's business is a response to these questions: How do we make money on the Web today? How can we take advantage of more widespread broadband access to the Internet and to new Web 2.0 technologies? Nexon pioneered in the microtransactions business model and became a leading provider of massively multiplayer online games. The company provides games replete with action and interactivity where players can socialize with friends or other players. By playing up social features of online games, and providing the ability to make online micropayments for small purchases, Nexon's games have huge numbers of users and a continuing stream of revenue.

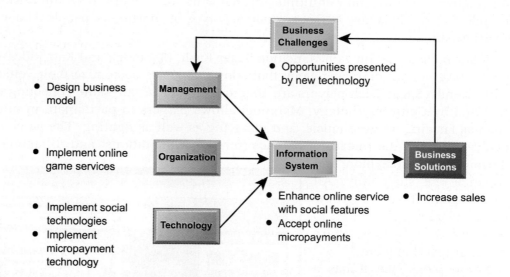

10.1 ELECTRONIC COMMERCE AND THE INTERNET

Have you ever purchased music over the Web? Have you ever used the Web to search for information about your sneakers before you bought them in a retail store? If so, you've participated in e-commerce. So have hundreds of millions of people around the globe. And although most purchases still take place through traditional channels, e-commerce continues to grow rapidly and to transform the way many companies do business.

E-COMMERCE TODAY

E-commerce refers to the use of the Internet and the Web to transact business. More formally, e-commerce is about digitally enabled commercial transactions between and among organizations and individuals. For the most part, this means transactions that occur over the Internet and the Web. Commercial transactions involve the exchange of value (e.g., money) across organizational or individual boundaries in return for products and services.

E-commerce began in 1995 when one of the first Internet portals, Netscape.com, accepted the first ads from major corporations and popularized the idea that the Web could be used as a new medium for advertising and sales. No one envisioned at the time what would turn out to be an exponential growth curve for e-commerce retail sales, which tripled and doubled in the early years. Only since 2006 has consumer e-commerce "slowed" to a 16-percent annual growth rate in 2008 (Figure 10-1).

Mirroring the history of many technological innovations, such as the telephone, radio, and television, the very rapid growth in e-commerce in the early years created a market bubble in e-commerce stocks. Like all bubbles, the "dot-com" bubble burst in March 2001. A large number of e-commerce companies failed during this process. Yet for many others, such as Amazon, e-Bay,

FIGURE 10-1   THE GROWTH OF E-COMMERCE

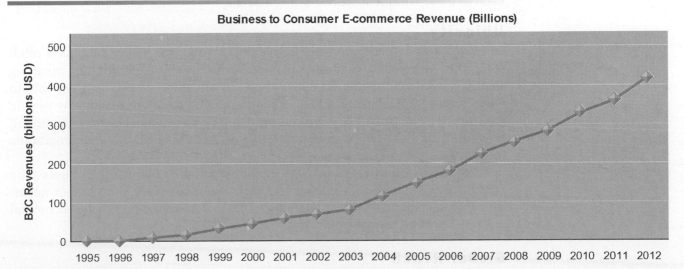

Retail e-commerce revenues have grown exponentially since 1995 and have only recently "slowed" to a very rapid 16-percent annual increase in 2008, which is projected to remain at this growth rate through 2010.

Expedia, and Google, the results have been more positive: soaring revenues, fine-tuned business models that produce profits, and rising stock prices. By 2006, e-commerce revenues returned to solid growth again, and have continued to be the fastest growing form of retail trade in the United States, Europe, and Asia.

- Online consumer sales increased by more than 15 percent in 2008 to an estimated $255 billion (including travel services), with 117 million people purchasing online and 138 million shopping and gathering information but not necessarily purchasing (eMarketer, 2008).

- The number of individuals online in the United States expanded to 173 million in 2008, up from 147 million in 2004. In the world, over 1.4 billion people are now connected to the Internet. Growth in the overall Internet population has spurred growth in e-commerce.

- On the average day, 112 million people go online, 97 million send e-mail, 71 million use a search engine, 67 million read a blog, 11 million write on their blogs, 12 million share music on peer-to-peer networks, 28 million work on their social network profile, 13 million visit Wikipedia, and 3 million use the Internet to rate a person, product, or service (Pew Internet, 2008).

- B2B e-commerce—use of the Internet for business-to-business commerce and collaboration among business partners expanded 17 percent to more than $3.6 trillion.

The e-commerce revolution is still unfolding. Individuals and businesses will increasingly use the Internet to conduct commerce as more products and services come online and households switch to broadband telecommunications. More industries will be transformed by e-commerce, including travel reservations, music and entertainment, news, software, education, and finance. Table 10-1 highlights these new e-commerce developments.

WHY E-COMMERCE IS DIFFERENT

Why has e-commerce grown so rapidly? The answer lies in the unique nature of the Internet and the Web. Simply put, the Internet and e-commerce technologies are much more rich and powerful than previous technology revolutions like radio, television, and the telephone. Table 10-2 describes the unique features of the Internet and Web as a commercial medium. Let's explore each of these unique features in more detail.

Ubiquity

In traditional commerce, a marketplace is a physical place, such as a retail store, that you visit to transact business. E-commerce is ubiquitous, meaning that is it available just about everywhere, at all times. It makes it possible to shop from your desktop, at home, at work, or even from your car, using mobile commerce. The result is called a **marketspace**—a marketplace extended beyond traditional boundaries and removed from a temporal and geographic location.

From a consumer point of view, ubiquity reduces **transaction costs**—the costs of participating in a market . To transact business, it is no longer necessary that you spend time or money traveling to a market, and much less mental effort is required to make a purchase.

Global Reach

E-commerce technology permits commercial transactions to cross cultural and national boundaries far more conveniently and cost effectively than is true in

TABLE 10-1 THE GROWTH OF E-COMMERCE

BUSINESS TRANSFORMATION

- E-commerce remains the fastest growing form of commerce when compared to physical retail stores, services, and entertainment.

- The first wave of e-commerce transformed the business world of books, music, and air travel. In the second wave, eight new industries are facing a similar transformation scenario: advertising, telephones, movies, television, jewelry, real estate, hotels, bill payments, and software.

- The breadth of e-commerce offerings grows, especially in the services economy of social networking, travel, information clearinghouses, entertainment, retail apparel, appliances, and home furnishings.

- The online demographics of shoppers broaden to match that of ordinary shoppers.

- Pure e-commerce business models are refined further to achieve higher levels of profitability, whereas traditional retail brands, such as Sears, JC Penney, L.L. Bean, and Wal-Mart, use e-commerce to retain their dominant retail positions.

- Small businesses and entrepreneurs continue to flood the e-commerce marketplace, often riding on the infrastructures created by industry giants, such as Amazon and eBay.

TECHNOLOGY FOUNDATIONS

- Wireless Internet connections (Wi-Fi, Wi-Max, and 3G smart mobile phones) grow rapidly.

- Powerful handheld mobile devices support music, Web surfing, and entertainment as well as voice communication. Podcasting takes off as a medium for distribution of video, radio, and user-generated content.

- The Internet broadband foundation becomes stronger in households and businesses as transmission prices fall. More than 75 million households had broadband cable or DSL access to the Internet in 2008—about 62% percent of all households in the United States (eMarketer, 2008).

- RSS grows to become a major new form of user-controlled information distribution that rivals e-mail in some applications.

- New Internet-based models of computing, such as .NET and Web services, expand B2B opportunities.

NEW BUSINESS MODELS EMERGE

- More than half the Internet user population join an online social network, contribute to social bookmarking sites, create blogs, and share photos. Together these sites create a massive online audience as large as television that is attractive to marketers.

- The traditional advertising business model is severely disrupted as Google and other technology players such as Microsoft and Yahoo! seek to dominate online advertising, and expand into offline ad brokerage for television and newspapers.

- Newspapers and other traditional media adopt online, interactive models but are losing advertising revenues to the online players despite gaining online readers.

traditional commerce. As a result, the potential market size for e-commerce merchants is roughly equal to the size of the world's online population (more than 1 billion, and growing rapidly).

In contrast, most traditional commerce is local or regional—it involves local merchants or national merchants with local outlets. Television and radio stations and newspapers, for instance, are primarily local and regional institutions with limited, but powerful, national networks that can attract a national audience but not easily cross national boundaries to a global audience.

Universal Standards

One strikingly unusual feature of e-commerce technologies is that the technical standards of the Internet and, therefore, the technical standards for conducting e-commerce are universal standards. They are shared by all nations around the

TABLE 10-2 EIGHT UNIQUE FEATURES OF E-COMMERCE TECHNOLOGY

E-COMMERCE TECHNOLOGY DIMENSION	BUSINESS SIGNIFICANCE
Ubiquity. Internet/Web technology is available everywhere: at work, at home, and elsewhere via mobile devices, anytime.	The marketplace is extended beyond traditional boundaries and is removed from a temporal and geographic location. "Marketspace" is created; shopping can take place anywhere. Customer convenience is enhanced, and shopping costs are reduced.
Global Reach. The technology reaches across national boundaries, around the earth.	Commerce is enabled across cultural and national boundaries seamlessly and without modification. The marketspace includes, potentially, billions of consumers and millions of businesses worldwide.
Universal Standards. There is one set of technology standards, namely Internet standards.	With one set of technical standards across the globe, disparate computer systems can easily communicate with each other.
Richness. Video, audio, and text messages are possible.	Video, audio, and text marketing messages are integrated into a single marketing message and consumer experience.
Interactivity. The technology works through interaction with the user.	Consumers are engaged in a dialog that dynamically adjusts the experience to the individual, and makes the consumer a co-participant in the process of delivering goods to the market.
Information Density. The technology reduces information costs and raises quality.	Information processing, storage, and communication costs drop dramatically, whereas currency, accuracy, and timeliness improve greatly. Information becomes plentiful, cheap, and more accurate.
Personalization/Customization. The technology allows personalized messages to be delivered to individuals as well as groups.	Personalization of marketing messages and customization of products and services are based on individual characteristics.
Social Technology. User content generation and social networking.	New Internet social and business models enable user content creation and distribution, and support social networks.

world and enable any computer to link with any other computer regardless of the technology platform each is using. In contrast, most traditional commerce technologies differ from one nation to the next. For instance, television and radio standards differ around the world, as does cell telephone technology.

The universal technical standards of the Internet and e-commerce greatly lower **market entry costs**—the cost merchants must pay simply to bring their goods to market. At the same time, for consumers, universal standards reduce **search costs**—the effort required to find suitable products.

Richness

Information **richness** refers to the complexity and content of a message. Traditional markets, national sales forces, and small retail stores have great richness: They are able to provide personal, face-to-face service using aural and visual cues when making a sale. The richness of traditional markets makes them powerful selling or commercial environments. Prior to the development of the Web, there was a trade-off between richness and reach: The larger the audience reached, the less rich the message. The Web makes it possible to deliver rich messages with text, audio, and video simultaneously to large numbers of people.

Interactivity

Unlike any of the commercial technologies of the twentieth century, with the possible exception of the telephone, e-commerce technologies are interactive, meaning they allow for two-way communication between merchant and consumer. Television, for instance, cannot ask viewers any questions or enter into conversations with them, and it cannot request that customer information be entered into a form. In contrast, all of these activities are possible on an e-commerce Web site. Interactivity allows an online merchant to engage a consumer in ways similar to a face-to-face experience but on a massive, global scale.

Information Density

The Internet and the Web vastly increase **information density**—the total amount and quality of information available to all market participants, consumers, and merchants alike. E-commerce technologies reduce information collection, storage, processing, and communication costs while greatly increasing the currency, accuracy, and timeliness of information.

Information density in e-commerce markets make prices and costs more transparent. **Price transparency** refers to the ease with which consumers can find out the variety of prices in a market; **cost transparency** refers to the ability of consumers to discover the actual costs merchants pay for products.

There are advantages for merchants as well. Online merchants can discover much more about consumers than in the past. This allows merchants to segment the market into groups who are willing to pay different prices and permits the merchants to engage in **price discrimination**—selling the same goods, or nearly the same goods, to different targeted groups at different prices. For instance, an online merchant can discover a consumer's avid interest in expensive, exotic vacations and then pitch high-end vacation plans to that consumer at a premium price, knowing this person is willing to pay extra for such a vacation. At the same time, the online merchant can pitch the same vacation plan at a lower price to a more price-sensitive consumer. Information density also helps merchants differentiate their products in terms of cost, brand, and quality.

Personalization/Customization

E-commerce technologies permit **personalization**: Merchants can target their marketing messages to specific individuals by adjusting the message to a person's name, interests, and past purchases. The technology also permits **customization**—changing the delivered product or service based on a user's preferences or prior behavior. Given the interactive nature of e-commerce technology, much information about the consumer can be gathered in the marketplace at the moment of purchase. With the increase in information density, a great deal of information about the consumer's past purchases and behavior can be stored and used by online merchants.

The result is a level of personalization and customization unthinkable with traditional commerce technologies. For instance, you may be able to shape what you see on television by selecting a channel, but you cannot change the content of the channel you have chosen. In contrast, the *Wall Street Journal*

Online allows you to select the type of news stories you want to see first and gives you the opportunity to be alerted when certain events happen.

You can see these features of e-commerce at work in the Interactive Session on Organizations. Turner Sports New Media operates a series of Web sites for NASCAR, the NBA, and other sports organizations. It uses interactivity and richness, and is able to combine the reach of cable TV with deep relationships with consumers.

Social Technology: User Content Generation and Social Networking

In contrast to previous technologies, the Internet and e-commerce technologies have evolved to be much more social by allowing users to create and share with their personal friends (and a larger worldwide community) content in the form of text, videos, music, or photos. Using these forms of communication, users are able to create new social networks and strengthen existing ones.

All previous mass media in modern history, including the printing press, use a broadcast model (one-to-many) where content is created in a central location by experts (professional writers, editors, directors, and producers) and audiences are concentrated in huge numbers to consume a standardized product. The new Internet and e-commerce empower users to create and distribute content on a large scale, and permit users to program their own content consumption. The Internet provides a many-to-many model of mass communications which is unique.

KEY CONCEPTS IN E-COMMERCE: DIGITAL MARKETS AND DIGITAL GOODS IN A GLOBAL MARKETPLACE

The location, timing, and revenue models of business are based in some part on the cost and distribution of information. The Internet has created a digital marketplace where millions of people all over the world are able to exchange massive amounts of information directly, instantly, and for free. As a result, the Internet has changed the way companies conduct business and increased their global reach.

The Internet shrinks information asymmetry. An **information asymmetry** exists when one party in a transaction has more information that is important for the transaction than the other party. That information helps determine their relative bargaining power. In digital markets, consumers and suppliers can "see" the prices being charged for goods, and in that sense digital markets are said to be more "transparent" than traditional markets.

For example, until auto retailing sites appeared on the Web, there was a pronounced information asymmetry between auto dealers and customers. Only the auto dealers knew the manufacturers' prices, and it was difficult for consumers to shop around for the best price. Auto dealers' profit margins depended on this asymmetry of information. Today's consumers have access to a legion of Web sites providing competitive pricing information, and three-fourths of U.S. auto buyers use the Internet to shop around for the best deal. Thus, the Web has reduced the information asymmetry surrounding an auto purchase. The Internet has also helped businesses seeking to purchase from other businesses reduce information asymmetries and locate better prices and terms.

Digital markets are very flexible and efficient because they operate with reduced search and transaction costs, lower **menu costs** (merchants' costs of

INTERACTIVE SESSION: ORGANIZATIONS

TURNER SPORTS NEW MEDIA MARRIES TV AND THE INTERNET

Turner Sports New Media is the online division of Turner Broadcasting System, a collection of TV networks assembled by billionaire Ted Turner. TBS was founded in the 1970s by Turner and has since grown into a prominent media company with diverse holdings, including CNN, TBS, TNT, and Cartoon Network. Turner Sports New Media was founded by Turner's sports division chief, David Levy, in response to the growing popularity of broadband video. Predicting that broadband video would damage Turner's TV business, Levy focused on making deals to manage the Web rights of various sports leagues and to unite TV and the Internet in creative ways.

Turner Sports New Media has established itself as an innovator through its ability to combine TV and the Web more successfully than rivals. Turner's success allows them to both sell more ads and persuade sports leagues such as the PGA Tour and NASCAR to pay Turner millions per year to run their Web operations. Turner's formula is to provide rich, interactive features that use TV and the Web simultaneously to enhance the viewer's experience.

In 2003, Turner lacked the number of Web clients it has today, with only NASCAR.com under their management. By 2006, they had added PGA.com and PGATour.com, and in early 2008 they reached an agreement with the NBA to jointly manage NBA.com, which has 5.5 million unique monthly visitors. Their latest target is Major League Soccer's Web operations, which, oddly enough, are managed by Major League Baseball. Turner earns fees for managing the sites and splits ad revenues with each league. With each site that Turner Sports New Media manages, their goal is to get fans switching between TV and unique features on their desktops or laptops. For example, PGATour.com visitors can watch play on certain holes, watch a certain player, aerial views of the course, and get tips from pros on the site while events are in progress.

Many sports leagues don't like to relinquish control of their Web sites to outside organizations, preferring to handle their Web operations themselves to avoid paying fees to organizations like Turner Sports New Media. The NFL recently reacquired rights to its Web site back from CBS. But Turner's value proposition to sports leagues is a compelling one. The league's official site will benefit from Turner's reach and the Web's relationship with consumers. Turner's experience with running Web sites is extensive, as is their track record for success in increasing site traffic and developing innovative interactive applications. Marketers can place ads in multiple formats (TV and the Internet).

Turner's oldest client is NASCAR, and the recent contract extension signed between the two suggests that NASCAR is more than happy with Turner's results. NASCAR.com has been one of the top three sports league sites on the Internet in the past few years. Since Turner assumed control of the league's Web rights, the site has seen double-digit growth in page views and an increase in average monthly unique visitors of 25 percent over the last 7 years. Over the past calendar year the site had 1.4 billion page views. Turner will continue to operate NASCAR.com through 2014, collaborating in content creation, e-commerce, and race ticket sales. Turner will continue to have oversight over news content, broadband coverage, wireless platforms, video downloads, and ad sales, and will seek to provide fans with better information and NASCAR merchandise.

Turner has implemented a wide array of cutting-edge applications and offerings to NASCAR.COM, including TrackPass, its most interactive feature. TrackPass is a premium service that consists of several interactive applications, including TrackPass Scanner, TrackPass PitCommand, and TrackPass RaceView. RaceView renders each car digitally and offers a multitude of camera angles and viewing options for each and every car and driver. Users can pause, rewind, and replay live races and listen to any driver's in-car audio, in addition to a variety of other features that give the viewer unparalleled customization over how they watch and enjoy each race.

Other features that Turner has implemented on NASCAR.com include a 24-hr news center, live streaming for some races, a social networking 'community' section, an extensive video library, live and interactive broadband shows, and a merchandise superstore.

Turner's contract extension with the NBA extends the longest-running partnership between a league and programming network in professional sports to a whopping 32 years. The contract also grants

Turner Sports New Media access to the NBA.com network, which includes WNBA.com and NBADleague.com in addition to the flagship site. Under the contract, TNT will continue televising NBA games, broaden their Internet involvement, and jointly manage NBA's digital businesses along with the league. These businesses include NBA TV (a 24-hr digital TV network), operating the NBA.com network of sites, NBA League Pass, advertising, and availability of TNT's on-air TV talent for NBA.com's interactive features. Turner is likely to develop features like TrackPass RaceView for NBA games to provide a similar level of richness and customizability to the viewer experience.

One feature that Turner hopes to further develop is TNT NBA Overtime—a broadband feature on NBA.com that streams TNT-televised games, highlights, exclusive interviews, expert analysis, and more, which users can get live, delayed, and on demand. Turner's contract with the NBA is slated to run through the 2015-16 NBA season. If Turner's track record continues, NBA.com will continue to be an example of rich, interactive media done right.

Sources: "Turner, NASCAR Announce Extension of Online Rights," NASCAR.com, January 22, 2008; "Turner Broadcasting and NBA Broaden Partnership with Digital Rights," NBA.com, January 17, 2008; Tom Lowry, "Turner's Secret WebWeapon," *BusinessWeek*, December 31, 2007/January 7, 2008; "NASCAR.COM: TrackPass," NASCAR.com, accessed July 2008.

CASE STUDY QUESTIONS

1. Describe the unique features of e-commerce technology illustrated in this case.

2. How does the Web enhance the TV businesses for the companies discussed in this case? How does it add value?

3. Why is NASCAR TrackPass a good example of Turner Sports New Media's value to sports league sites?

4. Do you think Turner Sports New Media will continue to grow steadily? Why or why not?

MIS IN ACTION

Visit PGA.com, PGATour.com, or NASCAR.com, explore the Web site, and then answer the following questions:

1. What unique features of e-commerce technology can you find on the site? What purposes do they serve?

2. How does the Web site promote TV viewing? How does it create value for the company?

changing prices), price discrimination, and the ability to change prices dynamically based on market conditions. In **dynamic pricing**, the price of a product varies depending on the demand characteristics of the customer or the supply situation of the seller.

These markets may either reduce or increase switching costs, depending on the nature of the product or service being sold, and they may cause some extra delay in gratification. Unlike a physical market, you can't immediately consume a product such as clothing purchased over the Web (although immediate consumption is possible with digital music downloads and other digital products.)

Digital markets provide many opportunities to sell directly to the consumer, bypassing intermediaries, such as distributors or retail outlets. Eliminating intermediaries in the distribution channel can significantly lower purchase transaction costs. To pay for all the steps in a traditional distribution channel, a product may have to be priced as high as 135 percent of its original cost to manufacture.

Figure 10-2 illustrates how much savings result from eliminating each of these layers in the distribution process. By selling directly to consumers or reducing the number of intermediaries, companies are able to raise profits while charging lower prices. The removal of organizations or business process layers responsible for intermediary steps in a value chain is called **disintermediation**.

Disintermediation is affecting the market for services. Airlines and hotels operating their own reservation sites online earn more per ticket because they have eliminated travel agents as intermediaries. Table 10-3 summarizes the differences between digital markets and traditional markets.

Digital Goods

The Internet digital marketplace has greatly expanded sales of digital goods. **Digital goods** are goods that can be delivered over a digital network. Music tracks, video, software, newspapers, magazines, and books can all be expressed, stored, delivered, and sold as purely digital products. Currently, most of these products are sold as physical goods, for example, CDs, DVDs, and hard copy books. But the Internet offers the possibility of delivering all these products on demand as digital products.

In general, for digital goods, the marginal cost of producing another unit is about zero (it costs nothing to make a copy of a music file). However, the cost of producing the original first unit is relatively high—in fact it is nearly the total cost of the product because there are few other costs of inventory and distribution. Costs of delivery over the Internet are very low, marketing costs remain the same, and pricing can be highly variable. (On the Internet, the merchant can change prices as often as desired because of low menu costs.)

The impact of the Internet on the market for these kinds of digital goods is nothing short of revolutionary, and we see the results around us every day. Businesses dependent on the physical products for sales—such as bookstores, book publishers, music labels, and film studios—face the possibility of declining sales and even destruction of their businesses. Newspapers and magazines are losing readers to the Internet, and losing advertisers. Record label companies are losing sales to Internet piracy and record stores are going out of business. Video rental firms, such as Blockbuster, based on a physical DVD

FIGURE 10-2   THE BENEFITS OF DISINTERMEDIATION TO THE CONSUMER

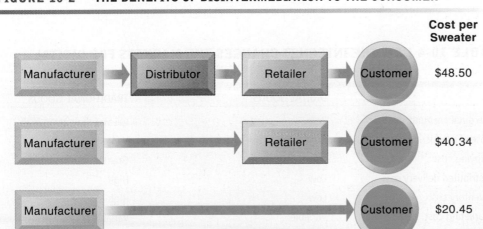

The typical distribution channel has several intermediary layers, each of which adds to the final cost of a product, such as a sweater. Removing layers lowers the final cost to the consumer.

TABLE 10-3 DIGITAL MARKETS COMPARED TO TRADITIONAL MARKETS

	DIGITAL MARKETS	TRADITIONAL MARKETS
Information asymmetry	Asymmetry reduced	Asymmetry high
Search costs	Low	High
Transaction costs	Low (sometimes virtually nothing)	High (time, travel)
Delayed gratification	High (or lower in the case of a digital good)	Lower: purchase now
Menu costs	Low	High
Dynamic pricing	Low cost, instant	High cost, delayed
Price discrimination	Low cost, instant	High cost, delayed
Market segmentation	Low cost, moderate precision	High cost, less precision
Switching costs	Higher/lower (depending on product characteristics)	High
Network effects	Strong	Weaker
Disintermediation	More possible/likely	Less possible/unlikely

market and physical stores have lost sales to NetFlix using an Internet model. Hollywood studios as well face the prospect that Internet pirates will distribute their product as a digital stream, bypassing Hollywood's monopoly on DVD rentals and sales, which now accounts for more than half of industry film revenues (see the Chapter 3 ending case). Table 10-4 describes digital goods and how they differ from traditional physical goods.

INTERNET BUSINESS MODELS

The bottom line result of these changes in the economics of information is nearly a revolution in commerce, with many new business models appearing and many old business models no longer tenable. Table 10-5 describes some of the most important Internet business models that have emerged. All, in one way or another, use the Internet to add extra value to existing products and services or to provide the foundation for new products and services.

TABLE 10-4 HOW THE INTERNET CHANGES THE MARKETS FOR DIGITAL GOODS

	DIGITAL GOODS	TRADITIONAL GOODS
Marginal cost/unit	Zero	Greater than zero , high
Cost of production	High (most of the cost)	Variable
Copying cost	Approximately 0	Greater than zero, high
Distributed delivery cost	Low	High
Inventory cost	Low	High
Marketing cost	Variable	Variable
Pricing	More variable (bundling, random pricing games)	Fixed, based on unit costs

TABLE 10-5 INTERNET BUSINESS MODELS

CATEGORY	DESCRIPTION	EXAMPLES
Virtual storefront	Sells physical products directly to consumers or to individual businesses.	Amazon.com RedEnvelope.com
Information broker	Provides product, pricing, and availability information to individuals and businesses. Generates revenue from advertising or from directing buyers to sellers.	Edmunds.com Kbb.com, Insweb.com, Realtor.com
Transaction broker	Saves users money and time by processing online sales transactions and generating a fee each time a transaction occurs. Also provides information on rates and terms.	Etrade.com Expedia.com
Online marketplace	Provides a digital environment where buyers and sellers can meet, search for products, display products, and establish prices for those products. Can provide online auctions or reverse auctions in which buyers submit bids to multiple sellers to purchase at a buyer-specified price as well as negotiated or fixed pricing. Can serve consumers or B2B e-commerce, generating revenue from transaction fees.	eBay.com Priceline.com ChemConnect.com
Content provider	Creates revenue by providing digital content, such as digital news, music, photos, or video, over the Web. The customer may pay to access the content, or revenue may be generated by selling advertising space.	WSJ.com GettyImages.com iTunes.com Games.com
Social network	Provides an online meeting place where people with similar interests can communicate and find useful information. Creates revenue through advertising.	Linkedin.com MySpace.com iVillage.com
Portal	Provides initial point of entry to the Web along with specialized content and other services. Revenue derives from advertising.	Yahoo.com MSN.com StarMedia.com
Service provider	Provides Web 2.0 applications such as photo sharing, video sharing, and user-generated content (in blogs and social networking sites) as services. Provide other services such as online data storage and backup. Uses either a subscription or advertising revenue model.	Google Maps Photobucket.com YouTube.com Xdrive.com

Communication and Social Networking

Some of these new business models take advantage of the Internet's rich communication capabilities. EBay is an online auction forum that uses e-mail and other interactive features of the Web, which we described in the Chapter 3 opening case. The system accepts bids entered on the Internet, evaluates the bids, and notifies the highest bidder. EBay collects a small commission on each listing and sale. EBay has become so popular that its site serves as a huge trading platform for other companies, hosting hundreds of thousands of "virtual storefronts."

Business-to-business auctions have also emerged. GoIndustry, for instance, features Web-based auction services for business-to-business sales of industrial equipment and machinery.

The Internet has created online communities, where people with similar interests are able to communicate with each other from many different locations. A major source of revenue for these communities involves providing ways for corporate clients to target customers, including the placement of banner ads and pop-up ads on their Web sites. A **banner ad** is a graphic display on a Web page used for advertising. The banner is linked to the advertiser's Web site so that a person clicking the banner is transported to a Web page with more information about the advertiser. **Pop-up ads** work in the opposite manner. They automatically open up when a user accesses a specific Web site, and the user must click the ad to make it disappear.

Social networking sites are a type of online community that has become extremely popular. Social networking is the practice of expanding the number of one's business or social contacts by making connections through individuals. Social networking sites link people through their mutual business or personal connections, enabling them to mine their friends (and their friends' friends) for sales leads, job-hunting tips, or new friends. MySpace, Facebook, and Friendster appeal to people who are primarily interested in extending their friendships, while LinkedIn.com focuses on job networking.

Members of social networking sites spend hours surfing pages, checking out other members, and exchanging messages, revealing a great deal of information about themselves. Businesses harvest this information to create carefully targeted promotions that far surpass the typical text and display ads found on the Web. They also use the sites to interact with potential customers. For example, Procter & Gamble set up a MySpace profile page for Crest toothpaste soliciting "friends" for a fictional character called "Miss Irresistable."

The most popular of these sites attract so many visitors and are so "sticky" that they have become very powerful marketing tools. The chapter-ending case study discusses Facebook as a business model.

Social networking is so appealing that it has inspired a new type of e-commerce experience called **social shopping**. Social shopping sites such as Kaboodle, ThisNext, and Stylehive.com provide online meeting places for people to swap shopping ideas. These sites provide tools for users to create their own Web pages with information and images about items they like to help other shoppers.

Digital Content, Entertainment, and Services

In 2008, perhaps no industry has experienced more Internet-driven change than the entertainment industry, roughly defined as television, movies, music, radio, and text content. The ability to deliver digital goods and digital content over the Web has created new alternatives to traditional print and broadcast media. There are Web sites for digital versions of print publications, such as the *New York Times* or the *Wall Street Journal*, and for new online journals such as Salon.com.

Some of the most popular Web sites deliver entertainment in digital form. Online games attract huge numbers of players. Nexon's games, described in the chapter-opening case, have millions of users.

You can listen to some of your favorite radio channels, such as Classic Rock or the BBC, on the Web as well as many independent channels. Because the radio signal is relayed over the Internet, it is possible to access stations from anywhere in the world. Services such as Yahoo!'s Launchcast even puts together individualized radio channels for listeners.

Broadband connections now make it possible for Web sites to display full-length films and television shows. Netflix, Apple, Amazon, Movielink, and CinemaNow have downloading services for full-length movies. MLB.com, the Web site for Major League Baseball, delivers live streaming video of MLB baseball games to paid subscribers. Some online television and video services, such as IVillage Live, provide instant messaging capabilities allowing viewers to discuss the show as its being broadcast.

Many of you use the Web to preview and download music. Although some of this Internet music is free of charge, Apple's iTunes and other sites are generating revenue by charging for each song or album downloaded from their Web sites. The phenomenal popularity of Apple's iTunes music service and Apple's iPod portable music player have inspired a new form of digital content delivery called *podcasting*. **Podcasting** is a method of publishing audio broadcasts via the Internet, allowing subscribing users to download audio files onto their personal computers or portable music players. Video clips designed to be downloaded and viewed on a portable device are called *vcasts*.

Podcasting enables independent producers to self-publish their own audio content and gives broadcast media a new distribution method. Podcasts also have internal uses for businesses who want to distribute information in audio form to their employees. Internet security firm SonicWALL uses podcats to demonstrate its expertise to customers and to provide new product information to its resellers.

The Web's information resources are so vast and rich that *portals* have emerged as an Internet business models to help individuals and organizations locate information more efficiently. In Chapter 2, we defined a portal as a Web interface for presenting integrated, personalized information from a variety of sources. As an e-commerce business model, a *portal* is a "supersite" that provides a comprehensive entry point for a huge array of resources and services on the Internet.

Yahoo! is an example. It provides capabilities for locating information on the Internet along with news, sports, weather, telephone directories, maps, games, shopping, e-mail, chat, discussion boards, and links to other sites. Also, specialized portals help users with specific interests. For example, StarMedia is a portal customized for Hispanic Internet users.

Yahoo! and other portals and Web content sites often combine content and applications from many different sources and service providers. Other Internet business models use syndication as well providing additional value. For example, E*TRADE, the discount Web trading site, purchases most of its content from outsider sources such as Reuters (news) and BigCharts.com (charts). Online **syndicators**, who aggregate content or applications from multiple sources, package them for distribution, and resell them to third-party Web sites, have emerged as another variant of the online content provider business model. The Web makes it much easier for companies to aggregate, repackage, and distribute information and information-based services.

Photobucket is an online photo-sharing service that works with other Web 2.0 applications and services. Other online service providers offer services such as remote storage of data (Xdrive.com). Online service providers generate revenue from subscription fees or from advertising.

Most of the business models described in Table 10-5 are called **pure-play** business models because they are based purely on the Internet. These firms did not have an existing bricks-and-mortar business when they designed their Internet business. However, many existing retail firms, such as L.L. Bean, Office Depot, R.E.I., and the *Wall Street Journal*, have developed Web sites as extensions of their traditional bricks-and-mortar businesses. Such businesses represent a hybrid **clicks-and-mortar** business model.

The Interactive Session on Technology describes another clicks-and-mortar business. J&R Electronics sells music, office equipment, cameras, computers, movies, and games through multiple channels: a massive retail store in New York City, a print catalog, and a Web site. As you read this case, try to determine the role of the Web in this company's business model and business strategy.

10.2 ELECTRONIC COMMERCE

Although most commercial transactions still take place through traditional retail channels, rising numbers of consumers and businesses are using the Internet for electronic commerce. Today, e-commerce revenue represents about 5 percent of all retail sales in the United States, and there is tremendous upside potential for growth.

TYPES OF ELECTRONIC COMMERCE

There are many ways to classify electronic commerce transactions. One is by looking at the nature of the participants in the electronic commerce transaction. The three major electronic commerce categories are business-to-consumer (B2C) e-commerce, business-to-business (B2B) e-commerce, and consumer-to-consumer (C2C) e-commerce.

- **Business-to-consumer (B2C)** electronic commerce involves retailing products and services to individual shoppers. BarnesandNoble.com, which sells books, software, and music to individual consumers, is an example of B2C e-commerce.

- **Business-to-business (B2B)** electronic commerce involves sales of goods and services among businesses. ChemConnect's Web site for buying and selling natural gas liquids, refined and intermediate fuels, chemicals, and plastics is an example of B2B e-commerce.

- **Consumer-to-consumer (C2C)** electronic commerce involves consumers selling directly to consumers. For example, eBay, the giant Web auction site, enables people to sell their goods to other consumers by auctioning the merchandise off to the highest bidder.

Another way of classifying electronic commerce transactions is in terms of the participants' physical connection to the Web. Until recently, almost all e-commerce transactions took place over wired networks. Now mobile phones and other wireless handheld digital appliances are Internet-enabled to send text messages and e-mail, access Web sites, and make purchases. Companies are offering new types of Web-based products and services that can be accessed by these wireless devices. The use of handheld wireless devices for purchasing goods and services from any location has been termed **mobile commerce** or **m-commerce**. Both business-to-business and business-to-consumer e-commerce transactions can take place using m-commerce technology, which we discuss in detail in Section 10.3.

INTERACTIVE SESSION: TECHNOLOGY

CAN J&R ELECTRONICS GROW WITH E-COMMERCE?

J&R Electronics is a mom-and-pop shop for the modern age. Joe and Rachelle Friedman started the business as an audio equipment store in 1971. Today, J&R Electronics encompasses a lucrative catalog business and 10 specialty electronics stores covering 300,000 square feet of retail space on Park Row in New York City. Among the stores are the famed J&R Music World and J&R Computer World.

The J&R empire sells nearly every type of electronic device imaginable. However, the Friedmans have resisted the advice of suppliers, such as record companies, who have told them the only way to compete with big box stores was to become a chain. Rachelle Friedman explained that "by staying on the block...we maintain control, which the chain stores lose."

How does J&R continue to survive with only one location in an industry dominated by Wal-Marts, Best Buy, and Circuit City? One reason is that the company found ways to make its Web site as popular a destination online as its bricks-and-mortar store.

J&R went online in 1998 using InterWorld's Commerce Exchange e-commerce software. InterWorld did not survive the dot-com bust in 2000, and J&R had to support its online presence on its own. The company's information systems staff managed to piece together a customized e-commerce application that could handle the 400,000 products that J&R sold. However, the solution did not support some of the features that online retail competitors offered, such as the ability to collect and display customer reviews and provide information on inventory statistics, and shipping time.

By that time, 30 percent of J&R's $400 million in revenue came from JR.com, and the company needed to inject new life into its Web site. For the new site, J&R chose an e-commerce platform from Blue Martini and a CRM package made by Loyalty Lab. In addition, management wanted to populate the site with videos and customer reviews. Those features were valuable tools that customers could use to educate themselves about products and comparison-shop before they committed to buying.

In May 2006, J&R unveiled an online loyalty program to encourage shoppers to visit JR.com directly rather than connect from a link on another site, such as a price comparison search engine.

The strategy intends to raise the number of unique visitors to the site and, as Jason Friedman put it, relieve J&R from "fighting over pennies with our competitors." For participating in the program, customers receive gift cards equaling 2 percent of their purchases. If successful, the loyalty program will keep past customers from giving their business to other stores, as well as entice new customers to join the J&R community. Catalog shoppers are also eligible for loyalty rewards.

Mark H. Goldstein, CEO of Loyalty Lab, noted that J&R already had a loyal customer base as a result of its top-notch customer service and focus on building relationships. All that the company lacked was a program that recognized customer loyalty. Loyalty Lab's CRM package helped fill that void by hosting the modules that enabled J&R customers to register for accounts, manage their accounts, and redeem the incentives they have earned. The Loyalty Lab program also reduces the Google tax." This is the 20 to 30 percent charge that J&R pays to search sites when visitors are directed to J&R from another site, a fee that J&R avoids when shoppers visit JR.com directly.

J&R selected Blue Martini as its new e-commerce platform because Blue Martini functions well with J&R's ERP software from a technical perspective. The two systems are able to exchange data easily. Blue Martini provides a better opportunity to share the strengths of J&R's bricks-and-mortar channels online.

J&R has plenty of advantages, or differentiators, to showcase. Its prices are very competitive, yet it maintains a vast inventory that rarely leaves customers disappointed. J&R also has a reputation for being at the leading edge of new technology. The company has a penchant for being the first retailer to sell new products or the latest versions of already popular products. J&R often caters to those trends before other stores are prepared to do so. Aside from good prices, perhaps the element of J&R that appeals to customers most is its sales staff. Customers who enter J&R stores know that the workers they encounter will be well informed and adept at explaining the features and specifications of even the newest and most high-tech products.

With Blue Martini, J&R will try to emulate the expertise of its sales staff online. The platform provides a Guided Selling application, which collects input from the shopper and produces a narrowed-down view of the product catalog that is tailored for the requirements and preferences of a particular customer. Customers are able to view products by brand, price, popularity, size, and availability of special offers. By providing interactive recommendations, J&R can put more information about products in the hands of the customers, which makes them more comfortable in their purchases.

Comprehensive product descriptions, product reviews from customers and other sources, and comparison grids will also make it easier for shoppers to understand and select products. Going a step further, Blue Martini enables J&R to deepen its Web content with videos, including hundreds of clips that feature staff members giving tutorials on specific products. The videos bring a personalization to the online shopping experience that normally would be available only in a bricks-and-mortar store. J&R even films the videos in its actual stores.

The new JR.com launched in March 2007 with a host of new customer conveniences. If a customer selects a product that is out of stock, the site is prepared with a list of similar products. The site also has real-time integration with store inventory, so onsite purchases are reflected in the availability of products online. J&R has also made the checkout process more efficient so shoppers arrive at final price more quickly. The shipping section has been restructured to improve the accuracy of delivery dates and shipping fees.

Jason Friedman recognizes that despite the increased functionality provided by Blue Martini, his company is still limited by having physical stores located solely in New York City. He notes that where chain stores can offer customers the option of ordering merchandise online and picking it up that day in person at the nearest store, J&R can only make that option available to customers in the New York City area. However, he feels that emphasizing e-commerce carries great potential for the business and represents the company's future.

In August 2008, J&R contracted with the Toy advertising agency to coordinate its TV, print, radio, events, digital, and in-store promotions. Although J&R spends millions of dollars each year on advertising through various channels, this is the first time it has worked with an advertising agency. Toy will further shape J&R's brand image of quality, customer service, and leading-edge technology offerings among new audiences in a rapidly changing retail environment.

Sources: "J&R Music Turns to Toy,"*Adweek*, August 19, 2008; www.jr.com, accessed August 28, 2008; Laton McCartney, "Mid-Market Case: J&R Electronics Pumps Up the Volume," *Baseline Magazine*, March 13, 2007; "J&R Electronics Taps Loyalty Lab's On-Demand Suite for First Shopper Loyalty Program," *Rtmilestones.com*, accessed May 1, 2007; and "J&R Electronics Migrating to Blue Martini E-Commerce Platform," *Internetretailer.com*, November 8, 2006.

CASE STUDY QUESTIONS

1. Analyze J&R Electronics using the competitive forces and value chain models. What is its business model and business strategy? How does it provide value?

2. What is the role of the Internet in J&R's business strategy? Is it providing a solution to J&R's problems? Why or why not?

3. Can J&R keep up with the competition since it is more or less a local brand competing with nationwide chains? How would you measure its success in keeping up with the competition?

MIS IN ACTION

Visit J&R's online store at JR.com, then answer the following questions:

1. What features described in this case are you able to find on the site?

2. How effective is the implementation of these features? Do they seem to be achieving the goals that J&R set for them?

3. Compare JR.com to the Web sites of Circuit City or Best Buy. Evaluate them in terms of product selection and availability, tools for providing product information and customer service, and ease of use. Which site would you use to purchase a computer or MP3 player? Why?

ACHIEVING CUSTOMER INTIMACY: INTERACTIVE MARKETING, PERSONALIZATION, AND SELF-SERVICE

The unique dimensions of e-commerce technologies that we have just described offer many new possibilities for marketing and selling. The Internet provides companies with additional channels of communication and interaction for closer yet more cost-effective relationships with customers in sales, marketing, and customer support.

Interactive Marketing and Personalization

The Internet and e-commerce have helped some merchants achieve the holy grail of marketing: making products for millions of consumers that are personal, an impossible task in traditional markets. Web sites, such as that for Lands' End (shirts and pants), Nike (athletic shoes), and VistaPrint (business cards, note cards, and labels), feature online tools that allow consumers to purchase products tailored to their individual specifications. Sites such as encourage customers to participate in designing products they want.

Web sites have become a bountiful source of detailed information about customer behavior, preferences, needs, and buying patterns that companies can use to tailor promotions, products, services, and pricing. Some customer information may be obtained by asking visitors to "register" online and provide information about themselves, but many companies also collect customer information using software tools that track the activities of Web site visitors.

Clickstream tracking tools collect data on customer activities at Web sites and store them in a log. The tools record the site that users visited prior to coming to a particular Web site and where these users go when they leave that site. They also record the specific pages visited on the particular site, the time spent on each page of the site, the types of pages visited, and what the visitors purchased (see Figure 10-3). Firms analyze this information about customer interests and behavior to develop precise profiles of existing and potential customers.

FIGURE 10-3   WEB SITE VISITOR TRACKING

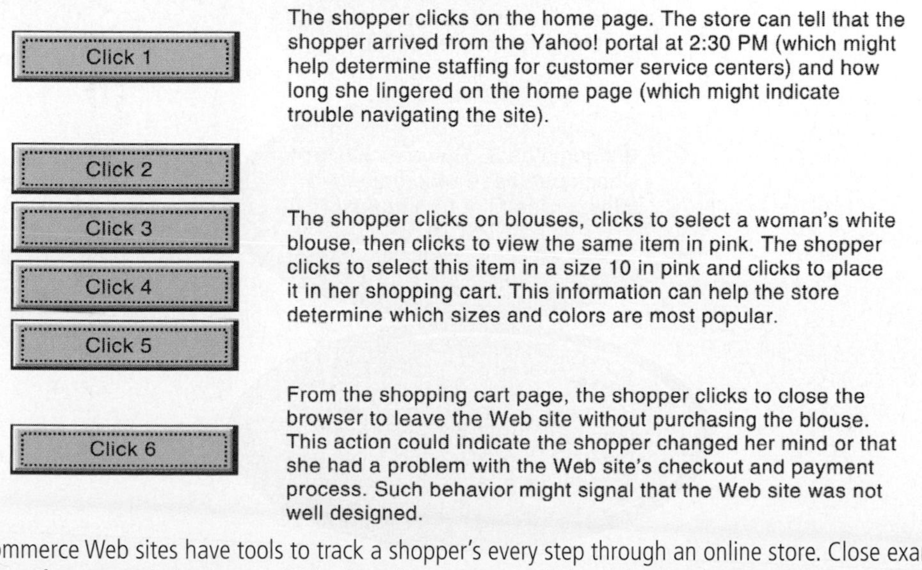

E-commerce Web sites have tools to track a shopper's every step through an online store. Close examination of customer behavior at a Web site selling women's clothing shows what the store might learn at each step and what actions it could take to increase sales.

Such information enables firms to create unique personalized Web pages that display content or ads for products or services of special interest to each user, improving the customer's experience and creating additional value (see Figure 10-4). By using personalization technology to modify the Web pages presented to each customer, marketers achieve the benefits of using individual salespeople at dramatically lower costs.

One technique for Web personalization is **collaborative filtering**, which compares information gathered about a specific user's behavior at a Web site to data about other customers with similar interests to predict what the user would like to see next. The software then makes recommendations to users based on their assumed interests. For example, Amazon.com and BarnesandNoble.com use collaborative filtering software to prepare personalized book recommendations: "Customers who bought this book also bought . . ." These recommendations are made just at the point of purchase, an ideal time to prompt a consumer into purchasing a related product.

Blogs and Wikis

Blogs, which we introduced in Chapter 7, have emerged as another promising Web-based tool for marketing. A blog, the popular term for a Weblog, is a personal Web page that typically contains a series of chronological entries (newest to oldest) by its author, and links to related Web pages.

The blog may include a blogroll (a collection of links to other blogs) and trackbacks (a list of entries in other blogs that refer to a post on the first blog). Most blogs allow readers to post comments on the blog entries as well.

FIGURE 10-4   WEB SITE PERSONALIZATION

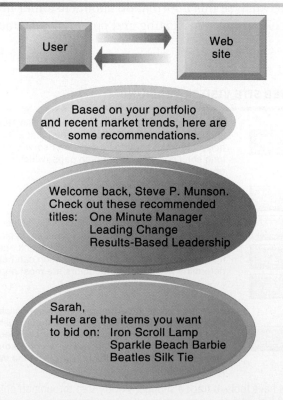

Firms can create unique personalized Web pages that display content or ads for products or services of special interest to individual users, improving the customer experience and creating additional value.

Blogs are either hosted by a third-party site such as Blogger.com, LiveJournal.com, Typepad.com, and Xanga.com, or prospective bloggers can download software such as Movable Type to create a blog that is housed by the user's ISP. Blogger and Twitter have added features to allow users to post short notes and photos to their blogs from cell phones.

Blog pages are usually variations on templates provided by the blogging service or software. Therefore, millions of people without HTML skills of any kind can post their own Web pages and share content with others. The totality of blog-related Web sites is often referred to as the **blogosphere**.

The content of blogs range from individual musings to corporate communications. Blogs have a significant impact on political affairs, and have gained increasing notice for their role in breaking and shaping the news. Blogs have become hugely popular. There are at least 70 million blogs on the Web and nearly 100,000 new ones added daily.

Companies that maintain public blogs use them as a new channel for reaching customers. These corporate blogs provide a personal and conversational way for businesses to present information to the public and prospective customers about new products and services. Readers are often invited to post comments. For example, Stonyfield Farm Inc., the world's third-largest organic food company, maintains blogs on childrearing and organic dairy farms to create a more personal relationship with consumers than the traditional selling relationship.

Marketers are analyzing blogs as well as chat groups and message boards to see what is being said online about new products, old brands, and ad campaigns. Blog-watching services that monitor popular blogs claim that "blog watching" can be cheaper and faster for analyzing consumer interests and sentiment than traditional focus groups and surveys. For example, Polaroid learned from blogs that consumers online frequently discuss photo longevity

Stonyfield Farms' Baby Babble blog provides a channel for the company to talk to customers with young children directly and hear back from them.

and archiving, prompting it to pay more attention to long-lasting photos in its product development. Companies are also posting ads on some of the most popular blogs published by individuals or by other organizations.

Customer Self-Service

Many companies use their Web sites and e-mail to answer customer questions or to provide customers with product information, reducing the need for human customer-support expert. For instance, American, Northwest, and other major airlines have created Web sites where customers can review flight departure and arrival times, seating charts, and airport logistics; check frequent-flyer miles; and purchase tickets online. Chapter 1 describes how customers of UPS use its Web site to track shipments, calculate shipping costs, determine time in transit, and arrange for a package pickup. FedEx and other package delivery firms provide similar Web-based services. Automated self-service or other Web-based responses to customer questions cost only a fraction of what a live customer service representative on the telephone would cost.

New software products are even integrating the Web with customer call centers, where customer service problems have been traditionally handled over the telephone. A **call center** is an organizational department responsible for handling customer service issues by telephone and other channels. For example, visitors to the Lands' End Web site can request a phone call from customer service by entering his or her telephone number. A call-center system directs a customer service representative to place a voice telephone call to the user's phone.

BUSINESS-TO-BUSINESS E-COMMERCE: NEW EFFICIENCIES AND RELATIONSHIPS

About 80 percent of B2B e-commerce is still based on proprietary systems for electronic data interchange (EDI). **Electronic data interchange (EDI)** enables the computer-to-computer exchange between two organizations of standard transactions such as invoices, bills of lading, shipment schedules, or purchase orders. Transactions are automatically transmitted from one information system to another through a network, eliminating the printing and handling of paper at one end and the inputting of data at the other. Each major industry in the United States and much of the rest of the world has EDI standards that define the structure and information fields of electronic documents for that industry.

EDI originally automated the exchange of documents such as purchase orders, invoices, and shipping notices. Although some companies still use EDI for document automation, firms engaged in just-in-time inventory replenishment and continuous production use EDI as a system for continuous replenishment. Suppliers have online access to selected parts of the purchasing firm's production and delivery schedules and automatically ship materials and goods to meet prespecified targets without intervention by firm purchasing agents (see Figure 10-5).

Although many organizations still use private networks for EDI, they are increasingly Web-enabled because Internet technology provides a much more flexible and low-cost platform for linking to other firms. Businesses are able to extend digital technology to a wider range of activities and broaden their circle of trading partners.

Take procurement, for example. **Procurement** involves not only purchasing goods and materials but also sourcing, negotiating with suppliers, paying for

FIGURE 10-5   ELECTRONIC DATA INTERCHANGE (EDI)

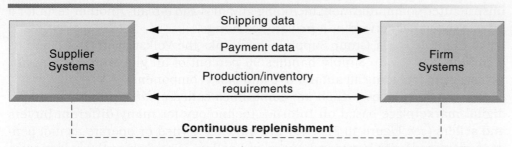

Companies use EDI to automate transactions for B2B e-commerce and continuous inventory replenishment. Suppliers can automatically send data about shipments to purchasing firms. The purchasing firms can use EDI to provide production and inventory requirements and payment data to suppliers.

goods, and making delivery arrangements. Businesses can now use the Internet to locate the most low-cost supplier, search online catalogs of supplier products, negotiate with suppliers, place orders, make payments, and arrange transportation. They are not limited to partners linked by traditional EDI networks.

The Internet and Web technology enable businesses to create new electronic storefronts for selling to other businesses with multimedia graphic displays and interactive features similar to those for B2C commerce. Alternatively, businesses can use Internet technology to create extranets or electronic marketplaces for linking to other businesses for purchase and sale transactions.

Private industrial networks typically consist of a large firm using an extranet to link to its suppliers and other key business partners (see Figure 10-6). The network is owned by the buyer, and it permits the firm and designated suppliers, distributors, and other business partners to share product design and

FIGURE 10-6   A PRIVATE INDUSTRIAL NETWORK

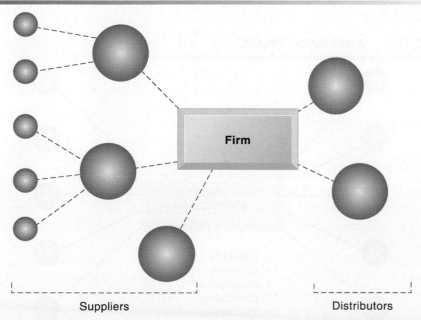

A private industrial network, also known as a private exchange, links a firm to its suppliers, distributors, and other key business partners for efficient supply-chain management and other collaborative commerce activities.

development, marketing, production scheduling, inventory management, and unstructured communication, including graphics and e-mail. Another term for a private industrial network is a **private exchange**.

An example is VW Group Supply, which links the Volkswagen Group and its suppliers. VW Group Supply handles 90 percent of all global purchasing for Volkswagen, including all automotive and parts components.

Net marketplaces, which are sometimes called *e-hubs*, provide a single, digital marketplace based on Internet technology for many different buyers and sellers (see Figure 10-7). They are industry owned or operate as independent intermediaries between buyers and sellers. Net marketplaces generate revenue from purchase and sale transactions and other services provided to clients. Participants in Net marketplaces can establish prices through online negotiations, auctions, or requests for quotations, or they can use fixed prices.

There are many different types of Net marketplaces and ways of classifying them. Some Net marketplaces sell *direct goods* and some sell indirect goods. *Direct goods* are goods used in a production process, such as sheet steel for auto body production. Indirect goods are all other goods not directly involved in the production process, such as office supplies or products for maintenance and repair. Some Net marketplaces support contractual purchasing based on long-term relationships with designated suppliers, and others support short-term spot purchasing, where goods are purchased based on immediate needs, often from many different suppliers.

Some Net marketplaces serve vertical markets for specific industries, such as automobiles, telecommunications, or machine tools, whereas others serve horizontal markets for goods and services that can be found in many different industries, such as office equipment or transportation.

Exostar is an example of an industry-owned net marketplace, focusing on long-term contract purchasing relationships and on providing common networks and computing platforms for reducing supply chain inefficiencies. This aerospace and defense industry-sponsored Net marketplace was founded

FIGURE 10-7   A NET MARKETPLACE

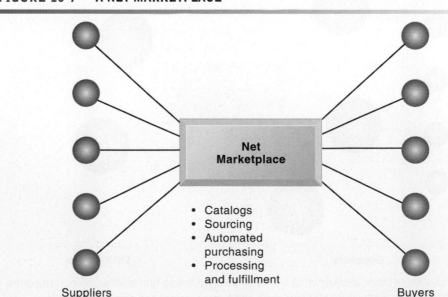

Net marketplaces are online marketplaces where multiple buyers can purchase from multiple sellers.

jointly by BAE Systems, Boeing, Lockheed Martin, Raytheon, and Rolls-Royce plc to connect these companies to their suppliers and facilitate collaboration. More than 16,000 trading partners in the commercial, military, and government sectors use Exostar's sourcing, e-procurement, and collaboration tools for both direct and indirect goods.

Exchanges are independently owned third-party Net marketplaces that connect thousands of suppliers and buyers for spot purchasing. Many exchanges provide vertical markets for a single industry, such as food, electronics, or industrial equipment, and they primarily deal with direct inputs. For example, FoodTrader.com automates spot purchases among buyers and sellers from more than 180 countries in the food and agriculture industry.

Exchanges proliferated during the early years of e-commerce, but many have failed. Suppliers were reluctant to participate because the exchanges encouraged competitive bidding that drove prices down and did not offer any long-term relationships with buyers or services to make lowering prices worthwhile. Many essential direct purchases are not conducted on a spot basis because they require contracts and consideration of issues such as delivery timing, customization, and quality of products.

10.3 M-COMMERCE

Wireless mobile devices are starting to be used for purchasing goods and services as well as for transmitting messages. In the United States, m-commerce is still in its infancy but is starting to grow as 3G cell phones become more common. In Asia and Europe, mobile commerce is much more widely adopted. Although m-commerce represents a small fraction of total e-commerce transactions, revenue has been steadily growing (see Figure 10-8). In 2008, there were an estimated 3 billion cell phone subscribers worldwide, with over 500 million in China alone. In the United States, there are about 255 million cell phone subscribers.

FIGURE 10-8   GLOBAL M-COMMERCE REVENUE, 2000–2012

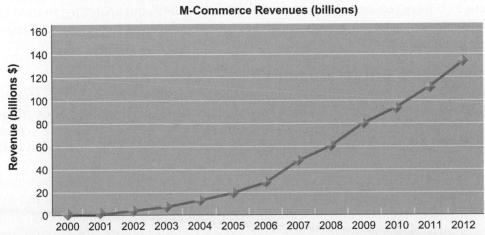

M-commerce sales represent a small fraction of total e-commerce sales, but that percentage is steadily growing.

Sources: eMarketer, 2008; Gartner, 2008; author estimates.

M-COMMERCE SERVICES AND APPLICATIONS

M-commerce applications have taken off for services that are time-critical, that appeal to people on the move, or that accomplish a task more efficiently than other methods. They are especially popular in Europe, Japan, South Korea, and other countries where fees for conventional Internet usage are very expensive. Here are some examples.

Location-Based Services

Services such as Verizon's VZ Navigator enable users to locate nearby restaurants, ATMs, and gasoline stations, find local entertainment, and send and receive location information with other Verizon users, providing maps showing how to reach the locations. MeetMoi provides a dating service that helps users identify people who are nearby and looking for dates. Smarter Agent enables users of cell phones with global positioning systems (GPS) to find nearby vacant apartments.

Banking and Financial Services

Banks are rolling out services that let customers manage their bank accounts from their cell phones or other mobile devices. Citibank and Bank of America customers can use their cell phones to check account balances, transfer funds, and pay bills.

Wireless Advertising

Cell phone service providers have information valuable to advertisers about where subscribers live, their location the moment they view ads, their age, and the games, music, and other services they use on their phones. Advertisers must find a way to deal with privacy issues and consumer reactions to ads on their phones. But when done right, mobile campaigns yield high response rates and increased consumer engagement.

Yahoo! displays ads on its mobile home page for companies such as Pepsi, Procter & Gamble, Hilton, Nissan, and Intel. The News Corporation has a mobile campaign to encourage people to vote for winners of its *American Idol* television show. Google is displaying ads linked to cell phone searches by users of the mobile version of its search engine, while Microsoft offers banner and text advertising on its MSN Mobile portal in the United States. Ads are starting to be embedded in downloadable applications such as games and videos. Less than $1 billion was spent on mobile advertising in 2007, but spending on mobile ads could surge to $10 billion to $20 billion over the next five years (Bellman and Engineer, 2008).

Games and Entertainment

Cell phones are quickly turning into portable entertainment platforms. Mobile phone services offer downloadable digital games, music, and **ringtones** (digitized snippets of music that play on mobile phones when a user receives or places a call). More and more handset models combine the features of a cell phone and a portable music player.

Users of broadband services from the major wireless vendors can download on-demand video clips, news clips, and weather reports. MobiTV, offered by Sprint and Cingular Wireless, features live TV programs, including MSNBC and Fox Sports. Film companies are starting to produce short films explicitly designed to play on mobile phones. News Corp., which owns the Fox Network, coined the trademark "mobisodes" for short cell phone videos.

User-generated content is also appearing in mobile form. A selection of YouTube videos are available to Verizon Wireless customers who subscribe to its VCast media service. MySpace arranged with Vodafone Group PLC and AT&T to allow European and American users to post comments, photos, and eventually videos to the MySpace Web site from their mobile phones.

ACCESSING INFORMATION FROM THE WIRELESS WEB

Although cell phones, PDAs, and other handheld mobile devices are able to access the Web at anytime and from any place, the amount of information that they can actually handle at one time is very limited. Until 3G broadband service comes into widespread use, these devices will not be able to transmit or receive large amounts data. The information must fit onto small display screens.

Major search providers Google, Yahoo!, and Microsoft have introduced search services for mobile phones that provide useful information with minimal typing. Their **wireless portals** (also known as *mobile portals*) feature content and services optimized for mobile devices to steer users to the information they are most likely to need. Google's mobile service remembers recent place names in searches, so that when users initiate a search for "movies," it returns a list of movies playing locally and makes it easy to find show times and purchase tickets. Microsoft's Tellme service allows uers to speak into their phones to search movie listings, stock quotes, news, and other information and then see the results on their phone screens.

10.4 ELECTRONIC COMMERCE PAYMENT SYSTEMS

Several electronic payment systems have been developed to pay for goods electronically on the Internet. Electronic payment systems for the Internet include systems for digital credit card payments, digital wallets, accumulated balance digital payment systems, online stored value payment systems, digital checking, and electronic billing presentment and payment systems.

TYPES OF ELECTRONIC PAYMENT SYSTEMS

Nearly all online payments in the United States (90 percent) use credit cards, or rely on the credit card system. Businesses can also contract with services that extend the functionality of existing credit card payment systems. **Digital wallets** make paying for purchases over the Web more efficient by eliminating the need for shoppers to enter their address and credit card information repeatedly each time they buy something. The digital wallet securely stores credit card and owner identification information and enters the shopper's name, credit card number, and shipping information automatically when invoked to complete a purchase. Google Checkout is an example.

Micropayment systems have been developed for purchases of less than $10, such as downloads of individual articles or music clips, which would be too small for conventional credit card payments. **Accumulated balance digital payment systems** enable users to make micropayments and purchases on the Web, accumulating a debit balance that they must pay periodically on their credit card or telephone bills. Examples are Valista's PaymentsPlus used by AOL, Vodafone, and NTT DoCoMo, and Clickshare, which is widely used by the online newspaper and publishing industry.

Online stored value payment systems enable consumers to make instant online payments to merchants and other individuals based on value stored in an online digital account. Some online stored value payment systems such as Valista are merchant platforms. Others are focused on peer-to-peer payments, such as PayPal. PayPal is owned by eBay and makes it possible for people to send money to vendors or individuals who are not set up to accept credit card payments.

Digital checking systems such as PayByCheck extend the functionality of existing checking accounts so they can be used for online shopping payments. Digital checks are processed much faster than traditional paper-based checking.

Electronic billing presentment and payment systems are used for paying routine monthly bills. They enable users to view their bills electronically and pay them through electronic fund transfers from bank or credit card accounts. These services notify purchasers about bills that are due, present the bills, and process the payments. Some of these services, such as CheckFree, consolidate subscribers' bills from various sources so that they can all be paid at one time. Table 10-6 summarizes the features of some of these e-commerce payment systems.

DIGITAL PAYMENT SYSTEMS FOR M-COMMERCE

Use of mobile handsets as payment devices is already well established in Europe, Japan, and South Korea. Three kinds of mobile payment systems are used in Japan, and these provide a glimpse of the future of mobile payment in the United States Japanese cell phones support stored value systems charged by credit cards or bank accounts, mobile debit cards (tied to personal bank accounts), and mobile

TABLE 10-6 EXAMPLES OF ELECTRONIC PAYMENT SYSTEMS FOR E-COMMERCE

PAYMENT DESCRIPTION	SYSTEM	COMMERCIAL EXAMPLE
Credit card payment systems	Protect information transmitted among users, merchant sites, and processing banks	Visa MasterCard American Express
Digital wallet	Software that stores credit card and other information to facilitate form completion and payment for goods on the Web	Google Checkout
Accumulated balance digital payment systems	Accumulates micropayment purchases as a debit balance that must be paid periodically on credit card or telephone bills	Valista PaymentsPlus Clickshare
Stored value payment systems	Enable consumers to make instant payments to merchants or individuals based on value stored in a digital account	PayPal, Valista
Digital checking	Provides electronic checks with a secure digital signature	PayByCheck
Electronic billing presentment and payment systems	Support electronic payments for online and physical store purchases of goods or services after the purchase have taken place	Yahoo! Bill Pay, CheckFree

credit cards. Japanese cell phones act like mobile wallets, containing a variety of payment mechanisms. Consumers can pay merchants by simply waving the cell phone at a merchant payment device that can accept payments. Japan's largest phone company NTT DoCoMo introduced wireless RFID cell phones and a related payment system (FeliCa) in 2004. Currently 10 million wallet phones are in use in Japan.

In the United States, the cell phone has not yet evolved into a fully capable mobile commerce and payment system. The cell phone in the United States is not connected to a wide network of financial institutions, but instead resides behind the walled garden of the telephone providers. In Europe and Asia, cell phone users can pay for a very wide variety of real goods and services, and there, phones are integrated into a large array of financial institutions.

10.5 HANDS-ON MIS PROJECTS

The projects in this section give you hands-on experience developing e-commerce strategies for businesses, using spreadsheet software to research the profitability of an e-commerce company, and using Web tools to research and evaluate e-commerce hosting services.

Management Decision Problems

1. Columbiana is a small, independent island in the Caribbean. It wants to develop its tourist industry and attract more visitors. The island has many historical buildings, forts, and other sites, along with rain forests and striking mountains. A few first-class hotels and several dozen less-expensive accommodations can be found along its beautiful white sand beaches. The major airlines have regular flights to Columbiana, as do several small airlines. Columbiana's government wants to increase tourism and develop new markets for the country's tropical agricultural products. How can a Web presence help? What Internet business model would be appropriate? What functions should the Web site perform?

2. Explore the Web sites of the following companies: Blue Nile, J.Crew, Circuit City, Black&Decker, Peet's Coffee & Tea, and Priceline. Determine which of these Web sites would benefit most from adding a company-sponsored blog to the Web site. List the business benefits of the blog. Specify the intended audience for the blog. Decide who in the company should author the blog, and select some topics for the blog.

Improving Decision Making: Using Spreadsheet Software to Analyze a Dot-Com Business

Software skills: Spreadsheet downloading, formatting, and formulas
Business skills: Financial statement analysis

Publicly traded companies, including those specializing in e-commerce, are required to file financial data with the U.S. Securities and Exchange Commission. By analyzing this information, you can determine the profitability of an e-commerce company and the viability of its business model.

Pick one e-commerce company on the Internet, for example, Ashford.com, Buy.com, Yahoo.com, or Priceline.com. Study the Web pages that describe the company and explain its purpose and structure. Use the Web to find articles that comment on the company. Then visit the Securities and Exchange Commission's Web site at www.sec.gov and select Filings & Forms to access the company's 10-K (annual report) form showing income statements and balance sheets. Select only the sections of the 10-K form containing the desired portions of financial statements that you need to examine, and download them into your spreadsheet. (The Laudon Web site for Chapter 10 provides more detailed instructions on how to download this 10-K data into a spreadsheet.) Create simplified spreadsheets of the company's balance sheets and income statements for the past three years.

- Is the company a dot-com success, borderline business, or failure? What information dictates the basis of your decision? Why? When answering these questions, pay special attention to the company's three-year trends in revenues, costs of sales, gross margins, operating expenses, and net margins.

- Prepare an overhead presentation (with a minimum of five slides), including appropriate spreadsheets or charts, and present your work to your professor and classmates.

Achieving Operational Excellence: Evaluating E-Commerce Hosting Services

Software skills: Web browser software
Business skills: Evaluating e-commerce hosting services

This project will help develop your Internet skills in commercial services for hosting an e-commerce site for a small startup company.

You would like to set up a Web site to sell towels, linens, pottery, and tableware from Portugal and are examining services for hosting small business Internet storefronts. Your Web site should be able to take secure credit card payments and to calculate shipping costs and taxes. Initially, you would like to display photos and descriptions of 40 different products. Visit Yahoo! Small Business, GoDaddy, and Volusion and compare the range of e-commerce hosting services they offer to small business, their capabilities, and costs. Also examine the tools they provide for creating an e-commerce site. Compare these services and decide which you would use if you were actually establishing a Web store. Write a brief report indicating your choice and explaining the strengths and weaknesses of each.

LEARNING TRACK MODULES

The following Learning Tracks provide content relevant to topics covered in this chapter:

1. E-Commerce Challenges: The Story of Online Groceries
2. Build an E-Commerce Business Plan
3. Hot New Careers in E-Commerce

Review Summary

1. **What are the unique features of e-commerce, digital markets, and digital goods?**

   E-commerce involves digitally enabled commercial transactions between and among organizations and individuals. Unique features of e-commerce technology include ubiquity, global reach, universal technology standards, richness, interactivity, information density, capabilities for personalization and customization, and social technology.

   Digital markets are said to be more "transparent" than traditional markets, with reduced information asymmetry, search costs, transaction costs, and menu costs, along with the ability to change prices dynamically based on market conditions. Digital goods, such as music, video, software, and books, can be delivered over a digital network. Once a digital product has been produced, the cost of delivering that product digitally is extremely low.

2. **How has Internet technology changed business models?**

   The Internet can help companies add extra value to existing products and services or create new products and services. Many different business models for electronic commerce on the Internet have emerged, including virtual storefronts, information brokers, transaction brokers, online marketplaces, content providers, social networks, service providers, and portals. Business models that take advantage of the Internet's capabilities for communication, community building, and digital goods distribution have become especially prominent.

3. **What are the various types of e-commerce and how has e-commerce changed consumer retailing and business-to-business transactions?**

   The three major types of electronic commerce are business-to-consumer (B2C), business-to-business (B2B), and consumer-to-consumer (C2C). Mobile commerce, or m-commerce, is the purchase of goods and services using handheld wireless devices.

   The Internet creates new channels for marketing, sales, and customer support and to eliminate intermediaries in buy-and-sell transactions. Interactive capabilities on the Web can be used to build closer relationships with customers in marketing and customer support. Web personalization technologies deliver Web pages with content geared to the specific interests of each user. Web sites and e-mail reduce transaction costs for placing orders and customer service.

   B2B e-commerce generates efficiencies by enabling companies to locate suppliers, solicit bids, place orders, and track shipments in transit electronically. Net marketplaces provide a single, digital marketplace for many buyers and sellers. Private industrial networks link a firm with its suppliers and other strategic business partners to develop highly efficient and responsive supply chains.

4. **What is the role of m-commerce in business and what are the most important m-commerce applications?**

   M-commerce is especially well-suited for location-based applications, such as finding local hotels and restaurants, monitoring local traffic and weather, and providing personalized location-based marketing. Mobile phones and handhelds are being used for mobile bill payment; banking; securities trading; transportation schedule updates; and downloads of digital content, such as music, games, and video clips. M-commerce requires wireless portals and special digital payment systems that can handle micropayments.

5. **What are the principal payment systems for electronic commerce?**

   The principal e-commerce payment systems are digital credit card payment systems, digital wallets, accumulated balance digital payment systems, stored value payment systems, digital checking, and electronic billing presentment and payment systems.

Key Terms

Review Questions

1. What are the unique features of e-commerce, digital markets, and digital goods?

   - Name and describe four business trends and three technology trends shaping e-commerce today.

   - List and describe the seven unique features of e-commerce.

   - Define a digital market and digital goods and describe their distinguishing features.

2. How has Internet technology changed business models?

   - Explain how the Internet is changing the economics of information and business models.

   - Name and describe six Internet business models for electronic commerce. Distinguish between a pure-play Internet business model and a clicks-and-mortar business model.

3. What are the various types of e-commerce and how has e-commerce changed consumer retailing and business-to-business transactions?

   - Name and describe the various categories of electronic commerce.

   - Explain how the Internet facilitates sales and marketing for individual customers and describe the role played by Web personalization.

   - Explain how the Internet can enhance customer service.

   - Explain how Internet technology supports business-to-business electronic commerce.

   - Define and describe Net marketplaces and explain how they differ from private industrial networks (private exchanges).

4. What is the role of m-commerce in business and what are the most important m-commerce applications?

- List and describe important types of m-commerce services and applications.
- Explain how wireless portals help users access information on the wireless Web.
- Describe some of the barriers to m-commerce.

5. What are the principal payment systems for electronic commerce?

- Name and describe the principal electronic payment systems used on the Internet.
- Describe the types of payment systems used in m-commerce.

Discussion Questions

1. How does the Internet change consumer and supplier relationships?

2. The Internet may not make corporations obsolete, but the corporations will have to change their business models. Do you agree? Why or why not?

Video Cases

You will find video cases illustrating some of the concepts in this chapter on the Laudon Web site along with questions to help you analyze the cases.

Collaboration and Teamwork: Performing a Competitive Analysis of E-Commerce Sites

Form a group with three or four of your classmates. Select two businesses that are competitors in the same industry and that use their Web sites for electronic commerce. Visit these Web sites. You might compare, for example, the Web sites for iTunes and Napster, Amazon.com and BarnesandNoble.com, or E*TRADE and Scottrade. Prepare an evaluation of each business's Web site in terms of its functions, user friendliness, and ability to support the company's business strategy. Which Web site does a better job? Why? Can you make some recommendations to improve these Web sites? If possible, use Google Sites to post links to Web pages, team communication announcements, and work assignments; to brainstorm; and to work collaboratively on project documents. Try to use Google Docs to develop a presentation of your findings for the class.

Facebook's Dilemma
CASE STUDY

Facebook is one of the largest social networking sites in the world, currently surpassed in the United States only by MySpace. Founded in 2004 by Mark Zuckerberg, the site had 118 million worldwide users as of June 2008. Facebook allows users to create a profile and join various types of self-contained networks, including college-wide, workplace, and regional networks. The site includes a wide array of tools that allow users to connect and interact with other users, including messaging, groups, photo-sharing, and user-created applications.

The site was originally open only to a small handful of colleges, but the site has grown explosively since it opened its doors to all college students and eventually the general public. Facebook is now one of the most recognizable sites on the Web. Compared to its rival, MySpace, Facebook's interface is simplistic and clean and tends to attract those looking for a crisp, more structured social networking environment.

Facebook represents a unique opportunity for advertisers to reach highly targeted audiences based on their demographic information, hobbies and personal preferences, geographical regions, and other narrowly specified criteria in a comfortable and engaging environment. Businesses can place advertisements that are fully integrated into primary features of the site, such as the News Feed, a continually updating list of news stories about members' friends' activities on Facebook. Firms also can create Facebook pages where users can learn more about and interact with their companies. For example, a restaurant can advertise by having Facebook place items in the News Feeds of its customers indicating that those people ate there recently. Blockbuster has recent rentals and reviews of its movies appearing in similar fashion. Many companies, including eBay, Sony Pictures, *The New York Times* and Verizon maintain Facebook pages where users can learn more about the company and its products.

For advertisers, Facebook presents unique and exciting opportunities. It represents a gold mine of opportunity because of the information the site has gathered and because of the richness of the social networking environment. The site has also benefited from its status as a first-mover in the social networking marketplace, amassing a large audience whose users are reluctant to leave for fear of leaving the rest of their friends behind.

Despite these advantages, Facebook's path to profitability has not been smooth. The company has encountered more than its fair share of controversy along its path to success, mostly concerning its handling and usage of the extensive information it collects from its users. Though users contribute most of their information to Facebook willingly, the privacy and user controls over the information granted to Facebook are the biggest concerns most users have with the site.

Facebook's dilemma is finding a way to turn a profit and to continue to increase revenues using the information its users voluntarily provide without violating the privacy of these users. Thus far, its attempts to do so have not been successful. Facebook's traffic continues to rise at a healthy rate, and the company's sales reached $150 million in 2007, but the company continues to spend more money than it earns. To truly capitalize on the massive audience and immersive environment of the site, Facebook needs to innovate and find new ways to grow revenue that do not alienate the very users that the company is depending on to spur its growth. The personal information collected on the site represents a mother lode to advertisers, but one that will remain largely untapped if Facebook users do not feel comfortable enough or have sufficient incentive to share it.

The launch of the company's Beacon advertising service was an example of Facebook grossly miscalculating the privacy demands of its users. Beacon was intended to inform users when their friends made purchases and engaged in other activities outside of Facebook. The trouble with the service is that it shared information about users that they had not explicitly intended or agreed to share. The service was opt-out, meaning users had to actively turn off Beacon or the service would share private personal information under the assumption that Facebook had the consent of the user to do so. As Facebook soon found out, this assumption was often mistaken. Not only that, Beacon was continuing to send information to Facebook even once the user had elected to opt out, regardless of whether or not the user was logged into Facebook at the time.

The civic action group MoveOn.org created a Facebook group to protest Beacon and grew to over 50,000 members in 10 days. In response to the media firestorm, Facebook changed Beacon to be an opt-in service and gave users the ability to disable it completely. Beacon represented Facebook's hopes to expand its sources of revenue by offering advertisers access to its users' information, but the company utterly failed to grasp the extent to which the service violated its users' privacy as well as the uproar such a service was likely to cause. Companies such as Coca-Cola and Overstock.com pulled out of the program when they learned about the privacy concerns it raised. The launch and subsequent embarrassment of Beacon damaged Facebook's reputation as a provider of a safe, secure environment for its users. Facebook has subsequently changed the privacy controls for the service, as well as for the rest of its site, to be more transparent.

The inception and handling of the News Feed feature of the site is another example of the company incorrectly anticipating its users' stance on the privacy of their personal information. News Feed is a feature which provides updates to your friends when you perform actions via Facebook, such as updating your profile, adding new friends, or adding new applications. When this feature was introduced, it was met with significant resistance from Facebook users, who considered the feature to be overly invasive. As with Beacon, users protested the feature through the Groups feature of the site, forming over 500 groups to protest it, with one group, 'Students Against Facebook News Feed', reaching well over 700,000 members at its peak.

In an open letter to Facebook members, Zuckerberg apologized for the abrupt introduction of the feature, but defended the feature itself as a positive thing, noting that users could control which types of items appeared on the News Feed and who could view those items. Also, the News Feed does not provide any additional details about users that are not already available—it simply collects profile updates and displays them in such a way that checking all of your friends' individual profiles isn't necessary to keep track of the updates they've made. In his letter, Zuckerberg said of News Feed: "This is information people used to dig for on a daily basis, nicely reorganized and summarized so people can learn about the people they care about." Now, the News Feed is one of the most popular features on the site, and has been imitated by MySpace and other competing social networking sites.

Facebook has also come under fire for its handling of the personal information of people who attempt to remove their profiles from the site. Facebook offers users the ability to deactivate their accounts, but the company's servers maintain copies of the information contained in those accounts indefinitely. The company's reasoning for this is that reactivating accounts is far easier if Facebook retains copies of profile content and other personal information. Users that attempted to delete their accounts were met with resistance and often required outside assistance from watchdog groups. One user, Nipon Das, a business consultant in Manhattan, spent two months attempting to delete his profile unsuccessfully while still receiving updates and messages through the site. Now, Facebook has joined MySpace, Friendster, and other social networking sites in offering a simpler process to permanently delete your account and the personal information it contains.

Currently, Facebook's most promising prospects to become more profitable involve the development of applications for use via Facebook Platform. In May 2007, Facebook announced the launch of Facebook Platform, which was an effort by the company to open up its site to third-party developers to become a 'platform' for their applications. These applications, sometimes also referred to as widgets, consist of games, plug-in features for user profiles, and other programs which are fully integrated with the Facebook site. They are independently developed. As of mid-2008, more than 24,000 applications had been created.

Facebook Platform has been beneficial for both Facebook as well as the developers who are creating applications for it: Facebook's environment has become even more engaging and self-sufficient, and developers gain unparalleled exposure for their applications. A small percentage of these applications have turned into viable businesses. Companies attracting large numbers of users to their applications on Facebook are able to sell goods, services, or advertising. For example, over 2 million people use FunSpace daily to post messages, videos, or cards on their friends' profile pages, and 1.6 million use Top Friends to highlight their closest friends in a box on their own Facebook pages. With over 400,000 daily users, Scrabulous allows Facebook users to play an adaptation of Scrabble. All of these applications earn advertising revenue.

Others are using the exposure on Facebook to raise their business visibility. Flixter, an online community for movie fans, has a Facebook application called Movies that allows people to tell their Facebook friends about the movies they've seen and share reviews. Flixter's management reports that this application, with about 482,000 daily users, has hugely expanded its customer base and business opportunities.

It's currently unclear as to whether there is significant revenue to be made through the development of these applications. Some believe that Facebook applications are 'the next big thing,' and that traditional advertisers will gravitate towards Facebook to reach highly targeted audiences with their applications. On the flip side, others believe Facebook's own popularity will injure its chances to attract advertisers to its site, claiming that the engaging and immersive environment that draws visitors to the site makes users less likely to click on ads. Skeptics also believe that the current application system, where applications tend to support one another via advertising through other applications without the aid of extensive outside advertising, is an unsustainable model over the long term. So far, only 200 Facebook applications have attracted more than 10,000 users per day and 60 percent failed to attract even 100 daily users.

There is little doubt that Facebook applications will make Facebook a 'stickier' destination for its users, as they will be able to do more of the things they like to do on the Web without having to leave Facebook. However, that may not necessarily translate to increased profitability.

In 2007, Microsoft purchased a small stake in Facebook, buying 1.6% of the company for $246 million. That investment put Facebook's valuation at approximately $15 billion. It remains to be seen whether or not the company can turn its heavy site traffic and trove of personal information into new revenue streams. The initial furor and subsequent acceptance of the News Feed feature shows that Facebook users' stances on their privacy may be subject to change or persuasion, and many users may not even be aware or care about the dissemination of their personal information. Even if they

did, the benefits of being a part of Facebook, thanks to its large audience and wealth of features and content, may outweigh the reservations its users have regarding their privacy. But it appears that enough Facebook users are concerned and aware of their privacy to prevent services as invasive as Beacon's initial incarnation from becoming realities.

In March 2008, Facebook launched a new series of privacy controls, including a feature that allows users to sort friends into groups and grant access to photo albums or parts of their profiles only to specific groups of friends. For example, users can post pictures of their family vacation and share them with just their family members on Facebook, or users can disable co-workers from seeing those embarrassing party pictures from a night out. This is a step in the right direction, but the toughest task for Facebook will be to continue to preserve the privacy of its members while monetizing the user data it has collected. Shortly after the launch of these new features, a Canadian computer technician uncovered a flaw in Facebook's security that allowed some photo albums and information, including party photos of Paris Hilton and a personal album of Zuckerberg's, to be accessed by any Facebook member. Although Facebook promptly corrected the flaw, the incident continued to damage the site's already shaky reputation regarding its user privacy controls. Only time will tell whether Facebook is able to make good on its tremendous potential for revenue growth, but one thing is for sure: the privacy concerns of its users will play a central role in its efforts to become profitable.

Sources: Riva Richmond, "Some Facebook Applications Thrive, Others Flop," *The Wall Street Journal*, June 16, 2008; Jim Carr, "Facebook Privacy Flap Should Spark Concern for Business," SCMagazineUS.com, March 26, 2008; Thomas Claburn, "Social Networks Find Ways to Monetize User Data," *InformationWeek*, November 10, 2007; Vauhini Vara, "Facebook CEO Seeks Help as Site Grows Up," *The Wall Street Journal*, March 5, 2008; Adam Cohen, "One Friend Facebook Hasn't Made Yet: Privacy Rights," *The New York Times*, February 18, 2008; Alan Krauss, "Piggybacking on Facebook," *The New York Times*, February 20, 2008; Maria Aspan, "How Sticky Is Membership on Facebook? Just Try Breaking Free," *The New York Times*, February 11, 2008; Maria Aspan, "Quitting Facebook Gets Easier," *The New York Times*, February 13, 2008; Brad Stone, "In Facebook, Investing In a Theory," *The New York Times*, October 4, 2007; and Randall Rothenberg, "Facebook's Flop," *The Wall Street Journal*, December 14, 2007.

CASE STUDY QUESTIONS

1. What concepts in this chapter are illustrated in this case?

2. What is the role of e-commerce and Web 2.0 technologies in Facebook's widespread popularity.

3. Describe the weaknesses of Facebook's privacy policies and features. What management, organization, and technology factors have contributed to those weaknesses?

4. Does Facebook have a viable business model? Explain your answer

5. If you were responsible for coordinating Facebook's advertising, how would you balance the desire to become increasingly profitable with the need to protect the privacy of your users?

Chapter 11

Managing Knowledge and Collaboration

LEARNING OBJECTIVES

After reading this chapter, you will be able to answer the following questions:

1. What is the role of knowledge management and knowledge management programs in business?

2. What types of systems are used for enterprise-wide knowledge management and how do they provide value for businesses?

3. What are the major types of knowledge work systems and how do they provide value for firms?

4. What are the business benefits of using intelligent techniques for knowledge management?

Interactive Sessions:

Managing with Web 2.0

Albassami

P&G MOVES FROM PAPER TO PIXELS FOR KNOWLEDGE MANAGEMENT

Procter & Gamble (P&G) is a global leader in the development of market-leading consumer and health care products. With 2007 sales of $76.5 billion, P&G has over 300 brands, including Crest, Tide, Folgers coffee, and Pampers. But there's another side to P&G that's less widely known: It is one of the world's great research organizations and holders of global patents. The company's research and development organization includes over 7,000 scientists and 20 research centers in 9 countries. P&G got to the top—and stays on top—by continually creating an ongoing stream of innovative new products. At this company, knowledge sharing is key to success and survival.

P&G's organizational culture explicitly promotes knowledge sharing. It supports numerous communities of practice that link people doing similar work in different business units. Researchers publish monthly reports on their projects. And P&G has undertaken a number of knowledge-sharing initiatives to connect its global knowledge community. An InnovationNet (INct) intranet houses over 5 million research-related documents in digital format that can be accessed from a browser-based portal. MyInet is an enhancement that helps researchers locate experts in the company who are doing related work and keep track of relevant innovations in other areas of the firm. MyInet users are able to specify topics of interest and be notified of any new documents pertaining to those topics.

Even with these leading-edge knowledge management efforts, P&G was still awash in paper documents. For companies developing drugs and over-the-counter medications, regulatory issues, research and development, and potential litigation create an avalanche of documents and files. Researchers, clinicians, quality-control staff, marketing specialists, and other internal P&G staff members and external partners must exchange and share these documents. In the past, storing all those documents meant filling up filing cabinets, producing microfiche, managing indexes, and renting warehouses to store the paperwork. Digging through these paper records to locate a document was a long and laborious process that threatened to slow down the pace of research and development work.

P&G recently rolled out an electronic document management system called eLab Notebook to store such information electronically. The new system uses Adobe LiveCycle software to create a searchable archive of PDF files and a common set of tools that can be used around the globe. After a researcher has collected all the data, the LiveCycle PDF generator creates a Portable Document Format (PDF) document and prompts the person who created the file to add a digital signature. Then LiveCycle Reader Extensions embed usage rights within the document, specifying which people in the company are allowed to access it.

The new system changed work flow. P&G had to train employees who had been accustomed to working with paper to use the eLab application and change the way they worked.

439

The eLab Notebook program is saving time and money. Researchers no longer have to spend several hours per week archiving paper files from their experiments. Other P&G employees are able to rapidly retrieve large volumes of data required by government regulators, outside partners, or buyers. An initial study showed that productivity increased between 5 and 10 percent.

Sources: Samuel Greengard, "A Document Management Case Study: Procter & Gamble," *Baseline Magazine*, September 2008 and Intel Corporation, "Enhancing Innovation: Intel Solution Services Helps Procter & Gamble Connect Its Global Knowledge Community," www.intel.com, accessed September 12, 2008.

P&G's experience shows how organizational performance can benefit by making organizational knowledge more easily available. Collaborating and communicating with practitioners and experts, facilitating access to knowledge, and using that knowledge to improve business processes and innovate are vital to success and survival.

The chapter-opening diagram calls attention to important points raised by this case and this chapter. Procter & Gamble is highly knowledge-intensive and has an innovation-driven business model. Much of the essential information and knowledge for research and development was not easily accessible because it was stored in many different paper documents. Delays in accessing research and development documents and other vital information created inefficiencies that threatened to impair P&G's business performance. In order to benefit from document management technology, P&G had to make changes in its work flow and train employees in the new system. By making R&D documents immediately available, the new system has made P&G much more efficient.

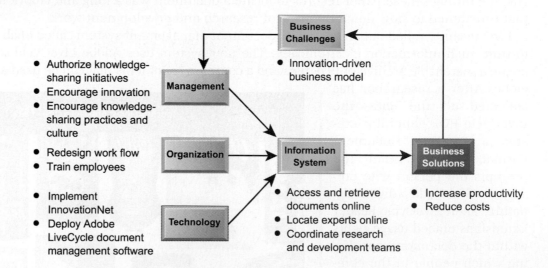

- Authorize knowledge-sharing initiatives
- Encourage innovation
- Encourage knowledge-sharing practices and culture
- Redesign work flow
- Train employees
- Implement InnovationNet
- Deploy Adobe LiveCycle document management software

Management

Organization

Technology

Business Challenges
- Innovation-driven business model

Information System
- Access and retrieve documents online
- Locate experts online
- Coordinate research and development teams

Business Solutions
- Increase productivity
- Reduce costs

11.1 THE KNOWLEDGE MANAGEMENT LANDSCAPE

Knowledge management and collaboration systems are among the fastest-growing areas of corporate and government software investment. Figure 11-1 shows that sales of enterprise content management software for knowledge management are expected to grow 15 percent annually through 2012. The past decade has likewise shown an explosive growth in research on knowledge and knowledge management in the economics, management, and information systems fields.

Knowledge management and collaboration are closely related. Knowledge that cannot be communicated and shared with others is nearly useless. Knowledge becomes useful and actionable when shared throughout the firm. As we described in Chapter 2, collaboration systems include Internet-based collaboration environments like Google Sites and IBM's Lotus Notes, social networking, e-mail and instant messaging, cell phones and wireless handhelds, wikis, and virtual worlds. In this chapter, we will be focusing on knowledge management systems, always mindful of the fact that communicating and sharing knowledge are becoming increasingly important.

We live in an information economy in which the major source of wealth and prosperity is the production and distribution of information and knowledge. About 55 percent of the U.S. labor force consists of knowledge and information workers, and 60 percent of the gross domestic product of the United States comes from the knowledge and information sectors, such as finance and publishing.

Knowledge management has become an important theme at many large business firms as managers realize that much of their firm's value depends on the firm's ability to create and manage knowledge. Studies have found that a

FIGURE 11-1 U.S. ENTERPRISE KNOWLEDGE MANAGEMENT SOFTWARE REVENUES, 2005–2012

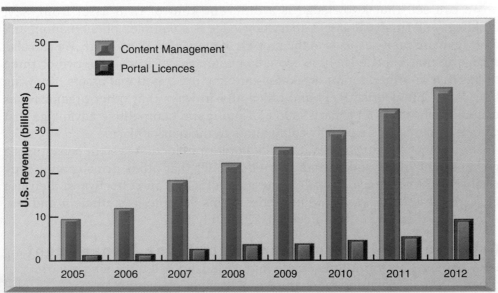

Enterprise knowledge management software includes sales of content management and portal licenses, which are growing at the rate of 15 percent annually, making it among the fastest-growing software applications. Data based on industry sources and author estimates.

substantial part of a firm's stock market value is related to its intangible assets, of which knowledge is one important component, along with brands, reputations, and unique business processes. Well-executed knowledge-based projects have been known to produce extraordinary returns on investment, although knowledge-based investments are difficult to measure (Gu and Lev, 2001; Blair and Wallman, 2001).

IMPORTANT DIMENSIONS OF KNOWLEDGE

There is an important distinction between data, information, knowledge, and wisdom. Chapter 1 defines **data** as a flow of events or transactions captured by an organization's systems that, by itself, is useful for transacting but little else. To turn data into useful *information*, a firm must expend resources to organize data into categories of understanding, such as monthly, daily, regional, or store-based reports of total sales. To transform information into **knowledge**, a firm must expend additional resources to discover patterns, rules, and contexts where the knowledge works. Finally, **wisdom** is thought to be the collective and individual experience of applying knowledge to the solution of problems. Wisdom involves where, when, and how to apply knowledge.

Knowledge is both an individual attribute and a collective attribute of the firm. Knowledge is a cognitive, even a physiological, event that takes place inside peoples' heads. It is also stored in libraries and records, shared in lectures, and stored by firms in the form of business processes and employee know-how. Knowledge residing in the minds of employees that has not been documented is called **tacit knowledge**, whereas knowledge that has been documented is called **explicit knowledge**. Knowledge can reside in e-mail, voice mail, graphics, and unstructured documents as well as structured documents. Knowledge is generally believed to have a location, either in the minds of humans or in specific business processes. Knowledge is "sticky" and not universally applicable or easily moved. Finally, knowledge is thought to be situational and contextual. For example, you must know when to perform a procedure as well as how to perform it. Table 11-1 reviews these dimensions of knowledge.

We can see that knowledge is a different kind of firm asset from, say, buildings and financial assets; that knowledge is a complex phenomenon; and that there are many aspects to the process of managing knowledge. We can also recognize that knowledge-based core competencies of firms—the two or three things that an organization does best—are key organizational assets. Knowing how to do things effectively and efficiently in ways that other organizations cannot duplicate is a primary source of profit and competitive advantage that cannot be purchased easily by competitors in the marketplace.

For instance, having a unique build-to-order production system constitutes a form of knowledge and perhaps a unique asset that other firms cannot copy easily. With knowledge, firms become more efficient and effective in their use of scarce resources. Without knowledge, firms become less efficient and less effective in their use of resources and ultimately fail.

Organizational Learning and Knowledge Management

Like humans, organizations create and gather knowledge using a variety of organizational learning mechanisms. Through collection of data, careful measurement of planned activities, trial and error (experiment), and feedback from customers and the environment in general, organizations gain experience. Organizations that learn then adjust their behavior to reflect that learning by

TABLE 11-1 IMPORTANT DIMENSIONS OF KNOWLEDGE

KNOWLEDGE IS A FIRM ASSET

Knowledge is an intangible asset.

The transformation of data into useful information and knowledge requires organizational resources.

Knowledge is not subject to the law of diminishing returns as are physical assets, but instead experiences network effects as its value increases as more people share it.

KNOWLEDGE HAS DIFFERENT FORMS

Knowledge can be either tacit or explicit (codified).

Knowledge involves know-how, craft, and skill.

Knowledge involves knowing how to follow procedures.

Knowledge involves knowing why, not simply when, things happen (causality).

KNOWLEDGE HAS A LOCATION

Knowledge is a cognitive event involving mental models and maps of individuals.

There is both a social and an individual basis of knowledge.

Knowledge is "sticky" (hard to move), situated (enmeshed in a firm's culture), and contextual (works only in certain situations).

KNOWLEDGE IS SITUATIONAL

Knowledge is conditional: Knowing when to apply a procedure is just as important as knowing the procedure (conditional).

Knowledge is related to context: You must know how to use a certain tool and under what circumstances.

creating new business processes and by changing patterns of management decision making. This process of change is called **organizational learning**. Arguably organizations that can sense and respond to their environments rapidly will survive longer than organizations that have poor learning mechanisms.

THE KNOWLEDGE MANAGEMENT VALUE CHAIN

Knowledge management refers to the set of business processes developed in an organization to create, store, transfer, and apply knowledge. Knowledge management increases the ability of the organization to learn from its environment and to incorporate knowledge into its business processes. Figure 11-2 illustrates the five value-adding steps in the knowledge management value chain. Each stage in the value chain adds value to raw data and information as they are transformed into usable knowledge.

In Figure 11-2, a line divides information systems activities and related management and organizational activities, with information systems activities on the top of the graphic and organizational and management activities below. One apt slogan of the knowledge management field is, "Effective knowledge management is 80 percent managerial and organizational, and 20 percent technology."

In Chapter 1, we define *organizational and management capital* as the set of business processes, culture, and behavior required to obtain value from investments in information systems. In the case of knowledge management, as with other information systems investments, supportive values, structures, and behavior patterns must be built to maximize the return on investment in knowledge management projects. In Figure 11-2, the management and organiza-

FIGURE 11-2 **THE KNOWLEDGE MANAGEMENT VALUE CHAIN**

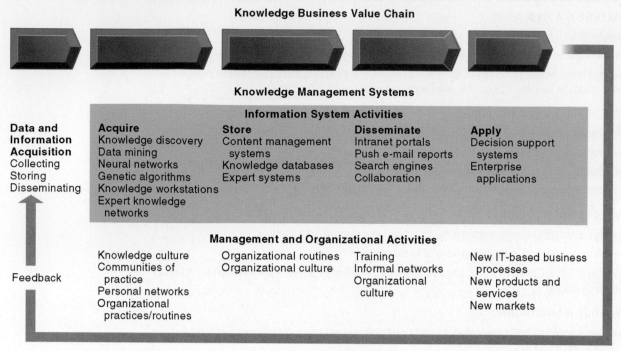

Knowledge management today involves both information systems activities and a host of enabling management and organizational activities.

tional activities in the lower half of the diagram represent the investment in organizational capital required to obtain substantial returns on the information technology (IT) investments and systems shown in the top half of the diagram.

Knowledge Acquisition

Organizations acquire knowledge in a number of ways, depending on the type of knowledge they seek. The first knowledge management systems sought to build corporate repositories of documents, reports, presentations, and best practices. These efforts have been extended to include unstructured documents (such as e-mail). In other cases, organizations acquire knowledge by developing online expert networks so that employees can "find the expert" in the company who has the knowledge in his or her head.

In still other cases, firms must create new knowledge by discovering patterns in corporate data or by using knowledge workstations where engineers can discover new knowledge. These various efforts are described throughout this chapter. A coherent and organized knowledge system also requires systematic data from the firm's transaction processing systems that track sales, payments, inventory, customers, and other vital data, as well as data from external sources such as news feeds, industry reports, legal opinions, scientific research, and government statistics.

Knowledge Storage

Once they are discovered, documents, patterns, and expert rules must be stored so they can be retrieved and used by employees. Knowledge storage generally involves the creation of a database. Document management systems that digitize, index, and tag documents according to a coherent framework are large databases adept at storing collections of documents. Expert systems also help corporations preserve the knowledge that is acquired by incorporating that knowledge into organizational processes and culture. Each of these is discussed later in this chapter and in the following chapter.

Management must support the development of planned knowledge storage systems, encourage the development of corporate-wide schemas for indexing documents, and reward employees for taking the time to update and store documents properly. For instance, it would reward the sales force for submitting names of prospects to a shared corporate database of prospects where all sales personnel can identify each prospect and review the stored knowledge.

Knowledge Dissemination

Portal, e-mail, instant messaging, wikis, social networks, and search engine technology have added to an existing array of collaboration technologies and office systems for sharing calendars, documents, data, and graphics (see Chapter 7). Contemporary technology seems to have created a deluge of information and knowledge. How can managers and employees discover, in a sea of information and knowledge, that which is really important for their decisions and their work? Here, training programs, informal networks, and shared management experience communicated through a supportive culture help managers focus their attention on the important knowledge and information.

Knowledge Application

Regardless of what type of knowledge management system is involved, knowledge that is not shared and applied to the practical problems facing firms and managers does not add business value. To provide a return on investment, organizational knowledge must become a systematic part of management decision making and become situated in decision-support systems (described in Chapter 12). Ultimately, new knowledge must be built into a firm's business processes and key application systems, including enterprise applications for managing key internal business processes and relationships with customers and suppliers. Management supports this process by creating—based on new knowledge—new business practices, new products and services, and new markets for the firm.

Building Organizational and Management Capital: Collaboration, Communities of Practice, and Office Environments

In addition to the activities we have just described, managers can help by developing new organizational roles and responsibilities for the acquisition of knowledge, including the creation of chief knowledge officer executive positions, dedicated staff positions (knowledge managers), and communities of practice. **Communities of practice (COPs)** are informal social networks of professionals and employees within and outside the firm who have similar work-related activities and interests. The activities of these communities include self- and group education, conferences, online newsletters, and day-to-day sharing of experiences and techniques to solve specific work problems. Many organizations, such as IBM, the U.S. Federal Highway Administration, and the World Bank have encouraged the development of thousands of online communities of practice. These communities of practice depend greatly on software environments that enable collaboration and communication.

COPs can make it easier for people to reuse knowledge by pointing community members to useful documents, creating document repositories, and filtering information for newcomers. COP members act as facilitators, encouraging contributions and discussion. COPs can also reduce the learning curve for new employees by providing contacts with subject matter experts and access to a community's established methods and tools. Finally, COPs can act as a spawning ground for new ideas, techniques, and decision-making behavior.

TYPES OF KNOWLEDGE MANAGEMENT SYSTEMS

There are essentially three major types of knowledge management systems: enterprise-wide knowledge management systems, knowledge work systems, and intelligent techniques. Figure 11-3 shows the knowledge management system applications for each of these major categories.

Enterprise-wide knowledge management systems are general-purpose firmwide efforts to collect, store, distribute, and apply digital content and knowledge. These systems include capabilities for searching for information, storing both structured and unstructured data, and locating employee expertise within the firm. They also include supporting technologies such as portals, search engines, collaboration tools (e-mail, instant messaging, wikis, blogs, and social bookmarking) and learning management systems.

The development of powerful networked workstations and software for assisting engineers and scientists in the discovery of new knowledge has led to the creation of knowledge work systems such as computer-aided design (CAD), visualization, simulation, and virtual reality systems. **Knowledge work systems (KWS)** are specialized systems built for engineers, scientists, and other knowledge workers charged with discovering and creating new knowledge for a company. We discuss knowledge work applications in detail in Section 11.3.

Knowledge management also includes a diverse group of **intelligent techniques**, such as data mining, expert systems, neural networks, fuzzy logic, genetic algorithms, and intelligent agents. These techniques have different

FIGURE 11-3   MAJOR TYPES OF KNOWLEDGE MANAGEMENT SYSTEMS

Enterprise-Wide Knowledge Management Systems	Knowledge Work Systems	Intelligent Techniques
General-purpose, integrated, firmwide efforts to collect, store, disseminate, and use digital content and knowledge	Specialized workstations and systems that enable scientists, engineers, and other knowledge workers to create and discover new knowledge	Tools for discovering patterns and applying knowledge to discrete decisions and knowledge domains
Enterprise content management systems Collaboration tools Learning management systems Knowledge network systems	CAD 3-D virtualization Virtual reality Investment workstations	Data mining Neural networks Expert systems Case-based reasoning Fuzzy logic Genetic algorithms Intelligent agents

There are three major categories of knowledge management systems, and each can be broken down further into more specialized types of knowledge management systems.

objectives, from a focus on discovering knowledge (data mining and neural networks), to distilling knowledge in the form of rules for a computer program (expert systems and fuzzy logic), to discovering optimal solutions for problems (genetic algorithms). Section 11.4 provides more detail about these intelligent techniques.

11.2 ENTERPRISE-WIDE KNOWLEDGE MANAGEMENT SYSTEMS

Firms must deal with at least three kinds of knowledge. Some knowledge exists within the firm in the form of structured text documents (reports and presentations). Decision makers also need knowledge that is semistructured, such as e-mail, voice mail, chat room exchanges, videos, digital pictures, brochures, or bulletin board postings. In still other cases, there is no formal or digital information of any kind, and the knowledge resides in the heads of employees. Much of this knowledge is tacit knowledge that is rarely written down. Enterprise-wide knowledge management systems deal with all three types of knowledge.

ENTERPRISE CONTENT MANAGEMENT SYSTEMS

Businesses today need to organize and manage both structured and semistructured knowledge assets. **Structured knowledge** is explicit knowledge that exists in formal documents, as well as in formal rules that organizations derive by observing experts and their decision-making behaviors. But, according to experts, at least 80 percent of an organization's business content is semistructured or unstructured—information in folders, messages, memos, proposals, e-mails, graphics, electronic slide presentations, and even videos created in different formats and stored in many locations.

Enterprise content management systems help organizations manage both types of information. They have capabilities for knowledge capture, storage, retrieval, distribution, and preservation to help firms improve their business processes and decisions. Such systems include corporate repositories of documents, reports, presentations, and best practices, as well as capabilities for collecting and organizing semistructured knowledge such as e-mail (see Figure 11-4). Major enterprise content management systems also enable users to access external sources of information, such as news feeds and research, and to communicate via e-mail, chat/instant messaging, discussion groups, and videoconferencing. Open Text Corporation, EMC (Documentum), IBM, and Oracle Corporation are leading vendors of enterprise content management software.

Central Vermont Public Service, which provides energy and energy-related services to nearly 160,000 people across Vermont, uses Open Text LiveLink Enterprise Content Management tools to manage the massive amounts of information it is required to maintain. The system organizes and stores both structured and unstructured content, including e-mail, spreadsheets, word processing documents, and PDF document files, from its moment of creation until its ultimate disposition. The system helps it comply with federal and state regulations for records management and also make better business use of the information (Open Text, 2008).

FIGURE 11-4   AN ENTERPRISE CONTENT MANAGEMENT SYSTEM

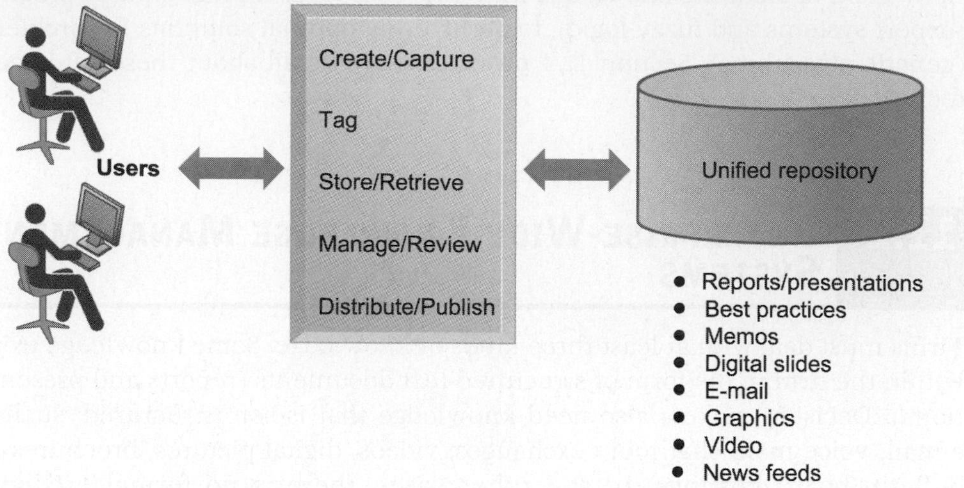

An enterprise content management system has capabilities for classifying, organizing and managing structured and semistructured knowledge and making it available throughout the enterprise.

A key problem in managing knowledge is the creation of an appropriate classification scheme, or **taxonomy**, to organize information into meaningful categories so that it can be easily accessed. Once the categories for classifying knowledge have been created, each knowledge object needs to be "tagged," or classified, so that it can be easily retrieved. Enterprise content management systems have capabilities for tagging, interfacing with corporate databases where the documents are stored, and creating an enterprise portal environment for employees to use when searching for corporate knowledge.

Firms in publishing, advertising, broadcasting, and entertainment have special needs for storing and managing unstructured digital data such as photographs, graphic images, video, and audio content. For example, Coca-Cola must keep track of all the images of the Coca-Cola brand that have been created in the past at all of the company's worldwide offices, to prevent both redundant work and variation from a standard brand image (see the chapter-ending case study). **Digital asset management systems** help companies classify, store, and distribute these digital objects.

KNOWLEDGE NETWORK SYSTEMS

Knowledge network systems, also known as *expertise location and management systems*, address the problem that arises when the appropriate knowledge is not in the form of a digital document but instead resides in the memory of expert individuals in the firm. Knowledge network systems provide an online directory of corporate experts in well-defined knowledge domains and use communication technologies to make it easy for employees to find the appropriate expert in a company. Some knowledge network systems go further by systematizing the solutions developed by experts and then storing the solutions in a knowledge database as a best practices or frequently asked questions (FAQ) repository (see Figure 11-5). AskMe and Tacit Software are leading knowledge network system vendors.

Intec Engineering Partnership, a project management company with more than 500 employees worldwide serving the global oil and gas industry uses the

FIGURE 11-5　AN ENTERPRISE KNOWLEDGE NETWORK SYSTEM

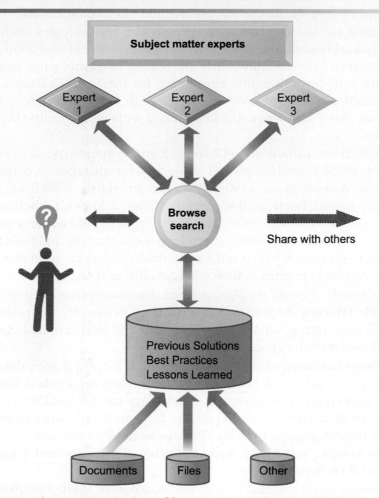

A knowledge network maintains a database of firm experts, as well as accepted solutions to known problems, and then facilitates the communication between employees looking for knowledge and experts who have that knowledge. Solutions created in this communication are then added to a database of solutions in the form of FAQs, best practices, or other documents.

AskMe enterprise knowledge network system. Using the system, an Intec engineer with a question could access relevant documents, Web links, and answers to previous related questions by initiating a keyword search. If no answer was found, that person could post a general question on a Web page for categories, such as Pipeline or Subsea, for other engineers accessing that page to answer. Alternatively, the person could review the profiles of all company engineers with relevant expertise and send a detailed e-mail query to experts who might have the answer. All questions and answers are automatically incorporated into the knowledge database.

COLLABORATION TOOLS AND LEARNING MANAGEMENT SYSTEMS

The major enterprise content management systems include powerful portal and collaboration technologies. Enterprise knowledge portals can provide access to external sources of information, such as news feeds and research, as well as to internal knowledge resources along with capabilities for e-mail, chat/instant messaging, discussion groups, and videoconferencing.

Companies are starting to use consumer Web technologies such as blogs, wikis, and social bookmarking for internal use to foster collaboration and information exchange between individuals and teams. Blogs and wikis help capture, consolidate, and centralize this knowledge for the firm. Collaboration tools from commercial software vendors, such as Microsoft SharePoint and Lotus Connections also offer these capabilities along with secure online collaborative workspaces.

Wikis, which we introduced in Chapters 2 and 7, are inexpensive and easy to implement. Wikis provide a central repository for all types of corporate data that can be displayed in a Web browser, including electronic pages of documents, spreadsheets, and electronic slides, and can embed e-mail and instant messages. Although users are able to modify wiki content contributed by others, wikis have capabilities for tracking these changes and tools for reverting to earlier versions. A wiki is most appropriate for information that is revised frequently but must remain available perpetually as it changes.

The Interactive Session on Management describes some of these corporate uses of Web 2.0 tools. As you read this case, try to identify the problem these companies were facing, what alternative solutions were available to management, and how well the chosen solution worked.

Social bookmarking makes it easier to search for and share information by allowing users to save their bookmarks to Web pages on a public Web site and tag these bookmarks with keywords. These tags can be used to organize and search for the documents. Lists of tags can be shared with other people to help them find information of interest. The user-created taxonomies created for shared bookmarks are called **folksonomies**. Delicious and Digg are two popular social bookmarking sites.

Suppose, for example, that you're on a corporate team researching wind power. If you did a Web search and found relevant Web pages on wind power, you'd click on a bookmarking button on a social bookmarking site and create a tag identifying each Web document you found to link it to wind power. By clicking on the "tags" button at the social networking site, you'd be able to see a list of all the tags you created and select the documents you need.

Companies need ways to keep track of and manage employee learning and to integrate it more fully into their knowledge management and other corporate systems. A **learning management system (LMS)** provides tools for the management, delivery, tracking, and assessment of various types of employee learning and training.

Contemporary LMS support multiple modes of learning, including CD-ROM, downloadable videos, Web-based classes, live instruction in classes or online, and group learning in online forums and chat sessions. The LMS consolidates mixed-media training, automates the selection and administration of courses, assembles and delivers learning content, and measures learning effectiveness.

For example, the Whirlpool Corporation uses CERTPOINT's learning management system to manage the registration, scheduling, reporting, and content for its training programs for 3,500 salespeople. The system helps Whirlpool tailor course content to the right audience, track the people who took courses and their scores, and compile metrics on employee performance.

INTERACTIVE SESSION: MANAGEMENT

MANAGING WITH WEB 2.0

Who's blogging? It's not just twenty-somethings who want to chronicle their experiences, vent about consumer products, or put out a political message. Today's blogger might very well be an employee at IBM, Intel, P&G, or any number of companies that have embraced Web 2.0 tools. Blogs, wikis, and social networking are emerging as powerful tools to boost communication and productivity in the corporate workforce. McKinsey & Co. consultants reported that approximately one-third of the top executives it polled use Web 2.0 tools or plan to deploy them.

Web 2.0 tools have made inroads into the business world because the software that supports them is generally inexpensive and user-friendly. A manager who wants to communicate with his or her team via a blog or have the progress of a project documented on a wiki can institute the technology without help from the IT department and without superiors worrying about high costs.

At Sun Microsystems, management instructed its engineers to create wiki pages that described their projects. Once the engineers were comfortable with the technology, it was easier for them to transition to using wikis for the company's formal software documentation. The use of wikis also spread to meeting notes, project plans, and software reports, resulting in a total four-fold increase in the amount of documented information at Sun.

At IBM, over 26,000 employees have created blogs on the company's network to post about technology and the work they are doing. Project team members use wikis to store information and share memos. IBM's Wiki Central manages over 20,000 company wikis with over 125,000 participants. The company created a wiki to help 50 of its experts on law, economics, government, and technology to collaborate on an intellectual property manifesto that services as the foundation of its new patent policy.

Web 2.0 tools are particularly valuable at IBM, where 42 percent of the workforce operates remotely, either from home or from client offices. Brian Goodman, who is the Connecticut-based manager of a software development team with members in New York and Massachusetts, says that the wikis give him "a single view of the projects and their status" without bombarding each worker every day with an instant message.

IBM employees engage in social networking internally through its corporate directory, BluePages, which is edited by employees and serves as a sort of internal corporate MySpace. The directory contains basic information on 400,000 employees and is accessed six million times daily. Employees have control of most of the content on their individual entries, and can post their own photos and resumes to their corporate "profiles."

IBM provides social networking capabilities to other companies through its IBM Lotus Connections software. Lotus Connections includes capabilities for user profiles, blogs, social bookmarking, and supporting communities of practice. The U.S. Federal Aviation Administration (FAA) uses a feature called Activities for disaster preparation. Should an emergency arise, the software channels RSS feeds from internal blogs, relevant documents, and plans into an Activities page for employees to see and discuss.

At Wachovia, the giant financial services company acquired by Wells Fargo, Web 2.0 technologies help link a worldwide network of offices with over 100,000 employees. Wachovia has rolled out wikis, blogs, instant messaging, personal profiles, and other collaboration tools anchored by Microsoft's SharePoint Server. Management believes a collaborative environment is essential for attracting and retaining young, energetic employees who expect to use Web 2.0 tools at work. These social networking tools, along with videoconferencing, have reduced travel expenditures and also helped the company preserve the experience of long-time knowledge workers as they retire.

Although some businesses block employee access to Facebook and other public networking sites, a number of businesses use them for limited purposes. Recruiters at Microsoft and Starbucks have used LinkedIn to search for potential job candidates. P&G employees use Facebook to keep interns in touch and share information with co-workers attending company events.

Two of the biggest challenges for companies using Web 2.0 technologies are convincing workers to embrace these tools and regulating their use. IBM reminds employees to remember the rules of privacy, respect, and confidentiality in its corporate code of conduct and does not allow any anonymous online communication. Companies using public social networking sites need to worry more about security and regulatory compliance because communications occur with parties outside the corporation. Employees chatting about their jobs could reveal sensitive information.

Some companies, such as Nokia and Frankfurt-based investment bank Dresdner Kleinwort, started wiki or blog implementations with a small group of employees. Once other managers and employees

saw the business benefits, ease of use, and versatility of the tools, their departments were quick to adopt the technology.

Sources: Paul McDougall, "The 'TLA Wiki' and Other Tips to Spark Enterprise 2.0 Efforts," *Information Week*, June 16, 2008; Judith Lamont, "Social Networking: KM and Beyond," *KM World*, June 2008; Michael Totty, "Social Studies," *The Wall Street Journal*, June 18, 2007; William M. Bulkeley, "Playing Well with Others," *The Wall Street Journal*, June 18, 2007; Vauhini Vara, "Wikis at Work," *The Wall Street Journal*, June 18, 2007; and Dan Carlin, "Corporate Wikis Go Viral," *BusinessWeek*, March 12, 2007.

CASE STUDY QUESTIONS

1. How do Web 2.0 tools help companies manage knowledge, coordinate work, and enhance decision making?

2. What business problems do blogs, wikis, and other social networking tools help solve?

3. Describe how a company such as Wal-Mart or Procter & Gamble would benefit from using Web 2.0 tools internally.

4. What challenges do companies face in spreading the use of Web 2.0? What issues should managers be concerned with?

MIS IN ACTION

Go to Sun Microsystems' Blogs home page at http://blogs.sun.com and click the Blog Directory tab. Select a blog from the directory and then answer the following questions:

1. What is the name of the blog you selected?

2. Who is the intended audience of this blog?

3. What subjects does the blog address?

4. Visit several more blogs in Sun's directory. If you were a Sun employee, do you think you would find the existence of these blogs helpful? Why or why not? Do you think there is value in blog entries that discuss the author's personal life instead of work-related matters?

11.3 KNOWLEDGE WORK SYSTEMS

The enterprise-wide knowledge systems we have just described provide a wide range of capabilities that can be used by many if not all the workers and groups in an organization. Firms also have specialized systems for knowledge workers to help them create new knowledge and to ensure that this knowledge is properly integrated into the business.

KNOWLEDGE WORKERS AND KNOWLEDGE WORK

Knowledge workers, which we introduced in Chapter 1, include researchers, designers, architects, scientists, and engineers who primarily create knowledge and information for the organization. Knowledge workers usually have high levels of education and memberships in professional organizations and are often asked to exercise independent judgment as a routine aspect of their work. For example, knowledge workers create new products or find ways of improving existing ones. Knowledge workers perform three key roles that are critical to the organization and to the managers who work within the organization:

- Keeping the organization current in knowledge as it develops in the external world—in technology, science, social thought, and the arts

- Serving as internal consultants regarding the areas of their knowledge, the changes taking place, and opportunities
- Acting as change agents, evaluating, initiating, and promoting change projects

REQUIREMENTS OF KNOWLEDGE WORK SYSTEMS

Most knowledge workers rely on office systems, such as word processors, voice mail, e-mail, videoconferencing, and scheduling systems, which are designed to increase worker productivity in the office. However, knowledge workers also require highly specialized knowledge work systems with powerful graphics, analytical tools, and communications and document management capabilities.

These systems require great computing power to handle the sophisticated graphics or complex calculations necessary for such knowledge workers as scientific researchers, product designers, and financial analysts. Because knowledge workers are so focused on knowledge in the external world, these systems also must give the worker quick and easy access to external databases. They typically feature user-friendly interfaces that enable users to perform needed tasks without having to spend a great deal of time learning how to use the system. Knowledge workers are highly paid—wasting a knowledge worker's time is simply too expensive. Figure 11-6 summarizes the requirements of knowledge work systems.

Knowledge workstations often are designed and optimized for the specific tasks to be performed; so, for example, a design engineer requires a different workstation setup than a financial analyst. Design engineers need graphics with enough power to handle three-dimensional (3-D) CAD systems. However, financial analysts are more interested in access to a myriad of external databases and optical disk technology for efficiently storing and accessing massive amounts of financial data.

FIGURE 11-6   REQUIREMENTS OF KNOWLEDGE WORK SYSTEMS

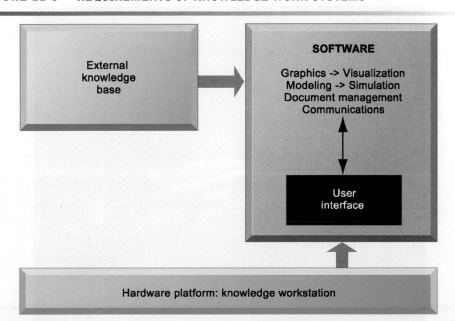

Knowledge work systems require strong links to external knowledge bases in addition to specialized hardware and software.

EXAMPLES OF KNOWLEDGE WORK SYSTEMS

Major knowledge work applications include CAD systems, virtual reality systems for simulation and modeling, and financial workstations. **Computer-aided design (CAD)** automates the creation and revision of designs, using computers and sophisticated graphics software. Using a more traditional physical design methodology, each design modification requires a mold to be made and a prototype to be tested physically. That process must be repeated many times, which is a very expensive and time-consuming process. Using a CAD workstation, the designer need only make a physical prototype toward the end of the design process because the design can be easily tested and changed on the computer. The ability of CAD software to provide design specifications for the tooling and manufacturing processes also saves a great deal of time and money while producing a manufacturing process with far fewer problems.

For example, architects from Skidmore, Owings, & Merrill LLP used a 3-D design program called Revit to work out the creative and technical details of the design for the Freedom Tower at the site of the former World Trade Center. The software enabled the architects to strip away the outer layer to manipulate the shape of the floors. Changes appeared immediately in the entire model, and the software automatically recalculated the technical details in the blueprints.

Virtual reality systems have visualization, rendering, and simulation capabilities that go far beyond those of conventional CAD systems. They use interactive graphics software to create computer-generated simulations that are so close to reality that users almost believe they are participating in a real-world situation. In many virtual reality systems, the user dons special clothing, headgear, and equipment, depending on the application. The clothing contains sensors that record the user's movements and immediately transmit that information back to the computer. For instance, to walk through a virtual reality simulation of a house, you would need garb that monitors the movement of your feet, hands, and head. You also would need goggles containing video

CAD systems improve the quality and precision of product design by performing much of the design and testing work on the computer.

screens and sometimes audio attachments and feeling gloves so that you can be immersed in the computer feedback.

Virtual reality is just starting to provide benefits in educational, scientific, and business work. For example, neuroradiologists at New York's Beth Israel Medical Center can use the Siemens Medical Systems 3D Virtuoso System to peek at the interplay of tiny blood vessels or take a fly-through of the aorta. Surgeons at New York University School of Medicine can use 3-D modeling to target brain tumors more precisely, thereby reducing bleeding and trauma during surgery.

Virtual reality applications developed for the Web use a standard called **Virtual Reality Modeling Language (VRML)**. VRML is a set of specifications for interactive, 3-D modeling on the World Wide Web that can organize multiple media types, including animation, images, and audio to put users in a simulated real-world environment. VRML is platform independent, operates over a desktop computer, and requires little bandwidth.

DuPont, the Wilmington, Delaware, chemical company, created a VRML application called HyperPlant, which enables users to access 3-D data over the Internet using Web browser software. Engineers can go through 3-D models as if they were physically walking through a plant, viewing objects at eye level. This level of detail reduces the number of mistakes they make during construction of oil rigs, oil plants, and other structures.

The financial industry is using specialized **investment workstations** to leverage the knowledge and time of its brokers, traders, and portfolio managers. Firms such as Merrill Lynch and UBS Financial Services have installed investment workstations that integrate a wide range of data from both internal and external sources, including contact management data, real-time and historical market data, and research reports. Previously, financial professionals had to spend considerable time accessing data from separate systems and piecing together the information they needed. By providing one-stop information faster and with fewer errors, the workstations streamline the entire investment process from stock selection to updating client records. Table 11-2 summarizes the major types of knowledge work systems.

11.4 INTELLIGENT TECHNIQUES

Artificial intelligence and database technology provide a number of intelligent techniques that organizations can use to capture individual and collective knowledge and to extend their knowledge base. Expert systems, case-based reasoning, and fuzzy logic are used for capturing tacit knowledge. Neural

TABLE 11-2 EXAMPLES OF KNOWLEDGE WORK SYSTEMS

KNOWLEDGE WORK SYSTEM	FUNCTION IN ORGANIZATION
CAD/CAM (computer-aided manufacturing)	Provides engineers, designers, and factory managers with precise control over industrial design and manufacturing
Virtual reality systems	Provide drug designers, architects, engineers, and medical workers with precise, photorealistic simulations of objects
Investment workstations	High-end PCs used in financial sector to analyze trading situations instantaneously and facilitate portfolio management

networks and data mining are used for **knowledge discovery**. They can discover underlying patterns, categories, and behaviors in large data sets that could not be discovered by managers alone or simply through experience. Genetic algorithms are used for generating solutions to problems that are too large and complex for human beings to analyze on their own. Intelligent agents can automate routine tasks to help firms search for and filter information for use in electronic commerce, supply chain management, and other activities.

Data mining, which we introduced in Chapter 6, helps organizations capture undiscovered knowledge residing in large databases, providing managers with new insight for improving business performance. It has become an important tool for management decision making, and we provide a detailed discussion of data mining for management decision support in Chapter 12.

The other intelligent techniques discussed in this section are based on **artificial intelligence (AI)** technology, which consists of computer-based systems (both hardware and software) that attempt to emulate human behavior. Such systems would be able to learn languages, accomplish physical tasks, use a perceptual apparatus, and emulate human expertise and decision making. Although AI applications do not exhibit the breadth, complexity, originality, and generality of human intelligence, they play an important role in contemporary knowledge management.

CAPTURING KNOWLEDGE: EXPERT SYSTEMS

Expert systems are an intelligent technique for capturing tacit knowledge in a very specific and limited domain of human expertise. These systems capture the knowledge of skilled employees in the form of a set of rules in a software system that can be used by others in the organization. The set of rules in the expert system adds to the memory, or stored learning, of the firm.

Expert systems lack the breadth of knowledge and the understanding of fundamental principles of a human expert. They typically perform very limited tasks that can be performed by professionals in a few minutes or hours, such as diagnosing a malfunctioning machine or determining whether to grant credit for a loan. Problems that cannot be solved by human experts in the same short period of time are far too difficult for an expert system. However, by capturing human expertise in limited areas, expert systems can provide benefits, helping organizations make high-quality decisions with fewer people. Today, expert systems are widely used in business in discrete, highly structured decision-making situations.

How Expert Systems Work

Human knowledge must be modeled or represented in a way that a computer can process. Expert systems model human knowledge as a set of rules that collectively are called the **knowledge base**. Expert systems have from 200 to many thousands of these rules, depending on the complexity of the problem. These rules are much more interconnected and nested than in a traditional software program (see Figure 11-7).

The strategy used to search through the knowledge base is called the **inference engine**. Two strategies are commonly used: forward chaining and backward chaining (see Figure 11-8).

In **forward chaining,** the inference engine begins with the information entered by the user and searches the rule base to arrive at a conclusion. The strategy is to fire, or carry out, the action of the rule when a condition is true. In Figure 11-8, beginning on the left, if the user enters a client's name with

FIGURE 11-7 RULES IN AN EXPERT SYSTEM

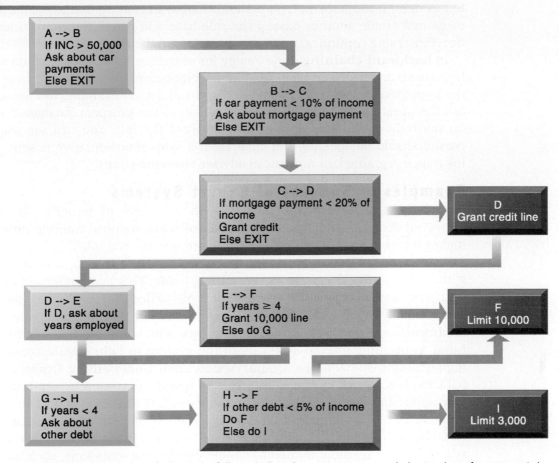

An expert system contains a number of rules to be followed. The rules are interconnected; the number of outcomes is known in advance and is limited; there are multiple paths to the same outcome; and the system can consider multiple rules at a single time. The rules illustrated are for simple credit-granting expert systems.

FIGURE 11-8 INFERENCE ENGINES IN EXPERT SYSTEMS

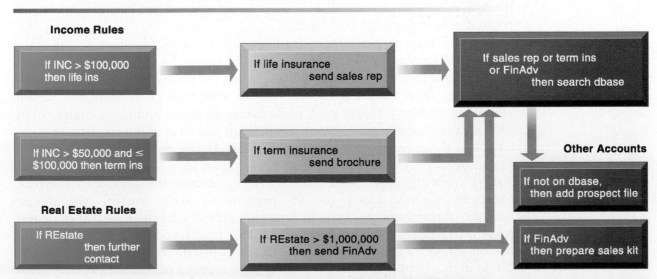

An inference engine works by searching through the rules and "firing" those rules that are triggered by facts gathered and entered by the user. Basically, a collection of rules is similar to a series of nested IF statements in a traditional software program; however, the magnitude of the statements and degree of nesting are much greater in an expert system.

income greater than $100,000, the engine will fire all rules in sequence from left to right. If the user then enters information indicating that the same client owns real estate, another pass of the rule base will occur and more rules will fire. Processing continues until no more rules can be fired.

In **backward chaining,** the strategy for searching the rule base starts with a hypothesis and proceeds by asking the user questions about selected facts until the hypothesis is either confirmed or disproved. In our example, in Figure 11-8, ask the question, "Should we add this person to the prospect database?" Begin on the right of the diagram and work toward the left. You can see that the person should be added to the database if a sales representative is sent, term insurance is granted, or a financial adviser visits the client.

Examples of Successful Expert Systems

Expert systems provide businesses with an array of benefits including improved decisions, reduced errors, reduced costs, reduced training time, and higher levels of quality and service. Here are several examples:

Countrywide Funding Corporation in Pasadena, California, uses an expert system to improve decisions about granting loans. This loan-underwriting firm employs about 400 underwriters in 150 offices around the country. The company developed a PC-based expert system in 1992 to make preliminary creditworthiness decisions on loan requests. The company had experienced rapid, continuing growth and wanted the system to help ensure consistent, high-quality loan decisions. Countrywide's Loan Underwriting Expert System (CLUES) has about 400 rules. Countrywide tested the system by sending every loan application handled by a human underwriter to CLUES as well. The system was refined until it agreed with the underwriters in 95 percent of the cases.

Countrywide does not rely on CLUES to reject loans because the expert system cannot be programmed to handle exceptional situations, such as those involving a self-employed person or complex financial schemes. An underwriter must review all rejected loans and makes the final decision. CLUES has other benefits. Traditionally, an underwriter could handle six or seven applications a day. Using CLUES, the same underwriter can evaluate at least 16 per day. "Countrywide illustrates the importance of managers and common sense in the use of expert systems. Countrywide made millions of faulty sub-prime mortgages in 2007 not because of the CLUES system, but because managers relaxed proper mortgage standards."

Con-Way Transportation built an expert system called Line-haul to automate and optimize planning of overnight shipment routes for its nationwide freight-trucking business. The expert system captures the business rules that dispatchers follow when assigning drivers, trucks, and trailers to transport 50,000 shipments of heavy freight each night across 25 states and Canada and when plotting their routes. Line-haul runs on a Sun platform and uses data on daily customer shipment requests, available drivers, trucks, trailer space, and weight stored in an Oracle database. The expert system uses thousands of rules and 100,000 lines of program code written in C++ to crunch the numbers and create optimum routing plans for 95 percent of daily freight shipments. Con-Way dispatchers tweak the routing plan provided by the expert system and relay final routing specifications to field personnel responsible for packing the trailers for their nighttime runs. Con-Way recouped its $3 million investment in the system within two years by reducing the number of drivers, packing more freight per trailer, and reducing damage from rehandling. The system also reduces dispatchers' arduous nightly tasks (Pastore, 2003).

Although expert systems lack the robust and general intelligence of human beings, they can provide benefits to organizations if their limitations are well understood. Only certain classes of problems can be solved using expert systems. Virtually all successful expert systems deal with problems of classification in limited domains of knowledge where there are relatively few alternative outcomes and these possible outcomes are all known in advance. Expert systems are much less useful for dealing with unstructured problems typically encountered by managers.

Many expert systems require large, lengthy, and expensive development efforts. Hiring or training more experts may be less expensive than building an expert system. Typically, the environment in which an expert system operates is continually changing so that the expert system must also continually change. Some expert systems, especially large ones, are so complex that in a few years the maintenance costs equal the development costs.

ORGANIZATIONAL INTELLIGENCE: CASE-BASED REASONING

Expert systems primarily capture the tacit knowledge of individual experts, but organizations also have collective knowledge and expertise that they have built up over the years. This organizational knowledge can be captured and stored using case-based reasoning. In **case-based reasoning (CBR)**, descriptions of past experiences of human specialists, represented as cases, are stored in a database for later retrieval when the user encounters a new case with similar parameters. The system searches for stored cases with problem characteristics similar to the new one, finds the closest fit, and applies the solutions of the old case to the new case. Successful solutions are tagged to the new case and both are stored together with the other cases in the knowledge base. Unsuccessful solutions also are appended to the case database along with explanations as to why the solutions did not work (see Figure 11-9).

Expert systems work by applying a set of IF-THEN-ELSE rules extracted from human experts. Case-based reasoning, in contrast, represents knowledge as a series of cases, and this knowledge base is continuously expanded and refined by users. You'll find case-based reasoning in diagnostic systems in medicine or customer support where users can retrieve past cases whose characteristics are similar to the new case. The system suggests a solution or diagnosis based on the best-matching retrieved case.

FUZZY LOGIC SYSTEMS

Most people do not think in terms of traditional IF-THEN rules or precise numbers. Humans tend to categorize things imprecisely using rules for making decisions that may have many shades of meaning. For example, a man or a woman can be *strong* or *intelligent*. A company can be *large*, *medium*, or *small* in size. Temperature can be *hot*, *cold*, *cool*, or *warm*. These categories represent a range of values.

Fuzzy logic is a rule-based technology that can represent such imprecision by creating rules that use approximate or subjective values. It can describe a particular phenomenon or process linguistically and then represent that description in a small number of flexible rules. Organizations can use fuzzy logic to create software systems that capture tacit knowledge where there is linguistic ambiguity.

FIGURE 11-9   HOW CASE-BASED REASONING WORKS

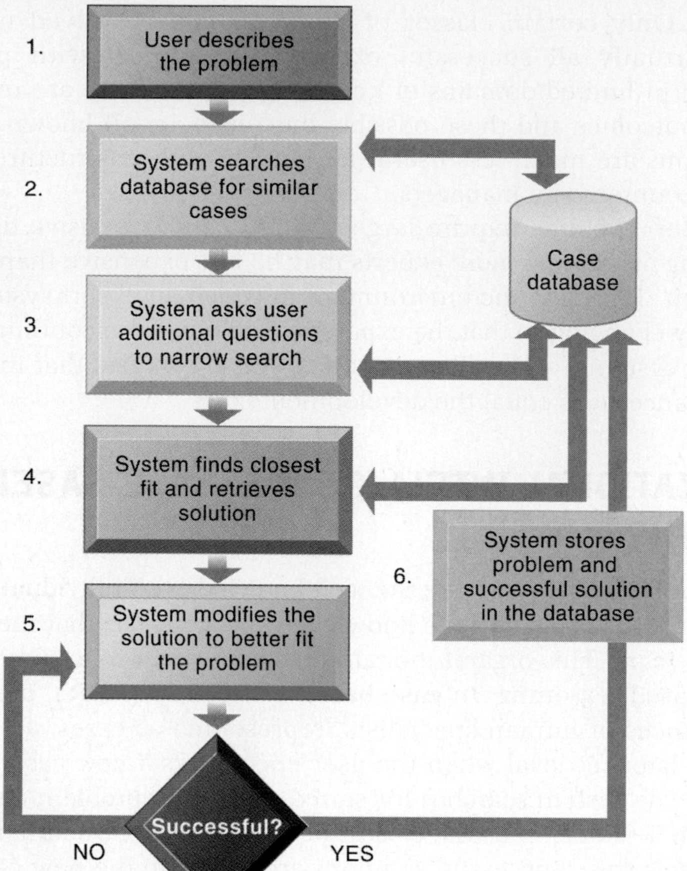

Case-based reasoning represents knowledge as a database of past cases and their solutions.
The system uses a six-step process to generate solutions to new problems encountered by the user.

Let's look at the way fuzzy logic would represent various temperatures in a computer application to control room temperature automatically. The terms (known as *membership functions*) are imprecisely defined so that, for example, in Figure 11-10, cool is between 45 degrees and 70 degrees, although the temperature is most clearly cool between about 60 degrees and 67 degrees. Note that *cool* is overlapped by *cold* or *norm*. To control the room environment using this logic, the programmer would develop similarly imprecise definitions for humidity and other factors, such as outdoor wind and temperature. The rules might include one that says: "If the temperature is *cool* or *cold* and the humidity is low while the outdoor wind is high and the outdoor temperature is low, raise the heat and humidity in the room." The computer would combine the membership function readings in a weighted manner and, using all the rules, raise and lower the temperature and humidity.

Fuzzy logic provides solutions to problems requiring expertise that is difficult to represent in the form of crisp IF-THEN rules. In Japan, Sendai's subway system uses fuzzy logic controls to accelerate so smoothly that standing passengers need not hold on. Mitsubishi Heavy Industries in Tokyo has been able to reduce the power consumption of its air conditioners by 20 percent by implementing control programs in fuzzy logic. The autofocus device in cameras is only possible because of fuzzy logic. In these instances, fuzzy logic allows incremental

FIGURE 11-10 FUZZY LOGIC FOR TEMPERATURE CONTROL

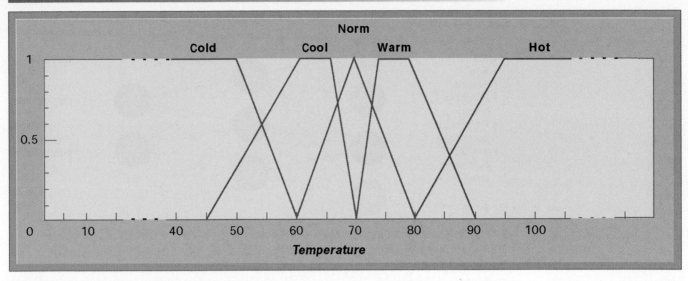

The membership functions for the input called temperature are in the logic of the thermostat to control the room temperature. Membership functions help translate linguistic expressions such as *warm* into numbers that the computer can manipulate.

changes in inputs to produce smooth changes in outputs instead of discontinuous ones, making it useful for consumer electronics and engineering applications.

Management also has found fuzzy logic useful for decision making and organizational control. A Wall Street firm created a system that selects companies for potential acquisition, using the language stock traders understand. A fuzzy logic system has been developed to detect possible fraud in medical claims submitted by health care providers anywhere in the United States.

NEURAL NETWORKS

Neural networks are used for solving complex, poorly understood problems for which large amounts of data have been collected. They find patterns and relationships in massive amounts of data that would be too complicated and difficult for a human being to analyze. Neural networks discover this knowledge by using hardware and software that parallel the processing patterns of the biological or human brain. Neural networks "learn" patterns from large quantities of data by sifting through data, searching for relationships, building models, and correcting over and over again the model's own mistakes.

A neural network has a large number of sensing and processing nodes that continuously interact with each other. Figure 11-11 represents one type of neural network comprising an input layer, an output layer, and a hidden processing layer. Humans "train" the network by feeding it a set of training data for which the inputs produce a known set of outputs or conclusions. This helps the computer learn the correct solution by example. As the computer is fed more data, each case is compared with the known outcome. If it differs, a correction is calculated and applied to the nodes in the hidden processing layer. These steps are repeated until a condition, such as corrections being less than a certain amount, is reached. The neural network in Figure 11-11 has learned how to identify a fraudulent credit card purchase. Also, self-organizing neural networks can be trained by exposing them to large amounts of data and allowing them to discover the patterns and relationships in the data.

FIGURE 11-11 HOW A NEURAL NETWORK WORKS

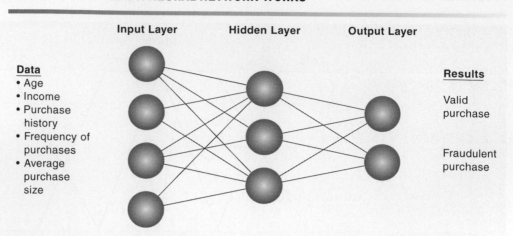

A neural network uses rules it "learns" from patterns in data to construct a hidden layer of logic. The hidden layer then processes inputs, classifying them based on the experience of the model. In this example, the neural network has been trained to distinguish between valid and fraudulent credit card purchases.

Whereas expert systems seek to emulate or model a human expert's way of solving problems, neural network builders claim that they do not program solutions and do not aim to solve specific problems. Instead, neural network designers seek to put intelligence into the hardware in the form of a generalized capability to learn. In contrast, the expert system is highly specific to a given problem and cannot be retrained easily.

Neural network applications in medicine, science, and business address problems in pattern classification, prediction, financial analysis, and control and optimization. In medicine, neural network applications are used for screening patients for coronary artery disease, for diagnosing patients with epilepsy and Alzheimer's disease, and for performing pattern recognition of pathology images. The financial industry uses neural networks to discern patterns in vast pools of data that might help predict the performance of equities, corporate bond ratings, or corporate bankruptcies. Visa International uses a neural network to help detect credit card fraud by monitoring all Visa transactions for sudden changes in the buying patterns of cardholders.

There are many puzzling aspects of neural networks. Unlike expert systems, which typically provide explanations for their solutions, neural networks cannot always explain why they arrived at a particular solution. Moreover, they cannot always guarantee a completely certain solution, arrive at the same solution again with the same input data, or always guarantee the best solution. They are very sensitive and may not perform well if their training covers too little or too much data. In most current applications, neural networks are best used as aids to human decision makers instead of substitutes for them.

Other types of applications have benefited from pattern recognition technology. These types of applications are based on **machine learning**, a related AI technology focusing on algorithms and techniques allowing computers to "learn" by extracting information using computation and statistical methods. Inductive machine learning methods extract rules and patterns out of massive data sets. Both neural networks and machine learning techniques are used in data mining.

INTERACTIVE SESSION:ORGANIZATIONS

ALBASSAMI'S JOB IS NOT FEASIBLE WITHOUT I.T.

If you live in a country with a diverse geography and a climate characterized as being harsh, with a dry desert and great temperature extremes like the Kingdom of Saudi Arabia (area: 2.1 million square km), and you need to move from one city to another, where the distance could be some thousand kilometers, you have two choices: to drive, or to fly and ship your car via a car transport carrier. Many people in the Kingdom prefer the second option. This has created a market for car transportation in the Kingdom that is the largest in the Middle East. Albassami was established to respond to these market needs. The Albassami International Group is considered one of the leading land transporters in the Middle East.

The estimated size of the car transportation market, both inside the Kingdom and with neighboring countries, is about two billion Saudi riyals and is increasing considerably annually. There are more than a million cars transported inside and outside the Kingdom. Albassami International Group owns the largest fleet of carriers in the Middle East.

At present, the group is operating all over the Kingdom and extends throughout the Gulf Cooperation Council (GCC) countries, Syria, Lebanon, and Jordan. Throughout these years the company has focused on how to maintain business leadership in order to achieve safe and fast transportation.

Every day there are more than 1,000 shipping contracts, including 2,000 to 2,500 bills of lading daily between the main branches. With the introduction of its new division of Express transportation in 2003, the group owns and allocates 170 heavy duty, medium and light vehicles of various types for its door-to-door courier services, which operate all over the Kingdom, covering more than 45 locations. It was therefore impossible to properly handle and control the endless number of daily work options and orders related to these operations at a perfect level of service without a robust computerized system. The system needed the facility to serve specific sectors in the organization, in addition to providing information throughout the group.

The system is based on clustered Dell servers running Windows 2003 and connected to over 270 Windows XP clients. The database management system, used as the backbone of the system, is Sybase Adaptive server, whereas clients use SQL Anywhere. There is replication between the server at headquarters and the client's branches. Throughout the replication, branches' data is sent to the server and aggregated to create the most updated database version, and then sent back to the branches. This means every branch has the most recent version of the client list, trucks' availability, and new shipping contracts so that any customer is able to deal with any branch at any time.

The business process starts when the customer goes to a branch to ship his car to a destination within shipping areas, and the branch then creates a shipping agreement. As the database is sent from the branch to HQ every 30 minutes, an aggregated version of the database of all branches is available at HQ and thereafter sent back to all branches. The recipient branch will create a receipt entry on the system upon arrival of the truck and then an Short Messaging Service communication (SMS) is created and sent to the customer, who will then go to the destination branch to receive the car.

The shipping information system used at Albassami maintains all the sender information such as the sent car, the truck number, the sender and receiving branches, and it also sends an SMS to the client acknowledging the arrival of the car. The system also records the client's data, and holds maintenance information. Linking the data of vehicle maintenance centers with the transportation service helps to enhance company performance and achieve better customer service. The system also enables standard reports to be provided to top management and head sectors about the productivity of each branch, resulting in accurate identification of needs for different regions and thus proper budget allocation. In addition, the system allowed a better audit on all drivers' behavior by using the output of the vehicles' tracking information. Proper performance monitoring resulted in adequate employees' appraisals and consequently loyal staff!

All business processes are facilitated by the shipping system, and the knowledge extracted from the central database has enabled the management team to make sound investment and operational decisions and therefore helped the business maintain its success and leadership in the Kingdom.

Sources: Michael Fitzgerald, "Predicting Where You'll Go and What You'll Like," *The New York Times*, June 22, 2008; Erick Schonfeld, "Location-Tracking Startup Sense Networks Emerges from Stealth to Answer the Question: Where Is Everybody?" TechCrunch.com, June 9, 2008; "Macrosense," sensenetworks.com, accessed July 2008; Caroline McCarthy, "Meet Sense Networks, the Latest Player in the Hot 'Geo' Market," news.cnet.com, June 9, 2008.

CASE STUDY QUESTIONS

1. What systems are described here? What valuable information do they provide?

2. What value did the IT/IS investments add to Albassami?

3. How did implementing the Shipping Information System address the business needs and information requirements of Albassami?

MIS IN ACTION

Please visit the IBM website (www.ibm.com) and read about IBM Enterprise Asset Management software and then answer the following questions:

1. Do you think that IBM enterprise asset management software could be beneficial to Albassami? Why or why not?

2. In case Albassami made the decision to implement the IBM software, what kind of extra investments would they need to make to enable the implementations?

3. Does IBM offer industry specific versions of their enterprise asset management software? If so, is the transportation industry one of them?

• Case contributed by Dr Ahmed Elragal, German University in Cairo

GENETIC ALGORITHMS

Genetic algorithms are useful for finding the optimal solution for a specific problem by examining a very large number of possible solutions for that problem. They are based on techniques inspired by evolutionary biology, such as inheritance, mutation, selection, and crossover (recombination).

A genetic algorithm works by representing information as a string of 0s and 1s. The genetic algorithm searches a population of randomly generated strings of binary digits to identify the right string representing the best possible solution for the problem. As solutions alter and combine, the worst ones are discarded and the better ones survive to go on to produce even better solutions.

In Figure 11-12, each string corresponds to one of the variables in the problem. One applies a test for fitness, ranking the strings in the population according to their level of desirability as possible solutions. After the initial population is evaluated for fitness, the algorithm then produces the next generation of strings, consisting of strings that survived the fitness test plus offspring strings produced from mating pairs of strings, and tests their fitness. The process continues until a solution is reached.

Genetic algorithms are used to solve problems that are very dynamic and complex, involving hundreds or thousands of variables or formulas. The problem must be one where the range of possible solutions can be represented genetically and criteria can be established for evaluating fitness. Genetic algorithms expedite the solution because they are able to evaluate

FIGURE 11-12 THE COMPONENTS OF A GENETIC ALGORITHM

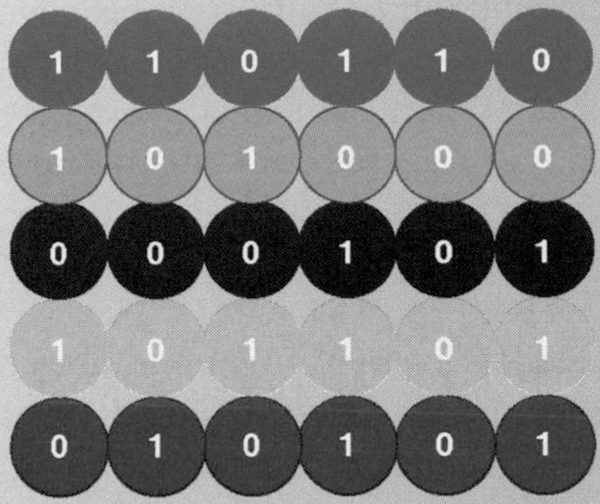

		Length	Width	Weight	Fitness
1 1 0 1 1 0	1	Long	Wide	Light	55
1 0 1 0 0 0	2	Short	Narrow	Heavy	49
0 0 0 1 0 1	3	Long	Narrow	Heavy	36
1 0 1 1 0 1	4	Short	Medium	Light	61
0 1 0 1 0 1	5	Long	Medium	Very light	74

A population of chromosomes | Decoding of chromosomes | Evaluation of chromosomes

This example illustrates an initial population of "chromosomes," each representing a different solution. The genetic algorithm uses an iterative process to refine the initial solutions so that the better ones, those with the higher fitness, are more likely to emerge as the best solution.

many solution alternatives quickly to find the best one. For example, General Electric engineers used genetic algorithms to help optimize the design for jet turbine aircraft engines, where each design change required changes in up to 100 variables. The supply chain management software from i2 Technologies uses genetic algorithms to optimize production-scheduling models incorporating hundreds of thousands of details about customer orders, material and resource availability, manufacturing and distribution capability, and delivery dates.

HYBRID AI SYSTEMS

Genetic algorithms, fuzzy logic, neural networks, and expert systems can be integrated into a single application to take advantage of the best features of these technologies. Such systems are called **hybrid AI systems**. Hybrid applications in business are growing. In Japan, Hitachi, Mitsubishi, Ricoh, Sanyo, and others are starting to incorporate hybrid AI in products such as home appliances, factory machinery, and office equipment. Matsushita has developed a "neurofuzzy" washing machine that combines fuzzy logic with neural networks. Nikko Securities has been working on a neurofuzzy system to forecast convertible-bond ratings.

INTELLIGENT AGENTS

Intelligent agent technology helps businesses navigate through large amounts of data to locate and act on information that is considered important. **Intelligent agents** are software programs that work in the background without direct human intervention to carry out specific, repetitive, and predictable tasks for an individual user, business process, or software application. The agent uses a limited built-in or learned knowledge base to accomplish tasks or make decisions on the user's behalf, such as deleting junk e-mail, scheduling appointments, or traveling over interconnected networks to find the cheapest airfare to California.

There are many intelligent agent applications today in operating systems, application software, e-mail systems, mobile computing software, and network tools. For example, the wizards found in Microsoft Office software tools have built-in capabilities to show users how to accomplish various tasks, such as formatting documents or creating graphs, and to anticipate when users need assistance.

Of special interest to business are intelligent agents for cruising networks, including the Internet, in search of information. Chapter 7 describes how shopping bots can help consumers find products they want and assist them in comparing prices and other features.

Many complex phenomena can be modeled as systems of autonomous agents that follow relatively simple rules for interaction. **Agent-based modeling** applications have been developed to model the behavior of consumers, stock markets, and supply chains and to predict the spread of epidemics (Samuelson and Macal, 2006).

Procter & Gamble used agent-based modeling to improve coordination among different members of its supply chain in response to changing business conditions (see Figure 11-13). It modeled a complex supply chain as a group of semiautonomous "agents" representing individual supply chain components, such as trucks, production facilities, distributors, and retail stores. The behavior of each agent is programmed to follow rules that mimic actual behavior, such as "order an item when it is out of stock." Simulations using the agents enable the company to perform what-if analyses on inventory levels, in-store stockouts, and transportation costs.

FIGURE 11-13 INTELLIGENT AGENTS IN P&G'S SUPPLY CHAIN NETWORK

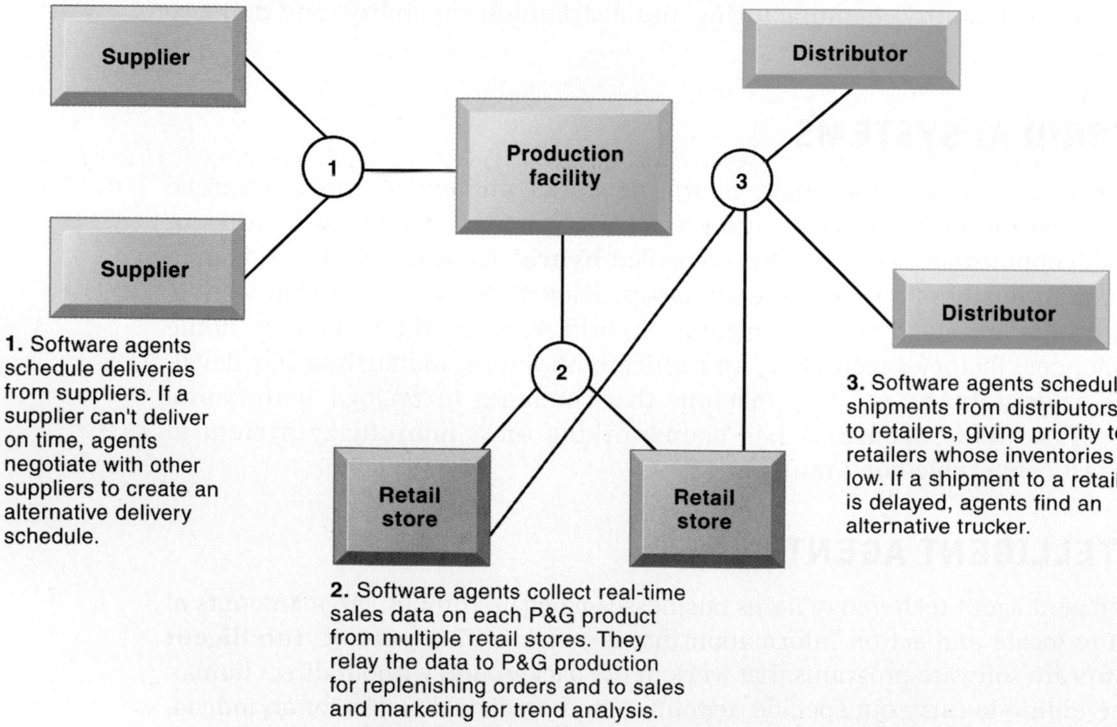
Supplier
Supplier
Production facility
Distributor
Distributor
Retail store
Retail store
1
2
3
1. Software agents schedule deliveries from suppliers. If a supplier can't deliver on time, agents negotiate with other suppliers to create an alternative delivery schedule.
2. Software agents collect real-time sales data on each P&G product from multiple retail stores. They relay the data to P&G production for replenishing orders and to sales and marketing for trend analysis.
3. Software agents schedule shipments from distributors to retailers, giving priority to retailers whose inventories are low. If a shipment to a retailer is delayed, agents find an alternative trucker.

Intelligent agents are helping P&G shorten the replenishment cycles for products such as a box of Tide.

Using intelligent agent models, P&G discovered that trucks should often be dispatched before being fully loaded. Although transportation costs would be higher using partially loaded trucks, the simulation showed that retail store stockouts would occur less often, thus reducing the amount of lost sales, which would more than make up for the higher distribution costs. Agent-based modeling has saved P&G $300 million annually on an investment of less than 1 percent of that amount (Anthes, 2003).

11.5   HANDS-ON MIS PROJECTS

The projects in this section give you hands-on experience designing a knowledge portal, applying collaboration tools to solve a customer retention problem, using an expert system or spreadsheet tools to create a simple expert system, and using intelligent agents to research products for sale on the Web.

Management Decision Problems

1. U.S. Pharma Corporation is headquartered in New Jersey but has research sites in Germany, France, the United Kingdom, Switzerland, and Australia. Research and development of new pharmaceuticals is the key to ongoing profits, and U.S. Pharma researches and tests thousands of possible drugs. The company's researchers need to share information with others within and outside the company, including the U.S. Food and Drug Administration, the World Health Organization, and the International Federation of Pharmaceutical Manufacturers & Associations. Also critical is access to health information sites, such as the U.S. National Library of Medicine and to industry conferences and professional journals. Design a knowledge portal for U.S. Pharma's researchers. Include in your design specifications relevant internal systems and databases, external sources of information, and internal and external communication and collaboration tools. Design a home page for your portal.

2. Sprint Nextel has the highest rate of customer churn (the number of customers who discontinue a service) in the cell phone industry, amounting to 2.45 percent. In the first quarter of 2008 alone, 1.1 million customers switched from Sprint to another cell phone carrier. Management wants to know why so many customers are leaving Sprint and what can be done to woo them back. Are customers deserting because of poor customer service, uneven network coverage, or the cost of Sprint cell phone plans? How can the company use tools for online collaboration and communication to help find the answer? What management decisions could be made using information from these sources?

Improving Decision Making: Building a Simple Expert System for Retirement Planning

Software skills: Spreadsheet formulas and IF function or expert system tool
Business skills: Benefits eligibility determination

Expert systems typically use a large number of rules. This project has been simplified to reduce the number of rules, but it will give you experience working with a series of rules to develop an application.

When employees at your company retire, they are given cash bonuses. These cash bonuses are based on the length of employment and the retiree's age. To receive a bonus, an employee must be at least 50 years of age and have worked for the company for five years. The following table summarizes the criteria for determining bonuses.

LENGTH OF EMPLOYMENT	BONUS
<5 years	No bonus
5–10 years	20 percent of current annual salary
11–15 years	30 percent of current annual salary
16–20 years	40 percent of current annual salary
20–25 years	50 percent of current annual salary
26 or more years	100 percent of current annual salary

Using the information provided, build a simple expert system. Find a demonstration copy of an expert system software tool on the Web that you can download. Alternatively, use your spreadsheet software to build the expert system. (If you are using spreadsheet software, we suggest using the IF function so you can see how rules are created.)

Improving Decision Making: Using Intelligent Agents for Comparison Shopping

Software skills: Web browser and shopping bot software
Business skills: Product evaluation and selection

This project will give you experience using shopping bots to search online for products, find product information, and find the best prices and vendors.

You have decided to purchase a new digital camera. Select a digital camera you might want to purchase, such as the Canon PowerShot SD 950 or the Olympus Stylus 1200. To purchase the camera as inexpensively as possible, try several of the shopping bot sites, which do the price comparisons for you. Visit My Simon (www.mysimon.com), BizRate.com (www.bizrate.com), and Google Product Search. Compare these shopping sites in terms of their ease of use, number of offerings, speed in obtaining information, thoroughness of information offered about the product and seller, and price selection. Which site or sites would you use and why? Which camera would you select and why? How helpful were these sites for making your decision?

LEARNING TRACK MODULE

The following Learning Track provides content relevant to topics covered in this chapter:

1. Challenges of Knowledge Management Systems

Review Summary

1. **What is the role of knowledge management and knowledge management programs in business?**

   Knowledge management is a set of processes to create, store, transfer, and apply knowledge in the organization. Much of a firm's value depends on its ability to create and manage knowledge. Knowledge management promotes organizational learning by increasing the ability of the organization to learn from its environment and to incorporate knowledge into its business processes. There are three major types of knowledge management systems: enterprise-wide knowledge management systems, knowledge work systems, and intelligent techniques.

2. **What types of systems are used for enterprise-wide knowledge management and how do they provide value for businesses?**

   Enterprise-wide knowledge management systems are firmwide efforts to collect, store, distribute, and apply digital content and knowledge. Enterprise content management systems provide databases and tools for organizing and storing structured documents and tools for organizing and storing semistructured knowledge, such as e-mail or rich media. Knowledge network systems provide directories and tools for locating firm employees with special expertise who are important sources of tacit knowledge. Often these systems include group collaboration tools (including wikis and social bookmarking), portals to simplify information access, search tools, and tools for classifying information based on a taxonomy that is appropriate for the organization. Enterprise-wide knowledge management systems can provide considerable value if they are well designed and enable employees to locate, share, and use knowledge more efficiently.

3. **What are the major types of knowledge work systems and how do they provide value for firms?**

   Knowledge work systems (KWS) support the creation of new knowledge and its integration into the organization. KWS require easy access to an external knowledge base; powerful computer hardware that can support software with intensive graphics, analysis, document management, and communications capabilities; and a user-friendly interface. Computer-aided design (CAD) systems and virtual reality systems, which create interactive simulations that behave like the real world, require graphics and powerful modeling capabilities. KWS for financial professionals provide access to external databases and the ability to analyze massive amounts of financial data very quickly.

4. **What are the business benefits of using intelligent techniques for knowledge management?**

   Artificial intelligence lacks the flexibility, breadth, and generality of human intelligence, but it can be used to capture, codify, and extend organizational knowledge. Expert systems capture tacit knowledge from a limited domain of human expertise and express that knowledge in the form of rules. Expert systems are most useful for problems of classification or diagnosis. Case-based reasoning represents organizational knowledge as a database of cases that can be continually expanded and refined.

   Fuzzy logic is a software technology for expressing knowledge in the form of rules that use approximate or subjective values. Fuzzy logic has been used for controlling physical devices and is starting to be used for limited decision-making applications.

   Neural networks consist of hardware and software that attempt to mimic the thought processes of the human brain. Neural networks are notable for their ability to learn without programming and to recognize patterns that cannot be easily described by humans. They are being used in science, medicine, and business to discriminate patterns in massive amounts of data.

   Genetic algorithms develop solutions to particular problems using genetically based processes such as fitness, crossover, and mutation. Genetic algorithms are beginning to be applied to problems involving optimization, product design, and monitoring industrial systems where many alternatives or variables must be evaluated to generate an optimal solution.

   Intelligent agents are software programs with built-in or learned knowledge bases that carry out specific, repetitive, and predictable tasks for an individual user, business process, or software application. Intelligent agents can be programmed to navigate through large amounts of data to locate useful information and in some cases act on that information on behalf of the user.

Key Terms

Review Questions

1. What is the role of knowledge management and knowledge management programs in business?

   - Define knowledge management and explain its value to businesses.

   - Describe the important dimensions of knowledge.

   - Distinguish between data, knowledge, and wisdom and between tacit knowledge and explicit knowledge.

   - Describe the stages in the knowledge management value chain.

2. What types of systems are used for enterprise-wide knowledge management and how do they provide value for businesses?

   - Define and describe the various types of enterprise-wide knowledge management systems and explain how they provide value for businesses.

   - Describe the role of the following in facilitating knowledge management: portals, wikis, social bookmarking, and learning management systems.

3. What are the major types of knowledge work systems and how do they provide value for firms?

   - Define knowledge work systems and describe the generic requirements of knowledge work systems.

   - Describe how the following systems support knowledge work: CAD, virtual reality, and investment workstations.

4. What are the business benefits of using intelligent techniques for knowledge management?

   - Define an expert system, describe how it works, and explain its value to business.

   - Define case-based reasoning and explain how it differs from an expert system.

   - Define a neural network, and describe how it works and how it benefits businesses.

   - Define and describe fuzzy logic, genetic algorithms, and intelligent agents. Explain how each works and the kinds of problems for which each is suited.

Discussion Questions

1. Knowledge management is a business process, not a technology. Discuss.
2. Describe various ways that knowledge management systems could help firms with sales and marketing or with manufacturing and production.

Video Cases

You will find video cases illustrating some of the concepts in this chapter on the Laudon Web site along with questions to help you analyze the cases.

Collaboration and Teamwork: Rating Knowledge Network Systems

With a group of classmates, select two knowledge network system products, such as AskMe Enterprise and Tacit ActiveNet™. Compare their features and capabilities. To prepare your analysis, use articles from computer magazines and the Web sites for the knowledge network software vendors. If possible, use electronic presentation software to present your find-ings to the class. If possible, use Google Sites to post links to Web pages, team communication announce-ments, and work assignments; to brainstorm; and to work collaboratively on project documents. Try to use Google Docs to develop a presentation of your find-ings for the class.

Knowledge Management and Collaboration at Tata Consulting Services
CASE STUDY

Tata Consultancy Services (TCS) is an IT-services, business-solutions and outsourcing organization that offers a portfolio of IT and IT-enabled services to clients all over the globe in horizontal, vertical, and geographical domains. A part of the Tata Group, India's largest industrial conglomerate, TCS has over 108,000 IT consultants in 47 countries.

The concept of knowledge management (KM) was introduced in TCS in 1995 and a dedicated KM team called "Corporate Groupware" was formed in 1998. This group launched the KM-pilot in mid-1999, which was implemented subsequently by a team comprising the steering committee, corporate GroupWare implanters, branch champions, application owners and the infrastructure group.

At that time, KM in TCS covered nearly every function, from quality assurance to HR management. While its 50 offices in India were linked through dedicated communication lines, overseas offices were connected through the Net and the Lotus Notes Domino Servers. The employees could access the knowledge repository that resided on the corporate and branch servers through the intranet, with a browser front-end or a Notes client. The knowledge repository, also called KBases contained a wide range of information about processes, line of business, line of technology, and projects.

Though the formal KM efforts started in TCS in the late 1990s, the informal, closely knit communities of practices (CoPs) had existed at TCS since the 1980s, when it had around a thousand employees. The earliest "group" was based on the migration of technologies. Later, teams were formed for mainframe, Unix, and databases. The groups, consisting of one or two experts in their respective fields, began formal documentation practices with the members writing down the best practices. Recollecting the group practices in the initial days, K Ananth Krishnan, technology consultant at that time said, "In the mid-eighties, we started documenting the problems and solutions. For mainframe, we had over 1,500 case studies.... Similarly, for quality area, we had around 40 reviewed case study documents way back in 1993."

The next step was to create Process Asset Libraries (PALs) which contained information related to technology, processes, and case studies for project lead-ers, which were made available to all development centers through the intranet.

Then Ultimatix, a web-based electronic knowledge management (EKM) portal, which made the knowledge globally available, was developed. The PAL library and KBases, which were hosted on the intranet, were merged with Ultimatix, which had sub-portals for a quality management system, software productivity improvement, training materials, and tools information. There were EKM administrators for each practice and subject group with defined responsibilities, such as editing the documents and approving them for publication. Commenting on the success of CoP, Krishnan said, "Between January 2003 and June 2003, CoP members had exchanged around 10,000 document transactions pertaining to the industry practices and 21,000 service practices via Ultimatix. The telecom CoP alone had 6,000 transactions. This excludes the intranet-based community activities."

To encourage employee conversations, TCS took considerable care in the architecture of its development centers, located across the country. Reflecting on the new design of one of its development centers in Sholinganallur, Chennai, CFO S Mahalingam said, "This center consists of modules, each dedicated to one particular technology or a client or an industry practice. These structures lead to garden terraces, where employees gather during their break for animated, informal conversations. ... When they converse with their colleagues, they often get solutions for problems they were vexed with."

TCS also launched a number of training programs such as the Initial Learning Program, targeted at new employees, the Continuous Learning Program for experienced employees, and the Leadership Development Program for employees with more than five years' experience. The integrated competency and learning management systems (iCALMS) that was deployed globally across all TCS offices promoted a culture of learning and growth in the organization. Equipped with data about competency definitions, role definitions, and online/classroom learning objectives it helped the consultants to enhance their skills in a customized manner. To gain cross-industry experience, TCS regularly rotated people across various functions and within other Tata Group companies. Employees were also encouraged to join outside bodies like the IEEE, and go in for certifications.

Knowmax, a knowledge management system, developed using Microsoft sharepoint portal server in 2007, gave TCS consultants access to nearly 40 years of experience and best practices, arranged by type of engagement, the technology in use, and customer requirements. It supported more than 60 knowledge assets and was accessible via Ultimatix to all TCS associates. Any associate could contribute to the K-Bank and Knowledge Officers were made responsible for maintaining the quality of content.

To maintain the work-life balance of its employees, TCS initiated Propel sessions which brought together employees with similar interests to conduct various activities such as reading books. Later, held every quarter through conferences and camps, this initiative also spurred knowledge transfer among the employees. The knowledge sharing at the project level was done through LiveMeeting application, where all the project meetings were recorded and stored in the project repository. Team members who missed the meeting, or any new members in the team, could listen to the recorded sessions and this enabled them to catch up with the rest of the team. Furthermore, Knowledge Transition sessions conducted weekly by the "Subject Matter Expert" helped the team to learn from the experience of the experts. "Tip of the Day" mail, comprising either technical, or conceptual, or human skills tips were also shared within the organization, almost daily.

Though Ultimatix, launched in 2002, digitized the entire organization from end to end and improved the business processes' efficiency, it still couldn't tap the knowledge of employees effectively. To improve collaboration among employees, Project Infinity was launched in 2007; this involved a number of technologies including IBM's Sametime, QuickPlace, Lotus Domino Collaboration tools, Avaya VOIP telephony, and Polycom IP videoconferencing.

As a result of adopting Infinity, collaboration of overseas and local offices improved as instant messaging (IM) got rid of cultural and pronunciation differences that could occur on the phone. Furthermore, corporate communications were able to run a 24-hour internal news broadcast to all TCS offices in the world. In addition, travel and telecommunications costs were reduced by 40 percent and 6 percent respectively.

Other than these channels, the company also used the JustAsk system (embedded into the KM), Blog platform, IdeaStorm, TIP, and My Site. Blogging had caught on rapidly since 2006 when it was first intro-

duced. Almost 40,000-50,000 TCS staff blogged on the intranet. While the JustAsk system allowed employees to post questions that others could answer, Idea Storm was a once-a-year event, where two to three topics were posted by the corporate team on which ideas were invited by everyone. TIP, an open portal for product innovation and potential new ideas was launched to promote the sharing of ideas. MySite, embedded into the KM portal, allowed each associate to have a personal page like Facebook or Orkut.

Sources: Sankaranarayanan G, "Building Communities, the TCS way," expressitpeople.com, September 2003; Kavita Kaur, "Give and Take," india-today.com, January 2000; Sunil Shah, "Network Wonder: Collaborative Tools Help TCS Grow," cio.com, July 2007; Shivani Shinde, "TCS Sees Synergy in Gen X Tools," rediff.com, July 2008.

CASE STUDY QUESTIONS

1. Analyze the knowledge management efforts at TCS using the knowledge management value chain model. Which tools or activities were used for managing tacit knowledge and which ones are used for explicit knowledge?

2. Describe the growth of knowledge management systems at TCS. How have these systems helped TCS in its business?

3. Describe the collaboration tools used at TCS? What benefits did TCS reap from these tools?

4. How did Web 2.0 tools help TCS to manage knowledge and collaboration among its employees?

5. How do you think KM tools have changed some key operational processes at TCS, such as bidding for new projects, project development and implementation, customer service, and so on?

• Case contributed by Neerja Sethi and Vijay Sethi, Nanyang Technological University

Chapter 12

Enhancing Decision Making

LEARNING OBJECTIVES

After reading this chapter, you will be able to answer the following questions:

1. What are the different types of decisions and how does the decision-making process work?

2. How do information systems support the activities of managers and management decision making?

3. How do decision-support systems (DSS) differ from MIS and how do they provide value to the business?

4. How do executive support systems (ESS) help senior managers make better decisions?

5. What is the role of information systems in helping people working in a group make decisions more efficiently?

CHAPTER OUTLINE

Interactive Sessions:

Too Many Bumped Fliers: Why?

Business Intelligence Turns Dick's Sporting Goods into a Winner

EASTERN MOUNTAIN SPORTS FORGES A TRAIL TO BETTER DECISIONS

Founded in 1967 by two rock climbers, Eastern Mountain Sports (EMS) has grown into one of the leading outdoor specialty retailers in the United States, with more than 80 retail stores in 16 states, a seasonal catalogue, and a growing online presence. EMS designs and offers a wide variety of gear and clothing for outdoor enthusiasts.

Until recently, however, the company's information systems for management reporting were dated and clumsy. It was very difficult for senior management to have a picture of customer purchasing patterns and company operations because data were stored in disparate sources: legacy merchandising systems, financial systems, and point-of-sale devices. Employees crafted most of the reports by hand, wasting valuable people resources on producing information rather than analyzing it.

After evaluating several leading business intelligence products, EMS selected WebFOCUS and iWay middleware from Information Builders Inc. EMS believed WebFOCUS was better than other tools in combining data from various sources and presenting the results in a user-friendly view. It is Web-based and easy to implement, taking EMS only 90 days to be up and running.

IWay extracts point-of-sale data from EMS's legacy enterprise system running on an IBM AS/400 midrange computer and loads them into a data mart running Microsoft's SQL Server database management system. WebFOCUS then creates a series of executive dashboards accessible through Web browsers, which provide a common view of the data to more than 200 users at headquarters and retail stores.

The dashboards provide a high-level view of key performance indicators such as sales, inventory, and margin levels, but enable users to drill down for more detail on specific transactions. Managers for merchandising monitor inventory levels and the rate that items turn over. E-commerce managers monitor hour-by-hour Web sales, visitors, and conversion rates. A color-coded system of red, yellow, and green alerts indicates metrics that are over, under, or at plan.

EMS is adding wikis and blogs to enable managers and employees to share tips and initiate dialogues about key pieces of data. For example, in identifying top-selling items and stores, EMS sales managers noticed that inner soles were moving very briskly in specialty stores. These stores had perfected a multi-step sales technique that included the recommendation of socks designed for specific uses, such as running or hiking, along with an inner sole custom-fit to each customer. Wikis and blogs made it easier for managers to discuss this tactic and share it with the rest of the retail network.

Longer term, EMS is planning for more detailed interactions with its suppliers. By sharing inventory and sales data with suppliers, EMS will be able to quickly restock inventory to meet customer demand, while suppliers will know when to ramp up production.

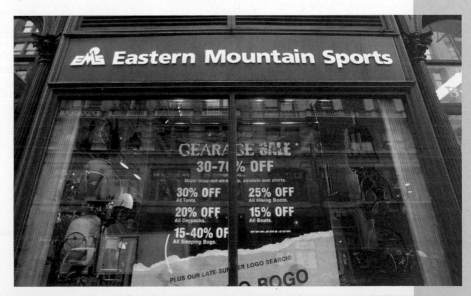

Sources: "Eastern Mountain Sports Forges a Trail to Merchandising Visibility," www.informationbuilders.com, accessed September 21, 2008; Jeffrey Neville, "X-treme Web 2.0," *Optimize Magazine*, January 2007; and "Web 2.0's Wild Blue Yonder," *Information Week*, January 1/8, 2007.

Eastern Mountain Sports' executive dashboards are a powerful illustration of how information systems improve decision making. Management was unable to make good decisions about how and where to stock stores because the required data were scattered in many different systems and were difficult to access. Management reporting was excessively manual. Bad decisions about how to stock stores and warehouses increased operating costs and prevented EMS stores from responding quickly to customer needs.

EMS management could have continued to use its outdated management reporting system or implemented a large-scale enterprise-wide database and software, which would have been extremely expensive and time-consuming to complete. Instead, it opted for a business intelligence solution that could extract, consolidate, and analyze sales and merchandising data from its various legacy systems. It chose a platform from Information Builders because the tools were user-friendly and capable of pulling together data from many different sources.

The chosen solution populates a data mart with data from point-of-sale and legacy systems and then pulls information from the data mart into a central series of executive dashboards visible to authorized users throughout the organization. Decision-makers are able to quickly access a unified high-level view of key performance indicators such as sales, inventory, and margin levels or drill down to obtain more detail about specific transactions. Increased availability of this information has helped EMS managers make better decisions about increasing sales, allocating resources, and propagating best practices.

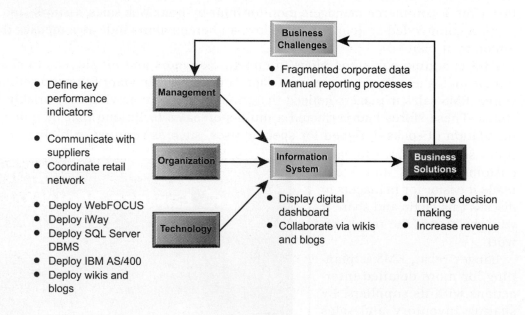

12.1   DECISION MAKING AND INFORMATION SYSTEMS

Decision making in businesses used to be limited to management. Today, lower-level employees are responsible for some of these decisions, as information systems make information available to lower levels of the business. But what do we mean by better decision making? How does decision making take place in businesses and other organizations? Let's take a closer look.

BUSINESS VALUE OF IMPROVED DECISION MAKING

What does it mean to the business to make better decisions? What is the monetary value of improved decision making? Table 12-1 attempts to measure the monetary value of improved decision making for a small U.S. manufacturing firm with $280 million in annual revenue and 140 employees. The firm has identified a number of key decisions where new system investments might improve the quality of decision making. The table provides selected estimates of annual value (in the form of cost savings or increased revenue) from improved decision making in selected areas of the business.

We can see from Table 12-1 that decisions are made at all levels of the firm and that some of these decisions are common, routine, and numerous. Although the value of improving any single decision may be small, improving hundreds of thousands of "small" decisions adds up to a large annual value for the business.

TYPES OF DECISIONS

Chapters 1 and 2 showed that there are different levels in an organization. Each of these levels has different information requirements for decision support and responsibility for different types of decisions (see Figure 12-1). Decisions are classified as structured, semistructured, and unstructured.

TABLE 12-1 BUSINESS VALUE OF ENHANCED DECISION MAKING

EXAMPLE DECISION	DECISION MAKER	NUMBER OF ANNUAL DECISIONS	ESTIMATED VALUE TO FIRM OF A SINGLE IMPROVED DECISION	ANNUAL VAUE
Allocate support to most valuable customers	Accounts manager	12	$ 100,000	$1,200,000
Predict call center daily demand	Call center management	4	150,000	600,000
Decide parts inventory levels daily	Inventory manager	365	5,000	1,825,000
Identify competitive bids from major suppliers	Senior management	1	2,000,000	2,000,000
Schedule production to fill orders	Manufacturing manager	150	10,000	1,500,000
Allocate labor to complete a job	Production floor manager	100	4,000	400,000

FIGURE 12-1 **INFORMATION REQUIREMENTS OF KEY DECISION-MAKING GROUPS IN A FIRM**

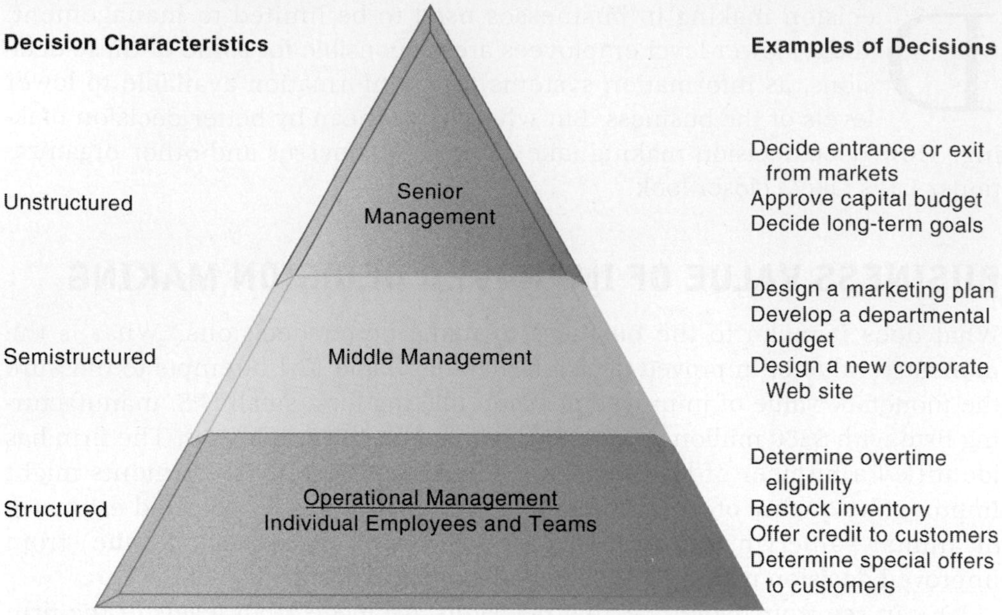

Decision Characteristics

Unstructured

Semistructured

Structured

Senior Management

Middle Management

Operational Management
Individual Employees and Teams

Examples of Decisions

Decide entrance or exit
  from markets
Approve capital budget
Decide long-term goals

Design a marketing plan
Develop a departmental
  budget
Design a new corporate
  Web site

Determine overtime
  eligibility
Restock inventory
Offer credit to customers
Determine special offers
  to customers

Senior managers, middle managers, operational managers, and employees have different types of decisions and information requirements.

Unstructured decisions are those in which the decision maker must provide judgment, evaluation, and insight to solve the problem. Each of these decisions is novel, important, and nonroutine, and there is no well-understood or agreed-on procedure for making them.

Structured decisions, by contrast, are repetitive and routine, and they involve a definite procedure for handling them so that they do not have to be treated each time as if they were new. Many decisions have elements of both types of decisions and are **semistructured**, where only part of the problem has a clear-cut answer provided by an accepted procedure. In general, structured decisions are more prevalent at lower organizational levels, whereas unstructured problems are more common at higher levels of the firm.

Senior executives face many unstructured decision situations, such as establishing the firm's five- or ten-year goals or deciding new markets to enter. Answering the question "Should we enter a new market?" would require access to news, government reports, and industry views as well as high-level summaries of firm performance. However, the answer would also require senior managers to use their own best judgment and poll other managers for their opinions.

Middle management faces more structured decision scenarios but their decisions may include unstructured components. A typical middle-level management decision might be "Why is the reported order fulfillment report showing a decline over the past six months at a distribution center in Minneapolis?" This middle manager will obtain a report from the firm's enterprise system or distribution management system on order activity and operational efficiency at the Minneapolis distribution center. This is the structured part of the decision. But before arriving at an answer, this middle manager will have to interview employees and gather more unstructured information from external sources about local economic conditions or sales trends.

Operational management and rank-and-file employees tend to make more structured decisions. For example, a supervisor on an assembly line has to decide whether an hourly paid worker is entitled to overtime pay. If the employee worked more than eight hours on a particular day, the supervisor would routinely grant overtime pay for any time beyond eight hours that was clocked on that day.

A sales account representative often has to make decisions about extending credit to customers by consulting the firm's customer database that contains credit information. If the customer met the firm's prespecified criteria for granting credit, the account representative would grant that customer credit to make a purchase. In both instances, the decisions are highly structured and are routinely made thousands of times each day in most large firms. The answer has been preprogrammed into the firm's payroll and accounts receivable systems.

THE DECISION-MAKING PROCESS

Making a decision is a multistep process. Simon (1960) described four different stages in decision making: intelligence, design, choice, and implementation (see Figure 12-2).

FIGURE 12-2   STAGES IN DECISION MAKING

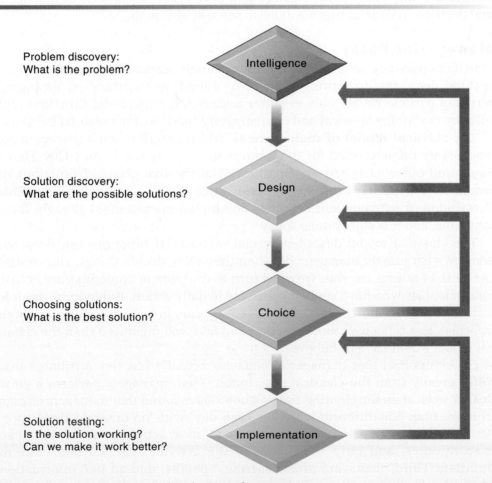

Problem discovery:
What is the problem?

Intelligence

Solution discovery:
What are the possible solutions?

Design

Choosing solutions:
What is the best solution?

Choice

Solution testing:
Is the solution working?
Can we make it work better?

Implementation

The decision-making process is broken down into four stages.

Intelligence consists of discovering, identifying, and understanding the problems occurring in the organization—why a problem exists, where, and what effects it is having on the firm.

Design involves identifying and exploring various solutions to the problem.

Choice consists of choosing among solution alternatives.

Implementation involves making the chosen alternative work and continuing to monitor how well the solution is working.

What happens if the solution you have chosen doesn't work? Figure 12-2 shows that you can return to an earlier stage in the decision-making process and repeat it if necessary. For instance, in the face of declining sales, a sales management team may decide to pay the sales force a higher commission for making more sales to spur on the sales effort. If this does not produce sales increases, managers would need to investigate whether the problem stems from poor product design, inadequate customer support, or a host of other causes that call for a different solution.

MANAGERS AND DECISION MAKING IN THE REAL WORLD

The premise of this book and this chapter is that systems to support decision making produce better decision making by managers and employees, above average returns on investment for the firm, and ultimately higher profitability. However, information systems cannot improve all the different kinds of decisions taking place in an organization. Let's examine the role of managers and decision making in organizations to see why this is so.

Managerial Roles

Managers play key roles in organizations. Their responsibilities range from making decisions, to writing reports, to attending meetings, to arranging birthday parties. We are able to better understand managerial functions and roles by examining classical and contemporary models of managerial behavior.

The **classical model of management**, which describes what managers do, was largely unquestioned for the more than 70 years since the 1920s. Henri Fayol and other early writers first described the five classical functions of managers as planning, organizing, coordinating, deciding, and controlling. This description of management activities dominated management thought for a long time, and it is still popular today.

The classical model describes formal managerial functions but does not address what exactly managers do when they plan, decide things, and control the work of others. For this, we must turn to the work of contemporary behavioral scientists who have studied managers in daily action. **Behavioral models** state that the actual behavior of managers appears to be less systematic, more informal, less reflective, more reactive, and less well organized than the classical model would have us believe.

Observers find that managerial behavior actually has five attributes that differ greatly from the classical description. First, managers perform a great deal of work at an unrelenting pace—studies have found that managers engage in more than 600 different activities each day, with no break in their pace. Second, managerial activities are fragmented; most activities last for less than nine minutes, and only 10 percent of the activities exceed one hour in duration. Third, managers prefer current, specific, and ad hoc information (printed information often will be too old). Fourth, they prefer oral forms of communication to written forms because oral media provide greater flexibility, require less effort, and bring a faster response. Fifth, managers give high priority to maintaining a diverse and complex web of contacts that acts as an informal information system and helps them execute their personal agendas and short- and long-term goals.

Analyzing managers' day-to-day behavior, Mintzberg found that it could be classified into 10 managerial roles. **Managerial roles** are expectations of the activities that managers should perform in an organization. Mintzberg found that these managerial roles fell into three categories: interpersonal, informational, and decisional.

Interpersonal Roles. Managers act as figureheads for the organization when they represent their companies to the outside world and perform symbolic duties, such as giving out employee awards, in their **interpersonal role**. Managers act as leaders, attempting to motivate, counsel, and support subordinates. Managers also act as liaisons between various organizational levels; within each of these levels, they serve as liaisons among the members of the management team. Managers provide time and favors, which they expect to be returned.

Informational Roles. In their **informational role**, managers act as the nerve centers of their organizations, receiving the most concrete, up-to-date information and redistributing it to those who need to be aware of it. Managers are therefore information disseminators and spokespersons for their organizations.

Decisional Roles. Managers make decisions. In their **decisional role**, they act as entrepreneurs by initiating new kinds of activities; they handle disturbances arising in the organization; they allocate resources to staff members who need them; and they negotiate conflicts and mediate between conflicting groups.

Table 12-2, based on Mintzberg's role classifications, is one look at where systems can and cannot help managers. The table shows that information systems do not yet contribute to some important areas of management life.

TABLE 12-2 MANAGERIAL ROLES AND SUPPORTING INFORMATION SYSTEMS

ROLE	BEHAVIOR	SUPPORT SYSTEMS
Interpersonal Roles		
Figurehead		None exist
Leader	Interpersonal	None exist
Liaison		Electronic communication systems
Informational Roles		
Nerve center		Management information systems, ESS
Disseminator	Information	Mail, office systems
Spokesperson	processing	Office and professional systems, workstations
Decisional Roles		
Entrepreneur	Decision	None exist
Disturbance handler	making	None exist
Resource allocator		DSS systems
Negotiator		None exist

Sources: Kenneth C. Laudon and Jane P. Laudon; and Mintzberg, 1971.

Real-World Decision Making

We now see that information systems are not helpful for all managerial roles. And in those managerial roles where information systems might improve decisions, investments in information technology do not always produce positive results. There are three main reasons: information quality, management filters, and organizational culture (see Chapter 3).

Information Quality. High-quality decisions require high-quality information. Table 12-3 describes information quality dimensions that affect the quality of decisions.

If the output of information systems does not meet these quality criteria, decision-making will suffer. Chapter 6 has shown that corporate databases and files have varying levels of inaccuracy and incompleteness, which in turn will degrade the quality of decision making.

Management Filters. Even with timely, accurate information, some managers make bad decisions. Managers (like all human beings) absorb information through a series of filters to make sense of the world around them. Managers have selective attention, focus on certain kinds of problems and solutions, and have a variety of biases that reject information that does not conform to their prior conceptions.

For instance, Wall Street firms such as Bear Stearns and Lehman Brothers imploded in 2008 because they underestimated the risk of their investments in complex mortgage securities, many of which were based on subprime loans that were more likely to default. The computer models they and other financial institutions used to manage risk were based on overly optimistic assumptions and overly simplistic data about what might go wrong. Management wanted to make sure that their firms' capital was not all tied up as a cushion against defaults from risky investments, preventing them from investing it to generate profits. So the designers of these risk management systems were encouraged to measure risks in a way that did not pick them all up. Some trading desks also oversimplified the information maintained about the mortgage securities to make them appear as simple bonds with higher ratings than were warranted by their underlying components (Hansell, 2008).

Organizational Inertia and Politics. Organizations are bureaucracies with limited capabilities and competencies for acting decisively. When environments change and businesses need to adopt new business models to survive,

TABLE 12-3 INFORMATION QUALITY DIMENSIONS

QUALITY DIMENSION	DESCRIPTION
Accuracy	Do the data represent reality?
Integrity	Are the structure of data and relationships among the entities and attributes consistent?
Consistency	Are data elements consistently defined?
Completeness	Are all the necessary data present?
Validity	Do data values fall within defined ranges?
Timeliness	Area data available when needed?
Accessibility	Are the data accessible, comprehensible, and usable?

strong forces within organizations resist making decisions calling for major change. Decisions taken by a firm often represent a balancing of the firm's various interest groups rather than the best solution to the problem.

Studies of business restructuring find that firms tend to ignore poor performance until threatened by outside takeovers, and they systematically blame poor performance on external forces beyond their control such as economic conditions (the economy), foreign competition, and rising prices, rather than blaming senior or middle management for poor business judgment (John, Lang, Netter, et al., 1992).

12.2 SYSTEMS FOR DECISION SUPPORT

There are four kinds of systems for supporting the different levels and types of decisions we have just described. We introduced some of these systems in Chapter 2. *Management information systems (MIS)* provide routine reports and summaries of transaction-level data to middle and operational level managers to provide answers to structured and semistructured decision problems. *Decision-support systems (DSS)* provide analytical models or tools for analyzing large quantities of data for middle managers who face semistructured decision situations. *Executive support systems (ESS)* are systems that provide senior management, making primarily unstructured decisions, with external information (news, stock analyses, and industry trends) and high-level summaries of firm performance.

In this chapter, you'll also learn about systems for supporting decision-makers working as a group. **Group decision-support systems (GDSS)** are specialized systems that provide a group electronic environment in which managers and teams are able to collectively make decisions and design solutions for unstructured and semistructured problems.

MANAGEMENT INFORMATION SYSTEMS (MIS)

MIS, which we introduced in Chapter 2 help managers monitor and control the business by providing information on the firm's performance. They typically produce fixed, regularly scheduled reports based on data extracted and summarized from the firm's underlying transaction processing systems (TPS). Sometimes, MIS reports are exception reports, highlighting only exceptional conditions, such as when the sales quotas for a specific territory fall below an anticipated level or employees have exceeded their spending limits in a dental care plan. Today, many of these reports are available online through an intranet, and more MIS reports are generated on demand. Table 12-4 provides some examples of MIS applications.

DECISION-SUPPORT SYSTEMS (DSS)

Whereas MIS primarily address structured problems, DSS support semistructured and unstructured problem analysis. The earliest DSS were heavily model-driven, using some type of model to perform "what-if" and other kinds of analyses. Their analysis capabilities were based on a strong theory or model combined with a good user interface that made the system easy to use. The voyage-estimating DSS and Air Canada maintenance system described in Chapter 2 are examples of model-driven DSS.

TABLE 12-4 EXAMPLES OF MIS APPLICATIONS

COMPANY	MIS APPLICATION
California Pizza Kitchen	Inventory Express application "remembers" each restaurant's ordering patterns and compares the amount of ingredients used per menu item to predefined portion measurements established by management. The system identifies restaurants with out-of-line portions and notifies their managers so that corrective actions will be taken.
PharMark	Extranet MIS identifies patients with drug-use patterns that place them at risk for adverse outcomes.
Black & Veatch	Intranet MIS tracks construction costs for various projects across the United States.
Taco Bell	Total Automation of Company Operations (TACO) system provides information on food, labor, and period-to-date costs for each restaurant.

The Interactive Session on Management describes another model-driven DSS. In this particular case, the system did not perform as well as expected because of the assumptions driving the model and user efforts to circumvent the system. As you read this case, try to identify the problem this company was facing, what alternative solutions were available to management, and how well the chosen solution worked.

Some contemporary DSS are data-driven, using online analytical processing (OLAP), and data mining to analyze large pools of data. The business intelligence applications described in Chapter 6 are examples of these data-driven DSS, as are the spreadsheet pivot table applications we describe in this section. **Data-driven DSS** support decision making by enabling users to extract useful information that was previously buried in large quantities of data. The Interactive Session on Technology provides an example.

Components of DSS

Figure 12-3 illustrates the components of a DSS. They include a database of data used for query and analysis; a software system with models, data mining, and other analytical tools; and a user interface.

The **DSS database** is a collection of current or historical data from a number of applications or groups. It may be a small database residing on a PC that contains a subset of corporate data that has been downloaded and possibly combined with external data. Alternatively, the DSS database may be a massive data warehouse that is continuously updated by major corporate TPS (including enterprise applications) and data generated by Web site transactions). The data in DSS databases are generally extracts or copies of production databases so that using the DSS does not interfere with critical operational systems.

The DSS user interface permits easy interaction between users of the system and the DSS software tools. Many DSS today have Web interfaces to take advantage of graphical displays, interactivity, and ease of use.

The **DSS software system** contains the software tools that are used for data analysis. It may contain various OLAP tools, data mining tools, or a collection of mathematical and analytical models that are accessible to the DSS user. A **model** is an abstract representation that illustrates the components or relationships of a phenomenon. A model may be a physical model (such as a model airplane), a mathematical model (such as an equation), or a verbal model (such as a description of a procedure for writing an order).

INTERACTIVE SESSION: MANAGEMENT

TOO MANY BUMPED FLIERS: WHY?

In a seemingly simpler and less hectic time, over-booked flights presented an opportunity. Frequent travelers regularly and eagerly chose to give up their seats and delay their departures by a few hours in exchange for rewards such as a voucher for a free ticket.

Today, fewer people are volunteering to give up their seats for a flight because there are fewer and fewer seats to be bumped to. Airlines are struggling to stay in business and look to save costs wherever possible. They are scheduling fewer flights and those flights are more crowded. Instead of delaying his or her trip by a few hours, a passenger that accepts a voucher for being bumped may have to wait several days before a seat becomes available on another flight. And passengers are being bumped from flights involuntarily more often.

Airlines routinely overbook flights to compensate for the millions of no-shows that cut into expected revenue. The purpose of overbooking is not to leave passengers without a seat, but to come as close as possible to filling every seat on every flight. The revenue lost from an empty seat is much greater than the costs of compensating a bumped passenger. Airlines are much closer today to filling every seat on flights than at any point in their history. The problem is, the most popular routes often sell out, so bumped passengers may be stranded for days.

The airlines do not approach overbooking haphazardly. They employ young, sharp minds with backgrounds in math and economics as analysts. The analysts use computer modeling to predict how many passengers will fail to show up for a flight. They recommend overbooking based on the numbers generated by the software.

The software used by US Airways, for example, analyzes the historical record of no-shows on flights and looks at the rate at every fare level available. The lowest-priced fares are generally nonrefundable, and passengers at those fare levels tend to carry their reservations through. Business travelers with the high-priced fares no-show more often. The software examines the fares people are booking on each upcoming flight and takes other data into account, such as the rate of no-shows on flights originating from certain geographic regions. Analysts then predict the number of no-shows on a particular

flight, based on which fares passengers have booked, and overbook the flight accordingly.

Of course, the analysts don't always guess correctly. And their efforts may be hampered by a number of factors. Ticket agents report that faulty computer algorithms result in miscalculations. Changes in weather can introduce unanticipated weight restrictions. Sometimes a smaller plane is substituted for the scheduled plane. All of these circumstances result in fewer seats being available for the same number of passengers, which might have been set too high already.

Regardless of how much support the analysts have from airline management, gate attendants complain because they are the ones who receive the brunt of overbooked passengers' wrath. Attendants have been known to call in sick to avoid dealing with the havoc caused by overbooked flights.

Some gate attendants have gone as far as creating phony reservations, sometimes in the names of airline executives or cartoon characters, such as Mickey Mouse, in an effort to stop analysts from overbooking. This tactic may save the attendants some grief in the short term, but their actions often come back to haunt them. The modeling software counts the phony reservations as no-shows, which leads the analysts to overbook the flight even more the next time. Thomas Trenga, vice president for revenue management at US Airways, refers to this game of chicken as "the death spiral." US Airways discourages the practice of entering phony reservations.

With fewer passengers volunteering to accept vouchers, tensions often escalate. The number of passengers bumped involuntarily in 2006 rose 23 percent from the previous year and has continued to rise. The encouraging statistic is that only 676,408 of the 555 million people who flew in 2006 were bumped, voluntarily or involuntarily.

W. Douglas Parker, CEO of US Airways, said that airlines have to overbook their flights as long as they allow passengers to no-show without penalty. US Airways has a no-show rate of between 7 and 8 percent. US Airways claimed that overbooking contributed to at least $1 billion of its 2006 revenue of $11.56 billion. With a profit of only $304 million, that extra revenue was critical to the survival of the business. Some airlines, such as JetBlue, have avoided the overbooking controversy by offering only nonrefundable tickets. No-shows cannot reclaim the price of their tickets. Business travelers often buy the most expensive seats, but also want the flexibility of refundable tickets, so JetBlue is considering a change in its policy.

The airlines are supposed to hold their analysts accountable for their work, but they are rarely subject to critical review. Some analysts make an effort to accommodate the wishes of the airport workers by finding a compromise in the overbooking rate. Unfortunately, analysts often leave their jobs for new challenges once they become proficient at overbooking.

Sources: Dean Foust and Justin Bachman, "You Think Flying Is Bad Now...," *Business Week*, May 28, 2008; "The Unfriendly Skies," *USA Today*, June 4, 2008; Jeff Bailey, "Bumped Fliers and Plan B," *The New York Times*, May 30, 2007; and Alice LaPlante, "Travel Problems? Blame Technology," *InformationWeek.com*, June 11, 2007.

CASE STUDY QUESTIONS

1. Is the decision support system being used by airlines to overbook flights working well? Answer from the perspective of the airlines and from the perspective of customers.
2. What is the impact on the airlines if they are bumping too many passengers?
3. What are the inputs, processes, and outputs of this DSS?
4. What people, organization, and technology factors are responsible for excessive bumping problems?
5. How much of this is a "people" problem? Explain your answer.

MIS IN ACTION

Visit the Web sites for US Airways, JetBlue, and Continental. Search the sites to answer the following questions:

1. What is the policy of each of these airlines for dealing with involuntary refunds (overbookings)? (Hint: These matters are often covered in the Contract of Carriage.)
2. In your opinion, which airline has the best policy? What makes this policy better than the others?
3. How are each of these policies intended to benefit customers? How do they benefit the airlines?

FIGURE 12-3   **OVERVIEW OF A DECISION-SUPPORT SYSTEM**

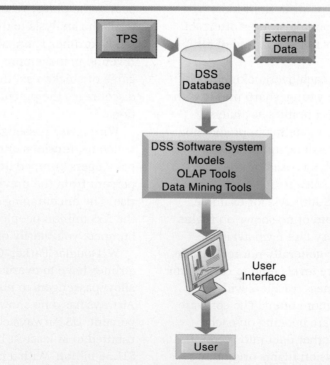

The main components of the DSS are the DSS database, the user interface, and the DSS software system. The DSS database may be a small database residing on a PC or a large data warehouse.

INTERACTIVE SESSION: TECHNOLOGY

BUSINESS INTELLIGENCE TURNS DICK'S SPORTING GOODS INTO A WINNER

Dick's Sporting Goods is a prominent retailer of sporting apparel and equipment based primarily in the eastern half of the United States. The company was founded in 1948 by Dick Stack, who was only 18 years old at the time. Stack's business initially sold only fishing supplies, but gradually expanded to sell general sporting goods. In the 1990s, under the stewardship of Stack's son Ed, the retailer began rapid growth in an effort to become a national sporting goods chain. Today, Dick's operates over 300 stores in 34 states and earns annual revenue of just under $4 billion. It also owns Golf Galaxy, a golf specialty retailer. The company planned to add 44 new stores in 2008 and has maintained a strong position during difficult economic conditions.

Dick's has flourished because it focuses on being an authentic sporting goods retailer by offering a broad selection of high-quality, competitively priced brand-name sporting goods equipment, apparel, and footwear that enhances its customers' performance and enjoyment of their sports activities. However, Dick's has had problems managing its inventory and making decisions about how to stock its stores. These problems stemmed from outdated merchandise management software and threatened to curtail Dick's lofty plans for the future.

The company initially used a merchandising system from STS as a basic reporting tool. The system wasn't well suited to the needs of the company. It was able to compile sales figures for athletic gear and clothing, but it wasn't able to analyze how a specific item, such as a Wilson Tennis n4 racquet, was performing regionally or in a particular store. Instead, it automatically aggregated information from all stores and combined it into a single report. Retrieving data from the database was a long, inefficient process, sometimes taking over an hour to complete, and wasn't satisfactory for answering questions requiring complex analysis.

Because there was no central repository for company information, it was also difficult to tell whether or not a particular report was accurate. There were no standard company-wide sales and inventory reports. The company lacked a unified database that all of the company's employees could access. Employees kept their own analyses of sales and inventory in their own departments and on

their own machines. Sometimes they lost their reports because they did not remember the names of their data files. Recognizing the problems, Dick's attempted to roll out new tools intended to update the company's data storage and information retrieval processes. But employees resisted the change, preferring the methods they were used to over new tools from Cognos, a maker of business intelligence software.

Dick's decided to perform a complete overhaul of their data storage system in 2003. The new system featured software from MicroStrategy and a database from Oracle. The database Dick's selected was Oracle's 8i database with customized capabilities to extract data and the ability to transform to meet different business requirements. It has since been upgraded to a more advanced 10g model. The new system was able to track the sale of apparel and equipment in each store and by region.

The new system was launched with a training program to promote user adoption, so that employees didn't persist in using the old system that they were more accustomed to. Even with the new training system, employee adoption was slow, but the company offered incentives to using the new system and gradually phased out the old one. Only when the old system was phased out completely did adoption of the new system increase tenfold. Some of the failings of previous information systems were attributed to lack of training programs to smooth the difficulties of adopting new systems, and this time around Dick's ensured that the proper programs were in place.

The MicroStrategy software was a key element of Dick's overhaul. What sets MicroStrategy apart from competing products is its ability to work with relational databases via relational online analytical processing (ROLAP). Multidimensional OLAP uses a multidimensional database for analysis (see Chapter 6), whereas ROLAP accesses data directly from data warehouses. It dynamically consolidates data for ad hoc and decision support analyses and scales to a large number of business analysis perspectives (dimensions) while MOLAP generally performs efficiently with 10 or fewer dimensions. The software allows Dick's employees to perform detailed analyses to track sales and inventory levels.

MicroStrategy allows Dick's employees to create different types of reports. For example, 'canned' reports are reports with settings frequently used by other employees. If an employee needs a report with commonly requested parameters, canned reports save workers the time and energy required to expressly set those parameters. On the other hand, 'self-service' reports have customized inputs and outputs for instances when a unique piece of information is sought. Processes that once took hours now take mere minutes because of the system's interaction with the master database, which consists of multiple terabytes of data.

Recent results suggest that the implementation has paid off for Dick's, as their earnings have doubled since the initiative began and their operating margin has been close to double that of their competitors going forward. Sales in Q1 2008 were up 11 percent to $912 million, and although the company hasn't been immune to the difficult economic conditions, the company is outperforming its competitors and has its sights set on gaining market share during the downturn. Although the company's stock price has not reached levels that it was expected to in the past several years, the company's future outlook remains positive, in large part due to their successful IT implementation.

Sources: MicroStrategy, "Success Story: Dick's Sporting Goods Inc.," 2008; Brian P. Watson, "Business Intelligence: Will It Improve Inventory?" www.baselinemag.com, May 14, 2007; "Dick's Sporting Goods Form 10-K Annual Report," March 27, 2008; "Dick's Sporting Goods Inc., Q1 2008 Earnings Call Transcript," www.seekingalpha.com, May 22, 2008.

CASE STUDY QUESTIONS

1. What problems did Dick's face with its data tracking and reporting? How did they affect decision making and business performance?

2. What did the company do to remedy those problems?

3. Was MicroStrategy an appropriate selection for Dick's? Why or why not?

4. Has improved reporting solved all of this company's problems? Explain your answer.

MIS IN ACTION

Explore the MicroStrategy Web site and then answer the following questions:

1. Describe the capabilities of MicroStrategy software. List the capabilities that would be most useful for supporting decisions about stocking Dick's stores. Explain how the software would help Dick's employees with these decisions.

2. Review the section on MicroStrategy's Dynamic Enterprise Dashboards. Then design a dashboard for a manager deciding how to stock Dick's stores.

Statistical modeling helps establish relationships, such as relating product sales to differences in age, income, or other factors between communities. Optimization models determine optimal resource allocation to maximize or minimize specified variables, such as cost or time. A classic use of optimization models is to determine the proper mix of products within a given market to maximize profits.

Forecasting models often are used to forecast sales. The user of this type of model might supply a range of historical data to project future conditions and the sales that might result from those conditions. The decision maker could vary those future conditions (entering, for example, a rise in raw materials costs or the entry of a new, low-priced competitor in the market) to determine how new conditions might affect sales.

Sensitivity analysis models ask "what-if" questions repeatedly to determine the impact on outcomes of changes in one or more factors. *What-if analysis*— working forward from known or assumed conditions—allows the user to vary certain values to test results to better predict outcomes if changes occur in those values. What happens if we raise product price by 5 percent or increase the advertising budget by $100,000? What happens if we keep the price and advertising budgets the same? Desktop spreadsheet software, such as Microsoft Excel, is often used for this purpose (see Figure 12-4). Backward-sensitivity analysis software helps decision makers with goal seeking: If I want to sell one million product units next year, how much must I reduce the price of the product?

Using Spreadsheet Pivot Tables to Support Decision Making

Managers also use spreadsheets to identify and understand patterns in business information. For instance, let's a take a look at one day's worth of transactions at an online firm Online Management Training Inc. (OMT Inc.) that sells online management training videos and books to corporations and individuals who want to improve their management techniques. On a single day the firm experienced 517 order transactions. Figure 12-5 shows the first 25 records of transactions produced at the firm's Web site on that day. The names of customers and other identifiers have been removed from this list.

You might think of this list as a database composed of transaction records (the rows). The fields (column headings) for each customer record are: customer ID, region of purchase, payment method, source of contact (e-mail versus Web banner ad), amount of purchase, the product purchased (either online training or a book), and time of day (in 24-hour time).

There's a great deal of valuable information in this transaction list that might help managers answer important questions and make important decisions:

- Where do most of our customers come from? The answer might tell managers where to spend more marketing resources, or to initiate new marketing efforts.

- Are there regional differences in the sources of our customers? Perhaps in some regions, e-mail is the most effective marketing tool, whereas in other regions, Web banner ads are more effective. The answer to this more complicated question might help managers develop a regional marketing strategy.

- Where are the average purchases higher? The answer might tell managers where to focus marketing and sales resources, or pitch different messages to different regions.

FIGURE 12-4   SENSITIVITY ANALYSIS

Total fixed costs	19000					
Variable cost per unit	3					
Average sales price	17					
Contribution margin	14					
Break-even point	1357					
			Variable Cost per Unit			
Sales	1357	2	3	4	5	6
Price	14	1583	1727	1900	2111	2375
	15	1462	1583	1727	1900	2111
	16	1357	1462	1583	1727	1900
	17	1267	1357	1462	1583	1727
	18	1188	1267	1357	1462	1583

This table displays the results of a sensitivity analysis of the effect of changing the sales price of a necktie and the cost per unit on the product's break-even point. It answers the question, "What happens to the break-even point if the sales price and the cost to make each unit increase or decrease?"

FIGURE 12-5 SAMPLE LIST OF TRANSACTIONS FOR ONLINE MANAGEMENT TRAINING INC.

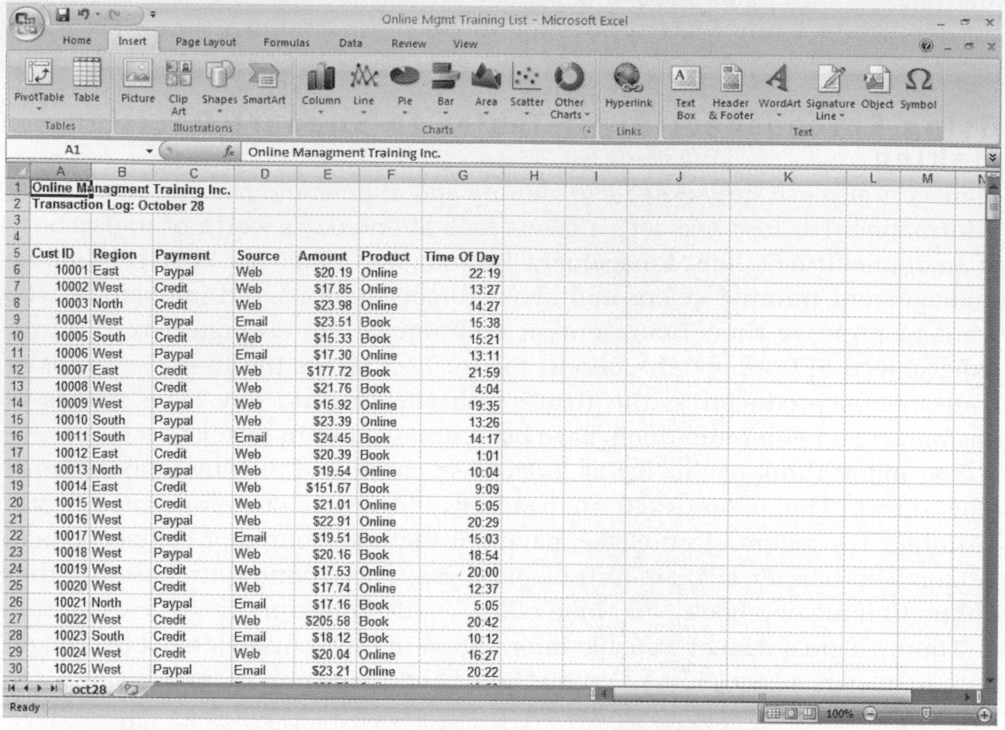

Cust ID	Region	Payment	Source	Amount	Product	Time Of Day
10001	East	Paypal	Web	$20.19	Online	22:19
10002	West	Credit	Web	$17.85	Online	13:27
10003	North	Credit	Web	$23.98	Online	14:27
10004	West	Paypal	Email	$23.51	Book	15:38
10005	South	Credit	Web	$15.33	Book	15:21
10006	West	Paypal	Email	$17.30	Online	13:11
10007	East	Credit	Web	$177.72	Book	21:59
10008	West	Credit	Web	$21.76	Book	4:04
10009	West	Paypal	Web	$15.92	Online	19:35
10010	South	Paypal	Web	$23.39	Online	13:26
10011	South	Paypal	Email	$24.45	Book	14:17
10012	East	Credit	Web	$20.39	Book	1:01
10013	North	Paypal	Web	$19.54	Online	10:04
10014	East	Credit	Web	$151.67	Book	9:09
10015	West	Credit	Web	$21.01	Online	5:05
10016	West	Paypal	Web	$22.91	Online	20:29
10017	West	Credit	Email	$19.51	Book	15:03
10018	West	Paypal	Web	$20.16	Book	18:54
10019	West	Credit	Web	$17.53	Online	20:00
10020	West	Credit	Web	$17.74	Online	12:37
10021	North	Paypal	Email	$17.16	Book	5:05
10022	West	Credit	Web	$205.58	Book	20:42
10023	South	Credit	Email	$18.12	Book	10:12
10024	West	Credit	Web	$20.04	Online	16:27
10025	West	Paypal	Email	$23.21	Online	20:22

This list shows a portion of the order transactions for Online Management Training Inc. (OMT Inc.) on October 28, 2008.

- What form of payment is the most common? The answer might be used to emphasize in advertising the most preferred means of payment.
- Are there any times of day when purchases are most common? Do people buy products while at work (likely during the day) or at home (likely in the evening)?
- Are there regional differences in the average purchase? If one region is much more lucrative, managers could focus their marketing and advertising resources on that region.

Notice that these questions often involve multiple dimensions: region and average purchase; time of day and average purchase; payment type and average purchase; and region, source of customer, and purchase. Also, some of the dimensions are categorical, such as payment type, region, and source. If the list were small, you might simply inspect the list and find patterns in the data. But this is impossible when you have a list of over 500 transactions.

Fortunately, the spreadsheet pivot table provides a powerful tool for answering such questions using large data sets. A **pivot table** is a table that displays two or more dimensions of data in a convenient format. Microsoft Excel's PivotTable capability makes it easy to analyze lists and databases by automatically extracting, organizing, and summarizing the data.

For instance, let's take the first question, "Where do our customers come from?" We'll start with region and ask the question, "How many customers come from each region?" To find the answer using Excel 2007, you would create a pivot table by selecting the range of data, fields you want to analyze, and a location for the PivotTable report, as illustrated in Figure 12-6. The PivotTable report shows most of our customers come from the Western region.

FIGURE 12-6   A PIVOT TABLE THAT DETERMINES THE REGIONAL DISTRIBUTION OF CUSTOMERS

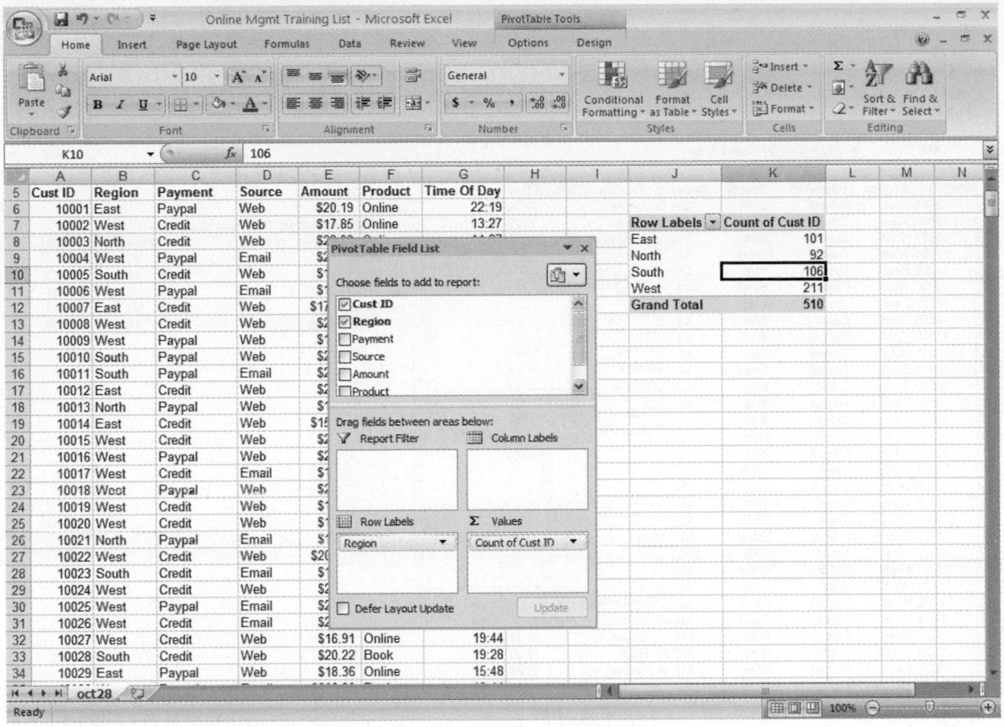

This PivotTable report was created using Excel 2007 to quickly produce a table showing the relationship between region and number of customers.

Does the source of the customer make a difference in addition to region? We have two sources of customers: e-mail campaigns and online banner advertising. In a few seconds you will find the answer shown in Figure 12-7. The pivot table shows that Web banner advertising produces most of the customers, and this is true of all the regions.

You can use pivot tables to answer all the questions we have posed about the Online Management Training data. The complete Excel file for these examples is available on our companion Web site. One of the Hands-on MIS Projects for this chapter asks you to find answers to a number of other questions regarding this data file.

DATA VISUALIZATION AND GEOGRAPHIC INFORMATION SYSTEMS

Data from information systems are made easier for users to digest and act on by using graphics, charts, tables, maps, digital images, three-dimensional presentations, animations, and other data visualization technologies. By presenting data in graphical form, **data visualization** tools help users see patterns and relationships in large amounts of data that would be difficult to discern if the data were presented as traditional lists of text. Some data visualization tools are interactive, enabling users to manipulate data and see the graphical displays change in response to the changes they make.

Geographic information systems (GIS) are a special category of DSS that use data visualization technology to analyze and display data for planning and decision making in the form of digitized maps. The software assembles, stores,

FIGURE 12-7 A PIVOT TABLE THAT EXAMINES CUSTOMER REGIONAL DISTRIBUTION AND ADVERTISING SOURCE

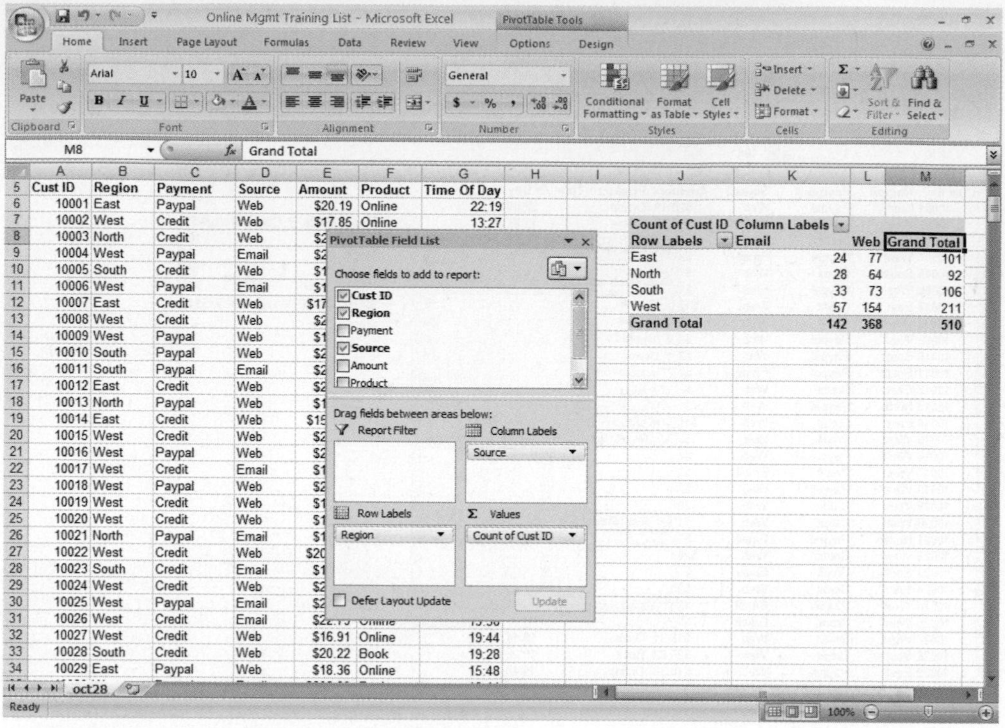

In this pivot table, we are able to examine where customers come from in terms of region and advertising source. It appears nearly 30 percent of the customers respond to e-mail campaigns, and there are some regional variations.

manipulates, and displays geographically referenced information, tying data to points, lines, and areas on a map. GIS have modeling capabilities, enabling managers to change data and automatically revise business scenarios to find better solutions.

GIS support decisions that require knowledge about the geographic distribution of people or other resources. For example, GIS might be used to help state and local governments calculate emergency response times to natural disasters, to help retail chains identify profitable new store locations, or to help banks identify the best locations for installing new branches or automatic teller machine (ATM) terminals.

WEB-BASED CUSTOMER DECISION-SUPPORT SYSTEMS

The growth of electronic commerce has encouraged many companies to develop DSS for customers that use Web information resources and capabilities for interactivity and personalization to help users select products and services. People are now using more information from multiple sources to make purchasing decisions (such as purchasing a car or computer) before they interact with the product or sales staff. For instance, nearly all automobile companies use customer decision-support systems that allow Web site visitors to configure their desired car. **Customer decision-support systems (CDSS)** support the decision-making process of an existing or potential customer.

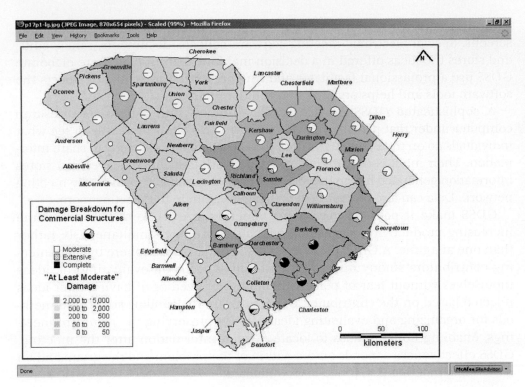

South Carolina used a GIS-based program called HAZUS to estimate and map the regional damage and losses resulting from an earthquake of a given location and intensity. HAZUS estimates the degree and geographic extent of earthquake damage across the state based on inputs of building use, type, and construction materials. The GIS helps the state plan for natural hazards mitigation and response.

People interested in purchasing a product or service are able to use Internet search engines, intelligent agents, online catalogs, Web directories, newsgroup discussions, e-mail, and other tools to help them locate the information they need to help with their decision. Companies have developed specific customer Web sites where all the information, models, or other analytical tools for evaluating alternatives are concentrated in one location.

Web-based DSS have become especially popular in financial services because so many people are trying to manage their own assets and retirement savings. For example, RiskGrades.com, a Web site run by RiskMetrics Group, lets users input all their stock, bond, and mutual fund holdings to determine how much their portfolios might decline under various conditions. Users see how the addition or subtraction of a holding might affect overall portfolio volatility and risk.

GROUP DECISION-SUPPORT SYSTEMS (GDSS)

The DSS we have just described focus primarily on individual decision making. However, so much work is accomplished in groups within firms that a special category of systems called group decision-support systems (GDSS) has been developed to support group and organizational decision making.

A GDSS is an interactive computer-based system for facilitating the solution of unstructured problems by a set of decision makers working together as a group in the same location or in different locations. Groupware and Web-based tools for videoconferencing and electronic meetings described earlier in this text support some group decision processes, but their focus is primarily on communication. GDSS, however, provide tools and technologies geared explicitly toward group decision making.

GDSS-guided meetings take place in conference rooms with special hardware and software tools to facilitate group decision making. The hardware includes computer and networking equipment, overhead projectors, and display screens. Special electronic meeting software collects, documents, ranks, edits, and stores the ideas offered in a decision-making meeting. The more elaborate GDSS use a professional facilitator and support staff. The facilitator selects the software tools and helps organize and run the meeting.

A sophisticated GDSS provides each attendee with a dedicated desktop computer under that person's individual control. No one will be able to see what individuals do on their computers until those participants are ready to share information. Their input is transmitted over a network to a central server that stores information generated by the meeting and makes it available to all on the meeting network. Data can also be projected on a large screen in the meeting room.

GDSS make it possible to increase meeting size while at the same time increasing productivity because individuals contribute simultaneously rather than one at a time. A GDSS promotes a collaborative atmosphere by guaranteeing contributors' anonymity so that attendees focus on evaluating the ideas themselves without fear of personally being criticized or of having their ideas rejected based on the contributor. GDSS software tools follow structured methods for organizing and evaluating ideas and for preserving the results of meetings, enabling nonattendees to locate needed information after the meeting. GDSS effectiveness depends on the nature of the problem and the group and on how well a meeting is planned and conducted.

12.3 EXECUTIVE SUPPORT SYSTEMS (ESS) AND THE BALANCED SCORECARD FRAMEWORK

The purpose of *executive support systems (ESS)*, introduced in Chapter 2, is to help managers focus on the really important performance information that affect the overall profitability and success of the firm. There are two parts to developing ESS. First, you will need a methodology for understanding exactly what is "the really important performance information" for a specific firm, and second, you will need to develop systems capable of delivering this information to the right people in a timely fashion.

Currently, the leading methodology for understanding the really important information needed by a firm's executives is called the **balanced scorecard method** (Kaplan and Norton, 2004; Kaplan and Norton, 1992). The balanced score card is a framework for operationalizing a firm's strategic plan by focusing on measurable outcomes on four dimensions of firm performance: financial, business process, customer, and learning and growth (Figure 12-8). Performance on each dimension is measured using **key performance indicators (KPIs),** which are the measures proposed by senior management for understanding how well the firm is performing along any given dimension. For instance, one key indicator of how well an online retail firm is meeting its customer performance objectives is the average length of time required to deliver a package to a consumer. If your firm is a bank, one KPI of business process performance is the length of time required to perform a basic function like creating a new customer account.

The balanced scorecard framework is thought to be "balanced" because it causes managers to focus on more than just financial performance. In this view, financial performance is past history—the result of past actions—and managers should focus on the things they are able to influence today, such as business process efficiency, customer satisfaction, and employee training.

FIGURE 12-8   THE BALANCED SCORECARD FRAMEWORK

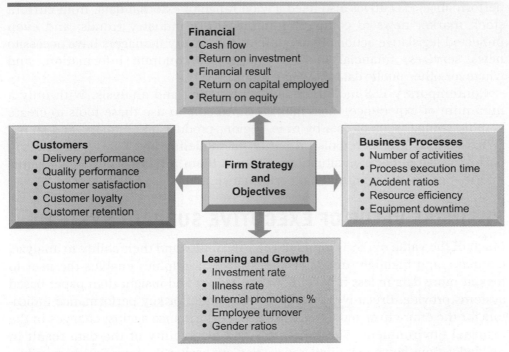

In the balanced scorecard framework, the firm's strategic objectives are operationalized along four dimensions: financial, business process, customer, and learning and growth. Each dimension is measured using several key performance indicators (KPIs).

Source: Authors.

Once a scorecard is developed by consultants and senior executives, the next step is automating a flow of information to executives and other managers for each of the key performance indicators. There are literally hundreds of consulting and software firms that offer these capabilities, which are described below. Once these systems are implemented, they are typically referred to as "executive support systems."

THE ROLE OF EXECUTIVE SUPPORT SYSTEMS IN THE FIRM

Use of ESS has migrated down several organizational levels so that the executive and subordinates are able to look at the same data in the same way. Today's systems try to avoid the problem of data overload by filtering data and presenting it in graphical or dashboard format. ESS have the ability to **drill down**, moving from a piece of summary data to lower and lower levels of detail. The ability to drill down is useful not only to senior executives but also to employees at lower levels of the firm who need to analyze data. OLAP tools for analyzing large databases provide this capability.

A major challenge of executive support systems has been to integrate data from systems designed for very different purposes so that senior executives are able to review organizational performance from a firm-wide perspective. Most ESS now rely on data provided by the firm's existing enterprise applications (enterprise resource planning, supply chain management, and customer relationship management) rather than entirely new information flows and systems.

While the balanced scorecard framework focuses on internal measures of performance, executives also need a wide range of external data, from current stock market news to competitor information, industry trends, and even projected legislative action. Through their ESS, many managers have access to news services, financial market databases, economic information, and whatever other public data they may require.

Contemporary ESS include tools for modeling and analysis. With only a minimum of experience, most managers are able to use these tools to create graphic comparisons of data by time, region, product, price range, and so on. (Whereas DSS use such tools primarily for modeling and analysis in a fairly narrow range of decision situations, ESS use them primarily to provide status information about organizational performance.)

BUSINESS VALUE OF EXECUTIVE SUPPORT SYSTEMS

Much of the value of ESS is found in their flexibility and their ability to analyze, compare, and highlight trends. The easy use of graphics enables the user to look at more data in less time with greater clarity and insight than paper-based systems provide. Executives are using ESS to monitor key performance indicators for the entire firm and to measure firm performance against changes in the external environment. The timeliness and availability of the data result in needed actions being identified and carried out earlier than previously possible. Problems will handled before they become too damaging, and opportunities will be identified earlier. These systems thus help businesses move toward a "sense-and-respond" strategy.

Well-designed ESS dramatically improve management performance and increase upper management's span of control. Immediate access to so much data increases executives' ability to monitor activities of lower units reporting to them. That very monitoring ability enables decision making to be decentralized and to take place at lower operating levels. Executives are often willing to push decision making further down into the organization as long as they are assured that all is going well. Alternatively, executive support systems based on enterprise-wide data potentially increase management centralization, enabling senior executives to monitor the performance of subordinates across the company and to take appropriate action when conditions change.

To illustrate the different ways in which ESS enhance decision making, we now describe important types of ESS applications for gathering business intelligence and monitoring corporate performance.

National Life: ESS for Business Intelligence

Headquartered in Toronto, Canada, National Life markets life insurance, health insurance, and retirement/investment products to individuals and groups. The company has more than 370 employees in Toronto and its regional offices. National Life uses an executive information system based on Information Builders' WebFOCUS, which allows senior managers to access information from corporate databases through a Web interface. The system provides statistical reporting and the ability to drill down into current sales information, which is organized to show premium dollars by salesperson. Authorized users are able to drill down into these data to see the product, agent, and client for each sale. They can examine the data many different ways—by region, by product, and by broker, accessing data for monthly, quarterly, and annual time periods (Information Builders, 2005).

Rohm and Haas and Pharmacia Corporation: Monitoring Corporate Performance with Digital Dashboards and Balanced Scorecard Systems

ESS are increasingly configured to summarize and report on key performance indicators for senior management in the form of a digital dashboard or "executive dashboard." The dashboard displays on a single screen all of the critical measurements for piloting a company, similar to the cockpit of an airplane or an automobile dashboard. The dashboard presents key performance indicators as graphs and charts in a Web browser format, providing a one-page overview of all the critical measurements necessary to make key executive decisions.

Rohm and Haas, a chemical and specialty materials firm headquartered in Philadelphia, has 13 different business units, each operating independently and using more than 300 disparate information systems. To obtain a company-wide overview of performance, it implemented a series of Web-based dashboards built with SAP tools atop an enterprise system and enterprise data warehouse.

Management defined a handful of key performance indicators to provide high-level measurements of the business and had the information delivered on dashboards. The KPIs may be broken down into their components. For example, a gross profit KPI can be broken down into figures for sales and cost of sales. A manager is able to drill down further to see that the cost of sales figures are based on manufacturing and raw materials costs. If raw materials costs appear to be problematic, the system allows the manager to drill down further to identify the costs of individual raw materials.

The dashboards are customized for multiple layers of management. An Executive Dashboard is geared toward the CEO, CFO, and other senior managers, and consists of Business Financials, which include all of the major KPIs. The Pulse is aimed at a wider range of users and displays only three KPIs: sales, standard gross profit, and volume. The Reporting and Analysis Toolkit provides a set of analysis tools that allow managers and business analysts to drill down into specifics to answer questions such as "Why are raw materials costs higher than expected?" The Analysis Accelerator focuses on standard sales and gross-profit analyses, allowing users to drill down to the individual customer level. The most popular dashboard is the daily sales report against Plan.

Rohm and Haas claims that the dashboards have made its management decision making more proactive. Managers are able to quickly anticipate problems before they erupt and take corrective action. For example, even though the cost of raw materials based on petrochemicals has escalated in recent years, the company has been able to maintain a high level of profitability by working out pricing changes and modifying its sales techniques (Maxcer, 2007).

Pharmacia Corporation, a global pharmaceutical firm based in Peapack, New Jersey, uses Oracle's Balanced Scorecard software and a data warehouse to ensure the entire organization is operating in a coordinated manner. Pharmacia spends about $2 billion annually on research and development, and the company wanted to make more effective use of the funds allocated for research. The balanced scorecard reports show, for example, how Pharmacia's U.S. or European clinical operations are performing in relation to corporate objectives and other parts of the company. Pharmacia uses the scorecard system to track the attrition rate of new compounds under study, to monitor the number of patents in clinical trials, and to see how funds allocated for research are being spent (Oracle, 2003).

12.4 HANDS-ON MIS PROJECTS

The projects in this section give you hands-on experience analyzing opportunities for DSS, using a spreadsheet pivot table to analyze sales data, and using online retirement planning tools for financial planning.

Management Decision Problems

1. Applebee's is the largest casual dining chain in the world, with 1,970 locations throughout the United States and nearly 20 other countries worldwide. The menu features beef, chicken, and pork items, as well as burgers, pasta, and seafood. The Applebee's CEO wants to make the restaurant more profitable by developing menus that are tastier and contain more items that customers want and are willing to pay for despite rising costs for gasoline and agricultural products. How might information systems help management implement this strategy? What pieces of data would Applebee's need to collect? What kinds of reports would be useful to help management make decisions on how to improve menus and profitability?

2. During the 1990s, the Canadian Pacific Railway used a tonnage-based operating model in which freight trains ran only when there was sufficient traffic to justify the expense. This model focused on minimizing the total number of freight trains in service and maximizing the size of each train. However, it did not necessarily use crews, locomotives, and equipment efficiently, and it resulted in inconsistent transit times and delivery schedules. Canadian Pacific and other railroads were losing business to trucking firms, which offered more flexible deliveries that could be scheduled at the times most convenient for customers. How could a DSS help Canadian Pacific and other railroads compete with trucking firms more effectively?

Improving Decision Making: Using Pivot Tables to Analyze Sales Data

Software skills: Pivot tables
Business skills: Analyzing sales data

This project gives you an opportunity to learn how to use Excel's PivotTable functionality to analyze a database or data list.

Use the data list for Online Management Training Inc. described earlier in the chapter. This is a list of the sales transactions at OMT for one day. You can find this spreadsheet file at the Companion Web site for this chapter.

Use Excel's PivotTable to help you answer the following questions:

- Where are the average purchases higher? The answer might tell managers where to focus marketing and sales resources, or pitch different messages to different regions.

- What form of payment is the most common? The answer might be used to emphasize in advertising the most preferred means of payment.

- Are there any times of day when purchases are most common? Do people buy products while at work (likely during the day) or at home (likely in the evening)?

- What's the relationship between region, type of product purchased, and average sales price?

Improving Decision Making: Using a Web-Based DSS for Retirement Planning

Software skills: Internet-based software
Business skills: Financial planning

This project will help develop your skills in using Web-based DSS for financial planning.

The Web sites for CNN Money and MSN Money Magazine feature Web-based DSS for financial planning and decision making. Select either site to plan for retirement. Use your chosen site to determine how much you need to save to have enough income for your retirement. Assume that you are 50 years old and plan to retire in 16 years. You have one dependant and $100,000 in savings. Your current annual income is $85,000. Your goal is to be able to generate an annual retirement income of $60,000, including Social Security benefit payments.

- To calculate your estimated Social Security benefit, use the Quick Calculator at the Social Security Administration Web site.
- Use the Web site you have selected to determine how much money you need to save to help you achieve your retirement goal.
- Critique the site—its ease of use, its clarity, the value of any conclusions reached, and the extent to which the site helps investors understand their financial needs and the financial markets.

LEARNING TRACK MODULE

The following Learning Track provides content relevant to topics covered in this chapter:

1. Building and Using Pivot Tables

Review Summary

1. *What are the different types of decisions and how does the decision-making process work?*

    The different levels in an organization (strategic, management, operational) have different decision-making requirements. Decisions can be structured, semistructured, or unstructured, with structured decisions clustering at the operational level of the organization and unstructured decisions at the strategic level. Decision making can be performed by individuals or groups and includes employees as well as operational, middle, and senior managers. There are four stages in decision making: intelligence, design, choice, and implementation. Systems to support decision making do not always produce better manager and employee decisions that improve firm performance because of problems with information quality, management filters, and organizational inertia.

2. *How do information systems support the activities of managers and management decision making?*

    Early classical models of managerial activities stress the functions of planning, organizing, coordinating, deciding, and controlling. Contemporary research looking at the actual behavior of managers has found that managers' real activities are highly fragmented, variegated, and brief in duration and that managers shy away from making grand, sweeping policy decisions.

Information technology provides new tools for managers to carry out both their traditional and newer roles, enabling them to monitor, plan, and forecast with more precision and speed than ever before and to respond more rapidly to the changing business environment. Information systems have been most helpful to managers by providing support for their roles in disseminating information, providing liaisons between organizational levels, and allocating resources. However, information systems are less successful at supporting unstructured decisions. Where information systems are useful, information quality, management filters, and organizational culture can degrade decision-making.

3. *How do decision-support systems (DSS) differ from MIS and how do they provide value to the business?*

Management information systems (MIS) provide information on firm performance to help managers monitor and control the business, often in the form of fixed regularly scheduled reports based on data summarized from the firm's transaction processing systems. MIS support structured decisions and some semistructured decisions.

DSS combine data, sophisticated analytical models and tools, and user-friendly software into a single powerful system that can support semistructured or unstructured decision making. The components of a DSS are the DSS database, the user interface, and the DSS software system. There are two kinds of DSS: model-driven DSS and data-driven DSS. DSS can help support decisions for pricing, supply chain management, and customer relationship management as well model alternative business scenarios. DSS targeted toward customers as well as managers are becoming available on the Web. A special category of DSS called geographic information systems (GIS) uses data visualization technology to analyze and display data for planning and decision making with digitized maps.

4. *How do executive support systems (ESS) help senior managers make better decisions?*

ESS help senior managers with unstructured problems that occur at the strategic level of the firm, providing data from both internal and external sources. ESS help senior executives monitor firm performance, spot problems, identify opportunities, and forecast trends. These systems can filter out extraneous details for high-level overviews, or they can drill down to provide senior managers with detailed transaction data if required. The balanced scorecard is the leading methodology for understanding the most important information needed by a firm's executives.

ESS help senior managers analyze, compare, and highlight trends so that the managers may more easily monitor organizational performance or identify strategic problems and opportunities. They are very useful for environmental scanning, providing business intelligence to help management detect strategic threats or opportunities from the organization's environment. ESS can increase the span of control of senior management, allowing them to oversee more people with fewer resources.

5. *What is the role of information systems in helping people working in a group make decisions more efficiently?*

Group decision-support systems (GDSS) help people working together in a group arrive at decisions more efficiently. GDSS feature special conference room facilities where participants contribute their ideas using networked computers and software tools for organizing ideas, gathering information, making and setting priorities, and documenting meeting sessions.

Key Terms

Balanced scorecard method, 494
Behavioral models, 480
Choice, 480
Classical model of management, 491
Customer decision-support systems (CDSS), 492
Data-driven DSS, 484
Data visualization, 491
Decisional role, 481
Design, 480
Drill down, 495
DSS database, 484
DSS software system, 484
Geographic information systems (GIS), 491

Group decision-support systems (GDSS), 483
Implementation, 480
Informational role, 481
Intelligence, 480
Interpersonal role, 481
Key performance indicators KPIs), 494
Managerial roles, 481
Model, 484
Pivot table, 490
Sensitivity analysis, 488
Semistructured decisions, 478
Structured decisions, 478
Unstructured decisions, 478

Review Questions

1. What are the different types of decisions and how does the decision-making process work?

   - List and describe the different levels of decision making and decision-making constituencies in organizations. Explain how their decision-making requirements differ.

   - Distinguish between an unstructured, semistructured, and structured decision.

   - List and describe the stages in decision making.

2. How do information systems support the activities of managers and management decision making?

   - Compare the descriptions of managerial behavior in the classical and behavioral models.

   - Identify the specific managerial roles that can be supported by information systems.

3. How do decision-support systems (DSS) differ from management information systems (MIS) and how do they provide value to the business?

   - Distinguish between DSS and MIS.

   - Compare a data-driven DSS to a model-driven DSS. Give examples.

   - Identify and describe the three basic components of a DSS.

   - Define a geographic information system (GIS) and explain how it supports decision making.

   - Define a customer decision-support system and explain how the Internet can be used for this purpose.

4. How do executive support systems (ESS) help senior managers make better decisions?

   - Define and describe the capabilities of an ESS.

   - Describe how the balanced scorecard helps managers identify important information requirements.

   - Explain how ESS enhance managerial decision making and provide value for a business.

5. What is the role of information systems in helping people working in a group make decisions more efficiently?

   - Define a group decision-support system (GDSS) and explain how it differs from a DSS.

   - Explain how a GDSS works and how it provides value for a business.

Discussion Questions

1. As a manager or user of information systems, what would you need to know to participate in the design and use of a DSS or an ESS? Why?

2. If businesses used DSS, GDSS, and ESS more widely, would managers and employees make better decisions? Why or why not?

Video Cases

You will find video cases illustrating some of the concepts in this chapter on the Laudon Web site along with questions to help you analyze the cases.

Collaboration and Teamwork: Designing a University GDSS

With three or four of your classmates, identify several groups in your university that might benefit from a GDSS. Design a GDSS for one of those groups, describing its hardware, software, and people elements. If possible, use Google Sites to post links to Web pages, team communication announcements, and work assignments; to brainstorm; and to work collaboratively on project documents. Try to use Google Docs to develop a presentation of your findings for the class.

Improving Business Intelligence Through Spend Visibility
CASE STUDY

According to its Web site, "ITWorx is the largest software professional services firm in Egypt. The company offers Portals, Business Intelligence, Service Oriented Architecture and Application Development Outsourcing services to Global 2000 companies. ITWorx serves financial service firms, educational institutions, telecommunication operators and independent software vendors (ISVs) in North America, Europe and the Middle East." Since 1994, it has amassed a list of industry-leading Fortune 500 repeat customers including United Technologies, Microsoft, Vodafone and Mellon Bank.

One of ITWorx's aims is to help decision makers rely on software systems to manage their spend data efficiently because managing a company's procurement information spend and procurement data has always been a problematic area. The benefits that managing spend data can yield are countless, and the costs of delay are immeasurable. The problem with accumulating and managing supplier and spend management information arises primarily from dispersed and scattered data. Most organizations store spend data in different locations and repositories, making it extremely difficult and time-consuming to draw analytical reports on spend data. This then becomes a tedious job that is usually confined to the spend data's financial aspect and is only carried out infrequently. These shortcomings often mean a lack of analytical reports, which in turn leads to disastrous effects on the company's daily operations, and problems in sourcing and supplier management, compliance, inventory management, and product management. Operational problems include missed savings, weak tracking and reporting, excess stock and redundant orders.

To maintain its competitiveness, it is crucial for any company to keep up to date with new advancements in Information Technology (IT). New applications in Business Intelligence (BI) have enabled organizations to realize millions in savings, let alone the competitive advantages gained in the market. It has perhaps become essential for any company planning to survive in today's competitive world to constantly update its IT and Information Systems (IS) infrastructure to keep pace with new advanced trends in the BI field.

Spend management software has been gaining in popularity over the last few years. Statistics have shown that a good spend visibility software can help to improve a company's efficiency and performance. Spend management software offers upper management clear visibility of three aspects: spend visibility by analyzing past spend; process visibility by providing management with the ability to analyze the process in order to identify any shortcomings or bottlenecks; and performance visibility, which is the ability to track the supplier's qualitative and quantitative performance indicators.

The increased operational efficiency that spend visibility triggers has a tremendous and quantifiable impact on a company's bottom line. Statistics show that companies are realizing savings in the millions of dollars. The advantages yielded by a professional spend management program help add credibility to procurement operations and is a key factor in its changeover from a cost center to a profit center. Needless to say, turning procurement into a profit center has helped a lot of companies acquire a unique competitive advantage.

A spend management program typically involves six steps, which might vary from one organization to the other and the maturity level of the program itself. Initially, all organizational data is extracted from different sources, whether from inside parties (Enterprise Resource Planning (ERP), e-Procurement) and outside parties (Partner systems, credit and procurement cards). The data is then validated to ensure accuracy and completeness. After the validation stage, the data undergoes a cleansing process, where errors and discrepancies are eliminated. Once all the data is collected, validated, and cleansed, it is classified according to an agreed upon standard schema. Classification can be based upon an internal schema or on a known industry standard, which is usually more comprehensive. Next, the organized data is enriched and enhanced with business information. This may include the supplier's financial status and performance information. This definitely helps companies relate figures to information, making more meaningful use of existing data. Now, information is ready to be subjected to advanced and multidimensional analysis. However, to make best use of such information, it should be widely accessible by different employees in the organization who are equipped with adequate analytical tools.

There are several approaches for implementing a spend management program. There is no one best approach but rather several of them, each accommodating different needs and facilities of the company.

The most primitive approach in Spend Data Management is the manual process. This approach focuses on manually collecting the information and feeding it into basic spreadsheet applications and then proceeding to make analyses. It is usually done by internal staff or external consultants. While this approach is generally considered the most inferior, it is a quick and cheap alternative for a limited amount of data. It fails to address several issues, the most significant being the lack of meaningful data. Classifications are inconsistent across different data sets and time span because different individuals classify subjective or incomplete data incoherently. Another problem is the lack of scalability.

The managed-service approach focuses on outsourcing the entire spend analysis program to a consulting firm/vendor. The company will usually provide the vendor with the data in an agreed upon format. The approach allows companies to focus on their core competencies, as resources do not need to be tied up and caged within tasks that fall out of their core job scale. In addition, this approach usually has a lower total cost of ownership (TCO), as the vendor is far more efficient and professional than the organization. However, there are negatives if a company adopts this approach such as losing data ownership and forfeiting proactive data practices. The software provided usually has minimal flexibility for customization and integration within the existing infrastructure, not to mention the periodical subscription and maintenance fees paid which might exceed what is incurred by the self-service approach over the long run. Finally, a critical negative point is security, as the organization's data is exposed to another entity.

The self-service approach is the third one. An organization actually buys a licensed specialized spend management software. One of the most important advantages is the company's ability to customize its spend management software according to needs and requirements, that is in addition to the capability of integrating this software with the existing applications and technologies infrastructure in the organization. However, this approach requires significant resource commitment. For the self-service approach to succeed, it is important to gain the support and

collaboration of the related departments and executives. Moreover, this approach takes the longest implementation period and hence the longest cycle to realize any benefits or Return on Investment (ROI).

The Hybrid approach is a combination of several of the above approaches. It can be the simultaneous use of more than one of the above approaches or a phased approach, where the project plan involves the transition from one type of approach to another.

Spend management has become one of the most important topics in BI, as it helps solve various procurement problems. Its low cost and high ROI justify the firm's investment.

Sources: www.itworx.com.

CASE STUDY QUESTIONS

1. What are the problems caused to organizations by poor spend management?
2. What is the relationship between BI and spend management?
3. Explain the value that spend management software offers to top management.
4. Discuss the various approaches used in implementing spend management.

• case contributed by Dr Ahmed Elragal, German University in Cairo

Building and Managing Systems

Part Four focuses on building and managing systems in organizations. This part answers questions such as: What activities are required to build a new information system? What alternative approaches are available for building system solutions? How should information systems projects be managed to ensure that new systems provide genuine business benefits and work successfully in the organization? What issues must be addressed when building and managing global systems?

Chapter 13

Building Information Systems

Interactive Sessions:

Dorfman Pacific Rolls Out a New Wireless Warehouse

Did Chrysler Make the Right Outsourcing Decision?

AL-MANSOUR AUTOMOTIVE: IT-ENABLED SUCCESS

Al-Mansour Automotive Company (MAC) is one of Egypt's largest importers, distributors and retailers of motor vehicles and was the largest General Motors dealer in the world in 2006 and 2007 consecutively. Today, MAC maintains a network of 12 national branches, over 35 authorized dealerships, with more than 750 employees and an annual turnover of about US$ 1 billion.

The management of MAC believes that IT builds the backbone of any great company. MAC has built a strong in-house Application Development team that understands the business in general and automotives specifically. In 2005 during efforts to align IT with business strategies and plans, the IT team realized that their running business applications (the third generation) were heading towards the end of their life-cycles and could hardly support the future plans of the company in an efficient, cost-effective and timely manner. They needed a new generation of software to play a role in shaping the company's future in the fast-changing and dynamic world of globalization and the era of information.

The IT-Steering Committee (ITSC) initiated an Enterprise Resource Planning (ERP) evaluation project. The results of the study showed that the ERP from SAP was the right technology base to support their current and future business plans in an efficient, cost-effective and timely manner.

The implementation project started mid-2006 with the objective of laying a new technology foundation by integrating the core modules of the SAP-Business Suite with the Industry Solution for Automotive (ISAutomotive). The benefits of this new technology would be gradually perceived by the consecutive implementations of further components and functions, and would be realized when business processes and strategic plans were optimized and supported.

As with any new system, there were accompanying changes: changes in duties and responsibilities, authorization, workflows and processes and, last but not least, changes in the presentation of data and information. Because of the history, size and structure of the company and the nature of its business, the team had to maintain their reporting standards and migrate a lot of data to meet the needs of the business units.

In one 72-hour exercise in the beginning of January 2008, the team extracted the data from the legacy systems, imported it into SAP, closed the doors to the company's legacy systems, opened the gates to SAP and went live. This required good planning, coordination, discipline, punctuality and the efforts of almost everyone in the company. With any new system, the productivity of users was expected to drop in the first weeks and months. However, most of the users returned to their normal productivity in a relatively short time and soon they will exceed the previous records.

'The introduction of ERP in our organization was the beginning of a new era for our company and an opportunity to enrich the experience of every individual using it', said

Khaled Ismail the IT Manager. He also added, 'a very important key success factor in this achievement was the management support. Without it we would hardly have been standing where we are today.'

Sources: -www.almansourauto.com, accessed December 2008; www.mansourgroup.com, accessed December 2008.

The experience of Al-Mansour in the building of an information system reflects at least two recurring themes. The first theme is the need to align strategic business objectives to the building of systems. In this case Al-Mansour has strong in-house capabilities so the main initial concern was to choose the appropriate technology. The second theme is the intermix of people, organization and technology components in the building of the ERP system, with the view that the project is a change management challenge that has to address a balance of all these aspects according to the context in order to achieve a successful outcome.

Therefore the building of the ERP is not just a technological challenge. The implementation team must ensure that the business is able to continue and transition to the new system on completion.

- Case contributed by Dr. Ahmed Elragal, German University in Cairo

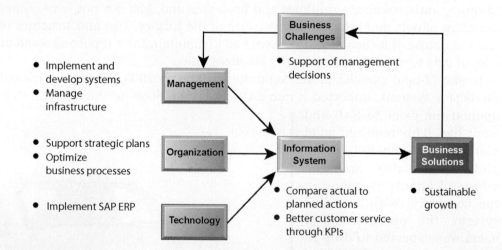

13.1 SYSTEMS AS PLANNED ORGANIZATIONAL CHANGE

B uilding a new information system is one kind of planned organizational change. The introduction of a new information system involves much more than new hardware and software. It also includes changes in jobs, skills, management, and organization. When we design a new information system, we are redesigning the organization. System builders must understand how a system will affect specific business processes and the organization as a whole.

SYSTEMS DEVELOPMENT AND ORGANIZATIONAL CHANGE

Information technology can promote various degrees of organizational change, ranging from incremental to far-reaching. Figure 13-1 shows four kinds of structural organizational change that are enabled by information technology: (1) automation, (2) rationalization, (3) reengineering, and (4) paradigm shifts. Each carries different rewards and risks.

The most common form of IT-enabled organizational change is **automation**. The first applications of information technology involved assisting employees with performing their tasks more efficiently and effectively. Calculating paychecks and payroll registers, giving bank tellers instant access to customer deposit records, and developing a nationwide network of airline reservation terminals for airline reservation agents are all examples of early automation.

FIGURE 13-1   ORGANIZATIONAL CHANGE CARRIES RISKS AND REWARDS

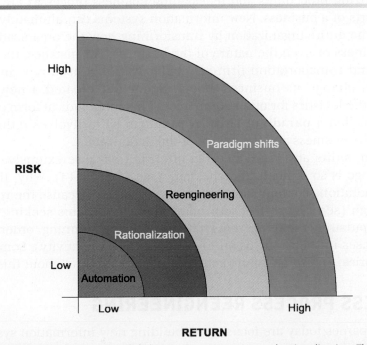

The most common forms of organizational change are automation and rationalization. These relatively slow-moving and slow-changing strategies present modest returns but little risk. Faster and more comprehensive change—such as reengineering and paradigm shifts—carries high rewards but offers substantial chances of failure.

A deeper form of organizational change—one that follows quickly from early automation—is **rationalization of procedures**. Automation frequently reveals new bottlenecks in production and makes the existing arrangement of procedures and structures painfully cumbersome. Rationalization of procedures is the streamlining of standard operating procedures. For example, PC Connections new order fulfillment system described in the chapter-opening case is effective not only because it uses fairly sophisticated and contemporary Web services software, but also because managers redesigned business processes, work flows, and user interfaces to the fulfillment software. Without this rationalization of procedures, the new Web services software and associated technology would not have been so useful.

A more powerful type of organizational change is **business process reengineering (BPR)**, in which business processes are analyzed, simplified, and redesigned. Using information technology, organizations can rethink and streamline their business processes to improve speed, service, and quality. Business reengineering reorganizes work flows, combining steps to cut waste and eliminating repetitive, paper-intensive tasks. (Sometimes the new design eliminates jobs as well.) It is much more ambitious than rationalization of procedures, requiring a new vision of how the process is to be organized.

A widely cited example of business reengineering is Ford Motor Company's invoiceless processing, which reduced headcount in Ford's North American accounts payable organization of 500 people by 75 percent. Accounts payable clerks used to spend most of their time resolving discrepancies between purchase orders, receiving documents, and invoices. Ford reengineered its accounts payable process so that the purchasing department enters a purchase order into an online database that can be checked by the receiving department when the ordered items arrive. If the received goods match the purchase order, the system automatically generates a check for accounts payable to send to the vendor. There is no need for vendors to send invoices.

Rationalizing procedures and redesigning business processes are limited to specific parts of a business. New information systems can ultimately affect the design of the entire organization by transforming how the organization carries out its business or even the nature of the business. For instance, the long-haul trucking and transportation firm Schneider National used new information systems to change its business model. Schneider created a new business managing the logistics for other companies. This more radical form of business change is called a **paradigm shift**. A paradigm shift involves rethinking the nature of the business and the nature of the organization.

Paradigm shifts and reengineering often fail because extensive organizational change is so difficult to orchestrate (see Chapter 14). Why, then, do so many corporations contemplate such radical change? Because the rewards are equally high (see Figure 13-1). In many instances, firms seeking paradigm shifts and pursuing reengineering strategies achieve stunning, order-of-magnitude increases in their returns on investment (or productivity). Some of these success stories, and some failure stories, are included throughout this book.

BUSINESS PROCESS REENGINEERING

Many companies today are focusing on building new information systems that will improve their business processes. Some of these system projects represent radical restructuring of business processes, whereas others entail more incremental process change.

If organizations rethink and radically redesign their business processes before applying computing power, they can potentially obtain very large payoffs from their investments in information technology. Let's look at how the home mortgage industry in the United States accomplished this.

The application process for a home mortgage used to take about six to eight weeks and cost about $3,000. Leading mortgage banks, such as Wells Fargo, Bank of America, and JP Morgan Chase, have redesigned the mortgage application process to reduce the cost to $1,000 and the time to obtain a mortgage to about one week (see Figure 13-2).

In the past, a mortgage applicant filled out a paper loan application. The bank entered the application into its computer system. Specialists, such as credit analysts and underwriters from perhaps eight different departments, accessed and evaluated the application individually. If the loan application was approved, the closing was scheduled. After the closing, bank specialists dealing with insurance or funds in escrow serviced the loan. This "desk-to-desk" assembly-line approach might take up to 17 days.

The banks replaced the sequential desk-to-desk approach with a speedier "work cell" or team approach. Now, loan originators in the field enter the mortgage application directly into laptop computers. Software checks the application transaction to make sure that all of the information is correct and complete. The loan originators transmit the loan applications over a network to regional production centers. Instead of working on the application individually, the credit analysts, loan underwriters, and other specialists convene electronically, working as a team to approve the mortgage.

After closing, another team of specialists sets up the loan for servicing. The entire loan application process can take as little as two days. Loan information is easier to access than before, when the loan application could be in eight or nine different departments. Loan originators also can dial into the bank's network to obtain information on mortgage loan costs or to check the status of a loan for the customer.

By radically rethinking their approaches to mortgage processing, mortgage banks have achieved remarkable efficiencies. They have not focused on redesigning a single business process, but instead they have reexamined the entire set of logically connected processes required to obtain a mortgage.

To support the new mortgage application process, the banks have implemented work flow and document management software. **Work flow management** is the process of streamlining business procedures so that documents can be moved easily and efficiently. Work flow and document management software automates processes such as routing documents to different locations, securing approvals, scheduling, and generating reports. Two or more people can work simultaneously on the same document, allowing much quicker completion time. Work need not be delayed because a file is out or a document is in transit. And with a properly designed indexing system, users will be able to retrieve files in many different ways, based on the content of the document.

Steps in Effective Reengineering

One of the most important strategic decisions that a firm can make is not deciding how to use information systems to improve business processes but rather understanding what business processes need improvement. Businesses are composed of hundreds, sometimes thousands of business processes. How can you decide which need to be changed and which could really benefit from information systems? When systems are used to strengthen the wrong business model or business processes, the business can become more efficient at doing

FIGURE 13-2   REDESIGNING MORTGAGE PROCESSING IN THE UNITED STATES

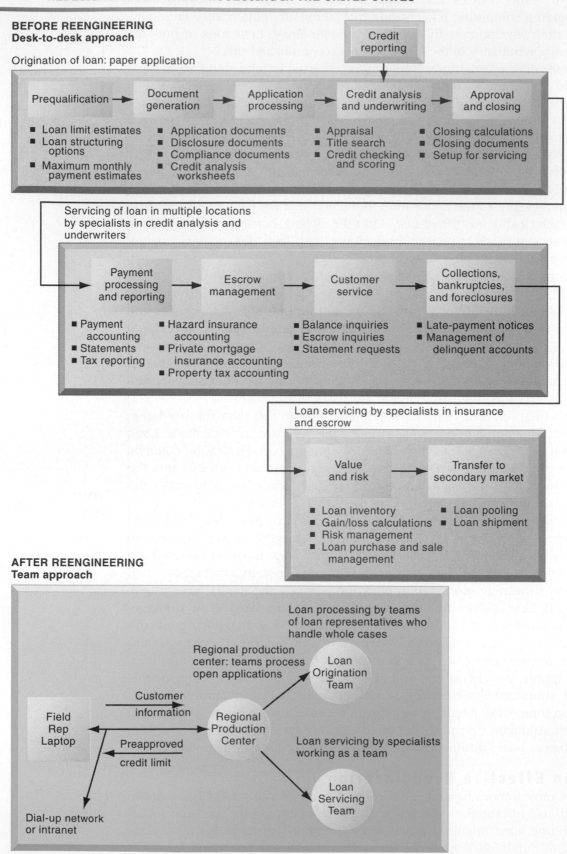

By redesigning their mortgage processing systems and the mortgage application process, many mortgage banks have reduced the costs of processing the average mortgage from $3,000 to $1,000 and reduced the time of approval from six weeks to one week or less. Some banks are even preapproving mortgages and locking interest rates on the same day the customer applies.

what it should not do (Hammer, 2002). As a result, the firm becomes vulnerable to competitors who may have discovered the right business model. Considerable time and cost can also be spent improving business processes that have little impact on overall firm performance and revenue. You will need to determine what business processes are the most important to focus on when applying new information technology and how improving these processes, will help the firm execute its strategy.

You will also need to understand and measure the performance of existing processes as a baseline. If, for example, the objective of process redesign is to reduce time and cost in developing a new product or filling an order, you will need to measure the time and cost consumed by the unchanged process. For example, before reengineering, Cemex, the international provider of cement and ready-mix concrete, required an average time of 3 hours to make a delivery. After Cemex's processes were reengineered, average delivery time dropped to 20 minutes. Without measuring the baseline original process, you will have no way to judge improvements.

Following these steps does not automatically guarantee that reengineering will always be successful. The majority of reengineering projects do not achieve breakthrough gains in business performance because the organizational changes are often very difficult to manage. Managing change is neither simple nor intuitive, and companies committed to reengineering need a good change management strategy (see Chapter 14).

Interorganizational processes, such as those for supply chain management, not only need to be streamlined but also coordinated and integrated with those of customers and suppliers. In such cases, reengineering will involve multiple companies working together to jointly redesign their shared processes. A Learning Track for this chapter explains business process redesign in greater detail.

PROCESS IMPROVEMENT: BUSINESS PROCESS MANAGEMENT, TOTAL QUALITY MANAGEMENT, AND SIX SIGMA

Business process reengineering is primarily a one-time effort, focusing on identifying one or two strategic business processes that need radical change. BPR projects tend to be expensive and organizationally disruptive. But organizations have many business processes and support processes that must be constantly revised to keep the business competitive. Business process management and quality improvement programs provide opportunities for more incremental and ongoing types of business process change.

Business Process Management

Mergers and acquisitions, changes in business models, new industry requirements, and changing customer expectations all pose multiple process-related problems that continually confront organizations. **Business process management (BPM)** enables organizations to manage incremental process changes that are required simultaneously in many areas of the business. It provides a methodology and tools for dealing with the organization's ongoing need to revise—and ideally optimize—its numerous internal business processes and processes shared with other organizations. It enables organizations to make continual improvements to many business processes simultaneously and to use processes as the fundamental building blocks of corporate information systems.

BPM includes work flow management, business process modeling, quality management, change management, and tools for recasting the firm's business processes into a standardized form where they can be continually manipulated. Companies practicing business process management use process-mapping tools to identify and document existing processes and to create models of improved processes that can then be translated into software systems. The process models might require entirely new systems or could be based on existing systems and data. BPM software tools automatically manage processes across the business, extract data from various sources and databases, and generate transactions in multiple related systems.

BPM also includes process monitoring and analytics. Organizations must be able to verify that process performance has been improved and measure the impact of process changes on key business performance indicators. A number of commercial software vendors, including IBM, Oracle-BEA Systems, Vitria, and TIBCO, supply business process management products.

American National Insurance Company, which offers life insurance, medical insurance, property casualty insurance, and investment services, used BPM to streamline customer service processes across four business groups. BPM built rules to guide customer service representatives through a single view of a customer's information across multiple systems. By eliminating the need to juggle multiple mainframe applications simultaneously to handle customer and agent requests, BPM increased customer service representative workload capacity by 192 percent (Cooper, 2006).

Total Quality Management and Six Sigma

Quality management is another area of continuous process improvement. In addition to increasing organizational efficiency, companies must fine-tune their business processes to improve the quality in their products, services, and operations. Many are using the concept of **total quality management (TQM)** to make quality the responsibility of all people and functions within an organization. TQM holds that the achievement of quality control is an end in itself. Everyone is expected to contribute to the overall improvement of quality—the engineer who avoids design errors, the production worker who spots defects, the sales representative who presents the product properly to potential customers, and even the secretary who avoids typing mistakes. TQM derives from quality management concepts developed by American quality experts such as W. Edwards Deming and Joseph Juran, but it was popularized by the Japanese.

Another quality concept that is being widely implemented today is six sigma. **Six sigma** is a specific measure of quality, representing 3.4 defects per million opportunities. Most companies cannot achieve this level of quality but use six sigma as a goal to implement a set of methodologies and techniques for improving quality and reducing costs. Studies have repeatedly shown that the earlier in the business cycle a problem is eliminated, the less it costs the company. Thus, quality improvements not only raise the level of product and service quality, but they can also lower costs.

How Information Systems Support Quality Improvements

TQM and six sigma are considered to be more incremental than business process reengineering. TQM typically focuses on making a series of continuous improvements rather than dramatic bursts of change. Six sigma uses statistical analysis tools to detect flaws in the execution of an existing process and make minor adjustments. Sometimes, however, processes may have to be fully reengineered to achieve a specified level of quality. Information systems can help firms achieve their quality goals by helping them simplify products or processes, make improvements based on customer demands, reduce cycle time, improve the quality and precision of design and production, and meet benchmarking standards.

Benchmarking consists of setting strict standards for products, services, and other activities, and then measuring performance against those standards. Companies may use external industry standards, standards set by other companies, internally developed high standards, or some combination of the three. L.L. Bean, the Freeport, Maine, outdoor clothing company, used benchmarking to achieve an order-shipping accuracy of 99.9 percent. Its old batch order fulfillment system could not handle the surging volume and variety of items to be shipped. After studying German and Scandinavian companies with leading-edge order fulfillment operations, L.L. Bean carefully redesigned its order fulfillment process and information systems so that orders could be processed as soon as they were received and shipped within 24 hours. You can find other examples of systems promoting quality improvements throughout this text.

13.2 OVERVIEW OF SYSTEMS DEVELOPMENT

New information systems are an outgrowth of a process of organizational problem solving. A new information system is built as a solution to some type of problem or set of problems the organization perceives it is facing. The problem may be one in which managers and employees realize that the organization is not performing as well as expected, or that the organization should take advantage of new opportunities to perform more successfully.

The activities that go into producing an information system solution to an organizational problem or opportunity are called **systems development**. Systems development is a structured kind of problem solving with distinct activities. These activities consist of systems analysis, systems design, programming, testing, conversion, and production and maintenance.

Figure 13-3 illustrates the systems development process. The systems development activities depicted here usually take place in sequential order. But some of the activities may need to be repeated or some may take place simultaneously, depending on the approach to system building that is being employed (see section 13.4).

SYSTEMS ANALYSIS

Systems analysis is the analysis of the problem that the organization will try to solve with an information system. It consists of defining the problem, identifying its causes, specifying the solution, and identifying the information requirements that must be met by a system solution.

The systems analyst creates a road map of the existing organization and systems, identifying the primary owners and users of data along with existing hardware and software. The systems analyst then details the problems of existing systems. By examining documents, work papers, and procedures; observing system operations; and interviewing key users of the systems, the analyst can identify the problem areas and objectives a solution would achieve.

FIGURE 13-3   THE SYSTEMS DEVELOPMENT PROCESS

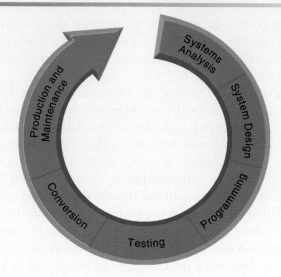

Building a system can be broken down into six core activities.

Often the solution requires building a new information system or improving an existing one.

The systems analysis would include a **feasibility study** to determine whether that solution was feasible, or achievable, from a financial, technical, and organizational standpoint. The feasibility study would determine whether the proposed system was a good investment, whether the technology needed for the system was available and could be handled by the firm's information systems specialists, and whether the organization could handle the changes introduced by the system.

Normally, the systems analysis process identifies several alternative solutions that the organization can pursue. The process then assesses the feasibility of each. A written systems proposal report describes the costs and benefits, advantages and disadvantages of each alternative. It is up to management to determine which mix of costs, benefits, technical features, and organizational impacts represents the most desirable alternative.

Establishing Information Requirements

Perhaps the most challenging task of the systems analyst is to define the specific information requirements that must be met by the system solution selected. At the most basic level, the **information requirements** of a new system involve identifying who needs what information, where, when, and how. Requirements analysis carefully defines the objectives of the new or modified system and develops a detailed description of the functions that the new system must perform. Faulty requirements analysis is a leading cause of systems failure and high systems development costs (see Chapter 14). A system designed around the wrong set of requirements will either have to be discarded because of poor performance or will need to undergo major modifications. Section 13.3 describes alternative approaches to eliciting requirements that help minimize this problem.

Some problems do not require an information system solution but instead need an adjustment in management, additional training, or refinement of existing organizational procedures. If the problem is information related, systems analysis still may be required to diagnose the problem and arrive at the proper solution.

SYSTEMS DESIGN

Systems analysis describes what a system should do to meet information requirements, and **systems design** shows how the system will fulfill this objective. The design of an information system is the overall plan or model for that system. Like the blueprint of a building or house, it consists of all the specifications that give the system its form and structure.

The systems designer details the system specifications that will deliver the functions identified during systems analysis. These specifications should address all of the managerial, organizational, and technological components of the system solution. Table 13-1 lists the types of specifications that would be produced during systems design.

Like houses or buildings, information systems may have many possible designs. Each design represents a unique blend of all technical and organizational components. What makes one design superior to others is the ease and efficiency with which it fulfills user requirements within a specific set of technical, organizational, financial, and time constraints.

The Role of End Users

User information requirements drive the entire system-building effort. Users must have sufficient control over the design process to ensure that the system reflects their business priorities and information needs, not the biases of the technical staff. Working on design increases users' understanding and acceptance of the system. As we describe in Chapter 14, insufficient user involvement in the design effort is a major cause of system failure. However, some systems require

TABLE 13-1 DESIGN SPECIFICATIONS

OUTPUT	PROCESSING	DOCUMENTATION
Medium	Computations	Operations documentation
Content	Program modules	Systems documents
Timing	Required reports	User documentation
	Timing of outputs	
INPUT		CONVERSION
Origins	MANUAL PROCEDURES	Transfer files
Flow	What activities	Initiate new procedures
Data entry	Who performs them	Select testing method
	When	Cut over to new system
USER INTERFACE	How	
Simplicity	Where	TRAINING
Efficiency		Select training techniques
Logic	CONTROLS	Develop training modules
Feedback	Input controls (characters, limit,	Identify training facilities
Errors	reasonableness)	
	Processing controls (consistency, record counts)	ORGANIZATIONAL CHANGES
DATABASE DESIGN	Output controls (totals, samples of output)	Task redesign
Logical data model	Procedural controls (passwords, special forms)	Job design
Volume and speed requirements		Process design
File organization and design	SECURITY	Organization structure design
Record specifications	Access controls	Reporting relationships
	Catastrophe plans	
	Audit trails	

more user participation in design than others, and section 13.3 shows how alternative systems development methods address the user participation issue.

The Interactive Session on Organizations demonstrates the importance of user involvement in designing and developing a successful solution. Dorfman Pacific, a manufacturer of headware and handbags, could not effectively expand its business because it was hampered by an outdated warehouse system and heavily manual processes. It decided to implement a new wireless warehouse that changed the way it worked. As you read this case, try to identify the problem this organization was facing, what alternative solutions were available to management, and how well the chosen solution worked.

COMPLETING THE SYSTEMS DEVELOPMENT PROCESS

The remaining steps in the systems development process translate the solution specifications established during systems analysis and design into a fully operational information system. These concluding steps consist of programming, testing, conversion, production, and maintenance.

Programming

During the **programming** stage, system specifications that were prepared during the design stage are translated into software program code. Today, many organizations no longer do their own programming for new systems. Instead, they purchase the software that meets the requirements for a new system from external sources such as software packages from a commercial software vendor, software services from an application service provider, or outsourcing firms that develop custom application software for their clients (see section 13.3).

Testing

Exhaustive and thorough **testing** must be conducted to ascertain whether the system produces the right results. Testing answers the question, "Will the system produce the desired results under known conditions?"

The amount of time needed to answer this question has been traditionally underrated in systems project planning (see Chapter 14). Testing is time-consuming: Test data must be carefully prepared, results reviewed, and corrections made in the system. In some instances, parts of the system may have to be redesigned. The risks resulting from glossing over this step are enormous.

Testing an information system can be broken down into three types of activities: unit testing, system testing, and acceptance testing. **Unit testing**, or program testing, consists of testing each program separately in the system. It is widely believed that the purpose of such testing is to guarantee that programs are error free, but this goal is realistically impossible. Testing should be viewed instead as a means of locating errors in programs, focusing on finding all the ways to make a program fail. Once they are pinpointed, problems can be corrected.

System testing tests the functioning of the information system as a whole. It tries to determine whether discrete modules will function together as planned and whether discrepancies exist between the way the system actually works and the way it was conceived. Among the areas examined are performance time, capacity for file storage and handling peak loads, recovery and restart capabilities, and manual procedures.

Acceptance testing provides the final certification that the system is ready to be used in a production setting. Systems tests are evaluated by users and reviewed by management. When all parties are satisfied that the new system meets their standards, the system is formally accepted for installation.

INTERACTIVE SESSION: ORGANIZATIONS

DORFMAN PACIFIC ROLLS OUT A NEW WIRELESS WAREHOUSE

You may not have heard of Dorfman Pacific, but you've probably seen its hats on celebrities featured in *People* and *InStyle* magazines. Dorfman Pacific, based in Stockton, California, has been manufacturing and distributing headwear and handbags for over 85 years. The company's philosophy has been to keep up with fashion trends while offering quality products with strong customer service, on-time deliveries, and competitive prices.

Traditionally, Dorfman served the mom-and-pop sector of the retail market. The company's warehouse processes reflected this. Warehouse activities relied on paper-based processes and tacit knowledge of the facility and Dorfman Pacific's customers.

In the 1980s and 1990s, Dorfman Pacific started adding big-box stores like Wal-Mart and JC Penney to its roster of customers. Such stores quickly came to represent half of Dorfman's business. More significantly, the large retailers had a much greater appetite for thousands of different items and box types.

Serving retailers like Wal-Mart with a paper-based order-picking process in a 100,000-square-foot warehouse was stressful and an ineffective means of doing business. During seasonal peaks in demand, Dorfman had to hire extra workers and pay hefty overtime wages to satisfy the demand. The extra wages amounted to $250,000 every year. The company's IT systems were spread out over various functional areas and did little to support a transparent inventory.

Dorfman eventually increased its warehouse space to 275,000 square feet, but the space alone was not enough to overcome flawed business processes. Top management at Dorfman realized that major changes were necessary if the company was going to expand its operations successfully. In 2001, CEO Douglass Highsmith committed to a complete overhaul of the technology in the warehouse. He wanted to eliminate the paper systems and replace them with wireless technology.

The traditional order-fulfillment process at Dorfman began with a warehouse worker, called a picker, receiving a paper pick ticket from a supervisor. The picker then drove a forklift to the area of the warehouse where he or she expected to find the bin that stored the product on the ticket. The worker manually picked boxes off of the shelf and then brought them to a packing area to be boxed, labeled, and loaded onto a truck. The warehouse was really set up only for picking, which left the remaining order-fulfillment processes as afterthoughts.

Confusing the process were bins that were labeled manually, making them difficult to read, and boxes that sometimes held more than one product. Additionally, each picker had his or her own preferred path to performing picking duties. The inefficiencies of these practices were magnified by special orders. The company's ERP system offered little help because it did not integrate well with other systems. Mark Dulle, Dorfman's IT Services Director, recognized that picking by order wasn't going to work in an era of expansion.

Dorfman approached the change as a business project rather than an IT project. A cross-functional team consisting of an outside consultant as project manager and managers from distribution, purchasing, customer service, and sales worked on the transformation. The IT department took responsibility for choosing hardware, installing the hardware and software for the wireless warehouse, and appointing an administrator for the new warehouse management system.

Highsmith's goals were to reduce labor costs and create the most efficient way for a streamlined warehouse staff to pick products with the smallest error rate. A successful implementation required a number of steps. First, the project team sought to learn everything it could about how Dorfman's 25,000 products were received, replenished, picked, packed, and shipped. This study included measuring the dimension and weight of each product, as well as the size of every bin and storage shelf, and determining whether products were stored in the correct places.

Next, Dorfman brought in Texas Bar Code Systems to test the feasibility of a wireless system in the warehouse. The project would have been fruitless if wireless signals did not function properly amidst the warehouse's concrete walls, steel doors, and metal storage shelves. The testing also helped to determine where the best wireless access points were located. Dorfman's warehouse required an unusually high number of access points, fifteen, because the floor space expansions over the years created an irregular layout, which was dense with inventory.

Dulle led the effort to revamp Dorfman's IT infrastructure, including replacing all of the old networking cables and switches with the most advanced networking technology available. He also reconfigured the ERP system and installed a new warehouse management system from HighJump Software complete with wireless capabilities and the ability to sort through warehouse and shipping data. To this system, which was based on a wireless LAN, Dulle added bar-coding equipment from Zebra Technologies, integration software, durable mobile computers, and additional computers mounted on forklifts.

With these components in place, paper was no longer necessary. The new ERP system and the warehouse management system used software to manage the picking, packing, and shipping processes. Pickers carrying mobile devices receive data telling them where to go, what to pick, and where to bring the merchandise using the most efficient route.

Dorfman employees had to change the way they worked. The new warehouse management system required a different warehouse floor configuration as well as new ways to pick, pack, and ship products. Dorfman took the job of selling the new systems to its workers very seriously, convincing them that the wireless warehouse would improve their lives and their job performance.

Once the new warehouse system was deployed, pickers armed with wireless scanning devices could be assured that the bar-code-labeled bins to which they were directed contained only one product type each. Tracking inventory became seamless. According to Dulle, Dorfman can now handle twice the number of orders during peak seasons, and labor costs are down almost 30 percent. Eliminating the need for temporary workers and overtime has saved the company $250,000 and counting.

Sources: Thomas Wailgum, "How to Take Your Warehouse Wireless," and "Wireless—Five Steps to a Successful Wireless Rollout," *CIO Magazine*, February 1, 2007; Jim Fulcher, "Rise of User-Friendly Devices Propels Strategic Use of Wireless Technology," *Manufacturing Business Technology*, February 18, 2007; Lisa M. Kempfer, "Hats Off to Wireless," *Material Handling Management*, January 2007; and "Hats-Off: Dorfman Pacific Implements Symbol Enterprise Mobility Solution for Paperless Warehouse Operations," www.symbol.com, September 13, 2006.

CASE STUDY QUESTIONS

1. Compare Dorfman Pacific's old and new order-picking processes. Diagram the processes.

2. What role did end users play in developing Dorfman's wireless warehouse system? What would have happened to the project if users hadn't been so involved? Explain your answer.

3. What types of system-building methods and tools did Dorfman use for building its wireless warehouse system?

4. How did the new system change the way Dorfman ran its business?

5. What problems did the new system solve? Was it successful?

MIS IN ACTION

Use your Web-searching capabilities to answer the following questions:

1. What are some of the components of a wireless warehouse system?

2. What companies manufacture these components?

3. What other businesses or organizations have implemented wireless warehouses?

4. If you were implementing a wireless warehouse, what potential problems would worry you most?

The systems development team works with users to devise a systematic test plan. The **test plan** includes all of the preparations for the series of tests we have just described.

Figure 13-4 shows an example of a test plan. The general condition being tested is a record change. The documentation consists of a series of test-plan screens maintained on a database (perhaps a PC database) that is ideally suited to this kind of application.

FIGURE 13-4   A SAMPLE TEST PLAN TO TEST A RECORD CHANGE

Procedure	Address and Maintenance "Record Change Series"		Test Series 2		
	Prepared By:		Date:	Version:	
Test Ref.	Condition Tested	Special Requirements	Expected Results	Output On	Next Screen
2.0	Change records				
2.1	Change existing record	Key field	Not allowed		
2.2	Change nonexistent record	Other fields	"Invalid key" message		
2.3	Change deleted record	Deleted record must be available	"Deleted" message		
2.4	Make second record	Change 2.1 above	OK if valid	Transaction file	V45
2.5	Insert record		OK if valid	Transaction file	V45
2.6	Abort during change	Abort 2.5	No change	Transaction file	V45

When developing a test plan, it is imperative to include the various conditions to be tested, the requirements for each condition tested, and the expected results. Test plans require input from both end users and information systems specialists.

Conversion is the process of changing from the old system to the new system. Four main conversion strategies can be employed: the parallel strategy, the direct cutover strategy, the pilot study strategy, and the phased approach strategy.

In a **parallel strategy,** both the old system and its potential replacement are run together for a time until everyone is assured that the new one functions correctly. This is the safest conversion approach because, in the event of errors or processing disruptions, the old system can still be used as a backup. However, this approach is very expensive, and additional staff or resources may be required to run the extra system.

The **direct cutover** strategy replaces the old system entirely with the new system on an appointed day. It is a very risky approach that can potentially be more costly than running two systems in parallel if serious problems with the new system are found. There is no other system to fall back on. Dislocations, disruptions, and the cost of corrections may be enormous.

The **pilot study** strategy introduces the new system to only a limited area of the organization, such as a single department or operating unit. When this pilot version is complete and working smoothly, it is installed throughout the rest of the organization, either simultaneously or in stages.

The **phased approach** strategy introduces the new system in stages, either by functions or by organizational units. If, for example, the system is introduced by functions, a new payroll system might begin with hourly workers who are paid weekly, followed six months later by adding salaried employees (who are paid monthly) to the system. If the system is introduced by organizational units, corporate headquarters might be converted first, followed by outlying operating units four months later.

Moving from an old system to a new one requires that end users be trained to use the new system. Detailed **documentation** showing how the system works from both a technical and end-user standpoint is finalized during conversion time for use in training and everyday operations. Lack of proper training and documentation contributes to system failure, so this portion of the systems development process is very important.

Production and Maintenance

After the new system is installed and conversion is complete, the system is said to be in **production**. During this stage, the system will be reviewed by both users and technical specialists to determine how well it has met its original objectives and to decide whether any revisions or modifications are in order. In some instances, a formal **postimplementation audit** document is prepared. After the system has been fine-tuned, it must be maintained while it is in production to correct errors, meet requirements, or improve processing efficiency. Changes in hardware, software, documentation, or procedures to a production system to correct errors, meet new requirements, or improve processing efficiency are termed **maintenance**.

Approximately 20 percent of the time devoted to maintenance is used for debugging or correcting emergency production problems. Another 20 percent is concerned with changes in data, files, reports, hardware, or system software. But 60 percent of all maintenance work consists of making user enhancements, improving documentation, and recoding system components for greater processing efficiency. The amount of work in the third category of maintenance problems could be reduced significantly through better systems analysis and design practices. Table 13-2 summarizes the systems development activities.

MODELING AND DESIGNING SYSTEMS: STRUCTURED AND OBJECT-ORIENTED METHODOLOGIES

There are alternative methodologies for modeling and designing systems. Structured methodologies and object-oriented development are the most prominent.

TABLE 13-2 SYSTEMS DEVELOPMENT

CORE ACTIVITY	DESCRIPTION
Systems analysis	Identify problem(s) Specify solutions Establish information requirements
Systems design	Create design specifications
Programming	Translate design specifications into program code
Testing	Unit test Systems test Acceptance test
Conversion	Plan conversion Prepare documentation Train users and technical staff
Production and maintenance	Operate the system Evaluate the system Modify the system

Structured Methodologies

Structured methodologies have been used to document, analyze, and design information systems since the 1970s. **Structured** refers to the fact that the techniques are step by step, with each step building on the previous one. Structured methodologies are top-down, progressing from the highest, most abstract level to the lowest level of detail—from the general to the specific.

Structured development methods are process-oriented, focusing primarily on modeling the processes, or actions that capture, store, manipulate, and distribute data as the data flow through a system. These methods separate data from processes. A separate programming procedure must be written every time someone wants to take an action on a particular piece of data. The procedures act on data that the program passes to them.

The primary tool for representing a system's component processes and the flow of data between them is the **data flow diagram (DFD)**. The data flow diagram offers a logical graphic model of information flow, partitioning a system into modules that show manageable levels of detail. It rigorously specifies the processes or transformations that occur within each module and the interfaces that exist between them.

Figure 13-5 shows a simple data flow diagram for a mail-in university course registration system. The rounded boxes represent processes, which portray the transformation of data. The square box represents an external entity, which is an originator or receiver of information located outside the boundaries of the system being modeled. The open rectangles represent data stores, which are either manual or automated inventories of data. The arrows represent data flows, which show the movement between processes, external entities, and data stores. They contain packets of data with the name or content of each data flow listed beside the arrow.

FIGURE 13-5   **DATA FLOW DIAGRAM FOR MAIL-IN UNIVERSITY REGISTRATION SYSTEM**

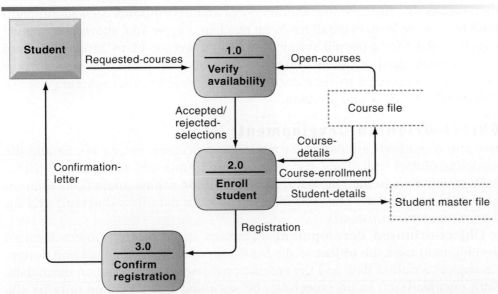

The system has three processes: Verify availability (1.0), Enroll student (2.0), and Confirm registration (3.0). The name and content of each of the data flows appear adjacent to each arrow. There is one external entity in this system: the student. There are two data stores: the student master file and the course file.

This data flow diagram shows that students submit registration forms with their name, identification number, and the numbers of the courses they wish to take. In process 1.0 the system verifies that each course selected is still open by referencing the university's course file. The file distinguishes courses that are open from those that have been canceled or filled. Process 1.0 then determines which of the student's selections can be accepted or rejected. Process 2.0 enrolls the student in the courses for which he or she has been accepted. It updates the university's course file with the student's name and identification number and recalculates the class size. If maximum enrollment has been reached, the course number is flagged as closed. Process 2.0 also updates the university's student master file with information about new students or changes in address. Process 3.0 then sends each student applicant a confirmation-of-registration letter listing the courses for which he or she is registered and noting the course selections that could not be fulfilled.

The diagrams can be used to depict higher-level processes as well as lower-level details. Through leveled data flow diagrams, a complex process can be broken down into successive levels of detail. An entire system can be divided into subsystems with a high-level data flow diagram. Each subsystem, in turn, can be divided into additional subsystems with second-level data flow diagrams, and the lower-level subsystems can be broken down again until the lowest level of detail has been reached.

Another tool for structured analysis is a data dictionary, which contains information about individual pieces of data and data groupings within a system (see Chapter 6). The data dictionary defines the contents of data flows and data stores so that systems builders understand exactly what pieces of data they contain. **Process specifications** describe the transformation occurring within the lowest level of the data flow diagrams. They express the logic for each process.

In structured methodology, software design is modeled using hierarchical structure charts. The **structure chart** is a top-down chart, showing each level of design, its relationship to other levels, and its place in the overall design structure. The design first considers the main function of a program or system, then breaks this function into subfunctions, and decomposes each subfunction until the lowest level of detail has been reached. Figure 13-6 shows a high-level structure chart for a payroll system. If a design has too many levels to fit onto one structure chart, it can be broken down further on more detailed structure charts. A structure chart may document one program, one system (a set of programs), or part of one program.

Object-Oriented Development

Structured methods are useful for modeling processes, but do not handle the modeling of data well. They also treat data and processes as logically separate entities, whereas in the real world such separation seems unnatural. Different modeling conventions are used for analysis (the data flow diagram) and for design (the structure chart).

Object-oriented development addresses these issues. Object-oriented development uses the **object** as the basic unit of systems analysis and design. An object combines data and the specific processes that operate on those data. Data encapsulated in an object can be accessed and modified only by the operations, or methods, associated with that object. Instead of passing data to procedures, programs send a message for an object to perform an operation that is already embedded in it. The system is modeled as a collection of objects and the relationships among them. Because processing logic resides within objects

FIGURE 13-6   HIGH-LEVEL STRUCTURE CHART FOR A PAYROLL SYSTEM

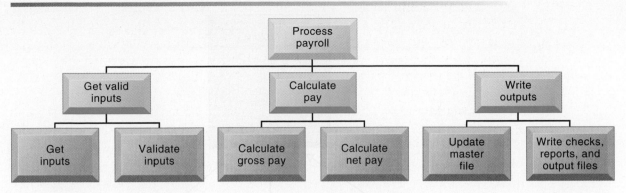

This structure chart shows the highest or most abstract level of design for a payroll system, providing an overview of the entire system.

rather that in separate software programs, objects must collaborate with each other to make the system work.

Object-oriented modeling is based on the concepts of *class* and *inheritance*. Objects belonging to a certain class, or general categories of similar objects, have the features of that class. Classes of objects in turn can inherit all the structure and behaviors of a more general class and then add variables and behaviors unique to each object. New classes of objects are created by choosing an existing class and specifying how the new class differs from the existing class, instead of starting from scratch each time.

We can see how class and inheritance work in Figure 13-7, which illustrates the relationships among classes concerning employees and how they are paid. Employee is the common ancestor, or superclass, for the other three classes. Salaried, Hourly, and Temporary are subclasses of Employee. The class name is in the top compartment, the attributes for each class are in the middle portion of each box, and the list of operations is in the bottom portion of each box. The features that are shared by all employees (id, name, address, date hired, position, and pay) are stored in the Employee superclass, whereas each subclass stores features that are specific to that particular type of employee. Specific to Hourly employees, for example, are their hourly rates and overtime rates. A solid line from the subclass to the superclass is a generalization path showing that the subclasses Salaried, Hourly, and Temporary have common features that can be generalized into the superclass Employee.

Object-oriented development is more iterative and incremental than traditional structured development. During analysis, systems builders document the functional requirements of the system, specifying its most important properties and what the proposed system must do. Interactions between the system and its users are analyzed to identify objects, which include both data and processes. The object-oriented design phase describes how the objects will behave and how they will interact with one other. Similar objects are grouped together to form a class, and classes are grouped into hierarchies in which a subclass inherits the attributes and methods from its superclass.

The information system is implemented by translating the design into program code, reusing classes that are already available in a library of reusable software objects and adding new ones created during the object-oriented design phase. Implementation may also involve the creation of an object-oriented database. The resulting system must be thoroughly tested and evaluated.

FIGURE 13-7 **CLASS AND INHERITANCE**

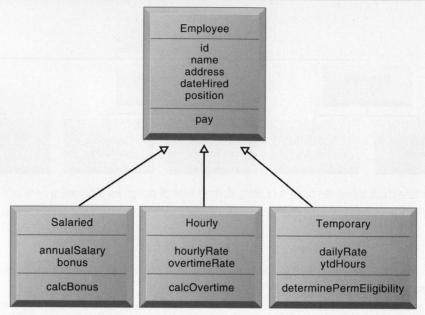

This figure illustrates how classes inherit the common features of their superclass.

Because objects are reusable, object-oriented development could potentially reduce the time and cost of writing software because organizations can reuse software objects that have already been created as building blocks for other applications. New systems can be created by using some existing objects, changing others, and adding a few new objects. Object-oriented frameworks have been developed to provide reusable, semicomplete applications that the organization can further customize into finished applications.

Computer-Aided Software Engineering

Computer-aided software engineering (CASE)—sometimes called *computer-aided systems engineering*—provides software tools to automate the methodologies we have just described to reduce the amount of repetitive work the developer needs to do. CASE tools also facilitate the creation of clear documentation and the coordination of team development efforts. Team members can share their work easily by accessing each other's files to review or modify what has been done. Modest productivity benefits can also be achieved if the tools are used properly.

CASE tools provide automated graphics facilities for producing charts and diagrams, screen and report generators, data dictionaries, extensive reporting facilities, analysis and checking tools, code generators, and documentation generators. In general, CASE tools try to increase productivity and quality by doing the following:

- Enforce a standard development methodology and design discipline
- Improve communication between users and technical specialists
- Organize and correlate design components and provide rapid access to them using a design repository
- Automate tedious and error-prone portions of analysis and design
- Automate code generation and testing and control rollout

CASE tools contain features for validating design diagrams and specifications. CASE tools thus support iterative design by automating revisions and changes and providing prototyping facilities. A CASE information repository stores all the information defined by the analysts during the project. The repository includes data flow diagrams, structure charts, entity-relationship diagrams, data definitions, process specifications, screen and report formats, notes and comments, and test results.

To be used effectively, CASE tools require organizational discipline. Every member of a development project must adhere to a common set of naming conventions and standards as well as to a development methodology. The best CASE tools enforce common methods and standards, which may discourage their use in situations where organizational discipline is lacking.

13.3 ALTERNATIVE SYSTEMS-BUILDING APPROACHES

Systems differ in terms of their size and technological complexity and in terms of the organizational problems they are meant to solve. A number of systems-building approaches have been developed to deal with these differences. This section describes these alternative methods: the traditional systems life cycle, prototyping, application software packages, end-user development, and outsourcing.

TRADITIONAL SYSTEMS LIFE CYCLE

The **systems life cycle** is the oldest method for building information systems. The life cycle methodology is a phased approach to building a system, dividing systems development into formal stages. Systems development specialists have different opinions on how to partition the systems-building stages, but they roughly correspond to the stages of systems development that we have just described.

The systems life cycle methodology maintains a very formal division of labor between end users and information systems specialists. Technical specialists, such as system analysts and programmers, are responsible for much of the systems analysis, design, and implementation work; end users are limited to providing information requirements and reviewing the technical staff's work. The life cycle also emphasizes formal specifications and paperwork, so many documents are generated during the course of a systems project.

The systems life cycle is still used for building large complex systems that require a rigorous and formal requirements analysis, predefined specifications, and tight controls over the systems-building process. However, the systems life cycle approach can be costly, time-consuming, and inflexible. Although systems builders can go back and forth among stages in the life cycle, the systems life cycle is predominantly a "waterfall" approach in which tasks in one stage are completed before work for the next stage begins. Activities can be repeated, but volumes of new documents must be generated and steps retraced if requirements and specifications need to be revised. This encourages freezing of specifications relatively early in the development process. The life cycle approach is also not suitable for many small desktop systems, which tend to be less structured and more individualized.

PROTOTYPING

Prototyping consists of building an experimental system rapidly and inexpensively for end users to evaluate. By interacting with the prototype, users can get a better idea of their information requirements. The prototype endorsed by the users can be used as a template to create the final system.

The **prototype** is a working version of an information system or part of the system, but it is meant to be only a preliminary model. Once operational, the prototype will be further refined until it conforms precisely to users' requirements. Once the design has been finalized, the prototype can be converted to a polished production system.

The process of building a preliminary design, trying it out, refining it, and trying again has been called an **iterative** process of systems development because the steps required to build a system can be repeated over and over again. Prototyping is more explicitly iterative than the conventional life cycle, and it actively promotes system design changes. It has been said that prototyping replaces unplanned rework with planned iteration, with each version more accurately reflecting users' requirements.

Steps in Prototyping

Figure 13-8 shows a four-step model of the prototyping process, which consists of the following:

Step 1: *Identify the user's basic requirements.* The system designer (usually an information systems specialist) works with the user only long enough to capture the user's basic information needs.

Step 2: *Develop an initial prototype.* The system designer creates a working prototype quickly, using tools for rapidly generating software.

Step 3: *Use the prototype.* The user is encouraged to work with the system to determine how well the prototype meets his or her needs and to make suggestions for improving the prototype.

Step 4: *Revise and enhance the prototype.* The system builder notes all changes the user requests and refines the prototype accordingly. After the prototype has been revised, the cycle returns to step 3. Steps 3 and 4 are repeated until the user is satisfied.

When no more iterations are required, the approved prototype then becomes an operational prototype that furnishes the final specifications for the application. Sometimes the prototype is adopted as the production version of the system.

Advantages and Disadvantages of Prototyping

Prototyping is most useful when there is some uncertainty about requirements or design solutions and often used for designing an information system's **end-user interface** (the part of the system with which end users interact, such as online display and data-entry screens, reports, or Web pages). Because prototyping encourages intense end-user involvement throughout the systems development life cycle, it is more likely to produce systems that fulfill user requirements.

However, rapid prototyping can gloss over essential steps in systems development. If the completed prototype works reasonably well, management may not see the need for reprogramming, redesign, or full documentation and testing to build a polished production system. Some of these hastily constructed systems may not easily accommodate large quantities of data or a large number of users in a production environment.

FIGURE 13-8   THE PROTOTYPING PROCESS

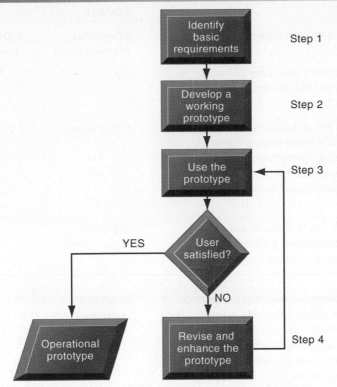

The process of developing a prototype can be broken down into four steps. Because a prototype can be developed quickly and inexpensively, systems builders can go through several iterations, repeating steps 3 and 4, to refine and enhance the prototype before arriving at the final operational one.

END-USER DEVELOPMENT

Some types of information systems can be developed by end users with little or no formal assistance from technical specialists. This phenomenon is called **end-user development**. A series of software tools categorized as fourth-generation languages makes this possible. **Fourth-generation languages** are software tools that enable end users to create reports or develop software applications with minimal or no technical assistance. Some of these fourth-generation tools also enhance professional programmers' productivity.

Fourth-generation languages tend to be nonprocedural, or less procedural, than conventional programming languages. Procedural languages require specification of the sequence of steps, or procedures, that tell the computer what to do and how to do it. Nonprocedural languages need only specify what has to be accomplished rather than provide details about how to carry out the task.

Table 13-3 shows that there are seven categories of fourth-generation languages: PC software tools, query languages, report generators, graphics languages, application generators, application software packages, and very high-level programming languages. The table shows the tools ordered in terms of ease of use by nonprogramming end users. End users are most likely to work with PC software tools and query languages. **Query languages** are software tools that provide immediate online answers to requests for information that are not predefined, such as "Who are the highest-performing sales representatives?" Query languages are often tied to data management software and to database management systems (see Chapter 6).

TABLE 13-3 CATEGORIES OF FOURTH-GENERATION LANGUAGES

FOURTH-GENERATION TOOL	DESCRIPTION	EXAMPLE	
PC software tools	General-purpose application software packages for PCs.	WordPerfect Microsoft Access	Oriented toward end users
Query language	Languages for retrieving data stored in databases or files. Capable of supporting requests for information that are not predefined.	SQL	
Report generator	Extract data from files or databases to create customized reports in a wide range of formats not routinely produced by an information system. Generally provide more control over the way data are formatted, organized, and displayed than query languages.	Crystal Reports	
Graphics language	Retrieve data from files or databases and display them in graphic format. Some graphics software can perform arithmetic or logical operations on data as well.	SAS Graph Systat	
Application generator	Contain preprogrammed modules that can generate entire applications, including Web sites, greatly speeding development. A user can specify what needs to be done, and the application generator will create the appropriate program code for input, validation, update, processing, and reporting.	WebFOCUS QuickBase	
Application software package	Software programs sold or leased by commercial vendors that eliminate the need for custom-written, in-house software.	Oracle PeopleSoft HCM mySAP ERP	
Very high-level programming language	Generate program code with fewer instructions than conventional languages, such as COBOL or FORTRAN. Designed primarily as productivity tools for professional programmers.	APL Nomad2	Oriented toward IS professionals

On the whole, end-user-developed systems can be completed more rapidly than those developed through the conventional systems life cycle. Allowing users to specify their own business needs improves requirements gathering and often leads to a higher level of user involvement and satisfaction with the system. However, fourth-generation tools still cannot replace conventional tools for some business applications because they cannot easily handle the processing of large numbers of transactions or applications with extensive procedural logic and updating requirements.

End-user computing also poses organizational risks because it occurs outside of traditional mechanisms for information systems management and control. When systems are created rapidly, without a formal development methodology, testing and documentation may be inadequate. Control over data can be lost in systems outside the traditional information systems department. To help organizations maximize the benefits of end-user applications development, management should control the development of end-user applications by requiring cost justification of end-user information system projects and by establishing hardware, software, and quality standards for user-developed applications.

APPLICATION SOFTWARE PACKAGES AND OUTSOURCING

Chapter 5 points out that the software for most systems today is not developed in-house but is purchased from external sources. Firms can rent the software from a software service provider, they can purchase a software package from a commercial vendor, or they can have a custom application developed by an outside outsourcing firm.

Application Software Packages

During the past several decades, many systems have been built on an application software package foundation. Many applications are common to all business organizations—for example, payroll, accounts receivable, general ledger, or inventory control. For such universal functions with standard processes that do not change a great deal over time, a generalized system will fulfill the requirements of many organizations.

If a software package can fulfill most of an organization's requirements, the company does not have to write its own software. The company can save time and money by using the prewritten, predesigned, pretested software programs from the package. Package vendors supply much of the ongoing maintenance and support for the system, including enhancements to keep the system in line with ongoing technical and business developments.

If an organization has unique requirements that the package does not address, many packages include capabilities for customization. **Customization** features allow a software package to be modified to meet an organization's unique requirements without destroying the integrity of the package software. If a great deal of customization is required, additional programming and customization work may become so expensive and time-consuming that they negate many of the advantages of software packages. PC Connection, described in the chapter-opening case, decided not to use a software package for these reasons.

When a system is developed using an application software package, systems analysis will include a package evaluation effort. The most important evaluation criteria are the functions provided by the package, flexibility, user friendliness, hardware and software resources, database requirements, installation and maintenance efforts, documentation, vendor quality, and cost. The package evaluation process often is based on a **Request for Proposal (RFP)**, which is a detailed list of questions submitted to packaged-software vendors.

When a software package solution is selected, the organization no longer has total control over the system design process. Instead of tailoring the system design specifications directly to user requirements, the design effort will consist of trying to mold user requirements to conform to the features of the package. If the organization's requirements conflict with the way the package works and the package cannot be customized, the organization will have to adapt to the package and change its procedures.

Outsourcing

If a firm does not want to use its internal resources to build or operate information systems, it can outsource the work to an external organization that specializes in providing these services. Cloud computing and SaaS providers, which we describe in Chapter 5, are one form of outsourcing. Subscribing companies would use the software and computer hardware provided by the service as the technical platform for their systems. In another form of outsourcing, a company could hire an external vendor to design and create the software for its system, but that company would operate the system on its own computers. The outsourcing vendor might be domestic or in another country.

Domestic outsourcing is driven primarily by the fact that outsourcing firms possess skills, resources, and assets which their clients do not have. Installing a new supply chain management system in a very large company might require hiring an additional 30-50 people with specific expertise in supply chain management software licensed, say, from i2 or another vendor. Rather than hire permanent new employees, most of whom would need extensive training in the software package, and then release them after the new system is built, it makes more sense, and is often less expensive, to outsource this work for a 12-month period.

In the case of **offshore outsourcing**, the decision tends to be much more cost-driven. A skilled programmer in India or Russia earns about U.S. $9,000 per year, compared to $65,000 per year for a comparable programmer in the United States. The Internet and low-cost communications technology have drastically reduced the expense and difficulty of coordinating the work of global teams in faraway locations. In addition to cost savings, many offshore outsourcing firms offer world-class technology assets and skills. Wage inflation outside the United States has recently eroded some of these advantages, and some jobs have moved back to the United States.

Nevertheless, there is a very strong chance that at some point in your career, you'll be working with offshore outsourcers or global teams. Your firm is most likely to benefit from outsourcing if it takes the time to evaluate all the risks and to make sure outsourcing is appropriate for its particular needs. Any company that outsources its applications must thoroughly understand the project, including its requirements, method of implementation, anticipated benefits, cost components, and metrics for measuring performance.

Many firms underestimate costs for identifying and evaluating vendors of information technology services, for transitioning to a new vendor, for improving internal software development methods to match those of outsourcing vendors, and for monitoring vendors to make sure they are fulfilling their contractual obligations. Companies will need to allocate resources for documenting requirements, sending out requests for proposal (RFPs), travel expenses, negotiating contracts, and project management. Experts claim it takes from three months to a full year to fully transfer work to an offshore partner and make sure the vendor thoroughly understands your business.

Outsourcing offshore incurs additional costs for coping with cultural differences that drain productivity and dealing with human resources issues, such as terminating or relocating domestic employees. All of these hidden costs undercut some of the anticipated benefits from outsourcing. Firms should be especially cautious when using an outsourcer to develop or to operate applications that give it some type of competitive advantage.

Figure 13-9 shows best- and worst-case scenarios for the total cost of an offshore outsourcing project. It shows how much hidden costs affect the total project cost. The best case reflects the lowest estimates for additional costs, and the worst case reflects the highest estimates for these costs. As you can see, hidden costs increase the total cost of an offshore outsourcing project by an extra 15 to 57 percent. Even with these extra costs, many firms will benefit from offshore outsourcing if they manage the work well. Under the worst-case scenario, a firm would still save about 15 percent.

FIGURE 13-9   TOTAL COST OF OFFSHORE OUTSOURCING

TOTAL COST OF OFFSHORE OUTSOURCING				
Cost of outsourcing contract			$10, 000, 000	
Hidden Costs	Best Case	Additional Cost ($)	Worst Case	Additional Cost ($)
1. Vendor selection	0%	20,000	2%	200,000
2. Transition costs	2%	200,000	3%	300,000
3. Layoffs & retention	3%	300,000	5%	500,000
4. Lost productivity/cultural issues	3%	300,000	27%	2,700,000
5. Improving development processes	1%	100,000	10%	1,000,000
6. Managing the contract	6%	600,000	10%	1,000,000
Total additional costs		1,520,000		5,700,000
	Outstanding Contract ($)	Additional Cost ($)	Total Cost ($)	Additional Cost
Total cost of outsourcing (TCO) best case	10,000,000	1,520,000	11,520,000	15.2%
Total cost of outsourcing (TCO) worst case	10,000,000	5,700,000	15,700,000	57.0%

If a firm spends $10 million on offshore outsourcing contracts, that company will actually spend 15.2 percent in extra costs even under the best-case scenario. In the worst-case scenario, where there is a dramatic drop in productivity along with exceptionally high transition and layoff costs, a firm can expect to pay up to 57 percent in extra costs on top of the $10 million outlay for an offshore contract.

The Interactive Session on Management describes a recent outsourcing arrangement between Chrysler LLC and Tata Consultancy Services (TCS), a global provider of information technology and business services based in India. As you read this case, try to apply what you have just read. Was outsourcing to TCS the right decision?

13.4   APPLICATION DEVELOPMENT FOR THE DIGITAL FIRM

In the digital firm environment, organizations need to be able to add, change, and retire their technology capabilities very rapidly to respond to new opportunities. Companies are starting to use shorter, more informal development processes that provide fast solutions. In addition to using software packages and external service providers, businesses are relying more heavily on fast-cycle techniques such as rapid application development (RAD), joint application design (JAD), agile development, and reusable standardized software components that can be assembled into a complete set of services for e-commerce and e-business.

RAPID APPLICATION DEVELOPMENT (RAD)

Object-oriented software tools, reusable software, prototyping, and fourth-generation language tools are helping systems builders create working systems much more rapidly than they could using traditional systems-building methods and software tools. The term **rapid application development (RAD)** is used to describe this process of creating workable systems in a very short period of time. RAD can include the use of visual programming and other tools for building graphical user interfaces, iterative prototyping of key system

INTERACTIVE SESSION: MANAGEMENT

DID CHRYSLER MAKE THE RIGHT OUTSOURCING DECISION?

On April 4, 2008, Tata Consultancy Services (TCS), a leading global information technology services provider, announced it had signed a multi-year, multi-million dollar outsourcing contract to provide Chrysler LLC with a comprehensive set of information technology services. Was this a good move for Chrysler?

Tata Consultancy Services is a unit of the Tata Group, and a sister division to Tata Motors, a company that will compete in India—and potentially other parts of the world—with Chrysler (see the Chapter 2 opening case). Tata Motors recently purchased the Jaguar and Land Rover brands from Ford Motor Company. One of TCS's focus markets is the automotive industry. TCS provides services for product development, manufacturing, supply chain, and customer service support to the leading auto manufacturers and suppliers in North America, Europe, and Japan. More than 15 percent of TCS's $4.3 billion in annual revenue came from services for auto manufacturers.

A preliminary version of the agreement had been announced earlier in February. Tata agreed to take over Chrysler's application maintenance and support services, particularly for Chrysler's sales, marketing, product development, shared services, and after sales functions.

In providing these services, TCS will leverage its Global Network Delivery Model, a collaborative best-of-class framework of people, processes, and infrastructure that uses TCS's tools, methodologies, and products to help customers reduce implementation time and realize business benefits. The Global Network Delivery Model is considered a benchmark of excellence in software development. TCS has over 108,000 IT consultants in 47 countries, including the United States.

According to N. Chandrasekaran, TCS executive director and chief operating officer, "The expertise and in-depth knowledge of the automotive industry and Chrysler's business, coupled with our ability to deliver certainty of results, will provide sustained value to Chrysler."

Chrysler declined to disclose the cost of the contract, but Tata officials indicated it might be worth around $100 million. They did not indicate how long the contract runs.

Jan Bertsch, Chrysler vice president and CIO, said that "This is really the next step in our continuous effort...to operate more efficiently and effectively... We do have the expectation of significant cost savings and that will allow future growth within this company." Bertsch declined to say exactly how much savings this outsourcing arrangement would produce.

Dennis Greathouse, third vice president of United Auto Workers Local 412, stated that Chrysler cost estimators—employees with technical backgrounds who examine competitive price issues involved in parts work—believe their jobs will eventually be taken over by Tata. Annual compensation for a cost estimator in the United States is around $70,000 to $80,000 per year. Greathouse said he was told that Tata could hire two to three people for the same price as one U.S. employee.

Chrysler's IT workers questioned how outside firms could be as efficient as people who had been working on Chrysler systems for years. But Bertsch asserted that the change will improve the company's IT operations. Chrysler's new management had determined that the company was spending too much of its IT budget on core maintenance of systems and not enough in reinvesting in the business.

Chrysler had about 2,100 people doing information systems work, of which 1,000 were full-time Chrysler employees and the rest supplemental workers on contract. Bertsch said that about 200 people, 20 percent of the full-time employees, were scheduled to lose their jobs because of the new outsourcing arrangement.

Detroit's automakers have struggled during the past few years as rising fuel prices and a housing meltdown hammered sales of pickup trucks and SUVs. Chrysler lost $2.9 billion on operations and restructuring costs in 2007. The company was spun off as a privately held company in 2007 when the venture capital firm Cerberus Capital Management bought it from Daimler for nearly $7 billion. Since that time, four products have been eliminated, thousands of jobs have been cut, and new executives have been appointed.

Cerberus puts a premium on not being bound by old practices. Chrysler was the first of the Detroit Three automakers to pull back on auto leasing in the tight credit market. Cerberus is betting it can get the company back to the break-even point by fixing its operational problems and cutting costs. Accoding to Jim McTevia, managing member of McTevia & Associates consultants, "There are only a couple of things they can do to turn this company around, and in this economy they have to keep chipping away at expenses."

Sources: Lawrence Walsh, "Tata Will Drive Chrysler's IT," *Baseline Magazine*, February 21, 2008; Patrick Thibodeau, "Chrysler Moves More IT Work to Offshore Giant Tata," *Computerworld*, February 21, 2008; "Tata Scores Again with Chrysler IT Outsourcing," *Detroit Free Press*, April 4, 2008; "Tata Consultancy Services Wins Multi-Year Deal with Chrysler LLC," *PR Newswire*, February 20, 2008.

CASE STUDY QUESTIONS

1. What management, organization, and technology issues should Chrysler have explored when deciding whether to outsource to TCS?
2. What points should Chrysler have addressed in its outsourcing contract with TCS?
3. Was Tata Consultancy Services a good outsourcing choice for Chrysler? Why or why not? Explain your answer.

MIS IN ACTION

Explore the Tata Consultancy Services Web site and then answer the following questions:

1. What kinds of services does TCS offer its clients?
2. Select one of the TCS offerings and describe how it could benefit Chrysler.

elements, the automation of program code generation, and close teamwork among end users and information systems specialists. Simple systems often can be assembled from prebuilt components. The process does not have to be sequential, and key parts of development can occur simultaneously.

Sometimes a technique called **joint application design (JAD)** is used to accelerate the generation of information requirements and to develop the initial systems design. JAD brings end users and information systems specialists together in an interactive session to discuss the system's design. Properly prepared and facilitated, JAD sessions can significantly speed up the design phase and involve users at an intense level.

Agile development focuses on rapid delivery of working software by breaking a large project into a series of small sub-projects that are completed in short periods of time using iteration and continuous feedback. Each mini-project is worked on by a team as if it were a complete project, including planning, requirements analysis, design, coding, testing, and documentation. Improvement or addition of new functionality takes place within the next iteration as developers clarify requirements. This helps to minimize the overall risk, and allows the project to adapt to changes more quickly. Agile methods emphasize face-to-face communication over written documents, encouraging people to collaborate and make decisions quickly and effectively.

COMPONENT-BASED DEVELOPMENT AND WEB SERVICES

We have already described some of the benefits of object-oriented development for building systems that can respond to rapidly changing business environments, including Web applications. To further expedite software creation, groups of objects have been assembled to provide software components for common functions such as a graphical user interface or online ordering capability that can be combined to create large-scale business applications. This approach to software development is called **component-based development**, and it enables a system to be built by assembling and integrating existing software components. Businesses are using component-based development to create their e-commerce applications by combining commercially available components for shopping carts, user authentication, search engines, and catalogs with pieces of software for their own unique business requirements.

Web Services and Service-Oriented Computing

Chapter 5 introduced *Web services* as loosely coupled, reusable software components deliverable using Extensible Markup Language (XML) and other open protocols and standards that enable one application to communicate with another with no custom programming required to share data and services. In addition to supporting internal and external integration of systems, Web services can be used as tools for building new information system applications or enhancing existing systems, as described in the chapter-opening case study. Because these software services use a universal set of standards, they promise to be less expensive and less difficult to weave together than proprietary components.

Web services can perform certain functions on their own, and they can also engage other Web services to complete more complex transactions, such as checking credit, procurement, or ordering products. By creating software components that can communicate and share data regardless of the operating system, programming language, or client device, Web services can provide significant cost savings in systems building while opening up new opportunities for collaboration with other companies.

13.5 HANDS-ON MIS PROJECTS

The projects in this section give you hands-on experience analyzing business process problems, designing and building a customer system for auto sales, and redesigning business processes for a company that wants to purchase goods over the Web.

Management Decision Problems

1. For an additional fee, a customer purchasing a Sears Roebuck appliance, such as a washing machine, can purchase a three-year service contract. The contract provides free repair service and parts for the specified appliance using an authorized Sears service provider. When a person with a Sears service contract needs to repair an appliance, such as a washing machine, he or she calls the Sears Repairs & Parts department to schedule an appointment. The department makes the appointment and gives the caller the date and approximate time of the appointment. The repair technician arrives during the designated time framework and diagnoses the problem. If the problem is caused by a faulty part, the technician either replaces the part if he is carrying the part with him or orders the replacement part from Sears. If the part is not in stock at Sears, Sears orders the part and gives the customer an approximate time when the part will arrive. The part is shipped directly to the customer. After the part has arrived, the customer must call Sears to schedule a second appointment for a repair technician to replace the ordered part. This process is very lengthy.

It make take 2 weeks to schedule the first repair visit, another 2 weeks to order and receive the required part, and another week to schedule a second repair visit after the ordered part has been received.

- Diagram the existing process.
- What is the impact of the existing process on Sears' operational efficiency and customer relationships?
- What changes could be made to make this process more efficient? How could information systems support these changes? Diagram the new improved process.

2. Management at your agricultural chemicals corporation has been dissatisfied with production planning. Production plans are created using best guesses of demand for each product, which are based on how much of each product has been ordered in the past. If a customer places an unexpected order or requests a change to an existing order after it has been placed, there is no way to adjust production plans. The company may have to tell customers it can't fill their orders, or it may run up extra costs maintaining additional inventory to prevent stock-outs.

At the end of each month, orders are totaled and manually keyed into the company's production planning system. Data from the past month's production and inventory systems are manually entered into the firm's order management system. Analysts from the sales department and from the production department analyze the data from their respective systems to determine what the sales targets and production targets should be for the next month. These estimates are usually different. The analysts then get together at a high-level planning meeting to revise the production and sales targets to take into account senior management's goals for market share, revenues, and profits. The outcome of the meeting is a finalized production master schedule.

The entire production planning process takes 17 business days to complete. Nine of these days are required to enter and validate the data. The remaining days are spent developing and reconciling the production and sales targets and finalizing the production master schedule.

- Draw a diagram of the existing production planning process.
- Analyze the problems this process creates for the company.
- How could an enterprise system solve these problems? In what ways could it lower costs? Diagram what the production planning process might look like if the company implemented enterprise software.

Improving Decision Making: Using Database Software to Design a Customer System for Auto Sales

Software skills: Database design, querying, reporting, and forms
Business skills: Sales lead and customer analysis

This project requires you to perform a systems analysis and then design a system solution using database software.

Ace Auto Dealers specializes in selling new vehicles from Subaru. The company advertises in local newspapers and also is listed as an authorized dealer on the Subaru Web site and other major Web sites for auto buyers. The company benefits from a good local word-of-mouth reputation and name recognition and is a leading source of information for Subaru vehicles in the Portland, Oregon, area.

When a prospective customer enters the showroom, he or she is greeted by an Ace sales representative. The sales representative manually fills out a form with information such as the prospective customer's name, address, telephone number, date of visit, and make and model of the vehicle in which the customer is interested. The representative also asks where the prospect heard about Ace—whether it was from a newspaper ad, the Web, or word of mouth—and this information is noted on the form also. If the customer decides to purchase an auto, the dealer fills out a bill of sale form.

Ace does not believe it has enough information about its customers. It cannot easily determine which prospects have made auto purchases, nor can it identify which customer touch points have produced the greatest number of sales leads or actual sales so it can focus advertising and marketing more on the channels that generate the most revenue. Are purchasers discovering Ace from newspaper ads, from word of mouth, or from the Web?

Prepare a systems analysis report detailing Ace's problem and a system solution that can be implemented using PC database management software. Then use database software to develop a simple system solution. Your systems analysis report should include the following:

- Description of the problem and its organizational and business impact.
- Proposed solution, solution objectives, and solution feasibility.
- Costs and benefits of the solution you have selected. The company has a PC with Internet access and the full suite of Microsoft Office desktop productivity tools.
- Information requirements to be addressed by the solution.
- Management, organization, and technology issues to be addressed by the solution, including changes in business processes.

On the basis of the requirements you have identified, design the database and populate it with at least 10 records per table. Consider whether you can use or modify Ace's existing customer database in your design. You can find this database on the Companion Web site for Chapter 13. Print out the database design. Then use the system you have created to generate queries and reports that would be of most interest to management. Create several prototype data input forms for the system and review them with your instructor. Then revise the prototypes.

Achieving Operational Excellence: Redesigning Business Processes for Web Procurement

Software skills: Web browser software
Business skills: Procurement

This project requires you to rethink how a business should be redesigned when it moves to the Web.

You are in charge of purchasing for your firm and would like to use the Grainger.com (www.grainger.com) B2B e-commerce site for this purpose. Find out how to place an order for painting supplies by exploring the Catalog, Order Form, and Repair Parts Order capabilities of this site. Do not register at the site. Describe all the steps your firm would need to take to use this system to place orders online for 30 gallons of paint thinner. Include a diagram of what you think your firm's business process for purchasing should be and the pieces of information required by this process.

In a traditional purchase process, whoever is responsible for making the purchase fills out a requisition form and submits it for approval based on the company's business rules. When the requisition is approved, a purchase order with a unique purchase order identification number is sent to the supplier. The purchaser might want to browse supplier catalogs to compare prices and features before placing the order. The purchaser might also want to determine whether the items to be purchased are available. If the purchasing firm were an approved customer, that company would be granted credit to make the purchase and would be billed for the total cost of the items purchased and shipped after the order was shipped. Alternatively, the purchasing company might have to pay for the order in advance or pay for the order using a credit card. Multiple payment options might be possible. How might this process have to change to make purchases electronically from the Grainger site?

LEARNING TRACK MODULES

The following Learning Tracks provide content relevant to topics covered in this chapter:

1. Unified Modeling Language (UML)

2. A Primer on Business Process Design and Documentation

Review Summary

1. How does building new systems produce organizational change?

Building a new information system is a form of planned organizational change. Four kinds of technology-enabled change are (a) automation, (b) rationalization of procedures, (c) business reengineering, and (d) paradigm shift, with far-reaching changes carrying the greatest risks and rewards. Many organizations are attempting business reengineering to redesign work flows and business processes in the hope of achieving dramatic productivity breakthroughs. Information systems can also be used to support business process management, total quality management (TQM), six sigma, and other initiatives for incremental process improvement.

2. What are the core activities in the systems development process?

The core activities in systems development are systems analysis, systems design, programming, testing, conversion, production, and maintenance. Systems analysis is the study and analysis of problems of existing systems and the identification of requirements for their solutions. Systems design provides the specifications for an information system solution, showing how its technical and organizational components fit together.

3. What are the principal methodologies for modeling and designing systems?

The two principal methodologies for modeling and designing information systems are structured methodologies and object-oriented development. Structured methodologies focus on modeling processes and data separately. The data flow diagram is the principal tool for structured analysis, and the structure chart is the principal tool for representing structured software design. Object-oriented development models a system as a collection of objects that combine processes and data. Object-oriented modeling is based on the concepts of class and inheritance.

4. What are the alternative methods for building information systems?

The oldest method for building systems is the systems life cycle, which requires that information systems be developed in formal stages. The stages must proceed sequentially and have defined outputs; each requires formal approval before the next stage can commence. The systems life cycle is useful for large projects that need formal specifications and tight management control over each stage of systems building, but it is very rigid and costly.

Prototyping consists of building an experimental system rapidly and inexpensively for end users to interact with and evaluate. Prototyping encourages end-user involvement in systems development and iteration of design until specifications are captured accurately. The rapid creation of prototypes can result in systems that have not been completely tested or documented or that are technically inadequate for a production environment.

Using a software package reduces the amount of design, programming, testing, installation, and maintenance work required to build a system. Application software packages are helpful if a firm does not have the internal information systems staff or financial resources to custom develop a system. To meet an organization's unique requirements, packages may require extensive modifications that can substantially raise development costs.

End-user development is the development of information systems by end users, either alone or with minimal assistance from information systems specialists. End-user-developed systems can be created rapidly and informally using fourth-generation software tools. However, end-user development may create information systems that do not necessarily meet quality assurance standards and that are not easily controlled by traditional means.

Outsourcing consists of using an external vendor to build (or operate) a firm's information systems instead of the organization's internal information systems staff. Outsourcing can save application development costs or enable firms to develop applications without an internal information systems staff. However, firms risk losing control over their information systems and becoming too dependent on external vendors. Outsourcing also entails "hidden" costs, especially when the work is sent offshore.

5. *What are new approaches for system-building in the digital firm era?*

Companies are turning to rapid application design, joint application design (JAD), agile development, and reusable software components to accelerate the systems development process. Rapid application development (RAD) uses object-oriented software, visual programming, prototyping, and fourth-generation tools for very rapid creation of systems. Agile development breaks a large project into a series of small sub-projects that are completed in short periods of time using iteration and continuous feedback. Component-based development expedites application development by grouping objects into suites of software components that can be combined to create large-scale business applications. Web services provide a common set of standards that enable organizations to link their systems regardless of their technology platform through standard plug-and-play architecture

Key Terms

Acceptance testing, 518

Agile development, 535

Automation, 509

Benchmarking, 515

Business process management, 513

Business process reengineering, 510

Component-based development, 536

Computer-aided software engineering (CASE), 526

Conversion, 521

Customization, 531

Data flow diagram (DFD), 523

Direct cutover, 521

Documentation, 521

End-user development, 529

End-user interface, 528

Feasibility study, 516

Fourth-generation languages, 529

Information requirements, 516

Iterative, 528

Joint application design (JAD), 535

Maintenance, 522

Object, 524

Object-oriented development, 524

Offshore outsourcing, 532

Paradigm shift, 510

Parallel strategy, 521

Phased approach, 521

Pilot study, 521

Postimplementation audit, 522

Process specifications, 524

Production, 522

Programming, 518

Prototype, 528

Prototyping, 528

Query languages, 529

Rapid application development (RAD), 533

Rationalization of procedures, 510

Request for Proposal (RFP), 531

Six sigma, 514

Structure chart, 524

Structured, 523

Systems analysis, 515

Systems design, 517

Systems development, 515

Systems life cycle, 527

System testing, 518

Test plan, 520

Testing, 518

Total quality management (TQM), 514

Unit testing, 518

Work flow management, 511

Review Questions

1. How does building new systems produce organizational change?

    • Describe each of the four kinds of organizational change that can be promoted with information technology.

    • Define business process reengineering and explain how it differs from business process management. Describe the steps required for effective reengineering.

    • Explain how information systems support process changes that promote quality in an organization.

2. What are the core activities in the systems development process?

    • Distinguish between systems analysis and systems design. Describe the activities for each.

    • Define information requirements and explain why they are difficult to determine correctly.

    • Explain why the testing stage of systems development is so important. Name and describe the three stages of testing for an information system.

    • Describe the role of programming, conversion, production, and maintenance in systems development.

3. What are the principal methodologies for modeling and designing systems?

- Compare object-oriented and traditional structured approaches for modeling and designing systems.

4. What are the alternative methods for building information systems?

- Define the traditional systems life cycle. Describe each of its steps and its advantages and disadvantages for systems building.

- Define information system prototyping. Describe its benefits and limitations. List and describe the steps in the prototyping process.

- Define an application software package. Explain the advantages and disadvantages of developing information systems based on software packages.

- Define end-user development and describe its advantages and disadvantages. Name some policies and procedures for managing end-user development.

- Describe the advantages and disadvantages of using outsourcing for building information systems.

5. What are new approaches for system-building in the digital firm era?

- Define rapid application development (RAD) and agile development and explain how they can speed up system-building.

- Explain how component-based development and Web services help firms build and enhance their information systems.

Discussion Questions

1. Why is selecting a systems development approach an important business decision? Who should participate in the selection process?

2. Some have said that the best way to reduce systems development costs is to use application software packages or fourth-generation tools. Do you agree? Why or why not?

Video Cases

You will find video cases illustrating some of the concepts in this chapter on the Laudon Web site along with questions to help you analyze the cases.

Collaboration and Teamwork: Preparing Web Site Design Specifications

With three or four of your classmates, select a system described in this text that uses the Web. Review the Web site for the system you select. Use what you have learned from the Web site and the description in this book to prepare a report describing some of the design specifications for the system you select. If pos-

sible, use Google Sites to post links to Web pages, team communication announcements, and work assignments; to brainstorm; and to work collaboratively on project documents. Try to use Google Docs to develop a presentation of your findings for the class.

Citizens National Bank Searches for a System Solution
CASE STUDY

Citizens National Bank of Texas is a private, full-service bank with headquarters in Waxahachie, Texas, and 200 employees. The bank has operated independently since 1868. Citizens National serves businesses and consumers in Ellis County and other nearby counties, primarily in communities with populations of 25,000 or less. The bank counts total assets of $400 million and is growing annually at a rate of 12 percent. Since 1999, the number of branches has increased from four to 15, with locations in 10 cities. Citizens National would like to increase its market share to at least 50 percent in eight counties south of the Dallas-Fort Worth area.

A major part of Citizen National's strategy for continuing growth was to implement customer relationship management (CRM) software. The CRM strategy targeted the bank's two main contact points with customers: the bank's call center and its sales force. The call center receives around 4,000 calls per day, which are handled by between 10 and 20 customer service representatives. The sales force consists of 16 representatives, who are known by the title of relationship bankers. It is the relationship bankers that drive business for Citizens National. Their contacts with customers generate loan sales and deposits that make money for the bank.

In 2001, CEO Mark Singleton oversaw the adoption of a CRM package from Siebel Systems (Siebel is now owned by Oracle). The main goal for the implementation was to increase sales by raising the number of contacts relationship bankers were making and improving the tracking of these activities so that the bank could learn more from them. The CRM package promised additional benefits. The bank would be able to approve credit and loan applications more quickly. It would also finally have a method for storing the interactions between relationship bankers and customers electronically.

Electronic records were key for two reasons. Under the old paper system, a salesperson that left Citizens National could take records of customer interaction with him or her, leaving the bank with no information to maintain the relationship. The paper system also created too much information for Singleton and his branch managers to process effectively.

For Singleton, the decision to move to a CRM system was not a slam dunk. While he recognized the great value that automated systems provided to businesses, he placed even greater value on the person-to-person interactions between his relationship bankers and their customers. He feared that an overreaching CRM system might interfere with those interactions and diminish the relationship bankers' rapport with customers. The track record for the old-fashioned way was impressive. For retail customers, the bank's cross-sale ratio was between 2 and 2.5, meaning that the average customer used at least two of the bank's products. The top commercial and personal customers were using between six and seven products.

With this strength in mind, Singleton insisted that any CRM implementation at Citizens National be able to fortify the relationship bankers' knowledge of their customers and potential customers, including their previous interactions with the bank. The Siebel package, which had a price tag of $150,000, was supposed to fulfill this goal. The bank contracted with a local consulting firm, The Small Business Solution, to help install the package. The union of old-fashioned business sensibility with powerful enterprise software was a mismatch almost immediately. The approach of Citizens National toward nearly all business functions, from tracking customer leads to generating reports about them, was very basic. The Siebel software was simply too rich in features. The bank spent an inordinate amount of time switching off features that hindered productivity.

For example, Siebel had a complex module for handling customer support cases. It included capabilities for detailed management of complaints from initial call through subsequent calls to options for resolving the issue. Customer complaints at Citizens National rarely went that far. A representative at the call center handled them immediately. In cases where a second interaction was necessary, the representative simply sent an e-mail to the employee responsible for carrying out the action.

Jim Davis, an expert on CRM from Deloitte Consulting, characterized the situation at Citizens National by saying, "The problem with Siebel is that it has everything." At Citizens National, the sheer size of the package was not the only issue.

Employees found the software to be too complicated. They were surprised to learn, for example, that the system did not automatically generate potential business opportunities for customers on their records. They had to assign the potential transaction to the customer. Furthermore, bankers were not able to view multiple relationships between a customer and the bank on the same screen. The extra navigation was confusing and inefficient. Not surprisingly, the relationship bankers resisted the new system. It didn't make sense for them to change their tried-and-true methods simply because new software required change.

According to Davis, the disconnect between the relationship bankers and the new system was at the crux of the implementation's failure. The relationship bankers were the key employees; the system was intended to be of value to them, and, in turn, provide value to the bank. However, they found no incentive in the Siebel environment because their compensation was based on sales, and sales had become harder to make.

Citizens National also experienced compatibility issues between the database formats in Siebel and those used by the bank's core banking application, developed by Kirchman. The Kirchman software combined customer first and last names into one field, whereas Siebel had separate fields for first and last names. As a result, the two systems had difficulty exchanging information properly. The bank was forced to spend a significant amount of time fixing such compatibility issues, which negatively impacted its ability to serve customers.

Citizens National spent three years trying to make its Siebel CRM implementation work. In 2004, having derived no quantifiable benefit from the effort, the bank finally decided to cut its losses. In addition to the initial $150,000 purchase, it had spent $350,000 on solving integration issues. Singleton referred to the process as "a $500,000 education."

David Furney, president and CEO of The Small Business Solution, began searching for another CRM solution for Citizens National. Furney happened upon a hosted online database system from Intuit called QuickBase, which was targeted toward small businesses and corporate work groups. It is especially well-suited for building simple database applications very quickly and does not require a great deal of training to use. Intuit was best known for its financial management applications such as Quicken and QuickBooks. The company did not have a defined reputation in the CRM market.

QuickBase included modules for databases, spreadsheets, and sales management, all of which could be easily manipulated for the bank's business functions. QuickBase was designed for organizing, tracking, and sharing information among team members in the workplace while encouraging progress by notifying workers via automated e-mails of updated files, new task assignments, and approaching deadlines. Intuit offered in the product ready-made applications for general purposes, such as project management, sales management, and marketing management, as well as more specific purposes, such as healthcare IT, legal, and real estate.

Furney referred to QuickBase as "the ultimate in rapid application development" and "a kind of do-it-yourself application." Citizens National people, including Singleton, would be able to customize the package themselves rather than having to solicit help from the manufacturer or an IT specialist. To make changes in the Siebel system, the bank had to request help from Siebel. Because QuickBase was not programmed as a specific business application, businesses could modify its database structure to meet specific business functions. The Citizens National staff were able to make changes to QuickBase themselves, so the cost of ownership and maintenance fees were much lower.

QuickBase offered Citizens National flexibility that it did not have previously. Because the system was Web-based, the relationship bankers were able to use it anywhere that they had access to a browser. In addition to the cost of ownership savings, Citizens National saved a small fortune with QuickBase, which started with a one-time fee of $249 for the first 10 users and increased by $3 per month for each additional user (the cost is now $249 per month plus $15 per month for every five additional users).

Singleton still had to deal with the fact that some relationship bankers would have preferred to push technology aside altogether. To give the system its best chance of success, Singleton permitted these bankers to dictate their activity to administrative assistants. The assistants then entered the information into QuickBase for the bankers. Davis observed that this may not have been the best practice, but it was fairly common and, more importantly, very worthwhile if the bankers were devoting their time to making money for the bank rather than wasting it wrestling with technology. Citizens National made the transition easier additionally by implementing QuickBase using a phased rollout, starting with the call center.

Also central to the success of QuickBase at Citizens National was Furney's ability to integrate the system with the Kirchman core banking application. Furney configured QuickBase to upload new account information to the core system every night via an XML interface. Relationship bankers and management received daily updated access to all interactions and transactions, enabling them to track business in a way that was never possible previously. For the first time, Citizens National was able to completely track sales opportunities and, as Singleton said, "where we lost business, so we know where we need to make those extra 10 or 15 sales calls."

Sources: Doug Bartholomew, "A Banker's $500,000 Lesson in CRM," *Baseline Magazine*, February 26, 2007; www.cnbwax.com, accessed September 23, 2008; www. quickbase.intuit.com, accessed September 21, 2008; Mark Singleton, as told to Colin Beasty, "Secret of My Success: Getting More for the Money," www.destinationcrm.com, March 1, 2006; and "Siebel Customer Relationship Management Applications," www.oracle.com, March 30, 2007.

CASE STUDY QUESTIONS

1. What was the initial problem that Mark Singleton was trying to solve at Citizens National?

2. What was the business case for implementing a new system? What were some of the tangible benefits? What were some of the intangible benefits?

3. Why didn't the implementation of the Siebel CRM solution work out for Citizens National? What were the biggest factors? How would you classify these factors in terms of organization, technology, and management issues?

4. Was QuickBase a better solution for Citizens National? If so, why? What factors suggest that the bank ended up with the right approach and the right choice of product?

5. Based on this case study, what kind of organization do you think would benefit from using the Siebel CRM package? Give an example of such an organization and justify your choice. You may use the Web to research your answer, including Oracle's Web site.

6. Could Citizens National have made a better choice of software for its CRM system the first time around? Explain your answer.

Chapter 14

Managing Projects

LEARNING OBJECTIVES

After reading this chapter, you will be able to answer the following questions:

1. What are the objectives of project management and why is it so essential in developing information systems?

2. What methods can be used for selecting and evaluating information systems projects and aligning them with the firm's business goals?

3. How can firms assess the business value of information systems projects?

4. What are the principal risk factors in information systems projects?

5. What strategics are useful for managing project risk and system implementation?

Interactive Sessions:

Kaiser Permanente Botches Its Kidney Transplant Center Project

Why Can't BioSense Take Off?

CHAPTER OUTLINE

14.1 THE IMPORTANCE OF PROJECT MANAGEMENT
Runaway Projects and System Failure
Project Management Objectives

14.2 SELECTING PROJECTS
Management Structure for Information Systems Projects
Linking Systems Projects to the Business Plan
Critical Success Factors
Portfolio Analysis
Scoring Models

14.3 ESTABLISHING THE BUSINESS VALUE OF INFORMATION SYSTEMS
Information System Costs and Benefits
Real Options Pricing Models
Limitations of Financial Models

14.4 MANAGING PROJECT RISK
Dimensions of Project Risk
Change Management and the Concept of Implementation
Controlling Risk Factors
Designing for the Organization
Project Management Software Tools

14.5 HANDS-ON MIS PROJECTS
Management Decision Problems
Improving Decision Making: Using Spreadsheet Software for Capital Budgeting for a New CAD System
Improving Decision Making: Using Web Tools for Buying and Financing a Home

LEARNING TRACK MODULES
Capital Budgeting Methods for Information System Investments
Information Technology Investments and Productivity
Enterprise Analysis (Business Systems Planning)

MCKESSON'S PRESCRIPTION FOR PROJECT MANAGEMENT

McKesson Corporation is the largest pharmaceutical distributor in the United States and was a leader in using information technology to make its operations more efficient and improve health care. Until recently, however, its McKesson Pharmaceutical business unit was grappling with inconsistent and fragmented data from multiple sources that hampered operational efficiency and decision making for order processing and inventory management. Logistics and finance personnel had to manually extract data from different distributed systems to achieve a company-wide view of inventory. In a business where high-value products sell at low profit margins, small losses due to outdated products in stock have a significant financial impact.

Management decided to replace its multiple data repositories and reporting systems with a common business intelligence infrastructure operating on a single integrated enterprise data warehouse for business intelligence and analytical reporting using SAP NetWeaver Business Intelligence tools. The system centrally houses and organizes critical company data that can be quickly accessed and analyzed using a series of Web-based scorecards, dashboards, and business intelligence performance tools. Operations and finance teams are able to spot and resolve inventory issues immediately as they arise.

It was a massive undertaking and a very ambitious project. A huge volume of transactional data, estimated at 15 million records per day, had to be extracted from multiple legacy systems as well as the company's new SAP enterprise system and loaded into the data warehouse. The system's business users were both sophisticated and demanding, which required a carefully designed user interface for analytical and reporting tools. McKesson's internal information systems staff had limited experience implementing SAP Business Intelligence software. McKesson Pharmaceutials had more than 30 business units. Amazingly, McKesson was able to complete this large and difficult implementation in less than two years, considered record time for a project of this magnitude. How did they do it?

One obvious reason McKesson was successful was because it used sound project management practices. At the highest level, project leadership defined the project requirements—what solutions would be delivered and when based on business requirements. The project's scope was clearly defined. Change leadership worked with management to promote adoption of the new system, trained user groups, and conducted in-depth workshops with analysts.

Although McKesson's Business Intelligence team had internal resources available, it used external consultants from SAP and other firms. Implementation teams led by internal McKesson staff members were organized around processes such as sell, finance, buy, profitability, compliance, and operations. Each implementation team was also assigned architects (internal technical resources) and developers (external consultants).

The consultants had specific technical knowledge and expertise in SAP Business Intelligence software and were charged with transferring this knowledge to internal team members. All the teams reported to a program management office that addressed cross-unit information requirements, coordinated development cycles across business units, and enforced standards.

Sources: Ben Worthen, "Prescription: Technology," *The Wall Street Journal*, June 9, 2008; "McKesson," www.mysap.com, accessed September 22, 2008; Michael Nadeau, "Keys to McKesson's Rapid BI Transformation," *SAP NetWeaver Magazine*, Spring 2005.

One of the principal challenges posed by information systems is ensuring they can deliver genuine business benefits. There is a very high failure rate among information systems projects because organizations have incorrectly assessed their business value or because firms have failed to manage the organizational change surrounding the introduction of new technology.

McKesson Pharmaceutical's management realized this when it authorized its business intelligence project. The project was massive and ambitious, but McKesson succeeded because it practiced sound project management.

The chapter-opening diagram calls attention to important points raised by this case and this chapter. McKesson Pharmaceutical is in a competitive industry where expensive products sell at low profit margins. Its inability to manage inventory raised operating costs and impacted profits. The company was able to improve inventory management by implementing a massive company-wide data warehouse with powerful analytical and business intelligence tools. Although the project was large and complex, management carefully defined the project goals, scope, requirements, and implementation team responsibilities. Strong management leadership and communication between information systems specialists and end users were essential.

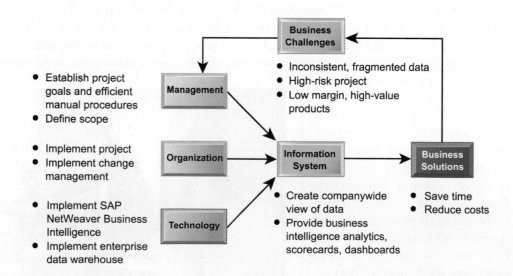

14.1 THE IMPORTANCE OF PROJECT MANAGEMENT

There is a very high failure rate among information systems projects. In nearly every organization, information systems projects take much more time and money to implement than originally anticipated or the completed system does not work properly. When an information system fails to work properly or costs too much to develop, companies may not realize any benefit from their information system investment, and the system may not be able to solve the problems for which it was intended. The development of a new system must be carefully managed and orchestrated, and the way a project is executed is likely to be the most important factor influencing its outcome. That's why it's essential to have some knowledge about managing information systems projects and the reasons why they succeed or fail.

RUNAWAY PROJECTS AND SYSTEM FAILURE

How badly are projects managed? On average, private sector projects are underestimated by one-half in terms of budget and time required to deliver the complete system promised in the system plan. A very large number of projects are delivered with missing functionality (promised for delivery in later versions). The Standish Group consultancy, which monitors IT project success rates, found that only 29 percent of all technology investments were completed on time, on budget, and with all features and functions originally specified (Levinson, 2006). Between 30 and 40 percent of all software projects are "runaway" projects that far exceed the original schedule and budget projections and fail to perform as originally specified.

As illustrated in Figure 14-1, a systems development project without proper management will most likely suffer these consequences:

- Costs that vastly exceed budgets
- Unexpected time slippage
- Technical performance that is less than expected
- Failure to obtain anticipated benefits

The systems produced by failed information projects are often not used in the way they were intended, or they are not used at all. Users often have to develop parallel manual systems to make these systems work.

The actual design of the system may fail to capture essential business requirements or improve organizational performance. Information may not be provided quickly enough to be helpful; it may be in a format that is impossible to digest and use; or it may represent the wrong pieces of data.

FIGURE 14-1   CONSEQUENCES OF POOR PROJECT MANAGEMENT

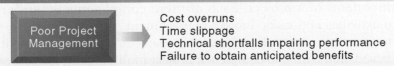

Without proper management, a systems development project takes longer to complete and most often exceeds the allocated budget. The resulting information system most likely is technically inferior and may not be able to demonstrate any benefits to the organization.

The way in which nontechnical business users must interact with the system may be excessively complicated and discouraging. A system may be designed with a poor user interface. The **user interface** is the part of the system with which end users interact. For example, an online input form or data entry screen may be so poorly arranged that no one wants to submit data or request information. System outputs may be displayed in a format that is too difficult to comprehend (Spier and Morris, 2003).

Web sites may discourage visitors from exploring further if the Web pages are cluttered and poorly arranged, if users cannot easily find the information they are seeking, or if it takes too long to access and display the Web page on the user's computer.

Additionally, the data in the system may have a high level of inaccuracy or inconsistency. The information in certain fields may be erroneous or ambiguous, or it may not be organized properly for business purposes. Information required for a specific business function may be inaccessible because the data are incomplete.

The Interactive Session on Management provides an example of a failed project. Kaiser Permanente, one of the largest health management organizations in the United States, was unable to establish its own center for handling kidney transplants. Kaiser opened its transplant center in 2004 but had to shut down the facility less than two years after it opened. A major factor was the company's mismanagement of information and information systems.

PROJECT MANAGEMENT OBJECTIVES

A **project** is a planned series of related activities for achieving a specific business objective. Information systems projects include the development of new information systems, enhancement of existing systems, or upgrade or replacement of the firm's information technology (IT) infrastructure.

Project management refers to the application of knowledge, skills, tools, and techniques to achieve specific targets within specified budget and time constraints. Project management activities include planning the work, assessing risk, estimating resources required to accomplish the work, organizing the work, acquiring human and material resources, assigning tasks, directing activities, controlling project execution, reporting progress, and analyzing the results. As in other areas of business, project management for information systems must deal with five major variables: scope, time, cost, quality, and risk.

Scope defines what work is or is not included in a project. For example, the scope of project for a new order processing system might be to include new modules for inputting orders and transmitting them to production and accounting but not any changes to related accounts receivable, manufacturing, distribution, or inventory control systems. Project management defines all the work required to complete a project successfully, and should ensure that the scope of a project not expand beyond what was originally intended.

Time is the amount of time required to complete the project. Project management typically establishes the amount of time required to complete major components of a project. Each of these components is further broken down into activities and tasks. Project management tries to determine the time required to complete each task and establish a schedule for completing the work.

Cost is based on the time to complete a project multiplied by the cost of human resources required to complete the project. Information systems project costs also include the cost of hardware, software, and work space. Project management develops a budget for the project and monitors ongoing project expenses.

INTERACTIVE SESSION: MANAGEMENT

KAISER PERMANENTE BOTCHES ITS KIDNEY TRANSPLANT CENTER PROJECT

Kaiser Permanente is one of the country's foremost health maintenance organizations (HMOs), also referred to as integrated managed care organizations. HMOs provide health care that is fulfilled by hospitals, doctors, and other providers with which the HMO has a contract. While Kaiser is a non-profit organization, the company earned $34.4 billion in revenues in 2007. Kaiser has approximately 170,000 employees, over 13,000 doctors, and serves 8.7 million members in 9 states. The company is headquartered in Oakland, California.

Kaiser is known for pioneering electronic medical records and currently boasts the world's largest electronic medical record storage system. The company also consistently ranks among the top HMOs in customer satisfaction. However, a 2004 attempt by Kaiser to handle kidney transplants on its own by setting up a transplant center was a public relations and information technology disaster. The company forced its members to transfer to its kidney transplant program without having adequately prepared to treat those patients.

In 2004, Kaiser implemented a kidney transplant program in Northern California under which transplants would be performed in-house at a transplant center owned and managed by Kaiser. Previously, the HMO had contracted with nearby university-affiliated California hospitals, such as UC San Francisco and UC Davis. The fledgling transplant center was shut down just two years later because of a litany of mistakes pertaining to paperwork, technology, and procedural planning. Through the duration of the doomed project, twice as many people died waiting for a transplant as received successful transplants. Patients now receive care from local hospitals once again.

Kaiser did very little correctly in its attempt to create its own kidney transplant program. The company lost track of records when transferring them to the new transplant center. More than 1,000 of the 1,500 patient records had incomplete or incorrect data, such as erroneous Social Security numbers and missing test results. Despite Kaiser's longtime experience with electronic medical records, the new center's records were stored primarily on paper. Kaiser had no comprehensive transplant patient master list or database. Many other transplant

programs have multiple IT professionals assigned to maintain the complicated databases required for a transplant program. Kaiser attempted to run such a program without similar resources. Kaiser employees dedicated to processing information on prospective transplant recipients were overworked, logging 10-to 16-hour days as they tried to keep up with the avalanche of information. The company did not accurately anticipate the personnel requirements of their undertaking.

These were by no means the company's only mistakes, however. There were no specific procedures for transferring data on the initial patients to the United Network for Organ Sharing (UNOS), which oversees national transplant waiting lists. There were no systematic processes for tracking or responding to patient complaints or requests. The Kaiser staff lacked guidance and training regarding their job requirements and uniformly lacked prior experience with transplant programs. And there was no executive governance to identify and correct any of these procedural problems that arose almost immediately after the beginning of the project. Kaiser had seemingly made no attempt to identify and define the processes required to ensure a smooth transition from external transplant programs to an in-house program.

Kaiser also failed to give patients credit for time spent on waiting lists at the other hospitals, sometimes dropping patients who had waited the longest down to the bottom of the list. Unlike other companies, IT mismanagement in health care companies can cost individuals their lives, and in Kaiser's case many plaintiffs seeking damages against the company believe the errors surrounding their transplant center have done just that.

At the outset of the transition, Kaiser mailed potential kidney recipients consent forms, but did not offer specific directions about what to do with the forms. Many patients failed to respond to the letter, unsure of how to handle it, and others returned the forms to the wrong entity. Other patients were unable to correct inaccurate information, and as a result UNOS was not able to approve those patients for inclusion on Kaiser's repopulated kidney wait list.

Despite all of the IT mishaps, the medical aspect of the transplant program was quite successful. All 56 transplant recipients in the first full year of business were still living one year later, which is considered to be strong evidence of high quality. But as the organizational woes continued to mount, Kaiser was forced to shut the program down in 2006, absorbing heavy losses and incurring what figures to be considerable legal expenses.

Kaiser paid a $2 million fine levied by the California Department of Managed Health Care (DMHC) for the various state and federal regulations it failed to adhere to in its attempt to set up a transplant program. Kaiser was also forced to make a $3 million charitable donation.

Many families of people who died waiting for kidneys from Kaiser are suing the company for medical negligence and wrongful death. Other patients, such as Bernard Burks, are going after Kaiser themselves for the same reasons. In March 2008, Burks won the right to have his case heard by a jury in a public courtroom, rather than a private judge or lawyer in arbitration. Most patient disputes with Kaiser are traditionally settled behind closed doors, presumably to minimize the damage to the company's reputation and increasing the likelihood of winning their cases. Burks was the first of over 100 patients on Kaiser's kidney transplant waiting list to win the right to a jury trial.

Sources: Marie-Anne Hogarth, "Kidney Patient Beats Kaiser Arbitration Rule," *East Bay Business Times,* March 21, 2008 and Kim S. Nash, "We Really Did Screw Up," *Baseline Magazine,* May 2007.

CASE STUDY QUESTIONS

1. Classify and describe the problems Kaiser faced in setting up the transplant center. What was the role of information systems and information management in these problems?
2. What were the management, organization, and technology factors responsible for those problems?
3. What steps would you have taken to increase the project's chances for success?
4. Were there any ethical problems created by this failed project? Explain your answer.

MIS IN ACTION

Explore the Web site for TeleResults, a provider of state-of-the-art electronic medical record (EMR) solutions and transplant software (www.teleresults.com), then answer the following question:

1. How could this company's products have helped Kaiser Permanente manage transplant information?

Quality is an indicator of how well the end result of a project satisfies the objectives specified by management. The quality of information systems projects usually boils down to improved organizational performance and decision making. Quality also considers the accuracy and timeliness of information produced by the new system and ease of use.

Risk refers to potential problems that would threaten the success of a project. These potential problems might prevent a project from achieving its objectives by increasing time and cost, lowering the quality of project outputs, or preventing the project from being completed altogether. Section 14.3 describes the most important risk factors for information systems.

14.2   SELECTING PROJECTS

Companies typically are presented with many different projects for solving problems and improving performance. There are far more ideas for systems projects than there are resources. Firms will need to select from this group the projects that promise the greatest benefit to the business. Obviously the firm's overall business strategy should drive project selection.

MANAGEMENT STRUCTURE FOR INFORMATION SYSTEMS PROJECTS

Figure 14-2 shows the elements of a management structure for information systems projects in a large corporation. It helps ensure that the most important systems projects are given priority.

At the apex of this structure is the corporate strategic planning group and the information system steering committee. The corporate strategic planning group is responsible for developing the firm's strategic plan, which may require the development of new systems.

The information systems steering committee is the senior management group with responsibility for systems development and operation. It is composed of department heads from both end-user and information systems areas. The steering committee reviews and approves plans for systems in all divisions, seeks to coordinate and integrate systems, and occasionally becomes involved in selecting specific information systems projects.

The project team is supervised by a project management group composed of information systems managers and end-user managers responsible for overseeing several specific information systems projects. The project team is directly responsible for the individual systems project. It consists of systems analysts, specialists from the relevant end-user business areas, application programmers, and perhaps database specialists. The mix of skills and the size of the project team depend on the specific nature of the system solution.

FIGURE 14-2   MANAGEMENT CONTROL OF SYSTEMS PROJECTS

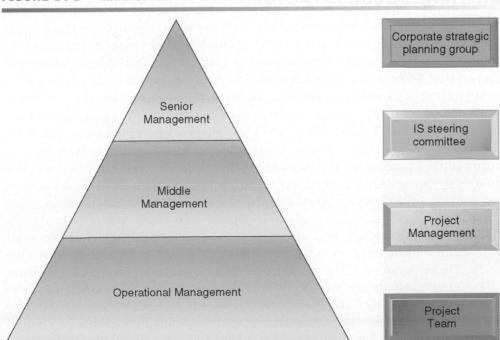

Each level of management in the hierarchy is responsible for specific aspects of systems projects, and this structure helps give priority to the most important systems projects for the organization.

LINKING SYSTEMS PROJECTS TO THE BUSINESS PLAN

In order to identify the information systems projects that will deliver the most business value, organizations need to develop an **information systems plan** that supports their overall business plan and in which strategic systems are incorporated into top-level planning. The plan serves as a road map indicating the direction of systems development (the purpose of the plan), the rationale, the current systems/situation, new developments to consider, the management strategy, the implementation plan, and the budget (see Table 14-1).

The plan contains a statement of corporate goals and specifies how information technology will support the attainment of those goals. The report shows how general goals will be achieved by specific systems projects. It identifies specific target dates and milestones that can be used later to evaluate the plan's progress in terms of how many objectives were actually attained in the time frame specified in the plan. The plan indicates the key management decisions concerning hardware acquisition; telecommunications; centralization/decentralization of authority, data, and hardware; and required organizational change. Organizational changes are also usually described, including management and employee training requirements; recruiting efforts; changes in business processes; and changes in authority, structure, or management practice.

In order to plan effectively, firms will need to inventory and document all of their information system applications and IT infrastructure components. For projects in which benefits involve improved decision making, managers should try to identify the decision improvements that would provide the greatest additional value to the firm. They should then develop a set of metrics to quantify the value of more timely and precise information on the outcome of the decision (see Chapter 12 for more detail on this topic).

CRITICAL SUCCESS FACTORS

To develop an effective information systems plan, the organization must have a clear understanding of both its long- and short-term information requirements. The strategic analysis, or critical success factors, approach argues that an organization's information requirements are determined by a small number of **critical success factors (CSFs)** of managers. If these goals can be attained, success of the firm or organization is assured (Rockart, 1979; Rockart and Treacy, 1982). CSFs are shaped by the industry, the firm, the manager, and the broader environment. For example, CSFs for the automobile industry might include styling, quality, and cost to meet the goals of increasing market share and raising profits. New information systems should focus on providing information that helps the firm meet these goals.

The principal method used in CSF analysis is personal interviews—three or four—with a number of top managers identifying their goals and the resulting CSFs. These personal CSFs are aggregated to develop a picture of the firm's CSFs. Then systems are built to deliver information on these CSFs. (For the method of developing CSFs in an organization, see Figure 14-3.)

Only top managers are interviewed, and the questions focus on a small number of CSFs rather than requiring a broad inquiry into what information is used in the organization. It is especially suitable for top management and for the development of decision-support systems (DSS) and executive support

TABLE 14-1 INFORMATION SYSTEMS PLAN

1. **Purpose of the Plan**
   Overview of plan contents
   Current business organization and future organization
   Key business processes
   Management strategy

2. **Strategic Business Plan Rationale**
   Current situation
   Current business organization
   Changing environments
   Major goals of the business plan
   Firm's strategic plan

3. **Current Systems**
   Major systems supporting business functions and processes
   Current infrastructure capabilities
      Hardware
      Software
      Database
      Telecommunications and Internet
   Difficulties meeting business requirements
   Anticipated future demands

4. **New Developments**
   New system projects
      Project descriptions
      Business rationale
      Applications' role in strategy
   New infrastructure capabilities required
      Hardware
      Software
      Database
      Telecommunications and Internet

5. **Management Strategy**
   Acquisition plans
   Milestones and timing
   Organizational realignment
   Internal reorganization
   Management controls
   Major training initiatives
   Personnel strategy

6. **Implementation Plan**
   Anticipated difficulties in implementation
   Progress reports

7. **Budget Requirements**
   Requirements
   Potential savings
   Financing
   Acquisition cycle

FIGURE 14-3   USING CSFs TO DEVELOP SYSTEMS

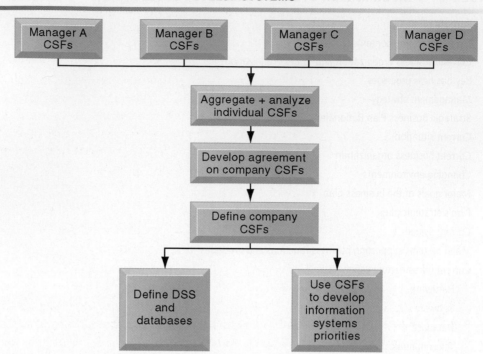

The CSF approach relies on interviews with key managers to identify their CSFs. Individual CSFs are aggregated to develop CSFs for the entire firm. Systems can then be built to deliver information on these CSFs.

systems (ESS). The CSF method focuses organizational attention on how information should be handled.

The method's primary weakness is that there is no particularly rigorous way in which individual CSFs can be aggregated into a clear company pattern. In addition, interviewees (and interviewers) often become confused when distinguishing between *individual* and *organizational* CSFs. These types of CSFs are not necessarily the same. What may be considered critical to a manager may not be important for the organization as a whole. This method is clearly biased toward top managers, although it could be extended to elicit ideas for promising new systems from lower-level members of the organization (Peffers and Gengler, 2003).

PORTFOLIO ANALYSIS

Once strategic analyses have determined the overall direction of systems development, **portfolio analysis** can be used to evaluate alternative system projects. Portfolio analysis inventories all of the organization's information systems projects and assets, including infrastructure, outsourcing contracts, and licenses. This portfolio of information systems investments can be described as having a certain profile of risk and benefit to the firm (see Figure 14-4) similar to a financial portfolio.

Each information systems project carries its own set of risks and benefits. (Section 14-4 describes the factors that increase the risks of systems projects.) Firms would try to improve the return on their portfolios of IT assets by balancing the risk and return from their systems investments. Although there is no ideal profile for all firms, information-intensive industries (e.g., finance) should have a few high-risk, high-benefit projects to ensure that they stay current with technology. Firms in non-information-intensive industries should focus on high-benefit, low-risk projects.

Most desirable, of course, are systems with high benefit and low risk. These promise early returns and low risks. Second, high-benefit, high-risk systems should be examined; low-benefit, high-risk systems should be totally avoided; and low-benefit, low-risk systems should be reexamined for the possibility of rebuilding and replacing them with more desirable systems having higher benefits. By using portfolio analysis, management can determine the optimal mix of investment risk and reward for their firms, balancing riskier high-reward projects with safer lower-reward ones. Firms where portfolio analysis is aligned with business strategy have been found to have a superior return on their IT assets, better alignment of information technology investments with business objectives, and better organization-wide coordination of IT investments (Jeffrey and Leliveld, 2004).

SCORING MODELS

A **scoring model** is useful for selecting projects where many criteria must be considered. It assigns weights to various features of a system and then calculates the weighted totals. Using Table 14-2, the firm must decide among two alternative enterprise resource planning (ERP) systems. The first column lists the criteria that decision makers will use to evaluate the systems. These criteria are usually the result of lengthy discussions among the decision-making group. Often the most important outcome of a scoring model is not the score but agreement on the criteria used to judge a system.

Table 14-2 shows that this particular company attaches the most importance to capabilities for sales order processing, inventory management, and warehousing. The second column in Table 14-2 lists the weights that decision makers attached to the decision criteria. Columns 3 and 5 show the percentage of requirements for each function that each alternative ERP system can provide. Each vendor's score can be calculated by multiplying the percentage of requirements met for each function by the weight attached to that function. ERP System B has the highest total score.

FIGURE 14-4 A SYSTEM PORTFOLIO

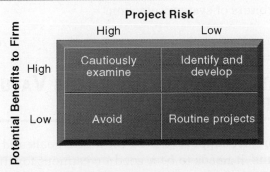

Companies should examine their portfolio of projects in terms of potential benefits and likely risks. Certain kinds of projects should be avoided altogether and others developed rapidly. There is no ideal mix. Companies in different industries have different profiles.

TABLE 14-2 EXAMPLE OF A SCORING MODEL FOR AN ERP SYSTEM

CRITERIA	WEIGHT	ERP SYSTEM A %	ERP SYSTEM A SCORE	ERP SYSTEM B %	ERP SYSTEM B SCORE
1.0 Order Processing					
1.1 Online order entry	4	67	268	73	292
1.2 Online pricing	4	81	324	87	348
1.3 Inventory check	4	72	288	81	324
1.4 Customer credit check	3	66	198	59	177
1.5 Invoicing	4	73	292	82	328
Total Order Processing			1,370		1,469
2.0 Inventory Management					
2.1 Production forecasting	3	72	216	76	228
2.2 Production planning	4	79	316	81	324
2.3 Inventory control	4	68	272	80	320
2.4 Reports	3	71	213	69	207
Total Inventory Management			1,017		1,079
3.0 Warehousing					
3.1 Receiving	2	71	142	75	150
3.2 Picking/packing	3	77	231	82	246
3.3 Shipping	4	92	368	89	356
Total Warehousing			741		752
Grand Total			3,128		3,300

As with all "objective" techniques, there are many qualitative judgments involved in using the scoring model. This model requires experts who understand the issues and the technology. It is appropriate to cycle through the scoring model several times, changing the criteria and weights, to see how sensitive the outcome is to reasonable changes in criteria. Scoring models are used most commonly to confirm, to rationalize, and to support decisions, rather than as the final arbiters of system selection.

14.3   ESTABLISHING THE BUSINESS VALUE OF INFORMATION SYSTEMS

Even if a system project supports a firm's strategic goals and meets user information requirements, it needs to be a good investment for the firm. The value of systems from a financial perspective essentially revolves around the issue of return on invested capital. Does a particular information system investment produce sufficient returns to justify its costs?

INFORMATION SYSTEM COSTS AND BENEFITS

Table 14-3 lists some of the more common costs and benefits of systems. **Tangible benefits** can be quantified and assigned a monetary value. **Intangible benefits**, such as more efficient customer service or enhanced decision making, cannot be immediately quantified but may lead to quantifiable gains in the long run. Transaction and clerical systems that displace labor and save space always produce more measurable, tangible benefits than management information systems, decision-support systems, and computer-supported collaborative work systems (see Chapters 2 and 11).

Chapter 5 introduced the concept of total cost of ownership (TCO), which is designed to identify and measure the components of information technology expenditures beyond the initial cost of purchasing and installing hardware and software. However, TCO analysis provides only part of the information needed

TABLE 14-3 COSTS AND BENEFITS OF INFORMATION SYSTEMS

COSTS

Hardware

Telecommunications

Software

Services

Personnel

TANGIBLE BENEFITS (COST SAVINGS)

Increased productivity

Lower operational costs

Reduced workforce

Lower computer expenses

Lower outside vendor costs

Lower clerical and professional costs

Reduced rate of growth in expenses

Reduced facility costs

INTANGIBLE BENEFITS

Improved asset utilization

Improved resource control

Improved organizational planning

Increased organizational flexibility

More timely information

More information

Increased organizational learning

Legal requirements attained

Enhanced employee goodwill

Increased job satisfaction

Improved decision making

Improved operations

Higher client satisfaction

Better corporate image

to evaluate an information technology investment because it does not typically deal with benefits, cost categories such as complexity costs, and "soft" and strategic factors discussed later in this section.

Capital Budgeting for Information Systems

To determine the benefits of a particular project, you'll need to calculate all of its costs and all of its benefits. Obviously, a project where costs exceed benefits should be rejected. But even if the benefits outweigh the costs, additional financial analysis is required to determine whether the project represents a good return on the firm's invested capital. **Capital budgeting** models are one of several techniques used to measure the value of investing in long-term capital investment projects.

Capital budgeting methods rely on measures of cash flows into and out of the firm; capital projects generate those cash flows. The investment cost for information systems projects is an immediate cash outflow caused by expenditures for hardware, software, and labor. In subsequent years, the investment may cause additional cash outflows that will be balanced by cash inflows resulting from the investment. Cash inflows take the form of increased sales of more products (for reasons such as new products, higher quality, or increasing market share) or reduced costs in production and operations. The difference between cash outflows and cash inflows is used for calculating the financial worth of an investment. Once the cash flows have been established, several alternative methods are available for comparing different projects and deciding about the investment.

The principal capital budgeting models for evaluating IT projects are: the payback method, the accounting rate of return on investment (ROI), net present value, and the internal rate of return (IRR). You can find out more about how these capital budgeting models are used to justify information system investments in the Learning Tracks for this chapter.

REAL OPTIONS PRICING MODELS

Some information systems projects are highly uncertain, especially investments in IT infrastructure. Their future revenue streams are unclear and their up-front costs are high. Suppose, for instance, that a firm is considering a $20 million investment to upgrade its IT infrastructure—its hardware, software, data management tools, and networking technology. If this upgraded infrastructure were available, the organization would have the technology capabilities to respond more easily to future problems and opportunities. Although the costs of this investment can be calculated, not all of the benefits of making this investment can be established in advance. But if the firm waits a few years until the revenue potential becomes more obvious, it might be too late to make the infrastructure investment. In such cases, managers might benefit from using real options pricing models to evaluate information technology investments.

Real options pricing models (ROPMs) use the concept of options valuation borrowed from the financial industry. An *option* is essentially the right, but not the obligation, to act at some future date. A typical *call option*, for instance, is a financial option in which a person buys the right (but not the obligation) to purchase an underlying asset (usually a stock) at a fixed price (strike price) on or before a given date.

For instance, on October 28, 2008, for $11.30 you could purchase the right (a call option) maturing in January 2009 to buy a share of P&G common stock for $50 per share. If, by the end of January 2009, the price of P&G stock did not rise above $50 per share, you would not exercise the option, and the value of the option would fall to zero on the strike date. If, however, the price of Procter & Gamble common stock rose to, say, $100 per share, you could purchase the stock for the strike price of $50 and retain the profit of $50 per share minus the cost of the option. (Because the option is sold as a 100-share contract, the cost of the contract would be 100 × $11.30 before commissions, or $1,130, and you would be purchasing and obtaining a profit from 100 shares of Procter & Gamble.) The stock option enables the owner to benefit from the upside potential of an opportunity while limiting the downside risk.

ROPMs value information systems projects similar to stock options, where an initial expenditure on technology creates the right, but not the obligation, to obtain the benefits associated with further development and deployment of the technology as long as management has the freedom to cancel, defer, restart, or expand the project. ROPMs give managers the flexibility to stage their IT investment or test the waters with small pilot projects or prototypes to gain more knowledge about the risks of a project before investing in the entire implementation. The disadvantages of this model are primarily in estimating all the key variables affecting option value, including anticipated cash flows from the underlying asset and changes in the cost of implementation. Models for determining option value of information technology platforms are being developed (Fichman, 2004; McGrath and MacMillan, 2000).

LIMITATIONS OF FINANCIAL MODELS

The traditional focus on the financial and technical aspects of an information system tends to overlook the social and organizational dimensions of information systems that may affect the true costs and benefits of the investment. Many companies' information systems investment decisions do not adequately consider costs from organizational disruptions created by a new system, such as the cost to train end users, the impact that users' learning curves for a new system have on productivity, or the time managers need to spend overseeing new system-related changes. Benefits, such as more timely decisions from a new system or enhanced employee learning and expertise, may also be overlooked in a traditional financial analysis (Ryan, Harrison, and Schkade, 2002).

14.4 MANAGING PROJECT RISK

We have already introduced the topic of information system risks and risk assessment in Chapter 8. In this chapter we describe the specific risks to information systems projects and show what can be done to manage them effectively.

DIMENSIONS OF PROJECT RISK

Systems differ dramatically in their size, scope, level of complexity, and organizational and technical components. Some systems development projects are more likely to create the problems we have described earlier or to suffer delays because they carry a much higher level of risk than others. The level of project risk is influenced by project size, project structure, and the level of technical expertise of the information systems staff and project team.

- *Project size.* The larger the project—as indicated by the dollars spent, the size of the implementation staff, the time allocated for implementation, and the number of organizational units affected—the greater the risk. Very large-scale systems projects have a failure rate that is 50 to 75 percent higher than that for other projects because such projects are complex and difficult to control. The organizational complexity of the system—how many units and groups use it and how much it influences business processes—contribute to the complexity of large-scale systems projects just as much as technical characteristics, such as the number of lines of program code, length of project, and budget (Xia and Lee, 2004; Concours Group, 2000; Laudon, 1989). In addition, there are few reliable techniques for estimating the time and cost to develop large-scale information systems.

- *Project structure.* Some projects are more highly structured than others. Their requirements are clear and straightforward so outputs and processes can be easily defined. Users know exactly what they want and what the system should do; there is almost no possibility of the users changing their minds. Such projects run a much lower risk than those with relatively undefined, fluid, and constantly changing requirements; with outputs that cannot be fixed easily because they are subject to users' changing ideas; or with users who cannot agree on what they want.

- *Experience with technology.* The project risk rises if the project team and the information system staff lack the required technical expertise. If the team is unfamiliar with the hardware, system software, application software, or database management system proposed for the project, it is highly likely that the project will experience technical problems or take more time to complete because of the need to master new skills.

Although the difficulty of the technology is one risk factor in information systems projects, the other factors are primarily organizational, dealing with the complexity of information requirements, the scope of the project, and how many parts of the organization will be affected by a new information system.

CHANGE MANAGEMENT AND THE CONCEPT OF IMPLEMENTATION

The introduction or alteration of an information system has a powerful behavioral and organizational impact. Changes in the way that information is defined, accessed, and used to manage the organization's resources often lead to new distributions of authority and power. This internal organizational change breeds resistance and opposition and can lead to the demise of an otherwise good system.

A very large percentage of information systems projects stumble because the process of organizational change surrounding system building was not properly addressed. Successful system building requires careful **change management**.

The Concept of Implementation

To manage the organizational change surrounding the introduction of a new information system effectively, you must examine the process of implementation. **Implementation** refers to all organizational activities working toward the adoption, management, and routinization of an innovation, such as a new information system. In the implementation process, the systems analyst is a **change agent**. The analyst not only develops technical solutions but also redefines the configurations, interactions, job activities, and power relationships of various organizational groups. The analyst is the catalyst for the entire change process and is responsible for ensuring that all parties involved accept the changes created by a new system. The change agent communicates with users, mediates between competing interest groups, and ensures that the organizational adjustment to such changes is complete.

The Role of End Users

System implementation generally benefits from high levels of user involvement and management support. User participation in the design and operation of information systems has several positive results. First, if users are heavily involved in systems design, they have more opportunities to mold the system according to their priorities and business requirements, and more opportunities to control the outcome. Second, they are more likely to react positively to the completed system because they have been active participants in the change process. Incorporating user knowledge and expertise leads to better solutions.

The relationship between users and information systems specialists has traditionally been a problem area for information systems implementation efforts. Users and information systems specialists tend to have different backgrounds, interests, and priorities. This is referred to as the **user-designer communications gap**. These differences lead to divergent organizational loyalties, approaches to problem solving, and vocabularies.

Information systems specialists, for example, often have a highly technical, or machine, orientation to problem solving. They look for elegant and sophisticated technical solutions in which hardware and software efficiency is optimized at the expense of ease of use or organizational effectiveness. Users prefer systems that are oriented toward solving business problems or facilitating organizational tasks. Often the orientations of both groups are so at odds that they appear to speak in different tongues.

These differences are illustrated in Table 14-4, which depicts the typical concerns of end users and technical specialists (information systems designers) regarding the development of a new information system. Communication problems between end users and designers are a major reason why user requirements are not properly incorporated into information systems and why users are driven out of the implementation process.

Systems development projects run a very high risk of failure when there is a pronounced gap between users and technical specialists and when these groups continue to pursue different goals. Under such conditions, users are often driven away from the project. Because they cannot comprehend what the technicians are saying, users conclude that the entire project is best left in the hands of the information specialists alone.

TABLE 14-4 THE USER-DESIGNER COMMUNICATIONS GAP

USER CONCERNS	DESIGNER CONCERNS
Will the system deliver the information I need for my work?	How much disk storage space will the master file consume?
How quickly can I access the data?	How many lines of program code will it take to perform this function?
How easily can I retrieve the data?	How can we cut down on CPU time when we run the system?
How much clerical support will I need to enter data into the system?	What is the most efficient way of storing these data?
How will the operation of the system fit into my daily business schedule?	What database management system should we use?

Management Support and Commitment

If an information systems project has the backing and commitment of management at various levels, it is more likely to be perceived positively by both users and the technical information services staff. Both groups will believe that their participation in the development process will receive higher-level attention and priority. They will be recognized and rewarded for the time and effort they devote to implementation. Management backing also ensures that a systems project receives sufficient funding and resources to be successful. Furthermore, to be enforced effectively, all the changes in work habits and procedures and any organizational realignments associated with a new system depend on management backing. If a manager considers a new system a priority, the system will more likely be treated that way by his or her subordinates.

Change Management Challenges for Business Process Reengineering, Enterprise Applications, and Mergers and Acquisitions

Given the challenges of innovation and implementation, it is not surprising to find a very high failure rate among enterprise application and business process reengineering (BPR) projects, which typically require extensive organizational change and which may require replacing old technologies and legacy systems that are deeply rooted in many interrelated business processes. A number of studies have indicated that 70 percent of all business process reengineering projects fail to deliver promised benefits. Likewise, a high percentage of enterprise applications fail to be fully implemented or to meet the goals of their users even after three years of work.

Many enterprise application and reengineering projects have been undermined by poor implementation and change management practices that failed to address employees' concerns about change. Dealing with fear and anxiety throughout the organization; overcoming resistance by key managers; changing job functions, career paths, and recruitment practices; and training have posed greater threats to reengineering than the difficulties companies faced visualizing and designing breakthrough changes to business processes. All of the enterprise applications require tighter coordination among different functional groups as well as extensive business process change (see Chapter 9).

Projects related to mergers and acquisitions have a similar failure rate. Mergers and acquisitions are deeply affected by the organizational characteristics of the merging companies as well as by their IT infrastructures. Combining the information systems of two different companies usually requires considerable organizational change and complex systems projects to manage. If the integration is not properly managed, firms can emerge with a tangled hodgepodge of inherited legacy systems built by aggregating the systems of one firm after another. Without a successful systems integration, the benefits anticipated from the merger cannot be realized, or, worse, the merged entity cannot execute its business processes effectively.

CONTROLLING RISK FACTORS

Various project management, requirements gathering, and planning methodologies have been developed for specific categories of implementation problems. Strategies have also been devised for ensuring that users play appropriate roles throughout the implementation period and for managing the organizational change process. Not all aspects of the implementation process can be easily controlled or planned. However, anticipating potential implementation problems and applying appropriate corrective strategies can increase the chances for system success.

The first step in managing project risk involves identifying the nature and level of risk confronting the project (Schmidt et al., 2001). Implementers can then handle each project with the tools and risk-management approaches geared to its level of risk (Iversen, Mathiassen, and Nielsen, 2004; Barki, Rivard, and Talbot, 2001; McFarlan, 1981).

Managing Technical Complexity

Projects with challenging and complex technology for users to master benefit from **internal integration tools**. The success of such projects depends on how well their technical complexity can be managed. Project leaders need both heavy technical and administrative experience. They must be able to anticipate problems and develop smooth working relationships among a predominantly technical team. The team should be under the leadership of a manager with a strong technical and project management background, and team members should be highly experienced. Team meetings should take place frequently. Essential technical skills or expertise not available internally should be secured from outside the organization.

Formal Planning and Control Tools

Large projects benefit from appropriate use of **formal planning tools** and **formal control tools** for documenting and monitoring project plans. The two most commonly used methods for documenting project plans are Gantt charts and PERT charts. A **Gantt chart** lists project activities and their corresponding start and completion dates. The Gantt chart visually represents the timing and duration of different tasks in a development project as well as their human resource requirements (see Figure 14-5). It shows each task as a horizontal bar whose length is proportional to the time required to complete it.

Although Gantt charts show when project activities begin and end, they don't depict task dependencies, how one task is affected if another is behind schedule, or how tasks should be ordered. That is where **PERT charts** are useful. PERT stands for Program Evaluation and Review Technique, a methodology developed by the U.S. Navy during the 1950s to manage the Polaris submarine missile program. A PERT chart graphically depicts project tasks and their interrelationships. The PERT chart lists the specific activities that make up a project and the activities that must be completed before a specific activity can start, as illustrated in Figure 14-6.

The PERT chart portrays a project as a network diagram consisting of numbered nodes (either circles or rectangles) representing project tasks. Each node is numbered and shows the task, its duration, the starting date, and the completion date. The direction of the arrows on the lines indicates the sequence of tasks and shows which activities must be completed before the commencement of another activity. In Figure 14-6, the tasks in nodes 2, 3, and 4 are not dependent on each other and can be undertaken simultaneously, but each is dependent on completion of the first task. PERT charts for complex projects can be difficult to interpret, and project managers often use both techniques.

These project management techniques can help managers identify bottlenecks and determine the impact that problems will have on project completion times. They can also help systems developers partition projects into smaller, more manageable segments with defined, measurable business results. Standard control techniques can successfully chart the progress of the project against budgets and target dates, so deviations from the plan can be spotted.

FIGURE 14-5   A GANTT CHART

HRIS COMBINED PLAN–HR	Da	Who
DATA ADMINISTRATION SECURITY		
QMF security review/setup	20	EF TP
Security orientation	2	EF JA
QMF security maintenance	35	TP GL
Data entry sec. profiles	4	EF TP
Data entry sec. views est.	12	EF TP
Data entry security profiles	65	EF TP
DATA DICTIONARY		
Orientation sessions	1	EF
Data dictionary design	32	EFWV
DD prod. coordn-query	20	GL
DD prod. coordn-live	40	EF GL
Data dictionary cleanup	35	EF GL
Data dictionary maint.	35	EF GL
PROCEDURES REVISION DESIGN PREP		
Work flows (old)	10	PK JL
Payroll data flows	31	JL PK
HRIS P/R model	11	PK JL
P/R interface orient. mtg.	6	PK JL
P/R interface coordn. 1	15	PK
P/R interface coordn. 2	8	PK
Benefits interfaces (old)	5	JL
Benefits interfaces (new flow)	8	JL
Benefits communication strategy	3	PK JL
New work flow model	15	PK JL
Posn. data entry flows	14	WV JL

RESOURCE SUMMARY

Name		Who	2008 Oct	Nov	Dec	2009 Jan	Feb	Mar	Apr	May	Jun	Jul	Aug	Sep	Oct	Nov	Dec	2010 Jan	Feb	Mar
Edith Farrell	5.0	EF	2	21	24	24	23	22	22	27	34	34	29	26	28	19	14			
Woody Vinton	5.0	WV	5	17	20	19	12	10	14	10	2							4	3	
Charles Pierce	5.0	CP		5	11	20	13	9	10	7	6	8	4	4	4	4	4			
Ted Leurs	5.0	TL		12	17	17	19	17	14	12	15	16	2	1	1	1	1			
Toni Cox	5.0	TC	1	11	10	11	11	12	19	19	21	21	21	17	17	12	9			
Patricia Knopp	5.0	PC	7	23	30	34	27	25	15	24	25	16	11	13	17	10	3	3	2	
Jane Lawton	5.0	JL	1	9	16	21	19	21	21	20	17	15	14	12	14	8	5			
David Holloway	5.0	DH	4	4	5	5	5	2	7	5	4	16	2							
Diane O'Neill	5.0	DO	6	14	17	16	13	11	9	4										
Joan Albert	5.0	JA	5	6		7	6	2	1					5	5	1				
Marie Marcus	5.0	MM	15	7	2	1	1													
Don Stevens	5.0	DS	4	4	5	4	5	1												
Casual	5.0	CASL		3	4	3			4	7	9	5	3	2						
Kathy Mendez	5.0	KM		1	5	16	20	19	22	19	20	18	20	11	2					
Anna Borden	5.0	AB						9	10	16	15	11	12	19	10	7	1			
Gail Loring	5.0	GL		3	6	5	9	10	17	18	17	10	13	10	10	7	17			
UNASSIGNED	0.0	X										9			236	225	230	14	13	
Co-op	5.0	CO		6	4				2	3	4	4	2	4	16			216	178	
Casual	5.0	CAUL								3	3	3								
TOTAL DAYS			49	147	176	196	194	174	193	195	190	181	140	125	358	288	284	237	196	12

The Gantt chart in this figure shows the task, person-days, and initials of each responsible person, as well as the start and finish dates for each task. The resource summary provides a good manager with the total person-days for each month and for each person working on the project to manage the project successfully. The project described here is a data administration project.

FIGURE 14-6   A PERT CHART

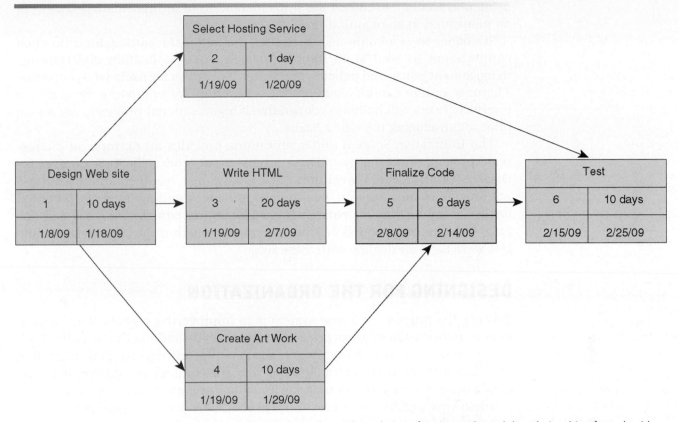

This is a simplified PERT chart for creating a small Web site. It shows the ordering of project tasks and the relationship of a task with preceding and succeeding tasks.

Increasing User Involvement and Overcoming User Resistance

Projects with relatively little structure and many undefined requirements must involve users fully at all stages. Users must be mobilized to support one of many possible design options and to remain committed to a single design. **External integration tools** consist of ways to link the work of the implementation team to users at all organizational levels. For instance, users can become active members of the project team, take on leadership roles, and take charge of installation and training. The implementation team can demonstrate its responsiveness to users, promptly answering questions, incorporating user feedback, and showing their willingness to help (Gefen and Ridings, 2002).

Participation in implementation activities may not be enough to overcome the problem of user resistance to organizational change. Different users may be affected by the system in different ways. Whereas some users may welcome a new system because it brings changes they perceive as beneficial to them, others may resist these changes because they believe the shifts are detrimental to their interests.

If the use of a system is voluntary, users may choose to avoid it; if use is mandatory, resistance will take the form of increased error rates, disruptions, turnover, and even sabotage. Therefore, the implementation strategy must not only encourage user participation and involvement, but it must also address the issue of counterimplementation (Keen, 1981). **Counterimplementation** is a deliberate strategy to thwart the implementation of an information system or an innovation in an organization.

Strategies to overcome user resistance include user participation (to elicit commitment as well as to improve design), user education and training, management edicts and policies, and better incentives for users who cooperate. The new system can be made more user friendly by improving the end-user interface. Users will be more cooperative if organizational problems are solved prior to introducing the new system.

The Interactive Session on Organizations provides an example of a large-scale project where many of these issues are at work. The U.S. Centers for Disease Control and Prevention (CDC) have had trouble implementing a nationwide system to alert health care providers and agencies to potential health crises such as flu pandemics or bioterrorist attacks. As you read this case, try to identify the risks of this project and whether the appropriate strategies were used for dealing with these risks.

DESIGNING FOR THE ORGANIZATION

Because the purpose of a new system is to improve the organization's performance, information systems projects must explicitly address the ways in which the organization will change when the new system is installed, including installation of intranets, extranets, and Web applications. In addition to procedural changes, transformations in job functions, organizational structure, power relationships, and the work environment should be carefully planned.

Areas where users interface with the system require special attention, with sensitivity to ergonomics issues. **Ergonomics** refers to the interaction of people and machines in the work environment. It considers the design of jobs, health issues, and the end-user interface of information systems. Table 14-5 lists the organizational dimensions that must be addressed when planning and implementing information systems.

Although systems analysis and design activities are supposed to include an organizational impact analysis, this area has traditionally been neglected. An **organizational impact analysis** explains how a proposed system will affect organizational structure, attitudes, decision making, and operations. To integrate information systems successfully with the organization, thorough and fully documented organizational impact assessments must be given more attention in the development effort.

TABLE 14-5 ORGANIZATIONAL FACTORS IN SYSTEMS PLANNING AND IMPLEMENTATION

Employee participation and involvement
Job design
Standards and performance monitoring
Ergonomics (including equipment, user interfaces, and the work environment)
Employee grievance resolution procedures
Health and safety
Government regulatory compliance

INTERACTIVE SESSION: ORGANIZATIONS

WHY CAN'T BIOSENSE TAKE OFF?

If you turn on the television, read a newspaper, or surf the Web, you're bound to find many dire predictions about large-scale loss of life from biological or chemical attacks or an avian influenza pandemic. Computer models estimate that between 2 and 100 million people could die in the event of a flu pandemic.

On May 3, 2006, the United States government issued an Implementation Plan for its National Strategy for Pandemic Influenza to improve coordination among federal, state, and local authorities and the private sector for pandemics and other public health emergencies. The implementation plan called for improving mechanisms for "real-time" clinical surveillance of hospital emergency rooms, intensive care units, and laboratories to inform local, state, and federal public health officials about rapidly spreading illness.

The centerpiece of this plan is the BioSense Real-Time Clinical Connections Program developed by the U.S. CDC. BioSense sits atop a hospital's existing information systems, continually gathering and analyzing their data as they are generated. Custom software developed by CDC monitors the facility's network traffic and captures relevant patient records, diagnoses, and prescription information. The data include patient age, sex, ZIP code of residence, ZIP code of the medical facility handling the patient, the principal medical complaint, symptoms, onset of illness, diagnoses, medical procedures, medications prescribed, and laboratory results. The software converts these data to the HL7 data messaging format, which is the standard for the health care industry, encrypts the data, and transmits them every 15 minutes over the Web to the CDC where they are maintained in a large data repository.

The system summarizes and presents analytical results by source, day, and syndrome for each ZIP code, state, and metropolitan area using maps, graphs, and tables. Registered state and local public health agencies as well as hospitals and health care providers are allowed to access data that pertain to their jurisdiction using a Web-based application over a secure data network. Information from BioSense could show early signs of a pandemic or biologic attack and alert local hospitals, health workers, and federal and state agencies to take preventive measures.

The traditional process for public health surveillance is manual and much slower. Hospitals, physicians, and laboratories would mail or fax paper reports to public health agencies, who would then call health care providers for more detailed information. This slow chain of person-to-person communication is not well-suited to a major public health emergency.

BioSense first became operational in 2004, when it began gathering daily data from U.S. Defense Department and Veterans Affairs (VA) hospitals and Laboratory Corporation of America (LabCorp) orders for medical tests. (LabCorp operates a large nationwide network of testing locations and service centers and is one of the largest clinical lab service providers in the United States.) Approximately 700 Defense Department and 1110 VA facilities report data to BioSense. In late 2005, CDC started to expand the BioSense network to civilian hospitals in major metropolitan areas.

However, in 2006 and 2007 Biosence encountered significant resistance from hospital administrators and physicians around the country. As of May, 2008, only 563 hospitals and state health organizations were participating. To transmit data to BioSense, each hospital must standardize its patient and other medical data. Most hospitals use their own coding systems for symptoms, diseases, and medications. CDC's contractors would have to work with each hospital to translate its data codes into the standards used by CDC's software. This is a massive task, given hospitals' limited IT staffs and resources.

Some in the medical community question whether the BioSense network is worth the effort. According to Dr. John Rosenberg, director of the Infectious Disease Laboratory at the State of California's Department of Health Services in Richmond, California, if an epidemic broke out, "You'd know it before the data rolled in. When your emergency rooms fill up you make a phone call; this is probably a better measure."

Although participation in BioSense is voluntary, physicians and health officials might resent the system because it enables the federal government to encroach on what has traditionally been the domain of local health care providers and organizations. They note that they and not the CDC have the responsibility for responding to and managing a pandemic. Additionally, hospitals are reluctant to sign up because of concerns about maintaining privacy and security of patient information. BioSense would let the CDC "listen in" on their treatment of patients on a real-time basis. The CDC does not use any data that would identify individual patients.

After investing an estimated $100 million on hospital recruitment and technology for BioSense in 2005 and 2006, the CDC decided in 2007 to work with state and local public health care systems instead of competing with them. It will continue to use BioSense in its limited form while simultaneously pursuing information-sharing measures with state health departments. CDC will not require states to

move their detailed data into a national repository but instead encourage them to link their databases with that of BioSense into some sort nationwide bio-surveillance system. The final design of the system is still unclear. CDC is piloting different strategies to determine the best approach. One effort, for example, focuses on building an alert system to notify state and regional public health care officials electronically about pandemic outbreaks instead of relying on e-mail or the telephone.

Sources: Doug Bartholomew and Chris Gonsalves, "CDC Issues Pandemic Systems Plan," *Baseline Magazine*, April 2008; Doug Bartholomew, "Second Opinions," *Baseline Magazine*, March 2006; and Wilson P. Dizard III, "CDC Weaving National Information Web," *Government Computer News*, April 3, 2006.

CASE STUDY QUESTIONS

1. Identify the risks in the BioSense project.
2. What management, organization, and technology factors explain why this project has been difficult to implement?
3. Is the CDC's new approach to improving pandemic warnings a viable solution? Why or why not?

MIS IN ACTION

Explore the BioSense Web site (www.cdc.gov/biosense/) and then answer the following question:

1. What information technologies do you see mentioned in the description of BioSense? Why would they be especially useful for this type of application?

Sociotechnical Design

One way of addressing human and organizational issues is to incorporate **sociotechnical design** practices into information systems projects. Designers set forth separate sets of technical and social design solutions. The social design plans explore different workgroup structures, allocation of tasks, and the design of individual jobs. The proposed technical solutions are compared with the proposed social solutions. The solution that best meets both social and technical objectives is selected for the final design. The resulting sociotechnical design is expected to produce an information system that blends technical efficiency with sensitivity to organizational and human needs, leading to higher job satisfaction and productivity.

PROJECT MANAGEMENT SOFTWARE TOOLS

Commercial software tools that automate many aspects of project management facilitate the project management process. Project management software typically features capabilities for defining and ordering tasks, assigning resources to tasks, establishing starting and ending dates to tasks, tracking progress, and facilitating modifications to tasks and resources. Many automate the creation of Gantt and PERT charts.

Some of these tools are large sophisticated programs for managing very large projects, dispersed work groups, and enterprise functions. These high-end tools can manage very large numbers of tasks and activities and complex relationships.

Microsoft Office Project 2007 has become the most widely used project management software today. It is PC-based, with capabilities for producing PERT and Gantt charts and for supporting critical path analysis, resource allocation, project tracking, and status reporting. Project also tracks the way changes in one aspect of a project affect others. Project Professional 2007 provides collaborative project management capabilities when used with Microsoft Office Project Server 2007. Project Server stores project data in a central SQL Server database, enabling authorized users to access and update the data over the Internet. Project Server 2007 is tightly integrated with the Microsoft Windows SharePoint Services collaborative workspace platform. These features help large enterprises manage projects in many different locations. Products such as EasyProjects.NET and Vertabase are also useful for firms that want Web-based project management tools.

14.5 HANDS-ON MIS PROJECTS

The projects in this section give you hands-on experience evaluating information systems projects, using spreadsheet software to perform capital budgeting analyses for new information systems investments, and using Web tools to analyze the financing for a new home.

Management Decision Problems

1. In 2001, McDonald's Restaurants undertook a project called Innovate to create an intranet connecting headquarters with its 30,000 restaurants in 120 countries to provide detailed operational information in real time. The new system would, for instance, inform a manager at the company's Oak Brook, Illinois, headquarters immediately if sales were slowing at a franchise in London, or if the grill temperature in a Rochester, Minnesota, restaurant wasn't hot enough. The idea was to create a global ERP application touching the workings of every McDonald's restaurant. Some of these restaurants were in countries that lacked network infrastructures. After spending over $1 billion over several years, including $170 million on consultants and initial implementation planning, McDonalds terminated the project. What should management have known or done at the outset to prevent this outcome?

2. Caterpillar is the world's leading maker of earthmoving machinery and supplier of agricultural equipment. Caterpillar wants to end its support for its Dealer Business System (DBS), which it licenses to its dealers to help them run their businesses. The software in this system is becoming out of date, and senior management wants to transfer support for the hosted version of the software to Accenture Consultants so it can concentrate on its core business. Caterpillar never required its dealers to use DBS, but the system had become a de facto standard for doing business with the company. The majority of the 50 Cat dealers in North America use some version of DBS, as do about half of the 200 or so Cat dealers in the rest of the world. Before Caterpillar turns the product over to Accenture, what factors and issues should it consider? What questions should it ask? What questions should its dealers ask?

Improving Decision Making: Using Spreadsheet Software for Capital Budgeting for a New CAD System

Software skills: Spreadsheet formulas and functions
Business skills: Capital budgeting

This project provides you with an opportunity to use spreadsheet software to use the capital budgeting models discussed in this chapter to analyze the return on an investment for a new CAD system.

Your company would like to invest in a new CAD system that requires purchasing hardware, software, and networking technology, as well as expenditures for installation, training, and support. The Laudon Web site for Chapter 14 contains tables showing each cost component for the new system as well as annual maintenance costs over a five-year period. It also features a Learning Track on capital budgeting models. You believe the new system will produce annual savings by reducing the amount of labor required to generate designs and design specifications, thus increasing your firm's annual cash flow.

- Using the data provided in these tables, create a worksheet that calculates the costs and benefits of the investment over a five-year period and analyzes the investment using the four capital budgeting models presented in this chapter's Learning Track.

- Is this investment worthwhile? Why or why not?

Improving Decision Making: Using Web Tools for Buying and Financing a Home

Software skills: Internet-based software
Business skills: Financial planning

This project will develop your skills using Web-based software for searching for a home and calculating mortgage financing for that home.

You have found a new job in Denver, Colorado, and would like to purchase a home in that area. Ideally, you would like to find a single-family house with at least three bedrooms and one bathroom that costs between $150,000 and $225,000 and finance it with a 30-year fixed rate mortgage. You can afford a down payment that is 20 percent of the value of the house. Before you purchase a house, you would like to find out what homes are available in your price range, find a mortgage, and determine the amount of your monthly payment. You would also like to see how much of your mortgage payment represents principal and how much represents interest. Use Yahoo!'s Real Estate site to help you with the following tasks:

- Locate homes in your price range in Denver, Colorado. Find out as much information as you can about the houses, including the real estate listing agent, condition of the house, number of rooms, and school district.

- Find a mortgage for 80 percent of the list price of the home. Compare rates from at least three sites (use search engines to find sites other than Yahoo!).

- After selecting a mortgage, calculate your closing costs.

- Calculate the monthly payment for the mortgage you select.

- Calculate how much of your monthly mortgage payment represents principal and how much represents interest, assuming you do not plan to make any extra payments on the mortgage.

When you are finished, evaluate the whole process. For example, assess the ease of use of the site and your ability to find information about houses and mortgages; the accuracy of the information you found; the breadth of choice of homes and mortgages; and how helpful the whole process would have been for you if you were actually in the situation described in this project.

LEARNING TRACK MODULES

The following Learning Tracks provide content relevant to topics covered in this chapter:

1. Capital Budgeting Methods for Information System Investments
2. Information Technology Investments and Productivity
3. Enterprise Analysis (Business Systems Planning)

Review Summary

1. *What are the objectives of project management and why is it so essential in developing information systems?*

    Good project management is essential for ensuring that systems are delivered on time, on budget, and provide genuine business benefits. Project management activities include planning the work, assessing the risk, estimating and acquiring resources required to accomplish the work, organizing the work, directing execution, and analyzing the results. Project management must deal with five major variables: scope, time, cost, quality, and risk.

2. *What methods can be used for selecting and evaluating information systems projects and aligning them with the firm's business goals?*

    Organizations need an information systems plan that describes how information technology supports the attainment of their business goals and documents all their system applications and IT infrastructure components. Large corporations will have a management structure to ensure the most important systems projects receive priority. Critical success factors, portfolio analysis, and scoring models can be used to identify and evaluate alternative information systems projects.

3. *How can firms assess the business value of information systems projects?*

    To determine whether an information systems project is a good investment, one must calculate its costs and benefits. Tangible benefits are quantifiable, and intangible benefits that cannot be immediately quantified may provide quantifiable benefits in the future. Benefits that exceed costs should be analyzed using capital budgeting methods to make sure a project represents a good return on the firm's invested capital. Real options pricing models, which apply the same techniques for valuing financial options to systems investments, can be useful when considering highly uncertain IT investments.

4. *What are the principal risk factors in information systems projects?*

    The level of risk in a systems development project is determined by (1) project size, (2) project structure, and (3) experience with technology. IS projects are more likely to fail when there is insufficient or improper user participation in the systems development process, lack of management support, and poor management of the implementation process. There is a very high failure rate among projects involving business process reengineering, enterprise applications, and mergers and acquisitions because they require extensive organizational change.

5. *What strategies are useful for managing project risk and system implementation?*

    Implementation refers to the entire process of organizational change surrounding the introduction of a new information system. User support and involvement and management support and control of the implementation process are essential, as are mechanisms for dealing with the level of risk in each new systems project. Project risk factors can be brought under some control by a contingency approach to project management. The risk level of each project determines the appropriate mix of external integration tools, internal integration tools, formal planning tools, and formal control tools to be applied.

Key Terms

Capital budgeting, 560
Change agent, 562
Change management, 562
Counterimplementation, 568
Critical success factors (CSFs), 554
Ergonomics, 568
External integration tools, 567
Formal control tools, 565
Formal planning tools, 565
Gantt chart, 565
Implementation, 562
Information systems plan, 554
Intangible benefits, 559

Internal integration tools, 565
Organizational impact analysis, 568
PERT chart, 565
Portfolio analysis, 556
Project, 550
Project management, 550
Real options pricing models (ROPMs), 560
Scope, 550
Scoring model, 557
Sociotechnical design, 570
Tangible benefits, 559
User-designer communications gap, 563
User interface, 550

Review Questions

1. What are the objectives of project management and why is it so essential in developing information systems?

   - Describe information system problems resulting from poor project management

   - Define project management. List and describe the project management activities and variables addressed by project management.

2. What methods can be used for selecting and evaluating information systems projects and aligning them with the firm's business goals?

   - Name and describe the groups responsible for the management of information systems projects.

   - Describe the purpose of an information systems plan and list the major categories in the plan.

   - Explain how critical success factors, portfolio analysis, and scoring models can be used to select information systems projects.

3. How can firms assess the business value of information systems projects?

   - List and describe the major costs and benefits of information systems.

   - Distinguish between tangible and intangible benefits.

   - Explain how real options pricing models can help manages evaluate information technology investments.

4. What are the principal risk factors in information systems projects?

   - Identify and describe each of the principal risk factors in information systems projects.

   - Explain why builders of new information systems need to address implementation and change management.

   - Explain why eliciting support of management and end users is so essential for successful implementation of information systems projects.

   - Explain why is there such a high failure rate for implementations involving enterprise applications, business process reengineering, and mergers and acquisitions.

5. What strategies are useful for managing project risk and system implementation?

   - Identify and describe the strategies for controlling project risk.

   - Identify the organizational considerations that should be addressed by project planning and implementation.

   - Explain how project management software tools contribute to successful project management.

Discussion Questions

1. How much does project management impact the success of a new information system?

2. It has been said that most systems fail because systems builders ignore organizational behavior problems. Why might this be so?

Video Cases

You will find video cases illustrating some of the concepts in this chapter on the Laudon Web site along with questions to help you analyze the cases.

Collaboration and Teamwork: Identifying Implementation Problems

Form a group with two or three other students. Write a description of the implementation problems you might expect to encounter in one of the systems described in the Interactive Sessions or chapter-ending cases in this text. Write an analysis of the steps you would take to solve or prevent these problems. If possible, use Google Sites to post links to Web pages, team communication announcements, and work assignments; to brainstorm; and to work collaboratively on project documents. Try to use Google Docs to develop a presentation of your findings for the class.

Structured Project Implementation Methodology at Focus
CASE STUDY

Focus is an Indian software company with headquarters in Dubai, UAE. Focus is primarily a product-based company that has developed and marketed packaged software for the last thirteen years. The company relies on a dual growth strategy: increased market share in existing markets and expansion to new markets. One of the company brands, Focus RT, was ranked in the top ten by IDC's ERP providers for the Middle East and North Africa.

The company has a portfolio of products including: FOCUS RT, which is a real-time ERP system; FOCUS 6, which is an enterprise-wide accounting system; FOCUS ARMS, which is an academic records management system; FOCUS WMS, a warehouse system; FOCUS STREAMLINE, a customer relationship management system, and finally FOCUS REACH, an off-the-shelf accounting solution for the SOHO Market.

Focus has witnessed many milestones to reach its current situation. In September 2001, Focus opened its branch in Dubai Internet City (DIC) in UAE. This proved to be a turning point in the success story of Focus. When Dubai announced the launch of Dubai Internet City, Focus was one of the first companies to decide to move its international headquarters to Dubai. The massive infrastructure support available in DIC has paved the way for Focus to grow and expand at a much faster rate. In 2005 they opened a branch in Qatar. The growth taking place in Qatar was being talked about everywhere in the Middle East and international markets from 2002 onwards. In fact, Focus realized that their decision to open a branch in Qatar, though a late one, was one of their best decisions, as it has now become one of the fastest growing branches within the last three years. Finally, in January 2006 the concentration on expansion moved from the Middle East to the USA.

Focus has a very structured implementation methodology which ensures their projects deliver to client's specifications, and are on time and budget. It is crucial that implementation is carried out in an organized manner so that the deliverables are clearly defined as milestones. On completion of each phase, a milestone certificate would be generated for the client to sign-off. To have a successful implementation, it is crucial that the implementation is a joint effort between the client and Focus.

During implementation, Focus maintains a one-point interface between Focus and the client. The key communicator is the project leader (PL) from Focus. In the event of a one-member team, the PL is Focus's software engineer. Focus recommends that the client should have a central coordinator (CC) for the entire project. A CC is essential and should be a driver for the entire project. He may decide to have other members in his central team. Along with these members, there should be rotating members, who are from departments where a particular module is being implemented.

The product is delivered incrementally, phase by phase. Some example phases are base product, screen customizations, business process customizations, MIS customizations and finally reports. The incremental deliveries ensure that users start using the software very early during the implementation time and do not have to wait for the entire product to go live. The approach taken by Focus is an output driven approach (i.e. reports). Focus believes that the implementation of the product equates with the usage of the software. It also believes that usage can be reasonably equated with having useful outputs from the system. These outputs normally take the form of onscreen or printed reports. As a result of this, Focus drives the product by focusing on the prioritized reports that can be taken out of the systems. For Focus, reports define the way the data is to be processed in the product. Once the output is clear, it is easy to visualize what inputs are needed to get to the output, what business rules need to be applied to the inputs, and the processing logic that needs to be followed to arrive at the final output.

Reports form the tangible deliverables and thus help drive the product implementation by clearly definable objectives. Without these tangible deliverables, the project tends to chase the bigger and unclear targets, jeopardizing the project's progress. This approach has been found to be extremely effective in situations where knowledge of the product is at its early stages in the user group.

The implementation is composed of the following stages. To begin with FOCUS needs to assess the client's infrastructure. Focus interviews end-users across the organization and draws out the total functional requirements and the objectives of implementing system integration solutions or an ERP solution. The boundaries of the scope of implementation are determined, as is an assessment of the computer awareness of end-users across the organization. User champions are identified from different business functions, and two implementation teams (one from Focus and the other from the client) are formed. A Pre-Implementation Report would be delivered.

At the initial business and architecture planning report (BAR) stage, a plan is developed describing the technical landscape, business processes, and organizational entities included in the project's scope. The project's context and boundaries are defined in order to ensure a clear understanding of the problem addressed by the system, and of the constraints that will be imposed on it. This provides a solid basis for collaboration with users in developing a solution that satisfies their business process requirements.

During the participatory data assessment (PDA) stage, users work with real data to determine its fitness for use within the system. Areas addressed include data quality issues, required cleansing rules, and possibilities for merging data drawn from multiple sources.

After developing customer-specific product extensions and customization and installing the final product, a roll-out plan is developed that lays out the full-scale functional implementation of the proposed solution. Effective deployment strategies ensure a smooth, effective, and efficient installation.

Once application training has been provided for User Champions and technical training for IT personnel, Focus provides knowledgeable and experienced professionals who validate the environment and recommend improvements. The team works with experts from the client side to review database performance, support issues, security, backup procedures, and all other aspects of the installation that impact on the operational effectiveness of the system. In this way, the review stage ensures that the client gets the maximum return on their investment.

Sources: www.focussoftnet.com

CASE STUDY QUESTIONS

1. From a project management point of view, how important is the implementation methodology?

2. Explain how Focus implementation methodology would help organizations to minimize and control project overall risks.

3. What modification would you make to the implementation methodology? Why?

• Case contributed by Dr. Ahmed Elragal, German University in Cairo

Chapter 15

Managing Global Systems

LEARNING OBJECTIVES

After reading this chapter, you will be able to answer the following questions:

1. What major factors are driving the internationalization of business?

2. What are the alternative strategies for developing global businesses?

3. How can information systems support different global business strategies?

4. What are the challenges posed by global information systems and management solutions for these challenges?

5. What are the issues and technical alternatives to be considered when developing international information systems?

Interactive Sessions:

Colgate-Palmolive Keeps the World Smiling

Can Cell Phones Close the Global Digital Divide?

CHAPTER OUTLINE

SEVERSTAL CREATES AN IT INFRASTRUCTURE FOR GLOBAL STEELMAKING

SeverStal ("Northern Steel") is one of Russia's largest steelmakers. It operates primarily in Russia but maintains facilities in Italy, the United Kingdom, France, and the United States. With more than 100,000 employees worldwide and more than US $15 billion in revenue in 2007, it's on its way to redefining global steel making.

Some U.S. firms have left the steel production market because it's very capital-intensive. SeverStal's not worried about that. This company's managers are convinced that they are at the helm of a global profitability leader in the steel and mining industry.

SeverStal's corporate strategy calls for providing high-margin value-added products in attractive niche markets worldwide while keeping costs low. The company is developing a global platform for best-practice sharing and competencies development. SeverStal company wants to leverage best practices and technologies across its global operations and improve efficiencies by locating mills closer to key automotive customers. In 2004, for example, SeverStal North America (SNA) purchased Rouge Industries in Dearborn, Michigan, originally part of Henry Ford's massive River Rouge manufacturing complex, to gain access to the U.S. market for automotive steel. SNA is now the fourth-largest integrated steelmaker in the United States.

Most of SeverStal's customers have operations throughout the world, and they want to be supplied with the same quality steel in North America, Europe, and Russia. SeverStal's strategy "is to create a global production platform that can supply high-quality steel to customers, wherever they are located," says Sergei Kuznetsov, SeverStal North America's chief financial officer.

All these plans call for a flexible IT infrastructure that is agile enough to meet changing global business requirements and support efficient growth. SNA's IT infrastructure was a hodgepodge of different systems, including Oracle PeopleSoft Enterprise for financials, Indus Enterprise PAC for purchasing and maintenance, and a variety of custom systems. Information was unable to flow freely across different functional areas.

Instead of upgrading its existing applications, SNA standardized on Oracle E-Business Suite 12, an enterprise applications suite that includes modules for financials, purchasing, enterprise asset management, manufacturing, and order management. The applications in Oracle E-Business Suite are integrated, making it easier to access data from different functional areas for decision making while creating more efficient work flows and enhancing productivity. Instead of optimizing individual business processes, the company is able to optimize end-to-end processes. For example, SNA's procure-to-pay processes are integrated with its purchasing system.

The new system also reduced the time required to close the company's books from 10 days to 5 days or less, providing more timely and

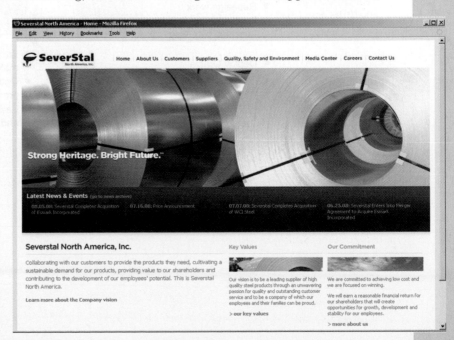

higher-quality information to the SeverStal parent company in Russia. Oracle iSupplier Portal, Oracle iProcurement, and Oracle Sourcing include capabilities for electronic quoting and self-service applications, facilitating communication and collaboration with SNA's suppliers and business partners. As SeverStal grows organically or through acquisitions, the Oracle software will help it integrate the new units on the same platform.

Sources: David A. Kelly, "Managing in a Global Economy: SeverStal," *Profit Magazine*, February 2008, and www.severstal.com/eng, accessed June 28, 2008.

Severstal's efforts to create a global IT infrastructure identifies some of the issues that organizations need to consider if they want to operate across the globe. In order to operate as a global business, the company had to have the right set of business processes and information systems in place.

The chapter-opening diagram calls attention to important points raised by this case and this chapter. SeverStal is trying to eke profits in a competitive and capital-intensive industry by providing products that can command higher prices in niche markets, but it still needs to keep its operating costs low. It adopted a global production model to meet this challenge. SeverStal's legacy information systems did not support global business processes and information flows, so the company replaced them with a set of enterprise applications from Oracle. The company is now able to respond flexibly to opportunities all over the world.

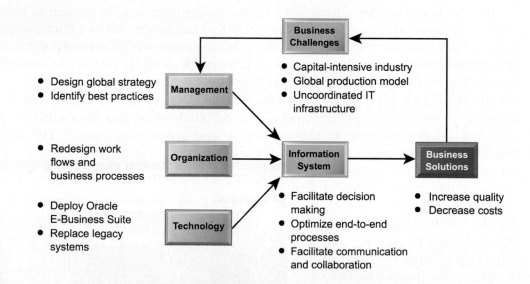

15.1 THE GROWTH OF INTERNATIONAL INFORMATION SYSTEMS

In earlier chapters we describe the emergence of a global economic system and global world order driven by advanced networks and information systems. The new world order is sweeping away many national corporations, national industries, and national economies controlled by domestic politicians. Many localized firms will be replaced by fast-moving networked corporations that transcend national boundaries. The growth of international trade has radically altered domestic economies around the globe.

Today, the production and design of many electronic products are parceled out to a number of different countries. Consider the path to market for a Hewlett-Packard (HP) laptop computer, which is illustrated in Figure 15-1. The idea for the product and initial design came from HP's Laptop Design Team in the United States. HP headquarters in Houston approved the concept. Graphics processors were designed in Canada and manufactured in Taiwan. Taiwan and South Korea provided the liquid-crystal display screens and many of the memory chips. The laptop's hard disk drive came from Japan. Sources in China, Japan, Singapore, South Korea, and the United States supplied other components. Laptop assembly took place in China. Contractors in Taiwan did the machine's engineering design and collaborated with the Chinese manufacturers.

DEVELOPING AN INTERNATIONAL INFORMATION SYSTEMS ARCHITECTURE

This chapter describes how to go about building an international information systems architecture suitable for your international strategy. An **international information systems architecture** consists of the basic information systems required by organizations to coordinate worldwide trade and other activities. Figure 15-2 illustrates the reasoning we follow throughout the chapter and depicts the major dimensions of an international information systems architecture.

FIGURE 15-1   AN HP LAPTOP'S PATH TO MARKET

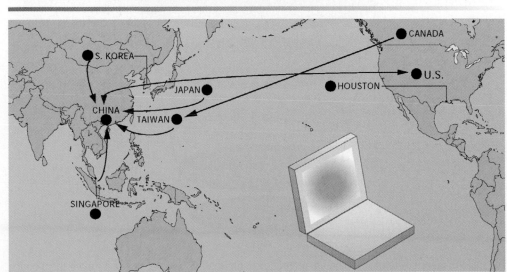

Hewlett-Packard and other electronics companies assign distribution and production of their products to a number of different countries.

The basic strategy to follow when building an international system is to understand the global environment in which your firm is operating. This means understanding the overall market forces, or business drivers, that are pushing your industry toward global competition. A **business driver** is a force in the environment to which businesses must respond and that influences the direction of the business. Likewise, examine carefully the inhibitors or negative factors that create *management challenges*—factors that could scuttle the development of a global business. Once you have examined the global environment, you will need to consider a corporate strategy for competing in that environment. How will your firm respond? You could ignore the global market and focus on domestic competition only, sell to the globe from a domestic base, or organize production and distribution around the globe. There are many in-between choices.

After you have developed a strategy, it is time to consider how to structure your organization so it can pursue the strategy. How will you accomplish a division of labor across a global environment? Where will production, administration, accounting, marketing, and human resource functions be located? Who will handle the systems function?

Next, you must consider the management issues in implementing your strategy and making the organization design come alive. Key here will be the design of business processes. How can you discover and manage user requirements? How can you induce change in local units to conform to international requirements? How can you reengineer on a global scale, and how can you coordinate systems development?

The last issue to consider is the technology platform. Although changing technology is a key driving factor leading toward global markets, you need to have a corporate strategy and structure before you can rationally choose the right technology.

FIGURE 15-2   INTERNATIONAL INFORMATION SYSTEMS ARCHITECTURE

The major dimensions for developing an international information systems architecture are the global environment, the corporate global strategies, the structure of the organization, the management and business processes, and the technology platform.

After you have completed this process of reasoning, you will be well on your way toward an appropriate international information systems portfolio capable of achieving your corporate goals. Let's begin by looking at the overall global environment.

THE GLOBAL ENVIRONMENT: BUSINESS DRIVERS AND CHALLENGES

Table 15-1 lists the business drivers in the global environment that are leading all industries toward global markets and competition.

The global business drivers can be divided into two groups: general cultural factors and specific business factors. Easily recognized general cultural factors have driven internationalization since World War II. Information, communication, and transportation technologies have created a *global village* in which communication (by telephone, television, radio, or computer network) around the globe is no more difficult and not much more expensive than communication down the block. The cost of moving goods and services to and from geographically dispersed locations has fallen dramatically.

The development of global communications has created a global village in a second sense: A **global culture** created by television, the Internet, and other globally shared media such as movies now permits different cultures and peoples to develop common expectations about right and wrong, desirable and undesirable, heroic and cowardly. The collapse of the Eastern bloc has speeded the growth of a world culture enormously, increased support for capitalism and business, and reduced the level of cultural conflict considerably.

A last factor to consider is the growth of a global knowledge base. At the end of World War II, knowledge, education, science, and industrial skills were highly concentrated in North America, western Europe, and Japan, with the rest of the world euphemistically called the *Third World*. This is no longer true. Latin America, China, India, southern Asia, and eastern Europe have developed powerful educational, industrial, and scientific centers, resulting in a much more democratically and widely dispersed knowledge base.

These general cultural factors leading toward internationalization result in specific business globalization factors that affect most industries. The growth of powerful communications technologies and the emergence of world cultures create the condition for *global markets*—global consumers interested in consuming similar products that are culturally approved. Coca-Cola, American sneakers (made in Korea but designed in Los Angeles), and Cable News Network (CNN) programming can now be sold in Latin America, Africa, and Asia.

TABLE 15-1 THE GLOBAL ENVIRONMENT: BUSINESS DRIVERS AND CHALLENGES

GENERAL CULTURAL FACTORS	SPECIFIC BUSINESS FACTORS
Global communication and transportation technologies	Global markets
Development of global culture	Global production and operations
Emergence of global social norms	Global coordination
Political stability	Global workforce
Global knowledge base	Global economies of scale

Responding to this demand, global production and operations have emerged with precise online coordination between far-flung production facilities and central headquarters thousands of miles away. At Sealand Transportation, a major global shipping company based in Newark, New Jersey, shipping managers in Newark can watch the loading of ships in Rotterdam online, check trim and ballast, and trace packages to specific ship locations as the activity proceeds. This is all possible through an international satellite link.

The new global markets and pressure toward global production and operation have called forth whole new capabilities for global coordination. Production, accounting, marketing and sales, human resources, and systems development (all the major business functions) can be coordinated on a global scale.

Frito Lay, for instance, can develop a marketing sales force automation system in the United States and, once provided, may try the same techniques and technologies in Spain. Micromarketing—marketing to very small geographic and social units—no longer means marketing to neighborhoods in the United States, but to neighborhoods throughout the world! These new levels of global coordination permit for the first time in history the location of business activity according to comparative advantage. Design should be located where it is best accomplished, as should marketing, production, and finance.

Finally, global markets, production, and administration create the conditions for powerful, sustained global economies of scale. Production driven by worldwide global demand can be concentrated where it can best be accomplished, fixed resources can be allocated over larger production runs, and production runs in larger plants can be scheduled more efficiently and precisely estimated. Lower cost factors of production can be exploited wherever they emerge. The result is a powerful strategic advantage to firms that can organize globally. These general and specific business drivers have greatly enlarged world trade and commerce.

Not all industries are similarly affected by these trends. Clearly, manufacturing has been much more affected than services that still tend to be domestic and highly inefficient. However, the localism of services is breaking down in telecommunications, entertainment, transportation, financial services, and general business services including law. Clearly, those firms within an industry that can understand the internationalization of the industry and respond appropriately will reap enormous gains in productivity and stability.

Business Challenges

Although the possibilities of globalization for business success are significant, fundamental forces are operating to inhibit a global economy and to disrupt international business. Table 15-2 lists the most common and powerful challenges to the development of global systems.

At a cultural level, **particularism**, making judgments and taking action on the basis of narrow or personal characteristics, in all its forms (religious, nationalistic, ethnic, regionalism, geopolitical position) rejects the very concept of a shared global culture and rejects the penetration of domestic markets by foreign goods and services. Differences among cultures produce differences in social expectations, politics, and ultimately legal rules. In certain countries, such as the United States, consumers expect domestic name-brand products to be built domestically and are disappointed to learn that much of what they thought of as domestically produced is in fact foreign made.

TABLE 15-2 CHALLENGES AND OBSTACLES TO GLOBAL BUSINESS SYSTEMS

GLOBAL	SPECIFIC
Cultural particularism: Regionalism, nationalism, language differences	Standards: Different Electronic Data Interchange (EDI), e-mail, telecommunications standards
Social expectations: Brand-name expectations, work hours	Reliability: Phone networks not uniformly reliable
Political laws: Transborder data and privacy laws, commercial regulations	Speed: Different data transfer speeds, many slower than United States
	Personnel: Shortages of skilled consultants

Different cultures produce different political regimes. Among the many different countries of the world are different laws governing the movement of information, information privacy of their citizens, origins of software and hardware in systems, and radio and satellite telecommunications. Even the hours of business and the terms of business trade vary greatly across political cultures. These different legal regimes complicate global business and must be considered when building global systems.

For instance, European countries have very strict laws concerning transborder data flow and privacy. **Transborder data flow** is defined as the movement of information across international boundaries in any form. Some European countries prohibit the processing of financial information outside their boundaries or the movement of personal information to foreign countries. The European Union Data Protection Directive, which went into effect in October 1998, restricts the flow of any information to countries (such as the United States) that do not meet strict European information laws on personal information. Financial services, travel, and health care companies could be directly affected. In response, most multinational firms develop information systems within each European country to avoid the cost and uncertainty of moving information across national boundaries.

Cultural and political differences profoundly affect organizations' business processes and applications of information technology. A host of specific barriers arise from the general cultural differences, everything from different reliability of phone networks to the shortage of skilled consultants.

National laws and traditions have created disparate accounting practices in various countries, which impact the ways profits and losses are analyzed. German companies generally do not recognize the profit from a venture until the project is completely finished and they have been paid. Conversely, British firms begin posting profits before a project is completed, when they are reasonably certain they will get the money.

These accounting practices are tightly intertwined with each country's legal system, business philosophy, and tax code. British, U.S., and Dutch firms share a predominantly Anglo-Saxon outlook that separates tax calculations from reports to shareholders to focus on showing shareholders how fast profits are growing. Continental European accounting practices are less oriented toward impressing investors, focusing rather on demonstrating compliance with strict rules and minimizing tax liabilities. These diverging accounting practices make it difficult for large international companies with units in different countries to evaluate their performance.

Language remains a significant barrier. Although English has become a kind of standard business language, this is truer at higher levels of companies and not throughout the middle and lower ranks. Software may have to be built with local language interfaces before a new information system can be successfully implemented.

Currency fluctuations can play havoc with planning models and projections. A product that appears profitable in Mexico or Japan may actually produce a loss because of changes in foreign exchange rates.

These inhibiting factors must be taken into account when you are designing and building international systems for your business. For example, companies trying to implement "lean production" systems spanning national boundaries typically underestimate the time, expense, and logistical difficulties of making goods and information flow freely across different countries.

STATE OF THE ART

One might think, given the opportunities for achieving competitive advantages as outlined previously and the interest in future applications, that most international companies have rationally developed marvelous international systems architectures. Nothing could be further from the truth. Most companies have inherited patchwork international systems from the distant past, often based on concepts of information processing developed in the 1960s—batch-oriented reporting from independent foreign divisions to corporate headquarters, manual entry of data from one legacy system to another, with little online control and communication. Corporations in this situation increasingly face powerful competitive challenges in the marketplace from firms that have rationally designed truly international systems. Still other companies have recently built technology platforms for international systems but have nowhere to go because they lack global strategy.

As it turns out, there are significant difficulties in building appropriate international architectures. The difficulties involve planning a system appropriate to the firm's global strategy, structuring the organization of systems and business units, solving implementation issues, and choosing the right technical platform. Let's examine these problems in greater detail.

15.2 ORGANIZING INTERNATIONAL INFORMATION SYSTEMS

Three organizational issues face corporations seeking a global position: choosing a strategy, organizing the business, and organizing the systems management area. The first two are closely connected, so we discuss them together.

GLOBAL STRATEGIES AND BUSINESS ORGANIZATION

Four main global strategies form the basis for global firms' organizational structure. These are domestic exporter, multinational, franchiser, and transnational. Each of these strategies is pursued with a specific business organizational structure (see Table 15-3). For simplicity's sake, we describe three kinds of organizational structure or governance: centralized (in the home country), decentralized (to local foreign units), and coordinated (all units participate as equals). Other types of governance patterns can be observed in specific

TABLE 15-3 GLOBAL BUSINESS STRATEGY AND STRUCTURE

BUSINESS FUNCTION	DOMESTIC EXPORTER	MULTINATIONAL	FRANCHISER	TRANSNATIONAL
Production	Centralized	Dispersed	Coordinated	Coordinated
Finance/Accounting	Centralized	Centralized	Centralized	Coordinated
Sales/Marketing	Mixed	Dispersed	Coordinated	Coordinated
Human Resources	Centralized	Centralized	Coordinated	Coordinated
Strategic Management	Centralized	Centralized	Centralized	Coordinated

companies (e.g., authoritarian dominance by one unit, a confederacy of equals, a federal structure balancing power among strategic units, and so forth).

The **domestic exporter** strategy is characterized by heavy centralization of corporate activities in the home country of origin. Nearly all international companies begin this way, and some move on to other forms. Production, finance/accounting, sales/marketing, human resources, and strategic management are set up to optimize resources in the home country. International sales are sometimes dispersed using agency agreements or subsidiaries, but even here foreign marketing is totally reliant on the domestic home base for marketing themes and strategies. Caterpillar Corporation and other heavy capital-equipment manufacturers fall into this category of firm.

The **multinational** strategy concentrates financial management and control out of a central home base while decentralizing production, sales, and marketing operations to units in other countries. The products and services on sale in different countries are adapted to suit local market conditions. The organization becomes a far-flung confederation of production and marketing facilities in different countries. Many financial service firms, along with a host of manufacturers, such as General Motors, Chrysler, and Intel, fit this pattern.

Franchisers are an interesting mix of old and new. On the one hand, the product is created, designed, financed, and initially produced in the home country, but for product-specific reasons must rely heavily on foreign personnel for further production, marketing, and human resources. Food franchisers such as McDonald's, Mrs. Fields Cookies, and KFC fit this pattern. McDonald's created a new form of fast-food chain in the United States and continues to rely largely on the United States for inspiration of new products, strategic management, and financing. Nevertheless, because the product must be produced locally—it is perishable—extensive coordination and dispersal of production, local marketing, and local recruitment of personnel are required.

Generally, foreign franchisees are clones of the mother country units, but fully coordinated worldwide production that could optimize factors of production is not possible. For instance, potatoes and beef can generally not be bought where they are cheapest on world markets but must be produced reasonably close to the area of consumption.

Transnational firms are the stateless, truly globally managed firms that may represent a larger part of international business in the future. Transnational firms have no single national headquarters but instead have many regional headquarters and perhaps a world headquarters. In a **transnational** strategy, nearly all the value-adding activities are managed from a global perspective without reference to national borders, optimizing sources of supply and demand wherever they appear, and taking advantage of any local competitive advantages. Transnational firms take the globe, not the home country, as their management frame of reference. The governance of these firms has been likened to a federal structure in which there is a strong central management core of decision making, but considerable dispersal of power and financial muscle throughout the global divisions. Few companies have actually attained transnational status, but Citicorp, Sony, Ford, and others are attempting this transition.

Information technology and improvements in global telecommunications are giving international firms more flexibility to shape their global strategies. Protectionism and a need to serve local markets better encourage companies to disperse production facilities and at least become multinational. At the same time, the drive to achieve economies of scale and take advantage of short-term local advantage moves transnationals toward a global management perspective and a concentration of power and authority. Hence, there are forces of decentralization and dispersal, as well as forces of centralization and global coordination.

GLOBAL SYSTEMS TO FIT THE STRATEGY

Information technology and improvements in global telecommunications are giving international firms more flexibility to shape their global strategies. The configuration, management, and development of systems tend to follow the global strategy chosen. Figure 15-3 depicts the typical arrangements. By *systems* we mean the full range of activities involved in building and operating information systems: conception and alignment with the strategic business plan, systems development, and ongoing operation and maintenance. For the sake of simplicity, we consider four types of systems configuration. *Centralized systems* are those in which systems development and operation occur totally at the domestic home base. *Duplicated systems* are those in which development occurs at the home base but operations are handed over to autonomous units in foreign locations. *Decentralized systems* are those in which each foreign unit designs its own unique solutions and systems. *Networked systems* are those in which systems development and operations occur in an integrated and coordinated fashion across all units.

FIGURE 15-3   GLOBAL STRATEGY AND SYSTEMS CONFIGURATIONS

SYSTEM CONFIGURATION	Strategy			
	Domestic Exporter	Multinational	Franchiser	Transnational
Centralized	X			
Duplicated			X	
Decentralized	x	X	x	
Networked		x		X

The large Xs show the dominant patterns, and the small Xs show the emerging patterns. For instance, domestic exporters rely predominantly on centralized systems, but there is continual pressure and some development of decentralized systems in local marketing regions.

As can be seen in Figure 15-3, domestic exporters tend to have highly centralized systems in which a single domestic systems development staff develops worldwide applications. Multinationals offer a direct and striking contrast: Here, foreign units devise their own systems solutions based on local needs with few if any applications in common with headquarters (the exceptions being financial reporting and some telecommunications applications). Franchisers have the simplest systems structure: Like the products they sell, franchisers develop a single system usually at the home base and then replicate it around the world. Each unit, no matter where it is located, has identical applications. Last, the most ambitious form of systems development is found in the transnational: Networked systems are those in which there is a solid, singular global environment for developing and operating systems. This usually presupposes a powerful telecommunications backbone, a culture of shared applications development, and a shared management culture that crosses cultural barriers. The networked systems structure is the most visible in financial services where the homogeneity of the product—money and money instruments—seems to overcome cultural barriers.

REORGANIZING THE BUSINESS

How should a firm organize itself for doing business on an international scale? To develop a global company and information systems support structure, a firm needs to follow these principles:

1. Organize value-adding activities along lines of comparative advantage. For instance, marketing/sales functions should be located where they can best be performed, for least cost and maximum impact; likewise with production, finance, human resources, and information systems.

2. Develop and operate systems units at each level of corporate activity— regional, national, and international. To serve local needs, there should be *host country systems units* of some magnitude. *Regional systems units* should handle telecommunications and systems development across national boundaries that take place within major geographic regions (European, Asian, American). *Transnational systems units* should be established to create the linkages across major regional areas and coordinate the development and operation of international telecommunications and systems development (Roche, 1992).

3. Establish at world headquarters a single office responsible for development of international systems—a global chief information officer (CIO) position.

Many successful companies have devised organizational systems structures along these principles. The success of these companies relies not only on the proper organization of activities, but also on a key ingredient—a management team that can understand the risks and benefits of international systems and that can devise strategies for overcoming the risks. We turn to these management topics next.

15.3 MANAGING GLOBAL SYSTEMS

Table 15-4 lists the principal management problems posed by developing international systems. It is interesting to note that these problems are the chief difficulties managers experience in developing ordinary domestic systems as well! But these are enormously complicated in the international environment.

TABLE 15-4 MANAGEMENT CHALLENGES IN DEVELOPING GLOBAL SYSTEMS

Agreeing on common user requirements
Introducing changes in business processes
Coordinating applications development
Coordinating software releases
Encouraging local users to support global systems.

A TYPICAL SCENARIO: DISORGANIZATION ON A GLOBAL SCALE

Let's look at a common scenario. A traditional multinational consumer-goods company based in the United States and operating in Europe would like to expand into Asian markets and knows that it must develop a transnational strategy and a supportive information systems structure. Like most multinationals, it has dispersed production and marketing to regional and national centers while maintaining a world headquarters and strategic management in the United States. Historically, it has allowed each of the subsidiary foreign divisions to develop its own systems. The only centrally coordinated system is financial controls and reporting. The central systems group in the United States focuses only on domestic functions and production.

The result is a hodgepodge of hardware, software, and telecommunications. The e-mail systems between Europe and the United States are incompatible. Each production facility uses a different manufacturing resources planning system (or a different version of the same ERP system), and different marketing, sales, and human resource systems. Hardware and database platforms are wildly different. Communications between different sites are poor, given the high cost of European intercountry communications. The central systems group at headquarters in the United States recently was decimated and dispersed to the U.S. local sites in the hope of serving local needs better and reducing costs.

What do you recommend to the senior management leaders of this company, who now want to pursue a transnational strategy and develop an information systems architecture to support a highly coordinated global systems environment? Consider the problems you face by reexamining Table 15-4. The foreign divisions will resist efforts to agree on common user requirements; they have never thought about much other than their own units' needs. The systems groups in American local sites, which have been enlarged recently and told to focus on local needs, will not easily accept guidance from anyone recommending a transnational strategy. It will be difficult to convince local managers anywhere in the world that they should change their business procedures to align with other units in the world, especially if this might interfere with their local performance. After all, local managers are rewarded in this company for meeting local objectives of their division or plant. Finally, it will be difficult to coordinate development of projects around the world in the absence of a powerful telecommunications network and, therefore, difficult to encourage local users to take on ownership in the systems developed.

GLOBAL SYSTEMS STRATEGY

Figure 15-4 lays out the main dimensions of a solution. First, consider that not all systems should be coordinated on a transnational basis; only some core systems are truly worth sharing from a cost and feasibility point of view. **Core systems** are systems that support functions that are absolutely critical to the organization. Other systems should be partially coordinated because they share key elements, but they do not have to be totally common across national boundaries. For such systems, a good deal of local variation is possible and desirable. A final group of systems is peripheral, truly provincial, and needed to suit local requirements only.

Define the Core Business Processes

How do you identify core systems? The first step is to define a short list of critical core business processes. Business processes are defined and described in Chapter 2, which you should review. Briefly, business processes are sets of logically related tasks to produce specific business results, such as shipping out correct orders to customers or delivering innovative products to the market. Each business process typically involves many functional areas, communicating and coordinating work, information, and knowledge.

The way to identify these core business processes is to conduct a business process analysis. How are customer orders taken, what happens to them once they are taken, who fills the orders, how are they shipped to the customers? What about suppliers? Do they have access to manufacturing resource planning

FIGURE 15-4   LOCAL, REGIONAL AND GLOBAL SYSTEMS

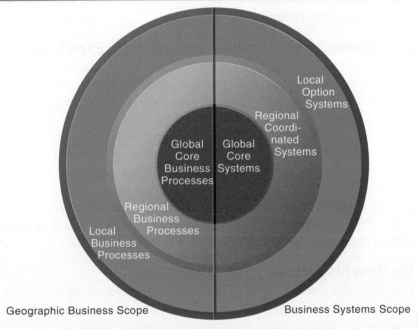

Agency and other coordination costs increase as the firm moves from local option systems toward regional and global systems. However, transaction costs of participating in global markets probably decrease as firms develop global systems. A sensible strategy is to reduce agency costs by developing only a few core global systems that are vital for global operations, leaving other systems in the hands of regional and local units.

Source: From *Managing Information Technology in Multinational Corporations* by Edward M. Roche, © 1993. Adapted by permission of Prentice Hall, Inc., Upper Saddle River, N.J.

systems so that supply is automatic? You should be able to identify and set priorities in a short list of 10 business processes that are absolutely critical for the firm.

Next, can you identify centers of excellence for these processes? Is the customer order fulfillment superior in the United States, manufacturing process control superior in Germany, and human resources superior in Asia? You should be able to identify some areas of the company, for some lines of business, where a division or unit stands out in the performance of one or several business functions.

When you understand the business processes of a firm, you can rank-order them. You then can decide which processes should be core applications, centrally coordinated, designed, and implemented around the globe, and which should be regional and local. At the same time, by identifying the critical business processes, the really important ones, you have gone a long way to defining a vision of the future that you should be working toward.

Identify the Core Systems to Coordinate Centrally

By identifying the critical core business processes, you begin to see opportunities for transnational systems. The second strategic step is to conquer the core systems and define these systems as truly transnational. The financial and political costs of defining and implementing transnational systems are extremely high. Therefore, keep the list to an absolute minimum, letting experience be the guide and erring on the side of minimalism. By dividing off a small group of systems as absolutely critical, you divide opposition to a transnational strategy. At the same time, you can appease those who oppose the central worldwide coordination implied by transnational systems by permitting peripheral systems development to progress unabated, with the exception of some technical platform requirements.

Choose an Approach: Incremental, Grand Design, Evolutionary

A third step is to choose an approach. Avoid piecemeal approaches. These surely will fail for lack of visibility, opposition from all who stand to lose from transnational development, and lack of power to convince senior management that the transnational systems are worth it. Likewise, avoid grand design approaches that try to do everything at once. These also tend to fail, because of an inability to focus resources. Nothing gets done properly, and opposition to organizational change is needlessly strengthened because the effort requires huge resources. An alternative approach is to evolve transnational applications incrementally from existing applications with a precise and clear vision of the transnational capabilities the organization should have in five years. This is sometimes referred to as the "salami strategy," or one slice at a time.

Make the Benefits Clear

What is in it for the company? One of the worst situations to avoid is to build global systems for the sake of building global systems. From the beginning, it is crucial that senior management at headquarters and foreign division managers clearly understand the benefits that will come to the company as well as to individual units. Although each system offers unique benefits to a particular budget, the overall contribution of global systems lies in four areas.

Global systems—truly integrated, distributed, and transnational systems—contribute to superior management and coordination. A simple price tag cannot be put on the value of this contribution, and the benefit will not show up in any capital budgeting model. It is the ability to switch suppliers on a moment's notice from one region to another in a crisis, the ability to move production in response to natural disasters, and the ability to use excess capacity in one region to meet raging demand in another.

A second major contribution is vast improvement in production, operation, and supply and distribution. Imagine a global value chain, with global suppliers and a global distribution network. For the first time, senior managers can locate value-adding activities in regions where they are most economically performed.

Third, global systems mean global customers and global marketing. Fixed costs around the world can be amortized over a much larger customer base. This will unleash new economies of scale at production facilities.

Last, global systems mean the ability to optimize the use of corporate funds over a much larger capital base. This means, for instance, that capital in a surplus region can be moved efficiently to expand production of capital-starved regions; that cash can be managed more effectively within the company and put to use more effectively.

These strategies will not by themselves create global systems. You will have to implement what you strategize.

THE MANAGEMENT SOLUTION

We now can reconsider how to handle the most vexing problems facing managers developing the global information systems architectures that were described in Table 15-4.

Agreeing on Common User Requirements

Establishing a short list of the core business processes and core support systems will begin a process of rational comparison across the many divisions of the company, develop a common language for discussing the business, and naturally lead to an understanding of common elements (as well as the unique qualities that must remain local).

Introducing Changes in Business Processes

Your success as a change agent will depend on your legitimacy, your authority, and your ability to involve users in the change design process. **Legitimacy** is defined as the extent to which your authority is accepted on grounds of competence, vision, or other qualities. The selection of a viable change strategy, which we have defined as evolutionary but with a vision, should assist you in convincing others that change is feasible and desirable. Involving people in change, assuring them that change is in the best interests of the company and their local units, is a key tactic.

Coordinating Applications Development

Choice of change strategy is critical for this problem. At the global level there is far too much complexity to attempt a grand design strategy of change. It is far easier to coordinate change by making small incremental steps toward a larger vision. Imagine a five-year plan of action rather than a two-year plan of action, and reduce the set of transnational systems to a bare minimum to reduce coordination costs.

The Interactive Session on Management describes how Colgate-Palmolive Company developed a strategy for coordinating information systems projects on a global basis. SAP's Resource and Portfolio Management software helped Colgate take a global perspective in selecting, staffing, and tracking projects.

COLGATE-PALMOLIVE KEEPS THE WORLD SMILING

Colgate-Palmolive Company is the second largest consumer products company in the world, whose products are marketed in over 200 countries and territories. The company has 36,000 employees worldwide and $13.7 billion annual revenue. Colgate has been keeping people smiling and clean around the world, with more than three-quarters of its sales in recent years coming from outside the United States. Colgate's brands in oral products, soap, and pet food are recognized around the world, including Colgate, Palmolive, Mennen, Softsoap, Irish Spring, Protex, Sorriso, Kolynos, Elmex, Tom's of Maine, Ajax, Axion, Fabuloso, Soupline, and Suavitel, as well as Hill's Science Diet and Hill's Prescription Diet.

The secret to continued growth and stability since 1990 has been Colgate's ability to move its brands off shore to Latin America, Europe, and Asia. Managing IT projects in a company operating in 200 countries poses unique challenges, not least of which is keeping track of who in the company is working on what IT projects, and how much money is being spent on all these projects. In the past, Colgate divided the world into geographic regions: Latin America, Europe, Asia, and North America. Each region planned its own IT projects and deployed available resources to build those systems. Within regions, IT resources (which included human and financial capital) were coordinated with spreadsheets being emailed among the operating companies and offices within each region. At the global corporate level, spreadsheets were also used to roll up the numbers to central planners in the United States. In other words, a state of global system disorganization existed at Colgate typical of firms that grew rapidly into multinational giants.

As long as the regions did not need to share resources or information and projects were localized, this patchwork system worked, more or less. Still, central executives in the United States had no idea who was working on which project, and had lost control over IT resources to the regions. This all changed as global operations became more integrated. A U.S. based team was building a factory in Poland, and Asian teams were working with their European counterparts on sharing IT systems. There was no mechanism for coordinating the Colgate global IT operation. Senior management realized that Colgate needed a coordinated, global approach to IT

resources, and that the regional system was terribly inefficient and ineffective.

In order to establish some control over IT projects worldwide, Colgate adopted SAP's Resource and Portfolio Management (RPM) software. SAP RPM is an integrated or "composite" application that uses the functions from SAP NetWeaver Business Intelligence (SAP NetWeaver BI) to report data. This application enables companies to inventory and track resources, skills, and budgets related to planning and managing of projects. It uses easy-to-understand dashboards with traffic light indicators to relay the status of budgets, schedules, and key performance indicators (KPIs). And because it is a composite application, it integrates with SAP ERP Human Capital Management (SAP ERP HCM) and other SAP systems. SAP claims that its RPM application will enable a company to achieve a "real-time" view of its IT project portfolio and better synchronize those projects with corporate strategy and priorities.

Here's how it works. Every year, Colgate's corporate IT department reviews a slate of projects submitted by various corporate groups, establishes priorities, and approves or disapproves projects. Monthly, IT personnel from around the world submit "Actuals reports" that identify the actual use of IT people and funds in that month. These data are rolled up into a comprehensive resource report for the entire company. One result is a listing of available people to work on new approved projects and who can be shared across the organization, as well as a comprehensive overview of who is working on maintenance programs, and who is developing new applications. One objective of the new application is to outsource as much maintenance work as possible to less expensive off-shore firms, while promoting more development work for internal IT staff in the regions that are closer to the customer.

The monitoring and reporting capabilities of SAP RPM enable the Colgate IT team to better align its priorities to business objectives. The measurement of actual time spent working on IT initiatives has enabled a clear understanding of the percentage of time spent on application development and support. Over a two-year period, CIO Tom Greene believes he has discovered a hidden 20 percent resource pool in the IT organization as it became apparent many people were not being used efficiently. Outsourcing of maintenance work has increased by 40 percent, allowing internal IT staff to focus on developing systems to serve customer needs.

Sources: Evan Albright, "Colgate-Palmolive Takes Control of Global IT with SAP RPM," *SAPNetWeaver Magazine*, October, 2008; Thomson, Inc. "SAP xApp Resource and Portofolio Management and SAP Consulting Enable Enterprise Wide Strategic and Operational R&D Portfolio Management." SAP White Paper, sap.com, accessed October 15, 2008; Colgate-Palmolive, Inc. Form 10K, filed with the Securities and Exchange Commission for the fiscal year ending December 31, 2007, filed February 28, 2008; ZDNet Australia, "Effective Management of Multiple Projects With SAP xApp Resource and Portfolio Management," August 28, 2007; and Bloomberg News, "New Products and Demand in Emerging Markets Fatten Profits at P.&G. and Colgate," *The New York Times*, January 31, 2007.

CASE STUDY QUESTIONS

1. Why was the traditional method of allocating IT resources to profits no longer effective?

2. Why is it important for central U.S. management to understand the global disposition of IT personnel and funds?

3. Which of the four global business strategies described in this chapter is Colgate pursuing, and how has this affected its selection of an IT resource management system?

4. What elements of "The Management Solution," described in this chapter, are mentioned in the case study? What elements are missing?

MIS IN ACTION

Explore the Colgate Web site and then answer the following questions:

1. Go to the SAP Web site and search on "RPM." Read SAP's description of the product and identify (a) other firms that use the product, and (b) how RPM integrates into ("snaps" into) larger SAP resource management applications.

2. Visit SAP's largest competitor, Oracle.com, and identify similar applications provided by Oracle. What do you think are the most important management and business considerations in deciding between Oracle and SAP solutions for global projects?

3. Visit HP.com and search on "Business Technology Optimization." BTO is a suite of products provided by HP to optimize the use of IT resources. Describe this suite of offerings and identify one global firm that uses this technology. Describe the global strategy of this firm, how it has changed in recent years, and the reasons for adopting this HP software.

Coordinating Software Releases

Firms can institute procedures to ensure that all operating units convert to new software updates at the same time so that everyone's software is compatible.

Encouraging Local Users to Support Global Systems

The key to this problem is to involve users in the creation of the design without giving up control over the development of the project to parochial interests. The overall tactic for dealing with resistant local units in a transnational company is cooptation. **Cooptation** is defined as bringing the opposition into the process of designing and implementing the solution without giving up control over the direction and nature of the change. As much as possible, raw power should be avoided. Minimally, however, local units must agree on a short list of transnational systems, and raw power may be required to solidify the idea that transnational systems of some sort are truly required.

How should cooptation proceed? Several alternatives are possible. One alternative is to permit each country unit the opportunity to develop one transnational application first in its home territory, and then throughout the world. In this manner, each major country systems group is given a piece of the action in developing a transnational system, and local units feel a sense of ownership in the transnational effort. On the downside, this assumes the ability to develop high-quality systems is widely distributed, and that, a German team, for example, can successfully implement systems in France and Italy. This will not always be the case.

A second tactic is to develop new transnational centers of excellence, or a single center of excellence. There may be several centers around the globe that focus on specific business processes. These centers draw heavily from local national units, are based on multinational teams, and must report to worldwide management. Centers of excellence perform the initial identification and specification of business processes, define the information requirements, perform the business and systems analysis, and accomplish all design and testing. Implementation, however, and pilot testing are rolled out to other parts of the globe. Recruiting a wide range of local groups to transnational centers of excellence helps send the message that all significant groups are involved in the design and will have an influence.

Even with the proper organizational structure and appropriate management choices, it is still possible to stumble over technology issues. Choices of technology platforms, networks, hardware, and software, are the final element in building transnational information system architectures.

15.4 TECHNOLOGY ISSUES AND OPPORTUNITIES FOR GLOBAL VALUE CHAINS

Once firms have defined a global business model and systems strategy, they must select hardware, software, and networking standards along with key system applications to support global business processes. Hardware, software, and networking pose special technical challenges in an international setting.

One major challenge is finding some way to standardize a global computing platform when there is so much variation from operating unit to operating unit and from country to country. Another major challenge is finding specific software applications that are user friendly and that truly enhance the productivity of international work teams. The universal acceptance of the Internet around the globe has greatly reduced networking problems. But the mere presence of the Internet does not guarantee that information will flow seamlessly throughout the global organization because not all business units use the same applications, and the quality of Internet service can be highly variable (just as with the telephone service). For instance, German business units may use an open source collaboration tool to share documents and communicate, which is incompatible with American headquarters teams, which use Lotus Notes. Overcoming these challenges requires systems integration and connectivity on a global basis.

COMPUTING PLATFORMS AND SYSTEMS INTEGRATION

The development of a transnational information systems architecture based on the concept of core systems raises questions about how the new core systems will fit in with the existing suite of applications developed around the globe by different divisions, different people, and for different kinds of computing hardware. The goal is to develop global, distributed, and integrated systems to support digital business processes spanning national boundaries. Briefly, these are the same problems faced by any large domestic systems development effort. However, the problems are magnified in an international environment. Just imagine the challenge of integrating systems based on the Windows, Linux, Unix, or proprietary operating systems running on IBM, Sun, Hewlett-Packard, and other hardware in many different operating units in many different countries!

Moreover, having all sites use the same hardware and operating system does not guarantee integration. Some central authority in the firm must establish data, as well as other technical standards, with which sites are to comply. For instance, technical accounting terms such as the beginning and end of the fiscal year must be standardized (review the earlier discussion of the cultural challenges to building global businesses), as well as the acceptable interfaces between systems, communication speeds and architectures, and network software.

CONNECTIVITY

Truly integrated global systems must have connectivity—the ability to link together the systems and people of a global firm into a single integrated network just like the phone system but capable of voice, data, and image transmissions. The Internet has provided an enormously powerful foundation for providing connectivity among the dispersed units of global firms. However, many issues remain. The public Internet does not guarantee any level of service (even in the U.S.). Few global corporations trust the security of the Internet and generally use private networks to communicate sensitive data, and Internet virtual private networks (VPN) for communications that require less security. Not all countries support even basic Internet service that requires obtaining reliable circuits, coordinating among different carriers and the regional telecommunications authority, obtaining bills in a common currency standard, and obtaining standard agreements for the level of telecommunications service provided. Table 15-5 lists the major challenges posed by international networks.

An increasingly attractive alternative is to create global networks based on the Internet and Internet technology. Companies can create global intranets for internal communication or extranets to exchange information more rapidly with business partners in their supply chains. They can use the public Internet to create global networks using VPNs from Internet service providers, which provide many features of a private network using the public Internet (see Chapter 7). However, VPNs may not provide the same level of quick and

TABLE 15-5 PROBLEMS OF INTERNATIONAL NETWORKS

Quality of service
Security
Costs and tariffs
Network management
Installation delays
Poor quality of international service
Regulatory constraints
Network capacity

predictable response as private networks, especially during times of the day when Internet traffic is very congested, and they may not be able to support large numbers of remote users.

The high cost of PCs, and low incomes, limit access to Internet service in many developing countries (see Figure 15-5). Where an Internet infrastructure exists in less-developed countries, it often lacks bandwidth capacity, and is unreliable in part due to power grid issues. The purchasing power of most people in developing countries makes access to Internet services very expensive in local currencies. In addition, many countries monitor transmissions. Governments in China, Singapore, Iran, and Saudi Arabia monitor Internet traffic and block access to Web sites considered morally or politically offensive. On the other hand, the rate of growth in the Internet population is far faster in Asia, Africa, and the Middle East than in North America and Europe, where the Internet population is growing slowly if at all. In 2009, China, for instance, has more than 200 million Internet users compared to the United States with about 180 million. Therefore, in the future, Internet connectivity will be much more widely available and reliable in less-developed regions of the world, and it will play a significant role in integrating these economies with the world economy.

The Interactive Session on Organizations describes how cell phones provide a partial solution to this problem. Their use is mushrooming in developing countries and they are starting to become engines for economic development.

SOFTWARE LOCALIZATION

The development of core systems poses unique challenges for application software: How will the old systems interface with the new? Entirely new

FIGURE 15-5   INTERNET PENETRATION BY REGION

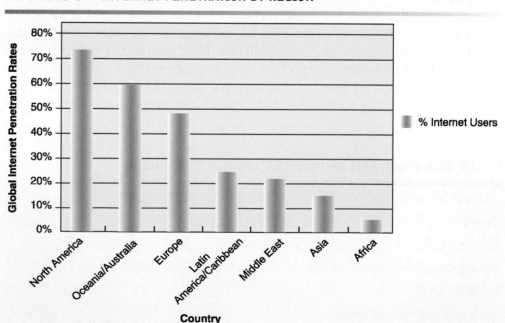

The percentage of the total population using the Internet in developing countries is much smaller than in the United States and Europe.

Source: Internetworldstats.com, 2008.

INTERACTIVE SESSION: ORGANIZATIONS

CAN CELL PHONES CLOSE THE GLOBAL DIGITAL DIVIDE?

As cell phones, the Internet, high-speed Internet connections, and other information and communication technologies become increasingly widespread, more and more people are experiencing the benefits each technology has to offer. Many of these technologies have not yet closed the 'digital divide' separating the world's well-developed and underdeveloped nations. Some countries, like the United States, have access to most new technologies, but most residents of poorer countries still struggle with challenges like obtaining reliable electricity and abject poverty. Recent trends in cell phone design and consumer research indicate that cellular phones are poised to cross the digital divide and become a truly ubiquitous technology, enhancing the quality of life for millions of people while also increasing the strength of the global economy.

Sixty-eight percent of the world's mobile phone subscriptions are in developing countries, compared with 20 percent of the world's Internet users. Because cell phones combine features of watches, alarm clocks, cameras and video cameras, stereos, televisions, and perhaps even wallets soon due to the growing popularity of mobile banking, they are growing in usefulness even as they decrease in price. Most importantly, cell phones are increasingly becoming the most convenient and affordable way to connect to the Internet and perform other tasks traditionally associated with computers.

The possession of a cell phone greatly increases efficiency and quality of life, so the global economy would stand to benefit on a proportionally large scale. Many economists believe that widespread cell phone usage in developing countries would have a profound and revolutionary effect on their economic well-being in a way that traditional methods of foreign aid have failed to achieve.

Cellular phone companies such as Nokia are sending what they call 'human-behavior researchers' or 'user anthropologists' to gather as much useful information as they can about consumer habits and the lives of potential cell phone buyers. They pass on that information to cell phone designers and technology architects. This process represents a new approach to designing phones known as 'human-centered design'. Human-centered design is important to high-tech companies trying to build products that people find appealing and easy to use, and are thus more likely to be bought.

Nokia and other companies face significant challenges in marketing their phones to the poorest segment of Africa and Asia's populations. Barriers include lack of electricity in many areas, incomes too low to afford a cell phone, and potential lack of service in non-urban areas. India currently leads the way in affordable cell phone subscriptions, with 226 million (19 percent of its total population), but many other countries lag far behind both in cell phone usage and rates of Internet access. For example, Morocco, one of Africa's leaders in cell phone and Internet usage, boasts 6.1 million Internet users, or 18.1 percent of its total population. By comparison, the U.S. has over 180 million Internet users, or 73 percent of its total population.

Despite this, the outlook for cell phones companies and the residents of Africa and Asia's poorest countries remains bright. Cell phones are spreading at a breakneck pace that shows little signs of slowing. It took 20 years for the first billion phones to sell, four years for the second billion, and only two years for the third billion. Eighty percent of the world's population lives within range of a cellular network, double the level in 2000.

The World Resources Institute published a report detailing how the poor in developing countries allocate their money. Even the poorest families dedicated significant portions of their small budgets to communication technologies such as cell phones. Having a cell phone is a tremendous advantage for members of populations that are constantly on the move due to war, drought, natural disasters, or extreme poverty, primarily because it allows people to remain reachable under practically any circumstances. Cell phones also have implications for medicine in these countries: patients can more easily reach doctors, and doctors can more easily acquire information pertaining to diseases and ailments they may need to treat.

In addition to the benefit of being able to stay in touch with others, cell phones are also useful as a business tool. Evidence suggests that possession of a cell phone increases profits on an individual level, allowing people to more easily identify and take advantage of business opportunities. A recent study by the Centre for Economic Policy Research also showed that for every additional 10 cellular phones per 100 people a country acquires, that country's gross domestic product (GDP) rises 0.5 percent.

Creative use of cell phones in developing countries includes 'phone ladies' in Bangladesh that charge small commissions for their fellow villagers to make and receive calls, and Ugandans using prepaid air time as an intermediary to transfer currency. Tradenet.biz in Ghana enables people in several West African countries to trade a variety of products using cell phone text messaging to communicate. Harvard University economics professor Robert Jensen found that when fishermen off the coast of Kerala in southern India started using cell phones to contact prospective buyers, their profits rose by an average of 8 percent while consumer prices in the local marketplace dropped 4 percent.

Many proponents of encouraging the growth of underdeveloped countries through commerce, as opposed to simply providing them with international aid money without changing their underlying economies, support the proliferation of cell phones because of this. Access to the Internet via cell phones also promises to bring about societal and political change in developing countries in which repressive governments exert control over all forms of media.

Sources: Nicole Ferraro, "Africa's Portal to the Internet," *Information Week*, February 4, 2008 and Sara Corbett, "Can the Cellphone Help End Global Poverty?" *The New York Times Magazine*, April 13 2008; "Top 20 Countries—Internet Usage," Internetworldstats.com, May 2008.

CASE STUDY QUESTIONS

1. What strategies are cell phone companies using to 'close the digital divide' and market phones to the poorest segment of the world's population?

2. Why do economists predict that widespread cell phone usage in developing countries would have an unprecedented effect on the growth of those countries?

3. What are some examples of how cell phones might increase quality of life for residents of developing countries?

4. Do you believe that cell phones will proliferate widely through Africa and Asia? Why or why not?

MIS IN ACTION

Explore the Web site for One Laptop Per Child (www.laptop.org) and then answer the following questions:

1. What are the capabilities of the XO laptop? How well-suited is this machine for developing countries?

2. How would use of the XO laptop narrow the global digital divide? Compare the potential impact of this machine to that of cell phones in developing nations.

interfaces must be built and tested if old systems are kept in local areas (which is common). These interfaces can be costly and messy to build. If new software must be created, another challenge is to build software that can be realistically used by multiple business units from different countries given these business units are accustomed to their unique business processes and definitions of data.

Aside from integrating the new with the old systems, there are problems of human interface design and functionality of systems. For instance, to be truly useful for enhancing productivity of a global workforce, software interfaces must be easily understood and mastered quickly. Graphical user interfaces are ideal for this but presuppose a common language—often English. When international systems involve knowledge workers only, English may be the assumed international standard. But as international systems penetrate deeper into management and clerical groups, a common language may not be assumed and human interfaces must be built to accommodate different languages and even conventions. The entire process of converting software to operate in a second language is called **software localization**.

This page from the Pearson Prentice Hall Web site was translated into Japanese. Web sites and software interfaces for global systems may have to be translated into multiple languages to accommodate users in other parts of the world.

What are the most important software applications? Many international systems focus on basic transaction and management reporting systems. Increasingly, firms are turning to supply chain management and enterprise systems to standardize their business processes on a global basis and to create coordinated global supply chains. However, these cross-functional systems are not always compatible with differences in languages, cultural heritages, and business processes in other countries (Martinons, 2004; Liang et al., 2004; Davison, 2002). Company units in countries that are not technically sophisticated may also encounter problems trying to manage the technical complexities of enterprise applications.

Electronic Data Interchange (EDI) systems and supply chain management systems are widely used by manufacturing and distribution firms to connect to suppliers on a global basis. Collaboration systems, e-mail, and videoconferencing are especially important worldwide collaboration tools for knowledge- and data-based firms, such as advertising firms, research-based firms in medicine and engineering, and graphics and publishing firms. Internet-based tools will be increasingly employed for such purposes.

15.5 HANDS-ON MIS PROJECTS

The projects in this section give you hands-on experience conducting international market research, analyzing international systems issues for an expanding business, and building a job posting database and Web page for an international company.

Management Decision Problems

1. United Parcel Service (UPS) has been expanding its package delivery and logistics services in China, serving both multinational companies and local businesses. UPS drivers in China need to use UPS systems and tools such as its handheld Driver Information Acquisition Device for capturing package delivery data. UPS wants to make its WorldShip, CampusShip, and other shipping management services accessible to Chinese and multinational customers via the Web. What are some of the international systems issues UPS must consider in order to operate successfully in China?

2. Your company manufactures and sells tennis rackets and would like to start selling outside the United States. You are in charge of developing a global Web strategy, and the first countries you are thinking of targeting are Brazil, China, Germany, Italy, and Japan. Using the statistics in the CIA World Factbook, which of these countries would you target first? What criteria would you use? What other considerations should you address in your Web strategy? What features would you put on your Web site to attract buyers from the countries you target?

Achieving Operational Excellence: Building a Job Database and Web Page for an International Consulting Firm

Software skills: Database and Web page design
Business skills: Human resources internal job postings

Companies with many overseas locations need a way to inform employees about available job openings in these locations. In this project, you'll use database software to design a database for posting internal job openings and a Web page for displaying this information.

KTP Consulting operates in various locations around the world. KTP specializes in designing, developing, and implementing enterprise systems for medium- to large-size companies. KTP offers its employees opportunities to travel, live, and work in various locations throughout the United States, Europe, and Asia. The firm's human resources department has a simple database that enables its staff to track job vacancies. When an employee is interested in relocating, he or she contacts the human resources department for a list of KTP job vacancies. KTP also posts its employment opportunities on the company Web site.

What type of data should be included in the KTP job vacancies database? What information should not be included in this database? Based on your answers to these questions, build a job vacancies database for KTP. Populate the database with at least 20 records. You should also build a simple Web page that incorporates job vacancy data from your newly created database. Send a copy of the KTP database and Web page to your professor.

Improving Decision Making: Conducting International Marketing and Pricing Research

Software skills: Internet-based software
Business skills: International pricing and marketing

When companies sell overseas, it's important to determine whether their products are priced properly for non-domestic markets. In this project, you'll use the Web to research overseas distributors and customs regulations and use Internet-based software to calculate prices in foreign currencies.

You are in charge of marketing for a U.S. manufacturer of office furniture that has decided to enter the international market. You have been given the name of Sorin SRL, a major Italian office furniture retailer, but your source had no other information. You want to test the market by contacting this firm to offer it a specific desk chair that you have to sell at about $125. Using the Web, locate the information needed to contact this firm and to find out how many European euros you would need to get for the chair in the current market. One source for locating European companies is the Europages Business Directory (www.europages.com). In addition, consider using the Universal Currency Converter Web site (www.xe.net/ucc/), which determines the value of one currency expressed in other currencies. Obtain both the information needed to contact the firm and the price of your chair in their local currency. Then locate and obtain customs and legal restrictions on the products you will export from the United States and import into Italy. Finally, locate a company that will represent you as a customs agent and gather information on shipping costs.

Review Summary

1. *What major factors are driving the internationalization of business?*

    The growth of cheap international communication and transportation has created a world culture with stable expectations or norms. Political stability and a growing global knowledge base that is widely shared contribute also to the world culture. These general factors create the conditions for global markets, global production, coordination, distribution, and global economies of scale.

2. *What are the alternative strategies for developing global businesses?*

    There are four basic international strategies: domestic exporter, multinational, franchiser, and transnational. In a transnational strategy, all factors of production are coordinated on a global scale. However, the choice of strategy is a function of the type of business and product.

3. *How can information systems support different global business strategies?*

    There is a connection between firm strategy and information systems design. Transnational firms must develop networked system configurations and permit considerable decentralization of development and operations. Franchisers almost always duplicate systems across many countries and use centralized financial controls. Multinationals typically rely on decentralized independence among foreign units with some movement toward development of networks. Domestic exporters typically are centralized in domestic headquarters with some decentralized operations permitted.

4. *What are the challenges posed by global information systems and management solutions for these challenges?*

    Global information systems pose challenges because cultural, political, and language diversity magnifies differences in organizational culture and business processes and encourages proliferation of disparate local information systems that are difficult to integrate. Typically, international systems have evolved without a conscious plan. The remedy is to define a small subset of core business processes and focus on building systems to support these processes. Tactically, managers will have to coopt widely dispersed foreign units to participate in the development and operation of these systems, being careful to maintain overall control.

5. *What are the issues and technical alternatives to be considered when developing international information systems?*

    Implementing a global system requires an implementation strategy that considers both business design and technology platforms. The main hardware and telecommunications issues are systems integration and connectivity. The choices for integration are to go either with a proprietary architecture or with open systems technology. Global networks are extremely difficult to build and operate. Firms can build their own global networks or they can create global networks based on the Internet (intranets or virtual private networks). The main software issues concern building interfaces to existing systems and selecting applications that can work with multiple cultural, language, and organizational frameworks.

Key Terms

Business driver, 582
Cooptation, 595
Core systems, 591
Domestic exporter, 587
Franchisers, 587
Global culture, 583
International information systems architecture, 581

Legitimacy, 593
Multinational, 587
Particularism, 584
Software localization, 600
Transborder data flow, 585
Transnational, 587

Review Questions

1. What major factors are driving the internationalization of business?

   - List and describe the five major dimensions for developing an international information systems architecture.

   - Describe the five general cultural factors leading toward growth in global business and the four specific business factors. Describe the interconnection among these factors.

   - List and describe the major challenges to the development of global systems.

   - Explain why some firms have not planned for the development of international systems.

2. What are the alternative strategies for developing global businesses?

   - Describe the four main strategies for global business and organizational structure.

3. How can information systems support different global business strategies?

   - Describe the four different system configurations that can be used to support different global strategies.

4. What are the challenges posed by global information systems and management solutions for these challenges?

   - List and describe the major management issues in developing international systems.

   - Identify and describe three principles to follow when organizing the firm for global business.

   - Identify and describe three steps of a management strategy for developing and implementing global systems.

   - Define cooptation and explain how can it be used in building global systems.

5. What are the issues and technical alternatives to be considered when developing international information systems?

   - Describe the main technical issues facing global systems.

   - Identify some technologies that will help firms develop global systems.

Discussion Questions

1. If you were a manager in a company that operates in many countries, what criteria would you use to determine whether an application should be developed as a global application or as a local application?
2. Describe ways the Internet can be used in international information systems.

Video Cases

You will find video cases illustrating some of the concepts in this chapter on the Laudon Web site along with questions to help you analyze the cases.

Collaboration and Teamwork: Identifying Technologies for Global Business Strategies

With a group of students, identify an area of information technology and explore how this technology might be useful for supporting global business strategies. For instance, you might choose an area such as digital telecommunications (e.g., e-mail, wireless communications, virtual private networks), enterprise systems, collaboration software, or the Web. It will be necessary to choose a business scenario to discuss the technology. You might choose an automobile parts franchise or a clothing franchise, such as Express, as example businesses. Which applications would you make global, which core business processes would you choose, and how would the technology be helpful? If possible, use Google Sites to post links to Web pages, team communication announcements, and work assignments; to brainstorm; and to work collaboratively on project documents. Try to use Google Docs to develop a presentation of your findings for the class.

Will a Global Strategy Save GM?
CASE STUDY

For many years, General Motors (GM) was the world's largest automaker. It is now second to Toyota. GM employs approximately 284,000 people worldwide to manufacture cars in 35 different countries and sells them under brands such as Buick, Cadillac, Chevrolet, Daewoo, GMC, Hummer, Pontiac, Saab, and Saturn. In recent years, GM has become increasingly unprofitable, with a $38 billion loss in 2007. One of the biggest reasons for GM's slow decline has been its inability to rapidly adjust to changing market trends, an issue exacerbated by the company's enormous size. However, GM hopes that it can reverse the trend via an IT transformation that has been years in the making.

GM's sheer size had traditionally been its strongest asset, but that bulk has now proved to be one of its greatest burdens. For 70 years, GM operated according to the philosophy of CEO Alfred Sloan, who divided the firm into five separate operating groups and divisions (Chevrolet, Pontiac, the now-defunct Oldsmobile, Buick, and Cadillac). Each division functioned as a semiautonomous company with its own product development, manufacturing, and marketing operations. This model of top-down control and decentralized execution had once been a powerful source of competitive advantage, enabling GM to build cars at lower cost than its rivals.

Over time, however, this policy worked against the company. GM was not able to move quickly to update its selection and styling, and the quality of its cars lagged behind Japanese and even U.S. rivals. It took GM more time and money than competitors to produce a car because the firm was saddled with a lumbering bureaucracy, inefficient production processes, and thousands of outdated "legacy" information systems that could not communicate with each other. GM's auto sales have steeply declined, from about 60 percent of the U.S. vehicle market in the 1970s to only 28.3 percent today.

GM has encountered several other problems sustaining its profitability. The company has a ratio of two and a half retirees to every active employee and provides retirees with significant pay and benefits. These additional expenses weigh the company down more than its competitors. GM plants are also predominantly located in high-cost areas due to the age of the company. Only relatively recently have companies began to take advantage of placing their manufacturing plants in lower-cost areas of the world.

GM is trying to address some of these problems by moving toward a global business model. It is aggressively expanding sales in China, Russia, and Latin America, while globalizing its production processes. GM's international units used to operate autonomously like its domestic divisions. In 2006, management launched an ambitious program to turn GM into a global company with standardized global business processes. The company is starting to operate as a global entity. Engineers and support people on three continents work in product development teams as if they are in the same room. GM can design cars for the United States from Brazil and take advantage of lower labor and materials costs throughout the world. Global logistics processes make it possible to build cars in Korea and easily distribute them in the Middle East. If GM runs out of production in one part of the world, it can shift to another country.

In order to make this global business model work, GM needs truly global systems capable of supporting the design, assembly, and sale of vehicles anywhere in the world. Since his appointment in 1996, CIO Ralph Szygenda has been standardizing IT systems, eliminating waste, and aggressively cutting costs, shaving billions off GM's annual IT budget. GM went from 7,000 different information systems down to 2,500.

For more than a decade, GM had relied on a single IT vendor—Electronic Data Systems (EDS), which GM purchased in 1984 and subsequently spun off as an independent entity in 1996. EDS handled all of GM's IT responsibilities. While GM owned the company, it had no direct involvement in its information systems. Relying on a single IT vendor drastically inflated GM's costs and led to few improvements. GM spent much more than any competing automaker on its information systems.

Szygenda decided to take back the strategic responsibility for information technology and began sourcing to multiple IT vendors—EDS, Oracle, IBM, HP. These GM technology partners share $7.5 billion in contracts. The other half of the $15 billion that GM has dedicated to its IT overhaul will be awarded over the next five years as GM meets its needs for new technology.

Getting these technology companies to work together was no small task. In the past, these companies only concerned themselves with making a particular product, allowing their customers to integrate the many products they had purchased. These vendors also had their own regional differences. Szygenda did not want to deal with "10 different IBMs" or "23 Ciscos." To turn things around, GM used its purchasing power to forge global contracts with these vendors and get disparate IT companies to work together on a combined, integrated series of solutions.

GM now has the infrastructure to keep its 160 global plants running smoothly. This includes standardized software and processes at every plant, updated networks, and four command centers in the United States, Latin America, and Europe. These command centers are designed to grant easy access to the relevant information at any factory and to help get lagging production up to speed faster.

GM oversaw global rollouts of two standardized software applications: a product routing and tracking system, which helps ensure that specific vehicles are produced as planned, and an in-plant order management system, which links suppliers into the assembly line. The product tracking system keeps track of even minute details about cars ready for assembly, and the order management system allows users access to information about any machine in use on the assembly line. GM's infrastructure consists of 500,000 devices, including 25,500 plant-floor computer terminals, 3,500 servers, 11,000 printers, 373,000 robots, and 14,000 network switches, routers, and access points Standardizing these is an enormous yet crucial task for a company of GM's size.

The automaker must also be very careful about the technologies it chooses to adopt. Once GM standardizes to a particular technology, it's tremendously expensive to go back. For example, the company still uses Windows XP rather than Vista because it is the 'conventional' choice, and it will very cautiously look into Bluetooth for wireless network technology while other companies have already taken the plunge. While it's critical that GM update its technology quickly and efficiently, GM executives are convinced that abandoning this cautious approach would create even more problems in the long run.

GM has explicitly defined processes to respond to technology mishaps. Eight expert centers based in key plants, staffed with specialists for particular applications, handle tech support issues at the company's plants. The four global command centers

also monitor and assist in the resolution of technology problems. Experts are on hand to solve these problems at all times. GM also uses a monitoring system called the Change Control Network. The system records IT changes at a plant, noting the size and impact of the change, assigning it a rating that describes the change's importance, and describing the potential risks.

The results of GM's technology upgrades are difficult to gauge amid the huge losses the company has sustained in recent quarters. But statistics suggest that they are having a decidedly positive impact. GM spends $1 billion less per year on information technology than it did in 1996. In 2006–2007, the number of vehicles on which production ceased because of IT-related issues decreased about 50 percent over 2005. In 2008, the number is less than 5 percent of the vehicles affected in all of 2005. 'Lost minutes' on the network, or periods of time during which devices were offline or malfunctioning, were down by 90 percent compared to 2005.

These figures may not appear impressive in the context of the company's staggering recent losses. GM's efforts to upgrade its IT will be just one of many improvements the company must make to return to profitability. The question is: will GM's globalization efforts pay off? To what extent can IT make GM a better automotive company?

Sources: Alex Taylor III, "Rick Wagoner Tries to Catch A Falling Knife - And Fails," CNNMoney.com, July 15, 2008; Stan Gibson, "GM Pens IT-Buying Bible," eWeek.com, July 23, 2006; David Welch, "GM Staggers Under Losses," Businessweek.com, August 1, 2008; Mary Hayes Weier, "GM's Factory IT Faces A Test," *Information Week*, June 21, 2008; John Soat, "CIOs Uncensored: GM's CIO: IT Vendors Aren't Helping With Globalization," *Information Week*, May 10, 2008; "GM's Ralph Szygenda Has the Biggest Stick in IT," CIOInsight.com, April 7, 2006; and Doug Bartholomew, "GM Outsourcing Overhaul, 1 Year Later," Baselinemag.com, January 7, 2007.

CASE STUDY QUESTIONS

1. Analyze GM using the competitive forces and value chain models.

2. What is the relationship between information systems and GM's business model? How are information systems related to the problems GM has been experiencing?

3. How have information systems helped GM transition to a global business model?

4. Do you think GM's global processes and upgraded information systems will be able to improve its business performance? Explain your answer.

References

CHAPTER 1

Belson, Ken. "Technology Lets High-End Hotels Anticipate Guests' Whims." *The New York Times* (November 16, 2005).

Brynjolfsson, Erik. "VII Pillars of IT Productivity." *Optimize* (May 2005).

Brynjolfsson, Erik and Lorin M. Hitt. "Beyond Computation: Information Technology, Organizational Transformation, and Business Performance." Journal of Economic Perspectives 14, no. 4 (2000).

Carr, Nicholas. "IT Doesn't Matter." *Harvard Business Review* (May 2003).

Davern, Michael J. and Robert J. Kauffman. "Discovering Potential and Realizing Value form Information Technology Investments." *Journal of Management Information Systems* 16, no. 4 (Spring 2000).

Dedrick, Jason, Vijay Gurbaxani, and Kenneth L. Kraemer. "Information Technology and Economic Performance: A Critical Review of the Empirical Evidence." Center for Research on Information Technology and Organizations, University of California, Irvine (December 2001).

Friedman, Thomas. *The World is Flat*. New York: Farrar, Straus, and Giroux (2006).

Garretson, Rob. "IT Still Matters." *CIO Insight* 81 (May 2007).

Greenspan Alan. "The Revolution in Information Technology." Boston College Conference on the New Economy (March 6, 2000).

Horrigan, John. "Mobile Access to Data and Information." Pew Internet and American Life Project (March 2008).

Hughes, Alan and Michael S. Scott Morton. "The Transforming Power of Complementary Assets." *MIT Sloan Management Review* 47. No. 4 (Summer 2006).

Ives, Blake, Joseph S. Valacich, Richard T. Watson, and Robert W. Zmud. "What Every Business Student Needs to Know about Information Systems." *CAIS* 9, Article 30 (December 2002).

Lamb, Roberta, Steve Sawyer, and Rob Kling. "A Social Informatics Perspective of Socio-Technical Networks." http://lamb.cba.hawaii.edu/pubs (2004).

Laudon, Kenneth C. *Computers and Bureaucratic Reform*. New York: Wiley (1974).

Lev, Baruch. "Intangibles: Management, Measurement, and Reporting." The Brookings Institution Press (2001).

Marchand, Donald A. "Exgtracting the Business Value of IT: IT Is Usage, Not Just Deployment that Counts!" The Copco Institute Journal of Financial Transformation (2004).

Pew Internet and American Life. "Internet Activities." (2008). wwwpewinternet.org, accessed 9/20/08.

Quinn, Francis J. "eBusiness Evangelist; An Interview with Erik Brynjolfsson." *Supply Chain Management Review* (May/June 2006).

Ross, Jeanne W., and Peter Weill. "Six IT Decisions Your IT People Shouldn't Make." *Harvard Business Review* (November 2002).

Teece, David. *Economic Performance and Theory of the Firm: The Selected Papers of David Teece*. London: Edward Elgar Publishing (1998).

Tuomi, Ilkka. "Data Is More Than Knowledge. *Journal of Management Information Systems* 16, no. 3 (Winter 1999–2000).

Verisign. "Domain Name Industry Brief." (June 2008). www.verisign.com, accessed October 2, 2008.

Weill, Peter, Jeanne Ross, and David Robertson. "Digitizing Down to the Core." *Optimize Magazine* (September 2006).

CHAPTER 2

Bernoff, Josh and Charlene Li. "Harnessing the Power of Social Applications." MIT Sloan Management Review (Spring 2008).

Basu, Amit and Chip Jarnagin. "How to Tap IT's Hidden Potential." *The Wall Street Journal* (March 10, 2008).

Broadbent, Marianne and Ellen Kitzis. *The New CIO Leader*. Boston, MA: Harvard Business Press (2004).

Cash, James I. Jr., Michael J. Earl, and Robert Morison. "Teaming Up to Crack Innovation and Enterprise Integration." Harvard Business Review (November 2008).

Cone, Edward. "The Accidental Strategist." *CIO Insight* (April 2008).

Hof, Robert. "The Coming Virtual Web." *Business Week* (April 16, 2007).

Huber, George P. "Organizational Information Systems: Determinants of Their Performance and Behavior." *Management Science* 28, no. 2 (1984).

Johnston, Russell, and Michael J. Vitale. "Creating Competitive Advantage with Interorganizational Information Systems." *MIS Quarterly* 12, no. 2 (June 1988).

Johnson, Bradfor, James Manyika, and Lareina Yee. "The Next Revolution in Interactions," McKinsey Quarterly No. 4 (2005).

Kalakota, Ravi, and Marcia Robinson. *e-Business2.0: Roadmap for Success*. Reading, MA: Addison-Wesley (2001).

Lamonica, Martin. "IBM Warms to Social Networking." *ZDNet News* (October 3, 2006).

Lardi-Nadarajan, Kamales. "Doing Business in Virtual Worlds." *CIO Insight* (March 2008).

Malone, Thomas M., Kevin Crowston, Jintae Lee, and Brian Pentland. "Tools for Inventing Organizations: Toward a Handbook of Organizational Processes." *Management Science* 45, no. 3 (March 1999).

Nolan, Richard, and F. Warren McFarland. "Information Technology and the Board of Directors." *Harvard Business Review* (October 1, 2005).

Oracle Corporation. "Alcoa Implements Oracle Solution 20% below Projected Cost, Eliminates 43 Legacy Systems." www.oracle.com, accessed August 21, 2005.

Picarelle, Lisa. Planes, Trains, and Automobiles. *Customer Relationship Management* (February 2004).

Raghupathi, W. "RP". "Corporate Governance of IT: A Framework for Development." *Communications of the ACM* 50, No. 8 (August 2007).

SAP. "Alcan Packaging Implements mySAP SCM to Increase Shareholder Value." www.mysap.com, accessed August 20, 2005.

SAP AG. "Air Liquide." (2007).

Shirky, Clay. "Social Media Changes the Enterprise." *CIO Insight* (May 2008).

Siebel Systems. "Saab Cars USA Increases Lead Follow-Up from 38 Percent to 50 Percent with Siebel Automotive." www.siebel.com, accessed October 15, 2005.

Soat, John. "Tomorrow's CIO." *Information Week* (June 16, 2008).

Sprague, Ralph H., Jr., and Eric D. Carlson. *Building Effective Decision Support Systems*. Englewood Cliffs, NJ: Prentice Hall (1982)

Tapscott, Don and Anthony D. Williams. "The Global Plant Floor." *Business Week* (March 20, 2007).

Vara, Vauhini. "Wikis at Work." *The Wall Street Journal* (June 18, 2007).

Telecommunications Industry Association. "TIA's 2008 Telecommunications Market Review and Forecast." www.tia.com, 2008.

Weill, Peter, and Jeanne Ross. "A Matrixed Approach to Designing IT Governance." *MIT Sloan Management Review* 46, no. 2 (Winter 2005).

Weill, Peter and Jeanne W. Ross. *IT Governance*. Boston: Harvard Business School Press (2004).

CHAPTER 3

Attewell, Paul, and James Rule. "Computing and Organizations: What We Know and What We Don't Know." *Communications of the ACM 27*, no. 12 (December 1984).

Beer, Michael, Russell A. Eisenstat, and Bert Spector. "Why Change Programs Don't Produce Change." *Harvard Business Review* (November-December 1990).

Bresnahan, Timohy F., Erik Brynjolfsson, and Lorin M. Hitt, "Information Technology, Workplace Organization, and the Demand for Skilled Labor," Quarterly Journal of Economics 117 (February 2002).

Bughin, Jacques, Michael Chui, and Brad Johnson. "The Next Step in Open Innovation." *The McKinsey Quarterly* (June 2008).

Cash, J. I., and Benn R. Konsynski. "IS Redraws Competitive Boundaries." *Harvard Business Review* (March-April 1985).

Christensen, Clayton. "The Past and Future of Competitive Advantage." *Sloan Management Review* 42, no. 2 (Winter 2001).

Clemons, Eric K. "Evaluation of Strategic Investments in Information Technology." *Communications of the ACM* (January 1991).

———. "Sustaining IT Advantage: The Role of Structural Differences." *MIS Quarterly* 15, no. 3 (September 1991).

Coase, Ronald H. "The Nature of the Firm."(1937) in Putterman, Louis and Randall Kroszner. *The Economic Nature of the Firm: A Reader*, Cambridge University Press, 1995.

Davenport, Thomas H. and Jeanne G. Harris. Competing on Analytics: The New Science of Winning. Boston: Harvard Business School Press (2007).

Drucker, Peter. "The Coming of the New Organization." *Harvard Business Review* (January-February 1988).

Feeny, David E., and Blake Ives. "In Search of Sustainability: Reaping Long-Term Advantage from Investments in Information Technology." *Journal of Management Information Systems* (Summer 1990).

Feeny, David. "Making Business Sense of the E-Opportunity." *Sloan Management Review* 42, no. 2 (Winter 2001).

Freeman, John, Glenn R. Carroll, and Michael T. Hannan. "The Liability of Newness: Age Dependence in Organizational Death Rates." *American Sociological Review* 48 (1983).

Fritz, Mary Beth Watson, Sridhar Narasimhan, and Hyeun-Suk Rhee. "Communication and Coordination in the Virtual Office." *Journal of Management Information Systems* 14, no. 4 (Spring 1998).

Fulk, Janet, and Geraldine DeSanctis. "Electronic Communication and Changing Organizational Forms." *Organization Science* 6, no. 4 (July-August 1995).

Gallaugher, John M. and Yu-Ming Wang. "Understanding Network Effects in Software Markets: Evidence from Web Server Pricing." *MIS Quarterly* 26, no. 4 (December 2002).

Garretson, Rob."IS IT Still Strategic?" *CIO Insight* (May 2007).

Gilbert, Clark and Joseph L. Bower, "Disruptive Change." *Harvard Business Review* (May 2002),

Gurbaxani, V., and S. Whang, "The Impact of Information Systems on Organizations and Markets." *Communications of the ACM* 34, no. 1 (Jan. 1991).

Hinds, Pamela, and Sara Kiesler. "Communication across Boundaries: Work, Structure, and Use of Communication Technologies in a Large Organization." *Organization Science* 6, no. 4 (July-August 1995).

Hitt, Lorin M. "Information Technology and Firm Boundaries: Evidence from Panel Data." *Information Systems Research* 10, no. 2 (June 1999).

Hitt, Lorin M., and Erik Brynjolfsson. "Information Technology and Internal Firm Organization: An Exploratory Analysis." *Journal of Management Information Systems* 14, no. 2 (Fall 1997).

Huber, George. "Organizational Learning: The Contributing Processes and Literature." *Organization Science*, 2 (1991), pp. 88-115.

———. "The Nature and Design of Post-Industrial Organizations." *Management Science* 30, no. 8 (August 1984).

Iansiti, Marco and Roy Levien, "Strategy as Ecology." *Harvard Business Review* (March 2004).

Ives, Blake and Gabriele Piccoli. "Custom Made Apparel and Individualized Service at Lands' End." *Communications of the AIS* 11 (2003).

Iyer, Bala and Thomas H. Davenport. "Reverse Engineering Google's Innovation Machine." *Harvard Business Review* (April 2008).

Jensen, M. C., and W. H. Meckling. "Specific and General Knowledge and Organizational Science." In *Contract Economics*, edited by L. Wetin and J. Wijkander. Oxford: Basil Blackwell (1992).

Jensen, Michael C., and William H. Meckling. "Theory of the Firm: Managerial Behavior, Agency Costs, and Ownership Structure." *Journal of Financial Economics* 3 (1976).

Kauffman, Robert J. and Yu-Ming Wang. "The Network Externalities Hypothesis and Competitive Network Growth." *Journal of Organizational Computing and Electronic Commerce* 12, no. 1 (2002).

Kettinger, William J., Varun Grover, Subashish Guhan, and Albert H. Segors. "Strategic Information Systems Revisited: A Study in Sustainability and Performance." *MIS Quarterly* 18, no. 1 (March 1994).

King, J. L., V. Gurbaxani, K. L. Kraemer, F. W. McFarlan, K. S. Raman, and C. S. Yap. "Institutional Factors in Information Technology Innovation." *Information Systems Research* 5, no. 2 (June 1994).

Kling, Rob. "Social Analyses of Computing: Theoretical Perspectives in Recent Empirical Research." *Computing Survey* 12, no. 1 (March 1980).

Kolb, D. A., and A. L. Frohman. "An Organization Development Approach to Consulting." *Sloan Management Review* 12, no. 1 (Fall 1970).

Kraemer, Kenneth, John King, Debora Dunkle, and Joe Lane. *Managing Information Systems*. Los Angeles: Jossey-Bass (1989).

Krishnan, M.S. "Moving Beyond Alignment: IT Grabs the Baton." *Optimize Magazine* (April 2007).

Lamb, Roberta and Rob Kling. "Reconceptualizing Users as Social Actors in Information Systems Research." *MIS Quarterly* 27, no. 2 (June 2003).

Laudon, Kenneth. "A General Model of the Relationship Between Information Technology and Organizations." Center for Research on Information Systems, New York University. Working paper, National Science Foundation (1989).

———. *Dossier Society: Value Choices in the Design of National Information Systems*. New York: Columbia University Press (1986).

———. "Environmental and Institutional Models of Systems Development." *Communications of the ACM* 28, no. 7 (July 1985).

———. "The Promise and Potential of Enterprise Systems and Industrial Networks." Working paper, The Concours Group. Copyright Kenneth C. Laudon (1999).

Laudon, Kenneth C. and Kenneth L. Marr, "Information Technology and Occupational Structure." (April 1995).

Lawrence, Paul, and Jay Lorsch. *Organization and Environment*. Cambridge, MA: Harvard University Press (1969).

Leavitt, Harold J. "Applying Organizational Change in Industry: Structural, Technological, and Humanistic Approaches." In *Handbook of Organizations*, edited by James G. March. Chicago: Rand McNally (1965).

Leavitt, Harold J., and Thomas L. Whisler. "Management in the 1980s." *Harvard Business Review* (November-December 1958).

Maier, Jerry L., R. Kelly Rainer, Jr., and Charles A. Snyder. "Environmental Scanning for Information Technology: An Empirical Investigation." *Journal of Management Information Systems* 14, no. 2 (Fall 1997).

Malone, Thomas W., JoAnne Yates, and Robert I. Benjamin. "Electronic Markets and Electronic Hierarchies." *Communications of the ACM* (June 1987).

March, James G., and Herbert A. Simon. *Organizations*. New York: Wiley (1958).

Markus, M. L. "Power, Politics, and MIS Implementation." *Communications of the ACM* 26, no. 6 (June 1983).

McAfee, Andrew and Erik Brynjolfsson. "Investing in the IT That Makes a Competitive Difference." Harvard Business Review (July/August 2008).

McFarlan, F. Warren. "Information Technology Changes the Way You Compete." *Harvard Business Review* (May-June 1984).

Mendelson, Haim, and Ravindra R. Pillai. "Clock Speed and Informational Response: Evidence from the Information Technology Industry." *Information Systems Research* 9, no. 4 (December 1998).

Mintzberg, Henry. *The Structuring of Organizations*. Englewood Cliffs, NJ: Prentice Hall (1979).

Orlikowski, Wanda J., and Daniel Robey. "Information Technology and the Structuring of Organizations." *Information Systems Research* 2, no. 2 (June 1991).

Pindyck, Robert S., and Daniel L. Rubinfeld. *Microeconomics, Seventh Ed*. Upper Saddle River, NJ: Prentice Hall (2009).

Porter, Michael E. and Scott Stern. "Location Matters." *Sloan Management Review* 42, no. 4 (Summer 2001).

Porter, Michael. *Competitive Strategy*. New York: Free Press (1980).

———. *Competitive Advantage*. New York: Free Press (1985).

———. "How Information Can Help You Compete." *Harvard Business Review* (August-September 1985a).

———."Strategy and the Internet." *Harvard Business Review* (March 2001).

Porter, Michael E. "The Five Competitive Forces that Shape Strategy." *Harvard Business Review* (January 2008).

Prahalad, C.K.and M.S.Krishnan. *The New Age of Innovation. Driving Cocreated Value Through Global Networks*. New York: McGraw Hill (2008).

Reich, Blaize Horner and Izak Benbasat. "Factors that Influence the Social Dimension of Alignment ween Business and Information Technology Objectives." *MIS Quarterly* 24, no. 1 (March 2000).

Robey, Daniel and Marie-Claude Boudreau. "Accounting for the Contradictory Organizational Consequences of Information Technology: Theoretical Directions and Methodological

Implications." *Information Systems Research* 10, no. 42 (June1999).

Shapiro, Carl, and Hal R. Varian. *Information Rules*. Boston, MA: Harvard Business School Press (1999).

Shpilberg, David, Steve Berez, Rudy Puryear, and Sachin Shah. "Avoiding the Alignment Trap in Information Technology." *MIT Sloan Management Review* 49, no. 1 (Fall 2007).

Starbuck, William H. "Organizations as Action Generators." *American Sociological Review* 48 (1983).

Tushman, Michael L., and Philip Anderson. "Technological Discontinuities and Organizational Environments." *Administrative Science Quarterly* 31 (September 1986).

Watson, Brian P. "Is Strategic Alignment Still a Priority?" *CIO Insight* (October 2007).

Weber, Max. *The Theory of Social and Economic Organization*. Translated by Talcott Parsons. New York: Free Press (1947).

Williamson, Oliver E. *The Economic Institutions of Capitalism*. New York: Free Press, (1985).

CHAPTER 4

Association of Computing Machinery. "ACM's Code of Ethics and Professional Conduct." *Communications of the ACM* 36, no. 12 (December 1993).

Barrett, Larry and Sean Gallagher. "What Sin City Can Teach Tom Ridge." Baseline Magazine (April 2004).

Bennett, Colin J."Cookies, Web Bugs, Webcams, and Cue Cats: Patterns of Surveillance on the World Wide Web." *Ethics and Information Technology* 3, no. 3 (2001).

Berdichevsky, Daniel and Erik Neunschwander. "Toward an Ethics of Persuasive Technology." *Communications of the ACM* 42, no. 5 (May 1999).

Bhattacharjee, Sudip, Ram D. Gopal, and G. Lawrence Sanders. "Digital Music and Online Sharing: Software Piracy 2.0?" *Communications of the ACM* 46, no.7 (July 2003).

Borland, John, "The Technology That Toppled Eliot Spitzer," *Technology Review* (March 19, 2008).

Bowen, Jonathan. "The Ethics of Safety-Critical Systems." *Communications of the ACM* 43, no. 3 (April 2000).

Brod, Craig. *Techno Stress-The Human Cost of the Computer Revolution*. Reading MA: Addison-Wesley (1982).

Brown Bag Software vs. Symantec Corp. 960 F2D 1465 (Ninth Circuit, 1992).

Business Software Alliance. "Fifth Annual BSA and IDC Global Software Piracy Study." (May 2008).

Carr, David F. and Sean Gallagher. "BofA's Direct-Deposit Debacle." *Baseline* (May 15, 2002).

Chellappa, Ramnath K. and Shivendu Shivendu. "An Economic Model of Privacy: A Property Rights Approach to Regulatory Choices for Online Personalization." *Journal of Management Information Systems* 24, no. 3 (Winter 2008).

Clarke, Roger. "Internet Privacy Concerns Confirm the Case for Intervention." *Communications of the ACM* 42, no. 2 (February 1999).

Collins, W. Robert, Keith W. Miller, Bethany J. Spielman, and Phillip Wherry. "How Good Is Good Enough? An Ethical Analysis of Software Construction and Use." *Communications of the ACM* 37, no. 1 (January 1994).

Day, George S., Adam J. Fein, and Gregg Ruppersberger, "Shakeouts in Digital Markets," *California Management Review* 45, no. 3 (Winter 2003).

Downes, Larry. "Avoiding Web Rocks and Shoals." *CIO Insight* (May 2008).

Farmer, Dan and Charles C. Mann. "Surveillance Nation." Part I *Technology Review* (April 2003) and Part II (*Technology Review* (May 2003)..

Foley, John. "P2P Peril." *Information Week* (March 17, 2008).

Goodman, Joshua, Gordon V. Cormack, and David Heckerman. "Spam and the Ongoing Battle for the Inbox." *Communications of the ACM* 50, No. 2 (February 2007).

Gorman, Siobhan. "NSA's Domestic Spying Grows As Agency Sweeps Up Data." *The Wall Street Journal* (March 10, 2008).

Grimes, Galen A. "Compliance with the CAN-SPAM Act of 2003." *Communications of the ACM* 50, No. 2 (February 2007).

Harrington, Susan J. "The Effect of Codes of Ethics and Personal Denial of Responsibility on Computer Abuse Judgments and Intentions." *MIS Quarterly* 20, no. 2 (September 1996).

Holmes, Allan. The Profits in Privacy." *CIO Magazine* (March 15, 2006).

Hsieh, J.J. Po-An, Arun Rai, and Mark Keil. "Understanding Digital Inequality: Comparing Continued Use Behavioral Models of the Socio-Economically Advantaged and Disadvantaged." *MIS Quarterly* 32, no. 1 (March 2008).

Jackson, Linda A., Alexander von Eye, Gretchen Barbatsis, Frank Biocca, Hiram E. Fitzgerald, and Yong Zhao. "The Impact of Internet Use on the Other Side of the Digital Divide." *Communications of the ACM* 47, no. 7 (July 2004).

Jackson, Thomas W., Ray Dawson, and Darren Wilson. "Understanding Email Interaction Increases Organizational Productivity." *Communications of the ACM* 46, no. 8 (August 2003).

Kling, Rob. "When Organizations Are Perpetrators: The Conditions of Computer Abuse and Computer Crime." In *Computerization & Controversy: Value Conflicts & Social Choices*, edited by Charles Dunlop and Rob Kling. New York: Academic Press (1991).

Kreie, Jennifer and Timothy Paul Cronan. "Making Ethical Decisions." *Communications of the ACM* 43, no. 12 (December 2000).

Laudon, Kenneth C. and Carol Guercio Traver. *E-Commerce: Business, Technology, Society* 5th *Edition*. Upper Saddle River, NJ: Prentice-Hall (2009).

Laudon, Kenneth C. *Dossier Society: Value Choices in the Design of National Information Systems*. New York: Columbia University Press (1986b).

Lee, Jintae. "An End-User Perspective on File-Sharing Systems," *Communications of the ACM* 46, no. 2 (February 2003).

Lohr, Steve. "Software Group Enters Fray over Proposed Piracy Law." *The New York Times* (July 19, 2004).

Mann, Catherine L. "What Global Sourcing Means for U.S. I.T. Workers and for the U.S. Economy." Communications of the ACM 47, no. 7 (July 2004).

Martin, Jr. David M., Richard M. Smith, Michael Brittain, Ivan Fetch, and Hailin Wu."The Privacy Practices of Web Browser Extensions." *Communications of the ACM* 44, no. 2 (February 2001).

Mason, Richard O. "Applying Ethics to Information Technology Issues." *Communications of the ACM* 38, no. 12 (December 1995).

Mason, Richard O. "Four Ethical Issues in the Information Age." *MIS Quarterly* 10, no. 1 (March 1986).

Mykytyn, Kathleen, Peter P. Mykytyn, Jr., and Craig W. Slinkman. "Expert Systems: A Question of Liability." *MIS Quarterly* 14, no. 1 (March 1990).

Nissenbaum, Helen. "Computing and Accountability." *Communications of the ACM* 37, no. 1 (January 1994).

Nord, G. Daryl, Tipton F. McCubbins, and Jeretta Horn Nord. "E-Monitoring in the Workplace: Privacy, Legislation, and Surveillance Software." *Communications of the ACM* 49, No. 8 (August 2006).

Okerson, Ann. "Who Owns Digital Works?" *Scientific American* (July 1996).

Payton, Fay Cobb."Rethinking the Digital Divide." *Communications of the ACM* 46, no. 6 (June 2003)

Reagle, Joseph, and Lorrie Faith Cranor. "The Platform for Privacy Preferences." *Communications of the ACM* 42, no. 2 (February 1999).

Redman, Thomas C. "The Impact of Poor Data Quality on the Typical Enterprise." *Communications of the ACM* 41, no. 2 (February 1998).

Rifkin, Jeremy. "Watch Out for Trickle-Down Technology." *The New York Times* (March 16, 1993).

Rigdon, Joan E. "Frequent Glitches in New Software Bug Users." *The Wall Street Journal* (January 18, 1995).

Rotenberg, Marc. "Communications Privacy: Implications for Network Design." *Communications of the ACM* 36, no. 8 (August 1993).

Samuelson, Pamela. "Computer Programs and Copyright's Fair Use Doctrine." *Communications of the ACM* 36, no. 9 (September 1993).

Sewell, Graham and James R. Barker. "Neither Good, nor Bad, but Dangerous: Surveillance as an Ethical Paradox." *Ethics and Information Technology* 3, no. 3 (2001).

Sipior, Janice C. "Unintended Invitation: Organizational Wi-Fi Use by External Roaming Users." *Communications of the ACM* 50, no.8 (August 2007).

Smith, H. Jeff, and John Hasnas. "Ethics and Information Systems: The Corporate Domain." *MIS Quarterly* 23, no. 1 (March 1999).

Smith, H. Jeff, Sandra J. Milberg, and Sandra J. Burke. "Information Privacy: Measuring Individuals' Concerns about Organizational Practices." *MIS Quarterly* 20, no. 2 (June 1996).

Smith, H. Jeff. "The Shareholders vs. Stakeholders Debate." *MIS Sloan Management Review* 44, no. 4 (Summer 2003).

Sophos Plc. "Security Threat Report//Q1 08." (2008).

Steel, Emily and Vishesh Kumar. "Targeted Ads Raise Privacy Concerns." *The Wall Street Journal* (July 8, 2008)

Straub, Detmar W., Jr., and Rosann Webb Collins. "Key Information Liability Issues Facing Managers: Software Piracy, Proprietary Databases, and Individual Rights to Privacy." *MIS Quarterly* 14, no. 2 (June 1990).

Story, Louise. "To Aim Ads, Web Is Keeping Closer Eye on You." *The New York Times* (March 10, 2008).

Tuttle, Brad, Adrian Harrell, and Paul Harrison. "Moral Hazard, Ethical Considerations, and the Decision to Implement an Information System." *Journal of Management Information Systems* 13, no. 4 (Spring 1997).

United States Department of Health, Education, and Welfare. *Records, Computers, and the Rights of Citizens*. Cambridge: MIT Press (1973).

Urbaczewski, Andrew and Leonard M. Jessup. "Does Electronic Monitoring of Employee Internet Usage Work?" *Communications of the ACM* 45, no. 1 (January 2002).

U.S. Sentencing Commiission. *U.S. Sentencing Commission's Sourcebook of Federal Sentencing Statistics.* (2004).

Vara, Vauhini. "New Sites Make It Easier to Spy on Your Friends." *The Wall Street Journal* (June 4, 2008).

Weitzner, Daniel J., Harold Abelson, Tim Berners-Lee, Joan Feigenbaum, James Hendler, and Gerald Jay Sussman. "Information Accountability." *Communications of the ACM* 51, no. 6 (June 2008).

Whiting, Rick. "Who's Buying and Selling Your Data? Everybody." *Information Week* (July 10, 2006).

Wolf, Christopher. "Dazed and Confused: Data Law Disarray." *Business Week* (June 8, 2006).

CHAPTER 5

Ante, Spencer E., Heather Green and Catherine Holahan. "The Next Small Thing." *Business Week* (July 23, 2007).

Babcock, Charles. "Linux No Longer the Cool New Kid on the Block. Now What?" *Information Week* (April 14, 2008).

Babcock, Charles. "Software Ecosystems." *Information Week* (May 28, 2007).

Babcock, Charles. "The Relentless Pace of Linux." *Information Week* (October 22, 2007).

Baum, David. "Moving Forward." *Oracle Magazine* (March 2008).

Bell, Gordon and Jim Gray. What's Next in High-Performance Computing? *Communications of the ACM* 45, no. 1 (January 2002).

Bowers, Brent. "It's Easy, and Expensive, to Forget About Old Equipment," *The New York Times* (March 13, 2008).

Bureau of Economic Analysis, National Income and Product Accounts. "Private Fixed Investment." Washington, D.C.(2008).

Carr, David F. "Scaling Up or Scaling Out?" *Baseline* (January 2008).

Carr, Nicholas. *The Big Switch*. Norton (2008).

Chickowski, Ericka. "How Good Are Your Service-Level Agreements?" *Baseline* (January 2008).

Chris Preimesberger, "Clouds in the Forecast," *eWeek*, March 3, 2008.

Clark, Don. "PC Makers Race to Market with Low-Cost 'Netbooks'." *The Wall Street Journal* (April 8, 2008).

Cone, Edward. "The Grid Wins." CIO Insight (January 2008).

Conklin, George, Mitch Lawrence and Mark Middleton. "Virtual Lifesaver." *Information Week* (January 28, 2008).

David, Julie Smith, David Schuff, and Robert St. Louis. "Managing Your IT Total Cost of Ownership." *Communications of the ACM* 45, no. 1 (January 2002).

Dempsey, Bert J.. Debra Weiss, Paul Jones, and Jane Greenberg. "What Is an Open Source Software Developer?" *Communications of the ACM* 45, no. 1 (January 2001).

Dornan, Andy. "I, Network." *Information Week* (February 11, 2008).

Driscoll, Sara. "AA: Friend or Foe?" *eWeek* (February 18, 2008).

Dubney, Abhijit and Dilip Wagle. "Delivering Software as a Service." *The McKinsey Quarterly* (June 2007).

Eisenberg, Anne. "Do the Mash (Even If You Don't Know All the Steps)." *The New York Times* (September 2, 2007).

Fitzgerald, Brian. "The Transformation of Open Source Software." *MIS Quarterly* 30, No. 3 (September 2006).

Ganek, A. G. and T.A. Corbi. "The Dawning of the Autonomic Computing Era." IBM Systems Journal. 42, No 1, (2003).

Gartner Research. "Worldwide Outsourcing Market to Grow 8.1 Percent in 2008." (January, 2008).

Gartner Research. "Worlwide PC Shipment to Grow 11 percent in 2008." (March 25, 2008).

Gerlach, James, Bruce Neumann, Edwin Moldauer, Martha Argo, and Daniel Frisby. "Determining the Cost of IT Services." *Communications of the ACM* 45, no. 9 (September 2002).

Hagel III, John and John Seeley Brown. "Your Next IT Strategy." *Harvard Business Review* (October, 2001).

Helft, Miguel. "Google and Salesforce Join to Fight Microsoft." *The New York Times* (April 14, 2008).

Hoover, J. Nicholas and Richard Martin. "Demystifying the Cloud." *Information Week* (June 23, 2008).

Hoover, J. Nicholas. "Ahead in the Cloud: Google, Others Expand Online Services." *Information Week* (April 14, 2008).

Hoover, J. Nicholas. "Ready to Launch?" *Information Week* (February 18, 2008)

IBM. "IBM Launches New Autonomic Offerings for Self-Managing IT Systems." IBM Media Relations (June 30, 2005).

King, John. "Centralized vs. Decentralized Computing: Organizational Considerations and Management Options." *Computing Surveys* (October 1984).

King, Rachael. "How Cloud Computing is Changing the World." *Business Week* (August 4, 2008).

Kontzer, Tony. "Taming the Cloud." *CIO Insight* (March 2008).

———. "Cloud Computing: Anything as a Service." *CIO Insight* (August 5, 2008).

———. "The Forecast for Cloud Computing." *CIO Insight* (March 2008)

Kurzweil, Ray. "Exponential Growth an Illusion?: Response to Ilkka Tuomi." KurzweilAI.net, September 23, 2003

Lawton, Christopher and Don Clark. "'Virtualization' is Pumping Up Servers." *The Wall Street Journal* (March 6, 2007).

Loo, Alfred W. "The Future of Peer-to-Peer Computing." *Communications of the ACM* 46, no. 9 (September 2003).

Markoff, John. "Intel Makes a Push into Pocket-Size Internet Devices." *The New York Times* (April 2, 2008).

Markoff, John. "Microsoft Reveals a Web-Based Software System." *The New York Times* (April 23, 2008).

Mearian, Lucas. "A Zettabyte by 2010: Corporate Data Grows Fiftyfold in Three Years." *Computerworld* (March 6, 2007). ms.

Merrill Lynch. "The Cloud Wars: $100+ billion at stake." Merrill Lynch Report, August 5, 2008.

Metrics 2.0. "Worldwide PC Shipments to Reach 334 Million in 2010." Metrics2.com, accessed October 2, 2008

Millard, Elizabeth. "The State of Mobile Applications." *Baseline* (August 20, 2008).

Moore, Gordon. "Cramming More Components Onto Integrated Circuits," Electronics 38, Number 8 (April 19, 1965).

Noffsinger, W. B., Robert Niedbalski, Michael Blanks, and Niall Emmart. "Legacy Object Modeling Speeds Software Integration." *Communications of the ACM* 41, no. 12 (December 1998).

Oskin, Mark. "The Revolution Inside the Box." *Communications of the ACM* 51, no. 7 (July 2008).

Patel, Samir and Suneel Saigal. "When Computers Learn to Talk: A Web Services Primer, " *The McKinsey Quarterly* (2002, No. 1).

Phillips, Charles. "Stemming the Software Spending Spree." *Optimize Magazine* (April 2002).

Rogow, Rruce."Tracking Core Assets." *Optimize Magazine* (April 2006).

Salkever, Alex with Olga Kharif. "Slowly Weaving Web Services Together." *Business Week* (June 24, 2003).

Schuff, David and Robert St. Louis. "Centralization vs. Decentralization of Application Software." *Communications of the ACM* 44, no. 6 (June 2001).

SOA in Action. "Rapid Growth Seen For "Software as a Service" Industry." (November 18, 2008).

Stango, Victor. "The Economics of Standards Wars." *Review of Network Economics* 3, Issue 1 (March 2004).

Tuomi, Ilkka. "The Lives and Death of Moore's Law." FirstMonday, Col 7, No. 11 (November 2002). www.firstmonday.org.

Walsh, Lawrence. "Outsourcing: A Means of Business Enablement." *Baseline* (May 2008).

Watson, Richard T., Marie-Claude Boudreau, Paul T. York, Martina E. Greiner, and Donald Wynn Jr. "The Business of Open Source." *Communications of the ACM* 51, no. 4 (April 2008).

Weier, Mary Hayes."Too Much Information," *Information Week*, April 9, 2007.

Weill, Peter, and Marianne Broadbent. *Leveraging the New Infrastructure*. Cambridge, MA: Harvard Business School Press (1998).

Weill, Peter, Mani Subramani and Marianne Broadbent. "Building IT Infrastructure for Strategic Agility." *Sloan Management Review* 44, no. 1 (Fall 2002).

Weitzel, Tim. *Economics of Standards in Information Networks*. Springer (2004).

Williams, Mark. "The Digital Utility." *Technology Review* (March/April 2008).

Zaino, Jennifer. "Client-Side Evolution." *Optimize Magazine* 81 (May 2007).

CHAPTER 6

Cappiello, Cinzia, Chiara Francalanci, and Barbara Pernici. "Time-Related Factors of Data Quality in Multichannel Information Systems." *Journal of Management Information Systems* 20, No. 3 (Winter 2004).

Chen, Andrew N.K., Paulo B. Goes, and James R. Marsden. "A Query-Driven Approach to the Design and Management of Flexible Database Systems." *Journal of Management Information Systems* 19, No. 3 (Winter 2002-2003).

Clifford, James, Albert Croker, and Alex Tuzhilin. "On Data Representation and Use in a Temporal Relational DBMS." *Information Systems Research* 7, no. 3 (September 1996).

Eckerson, Wayne W. "Data Quality and the Bottom Line." The Data Warehousing Institute (2002).

Fayyad, Usama, Ramasamy Ramakrishnan, and Ramakrisnan Srikant. "Evolving Data Mining into Solutions for Insights." *Communications of the ACM* 45, no.8 (August 2002).

Gartner Inc. "Dirty Data' is a Business Problem, not an IT Problem, Says Gartner." Sydney, Australia (March 2, 2007).

Goldstein, R. C., and J. B. McCririck. "What Do Data Administrators Really Do?" *Datamation* 26 (August 1980).

Goodhue, Dale L., Judith A. Quillard, and John F. Rockart. "Managing the Data Resource: A Contingency Perspective." *MIS Quarterly* (September 1988).

Goodhue, Dale L., Laurie J. Kirsch, Judith A. Quillard, and Michael D. Wybo. "Strategic Data Planning: Lessons from the Field." *MIS Quarterly* 16, no. 1 (March 1992).

Goodhue, Dale L., Michael D. Wybo, and Laurie J. Kirsch. "The Impact of Data Integration on the Costs and Benefits of Information Systems." *MIS Quarterly* 16, no. 3 (September 1992).

Grover, Varun, and James Teng. "How Effective Is Data Resource Management?" *Journal of Information Systems Management* (Summer 1991).

Helft, Miguel. "Google's New Tool Is Meant for Marketers." *The New York Times* (August 6, 2008).

Henschen, Doug. "The Data Warehouse Revised." *Information Week* (May 26, 2008).

Howson, Cindi. "The Road to Prevasive BI," Information Week (February 25, 2008).

Hirji, Karim K. "Exploring Data Mining Implementation." *Communications of the ACM* 44, no. 7 (July 2001).

Hoffer, Jeffrey A., Mary Prescott, and Heikki Toppi. *Modern Database Management*, 9th ed. Upper Saddle River, NJ: Prentice-Hall (2009)

Kahn, Beverly K. "Some Realities of Data Administration." *Communications of the ACM* 26 (October 1983).

King, John L., and Kenneth Kraemer. "Information Resource Management Cannot Work." *Information and Management* (1988).

Klau, Rick. "Data Quality and CRM," Line56.com (March 4, 2003).

Lee, Yang W. and Diane M. Strong. "Knowing-Why about Data Processes and Data Quality." *Journal of Management Information Systems* 20, No. 3 (Winter 2004).

McFadden, Fred R., Jeffrey A. Hoffer and Mary B. Prescott. *Modern Database Management*, Sixth Edition. Upper Saddle River, NJ: Prentice-Hall (2002).

Morrison, Mike, Joline Morrison, and Anthony Keys. "Integrating Web Sites and Databases." *Communications of the ACM* 45, no.9 (September 2002).

Pierce, Elizabeth M. "Assessing Data Quality with Control Matrices," *Communications of the ACM* 47, no. 2 (February 2004).

Redman, Thomas. *Data Driven: Profiting from Your Most Important Business Asset*. Boston: Harvard Business Press (2008).

Weier, Mary Hayes. "In Depth: Business Intelligence." *Information Week* (April 14, 2008).

CHAPTER 7

Ben Ameur, Walid, and Herve Kerivin. "New Economical Virtual Private Networks." *Communications of the ACM* 46, no 6 (June 2003).

Borland, John. "A Smarter Web." *Technology Review* (March/April 2007).

Brooks, Jason. "WiMax Back on the Map." *eWeek* (April 7, 2008).

Carr, David F. "How Google Works." *Baseline Magazine* (July 2006).

Chopra, Sunil and Manmohan S. Sodhi. "In Search of RFID's Sweet Spot." *The Wall Street Journal* (March 3, 2007).

Claburn, Thomas. "Google Revealed." *Information Week* (August 28,2006).

Dekleva, Sasha, J.P. Shim, Upkar Varshney, and Geoffrey Knoerzer. "Evolution and Emerging Issues in Mobile Wireless Networks." *Communications of the ACM* 50, No. 6 (June 2007).

Fish, Lynn A. and Wayne C. Forrest. "A Worldwide Look at RFID." *Supply Chain Management Review* (April 1, 2007).

Fish, Lynn A. and Wayne C. Forrest. "A Worldwide Look at RFID." *Supply Chain Management Review* (April 1, 2007).

Frauenfelder, Mark. "Sir Tim Berners-Lee." *Technology Review* (October 2004).

Ginevan, Sean. "Will WiMax Go the Distance?" *Information Week* (March 17, 2008).)

Greenemeier, Larry. "RFID Tags Are on the Menu." *Information Week* (February 5, 2007).

Greenemeier, Larry. "RFID Tags Are on the Menu." *Information Week* (February 5, 2007).

Greenstein, Howard. "Web 2.0 Meets the Enterprise." *Optimize Magazine* (May 2006)

Hof, Rob, with Ronald Grover, Peter Burrows, and Tom lowry. "Is Google Too Powerful?" Business Week (April 9, 2007).

Hof, Rob."You Tube Launches Video Ads." *Business Week* (August 21, 2007).

Hof, Robert. "Web 2.0 Has Corporate America Spinning." *Business Week* (June 5, 2006).

Hoover, J. Nicholas. "5 Things You Must Know About VoIP." *Information Week* (July 3, 2006)

Hoover, J. Nicholas. "Enterprise 2.0." *Information Week* (February 26, 2007).

Hoover, J. Nicholas. "Enterprise 2.0." Information Week (February 26, 2007).

Housel, Tom, and Eric Skopec. *Global Telecommunication Revolution: The Business Perspective*. New York: McGraw-Hill (2001).

Jesdanun, Anick. "Researchers Explore Scrapping Internet." Associated Press (April 13, 2007).

Lager, Marshall. "The Second Coming of 2.0." *Customer Relationship Management* (June 2008).

Mamberto, Carola. "Instant Messaging Invades the Office." *The Wall Street Journal* (July 24, 2007).

McGee, Marianne Kolbasuk. "Track This." *Information Week* (February 11, 2008).

National Research Council. *The Internet's Coming of Age*. Washington, DC: National Academy Press (2000).

Niemeyer, Alex, Minsok H. Pak, and Sanjay E. Ramaswamy. "Smart Tags for Your Supply Chain." *McKinsey Quarterly* no. 4 (2003).

Pottie, G. J., and W.J Kaiser. "Wireless Integrated Network Sensors." *Communications of the ACM* 43, no. 5 (May 2000).

Talbot, David. "The Internet Is Broken." *Technology Review* (December 2005/January 2006).

Trottman, Melanie. "In Search of the Cheaper Meeting." *The Wall Street Journal* (March 31, 2008).

Varshney, Upkar, Andy Snow, Matt McGivern, and Christi Howard. "Voice Over IP." *Communications of the ACM* 45, no. 1 (January 2002).

Vascellaro, Jessica E. "Coming Soon to a Phone Near You." *The Wall Street Journal* (March 31, 2008).

Vascellaro, Jessica E. and Amol Sharma. "Cellphones Get Wi-Fi, Adding Network Options." *The Wall Street Journal* (June 27, 2007).

Xiao, Bo and Izak Benbasat. "E-Commerce Product Recommendation Agents: Use, Characteristics, and Impact." *MIS Quarterly* 31, no. 1 (March 2007).

CHAPTER 8

Allan, Danny. "Managing A Growing Threat: An Executive's Guide to Web Application Security," IBM Corporation (2007).

Anti-Phishing Working Group. "Phishing Activity Trends Report for the Month of May, 2007." (May 2007).www.antiphishing.org, accessed July 24, 2007.

Austin, Robert D., and Christopher A. R. Darby. "The Myth of Secure Computing." *Harvard Business Review* (June 2003).

Australian IT News. "US China Main Sources of Malware." *News Limited* (January 23, 2007).

Baker, Wade H., Loren Paul Rees, and Peter S. Tippett: "Necessary Measures: Metric-Driven Information Security Risk Assessment and Decision Making." *Communications of the ACM* 50, no. 10 (October 2007).

Banham, Russ. "Personal Data for Sale: Calculating the Cost of Security Breaches." *The Wall Street Journal* (June 5, 2007).

Bartholomew, Doug. "IT Controls Yield Greater Productivity-and Revenue," *CIO Insight* (March 22, 2007).

Brandel, Mary."Keeping Secrets in a WikiBlogTubeSpace World." *Computerworld* (March19, 2007).

Brenner, Susan W. "U.S. Cygbercrime Law: Defining Offenses." *Information Systems Frontiers* 6, no. 2 (June 2004).

Byers, Simon, and Dave Kormann. "802.11b Access Point Mapping." *Communications of the ACM* 46, no. 5 (May 2003).

Cam Winget, Nancy, Russ Housley, David Wagner, and Jesse Walker. "Security Flaws in 802.11b Data Link Protocols." *Communications of the ACM* 46, no. 5 (May 2003).

Carvajal, Doreen. "High-Tech Crime is an Online Bubble that Hasn't Burst." *The New York Times* (April 7, 2008).

Cavusoglu, Huseyin, Birendra Mishra, and Srinivasan Raghunathan. "A Model for Evaluating IT Security Investments." *Communications of the ACM* 47, no. 7 (July 2004).

Claburn, Thomas. Botnet Maestro Pleads Guilty." *Information Week* (November 19, 2007).

Consumer Reports. "State of the Net 2008." (September 2008).

D'arcy, John and Anat Hovav. "Deterring Internal Information Systems Use." *Communications of the ACM* 50, no. 10 (October 2007).

Delaney, Kevin J. "'Evil Twins' and 'Pharming'." *The Wall Street Journal* (May 17, 2005).

Doug Bartholomew, "The Rhythm of Identity Management." *Baseline* (February 2008).

Duvall, Mel. "Virtual Project Yields Real-World Benefits." *Baseline* (August 2007).

Epstein, Keith. Defenseless on the Net." *Business Week* (April 16, 2008).

Foley, John. "P2P Peril." *Information Week* (March 17, 2008).

Fratto, Mike. "Precision Security." *Information Week* (June 30/July 7, 2008).

Gaudin, Sharon. "Prosecutors: Medco 'Bomber' Would have Wreaked Havoc." *Information Week* (January 1/8, 2007).

Gaur, Nalneesh and Bob Kiep. "Managing Mobile Menaces." *Optimize Magazine* (May 2007).

Giordano, Scott M. "Electronic Evidence and the Law." *Information Systems Frontiers* 6, no. 2 (June 2004).

Grow, Brian, Keith Epstein, and Chi-Chu Tschang. "The New E-spionage Threat." Business Week (April 10, 2008) and "An Evolving Crisis." *Business Week* (April 10, 2008).

Heng, Jared. "The War Against Malware." *CIO Asia* (February 2008).

Housley, Russ, and William Arbaugh. "Security Problems in 802.11b Networks." *Communications of the ACM* 46, no. 5 (May 2003).

Ives, Blake, Kenneth R. Walsh, and Helmut Schneider. "The Domino Effect of Password Reuse." *Communications of the ACM* 47, no.4 (April 2004).

Jagatic Tom, Nathaniel Johnson, Markus Jakobsson, and Filippo Menczer. "Social Phishing." *Communications of the ACM* 50, no. 10 (October 2007).

Kirk, Jeremy. "MySpace Users Struggle to Overcome Cybervandalism." *PC World* (June 30, 2008).

Keizer, Gregg. "Ex-Security Pro Admits Running Huge Botnet." *Computerworld* (November 12, 2007);

Loo, Alfred. "The Myths and Truths of Wireless Security." *Communications of the ACM* 51, no. 2 (February 2008).

Martin, Richard. "RIM Service Outage Leads to 'BlankBerrys' and Questions." *Information Week* (April 23, 2007).

McDougall, Paul. "High Cost of Data Loss." *Information Week* (March 20, 2006).

Meckbach, Greg. "MasterCard's Robust Data Centre: Priceless." *ComputerWorld Canada* (March 26, 2008).

Mercuri, Rebeca T. "Analyzing Security Costs." *Communications of the ACM* 46, no. 6 (June 2003).

Mitchell, Dan. "It's Here: It's There; It's Spyware." *The New York Times* (May 20, 2006).

Naraine, Ryan and Brian Prince. "Data Breaches Cause Concern." *eWeek*, April 7, 2008.

Naraine, Ryan. "Inside a Modern Malware System." *eWeek* (January 7, 2008).

NIST. "Software Vulnerabilities." Workshop on Software Security Assurance Tools, Techniques, and Metrics (November 2005).

Panko, Raymond R. *Corporate Computer and Network Security.* Upper Saddle River, NJ: Pearson Prentice Hall (2004).

Perez, Juan Carlos. "Facebook Stamps Out Malware Attack." *PC World* (August 8, 2008).

Prince, Brian. "The Growing E-Mail Security Challenge." *eWeek* (April 21, 2008).

Ransom, Diana. "Don't Fence Me In." *The Wall Street Journal* (January 28, 2008).

Richardson, Robert. "2007 CSI Computer Crime and Security Survey." Computer Security Institute (2007).

Richmond, Riva. "A New Battleground for Computer Security." *The Wall Street Journal* (March 6, 2007).

Robertson, Jordan. "Hackers: Social Networking Sites Flawed." Associated Press (August 3, 2007).

Roche, Edward M., and George Van Nostrand. *Information Systems, Computer Crime and Criminal Justice.* New York: Barraclough Ltd. (2004).

Ryan Naraine, "ActiveX Under Siege," *eWeek* (February 11, 2008).

Schmidt, Howard. "Cyber Anxiety." *Optimize Magazine* (May 2007).

Schwerha, Joseph J., IV. "Cybercrime: Legal Standards Governing the Collection of Digital Evidence." *Information Systems Frontiers* 6, no. 2 (June 2004).

Secure Computing. "White Paper: In Today's Web 2.0 Environment, Proactive Security is Paramount. Are You Protected?" (2007).

Shukla, Sudhindra, and Fiona Fui-Hoon Nah. "Web Browsing and Spyware Intrusion." *Communications of the ACM* 48, no. 8 (August 2005).

Sophos Plc. "Security Threat Report//Q1 08." (2008).

Stempel, Jonathan. "U.S. Identity Theft Losses Fall: Study." Reuters (February 1, 2007).

Straub, Detmar W., and Richard J. Welke. "Coping with Systems Risk: Security Planning Models for Management Decision Making." *MIS Quarterly* 22, no. 4 (December 1998).

Symantec Corporation. "Symantec Internet Threat Security Report." (March 2007).

Thompson, Roger. "Why Spyware Poses Multiple Threats to Security." *Communications of the ACM* 48, no. 8 (August 2005).

Vaas, Lisa. "The Rise of Badvertising." *eWeek* (November 27, 2007).

Volonino, Linda, and Stephen R. Robinson. *Principles and Practices of Information Security*. Upper Saddle River, NJ: Prentice Hall (2004).

Volonino, Linda., Reynaldo Anzaldua, and Jana Godwin: *Computer Forensics: Principles and Practices*. Upper Saddle River, NJ: Prentice Hall (2007).

Warkentin, Merrill, Xin Luo, and Gary F. Templeton. "A Framework for Spyware Assessement." *Communications of the ACM* 48, no. 8 (August 2005).

Watson, Brian P. "Botnets: How they Attack and How They Can Be Defeated." *Baseline Magazine* (June 2007).

West, Ryan. "The Psychology of Security." *Communications of the ACM* 51, no. 4 (April 2008).

Westerman, George and Richard Hunter. *IT Risk*. Boston, MA: Harvard Business Press (2007).

Westerman, George. *IT Risk: Turning Business Threats into Competitive Advantage*. Harvard Business School Publishing (2007).

White, Bobby. "A Question of Priorities." *The Wall Street Journal* (July 30, 2007).

Wiens, Jordan. "With Security, More Is Better." *Information Week* (March 10, 2008).

www.itl.nist.gov/div897/docs/samate.html, accessed August 1, 2005.

CHAPTER 9

Anderson, James C., and James A. Narus. "Selectively Pursuing More of Your Customer's Business." *MIT Sloan Management Review* 44, no. 3 (Spring 2003).

D'Avanzo, Robert, Hans von Lewinski, and Luk N. Van Wassenhove. "The Link between Supply Chain and Financial Performance." *Supply Chain Management Review* (November 1, 2003).

Davenport, Thomas H. *Mission Critical: Realizing the Promise of Enterprise Systems*. Boston: Harvard Business School Press (2000).

———. "Putting the Enterprise into Enterprise Systems." *Harvard Business Review* (July-August 1998).

Day, George S. "Creating a Superior Customer-Relating Capability." *MIT Sloan Management Review* 44, no. 3 (Spring 2003).

Ferrer, Jaume, Johan Karlberg, and Jamie Hintlian."Integration: The Key to Global Success." *Supply Chain Management Review* (March 1, 2007).

Fleisch, Elgar, Hubert Oesterle, and Stephen Powell. "Rapid Implementation of Enterprise Resource Planning Systems." *Journal of Organizational Computing and Electronic Commerce* 14, no. 2 (2004).

Garber, Randy and Suman Sarkar. "Want a More Flexible Supply Chain?" *Supply Chain Management Review* (January 1, 2007).

Goodhue, Dale L., Barbara H. Wixom, and Hugh J. Watson. "Realizing Business Benefits through CRM: Hitting the Right Target in the Right Way." *MIS Quarterly Executive* 1, no. 2 (June 2002).

Gosain, Sanjay, Arvind Malhotra, and Omar A. ElSawy. "Coordinating for Flexibility in E-Business Supply Chains." *Journal of Management Information Systems* 21, no. 3 (Winter 2004--2005).

Greenbaum, Joshiua. "Is ERP Dead? Or Has It Just Gone Underground?" *SAP NetWeaver Magazine* 3 (2007).

Greenfield, Dave. "CRM 2.0." *eWeek* (June 16, 2008).

Guinipero, Larry, Robert B. Handfield, and Douglas L. Johansen. "Beyond Buying." *The Wall Street Journal* (March 10, 2008).

Handfield, Robert B. and Ernest L. Nichols. *Supply Chain Redesign: Transforming Supply Chains into Integrated Value Systems*. Financial Times Press (2002).

Hitt, Lorin, D. J. Wu, and Xiaoge Zhou. "Investment in Enterprise Resource Planning: Business Impact and Productivity Measures." *Journal of Management Information Systems* 19, no. 1 (Summer 2002).

Jaiswal. M. P. "Implementing ERP Systems." *Dataquest* (June 30, 2003).

Kalakota, Ravi, and Marcia Robinson. *E-Business* 2.0. Boston: Addison-Wesley (2001).

———. *Services Blueprint: Roadmap for Execution*. Boston: Addison-Wesley (2003).

Kanakamedala, Kishore, Glenn Ramsdell, and Vats Srivatsan. "Getting Supply Chain Software Right." *McKinsey Quarterly* no. 1 (2003).

Kopczak, Laura Rock, and M. Eric Johnson. "The Supply-Chain Management Effect." *MIT Sloan Management Review* 44, no. 3 (Spring 2003).

Lee, Hau, L., V. Padmanabhan, and Seugin Whang. "The Bullwhip Effect in Supply Chains." *Sloan Management Review* (Spring 1997).

Lee, Hau. "The Triple-A Supply Chain." *Harvard Business Review* (October 2004).

Liang, Huigang, Nilesh Sharaf, Quing Hu, and Yajiong Xue. "Assimilation of Enterprise Systems: The Effect of Institutional Pressures and the Mediating Role of Top Management." *MIS Quarterly* 31, no. 1 (March 2007).

Malhotra, Arvind, Sanjay Gosain, and Omar A. El Sawy. "Absorptive Capacity Configurations in Supply Chains: Gearing for Partner-Enabled Market Knowledge Creation." *MIS Quarterly* 29, no. 1 (March 2005).

Maylett, Tracy and Kate Vitasek. "For Closer Collaboration, Try Education." *Supply Chain Management Review* (January 1, 2007).

Rai, Arun, Ravi Patnayakuni, and Nainika Seth. "Firm Performance Impacts of Digitally Enabled Supply Chain Integration Capabilities." *MIS Quarterly* 30 No. 2 (June 2006).

Ranganathan, C. and Carol V. Brown. "ERP Iinvestments and the Market Value of Firms: Toward an Understanding of Influential ERP Project Variables." *Information Systems Research* 17, No. 2 (June 2006).

Robey, Daniel, Jeanne W. Ross, and Marie-Claude Boudreau. "Learning to Implement Enterprise Systems: An Exploratory Study of the Dialectics of Change." *Journal of Management Information Systems* 19, no. 1 (Summer 2002).

Schwartz, Ephraim. "Does ERP Matter-Industry Stalwarts Speak Out." *InfoWorld* (April 10, 2007).

Scott, Judy E., and Iris Vessey. "Managing Risks in Enterprise Systems Implementations." *Communications of the ACM* 45, no. 4 (April 2002).

Sullivan, Laurie. "ERPZilla." *Information Week* (July 11, 2005).

Violino, Bob. "The Next-Generation ERP." *CIO Insight* (May 2008).

Whiting, Rick. "You Look Marvelous!" *Information Week* (July 24, 2006).

Zaino, Jennifer. "Valero Pumped on SOA." *Baseline* (July 2007).

CHAPTER 10

Adomavicius, Gediminas and Alexander Tuzhilin. "Personalization Technologies: A Process-Oriented Perspective." *Communications of the ACM* 48, no. 10 (October 2005).

Alboher, Marci. "Blogging's a Low-Cost, High-Return Marketing Tool." *The New York Times* (December 27, 2007).

Associated Press, "Netflix Launches Streaming Service," *The Wall Street Journal*, May 20, 2008.

Bakos, Yannis. "The Emerging Role of Electronic Marketplaces and the Internet." *Communications of the ACM* 41, no. 8 (August 1998).

Bellman, Eric and Tariq Engineer. "India Appears Ripe for Cellphone Ads." *The Wall Street Journal* (March 10, 2008.)

Bhargava, Hemant K. and Vidyanand Chourhary. "Economics of an Information Intermediary with Aggregation Benefits." *Information Systems Research* 15, no. 1 (March 2004).

Bo, Xiao and Izak Benbasat. "E-Commerce Product Recommendation Agents: Use, Characteristics, and Impact." *MIS Quarterly* 31, no. 1 (March 2007).

Boulton, Clint. "Apps Provide the MySpace Touch." *eWeek* (January 21, 2008).

Brynjolfsson, Erik, Yu Hu, and Michael D. Smith. "Consumer Surpus in the Digital Economy: Estimating the Value of Increased Product Variety at Online Booksellers." *Management Science* 49, no. 11 (November 2003).

Christiaanse, Ellen. "Performance Benefits Through Integration Hubs." *Communications of the ACM* 48, No.5 (April 2005).

Chua, Cecil Eng Huang, Jonathan Wareham, and Daniel Robey. "The Role of Online Trading Communities in Managing Internet Auction Fraud." *MIS Quarterly* 31, no. 4 (December 2007).

Cotteleer, Mark J., Christopher A. Cotteleer, and Andrew Prochmow. "Cutting Checks: Challenges and Choices in B2B E-Payments." *Communications of the ACM* 50, No. 6 (June 2007).

Dewan, Rajiv M., Marshall L. Freimer, and Jie Zhang. "Management and Valuation of Advertisement-Supported Web Sites." *Journal of Management Information Systems* 19, no. 3 (Winter 2002-2003).

EMarketer. "US Retail E-commerce: Slower But Steady Growth." (May 2008).

EMarketer. "US Broadband Population." (February, 2008).

eMarketer. "Mobile Spending: *US Non-Voice Services." September 2007).

Evans, Philip and Thomas S. Wurster. *Blown to Bits: How the New Economics of Information Transforms Strategy.* Boston, MA: Harvard Business School Press (2000).

Gartner. "Technology Barriers to Mobile Commerce are Coming Down." (February, 2008).

Helft, Miguel."Big Money in Little Screens." *The New York Times* (April 20, 2007).

Higgins, Michelle."A Guide to Anywhere, Right in Your Hand." The New York Times (June 17, 2007).

Junglas, Iris A. and Richard T. Watson. "Location-Based Services." *Communications of the ACM* 51, no. 3 (March 2008).

Kaplan, Steven and Mohanbir Sawhney. "E-Hubs: the New B2B Marketplaces." *Harvard Business Review* (May-June 2000).

Kauffman, Robert J. and Bin Wang. "New Buyers' Arrival Under Dynamic Pricing Market Microstructure: The Case of Group-Buying Discounts on the Internet, *Journal of Management Information Systems* 18, no. 2 (Fall 2001).

Kharif, Olga. "Mobile TV's Weak U.S. Signal." Business Week (March 3, 2008).

Kim, Jane J. "Mobile Banking Shifts into High Gear." *The Wall Street Journal* (February 21, 2007).

King, Rachael. "Tapping Wikis for Web Community-Building." *Business Week* (March 12, 2007).

Kleinberg, Jon. "The Convergence of Social and Technological Networks." *Communications of the ACM* 51, no. 11 (November 2008).

Kolbasuk-McGee, Marianne. "Track This." *Information Week* (February 11, 2008).

Laseter, Timothy M., Elliott Rabinovich, Kenneth K. Boyer, and M. Johnny Rungtusanatham. "Critical Issues in Internet Retailing." *MIT Sloan Management Review* 48, no. 3 (Spring 2007).

Laudon, Kenneth C. and Carol Guercio Traver. *E-Commerce: Business, Technology, Society,* 5th edition. Upper Saddle River, NJ: Prentice-Hall (2009).

Lawton, Christopher. "Once Wimpy, Cellphones Got Game," *The Wall Street Journal* (September 10, 2008).

Lee, Hau L. and Seungin Whang. "Winning the Last Mile of E-Commerce." *Sloan Management Review* 42, no. 4 (Summer 2001).

Magretta, Joan. "Why Business Models Matter." *Harvard Business Review* (May 2002).

Mc Knight, D. Harrison, Vivek Choudhury, and Charlea Kacmar. "Developing and Validating Trust Measures for e-Commerce: An Integrative Typology." *Information Systems Research* 13, no.3 (September 2002).

McKay, Lauren. "How UGC Can Benefit CRM." CRM Magazine (May 2008).

Patrick, Aaron O. "Tapping into Customers' Online Chatter." *The Wall Street Journal* (May 18, 2007).

Pavlou, Paul A., Huigang Liang, and Yajiong Xue. "Understanding and Mitigating Uncertainty in Online Exchange Relationships: A Principal-Agent Perspective." *MIS Quarterly* 31, no. 1 (March 2007).

Pew Internet and American Life. "Internet Activities." 2008.

Rayport, Jeffrey. "Demand-Side Innovation: Where IT Meets Marketing." Optimize Magazine (February 2007).

"Retailers Take a Tip from MySpace." *CIO Today* (February 13, 2007).

Sartain, Julie. "Opinion: Using MySpace and Facebook as Business Tools." *Computerworld* (May 23, 2008).

Sawhney, Mohanbir, Emanuela Prandelli, and Gianmario Verona. "The Power of Innomediation." *MIT Sloan Management Review* (Winter 2003).

Schiesel, Seth."In a Virtual Universe, the Politics Turn Real." *The New York Times* (June 7, 2007).

Schultze, Ulrike and Wanda J. Orlikowski. "A Practice Perspective on Technology-Mediated Network Relations: The Use of Internet-Based Self-Serve Technologies." *Information Systems Research* 15, no. 1 (March 2004).

Seybold, Patricia. "Customer-Controlled Innovation." *Optimize Magazine* (February 2007).

Smith, Michael D., Joseph Bailey and Erik Brynjolfsson. "Understanding Digital Markets: Review and Assessment" in Erik Brynjolfsson and Brian Kahin, ed. *Understanding the Digital Economy.* Cambridge, MA: MIT Press (1999).

Soat, John. "What Web 2.0 Has Taught Workforce 2.0," Information Week, February 26, 2007.

Story, Louise. "To Aim Ads, Web Is Keeping Closer Eye on You." *The New York Times* (March 10, 2008).

Story, Louise. "Yes, the Screen is Tiny, but the Plans Are Big." *The New York Times* (June 17, 2007).

Tan, Cheryl Lu-Lien. "That's So You! Just Click Here to Buy It," *The Wall Street Journal* (June 7, 2007).

Tedeschi, Bob. "Like Shopping? Social Networking? Try Social Shopping." *The New York Times* (September 11, 2006).

Tedeschi, Bob. "Small Merchants Gain Large Presence on Web." *The New York Times* (December 3, 2007).

Tedeschi, Bob. "Want to See That Shot Again? Download It for $3." *The New York Times* (May 7, 2007).

Tsai, Jessica. "The Moving Target." Customer Relationship Management (May 2008).

Urbaczewski, Andrew, Leonard M. Jessup, and Bradley Wheeler. "Electronic Commerce Research: A Taxonomy and Synthesis." *Journal of Organizational Computing and Electronic Commerce* 12, no. 2 (2002).

Vascellaro, Jessica E. "Finding a Date-on the Spot." *The Wall Street Journal* (June 6, 2007).

Vascellaro, Jessica E. and Kevin J. Delaney. "Search Engines Seek to Get Inside Your Head." *The Wall Street Journal* (April 25, 2007).

618   References

Vascellaro, Jessica. "Coming Soon to a Phone Near You." *The Wall Street Journal* (March 31, 2008).

Vauhini Vara, "'That Looks Great on You': Online Salespeople Get Pushy," Wall Street Journal, January 3, 2007-Ess8 file.

Vranica, Suzanne. "P&G Boosts Social-Networking Efforts." *The Wall Street Journal* (January 8, 2007).

Wagner, Christian and Ann Majchrzak. "Enabling Customer-Centricity Using Wikis and the Wiki Way." *Journal of Management Information Systems* 23, No. 3 (Winter 2006-7).

CHAPTER 11

Alavi, Maryam and Dorothy Leidner. "Knowledge Management and Knowledge Management Systems: Conceptual Foundations and Research Issues," *MIS Quarterly* 25, No. 1 ARTON (March 2001).

Alavi, Maryam, Timothy R. Kayworth, and Dorothy E. Leidner. "An Empirical Investigation of the Influence of Organizational Culture on Knowledge Management Practices." *Journal of Management Information Systems* 22, No.3 (Winter 2006).

Allen, Bradley P. "CASE-Based Reasoning: Business Applications." *Communications of the ACM* 37, no. 3 (March 1994).

Alter, Allan. "Unlocking the Power of Teams." *CIO Insight* (March 2008).

Anthes, Gary H. "Agents Change." *Computerworld* (January 27, 2003).

AskMe Corporation. "Select Customers: P&G Case Study." (August 2003), www.askmecorp.com/customers/default.asp.

Awad, Elias and Hassan M Ghaziri. *Knowledge Management*. Upper Saddle River, NJ: Prentice-Hall (2004).

Bargeron, David, Jonathan Grudin, Anoop Gupta, Elizabeth Sanocki, Francis Li, and Scott Le Tiernan."Asynchronous Collaboration Around Multimedia Applied to On-Demand Education." *Journal of Management Information Systems* 18, No. 4 (Spring 2002).

Barker, Virginia E., and Dennis E. O'Connor. "Expert Systems for Configuration at Digital: XCON and Beyond." *Communications of the ACM* (March 1989).

Becerra-Fernandez, Irma, Avelino Gonzalez, and Rajiv Sabhcrwal. *Knowledge Management*. Upper Saddle River, NJ: Prentice-Hall (2004).

Bieer, Michael, Douglas Englebart Richard Furuta, Starr Roxanne Hiltz, John Noll, Jennifer Preece, Edward A. Stohr, Murray Turoff, and Bartel Van de Walle. "Toward Virtual Community Knowledge Evolution." *Journal of Management Information Systems* 18, No. 4 (Spring 2002).

Birkinshaw, Julian and Tony Sheehan. "Managing the Knowledge Life Cycle." *MIT Sloan Management Review* 44, no. 1 (Fall 2002).

Blair, Margaret M. and Steven Wallman. "Unseen Wealth." Brookings Institution Press (2001).

Booth, Corey and Shashi Buluswar. "The Return of Artificial Intelligence," *The McKinsey Quarterly* No. 2 (2002).

Burtka, Michael. "Generic Algorithms." *The Stern Information Systems Review* 1, no. 1 (Spring 1993).

Carlin, Dan."Corporate Wikis Go Viral." *Business Week* (March 12, 2007).

Churchland, Paul M., and Patricia Smith Churchland. "Could a Machine Think?" *Scientific American* (January 1990).

Cole, R.E. "Introduction, Knowledge Management Special Issue." *California Management Review* (Spring 1998.)

Cone, Edward. "The Facebook Generation Goes to Work." *CIO Insight* (October 2007).

Cross, Rob and Lloyd Baird. "Technology is Not Enough: Improving Performance by Building Organizational Memory." *Sloan Management Review* 41, no. 3 (Spring 2000).

Cross, Rob, Nitin Nohria, and Andrew Parker. "Six Myths about Informal Networks-and How to Overcome Them," *Sloan Management Review* 43, no. 3 (Spring 2002)

Davenport, Thomas H., and Lawrence Prusak. *Working Knowledge: How Organizations Manage What They Know*. Boston, MA: Harvard Business School Press (1997).

Davenport, Thomas H., David W. DeLong, and Michael C. Beers. "Successful Knowledge Management Projects." *Sloan Management Review* 39, no. 2 (Winter 1998).

Davenport, Thomas H., Laurence Prusak, and Bruce Strong. "Putting Ideas to Work." *The Wall Street Journal* (March 10, 2008).

Davenport, Thomas H., Robert J. Thomas and Susan Cantrell. "The Mysterious Art and Science of Knowledge-Worker Performance." *MIT Sloan Management Review* 44, no. 1 (Fall 2002).

Davis, Gordon B. "Anytime/ Anyplace Computing and the Future of Knowledge Work." *Communications of the ACM* 42, no.12 (December 2002).

Desouza, Kevin C. "Facilitating Tacit Knowledge Exchange." *Communications of the ACM* 46, no. 6 (June 2003).

Dhar, Vasant, and Roger Stein. *Intelligent Decision Support Methods: The Science of Knowledge Work*. Upper Saddle River, NJ: Prentice Hall (1997).

Dhar, Vasant. "Plausibility and Scope of Expert Systems in Management." *Journal of Management Information Systems* (Summer 1987).

Du, Timon C., Eldon Y. Li, and An-pin Chang. "Mobile Agents in Distributed Network Management." *Communications of the ACM* 46, no.7 (July 2003).

Earl, Michael J., and Ian A. Scott. "What Is a Chief Knowledge Officer?" *Sloan Management Review* 40, no. 2 (Winter 1999).

Earl, Michael. "Knowledge Management Strategies: Toward a Taxonomy." *Journal of Management Information Systems* 18, no. 1 (Summer 2001).

Easley, Robert F., Sarv Devaraj, and J. Michael Crant."Relating Collaborative Technology Use to Teamwork Quality and Performance: An Empirical Analysis." *Journal of Management Information Systems* 19, no. 4 (Spring 2003).

El Najdawi, M. K., and Anthony C. Stylianou. "Expert Support Systems: Integrating AI Technologies." *Communications of the ACM* 36, no. 12 (December 1993).

Flash, Cynthia. "Who is the CKO?" *Knowledge Management* (May 2001).

Frangos, Alex. "New Dimensions in Design." *The Wall Street Journal* (July 7, 2004).

Gelernter, David. "The Metamorphosis of Information Management." *Scientific American* (August 1989).

Goldberg, David E. "Genetic and Evolutionary Algorithms Come of Age." *Communications of the ACM* 37, no. 3 (March 1994).

Gregor, Shirley and Izak Benbasat. "Explanations from Intelligent Systems: Theoretical Foundations and Implications for Practice." *MIS Quarterly* 23, no. 4 (December 1999).

Griffith, Terri L., John E. Sawyer, and Margaret A Neale. "Virtualness and Knowledge in Teams: Managing the Love Triangle of Organizations, Individuals, and Information Technology." *MIS Quarterly* 27, no. 2 (June 2003).

Grover, Varun and Thomas H. Davenport. "General Perspectives on Knowledge Management: Fostering a Research Agenda." *Journal of Management Information Systems* 18, no. 1 (Summer 2001).

Gu, Feng and Baruch Lev. "Intangible Assets. Measurements, Drivers, Usefulness." http://pages.stern.nyu.edu/~blev/.

Hansen, Morton T., Nitin Nohria, and Thomas Tierney. "What's Your Strategy for Knowledge Management?" *Harvard Business Review* (March-April 1999).

Hayes-Roth, Frederick, and Neil Jacobstein. "The State of Knowledge-Based Systems." *Communications of the ACM* 37, no. 3 (March 1994).

Hinton, Gregory. "How Neural Networks Learn from Experience." *Scientific American* (September 1992).

Holland, John H. "Genetic Algorithms." *Scientific American* (July 1992).

Hoover, J. Nicholas. "Enterprise 2.0." *Information Week* (February 26, 2007).

Housel Tom and Arthur A. Bell. *Measuring and Managing Knowledge*. New York: McGraw-Hill (2001).

Jarvenpaa, Sirkka L. and D. Sandy Staples. "Exploring Perceptions of Organizational Ownership of Information and Expertise." *Journal of Management Information Systems* 18, no. 1 (Summer 2001).

Jones, Quentin, Gilad Ravid, and Sheizaf Rafaeli. "Information Overload and the Message Dynamics of Online Interaction Spaces: A Theoretical Model and Empirical Exploration." *Information Systems Research* 15, no. 2 (June 2004).

Kankanhalli, Atreyi, Frasiska Tanudidjaja, Juliana Sutanto, and Bernard C.Y Tan. "The Role of IT in Successful Knowledge Management Initiatives." *Communications of the ACM* 46, no. 9 (September 2003).

Kuo, R.J., K. Chang, and S.Y.Chien. "Integration and Self-Organizing Feature Maps and Genetic-Algorithm-Based Clustering Method for Market Segmentation." *Journal of Organizational Computing and Electronic Commerce* 14, no. 1 (2004).

Lamont, Judith. "Communities of Practice Leverage Knowledge." *KMWorld* (July/August 2006).

Leonard-Barton, Dorothy and Walter Swap. "Deep Smarts." *Harvard Business Review* (September 1, 2004).

Leonard-Barton, Dorothy, and John J. Sviokla. "Putting Expert Systems to Work." *Harvard Business Review* (March-April 1988).

Lev, Baruch, and Theodore Sougiannis. "Penetrating the Book-to-Market Black Box: The R&D Effect," *Journal of Business Finance and Accounting* (April/May 1999).

Lev, Baruch. "Sharpening the Intangibles Edge." Harvard Business Review (June 1, 2004).

Maes, Patti. "Agents that Reduce Work and Information Overload." *Communications of the ACM* 38, no. 7 (July 1994).

Maglio, Paul P. and Christopher S. Campbell. "Attentive Agents." *Communications of the ACM* 46, no. 3 (March 2003).

Marks, Peter, Peter Polak, Scott McCoy, and Dennis Galletta. "Sharing Knowledge." *Communications of the ACM* 51, no. 2 (February 2008).

Markus, M. Lynne, Ann Majchrzak, and Less Gasser. "A Design Theory for Systems that Support Emergent Knowledge Processes." *MIS Quarterly* 26, no. 3 (September 2002).

Markus, M. Lynne. "Toward a Theory of Knowledge Reuse: Types of Knowledge Reuse Situations and Factors in Reuse Success." *Journal of Management Information Systems* 18, no. 1 (Summer 2001).

Maryam Alavi and Dorothy E. Leidner. "Knowledge Management and Knowledge Management Systems." *MIS Quarterly* 25, no. 1 (March 2001).

McCarthy, John. "Generality in Artificial Intelligence." *Communications of the ACM* (December 1987).

Moravec, Hans. "Robots, After All." *Communications of the ACM* 46, no. 10 (October 2003).

Munakata, Toshinori, and Yashvant Jani. "Fuzzy Systems: An Overview." *Communications of the ACM* 37, no. 3 (March 1994).

Ng, William R., Peter V. Marks, Jr. and Scott McCoy. "The Most Important Issues in Knowledge Management." *Communications of the ACM* 45, no.9 (September 2002).

Nidumolu, Sarma R. Mani Subramani and Alan Aldrich. "Situated Learning and the Situated Knowledge Web: Exploring the Ground Beneath Knowledge Management." *Journal of Management Information Systems* 18, no. 1 (Summer 2001).

O'Leary, Daniel, Daniel Kuokka, and Robert Plant. "Artificial Intelligence and Virtual Organizations." *Communications of the ACM* 40, no. 1 (January 1997).

Orlikowski, Wanda J. "Knowing in Practice: Enacting a Collective Capability in Distributed Organizing." *Organization Science* 13, no. 3 (May-June 2002).

Pastore, Richard. "Cruise Control." *CIO Magazine* (February 1, 2003).

Piccoli, Gabriele, Rami Ahmad, and Blake Ives. "Web-Based Virtual Learning Environments: A Research Framework and a Preliminary Assessment of Effectiveness in Basic IT Skills Training." *MIS Quarterly* 25, no. 4 (December 2001).

Ranft, Annette L. and Michael D. Lord. "Acquiring New Technologies and Capabilities: A Grounded Model of Acquisition Implementation." *Organization Science* 13, no. 4 (July-August 2002).

Rumelhart, David E., Bernard Widrow, and Michael A. Lehr. "The Basic Ideas in Neural Networks." *Communications of the ACM* 37, no. 3 (March 1994).

Sadeh, Norman, David W. Hildum, and Dag Kjenstad. "Agent-Based E-Supply Chain Decision Support." *Journal of Organizational Computing and Electronic Commerce* 13, no. 3 & 4 (2003)

Samuelson, Douglas A. and Charles M. Macal. "Agent-Based Simulation." OR/MS Today (August 2006).

Schultze, Ulrike and Dorothy Leidner. "Studying Knowledge Management in Information Systems Research: Discourses and Theoretical Assumptions." *MIS Quarterly* 26, no. 3 (September 2002).

Selker, Ted. "Coach: A Teaching Agent that Learns." *Communications of the ACM* 37, no. 7 (July 1994).

Spangler, Scott, Jeffrey T. Kreulen, and Justin Lessler. "Generating and Browsing Multiple Taxonomies over a Document Collection." *Journal of Management Information Systems* 19, no. 4 (Spring 2003)

Spender, J. C. "Organizational Knowledge, Learning and Memory: Three Concepts In Search of a Theory." *Journal of Organizational Change Management* 9, 1996.

Starbuck, William H. "Learning by Knowledge-Intensive Firms." *Journal of Management Studies* 29, no. 6 (November 1992).

Sviokla, John J. "An Examination of the Impact of Expert Systems on the Firm: The Case of XCON." *MIS Quarterly* 14, no. 5 (June 1990).

Tiwana, Amrit. "Affinity to Infinity in Peer-to-Peer Knowledge Platforms." *Communications of the ACM* 46, no. 5 (May 2003).

Trippi, Robert, and Efraim Turban. "The Impact of Parallel and Neural Computing on Managerial Decision Making." *Journal of Management Information Systems* 6, no. 3 (Winter 1989–1990).

Vara, Vauhini. "Offices Co-Opt Consumer Web Tools Like 'Wikis' and Social Networking." *The Wall Street Journal* (September 12, 2006).

Voekler, Michael. "Staying a Step Ahead of Fraud." *Intelligent Enterprise* (September 2006).

Wakefield, Julie. "Complexity's Business Model." *Scientific American* (January 2001).

Walczak, Stephen. "An Emprical Analysis of Data Requirements for Financial Forecasting with Neural Networks." *Journal of Management Information Systems* 17, no. 4 (Spring 2001).

Walczak, Steven. "Gaining Competitive Advantage for Trading in Emerging Capital Markets with Neural Networks." *Journal of Management Information Systems* 16, no. 2 (Fall 1999).

Wang, Huaiqing, John Mylopoulos, and Stephen Liao. "Intelligent Agents and Financial Risk Monitoring Systems." *Communications of the ACM* 45, no. 3 (March 2002).

Widrow, Bernard, David E. Rumelhart, and Michael A. Lehr. "Neural Networks: Applications in Industry, Business, and Science." *Communications of the ACM* 37, no. 3 (March 1994).

Wong, David, Noemi Paciorek, and Dana Moore. "Java-Based Mobile Agents." *Communications of the ACM* 42, no. 3 (March 1999).

Yimam-Seid, Dawit and Alfred Kobsa. "Expert-Finding Systems for Organizations: Problem and Domain Analysis and the DEMOIR Approach." *Journal of Organizational Computing and Electronic Commerce* 13, no. 1 (2003)

Zack, Michael H "Rethinking the Knowledge-Based Organization." *MIS Sloan Management Review* 44, no. 4 (Summer 2003).

Zadeh, Lotfi A. "Fuzzy Logic, Neural Networks, and Soft Computing." *Communications of the ACM* 37, no. 3 (March 1994).

Zadeh, Lotfi A. "The Calculus of Fuzzy If/Then Rules." *AI Expert* (March 1992).

CHAPTER 12

Badal, Jaclyne. "A Reality Check for the Sales Staff." *The Wall Street Journal* (October 16, 2006).

Bannan, Karen J. "Smart Selling." *Profit Magazine* (May 2006).

Bazerman, Max H. and Dolly Chugh. "Decisions Without Blinders." *Harvard Business Review* (January 2006).

Information Builders Inc. "Information Builders Underwrites New Enterprise Reporting System for National Life." www.informationbuilders.com, accessed August 7, 2005.

Alavi, Maryam and Erich A. Joachimsthaler. "Revisiting DSS Implementation Research. A Meta-Analysis of the Literature and Suggestions for Researchers." MIS Quarterly 16, no. 1 (March 1992).

Anson, Rob and Bjorn Erik Munkvold. "Beyond Face-to-Face: A Field Study of Electronic Meetings in Different Time and Place Modes." Journal of Organizational Computing and Electronic Commerce 14, no. 2 (2004).

Barkhi, Reza. "The Effects of Decision Guidance and Problem Modeling on Group Decision-Making." *Journal of Management Information Systems* 18, no. 3 (Winter 2001-2002).

Briggs, Robert O., Gert-Jan de Vreede, and Jay. F. Nunamaker Jr.: "Collaboration Engineering with ThinkLets to Pursue Sustained Success with Group Support Systems." *Journal of Management Information Systems* 19, no. 4 (Spring 2003).

Clark, Thomas D., Jr., Mary C. Jones, and Curtis P. Armstrong. "The Dynamic Structure of Management Support Systems: Theory Development, Research Focus, and Direction." *MIS Quarterly* 31, no. 3 (September 2007).

Dennis, Alan R. "Information Exchange and Use in Group Decision Making: You Can Lead a Group to Information, but You Can't Make It Think." *MIS Quarterly* 20, no. 4 (December 1996).

Dennis, Alan R., Barbara H. Wixom, and Robert J. Vandenberg. "Understanding Fit and Appropriation Effects in Group Support Systems Via Meta-Analysis." *MIS Quarterly* 25, no. 2 (June 2001).

Dennis, Alan R., Jay E. Aronson, William G. Henriger, and Edward D. Walker III. "Structuring Time and Task in Electronic Brainstorming." *MIS Quarterly* 23, no. 1 (March 1999).

Dennis, Alan R., Joey F. George, Len M. Jessup, Jay F. Nunamaker, and Douglas R. Vogel. "Information Technology to Support Electronic Meetings." *MIS Quarterly* 12, no. 4 (December 1988).

DeSanctis, Geraldine, and R. Brent Gallupe. "A Foundation for the Study of Group Decision Support Systems." *Management Science* 33, no. 5 (May 1987).

Dutta, Soumitra, Berend Wierenga, and Arco Dalebout. "Designing Management Support Systems Using an Integrative Perspective." *Communications of the ACM* 40, no. 6 (June 1997).

El Sawy, Omar. "Personal Information Systems for Strategic Scanning in Turbulent Environments." *MIS Quarterly* 9, no. 1 (March 1985).

El Sherif, Hisham, and Omar A. El Sawy. "Issue-Based Decision Support Systems for the Egyptian Cabinet." *MIS Quarterly* 12, no. 4 (December 1988).

Few. Stephen. "Dashboard Confusion." *Intelligent Enterprise* (March 20, 2004).

Fjermestad, Jerry. "An Integrated Framework for Group Support Systems." *Journal of Organizational Computing and Electronic Commerce* 8, no. 2 (1998).

Forgionne, Guiseppe. "Management Support System Effectiveness: Further Empirical Evidence." *Journal of the Association for Information Systems* 1 (May 2000).

Gallupe, R. Brent, Geraldine DeSanctis, and Gary W. Dickson. "Computer-Based Support for Group Problem-Finding: An Experimental Investigation." *MIS Quarterly* 12, no. 2 (June 1988).

George, Joey. "Organizational Decision Support Systems." *Journal of Management Information Systems* 8, no. 3 (Winter 1991–1992).

Ginzberg, Michael J., W. R. Reitman, and E. A. Stohr, eds. *Decision Support Systems*. New York: North Holland Publishing Co. (1982).

Gorry, G. Anthony, and Michael S. Scott Morton. "A Framework for Management Information Systems." *Sloan Management Review* 13, no. 1 (Fall 1971).

Hansell, Saul. "How Wall Street Lied to Its Computers." *The New York Times* (September 18, 2008).

Hogue, Jack T. "A Framework for the Examination of Management Involvement in Decision Support Systems." *Journal of Management Information Systems* 4, no. 1 (Summer 1987).

Houdeshel, George, and Hugh J. Watson. "The Management Information and Decision Support (MIDS) System at Lockheed, Georgia." *MIS Quarterly* 11, no. 2 (March 1987).

Kalakota, Ravi, Jan Stallaert, and Andrew B. Whinston. "Worldwide Real-Time Decision Support Systems for Electronic Commerce Applications." *Journal of Organizational Computing and Electronic Commerce* 6, no. 1 (1996).

Kaplan, Robert S. and David P. Norton. "The Balanced Scorecard: Measures that Drive Performance", *Harvard Business Review* (Jan - Feb 1992).

Kaplan, Robert S. and David P. Norton. *Strategy Maps: Converting Intangible Assets into Tangible Outcomes*. Boston: Harvard Business School Press (2004).

Keen, Peter G. W., and M. S. Scott Morton. *Decision Support Systems: An Organizational Perspective*. Reading, MA: Addison-Wesley (1982).

Kwok, Ron Chi-Wai, Jian Ma, and Douglas R. Vogel. "Effects of Group Support Systems and Content Facilitation on Knowledge Acquisition." *Journal of Management Information Systems* 19, no. 3 (Winter 2002-3).

Leidner, Dorothy E., and Joyce Elam. "Executive Information Systems: Their Impact on Executive Decision Making." *Journal of Management Information Systems* (Winter 1993–1994).

Leidner, Dorothy E., and Joyce Elam. "The Impact of Executive Information Systems on Organizational Design, Intelligence, and Decision Making." *Organization Science* 6, no. 6 (November-December 1995).

Lilien, Gary L., Arvind Rangaswamy, Gerrit H. Van Bruggen, and Katrin Starke. "DSS Effectiveness in Marketing Resource Allocation Decisions: Reality vs. Perception. "Information Systems Research 15, no. 3 (September 2004).

Maxcer, Chris. "Rohn and Haas: Dashboards to the Rescue." *SAP NetWeaver Magazine* 3 (2007).

Mintzberg, Henry. "Managerial Work: Analysis from Observation." *Management Science* 18 (October 1971).

Niederman, Fred, Catherine M. Beise, and Peggy M. Beranek. "Issues and Concerns about Computer-Supported Meetings: The Facilitator's Perspective." *MIS Quarterly* 20, no. 1 (March 1996).

Nunamaker, Jay, Robert O. Briggs, Daniel D. Mittleman, Douglas R. Vogel, and Pierre A. Balthazard. "Lessons from a Dozen Years of Group Support Systems Research: A Discussion of Lab and Field Findings." *Journal of Management Information Systems* 13, no. 3 (Winter 1997).

O'Keefe, Robert M., and Tim McEachern. "Web-based Customer Decision Support Systems." *Communications of the ACM* 41, no. 3 (March 1998).

Oracle Corporation. "Pharmacia Gains Discipline and Improves Corporate Performance Management Thanks to a Comprehensive, Strategic View of Research Operations," www.oracle.com, accessed August 31, 2003.

Pinsonneault, Alain, Henri Barki, R. Brent Gallupe, and Norberto Hoppen. "Electronic Brainstorming: The Illusion of Productivity." *Information Systems Research* 10, no. 2 (July 1999).

Reinig, Bruce A. "Toward an Understanding of Satisfaction with the Process and Outcomes of Teamwork." *Journal of Management Information Systems* 19, no. 4 (Spring 2003)

Rockart, John F., and David W. DeLong. *Executive Support Systems: The Emergence of Top Management Computer Use.* Homewood, IL: Dow-Jones Irwin (1988).

Schwabe, Gerhard. "Providing for Organizational Memory in Computer-Supported Meetings." *Journal of Organizational Computing and Electronic Commerce* 9, no. 2 and 3 (1999).

Silver, Mark S. "Decision Support Systems: Directed and Nondirected Change." *Information Systems Research* 1, no. 1 (March 1990).

Simon, H. A. *The New Science of Management Decision.* New York: Harper & Row (1960).

Sprague, R. H., and E. D. Carlson. *Building Effective Decision Support Systems.* Englewood Cliffs, NJ: Prentice Hall (1982).

Turban, Efraim, Jay E. Aronson. Ting-Peng Liang, and Ramesh Sharda. *Decision Support and Business Intelligence Systems*, 8th ed. Upper Saddle River, NJ: Prentice Hall (2007).

Volonino, Linda, and Hugh J. Watson. "The Strategic Business Objectives Method for EIS Development." *Journal of Management Information Systems* 7, no. 3 (Winter 1990-1991).

Walls, Joseph G., George R. Widmeyer, and Omar A. El Sawy. "Building an Information System Design Theory for Vigilant EIS." *Information Systems Research* 3, no. 1 (March 1992).

Watson, Hugh J., Astrid Lipp, Pamela Z. Jackson, Abdelhafid Dahmani, and William B. Fredenberger. "Organizational Support for Decision Support Systems." *Journal of Management Information Systems* 5, no. 4 (Spring 1989).

Watson, Hugh J., R. Kelly Rainer, Jr., and Chang E. Koh. "Executive Information Systems: A Framework for Development and a Survey of Current Practices." *MIS Quarterly* 15, no. 1 (March 1991).

Yoo, Youngjin and Maryam Alavi. "Media and Group Cohesion: Relative Influences on Social Presence, Task Participation, and Group Consensus." *MIS Quarterly* 25, no. 3 (September 2001).

CHAPTER 13

Agarwal, Ritu, Prabudda De, Atish P. Sinha, and Mohan Tanniru. "On the Usability of OO Representations." *Comunications of the ACM* 43, no. 10 (October 2000).

Alavi, Maryam, R. Ryan Nelson, and Ira R. Weiss. "Strategies for End-User Computing: An Integrative Framework." *Journal of Management Information Systems* 4, no. 3 (Winter 1987–1988).

Alavi, Maryam. "An Assessment of the Prototyping Approach to Information System Development." *Communications of the ACM* 27 (June 1984).

Albert, Terri C., Paulo B. Goes, and Alok Gupta. "GIST: A Model for Design and Management of Content and Interactivity of Customer-Centric Web Sites." *MIS Quarterly* 28, no. 2 (June 2004).

Alter, Allan E. "I.T. Outsourcing: Expect the Unexpected." *CIO Insight* (March 7, 2007).

Arinze, Bay and Murugan Anandarajan."A Framework for Using OO Mapping Methods to Rapidly Configure ERP Systems." *Communications of the ACM* 46, no.2 (February 2003).

Armstrong, Deborah J. and Bill C. Hardgrove. "Understanding Mindshift Learning: The Transition to Object-Oriented Development." *MIS Quarterly* 31, no. 3 (September 2007).

Aron, Ravi, Eric K.Clemons, and Sashi Reddi. "Just Right Outsourcing: Understanding and Managing Risk." *Journal of Management Information Systems* 22, no. 1 (Summer 2005).

Avison, David E. and Guy Fitzgerald."Where Now for Development Methodologies?" *Communications of the ACM* 41, no. 1 (January 2003).

Baily, Martin N. and Diana Farrell. "Exploding the Myths of Offshoring." *The McKinsey Quarterly* (July 2004).

Barthelemy, Jerome. "The Hidden Costs of IT Outsourcing." *Sloan Management Review* (Spring 2001).

Barua, Anitesh, Sophie C. H. Lee, and Andrew B. Whinston. "The Calculus of Reengineering." *Information Systems Research* 7, no. 4 (December 1996).

Broadbent, Marianne, Peter Weill, and Don St. Clair. "The Implications of Information Technology Infrastructure for Business Process Redesign." *MIS Quarterly* 23, no. 2 (June 1999).

Brown, Susan A., Norman L. Chervany, and Bryan A. Reinicke. "What Matters When Introducing New Technology." *Communications of the ACM* 50, No. 9 (September 2007).

Bullen, Christine, and John F. Rockart. "A Primer on Critical Success Factors." Cambridge, MA: Center for Information Systems Research, Sloan School of Management (1981).

Champy, James A. *X-Engineering the Corporation: Reinventing Your Business in the Digital Age.* New York: Warner Books (2002).

Curbera, Francisco, Rania Khalaf, Nirmal Mukhi, Stefan Tai, and Sanjiva Weerawarana. "The Next Step in Web Services." *Communications of the ACM* 46, no 10 (October 2003).

Davenport, Thomas H., and James E. Short. "The New Industrial Engineering: Information Technology and Business Process Redesign." *Sloan Management Review* 31, no. 4 (Summer 1990).

Davidson, Elisabeth J. "Technology Frames and Framing: A Socio-Cognitive Investigation of Requirements Determination. *MIS Quarterly* 26, no. 4 (December 2002).

Davidson, W. H. "Beyond Engineering: The Three Phases of Business Transformation." *IBM Systems Journal* 32, no. 1 (1993).

Davis, Gordon B. "Determining Management Information Needs: A Comparison of Methods." *MIS Quarterly* 1 (June 1977).

DeMarco, Tom. *Structured Analysis and System Specification.* New York: Yourdon Press (1978).

Den Hengst, Marielle and Gert-Jan DeVreede. "Collaborative Business Engineering: A Decade of Lessons from the Field." *Journal of Management Information Systems* 20, no. 4 (Spring 2004).

Dibbern, Jess, Jessica Winkler, and Armin Heinzl. "Explaining Variations in Client Extra Costs between Software Projects Offshored to India." *MIS Quarterly* 32, no. 2 (June 2008).

Ein Dor Philip and Eli Segev. "Strategic Planning for Management Information Systems." *Management Science* 24, no. 15 (1978).

El Sawy, Omar A. *Redesigning Enterprise Processes for E-Business.* McGraw-Hill (2001).

Feeny, David, Mary Lacity, and Leslie P. Willcocks. "Taking the Measure of Outsourcing Providers." *MIT Sloan Management Review* 46, No. 3 (Spring 2005).

Fingar, Peter. "Component-Based Frameworks for E-Commerce." *Communications of the ACM* 43, no. 10 (October 2000).

Fischer, G., E. Giaccardi. Y.Ye, A.G. Sutcliffe, and N. Mehandjiev. "Meta-Design: A Manifesto for End-User Development." *Communications of the ACM* 47, no. 9 (September 2004).

Gane, Chris, and Trish Sarson. *Structured Systems Analysis: Tools and Techniques*. Englewood Cliffs, NJ: Prentice Hall (1979).

Gefen, David and Erarn Carmel. "Is the World Really Flat? A Look at Offshoring in an Online Programming Marketplace." *MIS Quarterly* 32, no. 2 (June 2008).

Gefen, David and Catherine M. Ridings. "Implementation Team Responsiveness and User Evaluation of Customer Relationship Management: A Quasi-Experimental Design Study of Social Exchange Theory." *Journal of Management Information Systems* 19, no. 1 (Summer 2002).

Gemino, Andrew and Yair Wand." Evaluating Modeling Techniques Based on Models of Learning." *Communications of the ACM* 46, no. 10 (October 2003).

George, Joey, Dinesh Batra, Joseph S. Valacich, and Jeffrey A. Hoffer. *Object Oriented System Analysis and Design*, 2nd ed. Upper Saddle River, NJ: Prentice Hall (2007).

Grunbacher, Paul, Michael Halling, Stefan Biffl, Hasan Kitapci, and Barry W. Boehm. "Integrating Collaborative Processes and Quality Assurance Techniques: Experiences from Requirements Negotiation." *Journal of Management Information Systems* 20, no. 4 (Spring 2004).

Hammer, Michael, and James Champy. *Reengineering the Corporation*. New York: HarperCollins Publishers (1993).

Hammer, Michael. "Reengineering Work: Don't Automate, Obliterate." *Harvard Business Review* (July-August 1990).

Hammer, Michael. "Process Management and the Future of Six Sigma." *Sloan Management Review* 43, no.2 (Winter 2002)

Hickey, Ann M. and Alan M. Davis. "A Unified Model of Requirements Elicitation." *Journal of Management Information Systems* 20, no. 4 (Spring 2004)

Hirscheim, Rudy and Mary Lacity. "The Myths and Realities of Information Technology Insourcing." *Communications of the ACM* 43, no. 2 (February 2000).

Hoffer, Jeffrey, Joey George, and Joseph Valacich. *Modern Systems Analysis and Design*, 5th ed. Upper Saddle River, NJ: Prentice Hall (2008).

Hopkins, Jon. "Component Primer." *Communications of the ACM* 43, no. 10 (October 2000).

Iacovou, Charalambos L. and Robbie Nakatsu. "A Risk Profile of Offshore-Outsourced Development Projects." *Communications of the ACM* 51, no. 6 (June 2008).

Irwin, Gretchen. "The Role of Similarity in the Reuse of Object-Oriented Analysis Models." *Journal of Management Information Systems* 19, no. 2 (Fall 2002).

Ivari, Juhani, Rudy Hirscheim, and Heinz K. Klein. "A Dynamic Framework for Classifying Information Systems Development Methodologies and Approaches." *Journal of Management Information Systems* 17, no. 3 (Winter 2000-2001).

Iyer, Bala, Jim Freedman, Mark Gaynor, and George Wyner. "Web Services: Enabling Dynamic Business Networks." *Communications of the Association for Information Systems* 11 (2003).

Johnson, Richard A. "The Ups and Downs of Object-Oriented Systems Development." *Communications of the ACM* 43, no.10 (October 2000).

Keen, Peter G. W. *Shaping the Future: Business Design Through Information Technology*. Cambridge, MA: Harvard Business School Press (1991).

Kendall, Kenneth E., and Julie E. Kendall. *Systems Analysis and Design*, 8th ed. Upper Saddle River, NJ: Prentice Hall (2008).

Kindler, Noah B., Vasantha Krishnakanthan, and Ranjit Tinaikar. "Applying Lean to Application Development and Maintenance." *The McKinsey Quarterly* (May 2007).

Krishna, S., Sundeep Sahay, and Geoff Walsham. "Managing Cross-Cultural Issues in Global Software Outsourcing." *Communications of the ACM* 47, No. 4 (April 2004).

Lee, Jae Nam, Shaila M. Miranda, and Yong-Mi Kim. "IT Outsourcing Strategies: Universalistic, Contingency, and Configurational Explanations of Success." *Information Systems Research* 15, no. 2 (June 2004).

Lee, Jae-Nam, Minh Q. Huynh, Ron Chi-wai Kwok, and Shih-Ming Pi."IT Outsourcing Evolution-Past Present, and Future." *Communications of the ACM* 46, no. 5 (May 2003).

Levina, Natalia and Jeanne W. Ross. "From the Vendor's Perspective: Exploring the Value Proposition in Information Technology Outsourcing." *MIS Quarterly* 27, no. 3 (September 2003).

Lientz, Bennett P., and E. Burton Swanson. *Software Maintenance Management*. Reading, MA: Addison-Wesley (1980).

Limayem, Moez, Mohamed Khalifa, and Wynne W. Chin. "Case Tools Usage and Impact on System Development Performance." *Journal of Organizational Computing and Electronic Commerce* 14, no. 3 (2004).

Martin, James. *Application Development without Programmers*. Englewood Cliffs, NJ: Prentice Hall (1982).

Mazzucchelli, Louis. "Structured Analysis Can Streamline Software Design." *Computerworld* (December 9, 1985).

Nerson, Jean-Marc. "Applying Object-Oriented Analysis and Design." *Communications of the ACM* 35, no. 9 (September 1992).

Nidumolu, Sarma R. and Mani Subramani. "The Matrix of Control: Combining Process and Structure Approaches to Managing Software Development." *Journal of Management Information Systems* 20, no. 4 (Winter 2004).

Nissen, Mark E. "Redesigning Reengineering through Measurement-Driven Inference," *MIS Quarterly* 22, no. 4 (December 1998).

O'Donnell, Anthony. "BPM: Insuring Business Success." *Optimize Magazine* (April 2007).

Overby, Stephanie, "The Hidden Costs of Offshore Outsourcing," *CIO Magazine* (Sept.1, 2003).

Pancake, Cherri M. "The Promise and the Cost of Object Technology: A Five-Year Forecast." *Communications of the ACM* 38, no. 10 (October 1995).

Parsons, Jeffrey, and Yair Wand. "Using Objects for Systems Analysis." *Communications of the ACM* 40, no. 12 (December 1997).

Phillips, James and Dan Foody. "Building a Foundation for Web Services." *EAI Journal* (March 2002).

Pitts, Mitzi G. and Glenn J. Browne. "Stopping Behavior of Systems Analysts During Information Requirements Elicitation." *Journal of Management Information Systems* 21, no. 1 (Summer 2004).

Prahalad, C. K. and M.S.. Krishnan. "Synchronizing Strategy and Information Technology." *Sloan Management Review* 43, no. 4 (Summer 2002).

Ravichandran, T. and Marcus A. Rothenberger. "Software Reuse Strategies and Component Markets." *Communications of the ACM* 46, no. 8 (August 2003).

Rockart, John F. "Chief Executives Define Their Own Data Needs." *Harvard Business Review* (March-April 1979).

Rockart, John F., and Lauren S. Flannery. "The Management of End-User Computing." *Communications of the ACM* 26, no. 10 (October 1983).

Rockart, John F., and Michael E. Treacy. "The CEO Goes On-Line." *Harvard Business Review* (January-February 1982).

Sabherwahl, Rajiv. "The Role of Trust in IS Outsourcing Development Projects." *Communications of the ACM* 42, no. 2 (February 1999).

Sircar, Sumit, Sridhar P. Nerur, and Radhakanta Mahapatra. "Revolution or Evolution? A Comparison of Object-Oriented and Structured Systems Development Methods." *MIS Quarterly* 25, no. 4 (December 2001).

Smith, Howard and Peter Fingar. *Business Process Management: The Third Wave* Tampa, Florida: Meghan-Kiffer Press (2002).

Swanson, E. Burton and Enrique Dans. "System Life Expectancy and the Maintenance Effort: Exploring their Equilibration." *MIS Quarterly* 24, no. 2 (June 2000).

Turetken, Ozgur, David Schuff, Ramesh Sharda, and Terence T. Ow. "Supporting Systems Analysis and Design Through Fisheye Views." *Communications of the ACM* 47, no. 9 (September 2004).

Van Den Heuvel, Willem-Jan and Zakaria Maamar. "Moving Toward a Framework to Compose Intelligent Web Services." *Communications of the ACM* 46, no. 10 (October 2003).

Venkatraman, N. "Beyond Outsourcing: Managing IT Resources as a Value Center." *Sloan Management Review* (Spring 1997).

Vessey, Iris, and Sue Conger. "Learning to Specify Information Requirements: The Relationship between Application and Methodology." *Journal of Management Information Systems* 10, no. 2 (Fall 1993).

Vitharana, Padmal. "Risks and Challenges of Component-Based Software Development." *Communications of the ACM* 46, no. 8 (August 2003).

Watad, Mahmoud M. and Frank J. DiSanzo. "Case Study: The Synergism of Telecommuting and Office Automation." *Sloan Management Review* 41, no. 2 (Winter 2000).

Wulf, Volker and Matthias Jarke. "The Economics of End-User Development." *Communications of the ACM* 47, no. 9 (September 2004).

Yourdon, Edward, and L. L. Constantine. *Structured Design.* New York: Yourdon Press (1978).

CHAPTER 14

Aladwani, Adel M. "An Integrated Performance Model of Information Systems Projects." *Journal of Management Information Systems* 19, no.1 (Summer 2002).

Alleman, James. "Real Options Real Opportunities." *Optimize Magazine* (January 2002).

Alter, Steven, and Michael Ginzberg. "Managing Uncertainty in MIS Implementation." *Sloan Management Review* 20 (Fall 1978).

Andres, Howard P. and Robert W. Zmud. "A Contingency Approach to Software Project Coordination." *Journal of Management Information Systems* 18, no. 3 (Winter 2001–2002).

Armstrong, Curtis P. and V. Sambamurthy. "Information Technology Assimilation in Firms: The Influence of Senior Leadership and IT Infrastructures." *Information Systems Research* 10, no. 4 (December 1999).

Banker, Rajiv. "Value Implications of Relative Investments in Information Technology." Department of Information Systems and Center for Digital Economy Research, University of Texas at Dallas, January 23, 2001.

Barki, Henri and Jon Hartwick. "Interpersonal Conflict and Its Management in Information Systems Development." *MIS Quarterly* 25, no.2 (June 2001).

Barki, Henri, Suzanne Rivard, and Jean Talbot. "An Integrative Contingency Model of Software Project Risk Management." *Journal of Management Information Systems* 17, no. 4 (Spring 2001).

Beath, Cynthia Mathis, and Wanda J. Orlikowski. "The Contradictory Structure of Systems Development Methodologies: Deconstructing the IS-User Relationship in Information Engineering." *Information Systems Research* 5, no. 4 (December 1994).

Benaroch, Michel and Robert J. Kauffman. "Justifying Electronic Banking Network Expansion Using Real Options Analysis." *MIS Quarterly* 24, no. 2 (June 2000).

Benaroch, Michel, Sandeep Shah, and Mark Jeffrey. "On the Valuation of Multistage Information Technology Investments Embedding Nested Real Options." *Journal of Management Information Systems* 23, No. 1 (Summer 2006).

Benaroch, Michel. "Managing Information Technology Investment Risk: A Real Options Perspective." *Journal of Management Information Systems* 19, no. 2 (Fall 2002).

Bhattacherjee, Anol and G. Premkumar. "Understanding Changes In Belief and Attitude Toward Information Technology Usage: A Theoretical Model and Longitudinal Test." *MIS Quarterly* 28, no. 2 (June 2004).

Boer, F. Peter. "Real Options: The IT Investment Risk Buster." *Optimize Magazine* (July 2002).

Bostrom, R. P., and J. S. Heinen. "MIS Problems and Failures: A Socio-Technical Perspective. Part I: The Causes." *MIS Quarterly* 1 (September 1977); "Part II: The Application of Socio-Technical Theory." *MIS Quarterly* 1 (December 1977).

Bromlow, David. "Improve Your Odds of Project Success." *SAP NetWeaver Magazine* 04 (2008).

Brooks, Frederick P. "The Mythical Man-Month." *Datamation* (December 1974).

Brynjolfsson, Erik, and Lorin M. Hitt. "Information Technology and Organizational Design: Evidence from Micro Data." (January 1998).

Chatterjee, Debabroto, Carl Pacini, and V. Sambamurthy. "The Shareholder-Wealth and Trading Volume Effects of Information Technology Infrastructure Investments." *Journal of Management Information Systems* 19, no. 2 (Fall 2002).

Chatterjee, Debabroto, Rajdeep Grewal, and V. Sabamurthy. "Shaping Up for E-Commerce: Institutional Enablers of the Organizational Assimilation of Web Technologies." *MIS Quarterly* 26, no. 2 (June 2002).

Clement, Andrew, and Peter Van den Besselaar. "A Retrospective Look at PD Projects." *Communications of the ACM* 36, no. 4 (June 1993).

Concours Group. "Delivering Large-Scale System Projects." (2000).

Cooper, Randolph B. "Information Technology Development Creativity: A Case Study of Attempted Radical Change." *MIS Quarterly* 24, no. 2 (June 2000).

Datz, Todd. "Portfolio Management: How to Do It Right," *CIO Magazine* (May 1, 2003).

Davis, Fred R. "Perceived Usefulness, Ease of Use, and User Acceptance of Information Technology." *MIS Quarterly* 13, no. 3 (September 1989).

De Meyer, Arnoud, Christoph H. Loch and Michael T. Pich. "Managing Project Uncertainty: From Variation to Chaos." *Sloan Management Review* 43, no.2 (Winter 2002).

Delone, William H. and Ephraim R. McLean. "The Delone and McLean Model of Information Systems Success: A Ten-Year Update." *Journal of Management Information Systems* 19, no. 4 (Spring 2003).

Doll, William J. "Avenues for Top Management Involvement in Successful MIS Development." *MIS Quarterly* (March 1985).

Doll, William J., Xiaodung Deng, T. S. Raghunathan, Gholamreza Torkzadeh, and Weidong Xia. "The Meaning and Measurement of User Satisfaction: A Multigroup Invariance Analysis of End-User Computing Satisfaction Instrument." Journal of Management Information Systems 21, no. 1 (Summer 2004).

Ein-Dor, Philip, and Eli Segev. "Organizational Context and the Success of Management Information Systems." *Management Science* 24 (June 1978).

El Sawy, Omar, and Burt Nanus. "Toward the Design of Robust Information Systems." *Journal of Management Information Systems* 5, no. 4 (Spring 1989).

Fichman, Robert G. "Real Options and IT Platforms Adoption: Implications for Theory and Practice." Information Systems Research 15, no. 2 (June 2004).

Fichman, Robert G. "The Role of Aggregation in the Measurement of IT-Related Organizational Innovation." *MIS Quarterly* 25, no. 4 (December 2001).

Franz, Charles, and Daniel Robey. "An Investigation of User-Led System Design: Rational and Political Perspectives." *Communications of the ACM* 27 (December 1984).

Gefen, David and Catherine M. Ridings. "Implementation Team Responsiveness and User Evaluation of Customer Relationship Management: A Quasi-Experimental Design Study of Social Exchange Theory." *Journal of Management Information Systems* 19, no. 1 (Summer 2002).

Giaglis, George. "Focus Issue on Legacy Information Systems and Business Process Change: On the Integrated Design and Evaluation of Business Processes and Information Systems." *Communications of the AIS* 2, (July 1999).

Ginzberg, Michael J. "Early Diagnosis of MIS Implementation Failure: Promising Results and Unanswered Questions." *Management Science* 27 (April 1981).

Hitt, Lorin, D.J. Wu, and Xiaoge Zhou. "Investment in Enterprise Resource Planning: Business Impact and Productivity Measures." *Journal of Management Information Systems* 19, no. 1 (Summer 2002).

Housel, Thomas J., Omar El Sawy, JianfangJ. Zhong, and Waymond Rodgers. "Measuring the Return on e-Business Initiatives at the Process Level: The Knowledge Value-Added Approach." *ICIS* (2001).

Hunton, James E., and Beeler, Jesse D., "Effects of User Participation in Systems Development: A Longitudinal Field Study." *MIS Quarterly* 21, no. 4 (December 1997).

Iversen, Jakob H., Lars Mathiassen, and Peter Axel Nielsen. "Managing Risk in Software Process Improvement: An Action Research Approach." *MIS Quarterly* 28, no. 3 (September 2004).

Jeffrey, Mark and Ingmar Leliveld. "Best Practices in IT Portfolio Management." MIT Sloan Management Review 45, no. 3 (Spring 2004).

Jiang, James J., Gary Klein, Debbie Tesch, and Hong-Gee Chen. "Closing the User and Provider Service Quality Gap," *Communications of the ACM* 46, no.2 (February 2003).

Joshi, Kailash. "A Model of Users' Perspective on Change: The Case of Information Systems Technology Implementation." *MIS Quarterly* 15, no. 2 (June 1991).

Jun He and William R. King. "The Role of User Participation In Information Systems Development: Implications from a Meta-Analysis." *Journal of Management Information Systems* 25, no. 1 (Summer 2008).

Kalin, Sari. "Making IT Portfolio Management a Reality." *CIO Magazine* (June 1, 2006).

Keen, Peter W. "Information Systems and Organizational Change." *Communications of the ACM* 24 (January 1981).

Keil, Mark and Daniel Robey. "Blowing the Whistle on Troubled Software Projects." *Communications of the ACM* 44, no. 4 (April 2001).

Keil, Mark and Ramiro Montealegre. "Cutting Your Losses: Extricating Your Organization When a Big Project Goes Awry." *Sloan Management Review* 41, no. 3 (Spring 2000).

Keil, Mark, Bernard C.Y. Tan, Kwok-Kee Wei, Timo Saarinen, Virpi Tuunainen, and Arjen Waassenaar. "A Cross-Cultural Study on Escalation of Commitment Behavior in Software Projects." *MIS Quarterly* 24, no. 2 (June 2000).

Keil, Mark, Joan Mann, and Arun Rai. "Why Software Projects Escalate: An Empirical Analysis and Test of Four Theoretical Models." *MIS Quarterly* 24, no. 4 (December 2000).

Keil, Mark, Paul E. Cule, Kalle Lyytinen, and Roy C. Schmidt. "A Framework for Identifying Software Project Risks." *Communications of the ACM* 41, 11 (November 1998).

Keil, Mark, Richard Mixon, Timo Saarinen, and Virpi Tuunairen. "Understanding Runaway IT Projects." *Journal of Management Information Systems* 11, no. 3 (Winter 1994-95).

Kettinger, William J. and Choong C. Lee. "Understanding the IS-User Divide in IT Innovation." *Communications of the ACM* 45, no.2 (February 2002).

Klein, Gary, James J. Jiang, and Debbie B. Tesch. "Wanted: Project Teams with a Blend of IS Professional Orientations." *Communications of the ACM* 45, no. 6 (June 2002).

Kolb, D. A., and A. L. Frohman. "An Organization Development Approach to Consulting." *Sloan Management Review* 12 (Fall 1970).

Laudon, Kenneth C. "CIOs Beware: Very Large Scale Systems." Center for Research on Information Systems, New York University Stern School of Business, working paper (1989).

Levinson, Meridith. "When Failure Is Not an Option." *CIO Magazine* (June 1, 2006).

Liang, Huigang, Nilesh Sharaf, Qing Hu, and Yajiong Xue. "Assimilation of Enterprise Systems: The Effect of Institutional Pressures and the Mediating Role of Top Management." *MIS Quarterly* 31, no 1 (March 2007).

Lientz, Bennett P., and E. Burton Swanson. *Software Maintenance Management. Reading*, MA: Addison-Wesley (1980).

Lipin, Steven and Nikhil Deogun. "Big Mergers of 90s Prove Disappointing to Shareholders." *The Wall Street Journal* (October 30, 2000).

Lucas, Henry C., Jr. *Implementation: The Key to Successful Information Systems*. New York: Columbia University Press (1981).

Mahmood, Mo Adam, Laura Hall, and Daniel Leonard Swanberg, "Factors Affecting Information Technology Usage: A Meta-Analysis of the Empirical Literature." *Journal of Organizational Computing and Electronic Commerce* 11, no. 2 (November 2, 2001)

Markus, M. Lynne, and Mark Keil. "If We Build It, They Will Come: Designing Information Systems That People Want to Use." *Sloan Management Review* (Summer 1994).

Markus, M. Lynne, and Robert I. Benjamin. "Change Agentry-The Next IS Frontier." *MIS Quarterly* 20, no. 4 (December 1996).

Markus, M. Lynne, and Robert I. Benjamin. "The Magic Bullet Theory of IT-Enabled Transformation." *Sloan Management Review* (Winter 1997).

Matlin, Gerald. "What Is the Value of Investment in Information Systems?" *MIS Quarterly* 13, no. 3 (September 1989).

McFarlan, F. Warren. "Portfolio Approach to Information Systems." *Harvard Business Review* (September-October 1981).

McGrath, Rita Gunther and Ian C.McMillan. "Assessing Technology Projects Using Real Options Reasoning." *Industrial Research Institute* (2000)

Mumford, Enid, and Mary Weir. *Computer Systems in Work Design: The ETHICS Method*. New York: John Wiley (1979).

Nidumolu, Sarma R. and Mani Subramani. "The Matrix of Control: Combining Process and Structure Approaches to Management Software Development." *Journal of Management Information Systems* 20, no. 3 (Winter 2004).

Nolan, Richard. "Managing Information Systems by Committee." *Harvard Business Review* (July-August 1982).

Orlikowski, Wanda J., and J. Debra Hofman. "An Improvisational Change Model for Change Management: The Case of

Groupware Technologies." *Sloan Management Review* (Winter 1997).

Palmer, Jonathan W. "Web Site Usability, Design and Performance Metrics." *Information Systems Research* 13, no.3 (September 2002).

Peffers, Ken and Timo Saarinen. "Measuring the Business Value of IT Investments: Inferences from a Study of Senior Bank Executives." *Journal of Organizational Computing and Electronic Commerce* 12, no. 1 (2002).

Quan, Jin "Jim", Quing Hu, and Paul J. Hart."Information Technology Investments and Firms' Performance-A Duopoly Perspective." *Journal of Management Information Systems* 20, no. 3 (Winter 2004).

Rai, Arun, Sandra S. Lang, and Robert B. Welker. "Assessing the Validity of IS Success Models: An Empirical Test and Theoretical Analysis." *Information Systems Research* 13, no. 1 (March 2002).

Rapoza, Jim. "Next-Gen Project Management." *eWeek* (March 3, 2008).

Robey, Daniel, and M. Lynne Markus. "Rituals in Information System Design." *MIS Quarterly* (March 1984).

Robey, Daniel, Jeanne W. Ross, and Marie-Claude Boudreau. "Learning to Implement Enterprise Systems: An Exploratory Study of the Dialectics of Change." *Journal of Management Information Systems* 19, no. 1 (Summer 2002).

Rockart, John F. "Chief Executives Define Their Own Data Needs." *Harvard Business Review* (March-April 1979).

Rockart, John F. and Michael E. Treacy. "The CEO Goes Online." *Harvard Business Review* (January-February 1982).

Ross, Jeanne W. and Cynthia M. Beath." Beyond the Business Case: New Approaches to IT Investment." *Sloan Management Review* 43, no.2 (Winter 2002).

Ryan, Sherry D. and David A. Harrison. "Considering Social Subsystem Costs and Benefits in Information Technology Investment Decisions: A View from the Field on Anticipated Payoffs." *Journal of Management Information Systems* 16, no. 4 (Spring 2000).

Ryan, Sherry D., David A. Harrison, and Lawrence L Schkade." Information Technology Investment Decisions: When Do Cost and Benefits in the Social Subsystem Matter?" *Journal of Management Information Systems* 19, no. 2 (Fall 2002).

Sambamurthy, V., Anandhi Bharadwaj, and Varun Grover. "Shaping Agility Through Digital Options: Reconceptualizing the Role of Information Technology in Contemporary Firms." *MIS Quarterly* 27, no. 2 (June 2003).

Santhanam, Radhika and Edward Hartono. "Issues in Linking Information Technology Capability to Firm Performance." *MIS Quarterly* 27, no. 1 (March 2003).

Sauer, Chris and Leslie P. Willcocks, "The Evolution of the Organizational Architect." *Sloan Management Review* 43, no. 3 (Spring 2002).

Schmidt, Roy, Kalle Lyytinen, Mark Keil, and Paul Cule. "Identifying Software Project Risks: An International Delphi Study." *Journal of Management Information Systems* 17, no. 4 (Spring 2001)

Schneiderman, Ben." Universal Usability." *Communications of the ACM* 43, no. 5 (May 2000).

Schwalbe, Kathy. *Information Technology Project Management, 5/e.* Course Technology (2008).

Sharma, Rajeev and Philip Yetton. "The Contingent Effects of Training,Technical Complexity, and Task Interdependence on Successful Information System Implementation." *MIS Quarterly* 31, no. 2 (June 2007).

Shank, Michael E., Andrew C. Boynton, and Robert W. Zmud. "Critical Success Factor Analysis as a Methodology for MIS Planning." *MIS Quarterly* (June 1985).

Siewiorek, Daniel P. "New Frontiers of Application Design." Communications of the ACM 45, no.12 (December 2002.)

Smith, H. Jeff, Mark Keil, and Gordon Depledge. "Keeping Mum as the Project Goes Under." *Journal of Management Information Systems* 18, no. 2 (Fall 2001)

Speier, Cheri and Michael. G. Morris. "The Influence of Query Interface Design on Decision-Making Performance." *MIS Quarterly* 27, no. 3 (September 2003).

Straub, Detmar W., Arun Rai and Richard Klein. "Measuring Firm Performance at the Network Level: A Nomology of the Business Impact of Digital Supply Networks." *Journal of Management Information Systems* 21, no 1 (Summer 2004).

Swanson, E. Burton. *Information System Implementation.* Homewood, IL: Richard D. Irwin (1988).

Tallon, Paul P, Kenneth L. Kraemer, and Vijay Gurbaxani. "Executives' Perceptions of the Business Value of Information Technology: A Process-Oriented Approach." *Journal of Management Information Systems* 16, no. 4 (Spring 2000).

Taudes, Alfred, Markus Feurstein, and Andreas Mild. "Options Analysis of Software Platform Decisions: A Case Study." *MIS Quarterly* 24, no. 2 (June 2000).

Thatcher, Matt E. and Jim R. Oliver. "The Impact of Technology Investments on a Firm's Production Efficiency, Product Quality, and Productivity." *Journal of Management Information Systems* 18, no. 2 (Fall 2001).

Tornatsky, Louis G., J. D. Eveland, M. G. Boylan, W. A. Hetzner, E. C. Johnson, D. Roitman, and J. Schneider. *The Process of Technological Innovation: Reviewing the Literature.* Washington, DC: National Science Foundation (1983).

Venkatesh, Viswanath, Michael G. Morris, Gordon B Davis, and Fred D. Davis. "User Acceptance of Information Technology: Toward a Unified View." *MIS Quarterly* 27, No. 3 (September 2003).

Wallace, Linda and Mark Keil. "Software Project Risks and Their Effect on Outcomes." *Communications of the ACM* 47, no. 4 (April 2004).

Wang, Eric T.G., Gary Klein, and James J. Jiang. "ERP Misfit: Country of Origin and Organizational Factors." *Journal of Management Information Systems* 23, No. 1 (Summer 2006). "Winning the IT Portfolio Battle," Projects@Work (September 6, 2007).

Xia, Weidong and Gwanhoo Lee. "Grasping the Complexity of IS Development Projects." *Communications of the ACM* 47, no. 5 (May 2004).

Xue, Yajion, Huigang Liang, and William R. Boulton. "Information Technology Governance in Information Technology Investment Decision Processes: The Impact of Investment Characteristics, External Environment, and Internal Context." *MIS Quarterly* 32, no. 1 (March 2008).

Yin, Robert K. "Life Histories of Innovations: How New Practices Become Routinized." *Public Administration Review* (January-February 1981).

Zhu, Kevin and Kenneth L. Kraemer. "E-Commerce Metrics for Net-Enhanced Organizations: Assessing the Value of e-Commerce to Firm Performance in the Manufacturing Sector." *Information Systems Research* 13, no.3 (September 2002).

Zhu, Kevin, Kenneth L. Kraemer, Sean Xu, and Jason Dedrick. "Information Technology Payoff in E-Business Environments: An International Perspective on Value Creation of E-business in the Financial Services Industry." Journal of Management Information Systems 21, no. 1 (Summer 2004).

Zhu, Kevin. "The Complementarity of Information Technology Infrastructure and E-Commerce Capability: A Resource-Based Assessment of Their Business Value." Journal of Management Information Systems 21, no. 1 (Summer 2004).

CHAPTER 15

Biehl, Markus. "Success Factors For Implementing Global Information Systems." *Communications of the ACM* 50, No. 1 (January 2007).

Burkhardt, Grey E., Seymour E. Goodman, Arun Mehta, and Larry Press. "The Internet in India: Better Times Ahead?" *Communications of the ACM* 41, no. 11 (November 1998).

Cox, Butler. *Globalization: The IT Challenge.* Sunnyvale, CA: Amdahl Executive Institute (1991).

Davis. Bob. "Rise of Nationalism Frays Global Ties." *The Wall Street Journal* (April 28, 2008).

Davison, Robert. "Cultural Complications of ERP." *Communications of the ACM* 45, no. 7 (July 2002).

Deans, Candace P., and Michael J. Kane. *International Dimensions of Information Systems and Technology.* Boston, MA: PWS-Kent (1992).

Deans, Candace P., Kirk R. Karwan, Martin D. Goslar, David A. Ricks, and Brian Toyne. "Key International Issues in U.S.-Based Multinational Corporations." *Journal of Management Information Systems* 7, no. 4 (Spring 1991).

Ein-Dor, Philip, Seymour E. Goodman, and Peter Wolcott. "From Via Maris to Electronic Highway: The Internet in Canaan." *Communications of the ACM* 43, no. 7 (July 2000).

Farhoomand, Ali, Virpi Kristiina Tuunainen, and Lester W. Yee. "Barrier to Global Electronic Commerce: A Cross-Country Study of Hong Kong and Finland." *Journal of Organizational Computing and Electronic Commerce* 10, no. 1 (2000).

Ghislanzoni, Giancarlo, Risto Penttinen, an David Turnbull. "The Multilocal Challenge: Managing Cross-Border Functions." *The McKinsey Quarterly* (March 2008).

Ives, Blake, and Sirkka Jarvenpaa. "Applications of Global Information Technology: Key Issues for Management." *MIS Quarterly* 15, no. 1 (March 1991).

Ives, S. L. Jarvenpaa, R. O. Mason, "Global business drivers: Aligning Information Technology to Global Business Strategy," *IBM Systems Journal* Vol 32, No 1, 1993.

Jarvenpaa, Sirkka L., Kathleen Knoll, and Dorothy Leidner. "Is Anybody Out There? Antecedents of Trust in Global Virtual Teams." *Journal of Management Information Systems* 14, no. 4 (Spring 1998).

Jarvenpaa, Sirkka L., Thomas R. Shaw, and D. Sandy Staples."Toward Contextualized Theories of Trust: The Role of Trust in Global Virtual Teams." Information Systems Research 15, no. 3 (September 2004)

King, William R. and Vikram Sethi. "An Empirical Analysis of the Organization of Transnational Information Systems." *Journal of Management Information Systems* 15, no. 4 (Spring 1999).

Lai, Vincent S. and Wingyan Chung. "Managing International Data Communication." *Communications of the ACM* 45, no.3 (March 2002).

Liang, Huigang, Yajiong Xue, William R. Boulton, and Terry Anthony Byrd. "Why Western Vendors Don't Dominate China's ERP Market." *Communications of the ACM* 47, no. 7 (July 2004).

MacFarquhar, Neil. "Tunisia's Tangled Web Is Sticking Point for Reform." *The New York Times* (June 25, 2004).

Mann, Catherine L. "What Global Sourcing Means for U.S. I.T. Workers and for the U.S. Economy." *Communications of the ACM* 47, no. 7 (July 2004)

Martinsons, Maris G. "ERP In China: One Package Two Profiles," *Communications of the ACM* 47, no. 7 (July 2004).

Petrazzini, Ben, and Mugo Kibati. "The Internet in Developing Countries." *Communications of the ACM* 42, no. 6 (June 1999).

Quelch, John A., and Lisa R. Klein. "The Internet and International Marketing." *Sloan Management Review* (Spring 1996).

Roche, Edward M. *Managing Information Technology in Multinational Corporations.* New York: Macmillan (1992).

Shih, Eric, Kenneth L. Kraemer, and Jason Dedrick. "IT Diffusion in Developing Countries." *Communications of the ACM* 51, no.2 (February 2008).

Shore, Barry. "Enterprise Integration Across the Globally Dispersed Service Organization." *Communications of the ACM* 49, NO. 6 (June 2006).

Soh, Christina, Sia Siew Kien, and Joanne Tay-Yap. "Cultural Fits and Misfits: Is ERP a Universal Solution?" *Communications of the ACM* 43, no. 3 (April 2000).

Steel, Emily and Amol Sharma. "U.S. Web Sites Draw Traffic from Abroad but Few Ads." *The Wall Street Journal* (July 10, 2008).

Steinbart, Paul John, and Ravinder Nath. "Problems and Issues in the Management of International Data Networks." *MIS Quarterly* 16, no. 1 (March 1992).

Straub, Detmar W. "The Effect of Culture on IT Diffusion: E-Mail and FAX in Japan and the U.S." *Information Systems Research* 5, no. 1 (March 1994).

Tan, Zixiang, William Foster, and Seymour Goodman. "China's State-Coordinated Internet Infrastructure." *Communications of the ACM* 42, no. 6 (June 1999).

Tractinsky, Noam, and Sirkka L. Jarvenpaa. "Information Systems Design Decisions in a Global Versus Domestic Context." *MIS Quarterly* 19, no. 4 (December 1995).

Watson, Richard T., Gigi G. Kelly, Robert D. Galliers, and James C. Brancheau. "Key Issues in Information Systems Management: An International Perspective." *Journal of Management Information Systems* 13, no. 4 (Spring 1997).

Glossary

3G networks Cellular networks based on packet-switched technology with speeds ranging from 144 Kbps for mobile users to over 2 Mbps for stationary users, enabling users to transmit video, graphics, and other rich media, in addition to voice.

acceptable use policy (AUP) Defines acceptable uses of the firm's information resources and computing equipment, including desktop and laptop computers, wireless devices, telephones, and the Internet, and specifies consequences for noncompliance.

acceptance testing Provides the final certification that the system is ready to be used in a production setting.

access control Policies and procedures a company uses to prevent improper access to systems by unauthorized insiders and outsiders.

accountability The mechanisms for assessing responsibility for decisions made and actions taken.

accumulated balance digital payment systems Systems enabling users to make micropayments and purchases on the Web, accumulating a debit balance on their credit card or telephone bills.

agent-based modeling Modeling complex phenomena as systems of autonomous agents that follow relatively simple rules for interaction.

agency theory Economic theory that views the firm as a nexus of contracts among self-interested individuals who must be supervised and managed.

agile development Rapid delivery of working software by breaking a large project into a series of small sub-projects that are completed in short periods of time using iteration and continuous feedback.

Ajax Development technique for creating interactive Web applications capable of updating the user interface without reloading the entire browser page.

analog signal A continuous waveform that passes through a communications medium; used for voice communications.

analytical CRM Customer relationship management applications dealing with the analysis of customer data to provide information for improving business performance.

antivirus software Software designed to detect, and often eliminate, computer viruses from an information system.

application controls: Specific controls unique to each computerized application that ensure that only authorized data are completely and accurately processed by that application.

application server Software that handles all application operations between browser-based computers and a company's back-end business applications or databases.

application software package A set of prewritten, precoded application software programs that are commercially available for sale or lease.

application software Programs written for a specific application to perform functions specified by end users.

artificial intelligence (AI) The effort to develop computer-based systems that can behave like humans, with the ability to learn languages, accomplish physical tasks, use a perceptual apparatus, and emulate human expertise and decision making.

attribute A piece of information describing a particular entity.

authentication The ability of each party in a transaction to ascertain the identity of the other party.

authorization management systems Systems for allowing each user access only to those portions of a system or the Web that person is permitted to enter, based on information established by a set of access rules.

authorization policies Determine differing levels of access to information assets for different levels of users in an organization.

automation Using the computer to speed up the performance of existing tasks.

autonomic computing Effort to develop systems that can manage themselves without user intervention.

backward chaining A strategy for searching the rule base in an expert system that acts like a problem solver by beginning with a hypothesis and seeking out more information until the hypothesis is either proved or disproved.

balanced scorecard method Framework for operationalizing a firms strategic plan by focusing on measurable financial, business process, customer, and learning and growth outcomes of firm performance.

bandwidth The capacity of a communications channel as measured by the difference between the highest and lowest frequencies that can be transmitted by that channel.

banner ad A graphic display on a Web page used for advertising. The banner is linked to the advertiser's Web site so that a person clicking on it will be transported to the advertiser's Web site.

batch processing A method of collecting and processing data in which transactions are accumulated and stored until a specified time when it is convenient or necessary to process them as a group.

baud A change in signal from positive to negative or vice versa that is used as a measure of transmission speed.

behavioral models Descriptions of management based on behavioral scientists' observations of what managers actually do in their jobs.

benchmarking Setting strict standards for products, services, or activities and measuring organizational performance against those standards.

best practices The most successful solutions or problem-solving methods that have been developed by a specific organization or industry.

biometric authentication Technology for authenticating system users that compares a person's unique characteristics such as fingerprints, face, or retinal image, against a stored set profile of these characteristics.

bit A binary digit representing the smallest unit of data in a computer system. It can only have one of two states, representing 0 or 1.

blade server Entire computer that fits on a single, thin card (or blade) and that is plugged into a single chassis to save space, power and complexity.

blog Popular term for Weblog, designating an informal yet structured Web site where individuals can publish stories, opinions, and links to other Web sites of interest.

blogosphere Totality of blog-related Web sites.

Bluetooth Standard for wireless personal area networks that can transmit up to 722 Kbps within a 10-meter area.

botnet A group of computers that have been infected with bot malware without users' knowledge, enabling a hacker to use the amassed resources of the computers to launch distributed denial-of-service attacks, phishing campaigns or spam.

broadband High-speed transmission technology. Also designates a single communications medium that can transmit multiple channels of data simultaneously.

bugs Software program code defects.

bullwhip effect Distortion of information about the demand for a product as it passes from one entity to the next across the supply chain.

bus topology Network topology linking a number of computers by a single circuit with all messages broadcast to the entire network.

business continuity planning Planning that focuses on how the company can restore business operations after a disaster strikes.

business driver A force in the environment to which businesses must respond and that influences the direction of business.

business ecosystem Loosely coupled but interdependent networks of suppliers, distributors, outsourcing firms, transportation service firms, and technology manufacturers

business functions Specialized tasks performed in a business organization, including manufacturing and production, sales and marketing, finance and accounting, and human resources.

business intelligence Applications and technologies to help users make better business decisions.

business model An abstraction of what an enterprise is and how the enterprise delivers a product or service, showing how the enterprise creates wealth.

business process management Methodology for revising the organization's business processes to use business processes as fundamental building blocks of corporate information systems.

business process reengineering The radical redesign of business processes, combining steps to cut waste and eliminating repetitive, paper-intensive tasks in order to improve cost, quality, and service, and to maximize the benefits of information technology.

business processes The unique ways in which organizations coordinate and organize work activities, information, and knowledge to produce a product or service.

business-to-business (B2B) electronic commerce Electronic sales of goods and services among businesses.

business-to-consumer (B2C) electronic commerce Electronic retailing of products and services directly to individual consumers.

byte A string of bits, usually eight, used to store one number or character in a computer system.

cable Internet connections Internet connections that use digital cable lines to deliver high-speed Internet access to homes and businesses.

call center An organizational department responsible for handling customer service issues by telephone and other channels.

capacity planning The process of predicting when a computer hardware system becomes saturated to ensure that adequate computing resources are available for work of different priorities and that the firm has enough computing power for its current and future needs.

capital budgeting The process of analyzing and selecting various proposals for capital expenditures.

carpal tunnel syndrome (CTS) Type of RSI in which pressure on the median nerve through the wrist's bony carpal tunnel structure produces pain.

case-based reasoning (CBR) Artificial intelligence technology that represents knowledge as a database of cases and solutions.

cell phone A device that transmits voice or data, using radio waves to communicate with radio antennas placed within adjacent geographic areas called cells.

centralized processing Processing that is accomplished by one large central computer.

change agent In the context of implementation, the individual acting as the catalyst during the change process to ensure successful organizational adaptation to a new system or innovation.

change management Managing the impact of organizational change associated with an innovation, such as a new information system.

channel conflict Competition between two or more different distribution chains used to sell the products or services of the same company.

channel The link by which data or voice are transmitted between sending and receiving devices in a network.

chat Live, interactive conversations over a public network.

chief information officer (CIO) Senior manager in charge of the information systems function in the firm.

chief knowledge officer (CKO) Senior executive in charge of the organization's knowledge management program.

chief privacy officer (CPO) Responsible for ensuring the company complies with existing data privacy laws.

chief security officer (CSO) Heads a formal security function for the organization and is responsible for enforcing the firm's security policy.

choice Simon's third stage of decision making, when the individual selects among the various solution alternatives.

churn rate Measurement of the number of customers who stop using or purchasing products or services from a company. Used as an indicator of the growth or decline of a firm's customer base.

classical model of management Traditional description of management that focused on its formal functions of planning, organizing, coordinating, deciding, and controlling.

click fraud Fraudulently clicking on an online ad in pay per click advertising to generate an improper charge per click.

clicks-and-mortar Business model where the Web site is an extension of a traditional bricks-and-mortar business.

clickstream tracking Tracking data about customer activities at Web sites and storing them in a log.

client The user point-of-entry for the required function in client/server computing. Normally a desktop computer, workstation, or laptop computer.

client/server computing A model for computing that splits processing between clients and servers on a network, assigning functions to the machine most able to perform the function.

cloud computing Web-based applications that are stored on remote servers and accessed via the "cloud" of the Internet using a standard Web browser.

coaxial cable A transmission medium consisting of thickly insulated copper wire; can transmit large volumes of data quickly.

Code Division Multiple Access (CDMA) Major cellular transmission standard in the United States that transmits over several frequencies, occupies the entire spectrum, and randomly assigns users to a range of frequencies over time.

collaborative commerce The use of digital technologies to enable multiple organizations to collaboratively design, develop, build and manage products through their life cycles.

collaborative filtering Tracking users' movements on a Web site, comparing the information gleaned about a user's behavior against data about other customers with similar interests to predict what the user would like to see next.

collaborative planning, forecasting, and replenishment (CPFR) Firms collaborating with their suppliers and buyers to formulate demand forecasts, develop production plans, and coordinate shipping, warehousing, and stocking activities.

competitive forces model Model used to describe the interaction of external influences, specifically threats and opportunities, that affect an organization's strategy and ability to compete.

complementary assets Additional assets required to derive value from a primary investment.

component-based development Building large software systems by combining pre-existing software components.

computer Physical device that takes data as an input, transforms the data by executing stored instructions, and outputs information to a number of devices.

computer abuse The commission of acts involving a computer that may not be illegal but are considered unethical.

computer crime The commission of illegal acts through the use of a computer or against a computer system.

computer forensics The scientific collection, examination, authentication, preservation, and analysis of data held on or retrieved from computer storage media in such a way that the information can be used as evidence in a court of law.

computer hardware Physical equipment used for input, processing, and output activities in an information system.

computer literacy Knowledge about information technology, focusing on understanding of how computer-based technologies work.

computer software Detailed, preprogrammed instructions that control and coordinate the work of computer hardware components in an information system.

computer virus Rogue software program that attaches itself to other software programs or data files in order to be executed, often causing hardware and software malfunctions.

computer vision syndrome (CVS) Eyestrain condition related to computer display screen use; symptoms include headaches, blurred vision, and dry and irritated eyes.

computer-aided design (CAD) Information system that automates the creation and revision of designs using sophisticated graphics software.

computer-aided software engineering (CASE) Automation of step-by-step methodologies for software and systems development to reduce the amounts of repetitive work the developer needs to do.

computer-based information systems (CBIS) Information systems that rely on computer hardware and software for processing and disseminating information.

connectivity The ability of computers and computer-based devices to communicate with each other and share information in a meaningful way without human intervention..

consumer-to-consumer (C2C) electronic commerce Consumers selling goods and services electronically to other consumers.

controls All of the methods, policies, and procedures that ensure protection of the organization's assets, accuracy and reliability of its records, and operational adherence to management standards.

conversion The process of changing from the old system to the new system.

cookies Tiny file deposited on a computer hard drive when an individual visits certain Web sites. Used to identify the visitor and track visits to the Web site.

cooptation Bringing the opposition into the process of designing and implementing a solution without giving up control of the direction and nature of the change.

copyright A statutory grant that protects creators of intellectual property against copying by others for any purpose for a minimum of 70 years.

core competency Activity at which a firm excels as a world-class leader.

core systems Systems that support functions that are absolutely critical to the organization.

cost transparency the ability of consumers to discover the actual costs merchants pay for products.

counterimplementation A deliberate strategy to thwart the implementation of an information system or an innovation in an organization.

critical success factors (CSFs) A small number of easily identifiable operational goals shaped by the industry, the firm, the manager, and the broader environment that are believed to assure the success of an organization. Used to determine the information requirements of an organization.

cross-selling Marketing complementary products to customers.

culture The set of fundamental assumptions about what products the organization should produce, how and where it should produce them, and for whom they should be produced.

customer-decision-support system (CDSS) System to support the decision-making process of an existing or potential customer.

customer lifetime value (CLTV) Difference between revenues produced by a specific customer and the expenses for acquiring and servicing that customer minus the cost of promotional marketing over the lifetime of the customer relationship, expressed in today's dollars.

customer relationship management (CRM) Business and technology discipline that uses information systems to coordinate all of the business processes surrounding the firm's interactions with its customers in sales, marketing, and service.

customer relationship management systems Information systems that track all the ways in which a company interacts with its customers and analyze these interactions to optimize revenue, profitability, customer satisfaction, and customer retention.

customization The modification of a software package to meet an organization's unique requirements without destroying the package software's integrity.

cybervandalism Intentional disruption, defacement, or destruction of a Web site or corporate information system.

data Streams of raw facts representing events occurring in organizations or the physical environment before they have been organized and arranged into a form that people can understand and use.

data administration A special organizational function for managing the organization's data resources, concerned with information policy, data planning, maintenance of data dictionaries, and data quality standards.

data cleansing Activities for detecting and correcting data in a database or file that are incorrect, incomplete, improperly formatted, or redundant. Also known as data scrubbing.

data definition DBMS capability that specifies the structure and content of the database.

data dictionary An automated or manual tool for storing and organizing information about the data maintained in a database.

data-driven DSS A system that supports decision making by allowing users to extract and analyze useful information that was previously buried in large databases.

data element A field.

data flow diagram (DFD) Primary tool for structured analysis that graphically illustrates a system's component process and the flow of data between them.

data governance Policies and processes for managing the availability, usability, integrity, and security of the firm's data.

data inconsistency The presence of different values for same attribute when the same data are stored in multiple locations.

data management software Software used for creating and manipulating lists, creating files and databases to store data, and combining information for reports.

data manipulation language A language associated with a database management system that end users and programmers use to manipulate data in the database.

data mart A small data warehouse containing only a portion of the organization's data for a specified function or population of users.

data mining Analysis of large pools of data to find patterns and rules that can be used to guide decision making and predict future behavior.

data quality audit A survey and/or sample of files to determine accuracy and completeness of data in an information system.

data redundancy The presence of duplicate data in multiple data files.

data visualization Technology for helping users see patterns and relationships in large amounts of data by presenting the data in graphical form.

data warehouse A database, with reporting and query tools, that stores current and historical data extracted from various operational systems and consolidated for management reporting and analysis.

data workers People such as secretaries or bookkeepers who process the organization's paperwork.

database A group of related files.

database (rigorous definition) A collection of data organized to service many applications at the same time by storing and managing data so that they appear to be in one location.

database administration Refers to the more technical and operational aspects of managing data, including physical database design and maintenance.

database management system (DBMS) Special software to create and maintain a database and enable individual business applications to extract the data they need without having to create separate files or data definitions in their computer programs.

database server A computer in a client/server environment that is responsible for running a DBMS to process SQL statements and perform database management tasks.

dataconferencing Teleconferencing in which two or more users are able to edit and modify data files simultaneously.

decisional roles Mintzberg's classification for managerial roles where managers initiate activities, handle disturbances, allocate resources, and negotiate conflicts.

decision-support systems (DSS) Information systems at the organization's management level that combine data and sophisticated analytical models or data analysis tools to support semistructured and unstructured decision making.

dedicated lines Telephone lines that are continuously available for transmission by a lessee. Typically conditioned to transmit data at high speeds for high-volume applications.

deep packet inspection (DPI) Technology for managing network traffic by examining data packets, sorting out low-priority data from higher priority business-critical data, and sending packets in order of priority.

demand planning Determining how much product a business needs to make to satisfy all its customers' demands.

denial of service (DoS) attack Flooding a network server or Web server with false communications or requests for services in order to crash the network.

Descartes' rule of change A principle that states that if an action cannot be taken repeatedly, then it is not right to be taken at any time.

design Simon's second stage of decision making, when the individual conceives of possible alternative solutions to a problem.

digital asset management systems Classify, store, and distribute digital objects such as photographs, graphic images, video, and audio content.

digital certificate An attachment to an electronic message to verify the identity of the sender and to provide the receiver with the means to encode a reply.

digital checking Systems that extend the functionality of existing checking accounts so they can be used for online shopping payments.

digital credit card payment system Secure services for credit card payments on the Internet that protect information transmitted among users, merchant sites, and processing banks.

digital dashboard Displays all of a firm's key performance indicators as graphs and charts on a single screen to provide one-page overview of all the critical measurements necessary to make key executive decisions.

digital divide Large disparities in access to computers and the Internet among different social groups and different locations.

digital firm Organization where nearly all significant business processes and relationships with customers, suppliers, and employees are digitally enabled, and key corporate assets are managed through digital means.

digital goods Goods that can be delivered over a digital network.

digital market A marketplace that is created by computer and communication technologies that link many buyers and sellers.

Digital Millennium Copyright Act (DMCA) Adjusts copyright laws to the Internet Age by making it illegal to make, distribute, or use devices that circumvent technology-based protections of copy-righted materials.

digital signal A discrete waveform that transmits data coded into two discrete states as 1-bits and 0-bits, which are represented as on-off electrical pulses; used for data communications.

digital subscriber line (DSL) A group of technologies providing high-capacity transmission over existing copper telephone lines.

digital wallet Software that stores credit card, electronic cash, owner identification, and address information and provides this data automatically during electronic commerce purchase transactions.

direct cutover A risky conversion approach where the new system completely replaces the old one on an appointed day.

disaster recovery planning Planning for the restoration of computing and communications services after they have been disrupted.

disintermediation The removal of organizations or business process layers responsible for certain intermediary steps in a value chain.

disruptive technologies Technologies with disruptive impact on industries and businesses, rendering existing products, services and business models obsolete.

distance learning Education or training delivered over a distance to individuals in one or more locations.

distributed database A database that is stored in more than one physical location. Parts or copies of the database are physically stored in one location, and other parts or copies are stored and maintained in other locations.

distributed denial-of-service (DDoS) attack Numerous computers inundating and overwhelming a network from numerous launch points.

distributed processing The distribution of computer processing work among multiple computers linked by a communications network.

documentation Descriptions of how an information system works from either a technical or end-user standpoint.

domain name English-like name that corresponds to the unique 32-bit numeric Internet Protocol (IP) address for each computer connected to the Internet

Domain Name System (DNS) A hierarchical system of servers maintaining a database enabling the conversion of domain names to their numeric IP addresses.

domestic exporter Form of business organization characterized by heavy centralization of corporate activities in the home county of origin.

downsizing The process of transferring applications from large computers to smaller ones.

downtime Period of time in which an information system is not operational.

drill down The ability to move from summary data to lower and lower levels of detail.

DSS database A collection of current or historical data from a number of applications or groups. Can be a small PC database or a massive data warehouse.

DSS software system Collection of software tools that are used for data analysis, such as OLAP tools, datamining tools, or a collection of mathematical and analytical models.

due process A process in which laws are well-known and understood and there is an ability to appeal to higher authorities to ensure that laws are applied correctly.

dynamic pricing Pricing of items based on real-time interactions between buyers and sellers that determine what a item is worth at any particular moment.

e-government Use of the Internet and related technologies to digitally enable government and public sector agencies' relationships with citizens, businesses, and other arms of government.

e-learning Instruction delivered through purely digital technology, such as CD-ROMs, the Internet, or private networks.

efficient customer response system System that directly links consumer behavior back to distribution, production, and supply chains.

electronic billing and payment presentation system Systems used for paying routine monthly bills that allow users to view their bills electronically and pay them through electronic funds transfers from banks or credit card accounts.

electronic business (e-business) The use of the Internet and digital technology to execute all the business processes in the enterprise. Includes e-commerce as well as processes for the internal management of the firm and for coordination with suppliers and other business partners.

electronic commerce The process of buying and selling goods and services electronically involving transactions using the Internet, networks, and other digital technologies.

electronic data interchange (EDI) The direct computer-to-computer exchange between two organizations of standard business transactions, such as orders, shipment instructions, or payments.

electronic payment system The use of digital technologies, such as credit cards, smart cards and Internet-based payment systems, to pay for products and services electronically.

e-mail The computer-to-computer exchange of messages.

employee relationship management (ERM) Software dealing with employee issues that are closely related to CRM, such as setting objectives, employee performance management, performance-based compensation, and employee training.

encryption The coding and scrambling of messages to prevent their being read or accessed without authorization.

end-user development The development of information systems by end users with little or no formal assistance from technical specialists.

end-user interface The part of an information system through which the end user interacts with the system, such as on-line screens and commands.

end users Representatives of departments outside the information systems group for whom applications are developed.

enterprise applications Systems that can coordinate activities, decisions, and knowledge across many different functions, levels, and business units in a firm. Include enterprise systems, supply chain management systems, and knowledge management systems.

enterprise content management systems Help organizations manage structured and semistructured knowledge, providing corporate repositories of documents, reports, presentations, and best practices and capabilities for collecting and organizing e-mail and graphic objects.

enterprise portal Web interface providing a single entry point for accessing organizational information and services, including information from various enterprise applications and in-house legacy systems so that information appears to be coming from a single source.

enterprise software Set of integrated modules for applications such as sales and distribution, financial accounting, investment management, materials management, production planning, plant maintenance, and human resources that allow data to be used by multiple functions and business processes.

enterprise systems Integrated enterprise-wide information systems that coordinate key internal processes of the firm.

enterprise-wide knowledge management systems General-purpose, firmwide systems that collect, store, distribute, and apply digital content and knowledge.

entity A person, place, thing, or event about which information must be kept.

entity-relationship diagram A methodology for documenting databases illustrating the relationship between various entities in the database.

ergonomics The interaction of people and machines in the work environment, including the design of jobs, health issues, and the end-user interface of information systems.

ethical "no free lunch" rule Assumption that all tangible and intangible objects are owned by someone else, unless there is a specific declaration otherwise, and that the creator wants compensation for this work.

ethics Principles of right and wrong that can be used by individuals acting as free moral agents to make choices to guide their behavior.

evil twins Wireless networks that pretend to be legitimate to entice participants to log on and reveal passwords or credit card numbers.

exchange Third-party Net marketplace that is primarily transaction oriented and that connects many buyers and suppliers for spot purchasing.

executive support systems (ESS) Information systems at the organization's strategic level designed to address unstructured decision making through advanced graphics and communications.

expert system Knowledge-intensive computer program that captures the expertise of a human in limited domains of knowledge.

explicit knowledge Knowledge that has been documented.

external integration tools Project management technique that links the work of the implementation team to that of users at all organizational levels.

extranet Private intranet that is accessible to authorized outsiders.

Fair Information Practices (FIP) A set of principles originally set forth in 1973 that governs the collection and use of information about individuals and forms the basis of most U.S. and European privacy laws.

fault-tolerant computer systems Systems that contain extra hardware, software, and power supply components that can back a system up and keep it running to prevent system failure.

feasibility study As part of the systems analysis process, the way to determine whether the solution is achievable, given the organization's resources and constraints.

feedback Output that is returned to the appropriate members of the organization to help them evaluate or correct input.

fiber-optic cable A fast, light, and durable transmission medium consisting of thin strands of clear glass fiber bound into cables. Data are transmitted as light pulses.

field A grouping of characters into a word, a group of words, or a complete number, such as a person's name or age.

file transfer protocol (FTP) Tool for retrieving and transferring files from a remote computer.

file A group of records of the same type.

firewall Hardware and software placed between an organization's internal network and an external network to prevent outsiders from invading private networks.

focused differentiation Competitive strategy for developing new market niches for specialized products or services where a business can compete in the target area better than its competitors.

folksonomies User-created taxonomies for classifying and sharing information.

foreign key Field in a database table that enables users find related information in another database table.

formal control tools Project management technique that helps monitor the progress toward completion of a task and fulfillment of goals.

formal planning tools Project management technique that structures and sequences tasks, budgeting time, money, and technical resources required to complete the tasks.

forward chaining A strategy for searching the rule base in an expert system that begins with the information entered by the user and searches the rule base to arrive at a conclusion.

fourth-generation language A programming language that can be employed directly by end users or less-skilled programmers to develop computer applications more rapidly than conventional programming languages.

franchiser Form of business organization in which a product is created, designed, financed, and initially produced in the home country, but for product-specific reasons relies heavily on foreign personnel for further production, marketing, and human resources.

fuzzy logic Rule-based AI that tolerates imprecision by using nonspecific terms called membership functions to solve problems.

Gantt chart Visually representats the timing, duration, and resource requirements of project tasks.

general controls Overall control environment governing the design, security, and use of computer programs and the security of data files in general throughout the organization's information technology infrastructure.

genetic algorithms Problem-solving methods that promote the evolution of solutions to specified problems using the model of living organisms adapting to their environment.

geographic information system (GIS) System with software that can analyze and display data using digitized maps to enhance planning and decision-making.

global culture The development of common expectations, shared artifacts, and social norms among different cultures and peoples

global positioning system (GPS) Worldwide satellite navigational system.

graphical user interface (GUI) The part of an operating system users interact with that uses graphic icons and the computer mouse to issue commands and make selections.

Gramm-Leach-Bliley Act Requires financial institutions to ensure the security and confidentiality of customer data.

grid computing Applying the resources of many computers in a network to a single problem.

group decision-support system (GDSS) An interactive computer-based system to facilitate the solution to unstructured problems by a set of decision makers working together as a group.

hacker A person who gains unauthorized access to a computer network for profit, criminal mischief, or personal pleasure.

hertz Measure of frequency of electrical impulses per second, with 1 Hertz equivalent to 1 cycle per second.

high-availability computing Tools and technologies ,including backup hardware resources, to enable a system to recover quickly from a crash.

HIPAA Law outlining rules for medical security, privacy, and the management of health care records.

hotspot A specific geographic location in which an access point provides public Wi-Fi network service.

hubs Very simple devices that connect network components, sending a packet of data to all other connected devices.

hybrid AI systems Integration of multiple AI technologies into a single application to take advantage of the best features of these technologies.

hypertext markup language (HTML) Page description language for creating Web pages and other hypermedia documents.

hypertext transfer protocol (HTTP) The communications standard used to transfer pages on the Web. Defines how messages are formatted and transmitted.

identity theft Theft of key pieces of personal information, such as credit card or Social Security numbers, in order to obtain merchandise and services in the name of the victim or to obtain false credentials.

Immanuel Kant's Categorical Imperative A principle that states that if an action is not right for everyone to take it is not right for anyone.

implementation Simon's final stage of decision-making, when the individual puts the decision into effect and reports on the progress of the solution.

industry structure The nature of participants in an industry and their relative bargaining power. Derives from the competitive forces and establishes the general business environment in an industry and the overall profitability of doing business in that environment.

inference engine The strategy used to search through the rule base in an expert system; can be forward or backward chaining.

information Data that have been shaped into a form that is meaningful and useful to human beings.

information asymmetry Situation where the relative bargaining power of two parties in a transaction is determined by one party in the transaction possessing more information essential to the transaction than the other party.

information density The total amount and quality of information available to all market participants, consumers, and merchants.

information policy Formal rules governing the maintenance, distribution, and use of information in an organization.

information requirements A detailed statement of the information needs that a new system must satisfy; identifies who needs what information, and when, where, and how the information is needed.

information rights The rights that individuals and organizations have with respect to information that pertains to themselves.

information system Interrelated components working together to collect, process, store, and disseminate information to support decision making, coordination, control, analysis, and visualization in an organization.

information systems department The formal organizational unit that is responsible for the information systems function in the organization.

information systems literacy Broad-based understanding of information systems that includes behavioral knowledge about organizations and individuals using information systems as well as technical knowledge about computers.

information systems managers Leaders of the various specialists in the information systems department.

information systems plan A road map indicating the direction of systems development: the rationale, the current situation, the management strategy, the implementation plan, and the budget.

information technology (IT) All the hardware and software technologies a firm needs to achieve its business objectives.

information technology (IT) infrastructure Computer hardware, software, data, storage technology, and networks providing a portfolio of shared IT resources for the organization.

informational roles Mintzberg's classification for managerial roles where managers act as the nerve centers of their organizations, receiving and disseminating critical information.

informed consent Consent given with knowledge of all the facts needed to make a rational decision.

input The capture or collection of raw data from within the organization or from its external environment for processing in an information system.

instant messaging Chat service that allows participants to create their own private chat channels so that a person can be alerted whenever someone on his or her private list is on-line to initiate a chat session with that particular individual.

intangible benefits Benefits that are not easily quantified; they include more efficient customer service or enhanced decision making.

intellectual property Intangible property created by individuals or corporations that is subject to protections under trade secret, copyright, and patent law.

intelligence The first of Simon's four stages of decision making, when the individual collects information to identify problems occurring in the organization.

intelligent agent Software program that uses a built-in or learned knowledge base to carry out specific, repetitive, and predictable tasks for an individual user, business process, or software application.

internal integration tools Project management technique that ensures that the implementation team operates as a cohesive unit.

international information systems architecture The basic information systems required by organizations to coordinate worldwide trade and other activities.

Internet Global network of networks using universal standards to connect millions of different networks.

Internet Protocol (IP) address Four-part numeric address indicating a unique computer location on the Internet.

Internet Service Provider (ISP) A commercial organization with a permanent connection to the Internet that sells temporary connections to subscribers.

Internet telephony Technologies that use the Internet Protocol's packet-switched connections for voice service.

Internet2 Research network with new protocols and transmission speeds that provides an infrastructure for supporting high-bandwidth Internet applications.

interorganizational systems Information systems that automate the flow of information across organizational boundaries and link a company to its customers, distributors, or suppliers.

interpersonal roles Mintzberg's classification for managerial roles where managers act as figureheads and leaders for the organization.

intranet An internal network based on Internet and World Wide Web technology and standards.

intrusion detection system Tools to monitor the most vulnerable points in a network to detect and deter unauthorized intruders.

investment workstation Powerful desktop computer for financial specialists, which is optimized to access and manipulate massive amounts of financial data.

IT governance Strategy and policies for using information technology within an organization, specifying the decision rights and accountabilities to ensure that information technology supports the organization's strategies and objectives.

iterative A process of repeating over and over again the steps to build a system.

Java Programming language that can deliver only the software functionality needed for a particular task, such as a small applet downloaded from a network; can run on any computer and operating system.

Joint Application Design (JAD) Process to accelerate the generation of information requirements by having end users and information systems specialists work together in intensive interactive design sessions.

just-in-time Scheduling system for minimizing inventory by having components arrive exactly at the moment they are needed and finished goods shipped as soon as they leave the assembly line.

key field A field in a record that uniquely identifies instances of that record so that it can be retrieved, updated, or sorted.

key performance indicators Measures proposed by senior management for understanding how well the firm is performing along specified dimensions.

keylogger Spyware that records every keystroke made on a computer to steal personal information or passwords or to launch Internet attacks.

knowledge Concepts, experience, and insight that provide a framework for creating, evaluating, and using information.

knowledge—and information-intense products Products that require a great deal of learning and knowledge to produce.

knowledge base Model of human knowledge that is used by expert systems.

knowledge discovery Identification of novel and valuable patterns in large databases.

knowledge management The set of processes developed in an organization to create, gather, store, maintain, and disseminate the firm's knowledge.

knowledge management systems Systems that support the creation, capture, storage, and dissemination of firm expertise and knowledge.

knowledge network system Online directory for locating corporate experts in well-defined knowledge domains.

knowledge workers People such as engineers or architects who design products or services and create knowledge for the organization.

learning management system (LMS) Tools for the management, delivery, tracking, and assessment of various types of employee learning.

legacy system A system that has been in existence for a long time and that continues to be used to avoid the high cost of replacing or redesigning it.

legitimacy The extent to which one's authority is accepted on grounds of competence, vision, or other qualities. Making judgments and taking actions on the basis of narrow or personal characteristics.

liability The existence of laws that permit individuals to recover the damages done to them by other actors, systems, or organizations.

Linux Reliable and compactly designed operating system that is an offshoot of UNIX and that can run on many different hardware platforms and is available free or at very low cost. Used as alternative to UNIX and Windows NT.

local area network (LAN) A telecommunications network that requires its own dedicated channels and that encompasses a limited distance, usually one building or several buildings in close proximity.

mainframe Largest category of computer, used for major business processing.

maintenance Changes in hardware, software, documentation, or procedures to a production system to correct errors, meet new requirements, or improve processing efficiency.

malware Malicious software programs such as computer viruses, worms, and Trojan horses.

managed security service provider (MSSP) Company that provides security management services for subscribing clients.

management information systems (MIS) The study of information systems focusing on their use in business and management..

management-level systems Information systems that support the monitoring, controlling, decision-making, and administrative activities of middle managers.

managerial roles Expectations of the activities that managers should perform in an organization.

man-month The traditional unit of measurement used by systems designers to estimate the length of time to complete a project. Refers to the amount of work a person can be expected to complete in a month.

marketspace A marketplace extended beyond traditional boundaries and removed from a temporal and geographic location.

mashups Composite software applications that depend on high-speed networks, universal communication standards, and open-source code.

mass customization The capacity to offer individually tailored products or services using mass production resources..

megahertz A measure of cycle speed, or the pacing of events in a computer; one megahertz equals one million cycles per second.

menu costs Merchants' costs of changing prices.

metric A standard measurement of performance.

metropolitan area network (MAN) Network that spans a metropolitan area, usually a city and its major suburbs. Its geographic scope falls between a WAN and a LAN.

microbrowser Web browser software with a small file size that can work with low-memory constraints, tiny screens of handheld wireless devices, and low bandwidth of wireless networks.

micropayment Payment for a very small sum of money, often less than $10.

microprocessor Very large scale integrated circuit technology that integrates the computer's memory, logic, and control on a single chip.

microwave A high-volume, long-distance, point-to-point transmission in which high-frequency radio signals are transmitted through the atmosphere from one terrestrial transmission station to another.

middle management People in the middle of the organizational hierarchy who are responsible for carrying out the plans and goals of senior management.

midrange computer Middle-size computer that is capable of supporting the computing needs of smaller organizations or of managing networks of other computers.

minicomputer Middle-range computer used in systems for universities, factories, or research laboratories.

MIS audit Identifies all the controls that govern individual information systems and assesses their effectiveness.

mobile commerce (m-commerce) The use of wireless devices, such as cell phones or handheld digital information appliances, to conduct both business-to-consumer and business-to-business e-commerce transactions over the Internet.

mobile wallets (m-wallets) Store m-commerce shoppers' personal information and credit card numbers to expedite the purchase process.

moblog Specialized blog featuring photos with captions posted from mobile phones.

model An abstract representation that illustrates the components or relationships of a phenomenon.

model-driven DSS Primarily stand-alone system that uses some type of model to perform "what-if" and other kinds of analyses.

modem A device for translating a computer's digital signals into analog form for transmission over ordinary telephone lines, or for translating analog signals back into digital form for reception by a computer.

module A logical unit of a program that performs one or several functions.

Moore's Law Assertion that the number of components on a chip doubles each year

MP3 (MPEG3) Compression standard that can compress audio files for transfer over the Internet with virtually no loss in quality.

multicore processor Integrated circuit to which two or more processors have been attached for enhanced performance, reduced power consumption and more efficient simultaneous processing of multiple tasks.

multimedia The integration of two or more types of media such as text, graphics, sound, voice, full-motion video, or animation into a computer-based application.

multinational Form of business organization that concentrates financial management and control out of a central home base while decentralizing

multiplexing Ability of a single communications channel to carry data transmissions from multiple sources simultaneously.

multitiered (N-tier) client/server architecture Client/server network which the work of the entire network is balanced over several different levels of servers.

nanotechnology Technology that builds structures and processes based on the manipulation of individual atoms and molecules.

natural language Nonprocedural language that enables users to communicate with the computer using conversational commands resembling human speech.

net marketplace A single digital marketplace based on Internet technology linking many buyers to many sellers.

netbook Small low-cost, lightweight subnotebook optimized for wireless communication and Internet access.

network The linking of two or more computers to share data or resources, such as a printer.

network economics Model of strategic systems at the industry level based on the concept of a network where adding another participant entails zero marginal costs but can create much larger marginal gains.

network interface card (NIC) Expansion card inserted into a computer to enable it to connect to a network.

network operating system (NOS) Special software that routes and manages communications on the network and coordinates network resources.

networking and telecommunications technology Physical devices and software that link various computer hardware components and transfer data from one physical location to another.

neural network Hardware or software that attempts to emulate the processing patterns of the biological brain.

nonobvious relationship awareness (NORA) Technology that can find obscure hidden connections between people or other entities by analyzing information from many different sources to correlate relationships.

normalization The process of creating small stable data structures from complex groups of data when designing a relational database.

object Software building block that combines data and the procedures acting on the data.

object-oriented DBMS An approach to data management that stores both data and the procedures acting on the data as objects that can be automatically retrieved and shared; the objects can contain multimedia.

object-oriented development Approach to systems development that uses the object as the basic unit of systems analysis and design. The system is modeled as a collection o objects and the relationship between them.

object-oriented programming An approach to software development that combines data and procedures into a single object.

object-relational DBMS A database management system that combines the capabilities of a relational DBMS for storing traditional information and the capabilities of an object-oriented DBMS for storing graphics and multimedia.

offshore outsourcing Outsourcing systems development work or maintenance of existing systems to external vendors in another country.

on-demand computing Firms off-loading peak demand for computing power to remote, large-scale data processing centers, investing just enough to handle average processing loads and paying for only as much additional computing power as the market demands. Also called utility computing.

on-line analytical processing (OLAP) Capability for manipulating and analyzing large volumes of data from multiple perspectives.

online processing A method of collecting and processing data in which transactions are entered directly into the computer system and processed immediately.

online transaction processing Transaction processing mode in which transactions entered on-line are immediately processed by the computer.

open-source software Software that provides free access to its program code, allowing users to modify the program code to make improvements or fix errors.

operating system Software that manages the resources and activities of the computer.

operational CRM Customer-facing applications, such as sales force automation, call center and customer service support, and marketing automation.

operational management People who monitor the day-to-day activities of the organization.

operational-level systems Information systems that monitor the elementary activities and transactions of the organization.

opt-in Model of informed consent permitting prohibiting an organization from collecting any personal information unless the individual specifically takes action to approve information collection and use.

opt-out Model of informed consent permitting the collection of personal information until the consumer specifically requests that the data not be collected.

organization (behavioral definition) A collection of rights, privileges, obligations, and responsibilities that are delicately balanced over a period of time through conflict and conflict resolution.

organization (technical definition) A stable, formal, social structure that takes resources from the environment and processes them to produce outputs.

organizational and management capital Investments in organization and management such as new business processes, management behavior, organizational culture, or training.

organizational impact analysis Study of the way a proposed system will affect organizational structure, attitudes, decision making, and operations.

organizational learning Creation of new standard operating procedures and business processes that reflect organizations' experience.

output The distribution of processed information to the people who will use it or to the activities for which it will be used.

outsourcing The practice of contracting computer center operations, telecommunications networks, or applications development to external vendors.

P3P Industry standard designed to give users more control over personal information gathered on Web sites they visit. Stands for Platform for Privacy Preferences Project.

packet switching Technology that breaks messages into small, fixed bundles of data and routes them in the most economical way through any available communications channel..

paradigm shift Radical reconceptualization of the nature of the business and the nature of the organization.

parallel strategy A safe and conservative conversion approach where both the old system and its potential replacement are run together for a time until everyone is assured that the new one functions correctly.

particularism Making judgments and taking action on the basis of narrow or personal characteristics, in all its forms (religious, nationalistic, ethnic, regionalism, geopolitical position).

partner relationship management (PRM) Automation of the firm's relationships with its selling partners using customer data and analytical tools to improve coordination and customer sales.

patch Small pieces of software to repair the software flaws without disturbing the proper operation of the software.

patent A legal document that grants the owner an exclusive monopoly on the ideas behind an invention for 17 years; designed to ensure that inventors of new machines or methods are rewarded for their labor while making widespread use of their inventions.

peer-to-peer Network architecture that gives equal power to all computers on the network; used primarily in small networks.

personal area network (PAN) Computer network used for communication among digital devices (including telephones and PDAs) that are close to one person.

personal digital assistant (PDA) Small, pen-based, handheld computer with built-in wireless telecommunications capable of entirely digital communications transmission.

personalization Ability of merchants to target marketing messages to specific individuals by adjusting the message for a person's name, interests, and past purchases.

PERT chart Network diagram depicting project tasks and their interrelationships.

pharming Phishing technique that redirects users to a bogus Web page, even when an individual enters the correct Web page address.

phased approach Introduces the new system in stages either by functions or by organizational units.

phishing Form of spoofing involving setting up fake Web sites or sending e-mail messages that resemble those of legitimate businesses that ask users for confidential personal data.

pilot study A strategy to introduce the new system to a limited area of the organization until it is proven to be fully functional; only then can the conversion to the new system across the entire organization take place.

pivot table Spreadsheet tool for reorganizing and summarizing two or more dimensions of data in a tabular format.

podcasting Publishing audio broadcasts via the Internet so that subscribing users can download audio files onto their personal computers or portable music players.

pop-up ad Ad that opens automatically and does not disappear until the user clicks on it.

portal Web interface for presenting integrated personalized content from a variety of sources. Also refers to a Web site service that provides an initial point of entry to the Web.

portfolio analysis An analysis of the portfolio of potential applications within a firm to determine the risks and benefits, and to select among alternatives for information systems.

post-implementation audit Formal review process conducted after a system has been placed in production to determine how well the system has met its original objectives.

predictive analysis Use of datamining techniques, historical data, and assumptions about future conditions to predict outcomes of events.

price discrimination Selling the same goods, or nearly the same goods, to different targeted groups at different prices.

price transparency The ease with which consumers can find out the variety of prices in a market.

primary activities Activities most directly related to the production and distribution of a firm's products or services.

primary key Unique identifier for all the information in any row of a database table.

privacy The claim of individuals to be left alone, free from surveillance or interference from other individuals, organizations, or the state.

private exchange Another term for a private industrial network.

private industrial networks Web-enabled networks linking systems of multiple firms in an industry for the coordination of trans-organizational business processes.

process specifications Describe the logic of the processes occurring within the lowest levels of a data flow diagram.

processing The conversion, manipulation, and analysis of raw input into a form that is more meaningful to humans.

procurement Sourcing goods and materials, negotiating with suppliers, paying for goods, and making delivery arrangements.

product differentiation Competitive strategy for creating brand loyalty by developing new and unique products and services that are not easily duplicated by competitors.

production The stage after the new system is installed and the conversion is complete; during this time the system is reviewed by users and technical specialists to determine how well it has met its original goals.

production or service workers People who actually produce the products or services of the organization.

profiling The use of computers to combine data from multiple sources and create electronic dossiers of detailed information on individuals.

program-data dependence The close relationship between data stored in files and the software programs that update and maintain those files. Any change in data organization or format requires a change in all the programs associated with those files.

programmers Highly trained technical specialists who write computer software instructions.

programming The process of translating the system specifications prepared during the design stage into program code.

project Planned series of related activities for achieving a specific business objective.

project management Application of knowledge, tools, and techniques to achieve specific targets within a specified budget and time period.

protocol A set of rules and procedures that govern transmission between the components in a network.

prototype The preliminary working version of an information system for demonstration and evaluation purposes.

prototyping The process of building an experimental system quickly and inexpensively for demonstration and evaluation so that users can better determine information requirements.

public key encryption Uses two keys: one shared (or public) and one private.

public key infrastructure(PKI) System for creating public and private keys using a certificate authority (CA) and digital certificates for authentication.

pull-based model Supply chain driven by actual customer orders or purchases so that members of the supply chain produce and deliver only what customers have ordered.

pure-play Business models based purely on the Internet.

push-based model Supply chain driven by production master schedules based on forecasts or best guesses of demand for products, and products are "pushed" to customers.

query language Software tool that provides immediate online answers to requests for information that are not predefined.

radio-frequency identification (RFID) Technology using tiny tags with embedded microchips containing data about an item and its location to transmit short-distance radio signals to special RFID readers that then pass the data on to a computer for processing.

Rapid Application Development (RAD) Process for developing systems in a very short time period by using prototyping, fourth-generation tools, and close teamwork among users and systems specialists.

rational model Model of human behavior based on the belief that people, organizations, and nations engage in basically consistent, value-maximizing calculations.

rationalization of procedures The streamlining of standard operating procedures, eliminating obvious bottlenecks, so that automation makes operating procedures more efficient.

real options pricing models Models for evaluating information technology investments with uncertain returns by using techniques for valuing financial options.

record A group of related fields.

recovery-oriented computing Computer systems designed to recover rapidly when mishaps occur.

referential integrity Rules to ensure that relationships between coupled database tables remain consistent.

relational DBMS A type of logical database model that treats data as if they were stored in two-dimensional tables. It can relate data stored in one table to data in another as long as the two tables share a common data element.

Repetitive Stress Injury (RSI) Occupational disease that occurs when muscle groups are forced through repetitive actions with high-impact loads or thousands of repetitions with low-impact loads.

Request for Proposal (RFP) A detailed list of questions submitted to vendors of software or other services to determine how well the vendor's product can meet the organization's specific requirements.

resource allocation The determination of how costs, time, and personnel are assigned to different phases of a systems development project.

responsibility Accepting the potential costs, duties, and obligations for the decisions one makes.

richness Measurement of the depth and detail of information that a business can supply to the customer as well as information the business collects about the customer.

ring topology A network topology in which all computers are linked by a closed loop in a manner that passes data in one direction from one computer to another.

risk assessment Determining the potential frequency of the occurrence of a problem and the potential damage if the problem were to occur. Used to determine the cost/benefit of a control.

Risk Aversion Principle Principle that one should take the action that produces the least harm or incurs the least cost.

router Specialized communications processor that forwards packets of data from one network to another network.

routines Precise rules, procedures and practices that have been developed to cope with expected situations.

RSS Technology using aggregator software to pull content from Web sites and feed it automatically to subscribers' computers.

SaaS (Software as a Service) Services for delivering and providing access to software remotely as a Web-based service.

safe harbor Private self-regulating policy and enforcement mechanism that meets the objectives of government regulations but does not involve government regulation or enforcement.

Sarbanes-Oxley Act Law passed in 2002 that imposes responsibility on companies and their management to protect investors by safeguarding the accuracy and integrity of financial information that is used internally and released externally.

scalability The ability of a computer, product, or system to expand to serve a larger number of users without breaking down.

scope Defines what work is and is not included in a project.

scoring model A quick method for deciding among alternative systems based on a system of ratings for selected objectives.

search costs The time and money spent locating a suitable product and determining the best price for that product.

search engine A tool for locating specific sites or information on the Internet.

search engine marketing Use of search engines to deliver in their results sponsored links, for which advertisers have paid.

Secure Hypertext Transfer Protocol (S-HTTP) Protocol used for encrypting data flowing over the Internet; limited to individual messages.

Secure Sockets Layer (SSL) Enables client and server computers to manage encryption and decryption activities as they communicate with each other during a secure Web session.

security Policies, procedures, and technical measures used to prevent unauthorized access, alteration, theft, or physical damage to information systems.

security policy Statements ranking information risks, identifying acceptable security goals, and identifying the mechanisms for achieving these goals.

Semantic Web Ways of making the Web more "intelligent," with machine-facilitated understanding of information so that searches can be more intuitive, effective, and executed using intelligent software agents.

semistructured decisions Decisions in which only part of the problem has a clear-cut answer provided by an accepted procedure.

senior management People occupying the topmost hierarchy in an organization who are responsible for making long-range decisions.

sensitivity analysis Models that ask "what-if" questions repeatedly to determine the impact of changes in one or more factors on the outcomes.

server Computer specifically optimized to provide software and other resources to other computers over a network.

server farm Large group of servers maintained by a commercial vendor and made available to subscribers for electronic commerce and other activities requiring heavy use of servers.

service level agreement (SLA) Formal contract between customers and their service providers that defines the specific responsibilities of the service provider and the level of service expected by the customer.

service platform Integration of multiple applications from multiple business functions, business units, or business partners to deliver a seamless experience for the customer, employee, manager, or business partner.

service-oriented architecture Software architecture of a firm built on a collection of software programs that communicate with each other to perform assigned tasks to create a working software application

shopping bot Software with varying levels of built-in intelligence to help electronic commerce shoppers locate and evaluate products or service they might wish to purchase.

Simple Object Access Protocol (SOAP) Set of rules that allows Web services applications to pass data and instructions to one another.

six sigma A specific measure of quality, representing 3.4 defects per million opportunities; used to designate a set of methodologies and techniques for improving quality and reducing costs.

smart card A credit-card-size plastic card that stores digital information and that can be used for electronic payments in place of cash.

smartphone Wireless phone with voice, text, and Internet capabilities.

sniffer Type of eavesdropping program that monitors information traveling over a network.

social bookmarking Capability for users to save their bookmarks to Web pages on a public Web site and tag these bookmarks with keywords to organize documents and share information with others.

social engineering Tricking people into revealing their passwords by pretending to rrbe legitimate users or members of a company in need of information.

social networking sites Online community for expanding users' business or social contacts by making connections through their mutual business or personal connections.

social shopping Use of Web sites featuring user-created Web pages to share knowledge about items of interest to other shoppers.

sociotechnical design Design to produce information systems that blend technical efficiency with sensitivity to organizational and human needs.

sociotechnical view Seeing systems as composed of both technical and social elements.

software localization Process of converting software to operate in a second language.

software package A prewritten, precoded, commercially available set of programs that eliminates the need to write software programs for certain functions.

spam Unsolicited commercial e-mail.

spamming Form of abuse in which thousands and even hundreds of thousands of unsolicited e-mail and electronic messages are sent out, creating a nuisance for both businesses and individual users.

spyware Technology that aids in gathering information about a person or organization without their knowledge.

star topology A network topology in which all computers and other devices are connected to a central host computer. All communications between network devices must pass through the host computer.

storage area network (SAN) A high-speed network dedicated to storage that connects different kinds of storage devices, such as tape libraries and disk arrays so they can be shared by multiple servers.

storage technology Physical media and software governing the storage and organization of data for use in an information system.

stored value payment systems Systems enabling consumers to make instant on-line payments to merchants and other individuals based on value stored in a digital account.

strategic information systems Computer systems at any level of the organization that change goals, operations, products, services, or environmental relationships to help the organization gain a competitive advantage.

strategic transitions A movement from one level of sociotechnical system to another. Often required when adopting strategic systems that demand changes in the social and technical elements of an organization.

structure chart System documentation showing each level of design, the relationship among the levels, and the overall place in the design structure; can document one program, one system, or part of one program.

structured Refers to the fact that techniques are carefully drawn up, step by step, with each step building on a previous one.

structured decisions Decisions that are repetitive, routine, and have a definite procedure for handling them.

structured knowledge Knowledge in the form of structured documents and reports.

Structured Query Language (SQL) The standard data manipulation language for relational database management systems.

supply chain Network of organizations and business processes for procuring materials, transforming raw materials into intermediate and finished products, and distributing the finished products to customers.

supply chain execution systems Systems to manage the flow of products through distribution centers and warehouses to ensure that products are delivered to the right locations in the most efficient manner.

supply chain management Integration of supplier, distributor, and customer logistics requirements into one cohesive process.

supply chain management systems Information systems that automate the flow of information between a firm and its suppliers in order to optimize the planning, sourcing, manufacturing, and delivery of products and services.

supply chain planning systems Systems that enable a firm to generate demand forecasts for a product and to develop sourcing and manufacturing plans for that product.

support activities Activities that make the delivery of a firm's primary activities possible. Consist of the organization's infrastructure, human resources, technology, and procurement.

switch Device to connect network components that has more intelligence than a hub and can filter and forward data to a specified destination.

switching costs The expense a customer or company incurs in lost time and expenditure of resources when changing from one supplier or system to a competing supplier or system.

syndicator Business aggregating content or applications from multiple sources, packaging them for distribution, and reselling them to third-party Web sites.

system testing Tests the functioning of the information system as a whole in order to determine if discrete modules will function together as planned.

systems analysis The analysis of a problem that the organization will try to solve with an information system.

systems analysts Specialists who translate business problems and requirements into information requirements and systems, acting as liaison between the information systems department and the rest of the organization.

systems design Details how a system will meet the information requirements as determined by the systems analysis.

systems development The activities that go into producing an information systems solution to an organizational problem or opportunity.

systems life cycle A traditional methodology for developing an information system that partitions the systems development process into formal stages that must be completed sequentially with a very formal division of labor between end users and information systems specialists.

T lines High-speed data lines leased from communications providers, such as T-1 lines (with a transmission capacity of 1.544 Mbps).

tacit knowledge Expertise and experience of organizational members that has not been formally documented.

tangible benefits Benefits that can be quantified and assigned a monetary value; they include lower operational costs and increased cash flows.

taxonomy Method of classifying things according to a predetermined system.

teamware Group collaboration software that is customized for teamwork.

technology standards Specifications that establish the compatibility of products and the ability to communicate in a network.

technostress Stress induced by computer use; symptoms include aggravation, hostility toward humans, impatience, and enervation.

telecommunications system A collection of compatible hardware and software arranged to communicate information from one location to another.

teleconferencing The ability to confer with a group of people simultaneously using the telephone or electronic-mail group communication software.

Telnet Network tool that allows someone to log on to one computer system while doing work on another.

test plan Prepared by the development team in conjunction with the users; it includes all of the preparations for the series of tests to be performed on the system.

testing The exhaustive and thorough process that determines whether the system produces the desired results under known conditions.

text mining Discovery of patterns and relationships from large sets of unstructured data.

token Physical device similar to an identification card that is designed to prove the identity of a single user.

touch point Method of firm interaction with a customer, such as telephone, e-mail, customer service desk, conventional mail, or point-of-purchase.

topology The way in which the components of a network are connected.

Total Cost of Ownership (TCO) Designates the total cost of owning technology resources, including initial purchase costs, the cost of hardware and software upgrades, maintenance, technical support, and training.

Total Quality Management (TQM) A concept that makes quality control a responsibility to be shared by all people in an organization.

trade secret Any intellectual work or product used for a business purpose that can be classified as belonging to that business, provided it is not based on information in the public domain.

transaction costs Costs incurred when a firm buys on the marketplace what it cannot make itself.

transaction cost theory Economic theory stating that firms grow larger because they can conduct marketplace transactions internally more cheaply than they can with external firms in the marketplace.

transaction processing systems (TPS) Computerized systems that perform and record the daily routine transactions necessary to conduct the business; they serve the organization's operational level.

transborder data flow The movement of information across international boundaries in any form.

Transmission Control Protocol/Internet Protocol (TCP/IP) Dominant model for achieving connectivity among different networks. Provides a universally agree-on method for breaking up digital messages into packets, routing them to the proper addresses, and then reassembling them into coherent messages.

transnational Truly global form of business organization with no national headquarters; value-added activities are managed from a global perspective without reference to national borders, optimizing sources of supply and demand and local competitive advantage.

Trojan horse A software program that appears legitimate but contains a second hidden function that may cause damage.

tuple A row or record in a relational database.

twisted wire A transmission medium consisting of pairs of twisted copper wires; used to transmit analog phone conversations but can be used for data transmission.

Unified communications Integrates disparate channels for voice communications, data communications, instant messaging, e-mail, and electronic conferencing into a single experience where users can seamlessly switch back and forth between different communication modes.

Unified Modeling Language (UML) Industry standard methodology for analysis and design of an object-oriented software system.

unified threat management (UTM) Comprehensive security management tool that combines multiple security tools, including firewalls, virtual private networks, intrusion detection systems, and Web content filtering and anti-spam software.

uniform resource locator (URL) The address of a specific resource on the Internet.

unit testing The process of testing each program separately in the system. Sometimes called program testing.

UNIX Operating system for all types of computers, which is machine independent and supports multiuser processing, multitasking, and networking. Used in high-end workstations and servers.

unstructured decisions Nonroutine decisions in which the decision maker must provide judgment, evaluation, and insights into the problem definition; there is no agreed-upon procedure for making such decisions.

Usenet Forums in which people share information and ideas on a defined topic through large electronic bulletin boards where anyone can post messages on the topic for others to see and to which others can respond.

user interface The part of the information system through which the end user interacts with the system; type of hardware and the series of on-screen commands and responses required for a user to work with the system.

user-designer communications gap The difference in backgrounds, interests, and priorities that impede communication and problem solving among end users and information systems specialists.

Utilitarian Principle Principle that assumes one can put values in rank order and understand the consequences of various courses of action.

utility computing Model of computing in which companies pay only for the information technology resources they actually use during a specified time period. Also called on-demand computing or usage-based pricing.

value chain model Model that highlights the primary or support activities that add a margin of value to a firm's products or services where information systems can best be applied to achieve a competitive advantage.

value web Customer-driven network of independent firms who use information technology to coordinate their value chains to collectively produce a product or service for a market.

Value-Added Network (VAN) Private, multipath, data-only, third-party-managed network that multiple organizations use on a subscription basis.

videoconferencing Teleconferencing in which participants see each other over video screens.

virtual company Organization using networks to link people, assets and ideas to create and distribute products and services without being limited to traditional organizational boundaries or physical location.

Virtual Private Network (VPN) A secure connection between two points across the Internet to transmit corporate data. Provides a low-cost alternative to a private network.

Virtual Reality Modeling Language (VRML) A set of specifications for interactive three-dimensional modeling on the World Wide Web.

virtual reality systems Interactive graphics software and hardware that create computer-generated simulations that provide sensations that emulate real-world activities.

virtual world Computer-based simulated environment intended for its users to inhabit and interact via graphical representations called avatars.

virtualization Presenting a set of computing resources so that they can all be accessed in ways that are not restricted by physical configuration or geographic location.

Voice over IP (VoIP) Facilities for managing the delivery of voice information using the Internet Protocol (IP).

war driving Technique in which eavesdroppers drive by buildings or park outside and try to intercept wireless network traffic.

Web 2.0 Second-generation, interactive Internet-based services that enable people to collaborate, share information, and create new services online, including mashups, blogs, RSS, and wikis.

Web 3.0 Future vision of the Web where all digital information is woven together with intelligent search capabilities.

Web browser An easy-to-use software tool for accessing the World Wide Web and the Internet.

Web bugs Tiny graphic files embedded in e-mail messages and Web pages that are designed to monitor online Internet user behavior.

Web hosting service Company with large Web server computers to maintain the Web sites of fee-paying subscribers.

Web mining Discovery and analysis of useful patterns and information from the World Wide Web.

Web server Software that manages requests for Web pages on the computer where they are stored and that delivers the page to the user's computer.

Web services Set of universal standards using Internet technology for integrating different applications from different sources without time-consuming custom coding. Used for linking systems of different organizations or for linking disparate systems within the same organization.

Web site All of the World Wide Web pages maintained by an organization or an individual.

Wi-Fi Standards for Wireless Fidelity and refers to the 802.11 family of wireless networking standards.

Wide Area Network (WAN) Telecommunications network that spans a large geographical distance. May consist of a variety of cable, satellite, and microwave technologies.

widget Small software program that can be added to a Web page or placed on the desktop to provide additional functionality.

wiki Collaborative Web site where visitors can add, delete, or modify content, including the work of previous authors.

WiMax Popular term for IEEE Standard 802.16 for wireless networking over a range of up to 31 miles with a data transfer rate of up to 75 Mbps. Stands for Worldwide Interoperability for Microwave Access.

Windows Microsoft family of operating systems for both network servers and client computers. The most recent version is Windows Vista.

Wintel PC Any computer that uses Intel microprocessors (or compatible processors) and a Windows operating system.

wireless portals Portals with content and services optimized for mobile devices to steer users to the information they are most likely to need.

wireless sensor networks (WSNs) Networks of interconnected wireless devices with built-in processing, storage, and radio frequency sensors and antennas that are embedded into the physical environment to provide measurements of many points over large spaces.

wisdom The collective and individual experience of applying knowledge to the solution of problems.

WML (Wireless Markup Language) Markup language for Wireless Web sites; based on XML and optimized for tiny displays.

workflow management The process of streamlining business procedures so that documents can be moved easily and efficiently from one location to another.

World Wide Web A system with universally accepted standards for storing, retrieving, formatting, and displaying information in a networked environment.

worms Independent software programs that propagate themselves to disrupt the operation of computer networks or destroy data and other programs.

XML (eXtensible Markup Language) General-purpose language that describes the structure of a document and supports links to multiple documents, allowing data to be manipulated by the computer. Used for both Web and non-Web applications.

Photo and Screen Shot Credits

Index

International Organizations Index

Subject Index

REVIEWERS AND CONSULTANTS

CONSULTANTS

AUSTRALIA
Robert MacGregor, *University of Wollongong*
Alan Underwood, *Queensland University of Technology*

CANADA
Wynne W. Chin, *University of Calgary*
Len Fertuck, *University of Toronto*
Robert C. Goldstein, *University of British Columbia*
Rebecca Grant, *University of Victoria*
Kevin Leonard, *Wilfrid Laurier University*
Anne B. Pidduck, *University of Waterloo*

GERMANY
Lutz M. Kolbe, *University of Göttingen*
Dctlcf Schoder, *University of Cologne*

GREECE
Anastasios V. Katos, *University of Macedonia*

HONG KONG
Enoch Tse, *Hong Kong Baptist University*

INDIA
Sanjiv D. Vaidya, *Indian Institute of Management, Calcutta*

ISRAEL
Phillip Ein-Dor, *Tel-Aviv University*
Peretz Shoval, *Ben Gurion University*

MEXICO
Noe Urzua Bustamante, *Universidad Tecnológica de México*

NETHERLANDS
E.O. de Brock, *University of Groningen*
Theo Thiadens, *University of Twente*
Charles Van Der Mast, *Delft University of Technology*

PUERTO RICO,
Commonwealth of the United States
Brunilda Marrero, *University of Puerto Rico*

SOUTH AFRICA
Daniel Botha, *University of Stellenbosch*

SWEDEN
Mats Daniels, *Uppsala University*

SWITZERLAND
Andrew C. Boynton, *International Institute for Management Development*
Walter Brenner, *University of St. Gallen*
Donald A. Marchand, *International Institute for Management Development*

UNITED KINGDOM

ENGLAND
G.R. Hidderley, *University of Central England, Birmingham*
Christopher Kimble, *University of York*
Jonathan Liebenau, *London School of Economics and Political Science*
Kecheng Liu, *Staffordshire University*

SCOTLAND
William N. Dyer, *Falkirk College of Technology*

UNITED STATES OF AMERICA
Tom Abraham, *Kean University*
Evans Adams, *Fort Lewis College*
Kamal Nayan Agarwal, *Howard University*
Roy Alvarez, *Cornell University*
Chandra S. Amaravadi, *Western Illinois University*
Beverly Amer, *Northern Arizona University*
John Anderson, *Northeastern State University*
Arben Asllani, *Faytetteville State University*
David Bahn, *Metropolitan State University of Minnesota*
Rahul C. Basole, *Georgia Institute of Technology*
Jon W. Beard, *University of Richmond*
Patrick Becka, *Indiana University Southeast*
Michel Benaroch, *Syracuse University*
Cynthia Bennett, *University of Arkansas at Pine Bluff*
David Bradbard, *Winthrop University*
Nancy Brome, *Southern NH University*
Kimberly Cass, *University of Redlands*
Jason Chen, *Gonzaga University*
P. C. Chu, *Ohio State University, Columbus*
Kungwen Chu, *Purdue University, Calumet*
Richard Clemens, *West Virginia Wesleyan College*
Lynn Collen, *St. Cloud State University*
Daniel Connolly, *University of Denver*
Jakov Crnkovic, *SUNY Albany*
Albert Cruz, *National University*
John Dalphin, *SUNY Potsdam*
Marica Deeb, *Waynesburg College*
William DeLone, *American University*
Vasant Dhar, *New York University*
Cindy Drexel, *Western State College of Colorado*
Warren W. Fisher, *Stephen F. Austin State University*
William B. Fredenberger, *Valdosta State University*
Bob Fulkerth, *Golden Gate University*

Mark A. Fuller, *Baylor University*
Minnie Ghent, *Florida Atlantic University*
Amita Goyal, *Virginia Commonwealth University*
Bobby Granville, *Florida A&M University*
Jeet Gupta, *Ball State University*
Vijay Gurbaxani, *University of California, Irvine*
Rassule Hadidi, *University of Illinois, Springfield*
Jeff Harper, *Indiana State University*
William L. Harrison, *Oregon State University*
Joe Harrison, *Union University*
Albert M. Hayashi, *Loyola Marymount University*
Anthony Hendrickson, *Iowa State University*
Michelle Hepner, *University of Central Oklahoma*
Rick Hicks, *Florida Atlantic University*
Marianne Hill, *Furman University*
Bart Hodge, *Virginia Commonwealth University*
Jack Hogue, *University of North Carolina, Charlotte*
Rui Huang, *Binghamton University, SUNY*
George Jacobson, *California State University, Los Angeles*
Carolyn Jacobson, *Marymount University*
Murray Jennex, *University of Phoenix*
Rob Kauffman, *University of Minnesota*
Timothy Kayworth, *Baylor University*
Robert W. Key, *University of Phoenix*
Stephen Klein, *Ramapo College*
Virginia Kleist, *West Virginia State University*
Cenk Kocas, *Michigan State University*
Brian Kovar, *Kansas State University*
Al Lederer, *University of Kentucky*
Robert Lee, *Chapman University*
Roger Letts, *Fairleigh Dickinson University*
Stanley Lewis, *The University of Southern Mississippi*
Teresita Leyell, *Washburn University*
Susan K. Lippert, *George Washington University*
Bruce Lo, *University of Wisconsin-Eau Claire*
Carl Longnecker, *Loyola University*
Treise Lynn, *Wingate University*
Jane Mackay, *Texas Christian University*
Efrem G. Mallach, *University of Massachusetts, Lowell*
Gary Margot, *Ashland University*
Kipp Martin, *University of Chicago*
Richard O. Mason, *Southern Methodist University*
Khris McAlister, *University of Alabama, Birmingham*
Ronald E. McGaughey, *Arkansas Tech University*
Roger McHaney, *Kansas State University*
Patricia McQuaid, *California Polytechnic State Institute*
Charles Menifield, *University of Memphis*
Lisa Miller, *University of Central Oklahoma*
Cindi Nadelman, *New England College*
Peter J. Natale, *Regent University*
Denise Nitterhouse, *DePaul University*
Alan Graham Peace, *West Virginia University*
Leah R. Pietron, *University of Nebraska*
Jack Powell, *University of South Dakota*
Leonard Presby, *William Patterson University*

Sheizaf Rafaeli, *University of Michigan*
Sasan Rahmatian, *California State University, Fresno*
Mary Reed, *Jamestown College*
Brian Reithel, *University of Mississippi*
Eliot Rich, *University at Albany, SUNY*
Leasa Richards-Mealy, *Columbia College*
James Riha, *Northern Illinois University*
Stephanie Robbins, *University of North Carolina, Charlotte*
Marcel Robelis, *University of North Dakota*
Juan Robertson, *Central Washington University*
Ian Robinson, *University of San Francisco*
Alan Roper, *Golden Gate University*
Paula Ruby, *Arkansas State University*
Naveed Saleem, *University of Houston, Clear Lake*
Joko W. Saputro, *University of Wisconsin, Madison*
David Scanlan, *California State University, Sacramento*
Werner Schenk, *University of Rochester*
Kala Chand Seal, *Loyola Marymount University*
Richard S. Segall, *Arkansas State University*
Sherri Shade, *Kennesaw State University*
Ivan J. Singer, *University of Hartford*
Rod Sink, *Northern Illinois University*
Jill Y. Smith, *University of Denver*
Guy Smith, *Embry-Riddle Aeronautical University*
Kathy Stevens, *Merrimack College*
Troy Strader, *Drake University*
Dennis Strouble, *Bowling Green State University*
Michael JD Sutton, *Kent State University*
E. Burton Swanson, *University of California, Los Angeles*
Gladys Swindler, *Fort Hays State University*
Bernadette Szajna, *Texas Christian University*
John Tarjan, *California State University, Bakersfield*
Pam Taylor, *University of Tennessee at Chattanooga*
David Teneyuca, *Schreiner University*
Claire Theriault-Perkins, *University of Maine at Augusta*
Jennifer Thomas, *Pace University*
Kranti Toraskar, *Penn State University*
Goran Trajkovski, *Towson University*
Duane Truex, *Georgia State University*
Douglas Turner, *State University of West Georgia*
B.S. Vijayaraman, *University of Akron*
Patrick J. Walsh, *State University of New York, Binghamton*
Diane Walz, *University of Texas, San Antonio*
Peter Weill, *Massachusetts Institute of Technology*
Frederick Wheeler, *University of Maryland, University College*
Lanny Wilke, *Montana State University-Northern*
Karen L. Williams, *University of Texas at San Antonio*
Jennifer Williams, *University of Southern Indiana*
Paul Witman, *California Lutheran University*
Erma Wood, *University of Arkansas, Little Rock*
Kathie Wright, *Purdue University*